DOES OWNERSHIP MATTER?

Japanese Multinationals in Europe

DOES OWNERSHIP MATTER?

Japanese Multinationals in Europe

Edited by

MARK MASON
AND
DENNIS ENCARNATION

CLARENDON PRESS · OXFORD

6-6-01

Oxford University Press, Walton Street, Oxford OX2 6DP
Oxford New York
Athens Auckland Bangkok Bombay
Calcutta Cape Town Dar es Salaam Delhi
Florence Hong Kong Istanbul Karachi
Kuala Lumpur Madras Madrid Melbourne
Mexico City Nairobi Paris Singapore
Taipei Tokyo Toronto
and associated companies in
Berlin Ibadan

Oxford is a trade mark of Oxford University Press

Published in the United States
by Oxford University Press Inc., New York

© *M. Mason and D. Encarnation 1994*

First published in hardback 1994
First published in paperback 1995

British Library Cataloguing in Publication Data
Data available

Library of Congress Cataloging in Publication Data
Does ownership matter? : Japanese multinationals in Europe / edited by
Mark Mason and Dennis Encarnation.
Revised papers initially presented at a conference hosted by the
Euro-Asia Centre of the European Institute of Business
Administration (INSEAD), plus subsequent presentations at the
Academy of International Business in Brussels and at the Council on
Foreign Relations in New York. Includes bibliographical references.
1. Corporations, Japanese—Europe—Congresses. 2. Investments,
Japanese—Europe—Congresses. 3. Corporations, American—Europe—
Congresses. 4. Investments, American—Europe—Congresses.
5. Corporations, Japanese—United States—Congresses.
6. Investments, Japanese—United States—Congresses.
7. International business enterprises—Japan—Congresses.
8. International business enterprises—Europe—Congresses.
9. International business enterprises—United States—Congresses.
I. Mason, Mark, 1955- . II. Encarnation, Dennis J.
HD2844.D63 1994 338.8'895204—dc20 93–37553
ISBN 0–19–828827–1
ISBN 0–19–829026–8 (Pbk)

Printed in Great Britain
on acid-free paper by
Biddles Ltd., Guildford & King's Lynn

To Roz and Kathy

LIST OF CONTENTS

LIST OF CONTRIBUTORS

PETER BUCKLEY. Professor, Management Centre, University of Bradford, UK.

PIERRE BUIGUES. Head of Unit, Directorate General for Economic and Financial Affairs (DG II), Commission of the European Communities, Belgium.

ARNOUD DE MEYER. Professor, INSEAD, France.

GUNTER DUFEY. Professor, School of Business Administration, University of Michigan, USA.

JOHN DUNNING. Professor, Department of Economics, University of Reading, UK and Graduate School of Management, Rutgers University, USA.

DENNIS ENCARNATION. Associate Professor, Graduate School of Business Administration, Harvard University, USA.

TAKAHIRO FUJIMOTO. Assistant Professor, Department of Economics, University of Tokyo, Japan.

LANDIS GABEL. Professor, INSEAD, France.

MICHELLE GITTELMAN. Doctoral Candidate, Wharton School, University of Pennsylvania, USA.

EDWARD GRAHAM. Senior Fellow, Institute for International Economics, USA.

GABRIEL HAWAWINI. Professor and Director, INSEAD Euro-Asia Centre, France.

ALEXIS JACQUEMIN. Professor, Department of Economics, Catholic University of Louvain, and Head, Cellule de Perspective, Commission of the European Communities, Belgium.

GEOFFREY JONES. Professor, Department of Economics, University of Reading, UK.

YUI KIMURA. Associate Professor, Graduate School of International Management, International University of Japan.

BRUCE KOGUT. Associate Professor, Wharton School, University of Pennsylvania, USA.

AKIRA KUDO. Professor, Institute of Social Sciences, University of Tokyo, Japan.

MARK MASON. Assistant Professor, School of Organization and Management, Yale University, USA.

TOSHIHIRO NISHIGUCHI. Assistant Professor, Wharton School, University of Pennsylvania, USA.

MICHAEL SCHILL. Research Associate, INSEAD Euro-Asia Centre, France.

SHOICHIRO SEI. Professor, Faculty of Economics, Kanto Gakuin University, Japan.

JONATHAN STORY. Professor, INSEAD, France.

SUSAN STRANGE. Professor, European University Institute, Italy.

STEPHEN THOMSEN. Research Fellow, Royal Institute of International Affairs, UK.

RAYMOND VERNON. Professor Emeritus, John F. Kennedy School of Government, Harvard University, USA.

MIRA WILKINS. Professor, Department of Economics, Florida International University, USA.

KOZO YAMAMURA. Professor, Jackson School of International Studies, University of Washington, Seattle, USA.

HIDEKI YAMAWAKI. Assistant Professor, Department of Economics, Catholic University of Louvain, Belgium.

JOHN ZYSMAN. Professor, Department of Political Science, University of California, Berkeley, USA.

LIST OF FIGURES

LIST OF TABLES

PREFACE

Do Japanese multinationals in Europe operate differently? Compared to what? Historically? Cross-sectionally? With what consequences for economics and politics? For corporate strategy and public policy? In Europe and elsewhere? In the end, then, can we conclude that ownership matters?

During 1992, these questions guided an interrelated series of benchmark conferences, all examining Japanese multinationals in Europe. The Euro-Asia Centre of the European Institute of Business Administration (INSEAD) hosted the first and largest of these conferences, entitled 'Japanese Direct Investment in a Unifying Europe: Impacts on Japan and the European Community'. Here, an inter-disciplinary and multinational gathering of economists, historians, political scientists, and business administration specialists—drawn from Europe, Japan, and the USA—initially presented and discussed most of the papers subsequently edited for the present volume.

The INSEAD conference also identified other issues in need of additional research, which the co-editors sought to address in part during subsequent presentations both at the Academy of International Business in Brussels and at the Council on Foreign Relations in New York. From these additional perspectives flowed a greater attention to the interdependence both of trade and investment, and of economics and politics. When combined, these subsequent presentations, together with the revised INSEAD conference papers and related comments, provide a timely benchmark for ongoing discussions of Japanese multinationals in Europe.

The dramatic rise of Japan's foreign direct investment (FDI) in Europe in recent years has stimulated enormous interest among managers, policymakers, and scholars eager to discern the real significance of what many Europeans now call the 'Japanese challenge'. That emotionally-charged label has as its much-publicized antecedent the earlier 'American challenge' to Europe. At the centre of both sets of challenges are the direct investments of multinational corporations: for the Americans, these investments surged during the 1950s and 1960s; while for the Japanese, a comparable surge came two decades later. Recognizing these two challenges, several of the papers collected in this edited volume directly compare and contrast the European operations of American and Japanese multinationals.

As these papers testify, the 'Japanese challenge' greatly escalated during the mid- to late 1980s, when Europe finally rushed past East Asia to rank second among foreign hosts to fresh flows of Japanese investment. By comparison, the USA had surpassed East Asia more than a decade earlier, and subsequently retained its Number One ranking as Japanese investment grew worldwide. Even though that growth fell off dramatically as we entered the 1990s, Europe and the USA remained the top two destinations for new Japanese investment globally. This simple fact invites cross-national comparisons, as several of our authors expressly compare and contrast the foreign operations of Japanese multinationals investing in both Europe and the USA.

In Europe, Japanese multinationals by 1991 concentrated roughly two-fifths of their direct investments in two broad sectors, finance and insurance. Another one-fifth operated in the manufacturing sector, principally in the production of electrical machinery and transportation equipment. But for Japanese car manufacturers and electronics companies, the figure does not adequately capture the broad operations of their direct investments in Europe—for Japanese manufacturers have joined general trading companies (*sogo shosha*) with large investments in European commerce, mainly for sales and service. To mirror these facts, we have included in this edited volume industry studies that reflect the industrial concentration (in finance, electronics, and car production) of Japanese FDI in Europe, as well as the broad operations (from services to manufacturing) of that investment.

1. OVERVIEW

The sectoral distribution of Japanese FDI in Europe today actually follows a well-established pattern, according to Mark Mason, who, in his role as conference chairman, led off the INSEAD Conference (and this volume). In 'Historical Perspectives on Japanese Direct Investment in Europe', Mason charts the historical development of Japanese direct investment in Europe, and then analyses the numerous continuities and changes that have characterized this investment. Specifically, in addition to sectoral distribution, Mason finds that the relative value, geographical location, and other related characteristics of Japanese FDI in Europe all remained remarkably constant for most of the five distinct periods he identifies over the past century. But over the past two decades, many of these characteristics altered dramatically. These recent changes, Mason concludes from his earlier research, have reversed earlier asymmetries in bilateral investment flows between Europe and Japan, leaving the Japanese with far more direct investment in Europe than the Europeans now own in Japan.

To comment on Mason's presentation, and then to offer their own historical perspectives, came three rapporteurs deliberately drawn from Europe, Japan, and the USA. First, from Europe, Geoffrey Jones reminded us that the historical development of Japanese direct investment in Europe generally conforms to larger, well-established patterns of FDI inflows to

that region. Next, from Japan, Akira Kudo underscored the historical significance of direct investments by Japanese trading companies operating in
Europe, and then offered an alternative periodization to Mason's largely
policy-driven analysis. Finally, from the USA, Mira Wilkins highlighted
numerous similarities between the historical development of Japanese FDI
in Europe and the USA, all of which raise additional questions for future
research on the general operations of multinational enterprises.

2. GENERAL CAUSES AND CONSEQUENCES

After establishing several historical baselines, the INSEAD conference
(and this volume) proceeded to examine the general causes and overall
consequences of Japanese direct investment in Europe. Leading off this
discussion was a paper written by John Dunning, entitled 'The Strategy of
Japanese and US Manufacturing Investment in Europe'. Here, Dunning
begins by documenting wide variation in the sectoral distribution of US
and Japanese FDI. To account for that variation, Dunning first surveys a
broad range of existing hypotheses, including his now-familiar 'eclectic
paradigm', all positing common investment motivations. Then, to account
for remaining differences in FDI patterns, Dunning draws on his earlier
research on Japanese multinationals in Europe to generate and test original hypotheses based on a broad range of ownership-specific advantages
(including governance structures and inter-firm relationships) available to
Japanese multinationals.

In his comment on Dunning's paper, Kozo Yamamura raises issues also
germane to the entire conference. Namely, he urges Dunning and others
to include in their analyses of Japanese FDI two additional sets of variables: the peculiar institutional characteristics of Japanese corporations,
together with Japanese government policies and practices which crucially
affect the foreign operations of these corporations. Taken together, such
variables can greatly enrich existing theoretical constructs that attempt to
explain variations in the general motivations underlying all foreign direct
investment.

Shifting our focus from causes to consequences, Hideki Yamawaki
examines the initial entry strategies pursued by Japanese multinationals
seeking to invest in both Europe and the USA. In his 'Entry Patterns of
Japanese Multinationals in US and European Manufacturing', Yamawaki
assembles a unique data set from which he distils a number of findings
which run counter to long-standing propositions. Notable here is the growing propensity over time of Japanese multinationals to pursue mergers and
acquisitions (M&As) abroad. That propensity, Yamawaki finds, is greater
in the USA than it is in Europe, and is most commonly used to diversity
abroad into new products and markets. What does not vary across host

countries or product sectors, according to Yamawaki, is the consistent objective of Japanese multinationals to own an uncontested majority of the equity shares in their foreign subsidiaries.

To discern the broader implications of this analysis, Bruce Kogut in part turns to Yamawaki's earlier research on Japanese multinationals in Europe. These previous findings, Kogut suggests, point to the important ways in which the technological strengths of potential host countries 'pull' FDI into specific industries. This stands in marked contrast to more traditional theories that focus on existing rivalries back in the home country that 'push' FDI abroad. In addition, Kogut underlines the importance of what Yamawaki calls the 'sequential entry process', but cautions that this and other patterns noted throughout the paper may be critically influenced by the effects of time, as variation in the age of American and Japanese investments produces different vintage effects.

These same vintage effects may also help explain wide variation in the subsequent operations of American and Japanese multinationals operating in the same location (Europe), and of Japanese multinationals operating in different locations (Europe and the USA). Detailing and analysing these operational differences falls to Michelle Gittelman and Edward Graham, who extend their earlier research by assembling and analysing a broad survey of available data. In 'The Performance and Structure of Japanese Affiliates in the European Community', Gittelman and Graham first compare and contrast the European operations of American and Japanese multinationals. They find, for example, that Japanese subsidiaries are generally more capital-intensive, yet no more regionally integrated, than their American couterparts. From a study of economic performance, Gittelman and Graham next turn to examine industrial organization of Japanese multinationals abroad, by comparing the cross-national development of Japanese *keiretsu*. These structures, they conclude, are more fully developed in the USA than in Europe, and more in car production than in electronics. To each of these findings, however, Gittelman and Graham attach a word of caution, given the numerous data problems they encounter.

While expressing sympathy for the problems faced by Gittelman and Graham, Raymond Vernon raises several additional questions. Specifically, he asks for an explicit examination of the likely impact of *keiretsu* structures on the overseas performance of Japanese multinationals. Such an examination, for example, would address the economic efficiency of these peculiar Japanese structures, and would estimate the economic costs and benefits they generate for their host countries. In the end, Vernon reminds us all that the local performance of any foreign subsidiary is a direct function of the larger global structure of the multinational corporation.

Among the several differences between American and Japanese multinationals identified by Gittelman and Graham, trade figures prominently—

a fact meriting the special attention of Pierre Buigues and Alexis Jacquemin in 'Foreing Direct Investment and Exports to the European Community'. Here, Buigues and Jacquemin draw on their earlier research to argue that exports and FDI often act as complements rather than substitutes—a point they seek to illustrate empirically by charting for the 1980s the simultaneous rise of exports and investments from both Japan and America to the European Community. Based on this analysis, the authors go on to review a broad range of policy options available to the EC which, they conclude, must better co-ordinate and integrate competition policies across member states.

While not disputing that investment and trade are interrelated, Stephen Thomsen does dispute the causation imputed by Buigues and Jacquemin. In addition to trade, other possible explanations for the rapid rise of Japanese FDI in Europe include the strong motivation of Japanese multinationals to acquire advanced technology and to source skilled labour. Moreover, strong correlations between trade and investment may also mask large sectoral shifts in the corporate strategies pursued by Japanese multinationals to gain access to EC markets. These and other reservations aside, however, Thomsen applauds the authors' advocacy of generally open and liberal EC policies towards FDI from Japan and elsewhere.

The interdependence between trade and investment stimulated much discussion at the INSEAD conference, and subsequently led Dennis Encarnation to test empirically several of the arguments he had made rhetorically. In 'Investment and Trade by American, European, and Japanese Multinationals across the Triad', which he later prepared for the Academy of International Business, Encarnation builds on his earlier research to argue that the foreign investment and related trade strategies of American, European, and Japanese multinationals have developed in strikingly similar ways, and that such strategies are closely interrelated. However, in contrast both to the Americans in Europe and the Europeans in America, the Japanese in both America and Europe still sell more manufactured goods in the markets of their Triad partners through international trade than through local production. This they accomplish through massive investment in local distribution, which affords them unparalleled control over USA–Japan and EC–Japan trade flows. In this respect, at least, Encarnation argues that ownership can and does matter.

The central importance of foreign direct investment in determining patterns of international economic activity suggests that ownership does indeed matter, Peter Buckley says, although the apparent convergence of trade and investment strategies among multinationals across the Triad requires careful qualification. FDI can enable firms to obtain greater shares of overseas markets than through exports alone, to cross-subsidize between internal units and economize on tax payments through transfer pricing, and to reduce costs by locating production abroad. In all these ways, ownership surely makes a significant difference to the operation of multinationals, and suggests vital links between the trade and investment strategies of such firms. At the same time, however, there remain important differences between these interrelated strategies as practised by multinationals based in different points of the Triad. Contrasting conditions in specific host markets, varying institutional arrangements in home countries, and the effects of time all contribute to such differences, and suggest that convergence will never be complete.

3. INDUSTRY STUDIES

Having thus identified the general causes and overall consequences of Japanese direct investment in Europe, the INSEAD Conference (and this edited volume) shifted the level of analysis, with a series of industry studies designed to explore variation in the broad conclusions outlined above. In this volume, we begin with one sector—financial services—that has long hosted significant shares of Japanese direct investment in Europe (see Fig. 1.2 above). From here, we move to electronics and then to automobiles, the two industries which in more recent years have attracted the greatest attention of both Japanese manufacturers and European policymakers.

Leading off these industry studies are Gabriel Hawawini and Michael Schill, who assembled and analysed a broad array of data in their 'The Japanese Presence in the European Financial Services Sector'. Here, drawing on earlier research, Hawawini and Schill identify at least two main factors to explain the rapid growth of EC investments by Japanese banks and securities houses during the 1980s: first, rising demands by Japanese clients to service their new European operations; and second, emerging opportunities in one of the world's most important financial centres, especially in the area of wholesale banking, where lower (capital and related) costs granted Japanese banks significant competitive advantages. These advantages, however, may be eroding, according to Hawawini and Schill, as banking crises back home combine with escalating competition abroad to challenge Japanese banks and securities houses in Europe.

Responding to this analysis we have Gunter Dufey, who offers a different perspective. According to Dufey, Japanese government regulation of financial services back home merits special attention among the several factors that help explain the European expansion of Japanese banks and securities houses. That regulation has forced Japanese banks to shift operations overseas, to both Europe and America, where they can more easily secure access to US dollars, hide non-performing assets in the balance sheets of unconsolidated subsidiaries, and generally pursue sources and uses of funds denied to them back in Japan. These, Dufey concludes, are the principal motivations of Japanese financial institutions as they invest directly abroad in order to 'catch up' with their formidable American and European competitors.

From financial services we move to the electronics industry, among the first manufacturing sectors to attract sizeable Japanese investments. Here, in 'Japanese Direct Investment in the European Semiconductor Industry', Yui Kimura draws on his earlier research to examine an advanced technology essential to the future growth of the electronics industry. Specifically, through cross-national comparisons, Kimura illustrates that Japanese semiconductor producers established more advanced, fully integrated production operations in the European Community than in either East Asia or the United States. Expected sales growth, threatened market access, and heightened customer demands all served to attract Japanese FDI in the EC semiconductor industry. Kimura predicts that these investments will significantly benefit EC industry, but warns that such benefits will be fully realized only if the Community pursues liberal economic policies which encourage collaboration between domestic and foreign firms.

While acknowledging the potential benefits which Japanese FDI in the European semiconductor industry can create for host economies, Arnoud De Meyer suggests that Kimura's optimism requires careful qualification. The increased presence of efficient Japanese firms operating in open European markets, Kimura argues, will force EC firms to behave more competitively and thereby produce economic benefits for the Community as a whole. Yet such benefits will accrue only if European firms remain viable competitors, De Meyer maintains, which may require that the EC apply anti-trust and anti-monopoly measures in addition to collaborative R&D projects as advocated by Kimura. In addition, De Meyer questions the degree to which the Japanese semiconductor industry has been and will continue to be successful both at home and abroad. With regard to past performance, De Meyer points out that Japanese companies have been far less successful in producing sophisticated integrated circuits (ICs) than in manufacturing memories. And with regard to future performance, De Meyer speculates that even those strengths which benefitted Japanese producers in earlier times may well prove far less advantageous in coming years.

Semiconductors appear early in the value-added process that forms the electronics industry as broadly defined by John Zysman. Drawing on his previous research, Zysman uses the title of his paper to ask the one question that must be answered by European managers and policymakers alike: 'Can Japanese Direct Investment Sustain European Development in Electronics?' His answer is a qualified yes, but only if Europe sheds the failed government policies and corporate strategies of the past. Earlier, as Zysman documents, Europe sought to shore up its declining position in the electronics industry by subsidizing and protecting semiconductors, computers, and other key subsectors where European firms remained weak in relation to their foreign competitors. As a preferred alternative, Zysman proposes that Europe build directly on local strengths in telecommunications, and industrial electronics, while at the same time maintaining access to the critical technology networks (what he calls 'regional supply bases') centred principally in Japan and the USA. Such European access, Zysman concludes, can be secured in part through the active encouragement of both Japanese and US direct investments in the EC electronics industry.

While in broad agreement with Zysman's analysis, Susan Strange does question one of his key assumptions. From the perspective of concerned host countries, Zysman implicitly assumes that it is generally preferable for Europeans themselves to own electronics (and other) companies operating in the Community, rather than to relinquish that ownership to non-Europeans. However, far more important to the health of European industry, according to Strange, is the intensity of inter-firm rivalries, which operate largely independent of each firm's national origins. Except, it seems, when these firms are Japanese: for Strange detects a strong streak of xenophobia which, she argues, leads Japanese firms to operate differently from their foreign competitors. Until that xenophobia subsides, Strange finds Zysman's policy recommendations both reasonable and persuasive.

From electronics we move to automobiles, and specifically to the organizational behaviour of Japanese transplants and their parts suppliers in both America and Europe. In 'The Strategy and Structure of Japanese Automobile Manufactures in Europe', a team of three authors—Takahiro Fujimoto, Toshihiro Nishiguchi, and Shoichiro Sei—assembled a unique data set that combined extensive interviews with survey questionnaires of Japanese managers in both America and Europe. With these data, our team was able to test empirically numerous conceptual models derived from their earlier research. Their tests confirm the authors' initial suspicion that no single model can explain different patterns of management control and information flow apparent across a broad range of operational issues. Moreover, such patterns seem to vary systematically across different geographical locations, thereby blunting the transferability of information and control systems.

This largely empirical description of Japanese automobile transplants in America and Europe offers valuable new information on their post-investment operations, according to Landis Gabel, but demands further analytical treatment. Through their survey questionnaires and other research, Fujimoto, Nishiguchi, and Sei have obtained original information on the important yet largely neglected topic of post-investment transplant operations of Japanese auto parts producers as well as of the automobile manufactures themselves. Although the authors then explore the suitability of various conceptual 'models' they develop to describe these observed operations, these models in no way explain the causal relationships between differing observed patterns of resource flows and operational outcomes.

Recourse to the considerable literature on international trade, foreign direct investment, and management of multinational enterprise would provide a substantive basis for explaining some of these important 'Whys'.

Shifting from internal operations to external politics in his analysis of Japanese investment in the EC automobile industry, Mark Mason responds to a perceived gap at the INSEAD conference, one that he sought to fill through a later presentation at the Academy of International Business. There, in his 'The Political Economy of Japanese Automobile Investment in Europe', Mason analysed the evolution of European policymaking in this critically important industry. That policy process culminated in a series of EC–Japanese understandings which placed important limits on Japan's penetration of Community markets until the year 2000. Those understandings included Japanese acceptance not only of explicit restrictions on automobile imports to the Community as a whole and to several specified EC member states until the year 2000, but also of implicit constraints on the operation of Japanese transplants functioning within the region. While formally negotiated on the European side by the EC Commission, this extraordinary (though somewhat ambiguous) arrangement with Japan was largely determined by critically affected member states. At least in this key industry, such EC policy initiatives, driven by national politics, greatly influence the character and operation of Japanese FDI as well as trade throughout the region.

Responding to Mason is Jonathan Story, who argues that the character of the EC–Japanese understanding on car imports and production reflects a broader pattern of European policymaking. Specifically, Story finds that the Commission is often forced to craft vague or partially ambiguous arrangements with non-Community actors when the interests of EC member states significantly diverge. Such outcomes may well be endemic to this EC policymaking process, where states, rather than the European Commission, still prevail.

4. IMPLICATIONS

Having moved from general causes and consequences to specific industry studies, we are ready in our concluding chapter to answer the overarching questions that permeated the otherwise diverse papers collected in this volume. In 'Does Ownership Matter? Answers and Implications for Europe and America', Dennis Encarnation and Mark Mason conclude that ownership can—and does—matter. But their conclusions require careful qualification, given the often competing facts and differing analyses presented by our several authors. Specifically, from a corporate perspective, important differences remain in both the structure and performance of Japanese multinationals abroad, even as they rapidly evolve along an otherwise common path charted earlier by their American and European counterparts. Such persistent differences cannot be discounted as mere 'vintage effects', vestigial remnants reflecting an earlier stage in a multinational's evolution, but instead may actually grow larger with the proliferation and maturation of Japanese investment abroad. Next, from a government perspective, ownership again matters, as individual European states and the European Community as a whole continue to enact numerous policies that specifically respond to the much-vaunted Japanese challenge. From these responses we see an emerging European policy model that has important implications for Japan's future relations, not only with Europe, but also with the USA.

Along the way to discerning these several implications, numerous individuals and institutions provided critical support. At the INSEAD conference, we wish to thank in particular: Professor Henri-Claude de Bettignies, INSEAD; Dr. Kenneth Courtis, Deutsche Bank (Asia); Professor Jean Dermine, INSEAD; Professor Yves Doz, INSEAD; Professor Kasra Ferdows, Georgetown University; Ms. Noriko Hama, Mitsubishi Research Institute; Professor Kenichi Imai, Hitotsubashi University; Mr. Takashi Kiuchi, Long-Term Credit Bank of Japan; Professor Robert Lawrence, Harvard University; Mr. Simon Nuttall, Commission of the European Communities; Professor Lars-Hendrick Roller, INSEAD; Mr. Makoto Sakurai, Mitsui Marine Research Institute; Professor Gianfranco Viesti, CERPEM; and Professor George Yannopolous, University of Reading.

We are also indebted to a number of other experts who commented on one or more draft book chapters at additional meetings we organized to explore Japanese FDI in Europe. At the 1992 Annual Meetings of the Academy of International Business held in Brussels, Professor Louis Wells provided important perspectives on the general phenomenon of foreign direct investment. And at a seminar sponsored by the Council on Foreign Relations in New York, Professors Hugh Patrick of Columbia University, Michael Smitka of Washington and Lee University, and Ezra Vogel of Harvard University all offered helpful comments. We also wish to thank Dr. Shafiqul Islam and Ms. Radha Mutiah of the Council for their help in organizing the seminar.

In addition, we wish to acknowledge the support of a number of institutions. These include the Research Division of the Graduate School of Business Administration at Harvard University, the School of Organization and Management at Yale University, and the Alex C. Walker Educational and Charitable Foundation. Finally, we thank INSEAD and the Euro-Asia Centre for their considerable financial and logistical assistance in connection with the INSEAD conference, and express our special gratitude to Centre Director and INSEAD Professor Gabriel Hawawini, to Conference Co-ordinator Hillary Lassis, and to other staff at the Centre.

PART I
OVERVIEW

1

Historical Perspectives on Japanese Direct Investment in Europe*

Mark Mason

Contrary to popular notions and much of the relevant scholarship, Japan's foreign direct investment (FDI) in Europe enjoys a long history. Lay discussions in the Japanese and European media are filled with references to the surge in Japan's FDI to Europe in recent years, but they ignore accrued experience from the past.[1] This surge has also prompted considered analyses within the scholarly community, but here again references to the past tend to be superficial or altogether lacking.[2] Even historians of Japanese FDI have generally ignored the record of such investment in Europe, concentrating instead on the development of Japan's direct investments in Asia during the pre-war period, and on Japan's direct investments in Asia, Latin America, and the USA during the post-war period.[3]

* The author gratefully acknowledges the comments of Geoffrey Jones, Nobuo Kawabe, Akira Kudo, Ian Nish, Erich Pauer, Mira Wilkins, and two anonymous reviewers on earlier drafts of this paper. An earlier version was published as 'The Origins and Evolution of Japanese Direct Investment in Europe', *Business History Review*, 66 (Autumn 1992), 435–74.

[1] On representative Japanese perspectives see e.g. the Special Edition of *Toyo Keizai* (28 Feb. 1992) entitled 'Jipangu in yoroppa' [Japan in Europe]; typical of one viewpoint expressed by many Europeans is P.-A. Donnet, *Le Japon achete le monde* [Japan Buys the World] (Paris: Editions du Seuil, 1991).

[2] See e.g. S. Micossi and G. Viesti, 'Japanese Direct Manufacturing Investment in Europe', in L. Alan Winters and A. J. Venables, eds., *European Integration: Trade and Industry* (New York: Cambridge University Press, 1991), 200–33; S. Thomsen and P. Nicolaides, *The Evolution of Japanese Direct Investment in Europe: Death of a Transistor Salesman* (London: Harvester Wheatsheaf, 1991); and M. Yoshitomi, *et al., Japanese Direct Investment in Europe: Motives, Impact and Policy Implications* (Aldershot: Avebury, n.d.).

[3] Virtual or total neglect of the history of Japanese FDI in pre-war Europe is evident in the otherwise excellent historical studies of e.g. M. Fujii *et al.*, eds., *Nihon takokuseki kigyo no shiteki tenkai* [The Historical Development of Japanese Multinational Enterprise] (Tokyo: Otsuki Shoten, 1979), i; M. Miyamoto *et al.*, eds., *Sogo shosha no keieishi* [The Business History of General Trading Companies] (Tokyo: Toyo keizai shinposha, 1976); and G. Numaguchi, 'Nihon no kaigai jigyo katsudo: sono rekishiteki katei to keieiteki sho yoin' [The Overseas Activities of Japanese Enterprise: The Historical Process and Various Managerial Factors], in *Chiba shodai ronso*, 13-B (June 1970), 244–68. For an overview of recent work on Japanese FDI before World War II, see T. Kuwahara, 'Trends in Research on Overseas Expansion by Japanese Enterprises prior to World War Two', in *Japanese Yearbook on Business History*, 7 (1990), 61–81.

The development of Japanese FDI in post-war Europe gets short shrift in such analyses as R. Komiya, 'Japan's Foreign Direct Investment', in R. Komiya, *The Japanese Economy: Trade, Industry and Government* (Tokyo: University of Tokyo Press, 1990), ch. 3; M. Yoshino, *Japan's Multinational Enterprises* (Cambridge: Harvard University Press, 1976), and id., 'The Multinational Spread of Japanese Manufacturing Investment since World War II', *Business*

Yet the history of Japanese FDI in Europe extends back over more than a century of modern experience, and merits more serious consideration than it has heretofore received.[4]

To fill this gap in the literature and to place current trends in longer-term perspective, this paper will explore the origins and development of Japanese direct investment in modern Europe. The paper will first examine the evolution of this investment in chronological fashion, then analyse some of the major continuities as well as changes evident from the historical record, and finally compare this record with the development of European direct investment in Japan.

1. THE DEVELOPMENT OF JAPANESE FDI IN EUROPE

At least in terms of relevant political changes, the modern history of Japanese direct investment in Europe breaks down into five principal periods. These changes either represent important shifts in government policies or major international political events which critically affected Japanese investment flows to Europe. As we shall see, however, continuity rather than change best characterizes key features of Japanese FDI in Europe, at least through most of its first century of development.

History Review, 48/3 (Autumn 1974), 357–81; and H. Yoshihara, 'Multinational Growth of Japanese Manufacturing Enterprises in the Postwar Period', in A. Okochi and T. Inoue, eds., *Overseas Business Activities* (Tokyo: Tokyo University Press, 1984), 95–120. T. Ozawa, to his credit, does provide a brief overview of Japanese FDI in Europe in his *Multinationalism, Japanese Style: The Political Economy of Outward Dependency* (Princeton: Princeton University Press, 1979), 154–6.

In recent years, a number of scholars in Japan and elsewhere have contributed to our understanding of the history of Japanese FDI in the industrialized nations by examining in particular the development of such investment in the USA. See e.g. Mira Wilkins, 'Japanese Multinationals in the United States: Continuity and Change, 1879–1990', in *Business History Review*, 64 (Winter 1990), 585–629—which offers findings on the development of Japanese FDI in the USA in many respects parallel to those presented in the current paper on Japanese FDI in Europe—and relevant portions of id., 'Japanese Multinational Enterprise before 1914', *Business History Review*, 60 (Summer 1986), 199–231; N. Kawabe, 'Japanese Business in the United States before World War II: The Case of Mitsubishi Shoji Kaisha, the San Francisco and Seattle Branches' (unpublished Ph.D. thesis, Ohio State University, 1980) (largely summarized in id., 'Senzen ni okeru sogo shosha no zaibei shiten katsudo: Mitsubishi Shoji san furanshisuko, shiattoru ryo shiten no jirei kenkyu' [The Pre-war Activities of the American Branches of the General Trading Companies: Case Studies of the Mitsubishi Corporation's Branch Offices in San Francisco and Seattle], *Keiei shi gaku*, 16/3 (Oct. 1981), 26–49) and id., 'Development of Overseas Operations by General Trading Companies, 1868–1945', in S. Yonekawa and H. Yoshihara, eds., *Business History of General Trading Companies* (Tokyo: Tokyo University Press, 1987), 71–103.

[4] Although it is rarely the focus of their attention, some business historians of Japanese trading companies such as Mitsui & Co. and the Mitsubishi Corporation, of Japanese banks such as the Yokohama Specie Bank, and of other Japanese firms that historically have invested abroad do mention Japanese FDI in Europe in their studies. For references to many of these studies, see below.

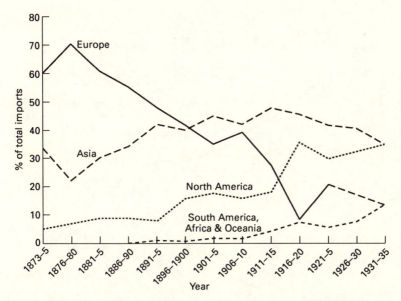

Source: S. Shinya, *Japan's Industrialization in the World Economy, 1859–1899: Export Trade and Overseas Competition* (London: Athlone Press, 1988), table A-2, n.p.

FIG. 1.1. Average annual shares of Japanese imports, by region, 1873–1935

1.1. Origins (to 1914)

Japan's earliest direct investments in Europe began in the late nineteenth century, and were aimed primarily at facilitating bilateral trade flows. These flows proved critically important to Japan, which in its strategy to industrialize sought to import machinery and other advanced capital equipment from the West and export in exchange raw silk, and textiles and other relatively simple manufactured products to this same region. Rather than America, Europe initially represented Japan's principal Western trading partner. Europe supplied a far greater proportion of Japanese imports than did its Atlantic counterpart for at least the four decades preceding World War I, for example, and Europe consumed a greater proportion of Japanese exports than did North America at least through the 1870s (see Figs. 1.1 and 1.2). The UK far outstripped other European countries as a supplier of Japanese imports, which mainly comprised manufacturing machinery and other capital goods, until World War I (and beyond) (see Fig. 1.3). Among European nations, France from the mid-1870s until 1914 was the largest recipient of Japanese exports, which consisted largely of raw silk and silk products (see Fig. 1.4).

To facilitate this trade, Japanese enterprise set up European affiliates in at least four different commercial fields: trade, banking, shipping, and

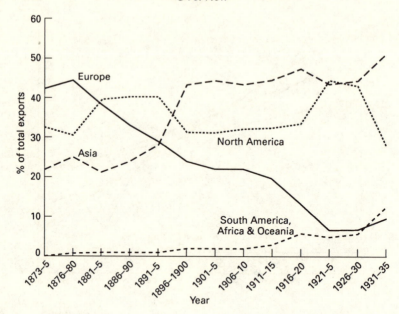

Source: as Fig. 1.1.

FIG. 1.2. Average annual shares of Japanese exports, by region, 1873–1935

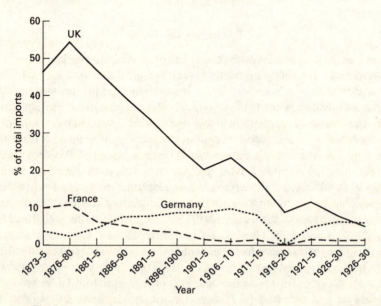

Source: as Fig. 1.1.

FIG. 1.3. Average annual shares of Japanese imports, by principal European sources, 1873–1935

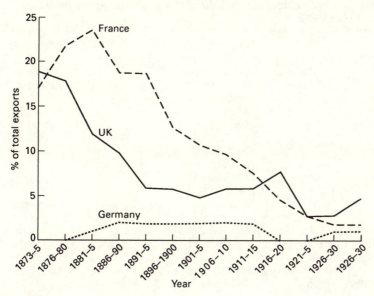

Source: as Fig. 1.1.

FIG. 1.4. Average annual shares of Japanese exports, by principal European markets, 1873–1935

insurance. Trading companies established local offices to import and sell Japanese goods in Europe, and to acquire European products and technology and export them to Japan.[5] Unquestionably the most important Japanese trading firm in Europe during this period was Mitsui & Co., which in 1878 chose Paris as the site for its first branch office in the Western world.[6] Although Mitsui & Co. apparently judged that business did not warrant the continued operation of the Paris (or of the 1880-established Milan) office for long, the trading company did identify other European regions as sufficiently important to justify a local presence, and soon operated branch offices in London (established in 1880), Lyons (established in 1880, closed in 1881, and reopened in 1908), and Hamburg (1899) (see Table 1.1). Nor was Mitsui & Co. the only Japanese trading firm which directly invested in Europe during this period. Okura Gumi, for example, operated branch or sub-branch offices in London and Hamburg after the (1904–5) Russo-Japanese War, and Nihon Menka established Menka Gesellschaft

[5] According to A. Kudo, the trading companies' role as importer into Japan was apparently more important than their role as exporter to Europe during these years, which helps to explain why they were often referred to as '*import* trading companies' in this era.

[6] In 1881, just three years after its establishment, however, the Paris branch was closed. See Y. Togai, 'Saisho ni shutsugen shita sogo shosha: Mitsui Bussan' [The First General Trading Company to Move Abroad: Mitsui & Co.], in M. Miyamoto *et al.*, eds., *Sogo shosha no keieishi*, 91.

TABLE 1.1. *The establishment of Mitsui & Co. branch offices in Europe and the USA, 1878–1908*

Year	Location	Comments
1878	Paris	Closed in 1881
1879	New York	Closed in 1882
1880	London	
1880	Lyons	Closed in 1881
1880	Milan	Closed in 1881
1896	New York	Reopened
1898	San Francisco	
1899	Hamburg	
1906	Oklahoma City	
1907	Portland	
1908	Lyons	Reopened

Note: Mitsui & Co. also established a wholly owned subsidiary, Southern Products Company, in Houston, Texas in 1911. See Mitsui & Co., *The 100-Year History of Mitsui & Co., Ltd.* (Tokyo: Mitsui & Co., 1977), 50. Soon after its founding, this subsidiary apparently took over the functions of the Oklahoma City office, which closed shortly thereafter.

Source: M. Miyamoto *et al.*, eds., *Sogo shosha no keieishi* [The Business History of General Trading Companies], 91.

in Bremen, Germany, and set up branches in, or dispatched employees to, Liverpool, London, and Milan well before the start of World War I.[7]

In addition to trading companies, Japanese enterprise established European operations in at least three other main business lines to enhance bilateral trade. For example, the Yokohama Specie Bank (YSB; predecessor of the Bank of Tokyo), which was established in 1880, the very next year set up its first European representative office in London largely to provide foreign exchange, export and import financing, and other financial services related to such trade, and later established a Hamburg office as well.[8] In addition, the YSB's London branch served as a vital conduit of foreign capital, for through this branch the Bank marketed Japanese government-backed securities to European (principally British) investors.[9]

[7] H. Yamazaki, 'The Logic of the Formation of General Trading Companies in Japan', in S. Yonekawa and H. Yoshihara, eds., *Business History of General Trading Companies*, 53; and N. Kawabe, 'Overseas Operations, 1868–1945', 77.

[8] S. Hijikata, *Yokohama shokin ginko* [The Yokohama Specie Bank] (Tokyo: Kyoikusha, 1980), 67, 237. According to Hijikata, the YSB's earliest overseas offices were located in New York (1880), London (1881), San Francisco (1886), Honolulu (1892), and Shanghai (1893). Ibid. 237–8. N. Tamaki reports that, in addition, the YSB had established an agent's office in Lyons by 1889. See N. Tamaki, 'The Yokohama Specie Bank: A Multinational in the Japanese Interest 1879–1931', in Geoffrey Jones, ed., *Banks as Multinationals* (London: Routledge, 1990), 196.

[9] In March 1905, for example, the London branch of the YSB distributed prospectuses and application forms, and handled subsequent business, for a $4^{1}/_{2}$% sterling loan of £30 million for the Japanese Imperial Government. Yokohama shokin ginko (Yokohama Specie Bank),

Japanese affiliates in Europe also facilitated trade through provision of shipping and insurance services. The great Japanese shipping company Nippon Yusen Kaisha (NYK), established in 1885, inaugurated shipping lines between Japan and Europe just eleven years later. In terms of freight income and value of owned tonnage, these lines had become NYK's most important international routes—far surpassing the American lines—by the turn of the century. To facilitate this rapidly expanding business, NYK apparently set up offices in its European ports of Hamburg, Bremen, and Antwerp and, in Britain, in Middlesbrough, Liverpool, Southampton, and London.[10]

The Tokio Marine Insurance Company, for its part, soon became the most important Japanese supplier of shipping and other insurance services principally to cover the transportation of goods between Japan and Europe during these years. In 1880, Tokio Marine entrusted Mitsui & Co. agencies in Paris and London with representing its European interests, but the company later chose to create its own London office.[11] Already experiencing rapid growth through contract sales for accident insurance through this office, in 1898 Tokio Marine chose to expand its British-based activities to include international cargo insurance and other trade-related business. Several other Japanese insurance companies also operated London offices to conduct such business, although Tokio Marine clearly dominated the field.[12] Through trading company branches, financial services outlets, shipping offices, and insurance agencies, European affiliates of Japanese-based enterprises promoted two-way trade vital to Japan's industrializing economy.

The intimate involvement of the Japanese government stands out as a particularly striking feature of the nation's earliest direct investments in Europe. Indeed, the government directly supported the European activities of each of the four leading Japanese companies involved in these bilateral trade-facilitating activities. To NYK, for example, the Japanese authorities provided substantial subsidies to cover the costs of operating the European shipping line.[13] In the YSB, the government initially provided one-third of the capital and determined the appointments of the President and Vice-President and, later, took effective control of the

Yokohama shokin ginko shi furoku [Supplement to the History of the Yokohama Specie Bank] (Tokyo: Nihon keizai hyoronsha, 1976), iii. 719–24. According to I. Nish, the YSB arranged a number of other such loans in London at the time of the Russo-Japanese War.

[10] W. D. Wray, *Mitsubishi and the N.Y.K., 1870–1914: Business Strategy in the Japanese Shipping Industry* (Cambridge: Harvard University Press, 1984), 14, 248–9, 290, 308–11, 523–9.

[11] Tokio Marine later (1899) closed this London office, and entrusted its local representation to Wills Trading Company. Nihon keieishi kenkyujo (Japan Business History Institute), ed., *Tokyo kaijo no 100 nen* [One Hundred Years of Tokio Marine] (Tokyo: Tokyo kaijo kasai hoken, 1979), 344–6.

[12] Nihon keieishi kenkyujo, ed., *Tokyo kaijo no 100 nen*, 79–86.

[13] W. D. Wray, *Mitsubishi and the N.Y.K.*, 289, 308, 529.

entire organization.[14] In Tokio Marine, the government initially held a substantial number of the firm's shares.[15] And for Mitsui & Co., the authorities provided subsidies and interest-free loans to encourage exports to Europe, and at one point even granted the trading company's Paris office the exclusive right to market throughout France silk manufactured in Japan's state-run spinning-mills.[16]

Despite the relatively early entry of Japanese FDI into Europe, however, overall investment levels—together with the European impacts of such investment—remained extremely modest. Although detailed statistical figures do not exist, anecdotal and other evidence suggests that Japanese FDI in Europe before World War I was limited to the modest sums required to establish the kinds of service organizations outlined above.[17] And although the impacts of such investments surely were important to Japan, these investments constituted only a tiny proportion of the FDI which entered any of the European countries in this period, and generally had little effect on the operation of their economies[18] Reflecting this limited presence, European attitudes towards Japan and its local investments, to the extent that they even existed, generally were characterized by indifference, if not condescension.

1.2. Interwar Expansion (1914–1941)

Following a brief hiatus created by the start of World War I, Japanese firms generally expanded their investments in Europe during the decades preceding World War II. The outbreak of war in 1914 initially slowed Japan's trade with Europe.[19] As a result, the European operations of Japanese-based trading, finance, transportation, and insurance companies at first declined, and few new investments were undertaken. Instead, Japanese investors increasingly concentrated their efforts on other Asian markets, where they could partially fill the void created by the drop in trade

---

[14] See H. Patrick, 'Japan 1868–1914', in R. Cameron, ed., *Banking in the Early Stages of Industrialization* (New York: Oxford University Press, 1967), 267–8; and G. C. Allen, *A Short Economic History of Modern Japan* (London: 1962), 53, as cited in Wilkins, 'Japanese Multinational Enterprise before 1914', 215 n.

[15] Nihon keieishi kenkyujo, ed., *Tokyo kaijo no 100 nen*, 345.

[16] Mitsui & Co., *The 100-Year History of Mitsui & Co., Ltd.* (Tokyo: Mitsui & Co., 1977), 31–2.

[17] Indeed, a Bank of Japan survey of Japanese business abroad reports that total foreign investments of Japanese companies stood at roughly $197 million in 1914. Of that amount, China accounted for roughly $152.7 million, followed by $24.6 million in the USA and Hawaii, and $19.7 million in the rest of the world. Apparently due to the small amounts involved, neither individual European countries nor even the European region as a whole are mentioned by name in this official survey. Bank of Japan data, as reported in Wilkins, 'Japanese Multinational Enterprise before 1914', 209.

[18] Exceptions include the impacts of Japanese FDI on the pre-World War II French silk industry and on the turn-of-the-century London money markets. See below.

[19] Mitsui & Co., *The 100-Year History of Mitsui & Co., Ltd.*, 81–2.

with Europe, and on the USA, which became an increasingly important alternative Western trading partner.[20]

Well before the end of World War I, however, trade with Europe once again increased, and Japanese trading firms and others responded to this renewed activity by expanding their investments in Europe.[21] Indeed, compared with earlier years, evidence suggests that a far greater number of Japanese trading companies chose to set up offices in Europe during this period. By the mid-1920s, for example, leading traders such as Nihon Menka, Mitsubishi Shoji, Suzuki Shoten, Iwai Shoten, Okura Shoji, Takashimaya Iida, and Ataka Shokai in addition to Mitsui & Co. had established branch offices in London alone.[22] Before World War II they were joined in London by Naniwa Boeki Shokai and Showa Menka.[23] Some of these same firms also operated offices elsewhere in Europe during this period, such as Mitsui & Co.'s French and German subsidiaries, and Mitsubishi Shoji's branches or offices in Berlin, Lyons, Marseilles, Paris, and Rome.[24]

Not only did the number of Japanese trading firms expand significantly in inter-war Europe, but they also took on an increasing range of functions. Initially, such firms principally engaged in the bilateral import and export of a relatively small number of products such as machinery, textiles,

[20] See e.g. Wilkins, 'Japanese Multinationals in the United States: Continuity and Change, 1879–1990', 588–99; and N. Kawabe, 'Overseas Operations, 1868–1945', 79–80.

[21] Y. Ando, *Kindai nihon keizai shi yoran* [An Overview of Modern Japanese Economic History] (Tokyo: Tokyo University Press, 1975), 23.

[22] H. Yamazaki , 'General Trading Companies in Japan', 34, 57; and Archives, Public Record Office [hereinafter, PRO], Board of Trade [hereinafter, BT] 271/430. These firms, which included specialists in the textile trade together with generalists dealing in a wider range of commodities, all ranked among the top twenty Japanese trading companies in terms of paid-up capital during the mid-1920s. For a more detailed description of some of the chief activities of these companies, see H. Yamazaki, 'General Trading Companies in Japan', 24–31.   [23] Archives, PRO, BT 271/430.

[24] Y. Mishima, 'Sekitan kaisha kara sogo shosha e: Mitsubishi Shoji' [From Coal Company to General Trading Company: Mitsubishi Corporation], in M. Miyamoto *et al.*, eds., *Sogo shosha no keiei shi* [A Business History of General Trading Companies] (Tokyo: Toyo keizai shinposha, 1976), 132; H. Yamazaki, 'General Trading Companies in Japan', 33; Mitsubishi Shoji (Mitsubishi Corporation), *Mitsubishi Shoji: sono ayumi* [Mitsubishi Corporation: Its Development] (Tokyo: Mitsubishi Shoji, n.d.), 94; N. Kawabe, 'Senzen ni okeru sogo shosha no zaibei shiten katsudo', 33; Y. Nagasawa, 'The Overseas Branches of Mitsubishi Limited during the First World War: With Particular Reference to the London Branch', *Japanese Yearbook on Business History*, 6 (1989), 132–3. Nagasawa reports that Mitsubishi Goshi (Mitsubishi Ltd.) established between 1915 and 1919 the trading operations throughout Europe later (1921) taken over by Mitsubishi Shoji (Mitsubishi Trading Co.). Ibid. 133, 139.

According to French records, Mitsubishi's Paris office operated continuously until 1945. Archives Économiques et Financières, Ministère de L'Industrie, Cote 79, 0720/185, Compte rendu no. 204 of the Comité des Investissements Étrangers. In the inter-war period, according to A. Kudo, Mitsubishi Shoji apparently became the dominant Japanese trading firm in Germany, whereas Mitsui & Co. was key in the UK.

A. Kudo reports that Okura Shoji also maintained an office in Germany during the years preceding World War II. See A. Kudo, *Nichidoku kigyo kankeishi* [A History of Japanese-German Industrial Relations] (Tokyo: Yuhikaku, 1992), 30, 32.

and raw silk, and in the transfer to Japan of various European technologies. In the inter-war period, however, these companies expanded the range of traded products to include coal, metal, produce, oils and fats, marine products, chemicals, and other goods.[25] Moreover, an ever larger number of these firms engaged in third-country trade, such as Mitsui & Co.'s active trade in Indian jute, which the firm purchased from its Calcutta branch and sold to its London office.[26] And finally, the European operations of Japanese trading firms played increasingly important roles as sources of market intelligence in the UK, France, Germany, and elsewhere. Often, these European-based subsidiaries became the eyes and ears not only of Japanese business, but of the Japanese government as well.[27]

Other Japanese service organizations also expanded their European presence during the decades preceding World War II. The Mitsubishi Bank and, apparently, the Mitsui Bank as well set up London branches in the inter-war era, for example, although the Sumitomo Bank lived up to its reputation—'The Yokohama Specie Bank aside, the Sumitomo Bank was the earliest [Japanese] bank to develop overseas,' according to common wisdom—by establishing its own London branch in 1918, which pre-dated these Mitsubishi and Mitsui operations.[28] The Yokohama Specie Bank, for its part, opened branches in Paris and Berlin (both in 1931) in addition to previously established offices in London and Hamburg.[29] And numerous Japanese shipping companies apparently set up agencies in Europe to support the expansion of their services to that region in the inter-war period.[30]

In the insurance industry, at least ten Japanese companies operated

[25] See e.g. N. Kawabe, 'Overseas Operations, 1868–1945', 84; Y. Nagasawa, 'The Overseas Branches of Mitsubishi Limited during the First World War', 126–8, 132.

[26] Mitsui & Co., *The 100-Year History of Mitsui & Co., Ltd.*, 91. On Mitsubishi Shoji's third-country trade, see Y. Nagasawa, 'The Overseas Branches of Mitsubishi Limited during the First World War', 127–8, 132.

[27] See e.g. Mitsui & Co., *The 100-Year History of Mitsui & Co., Ltd.*, 113; and Mark Mason, 'United States Direct Investment in Japan: Studies in Government Policy and Corporate Strategy' (Ph.D. diss., Harvard University, 1988), ch. 4.

[28] M. Fujii *et al.*, eds., *Nihon takokuseki kigyo no shiteki tenkai*, 153; Bank of England Archive OV 16/31. Mitsubishi Goshi operated a foreign exchange business out of its London office from 1916. This business was taken over by Mitsubishi Bank when the latter opened its London branch for business in 1920. Y. Nagasawa, 'The Overseas Branches of Mitsubishi Limited during the First World War', 123, 137–8.

[29] S. Hijikata, *Yokohama shokin ginko*, 229. The YSB also operated an office in Lyons, but closed this office the same year it established the Paris and Berlin offices. N. Tamaki, 'The Yokohama Specie Bank', 196–7, 212. In addition, the Bank of Chosen operated a London branch by 1931. Comments of Mira Wilkins.

[30] On those companies see e.g. K. Nakagawa, 'Ryotaisenkan no nihon kaiungyo' [The Japanese Shipping Industry in the Inter-war Period], in K. Nakagawa, ed., *Ryotaisenkan no nihon kaiji sangyo* [The Inter-War Japanese Maritime Industry] (Tokyo: Chuo daigaku shuppanbu, 1985), ch. 1. Also, see William Wray, 'NYK and the Commercial Diplomacy of the Far Eastern Freight Conference, 1896–1956', in T. Yui and K. Nakagawa, eds., *Business History of Shipping: Strategy and Structure* (Tokyo: University of Tokyo Press, 1985), 279–305.

offices in pre-war Britain alone. In addition to Tokio Marine, these offices represented, among others, the Mitsubishi, Sumitomo, and Taisho interests.[31] Some of these London-based operations, such as the Taisho Marine and Fire Insurance Company, developed rather extensive business relationships with numerous British reinsurance firms during this period.[32]

Despite these examples of increasing Japanese direct investment in inter-war Europe, however, available evidence suggests that the amounts of such investment were quite small throughout the period. The few official Japanese statistics on foreign investment before World War II, for example, do not even mention the existence of Japanese FDI in Europe. Rather, these and other limited data emphasize the considerable buildup of Japanese FDI in Asia primarily, and in the South Pacific, Hawaii, and North America secondarily.[33]

1.3. War- and Occupation-Induced Disruption (1941–1951)

The decade of war and occupation from 1941 generally froze and then erased the pre-war investments of Japanese companies in Europe. Like the US government, for example, many European states froze Japanese assets in their territories before Pearl Harbor. Many of Japan's European investments remained frozen or were transferred to native control in the Allied nations during the War, and the operations of Japanese firms virtually ceased to function in most of the other countries of Europe as well.[34] In Great Britain, the authorities ordered the freezing of Japanese assets on 26 July 1941, which led Japan to freeze British assets in its territory two days later.[35] The British government designated Japanese firms 'enemy' concerns on 8 December 1941, and shifted control of their assets to the official Custodian of Alien Property. In many cases—such as those of Mitsui & Co., Tokio Marine, NYK, and the YSB—the Board of Trade, under the

---

[31] *Tokio Kaijo no 100 nen*, 350–1; Archives, PRO, BT 271/488. The other Japanese insurance companies were Imperial, Kyodo, Nippon, Osaka, Tomei, and Yokohama.

[32] For details, see Archives, PRO, BT 271/637.

[33] See e.g. I. Yamazawa and Y. Yamamoto, *Boeki to kokusai shushi* [Foreign Trade and Balance of Payments: Estimates of Long-Term Economic Statistics of Japan Since 1868] (Tokyo, 1979), as cited in K. Yasumuro, 'The Contribution of Sogo Shosha to the Multinationalization of Japanese Industrial Enterprises in Historical Perspective', in A. Okochi *et al.*, eds., *Overseas Business Activities*, 84; and Harold Moulton, *Japan: An Economic and Financial Appraisal* (Washington, DC: Brookings Institution, 1931), 282–6. Indeed, in his extensive survey of foreign multinationals in British manufacturing and utilities before 1945, Geoffrey Jones lists a total of more than 120 such firms from 11 countries—but found that not even one came from Japan. See G. Jones, 'Foreign Multinationals and British Industry before 1945', in *Economic History*, 2nd ser. 41/3 (1988), 429–53.

[34] N. Kawabe, 'Overseas Operations, 1868–1945', 92; *New York Times*, various issues.

[35] Bank of England Archive OV16/117. Although located British records do not provide estimates of the total value of Japanese assets in the UK frozen by the British authorities in 1941, estimates of the value of all Japanese assets in the UK in 1952 (see below) and other related evidence suggests that the value of these frozen assets was not large.

authority of the Trading with the Enemy Act of 1939, then appointed British nationals to act as 'controllers' of individual 'enemy' companies to oversee taxation and other matters.[36]

The German case constituted the one important exception to Europe's treatment of Japanese investment during World War II. In fact, rather than impound or appropriate Japan's direct investments in its territories, Axis partner Germany actively *encouraged* the growth of Japanese investment there. This policy of encouragement was formally adopted when the German and Japanese governments signed a bilateral economic treaty on 20 January 1943. 'Japan and Germany shall devote their total strength to promote economic interchange in every field between their respective countries,' read the First Article of the Agreement Between Japan and Germany Concerning Economic Cooperation. 'Each nation shall assist the other in procuring goods and establishing facilities in its domain, and the two nations shall furthermore engage in close and intimate technical cooperation.'[37] Despite this official policy, Japanese investments in Germany apparently remained quite small throughout the war years.[38]

Virtually from the start of the Allied Occupation of Japan (1945–52), the Supreme Commander for the Allied Powers (SCAP) prohibited almost all transactions involving Japanese investment abroad by persons located in Japan.[39] Indeed, in September 1945 SCAP forbade the transfer of Japan's external assets belonging not only to Japanese corporations and financial institutions, but also to government agencies and private individuals. The

---

[36] Archives, PRO, BT 271/385, BT 271/637, and BT 271/654.

[37] Article 1, Agreement Between Japan and Germany Concerning Economic Cooperation, as cited in Mason, 'United States Direct Investment in Japan', 232. According to an official analysis of the Allied Occupation of Japan's Supreme Commander for the Allied Powers, by this treaty '[b]oth governments [would] consider favorably applications for capital investments in industrial enterprises of the treaty partner's country'.

[38] At least two factors help explain the apparent paucity of Japanese direct investment in wartime Germany. First, Japan took a far greater interest in investing in China, Manchuria, and elsewhere in Asia during the war years. And second, significant economic tensions between Germany and Japan also served to limit bilateral investment flows. (Similar to Japanese FDI trends in wartime Germany, German FDI apparently did not grow significantly in wartime Japan.) On (often cool) German–Japanese economic relations from the late 1930s, see esp. A. Kudo, 'The Tripartite Pact and Synthetic Oil: The Ideal and Reality of Economic and Technical Cooperation between Japan and Germany', in *Occasional Papers in Social and Economic History*, Institute of Social Science, University of Tokyo, 4 (Mar. 1992) and A. Kudo, *Nichidoku kigyo kankeishi*; Mason, 'United States Direct Investment in Japan', 232–3; and Erich Pauer, 'Lots of Friendship, but Few Orders: German–Japanese Economic Relations in the Late 1930's', in Ian Nish, ed., *German–Japanese Relations in the 1930's* (London: London School of Economics and Political Science, 1986), 10–37. Japan and Italy presumably entered into a similar co-operative economic arrangement in wartime, although the relative importance of such an accord surely would have been far less significant than the German–Japanese tie.

[39] Certain minor exceptions were permitted. See General Headquarters, Supreme Commander for the Allied Powers, 'Japanese Property Administration', in *History of the Nonmilitary Activities of the Occupation of Japan*, ii. *Reparations and Property Administration*, Part C (unpublished), 65. (This report is available on microfilm at Yale University.)

Allied authorities then systematically inventoried these external assets.[40] In Europe and elsewhere, Japan's foreign investments remained blocked until the close of the Occupation. Investments made before or during World War II in general were controlled at the conclusion of hostilities by the government of the territory in which they were located, although some of these investments were liquidated (and others, principally those located in Manchuria, were literally carried off by the Soviet military).[41]

At the signing of the Peace Treaty in September 1951, signatory countries adopted a definitive policy towards the disposition of Japan's pre-war and wartime foreign investments and other external assets located within their territories. Under the terms of the Treaty, those nations that had been at war with Japan were allowed to confiscate and liquidate virtually all Japanese assets in their respective jurisdictions.[42] According to an internal British government report at the end of the Occupation, the British authorities chose to use proceeds from the sale of Japanese assets in their territory 'for the benefit of former prisoners-of-war and internees who suffered in Japanese hands'.[43] Yet, according to another internal government memorandum, many intended beneficiaries became deeply dissatisfied with the process, for 'Japanese assets [were] so small in relation to the claims against Japan'.[44] Japan's assets located in former Axis and officially neutral countries apparently were transferred by Japan to the International Committee of the Red Cross, which later sold them off. Proceeds from the sale of these assets, as in the British case, later were used to compensate certain former Allied prisoners of war.[45] In short, soon after the turn of the decade Japan had lost almost its entire range of foreign direct investments located in Europe (and elsewhere).

Under the circumstances of war and occupation, it is hardly surprising that Japanese direct investment in 1940s Europe remained extremely limited before its virtual elimination at the turn of the new decade. Indeed, evidence suggests that the vast majority of Japanese FDI during this period was located in nearby Asian territories, which, in the early part of the decade, generally were controlled by the Japanese government. Based on its own investigations, for example, SCAP calculated that no less than 93.69 per cent of all Japanese external assets were located in China, Manchuria, Korea, and Formosa (Taiwan) in August 1945; just 6.31 per cent reportedly were situated elsewhere at that time.[46] And the British government estimated that total Japanese assets of all types in Great Britain

---

[40] Ibid. 64 ff. On the general results of this inventory, see ibid. 65–75.
[41] Ibid. 74.   [42] For the limited exceptions, see ibid. 74–5.
[43] Archives, PRO, BT 271/385.   [44] Ibid.
[45] General Headquarters, Supreme Commander for the Allied Powers, 'Japanese Property Administration', 75.
[46] Ibid. 71. These estimates of external assets do not include Japanese military and naval *materiel* located abroad.

as of 1952 stood at less than £1 million.[47] A vast amount of anecdotal evidence supports these overall SCAP and British government figures.[48]

1.4. Post-war Resumption (1951–1971)

The Japanese government established a new era in the history of Japan's foreign direct investment in Europe towards the close of the Allied Occupation. Less than one year after the limited reopening of Japan to FDI from abroad, in 1951 the local authorities—increasingly independent of SCAP regulation—revoked the blanket ban on outward investment that had been operative throughout much of the 1940s.

As they had in their treatment of inward flows, however, Japanese officials carefully regulated all overseas investments through powers contained in the 1949 Foreign Exchange and Foreign Trade Control Law (FEFTCL). Specifically, the Ministry of Finance (MOF), often in concert with other interested agencies such as the Ministry of International Trade and Industry (MITI), carried out an 'individual examination' (*kobetsu shinsa*) of every potential Japanese direct investment abroad over roughly the next two decades, and denied requisite foreign exchange to those investment proposals that did not gain their approval. The authorities undertook these examinations by calling together a liaison conference of concerned ministries to deliberate the merits of every proposed case.[49]

Official motives and standards were not publicly clarified, but the pattern of decisions suggests the authorities' underlying intent. The government apparently instituted its control policy both to conserve scarce foreign exchange reserves and to prevent 'reverse imports' of manufactured products from Japanese affiliates abroad back to the home market. (The latter eventuality, it was feared, could damage smaller, less efficient Japanese producers without access to the advantages of overseas production.[50]) Specific screening criteria, however, varied by industry, were vaguely worded, and often became subject to differing interpretations.[51] As we

---

[47] Archives, PRO, BT 271/429. By contrast, the British estimated that total Japanese assets in British territories in the Far East as of 1952 amounted to about £10 million. Ibid.

[48] See e.g. G. Numaguchi, 'Nihon no kaigai jigyo katsudo', 252–7.

[49] *Nihon Keizai Shimbun* (English edn.), 17 Nov. 1970.

[50] According to one expert, during at least part of this era MITI required that prospective Japanese direct investors sign a written pledge that they would not export back to Japan goods which they might produce in overseas factories. See Yoshino, 'The Multinational Spread of Japanese Manufacturing Investment since World War II', 370–1.

[51] On Japanese government policies and practices towards outward direct investment in this period, see Dennis Encarnation, *Rivals beyond Trade: America versus Japan in Global Competition* (Ithaca: Cornell University Press, 1992), 108; *Zaisei kinyu tokei geppo*, 452 (Dec. 1989), 3; R. Komiya, 'Japan's Foreign Direct Investment', 117–18; and K. Hamada, 'Japanese Investment Abroad', in Peter Drysdale, ed., *Direct Foreign Investment in Asia and the Pacific* (Sydney: ANU, 1972), 188–9. Hamada suggests that concerns over loss of autonomous control over domestic monetary policy also may have figured among the government's motivations.

shall see, in practice the authorities approved limited numbers of direct investments in Europe, generally by those domestic firms best positioned to enhance Japanese exports to European markets.

The verdict of the government's deliberations, however, affected more than an applicant's access to foreign exchange. In addition, those investments that did receive government approval often benefited from official support such as low-interest loans and special tax advantages. In short, through positive as well as negative measures the Japanese government played a critical role in the post-war development of Japan's FDI in Europe.[52]

Responding to these new—though still severely circumscribed—investment freedoms, numerous Japanese firms managed to gain the government's consent to directly invest in Europe during this era. Mimicking the pre-war investment pattern, many of the early post-war entrants were trading companies that set up wholly owned subsidiaries. Mitsui & Co., the Mitsubishi Corporation (successor to Mitsubishi Shoji), Marubeni, C. Itoh, and other general trading firms established or re-established offices in Europe throughout the 1950s. The very first such office set up by a major trading firm was the Mitsui & Co. branch in London (1953), but official Japanese data suggest that the vast majority of such trading offices in the 1950s were located in West Germany rather than the UK (see Table 1.2). The Mitsubishi Corporation apparently became the first important Japanese direct investor in post-war France when, in 1960, it established a limited corporation in Paris to import and export metals and other goods. Mitsubishi invested 94 per cent of the capital, and French interests put up the remainder.[53]

In addition, numerous trading firms established joint ventures in Europe, principally during the 1960s, often investing with Japanese manufacturers to market the latter's products in European countries. By the end of that decade, for example, Marubeni had established joint ventures with Japanese firms to market chemicals in West Germany (Sekisui Chemical GmbH; set up in 1962) as well as electrical goods in the UK (Sanyo Marubeni [UK] Ltd.; 1969). In addition, Marubeni joint-ventured with European capital to create local companies such as Promotors de Inversiones, SA in Spain (1964).[54] Mitsui & Co. also went beyond mere

[52] Encarnation, *Rivals beyond Trade*, 110; and R. Komiya, 'Japan's Foreign Direct Investment', 118.

[53] Archives Économiques et Financières, Ministère de l'Industrie, Cote 79, 0720/185, Compte rendu no. 204 of the Comité des Investissements Étrangers. It is possible that certain Japanese banks and insurance companies directly invested in post-war France prior to the entry of the Mitsubishi Corporation, yet such investments apparently were not recorded in the Bank of Japan data as cited in Table 1.2.

[54] Keizai hatten kyokai (Economic Development Association), *Fuyo Guruupu kigyo no kaigai jigyo* [The Overseas Enterprises of the Fuyo Group] (Tokyo: Keizai hatten kyokai, 1972), 112–13 ff.

TABLE 1.2. *Japanese FDI in Europe, by firm and host country, 1951–1961 (notifications basis)*

Japanese Parent	European Affiliate	Date	Industry	Location
Belgium				
Marubeni Iida	Société Belge Marubeni-Iida SPRL	1957	Trading	Brussels
England				
Mitsui & Co.	Mitsui & Co., Ltd., London	1953	Trading	London
Kawasaki Steamship	Kawasaki SS Co. (London)	1956	Trading	London
Takaraisu Sales	Belmont Chairs (London), Ltd.	1959	Trading	London
France				
Mitsubishi Corp.	Mitsubishi France	1960	Trading	Paris
Germany				
Mitsubishi Corp.	Deutsche Mitsubishi	1955	Trading	Düsseldorf
Mitsui & Co.	Deutsche Bussan	1955	Trading	Hamburg
Marubeni Iida	Marubeni Iida, GmbH	1955	Trading	Hamburg
Toyo Menka	Toyo Menka, GmbH	1956	Trading	Hamburg
Gosho	Gosho, GmbH	1956	Trading	Hamburg
C. Itoh & Co.	C. Itoh & Co.	1956	Trading	Hamburg
Nissho	Deutsche Nissho Import & Export, GmbH	1956	Trading	Hamburg
Okura Trading	Okura Trading Co., GmbH	1957	Trading	Düsseldorf
Kanematsu	F. Kanematsu & Co., GmbH	1957	Trading	Hamburg
Atake Industries	Deutsche Atake, GmbH	1957	Trading	Hamburg
Sumitomo Trading	Deutsche Sumitomo Export & Import, GmbH	1958	Trading	Düsseldorf
Far East Trading	Far East Mercantile, GmbH	1958	Trading	Frankfurt
Nichimen Industries	Deutsche Nichimen, GmbH	1959	Trading	Hamburg
Kinoshita Trading	Deutsche Kinoshita, GmbH	1959	Trading	Düsseldorf
Osaka Trade Association	UTO Import & Export, GmbH	1960	Trading	Hamburg
Momoi Textile	Deutsche Momoi Co., GmbH	1960	Trading	Hamburg
Iwai Industries	Iwai & Co., GmbH	1961	Trading	Düsseldorf
Honda Giken Industries	European Honda Motor, GmbH	1961	Trading	Hamburg

TABLE 1.2 *(cont.)*.

Japanese Parent	European Affiliate	Date	Industry	Location
Ireland				
Brother International	Brother International Corp. (Europe)	1958	Trading	Dublin
Sony	Sony Ltd. (Shannon)	1959	Machinery	Shannon
Toyo Menka Feather Working Machine	Tomen (Ireland) Ltd.	1960	Machinery	Dublin
Portugal				
Mitsui & Co. Shinetsu Chemical Industries	Uniao Electrica Portuguesa SARL	1960	Other	Porto
Switzerland				
Chugai Pharmaceutical	Yoroppa Chugai	1958	Trading	Zurich
Taiyo Fishery Industries	Taiyo & Suisse & ARL	1960	Trading	Geneva
Sony	Sony Overseas SA	1960	Trading	Zug

Note: This list does not include banks and insurance companies.
Source: Bank of Japan.

investments in its own trading branches to participate in a wide range of joint ventures throughout Europe in the 1960s.

A limited number of Japanese banks also gained MOF approval and chose to invest. Fuji Bank and Teikoku Bank, in addition to the Bank of Tokyo, managed to establish representative offices in London by September 1952. A number of other Japanese banks also sought permission to set up offices in London at the end of the Occupation, but MOF initially permitted them to start business only in New York.[55] In 1956, however, the Ministry modified its position to allow the Mitsubishi Bank and the Sumitomo Bank to resume business in London.[56]

Yet trading companies and banks were not the only Japanese firms that directly invested in post-war Europe. In addition, from about 1960 an

[55] Bank of England Archive, OV 16/83; R. Komiya, 'Japan's Foreign Direct Investment', 248. The European investments of these banks had been preceded by that of the Bank of Japan, however, which managed to open for business in London in late 1951. 'A very important position is occupied by England and other countries of the Sterling Area in Japan's progress toward realization of a self-supporting economy,' Bank of Japan Governor Hisato Ichimada had written to the British Government in June 1951, explaining the reasons for his institution's interest in returning to London. 'It has been our earnest desire for some time to station a representative of this bank, a central bank, in London,' he went on, 'which is the nucleus of these areas and the economic and financial centre of Europe.' Bank of England Archive, OV 16/109.   [56] Bank of England Archive, OV 16/83.

increasing number of Japan's major manufacturers began to set up local operations on their own, principally to distribute and sell their wares directly to European consumers. Electronics producers were some of the first to do so. Among this group Sony apparently was the pioneer, for it managed to establish not only the first post-war direct investment in Europe by a Japanese electronics maker, but also the first post-war direct *manufacturing* investment in Europe by *any* major Japanese corporation. This Sony accomplished when in 1959 it set up a small plant in Shannon, Ireland to produce transistor radios.[57] To support the company's European efforts and take advantage of local tax laws, Sony then established a regional office in Zug, Switzerland (Sony Overseas, SA) the following year.[58] Sony steadily built up its European presence, gradually shifting from local sales agents to wholly Sony-owned marketing operations (in addition to limited production facilities) during the 1960s.[59] Matsushita soon followed Sony's lead, creating sales subsidiaries for radios, televisions, tape recorders, and other products in West Germany (1962) and France (1968).[60]

Japanese car manufacturers also began their move into Europe during the 1960s. Toyota, for example, established marketing organizations in some of its principal European markets starting early in the decade. The first such organization Toyota set up in Denmark (1963), followed by the creation of similar operations in the Netherlands (1964), Finland (1964), the UK (1965), Belgium (1966), Switzerland (1966), Portugal (1968), and Sweden (1968).[61] Nissan created similar marketing operations in Europe during these same years, followed by the company's first European assembly arrangement—the establishment of Entreposto Comercial Veiculos e Macquinas, SA, a Nissan-created and wholly owned importer of knocked-down commercial vehicle kits, with assembly entrusted to the locally owned Entreposto Comercial de Automoveis—in Portugal in July 1968.[62] Toyota set up its own importing and assembly operation to produce commercial vehicles in Portugal—in Toyota's case, in concert with the local firm Salvador Caetano IMVT, SA—just three months later.[63] Both of these Japanese motor-vehicle producers had been preceded in Europe, however, by Honda, which in 1961 had created a European regional sales office in

[57] A. Morita, *Made in Japan* (New York: Signet, 1988), 329. Also, see Table 1.2.

[58] Ibid. 137–8. Also, see Table 1.2.   [59] Ibid. 137–41, 324–30.

[60] Y. Kinugasa, 'Japanese Firms' Foreign Direct Investment in the U.S.: The Case of Matsushita and Others', in A. Okochi *et al.*, eds., *Overseas Business Activities* (Tokyo: Tokyo University Press, 1984), 30–1.

[61] Toyota Motor Corporation, 'EC Market Unification and Toyota Activity in Europe' (unpublished report), 5.

[62] Keizai hatten kyokai (Economic Development Association), *Fuyo Guruupu kigyo no kaigai jigyo* [The Overseas Enterprises of the Fuyo Group] (Tokyo: Keizai hatten kyokai, 1972), 100–1; and Nissan Motor Co., Ltd., 'Facts File 1991', 28–29.

[63] Toyota Motor Company, 'EC Market Unification', 5.

Hamburg, West Germany (European Honda Motor GmbH) followed by a British sales branch in London in 1962, both principally to support its burgeoning motorcycle sales.[64]

Despite these and other examples of Japanese FDI in post-war Europe, however, the quantity and impact of such investment remained quite limited. According to official Japanese statistics, for example, Japan's total FDI outflows to Europe from 1951 to 1970 amounted to just $636 million.[65] As in earlier periods, these modest amounts of investment remained concentrated primarily in larger European markets such as those of the UK, West Germany, and France. Yet such investments seem to have created little impact on any of these European economies.

1.5. Growth and Diversification (1971–Present)

Japanese direct investment in Europe entered a new era in the early 1970s, and once again the Japanese government played a critical role in fostering the transition. Roughly paralleling its progressive liberalization of controls over *inward* direct investment,[66] from 1969 the government inaugurated a five-stage process to deregulate controls over *outward* direct investment as well (see Table 1.3). Although the final stage of this process was not implemented until 1978, the government undertook its critical third-stage liberalization in mid-1971. From that time onward, with few exceptions the Ministry of Finance automatically validated proposals by Japanese companies to establish greenfield investments abroad without financial limit. This key change in government policy—essentially motivated not only by rising balance-of-payments surpluses but also by increasing pressures from Japanese business—created important new opportunities for domestic firms to invest abroad that were without precedent in the post-war period.[67]

Japanese FDI in Europe increased significantly from the early 1970s in response to these changes in government policies as well as to numerous economic and other political developments. Shortly after the turn of the decade, for example, the appreciation of the yen, a rise in real domestic

[64] Z. Katagata, *Tatakau nihon kigyo* [Fighting Japanese Enterprise] (Tokyo: Nihon Keizai shinbunsha, 1967), 51 ff.; and Jiji shinsho (Jiji Press), *Nihon kigyo no kaigai shinshutsu: obei hen* [The Overseas Advance of Japanese Enterprise: Europe and America) (Tokyo: Jiji Press, 1969), 172. Also, see Table 1.2.

[65] MOF data, as cited in M. Yoshitomi *et al.*, *Japanese Direct Investment in Europe*, 9.

[66] For a description of the inward capital liberalization process, see M. Mason, *American Multinationals and Japan: The Political Economy of Japanese Capital Controls, 1899–1980* (Cambridge: Harvard University Press, 1992), 5; and D. Encarnation and M. Mason, 'Neither MITI nor America: The Political Economy of Capital Liberalization in Japan', in *International Organization*, 44/1 (Winter 1990), 42–51.

[67] R. Komiya, 'Japan's Foreign Direct Investment', 118–20; L. B. Krause and S. Sekiguchi, 'Japan and the World Economy', in H. Patrick and H. Rosovsky, eds., *Asia's New Giant: How the Japanese Economy Works* (Washington, DC: Brookings Institution, 1976), 447.

TABLE 1.3. *The liberalization of Japanese FDI, 1969–1978*

Stage	Date	Chief Measures
First Liberalization	1 Oct. 1969	Automatic validation for [greenfield] FDI: up to $200,000.
		[Conditions for] automatic validation for investments which augment the capital of foreign juridical persons: Japanese capital must constitute 25% or more of the total, and there must be at least one full-time manager sent from Japan.
		Exceptions to the above (designated industries and so forth): (1) the fisheries industry as reflected in international fisheries treaties; (2) the fisheries industry as designated in the Fisheries Industry Law or as approved by the Minister of Agriculture and Forestry; (3) the pearl farming industry; (4) the banking and securities industries; (5) cases which may cause problems in terms of international co-operation or foreign affairs; (6) cases which may create a very negative effect on the Japanese economy; (7) direct investments by banks or securities companies.
Second Liberalization	1 Sept. 1970	Automatic validation for [greenfield] FDI: up to $1 million.
		[Conditions for] automatic validation for investments which augment the capital of foreign juridical persons: (1) Japanese capital must constitute 50% or more of the total capital of the foreign juridical person; (2) the Japanese capital share is 25% or more but less than 50% and there is more than one full-time manager sent from Japan.
		Exceptions to the above (designated industries and so forth): [(1), (3) – (7): same as above]; (2) the fisheries industry as designated in the Fisheries Industry Law.
Third Liberalization	1 July 1971	Automatic validation for [greenfield] FDI: No financial limit.
		[Conditions for] automatic validation for investments which augment the

TABLE 1.3 *(cont.)*.

Stage	Date	Chief Measures
		capital of foreign juridical persons: (1) the Japanese capital share must constitute 25% or more of the total capital; (2) the Japanese capital share is 10% or more but less than 25%, and it is a foreign juridical person which is characterized by one of the following: (*a*) Japanese managers; (*b*) manufacturing technology assistance; (*c*) purchases basic materials; (*d*) purchases manufactured products and so forth; (*e*) capital subsidies; (*f*) tie-up through a contract for a general agent's office.
		Exceptions to the above (designated industries and so forth): [same as above].
Fourth Liberalization	8 June 1972	Automatic validation for [greenfield] FDI: no financial limit.
		[Conditions for] automatic validation for investments which augment the capital of foreign juridical persons: (1) [same as above]; (2) if the Japanese capital share is below 25% and it is a foreign juridical person which is characterized by one of the following: [(a) – (f): same as above]; (g) in addition, there is a permanent economic relationship with the industry into which the capital will be invested.
		Exceptions to the above (designated industries and so forth): [same as above].
Fifth Liberalization	1 April 1978	Automatic validation for [greenfield] FDI: no financial limit.
		[Conditions for] automatic validation for investments which augment the capital of foreign juridical persons: (1) [same as above]; (2) [same as above]. Note: acquisition of foreign securities is now placed under a notification system with the Bank of Japan. (However, the below-enumerated items are subject to a system of compulsory validation.)
		Exceptions to the above (designated industries and so forth): [(1) – (4), (7): same as above]; (5) the manufacture of

TABLE 1.3 *(cont.)*.

Stage	Date	Chief Measures
		textile products; (6) manufacturing industries engaged in the production of weapons and narcotics, etc.; (8) investment in South Africa or Namibia.

Note: All dollar amounts in US dollars.
Source: *Zaisei kinyu tokei geppo*, 452 (Dec. 1989), 3–6.

wages, and the prospect of greater competition at home as controls over inward direct investment eased all created powerful motivations for Japanese firms to invest directly abroad.[68] Indeed, the year 1972 is often referred to metaphorically as the 'gannen' of Japanese foreign direct investment (the term 'gannen' signifies the first year of a new imperial reign), for beginning that year Japanese FDI in Europe (but especially in North America and Asia) grew considerably as compared to earlier periods. And from the mid-1980s, still larger trade surpluses, major new increases in the value of the yen, and growing fears of European protectionism as the 1992 EC unification programme progressed, all combined to produce yet greater pressures for Japanese business to invest far greater sums in the Community. These and other pressures led to truly dramatic surges in Japanese FDI in Europe from about 1986.[69] (See Fig. 1.5 for trends in Japanese FDI in major recipient regions from 1971 to 1991.)

As in earlier periods, service-sector enterprises accounted for a substantial part of the increase in Japanese FDI to Europe during these years, although the relative importance of at least one major group of such Japanese enterprises changed significantly. Financial services firms established or expanded their direct investments in Europe from the 1970s. Japanese banks, for example, began to follow the growing numbers of their customers who invested in Europe, and by the late 1970s many such banks operated subsidiaries, branches, and offices in London, Frankfurt, Düsseldorf, Brussels, and elsewhere in the region.[70] Major investors in Europe by that time included the Bank of Tokyo, and the Dai Ichi Kangyo, Fuji, Sumitomo, Mitsubishi, Sanwa, and Mitsui Banks.[71] The large Japanese securities firms

---

[68] R. Komiya, 'Japan's Foreign Direct Investment', 120. Rising trade protectionism in the key American market and elsewhere also motivated Japanese business to invest more abroad during this period. See Encarnation, *Rivals beyond Trade*, 110.

[69] Japan continued to directly invest large sums into Europe during the early 1990s, although neither during the 1990 nor 1991 Japanese fiscal years did annual outflows reach levels registered in the peak (fiscal) year of 1989. (See Fig. 1.5.)

[70] F. N. Burton and F. H. Saelens, 'The European Investments of Japanese Financial Institutions', in *Columbia Journal of World Business* (Winter 1986), 32; and M. Fujii *et al.*, eds., *Nihon takokuseki kigyo no shiteki tenkai*, ii. 92–3.

[71] M. Fujii *et al.*, eds., *Nihon takokuseki kigyo no shiteki tenkai*, ii. 94–5.

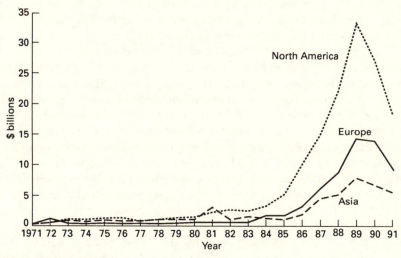

Source: Bank of Japan.

FIG. 1.5. Japanese FDI flows to Asia, Europe, and North America, 1971–91

also established operations in Europe during these years. The 'Big Four' securities houses all set up offices in London at the start of this period— Nikko and Yamaichi in 1971, followed by Nomura and Daiwa in 1972— together with most other major firms in the securities industry by the end of the decade. Moreover, all or most of the 'Big Four' also created establishments in Paris, Frankfurt, and Amsterdam during these same years.[72] Numerous Japanese insurance companies similarly inaugurated or increased their European investments.

The Japanese government's 1980 revision of the Foreign Exchange and Foreign Trade Control Law encouraged many of these same financial services firms further to augment their presence in Europe.[73] Largely exempted from the capital liberalization process begun in 1969, Japan's financial services industry now invested in the UK and on the Continent still more aggressively. Major Japanese bank investments following the 1980 liberalization included Fuji Bank's 1982 buy-out of its erstwhile equal partnership joint venture with Kleinwort Benson in Fuji International Finance Bank (London), the Long-Term Credit Bank of Japan's 1983 acquisition which led to full ownership in the Nippon European Bank (Brussels), and Sumitomo Bank's 1984 majority acquisition of Banca del Gottardo (Zurich).[74] These and other such investments were followed in part by bank acquisitions in Southern Europe later in the decade, apparently

---

[72] Ibid. 104–5.   [73] R. Komiya, 'Japan's Foreign Direct Investment', 126.
[74] Burton and Saelens, 'The European Investments of Japanese Financial Institutions', 30.

to diffuse the Japanese presence to a wider number of European countries.[75] Japan's securities houses and insurance companies also increased their European direct investments in the 1980s.[76]

There are indications that the historically important investment roles of the general trading companies (*sogo shosha*) may have undergone a relative decline during this era. Following a brief burst of direct investment activity by the *sogo shosha* in Europe following the Japanese government's liberalization of outward FDI in the early 1970s, the number of their new investments declined dramatically thereafter. Indeed, the top nine general trading companies participated in just four new direct investments throughout Europe in 1977 and 1978, and none at all from 1979 to 1982.[77] Other data similarly suggest that, as compared with other Japanese investors, the activities of these firms in Europe became less significant. During the period 1978–81, for example, seven of the nine *sogo shosha* reported absolute *declines* in employment at their European-based trading subsidiaries. And at least one study indicates that these traders reduced their investments in sales companies and manufacturing firms in Europe during the late 1970s.[78] None the less, the *sogo shosha* continued to play important roles in Europe as facilitators of trade and other economic activities throughout the 1970s, 1980s, and beyond.[79]

Similar to the record of many financial services firms, from the early 1970s Japanese manufacturing companies also greatly increased their direct investments in Europe. Many such investments took the form of importing, sales, and service organizations that bypassed the traditional role of the general trading company. Matsushita, for example, continued its earlier build-up of European-based sales subsidiaries by establishing wholly owned affiliates in virtually every large and even many smaller European markets during the 1970s and early 1980s.[80] Toyota added to its earlier network of European sales affiliates by setting up marketing organizations in Austria, France, Ireland, Italy, Germany, Greece, Norway, and Spain between 1970 and 1987.[81] Numerous other Japanese manufacturers pursued similar investment strategies in Europe from the early 1970s.

---

[75] See e.g. A. Rowley, 'A Southern Spree', in *Far Eastern Economic Review* (3 Aug. 1989), 55.

[76] See e.g. Burton and Saelens, 'The European Investments of Japanese Financial Institutions', 30–2; J.-M. Dinand, 'Séduire les banquiers japonais', in *France Japon Eco*, 45 (1991), 45–8; and N. MacKinnon, 'Japanese Corporate and Financial Strategy in the Single European Market', *European Management Journal*, 8/3 (Sept. 1990), 313–20.

[77] M. Fujii *et al.*, eds., *Nihon takokuseki kigyo no shiteki tenkai*, ii. 40–1.

[78] F. N. Burton and F. H. Saelens, 'Direct Investment by Sogo-Shosha in Europe', *Journal of World Trade Law*, 17/3 (May–June 1983), 249–58.

[79] On the significance of the *sogo shosha* in bilateral trade between the EC and Japan during the 1980s see e.g. S. Thomsen and P. Nicolaides, *The Evolution of Japanese Direct Investment in Europe*, 79–80.

[80] Y. Kinugusa, 'Japanese Firms' Foreign Direct Investment in the U.S.: The Case of Matsushita and Others', 31; and Panasonic Europe (Headquarters) Ltd., 'Panasonic: Integrating With Europe' (Panasonic Europe, Ltd.: Uxbridge, Middlesex, UK, n.d.), 18–20.

[81] Toyota Motor Corporation, unpublished report, n.d.

At the same time, however, an increasing number of Japanese producers chose to establish assembly or manufacturing operations in Europe. The official Invest in Britain Bureau, for example, calculated that from 1972 through early 1991 major Japanese companies established no fewer than 158 manufacturing companies in the UK, beginning with the first recorded instance (YKK, to produce zip fasteners, in 1972), up to the last-recorded investment in its survey (Yokogawa Electric, to produce process control systems and related equipment, in 1991).[82] And in France, the functionally equivalent public agency DATAR estimated that Japanese firms had established no fewer than 144 local manufacturing concerns between 1970 and 1990, to produce goods ranging from perfume to photocopiers.[83]

Electronics and motor vehicle firms both numbered significantly among the range of Japanese manufacturing investors which entered Europe during this period. In the electronics industry, for example, virtually all of the major Japanese producers created or expanded their local manufacturing bases from the 1970s. Indeed, in this era Matsushita alone established sixteen manufacturing companies in diverse locations within Europe to produce everything from batteries (in a joint venture with Philips; Belgium; 1970), to vacuum cleaners, VCRs, and 'Hi-Fi's (Spain; 1973), to passive electronic components (in a joint venture with Siemens; headquartered in Germany; 1989).[84] Yet Matsushita was hardly alone: Hitachi, JVC, Mitsubishi Electric, NEC, Sanyo, Sharp, Sony, and Toshiba all had significant manufacturing investments in the European electronics industry by the end of the 1980s.

Japanese automobile companies also established assembly and manufacturing operations in Europe starting in the early 1970s. In 1972, for example, Toyota acquired a 27 per cent stake in Salvador Caetano, the Portuguese company to which it had already consigned assembly of vehicles imported by a wholly Toyota-owned subsidiary (see above).[85] Indeed, Hino, Honda, Isuzu, Mitsubishi Motors, Nissan, and Toyo Kogyo (now Mazda) as well as Toyota had all established assembly operations in Europe by 1977—though by that date not one had begun full-scale manufacturing in the region. These assembly operations were all located in Greece, Portugal, and Ireland, apparently to take advantage of low labour costs within the unifying European Community (see Table 1.4). This pattern contrasted with that of the American 'Big Three', which by this date had established comprehensive manufacturing plants as well as assembly operations in a number of the higher-wage European countries.[86] Yet this

[82] Invest in Britain Bureau, 'List of Japanese Manufacturing Companies in the UK', (unpublished report, n.d.).

[83] DATAR, 'Liste des unités de production japonaises en France' (unpublished report, n.d.).

[84] Panasonic Europe (Headquarters) Ltd., 'Panasonic: Integrating with Europe' (company pamphlet, n.d.), 8–11, 18–20.

[85] Toyota Motor Corporation, *Toyota: History of the First 50 Years*, 494.

[86] M. Fujii *et al.*, eds., *Nihon takokuseki kigyo no shiteki tenkai*, ii. 166.

TABLE 1.4. *Japanese and US automobile assembly and manufacturing plants in Europe by country, as of 1977*

	UK	France	Germany	Belgium	Switzerland	Holland	Denmark	Spain	Greece	Portugal	Ireland
Japanese Producers											
Nissan										A	A
Toyota									A	A	A
Toyo Kogyo									A	A	A
Mitsubishi										A	
Isuzu									A		
Honda										A	
Hino									A	A	A
American Producers											
GM	M		M	A	A		A				
Ford	M		M	A		A	A			A	A
Chrysler		M		A	A	A		M	A	A	A

Note: 'A' denotes assembly plant; 'M' denotes full manufacturing plant. Toyo Kogyo is now Mazda.

Source: Adapted from M. Fujii *et al.*, eds., *Nihon takokuseki kigyo no shiteki tenkai* [The historical development of Japanese multinational enterprise]. ii. 166.

situation changed dramatically during the 1980s, during which time Nissan (1983, Spain; 1984, UK), Honda (1985, UK), Isuzu (1987, UK), and Toyota (1989, West Germany; 1992, UK) all committed substantial resources to direct investment in European manufacturing plants.[87]

These and other investments vastly expanded Japan's FDI presence in Europe. Indeed, as compared to the relatively small amounts of such FDI in previous decades, from the 1970s the growth rate of Japanese direct investment in Europe increased dramatically. MOF data indicate that this investment grew more than sixfold between 1971 and 1980, for example, and more than tenfold between 1981 and 1990.[88] Recent trends in Japanese FDI to Europe are also striking when compared with trends to other major recipient regions. Beginning in 1984, for example, Japanese direct investment flows to Europe exceeded those to Asia on a sustained basis for the first time in history (see Fig. 1.5). And although annual Japanese FDI outflows as well as accumulated direct investments in the USA still exceed such investments in Europe, the difference between the proportion of total Japanese FDI flowing to the USA versus that going to Europe has been declining steadily in recent years.[89] In short, from numerous perspectives the last two decades have witnessed a huge and unprecedented build-up of Japanese direct investment in Europe. Among other results, this build-up has led to a new geographical pattern of distribution within Europe, and to major new impacts on Europe.

2. CONTINUITY AND CHANGE

A close look at the development of Japanese direct investment in Europe reveals at least eight striking continuities that generally characterize the first century or so of this development. However, since the early 1970s new features of this investment reveal striking contrasts with these longer-term historical patterns. In this section, we shall consider each of these longer-term continuities together with the significance of recent changes.

2.1. Investment Levels

One of the most striking features of Japanese direct investment in Europe from its beginnings in the late nineteenth century through the 1960s is its paucity. During the decades before World War II, for example, available

---

[87] Japan Automobile Manufacturers Association, various pamphlets; company brochures. The *start-up* dates of these several Japanese auto plants in Europe naturally succeeded the dates on which their parent companies *committed capital* to build these operations.

[88] MOF data, as cited in various MOF and BOJ publications, and in M. Yoshitomi *et al.*, *Japanese Direct Investment in Europe*, 9.

[89] Calculated on the basis of Japanese FDI data as reported by MOF through March 1992.

evidence suggests that the overall quantities of FDI that entered Europe were very small. These modest amounts then declined during World War II, and by the end of the Allied Occupation the systematic elimination of Japan's pre-war FDI in Europe had virtually wiped the slate clean. Nor did renewed independence usher in a period of large-scale investment in Europe, for during the 1950s and 1960s the Japanese government severely restricted FDI outflows to the region.

In contrast to the meagre amounts of Japanese FDI that entered Europe during the first century or so of its development, however, comparatively great amounts of Japanese investment have accumulated there in more recent times. The Japanese government's capital liberalization programme begun in 1969 marked a watershed in the nation's regulation of invest- ment outflows, and in succeeding years this liberalization programme together with powerful economic as well as other political forces led to substantial increases in the nation's direct investments in Europe. As a result, accumulated Japanese FDI in Europe during the 1970s and 1980s increased dramatically when compared to earlier periods.

2.2. Sectoral Composition

A pronounced bias towards direct investment in the service sector consti- tutes a second major continuity in the historical development of Japanese FDI in Europe. From Japan's very first investments in the 1870s down to the present, firms in such industries as trade, banking, and insurance have been among the most active Japanese direct investors in the region. The relative importance of specific industries within the service sector has varied over time, but the general predominance of services has not.

Although the sectoral breakdown of more recent Japanese direct invest- ments in Europe still clearly favours the service sector, an increasing range of companies in other sectors has also invested there in recent years. Indeed, even though a majority of accumulated Japanese FDI in Europe remained in services in 1991, direct investments in the machinery, chem- ical, and other manufacturing industries, together with FDI in other non- service fields such as property and mining, accounted for a growing proportion of all Japanese direct investment in the region. (See Fig. 1.6 for a breakdown by sector of Japan's FDI in Europe as of 1991.)

2.3. Location

From its first appearance in modern Europe and for many decades there- after, Japanese direct investment was highly concentrated in a few major European markets. In fact, the record of Mitsui & Co.'s establishment of branch offices in nineteenth-century Europe—all but one of which were located in England, France, or Germany—reflects a pattern of Japanese

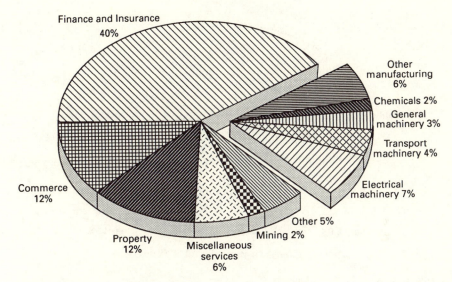

Finance and Insurance
40%

Other
manufacturing
6%

Chemicals 2%

General
machinery 3%

Transport
machinery 4%

Electrical
machinery 7%

Commerce
12%

Other 5%

Mining 2%

Property
12%

Miscellaneous
services
6%

Note: Broken-out slices of the pie represent manufacturing FDI.
Source: Japan, Ministry of Finance.

Fig. 1.6. Accumulated Japanese FDI in Europe, by sector, 1991

investments in the region that endured for nearly a century. That pattern not only held for trading companies, but also for banking, insurance, and many other types of direct investments as well.

In more recent times, however, there has been a shift in Japanese FDI in Europe from geographical concentration to geographical dispersion. In contrast to the pre-war anecdotal evidence and the post-war statistical evidence, both of which point up the high concentration of Japanese investment in just a few of the principal European economies, since the 1970s substantial amounts of Japanese FDI have flowed to a far wider range of countries in the region. Indeed, this change has led to a major locational redistribution of such investment, which by 1991 had rendered the Netherlands and Luxemburg (largely for tax and other legal reasons) the second- and third-ranking recipients respectively of accumulated stocks of Japanese FDI in Europe, and which had measurably raised the levels of such FDI in Spain, Belgium, and Italy (for economic but also for political reasons).[90] (See Fig. 1.7 for a breakdown by principal recipient of Japan's FDI in Europe as of 1991.)

[90] Micossi and Viesti, 'Japanese Direct Manufacturing Investment in Europe', 207–8; Crowley, 'A Southern Spree', 55. Indeed, Crowley echoed the author's own interview findings that, at least by 1989, there had developed a 'growing awareness' among Japanese managers and policy-makers that a 'diffusion of Japanese investment throughout Europe, especially into the poorer southern states of the Continent' might well produce '*political* as well as economic rewards' (emphasis added).

Overview

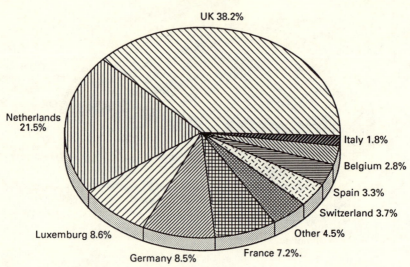

Source: Japan, Ministry of Finance.

Fig. 1.7. Accumulated Japanese FDI, principal European recipients, 1991

2.4. Motivation

Yet another clear historical continuity in the development of Japanese FDI in Europe until the recent past has been the underlying motivation to invest: from the earliest investments in the 1870s and for many decades thereafter, Japanese investors sought principally to enhance bilateral trade flows. In the pre-war period Japanese investors in the trade, shipping, banking, and insurance sectors generally sought to facilitate trade flows in both directions, and in the post-war era these investors principally concentrated on increasing Japanese exports to Europe. Yet at both times trade enhancement was the central motive.

Here again, however, the record since 1970 contrasts significantly with this longer-term historical pattern. Although much Japanese FDI in Europe is still aimed at facilitating bilateral trade, in recent times an increasing amount of such investment has been aimed rather at defending or enhancing European market share by providing goods and services locally through European-based assembly, manufacturing, and other investments. Threats or perceived threats of European protectionism in the approach to market unification have contributed powerfully to the increasing importance of this latter motive.[91]

[91] Ironically, however, if Europe follows the American example, total Japanese exports to Europe may substantially *increase* because of the potential import-stimulating effects of Japanese affiliates operating in the region. See Encarnation, *Rivals beyond Trade*, ch. 1.

2.5. The Role of General Trading Companies

Over the course of the more than 110 years that Japan's general trading companies have operated in Europe, they have fulfilled at least four critically important functions. First, the general traders facilitated exports of Japanese products to Europe and imports of European products to Japan. Second, these firms transferred numerous European technologies to Japanese industry. Third, many of these same companies provided critical information to Japanese business and government concerning economic, political, and other conditions in Europe. And fourth, principally during the post-war period, the *sogo shosha* acted as joint-venture partners with both Japanese and local manufacturing companies. Indeed, for many years the general traders constituted the largest single category of Japanese direct investors in Europe.[92]

In contrast to this long-standing importance of the *sogo shosha*, however, in recent times the relative significance of the general trading companies as investors in Europe has apparently declined. Although these firms still play important roles in bilateral (and, indeed, multilateral) economic ties, since at least the mid-1970s Japanese manufacturing companies in particular have begun to directly invest in and otherwise transact economically with the markets of Europe without the same degree of involvement by the general traders that was common in years past. The manufacturing investments of Japanese motor vehicle companies in the UK during the 1980s provide only some of the more recent and vivid examples of this recent trend.

2.6. The Role of the Japanese Government

From Japan's earliest direct investments in Europe and for decades afterwards, the Japanese government participated as an intimate and often highly influential player. One key government role was to provide various types of assistance to Japanese investors in Europe. This assistance dates back to the nineteenth century, and includes capital participation, subsidies, low-interest loans, and preferential or exclusive rights to market goods produced in Japan by government-owned factories to select European markets through local affiliates. Another central government role was to control the types and amounts of Japanese FDI that entered Europe. In the post-World War II period, most notably, the government strictly regulated investment outflows to Europe and other regions, and both before and after World War II the authorities managed to influence Japan's direct investments in Europe by denying assistance to some potential investors even as they granted help to others.

[92] See e.g. M. Fujii *et al.*, eds., *Nihon takokuseki kigyo no shiteki tenkai*, ii. 2.

Since the completion of the capital liberalization programme in the 1970s, however, the role of the Japanese government has become much less important. In fact, as early as 1971 the authorities had removed many of the key public controls on outward direct investments that had operated for the previous two decades. And by 1980, following revision of the Foreign Exchange and Foreign Trade Control Law, the government greatly eased regulations governing the external investments of numerous types of Japanese financial institutions, which had been largely exempted from earlier de-control measures. These important changes do not mean, of course, that governments no longer have any influence on Japan's FDI in Europe. For one thing, certain Japanese public agencies still provide limited financial assistance such as low-interest loans to select Japanese investors in Europe. And for another, European-based public agencies continue to affect the level, location, and character of Japan's direct investment in the area.

2.7. European Impacts

The extremely modest impacts of Japanese direct investment on the economies of Europe constitute yet another long-term continuity in the development of Japan's FDI in the region. It is true that, in certain periods and specific industries, the impacts of such investment have been rather considerable.[93] Japanese investments in the Lyons-based French silk trade before World War II stand out as one important historical case in point, as does the role played by the YSB's London branch in holding (and shifting) Japanese government balances at times so 'exceptionally large' that on occasion they caused significant 'disturbances' on the London money markets, especially in the late 1890s and early 1900s. Yet such cases constitute the exception rather than the rule, and although Japanese FDI in

---

[93] R. S. Sayers, *Bank of England Operations, 1890–1914* (London: P. S. King & Son, Ltd., 1936), 40–2; I. Kanji, 'Japan', in R. Cameron and V. I. Bovykin, eds., *International Banking, 1870–1914* (New York: Oxford University Press, 1991), 220–1. I am grateful to Geoffrey Jones for alerting me to the significant impacts of the YSB's London activities on the financial markets of the pre-1914 City of London. On the importance of the silk trade for Japan, see e.g. Yokohama Shokin Ginko Chosabu (Research Section, Yokohama Specie Bank), *Kiito kinyu to gaikoku kawase* (Trade in Raw Silk Thread and Foreign Exchange) (May 1926), 1–9.

　On some of the early effects of the silk trade on France as well as Japan, see e.g. J.-P. Lehmann, 'The Silk Trade in the Bakumatsu Era and the Pattern of Japanese Economic Development', in Ian Nish, ed., *Bakumatsu and Meiji: Studies in Japan's Economic and Social History* (London: London School of Economics and Political Science, 1982), 39–55. According to Lehmann, Japan became a key source of raw silk and silkworm eggs for the Lyons-based silk industry as early as the mid-1860s. The silk industry, Lehmann reports, constituted a 'vital sector of the French economy' for many years thereafter—silken fabrics produced in Lyons alone, for example, accounted for no less than 7% of France's total exports in 1880—and Japan acted as a critical supplier to that industry.

Europe often had a great impact on the *Japanese* economy, the reverse was rarely true.

Yet here again the decades-old pattern has been overturned, for in contemporary Europe the impacts of Japanese FDI have become highly significant in a number of important sectors. The growth of Japanese investments in the motor vehicle and electronics industries, to name just two of the more obvious examples, has greatly influenced the competitive positions of many European-based producers, led to important technology flows in both directions, and has significantly affected Europe's trade patterns as well. Japan's investments in the European financial services and property sectors have also had important impacts, both economic and psychological. Finally, many of these same investments have created important political effects, with regard to relations both between Japan and Europe and to those between individual European states.[94]

2.8. European Attitudes

Finally, European attitudes of indifference or even condescension towards Japan's direct investments in Europe endured for many decades from the first such investments in the 1870s. The extremely limited amounts of Japanese FDI in pre-war Europe undoubtedly encouraged such attitudes, as did Japan's status as a late industrial developer. Increased Japanese penetration during World War I of Asian markets previously supplied by European producers, conflicts between British and Japanese textile-makers between the two world wars, and the pronounced rise of Japanese military and industrial power in the 1930s at times seriously challenged these long-held views, yet wartime defeat and subsequent occupation once again encouraged their return.[95]

In the last two decades or so, however, European attitudes have changed quite markedly. Although specific attitudes differ by country and by many other factors, in recent years European business and government leaders and often the general public as well have become far more concerned about direct investment and other types of economic relationships with Japan. In many cases this concern has turned into preoccupation and even

---

[94] Consider e.g. the highly complex political ramifications of Japan's negotiations with the European Community over the issue of Japanese automobile exports to—but also *transplant* production in—the EC. See, for details, ch. 12.

[95] On past European attitudes see e.g. R. P. T. Davenport-Hines and G. Jones, 'British Business in Japan since 1868', in Davenport-Hines and Jones, ed., *British Business in Asia since 1860* (New York: Cambridge University Press, 1989), 232; I. Nish, 'Europe and Japan: A British Historian Looks at Misperceptions in the Inter-War Years' (paper presented at the conference 'Europe and Japan: Cooperation and Conflict', European Policy Unit, European University Institute, Florence, June 1992); and E. Wilkinson, *Japan versus the West: Image and Reality* (New York: Penguin Books, 1990), pt. 3.

outright fear, as is evident in recent statements by some leading figures in France and elsewhere.[96]

In sum, the development of Japanese direct investment in Europe exhibits striking continuities across its first century of development but important changes in more recent years. Many aspects of Japanese direct investment in modern Europe remained virtually constant from the late nineteenth century through the mid- to late twentieth century. As the foregoing analysis has shown, important elements of continuity during this period include investment levels, sectoral composition, location, motivation, the role of the general trading companies, the role of the Japanese government, European impacts, and European attitudes. There are exceptional examples of discontinuities for most of these categories, yet the overall historical pattern is clear.

Since roughly the 1970s, however, the character of Japanese FDI in Europe has undergone a number of profound changes. Investment levels have surged far beyond the trajectory suggested by earlier trends, an increasing number of Japanese firms have undertaken direct manufacturing investments in the region, there has developed a tendency towards greater geographical dispersion of this investment, and the overriding motivation has shifted from trade creation to defence and enhancement of European market share through local value-added activities. Nor are these the only significant changes of the last two decades. In addition, recent trends suggest far less significant roles for both the general trading companies and the Japanese government, growing Japanese FDI impacts on the economies of Europe, and a transformation in European attitudes from apathy to interest and, among some, to fear.

3. CROSS FLOWS: JAPANESE FDI IN EUROPE VERSUS EUROPEAN FDI IN JAPAN

If change marks recent as compared to earlier patterns of Japanese FDI in Europe, then asymmetry characterizes numerous aspects of the history of Japanese FDI in Europe as compared to the history of European FDI in Japan. Consider, for example, reciprocal levels of foreign direct investment. Although lack of data prevents a thoroughgoing analysis of

---

[96] On recent French reactions, see e.g. 'Japon: La Bataille d'Europe' [Japan: The Battle of Europe], in *Le Point*, 975 (27 May 1991), 87–92; 'L'Invasion japonais' [The Japanese Invasion], in *Le Monde* (10 July 1991), 1; and 'Edith peut-elle sauver nos industries: L'Obsession japonaise du Premier ministre' [Can Edith [Cresson] Save Our Industries: The Japanese Obsession of the Prime Minister], *Le Nouvel Observateur* (23–9 May, 1991), 93. For an informative overview of current (but also historical) French perceptions of Japan and its economic position, see F. Crouzet, 'Some French Views of Japan Today' (paper presented at the conference 'Europe and Japan: Cooperation and Conflict', European Policy Unit, European University Institute, Florence, June 1992).

comparative accumulations of FDI, anecdotal evidence suggests that the European presence in Japan was substantially greater than the Japanese presence in Europe at least from the 1870s to the 1920s. European (especially British) businesses managed to establish numerous trading companies in Japan's so-called Treaty Ports in the late nineteenth century, and to set up manufacturing and other firms in the interior of the country once (in 1899) the Japanese government had partially deregulated inward direct investment.[97] These investments almost certainly exceeded Japan's limited FDI in Europe throughout this era.

The European advantage in reciprocal FDI levels apparently persisted throughout most of the next four decades from 1930, but this asymmetry then swung decisively in Japan's favour in the 1970s. Evidence does point to a modest increase in Japanese FDI in Europe and to a corresponding decrease in European FDI in Japan during the 1930s, but these trends did not continue during the virtual two-way investment freeze which lasted throughout much of the 1940s.[98] Beginning in the 1950s, however, European (once more, principally British) FDI in Japan again accumulated more rapidly than did Japanese FDI in Europe, although Japanese government regulations and other factors severely limited the absolute quantities of such investment flows in both directions. From 1972, however, accumulated Japanese FDI in Europe has exceeded accumulated European FDI in Japan in every year.[99] Indeed, by 1990 the powerful surge in Japanese direct investment in Europe had resulted in an investment imbalance roughly 11 : 1 in Japan's favour.[100]

[97] On the development of European FDI in pre-war Japan see esp. the several articles in T. Yuzawa and M. Udagawa, eds., *Foreign Business in Japan Before World War II* (Tokyo: University of Tokyo Press, 1990); on the development of British FDI in Japan both before and after World War II, see Davenport-Hines and Jones, 'British Business in Japan since 1868', 217–44. For a discussion of changes in Japanese government policies towards inward direct investment at the turn of the century, see Mason, *American Multinationals and Japan*, ch. 1.

[98] Indeed, it is possible that Japanese FDI in Europe briefly *exceeded* European FDI in Japan during the late 1930s. Such an occurrence, if true, would mirror M. Wilkins's findings that the dollar value of Japanese FDI in the USA came to exceed that of US FDI in Japan as World War II approached. On the US–Japan comparison, see M. Wilkins, 'American–Japanese Direct Foreign Investment Relationships, 1930–1952', in *Business History Review*, 61 (Winter 1982), 505–6. For estimates of overall levels of FDI in 1930s Japan, see W. Lockwood, *The Economic Development of Japan: Growth and Structural Change, 1868–1938* (Princeton: Princeton University Press, 1954), 260.

[99] Ministry of Finance data, as cited in Booz, Allen, & Hamilton, Inc., *Direct Foreign Investment in Japan: The Challenge for Foreign Firms* (Tokyo: American Chamber of Commerce in Japan, Council of the European Business Community and Booz, Allen, & Hamilton, Inc., 1987), 10.

[100] MOF data, as cited in HEC Eurasia Institute, *Japan and Europe: Overcoming the Imbalances* (Jouy-en-Josas, France: Autumn, 1991), 13. On the corresponding imbalance in reciprocal US–Japanese FDI levels in recent years, see Mark Mason, 'United States Direct Investment in Japan: Trends and Prospects', in *California Management Review*, 35/1 (Fall 1992), 98–115.

Other important asymmetries also apparently characterize the development of European–Japanese cross direct investments. In contrast to the historically high concentration of Japanese FDI in Europe's services industries, for example, available evidence suggests that, at least during the twentieth century, European FDI generally has been more concentrated in Japan's manufacturing sector.[101] And, at least until recently, there has been a striking asymmetry in attitude. During the first century of Japan's FDI in Europe, as we have already seen, Europeans in general displayed a striking lack of interest in Japanese direct investments in their midst. From the earliest instances of European FDI in Japan, by contrast, the Japanese have demonstrated an extraordinary degree of interest in this investment.[102]

Recent trends suggest that historical asymmetries in sectoral composition and attitude are now disappearing, but that the gap between levels of Japanese FDI in Europe as compared to levels of European FDI in Japan is becoming wider rather than narrower.

[101] Historical evidence on European FDI in Japan does suggest, however, that, prior to the Japanese government's 1899 capital liberalization, European business probably invested more in trade, finance, and other service industries than in manufacturing. See e.g. T. Yuzawa and M. Udagawa, eds., *Foreign Business in Japan Before World War II*; Davenport-Hines and Jones, 'British Business in Japan since 1868'; George C. Allen and A. G. Donnithorne, *Western Enterprise in Far Eastern Economic Development: China and Japan* (New York: MacMillan, 1954); and EC Delegation, *EC Investment in Japan* (Tokyo: 1985). In many cases, European companies doing business in 20th-cent. Japan undoubtedly would have preferred to invest in trade-facilitating sectors such as distribution, but instead invested in manufacturing to avoid the pronounced difficulties of investing in such sectors in that country.

[102] Mimicking current European debates, this Japanese interest at times turned into profound fear. On the historical devolvement of Japanese attitudes towards European (and other foreign) direct investment in Japan, see Mason, *American Multinationals and Japan*, Conclusion.

RAPPORTEUR

Geoffrey Jones

This comment seeks to put Mark Mason's paper in a wider perspective by sketching the evolution of Europe as a home and host economy for multinationals over the last hundred years. This is not an easy task because of the lack of statistics until the very recent past. Although the Americans began to distinguish between FDI and portfolio investments in the interwar years, and to publish data on the former, European governments took much longer to follow this route. Most European governments did not collect data on inward and outward FDI until the 1960s. An extreme case was Switzerland, which published its first official figures on FDI only in 1985. As a result, although the first modern-style multinationals appeared in Europe in the 1850s and 1860s, our knowledge of the first hundred years of international business in Europe remains desperately patchy. For some countries, such as Switzerland and even France, our knowledge of historical flows of inward and outward FDI barely rise above the acecdotal. We are left with the pioneering historical estimates of John Dunning of changes in the level of international production, supplemented by case studies by business historians.[103]

The following generalizations rest, therefore, on a fragile base. Before World War I, it would seem that Western Europe was home to around 75 per cent of world FDI: of this the UK represented around 45 per cent, and the other Western European economies around 30 per cent. The remainder of world FDI was mostly American, while the Japanese share was minimal. Thereafter Western Europe's relative importance as a home economy declined to a low of just under 40 per cent in the early 1970s. This trend reflected both the extremely subdued levels of German FDI between 1914 and the 1960s, and the replacement of the UK by the USA as the world's largest multinational investor after World War II. From the 1970s, the relative importance of European FDI began to grow. In the 1980s European FDI grew faster than that of the USA, and by the late 1980s the EC stock of outward FDI was around 45 per cent of the world total, or 34–5 per cent (equal to the US share) if intra-EC FDI was excluded.[104] Within Europe, there were wide variations in propensities to

---

[103] J. H. Dunning, 'Changes in the Level and Structure of International Production: The Last 100 Years', in J. H. Dunning, *Explaining International Production* (London: Unwin Hyman, 1988); G. Jones and H. G. Schröter, eds., *The Rise of Multinationals in Continental Europe* (Aldershot: Edward Elgar, 1993); H. G. Schröter, *Multinationale Unternehmen aus kleinen Staaten 1870 bis 1914* (Free University of Berlin, 1991).

[104] United Nations Centre on Transnational Corporations (UNCTC), *World Investment Report: The Triad in Foreign Direct Investment* (1991).

engage in FDI. The UK, and certain smaller European economies such as the Netherlands, Switzerland, and Sweden, have been continuously active in FDI over the long term. For over a hundred years the UK has been by far the most important European outward investor. It continues to hold the largest stock of foreign direct investment in the USA of any nationality. A small economy such as the Netherlands also had a remarkable propensity to invest abroad. Until the late 1970s it was the largest Continental European direct investor, with a stock of FDI considerably above that of Germany. In contrast, other European economies, such as Italy or Belgium after 1914, have been very modest outward investors.

Europe's evolution as a host economy was rather different. Partly because before 1945 at least a half of world FDI was in the extractive sector, Western Europe received a relatively small share of world FDI flows before World War II. Dunning estimated that in 1938 Western Europe held just over 7 per cent of the stock of world FDI, about the same proportion as the USA, though recent research has suggested considerable intra-European FDI in the pre-1945 period which may need to be taken into account. Thereafter the Western European share rose quickly and was over one-third by 1973, with the UK particularly prominent as a host economy. The USA had a 10 per cent share of world FDI in that year. The subsequent development of the USA as a major host economy radically changed these proportions. By the late 1980s the EC stock of inward FDI was around 23 per cent of the world total, or 34 per cent (just over the US share) if intra-EC FDI was included.[105] Once again, there would appear to have been substantial long-term differences in the attractiveness of individual European economies as host economies. The UK and Germany appear to have been attractive as host economies over a very long period, while Belgium was prominent as a host economy from the late 1950s. Conversely a number of countries, including Italy and Sweden, attracted relatively less inward FDI. The result is wide variations between European countries in their ratio of inward FDI stock to their gross domestic products. At the beginning of the 1990s, this ratio was less than 5 per cent for some countries (such as France and Norway), between 5 and 10 per cent for others (such as Germany and Spain), and approaching 20 per cent for the UK.

Within this context, Mark Mason's story holds only a few surprises. It is hardly surprising, given the overall dimensions and sectoral distribution of Japanese FDI, that Japanese investment in Europe was very modest before the 1970s, and that it was largely concentrated in the service sector. Nor is it surprising that Japanese investors preferred the USA to Europe in the inter-war years. The political and economic situation of Europe in that period was not attractive, and British FDI also steered clear of Continental Europe. Possibly the geographical distribution of Japanese

---

[105] Dunning, 'Changes'; UNCTC, *World Investment Report*.

investment is more intriguing. The Japanese interest in France seems higher than might have been expected, although as observed earlier the overall importance of FDI in the French economy before the recent past is very unclear. The extensive Japanese trading company investment in Germany in the 1950s is also interesting. It would be helpful to know more about the motivations and activities of these firms.

Given the importance of Europe as a home economy before 1914, it is not surprising that European investment in Japan was greater than vice versa, and that Europeans on occasion made a significant impact on Japanese manufacturing, as in the case of the British company Dunlop's establishment of the first factory of modern type in Japan before 1914.[106] Perhaps it is rather more surprising that European FDI in Japan has been so subdued since the 1970s. It is striking that the rapid growth of German FDI over the last twenty years has not resulted in a flow of investment to Japan. In 1990 a mere 1.9 per cent of the stock of German FDI was in Japan.[107]

Mark Mason is surely right to argue that before the 1970s Europe's importance to Japan was far greater than the other way round. Any search for the impact of Japanese FDI in Europe before the 1970s must inevitably focus on very specific niches. Mason mentions the case of the Lyons-based French silk trade. The role of the Yokohama Specie Bank in the pre-1914 City of London should also be highlighted. By the 1890s this bank's London branch had assumed the role of regional headquarters, supervising other YSB offices in gold-standard countries. The London branch performed the financial activities of the Japanese government and the Bank of Japan in London, which had a considerable importance for the UK. The Japanese government kept much of its gold reserve in London, and these balances played a significant role in the Bank of England's control over the London money markets and the maintenance of the gold standard.[108] The YSB London branch also participated with British banks in the issue of Japanese government loans on the London market before 1914. This was a unique role for an Asian financial institution before 1914. It can be seen as a precedent for the use of the City of London by Japanese banks in the 1980s.[109]

---

[106] M. Mason, 'Foreign Direct Investment and Japanese Economic Development, 1899–1931', *Business and Economic History*, 16 (1987); G. Jones, 'The Multinational Expansion of Dunlop, 1890–1939', in G. Jones, ed., *British Multinationals: Origins, Management and Performance* (Aldershot: Gower, 1986); Takeshi Yuzawa and Masaru Udagawa, eds., *Foreign Business in Japan before World War II* (Tokyo: University of Tokyo Press, 1990).

[107] H. G. Schröter, 'Continuity and Change: German Multinationals since 1850', in Jones and Schröter, *Rise*, 41.

[108] R. S. Sayers, *The Bank of England, 1891–1944* (Cambridge: Cambridge University Press, 1976), i. 40–1.

[109] N. Tamaki, 'The Yokohama Specie Bank: A Multinational in the Japanese Interest, 1879–1931', in Geoffrey Jones, ed., *Banks as Multinationals* (London: Routledge, 1990); Kanji Ishii, 'Japan', in R. Cameron and V. I. Bovykin, eds., *International Banking, 1870–1914* (New York: Oxford University Press, 1991).

The extremely modest scale of Japanese FDI in pre- and, indeed, post-World War II Europe did not mean, however, that all Europeans necessarily viewed Japan 'as little more than an exotic and far-away land'. The first major conflict between European manufacturers and the Japanese occurred in the inter-war years, when British cotton textile firms faced an onslaught on their Asian markets from the Japanese. British manufacturers complained loudly about the 'unfair' nature of Japanese competition, which allegedly rested on cheap and exploited labour, copying, and an undervalued currency.[110] Today, William Lazonick and other scholars have argued that the Japanese competitive advantage in cotton textiles rested on superior organizational capabilities compared to the British. Japanese firms were better managed and more efficient than their Lancashire rivals. They have seen the competition between British and Japanese cotton textile firms in the inter-war years as the first round of the struggle between Western and Japanese business that was to resume over automobiles and electronics from the 1960s.[111] Certainly the British comments on the strategies of their Japanese competitors had a very similar tone to those of American critics of contemporary Japanese business.

Although the UK lost the cotton textiles struggle, as it did later on in shipbuilding and other industries, this did not translate into any hostility towards Japanese FDI when it began to accelerate from the 1970s. As Mason shows, the Japanese had around 40 per cent of their total European FDI in 1990 in the UK.

The UK's attractiveness to Japanese investors reflected, as has already been noted, a long-term tradition of acting as a leading European host economy. In the inter-war years and beyond Britain was a favoured location of US multinationals. In the 1950s the UK attracted 56 per cent of US manufacturing FDI in Europe, and in the 1960s 43 per cent.[112] A number of common factors attracted both US and Japanese investors, including the use of the English language, the importance of London as an international financial centre, and political stability. British government policy towards inward investors has been very liberal throughout the twentieth century, with almost no restrictions on foreign ownership of assets, except in a number of strategic sectors such as banking and defence, and even these were relaxed in the 1980s. Historically, there has been a wide divergence between European governments in their attitudes to inward FDI. Many European governments held more restrictive views than the British on foreign investment in their countries. However Germany—for example—

[110] R. P. T. Davenport-Hines and G. Jones, 'British Business in Japan since 1868', in R. P. T. Davenport-Hines and G. Jones, eds., *British Business in Asia since 1860* (Cambridge: Cambridge University Press, 1989), 232.

[111] W. Mass and W. Lazonick, 'The British Cotton Industry and International Competitive Advantage: The State of the Debates', *Business History*, 4 (1990), 58–9.

[112] Calculated from M. D. Steuer, *The Impact of Foreign Direct Investment on the United Kingdom* (Department of Trade and Industry, 1973), 204–5.

also had a long tradition, dating from the late nineteenth century, of a welcoming and neutral stance towards foreign companies.[113]

The British welcomed foreign multinationals because of their generally liberal industrial policy and because of their own large outward investment. The latter was also a considerable influence on German policy before 1914. The British also held an almost naïve belief that foreigners could improve the performance of their industry. In the 1980s the British government welcomed Japanese multinationals not only as providers of employment, but because it was hoped that their production management and human resource management policies would 'spill over' into UK industry. The collapse of the British motor car industry in the 1970s naturally predisposed the British to take a favourable view of Japanese firms who promised to build them a new one, but it is also noteworthy that the British had also greeted American multinationals in the inter-war years as their saviours. American firms were widely praised for superior organizational and technological skills, and welcomed as providing necessary competition and a valuable role model to their sluggish British competitors.[114] Interestingly, the British admiration for American or Japanese business almost never—and perhaps never at all—was matched by praise for other European multinationals, and what they might contribute to British competitiveness.

When we look at the history of inward and outward FDI in Europe before the 1960s we enter a world without aggregate data in which contemporaries did not even distinguish between FDI and portfolio investment. There were, however, obviously marked differences between individual European economies in both their inward and outward FDI propensities, though the scale of those differences, let alone the reasons for them, remain the subject for speculation. When we examine the cross-investment patterns between Japan and Europe over the last hundred years, we need to remember the strong differences in the patterns of FDI in different European countries until recently, and also the strong differences in public policy and public attitudes. The process of convergence within Europe in these matters has been slow. By exploring the historical evolution of Japanese FDI in Europe, Mark Mason has made a pioneering contribution to our knowledge of a much-neglected subject.

---

[113] See e.g. F. Blaich, *Amerikanische Firmen in Deutschland, 1890–1918* (Wiesbaden: Steiner, 1984), 96–8.

[114] G. Jones, 'Foreign Multinationals and British Industry before 1945', *Economic History Review*, 41 (1988), 440; id., 'The British Government and Foreign Multinationals before 1970', in M. Chick, ed., *Governments, Industries and Markets* (Aldershot: Edward Elgar, 1990).

RAPPORTEUR

Akira Kudo

My comments on Mark Mason's paper have two points. The first one concerns Japan's trading companies (*shosha*) as the main Japanese investors abroad. It is evident, as Mason writes, that until the 1970s Japanese direct investment in Europe was almost negligible so far as its volume is concerned. It is, however, also clear that trading companies were the most important Japanese investors in Europe, as well as in other regions, even during the early post-war era, both quantitatively and qualitatively. It is evident that this feature of Japanese direct investment abroad is critical to understanding almost all of its other characteristics, which Mason describes as the 'striking continuities' of Japanese direct investment in Europe until the 1970s.

The following points should be emphasized about the historical importance of trading companies as the main Japanese foreign investors. Firstly, it is true that Japanese trading companies began to establish their liaison offices or branches as early as the end of the nineteenth century. The most important turning-point in their activities abroad, however, came during and soon after World War I. For example, the predecessor of the present Mitsubishi Shoji's London branch was established in 1915 as an arm of Mitsubishi Goshi, the headquarters and holding company of the Mitsubishi *zaibatsu*.

Secondly, the most decisive motive in the establishment of those offices or branches, as well as their most important function, was to import rather than export machinery and other capital goods, advanced technologies, and technological information and know-how. These were essential to Japanese heavy and chemical industrialization stimulated by the impact of World War I, and could not be supplied by the recently born Japanese heavy and chemical industries. Indeed, at that time trading companies were called 'import trading companies' in recognition of their role.

Thirdly, it needs to be explained why Japanese trading companies could seize the business opportunity and dominate the trade of machinery, other capital goods, advanced technologies, and technological information and know-how from Europe to Japan, and why their European competitors could not exploit their advantages as dominant traders, and so failed to make use of this opportunity. My own case studies[115] suggest that some

---

[115] A. Kudo, *A History of Japan–German Business Relations* (Tokyo: Yuhikaku, 1992), ch. 2 (in Japanese).

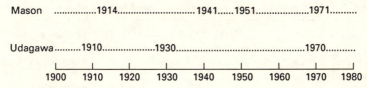

Fig. 1.8. Alternative perspectives on the historical evolution of Japanese policy toward inward FDI

Japanese trading companies could rely on their managerial and technological relations with industrial enterprises and/or their relations with the Japanese government to exploit economies of scale and scope, and that some of them could diversify their business regions, products and functions to become general trading companies (*sogo shosha*). It is worthwhile to note in this context that medium- and small-scale trading companies, whether European or Japanese, dominated the Japanese export trade, where economies of scale and scope were much smaller than in the Japanese import trade.

One related question could be raised on the decreasing relative importance of general trading companies (*sogo shosha*) as investors in Europe in the 1970s and later. Why did *sogo shosha* lose their relative importance, and how far was it related to the so-called coming of the winter season for *sogo shosha*? Mason refers to the increasing establishment of sales outlets as well as production sites by manufacturing companies. It is also possible to stress the declining importance of European countries as suppliers of capital goods and technologies to Japan, as well as the declining importance of Japanese trading companies in import and export transactions.

2 JAPAN AND EUROPE AS INVESTMENT PARTNERS

As is seen in Fig. 1.8, Mason's periodization, according to his rather policy-oriented approach, consists of five periods: pre-1914, 1914–41, 1941–51, 1951–71, and 1971–present. Masaru Udagawa made a periodization on inward direct investment into Japan according to the foreign capital policy of the Japanese government as follows: closed-door policy to 1900; open-door policy in 1900–30; closed-door policy again in 1930–70; and open-door policy again from 1970 to present.[116] Only one coincidence is found in the rival periodizations of Mason and Udagawa, in 1970/1.

If both policies of outward and inward direct investment have a linkage, and provided that Japanese direct investment in Europe increased in the

---

[116] M. Udagawa, 'Business Management and Foreign Affiliated Companies in Japan before World War II', in T. Yuzawa and M. Udagawa, eds., *Foreign Business in Japan before World War II*, International Conference on Business History, 16 (Tokyo: University of Tokyo Press, 1990).

TABLE 1.5. *Two periods of increasing Japanese direct investment in Europe*

	1900–1930	1970/1–present
Main investor from Japan	Trading companies	Manufactures, trading companies, financial institutions
Investment balance	European surplus	Japanese surplus
Trade balance	Japanese deficit	European deficit
Main trade	Capital goods	Consumer goods

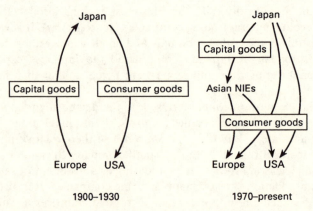

FIG. 1.9. Changing patterns of Japanese trade, early 1900s *v.* recent decades

years 1900–30, the same periodization as Udagawa's is applicable to the Japanese direct investment in Europe. Then, as is seen in Table 1.5, two periods of increasing Japanese direct investment in Europe are comparable, that is, 1900–30 and 1970/1–present. In both periods direct investment functioned as a balancing factor to trade imbalance. In both periods, however, conflicts occurred in investment as well as in trade.

As Fig. 1.9 can show, Europe–Japan–USA relations in the former period are comparable to today's relations of Japan–Asian NIEs–Europe. Some part of Asian NIEs' exports to Europe may well be regarded as Japanese 'indirect' FDI in Europe, because Japanese direct investment in Asia contributes mostly to strengthening the competitiveness of East and South-East Asian countries in some consumer goods industries. In the former period, however, consumer goods from Japan flowed mainly to the USA, not to Europe, while from 1970/1 on, consumer goods have been flowing into the European market not only from Asian NIEs, but also from Japan. This may be part of the reason for today's apparently worsening conflict between Japan and the EC. Such a historical comparison stimulates us to raise a further question: should Europe close the door to Japanese investment, just as Japan did to Europe half a century ago, or can we find other outlets for Japanese consumer goods?

RAPPORTEUR

Mira Wilkins

I am delighted to comment on this excellent opening paper. In the USA there has been immense concern over Japanese multinationals. In part this attention has been based on symbols: the takeover of Rockefeller Center and the Hollywood movie studios. Now, Sony has bought land in the 'heart' of Berlin; where once there was the Berlin Wall, there will be a Sony headquarters. More serious as a symbol, a major Paris restaurant—Lucas Carton—recently passed to Japanese ownership. And when rumours circulated that Fiat might sign a strategic alliance with Toyota, Giovanni Agnelli was vehement in his denial: 'My Fiat will never be Japanese,' he declared.[117]

Yet it is important to go beyond the fears and rhetoric. Mark Mason's paper gives us the opportunity to do this. Clearly, history matters. As I read Mason's superb essay, I had a sense of *déjà vu*. In tracking Japanese stakes in Europe, Mason has found a pattern extraordinarily similar to what I uncovered on the history of Japanese business in the USA. In both instances, the public—and most scholars—have assumed a novelty in the current Japanese presence. In both cases, Japanese trading companies, banks, shipping-lines, and insurance firms stand out with long histories; and with some few exceptions, the same enterprises are in evidence in each host locale.

The Conference sponsors have asked me to limit my remarks to the historical data; thus, I will not venture past 1971. We should not forget, however, how rapidly the Japanese economy has developed over the course of the twentieth century and especially in the last two decades; indeed, the approval pattern 1971–91 of the Invest in Britain Bureau (provided in Mason's article) captures the very essence of the change: from zipfasteners to high-tech investments.

Multinational enterprise has a long history, and Japanese multinationals are no exception. What the history of multinationals tells us is that it is important to consider *channels* of trade, capital movements, and technology—and not simply macroeconomic statistics. And this brings me to the first general point I want to make, on what I have called the 'truncation problem', that is, when 'area' specialists look at multinationals in host countries, by definition they break into the growth of the firm—cutting into

---

[117] *Wall Street Journal*, 27 June 1991, on Sony; I wish to thank M. Mason for pointing out the symbolic aspect of the Japanese takeover of the famous French restaurant; *Wall Street Journal*, 15 Jan. 1993 (Agnelli quotation).

a holistic, dynamic, expansion pattern.[118] Once we acknowledge the truncation problem, it is not at all odd that the identical Japanese multinational enterprises appeared in the USA and Europe and that they behaved historically in a similar manner. If we start with the multinational firm rather than the country (or regional) recipients of its 'investments' then this makes good sense.

As I read Mason's wonderful material on Japanese FDI in Europe and compared it with my research on Japanese multinationals in the USA, the coincidence of the early activities in the USA and Europe is striking.[119] My reading of the data suggests that the size of Japanese direct investments in Europe seems from the late nineteenth century to today to have been smaller than in the USA.[120]

As I have pointed out elsewhere, in the years 1880–1914, increasingly, Japanese firms took over from foreigners the conduct of their nation's overseas trade.[121] As late as 1887, nine-tenths of Japan's external trade was handled by foreigners, principally British trading-houses.[122] Over time, Japanese multinationals—trading companies, shipping companies, banks, and insurance companies—developed an infrastructure that could return to Japan more of the benefits from its foreign trade. This is now clear; what we need, however, are many more studies on specifically what the Japanese 'took over', that is, was it new trading activities, or was the expansion principally to substitute for foreign houses in existing commerce?

By 1914, one Japanese trading company alone, Mitsui Bussan, moved 27.3 per cent of Japan's exports and 23.9 per cent of its imports.[123] By 1913, 52 per cent of Japanese exports were carried on Japanese ships and 47 per cent of Japanese imports arrived on Japanese vessels.[124] FDI by Japanese trading companies, shipping-lines, banks, and cargo insurers made such involvements possible.

This growing control by the Japanese over their own trade was all the more remarkable when we consider how far behind Japan was in manufacturing relative to other industrial and industrializing nations. In 1913,

[118] I explore this idea in M. Wilkins, 'Hosts to Transnational Investments: A Comparative Analysis', a paper delivered at the Joint US/German Business History Conference, Munich, Aug. 1992; publication is forthcoming in a volume edited by Hans Pohl, in the *Zeitschrift für Unternehmensgeschichte* series.

[119] See esp. M. Wilkins, 'Japanese Multinationals in the United States: Continuity and Change, 1879–1990', *Business History Review*, 64 (Winter 1990), 585–629.

[120] This is based on all evidence that I have seen. For the early period the comments are based on figures for 1913, provided by the Bank of Japan to Harold Moulton in 1931, and reprinted in M. Wilkins, 'Japanese Multinational Enterprise before 1914', *Business History Review*, 60 (Summer 1986), 209. See also other figures, ibid.

[121] Wilkins, 'Japanese Multinationals in the United States . . . 1879–1990', 586.

[122] Wilkins, 'Japanese Multinational Enterprise before 1914', 206 n. See also H. Yamazaki, 'The Logic of the Formation of General Trading Companies in Japan', in S. Yonekawa and H. Yoshihara, eds., *Business History of General Trading Companies* (Tokyo: University of Tokyo Press, 1987), 37.   [123] Yamazaki, 'The Logic', 36.

[124] Wilkins, 'Japanese Multinational Enterprise before 1914', 219–20.

the USA produced 35.8 per cent of world manufactures, Germany 14.3 per cent, the UK 14.1 per cent, Russia 4.4 per cent, Japan 1.2 per cent, and India 1.1 per cent.[125] Yet it is interesting that at least one branded Japanese good was early marketed in the USA and Europe: the Kikkoman trade mark had been registered in California in 1879 and in Germany in 1886.[126]

During World War I and throughout the inter-war years, Japanese development made giant strides. None the less, in 1936–8, while the Japanese 3.5 per cent of world manufacturing was almost triple its share in 1913, Japan was still a minor factor in world industry. The percentages for the leaders were: the USA 32.2; the Soviet Union 18.5; Germany 10.7; and the UK 9.2.[127]

Through World War I and the inter-war years, as Japan industrialized, Japanese firms increased their control over the essential service activities related to international trade—albeit the concentration in control by particular individual Japanese firms appears to have diminished. Thus, by 1937–42, it was two major trading companies (Mitsui Bussan and Mitsubishi Shoji) that accounted for 28.6 per cent of Japan's foreign trade.[128] (In 1913, Mitsui Bussan alone had handled almost that much of Japan's overseas commerce.) By the end of the inter-war period, Japanese firms had become conduits for a sizeable proportion of their nation's foreign trade. In addition, a number of Japanese banks other than the earliest leader, the Yokohama Specie Bank, pursued business abroad. There appears, however, to have been no Japanese investment in manufacturing plants in Europe in the inter-war period, which is not surprising given Japan's position in the world economy.

Because for many years raw silk had been Japan's major export, this had a significant impact on the activities of the Japanese service sector firms—in the USA and Europe. More research needs to be done on both the pre-World War I and pre-World War II Japanese role in Lyons, Europe's centre for luxury silk goods. Likewise, I would like to see this associated with studies on the artificial silk (the rayon) industry. In the inter-war years, the development of substitutes for silk—the activities of the Gillet family business in France and Courtaulds in Britain—must have alarmed the Japanese. What was the trading companies' role as a conduit for information, technology transfer, and so forth in this new and threatening industrial development?

[125] League of Nations, *Industrialization and Foreign Trade* (Geneva: League of Nations, 1945), 13.
[126] Y. Kinugasa, 'Japanese Firms' Foreign Direct Investment in the U. S.', in A. Okochi and T. Inoue, eds., *Overseas Business Activities* (Tokyo: University of Tokyo Press, 1984), 54.
[127] League of Nations, *Industrialization and Foreign Trade*, 13.
[128] H. Yoshihara, 'Some Questions on Japan's Sogo Shosha', in Yonekawa and Yoshihara, eds., *Business History*, 4.

The story of Japanese stakes in the USA from 1879 to 1939—apart from some details on timing—diverges very little from the European chronology as presented by Mason. Only one basic difference seems to loom large: Japan became a major purchaser (importer) of raw cotton from the USA, and Japanese firms' FDI in relation to commerce in this commodity seem to have had no European counterpart—although there are some issues that are still unclear. We need to know, for example, how the involvement of the trading companies and the Yokohama Specie Bank in London affected the Japanese trade in *Indian* cotton. As Mason points out, Mitsui & Co. did carry on an active trade in Indian jute, which went from Mitsui & Co., Calcutta, to Mitsui & Co., London. Japanese service companies handled much more than bilateral trade. Japanese FDI in Europe must be viewed in the context of global commercial relationships.

The amounts invested in the pre-World War II (as in the pre-World War I) extension of the Japanese service multinationals were not large—neither in the USA nor in Europe. Yet much more important, and much more interesting, than the size of the FDI was the existence of, and very extensive creation by the Japanese of, this organizational and institutional network structure to provide for Japanese requirements; it is this that cries out for study.

What my research has shown was that these Japanese multinational enterprise conduits for trade (and also apparently technology transfer) *were* historically of growing importance in Japanese–US economic relationship. Mason reminds us (and indeed pushes us) to look at this matter more broadly. It seems that Japanese multinational enterprises were also vital for the Japanese in Japanese–European economic transactions. In demonstrating this, Mason is making a very significant contribution. In both the USA and Europe, Japanese direct investments were from the earliest days on heavily concentrated in the service sector.

It is useful to look—as Mason does—at the specific host locations of the Japanese multinationals. In the USA, before World War II, the principal Japanese presence was in New York, on the west coast, and in Texas (to buy raw cotton).[129] In 1923 the Yokohama Specie Bank (the predecessor of the Bank of Tokyo) ran regular advertisements in *Bankers Magazine*, New York. It advertised its four US 'agencies' and its numerous branches and agencies around the world (from Batavia to Vladivostok). In Europe, however, in 1923 the Yokohama Specie Bank had only three branches: in London, Hamburg, and Lyons. The places deserve notice: London was a financial centre; Hamburg, a key trading and shipping centre; and Lyons, the centre of the European silk industry.[130] Not until 1931 did the Yokohama Specie Bank set up branches in Paris and Berlin (and that year it closed

---

[129] Wilkins, 'Japanese Multinationals in the United States . . . 1879–1990', 594.
[130] Ibid. 591.

its branch in Lyons).[131] What could be more logical? With major worldwide foreign exchange problems in 1931, the Yokohama Specie Bank needed to be in Paris and Berlin; with the precipitous decline in the silk trade in 1931, it no longer had to be in Lyons.

Before World War II, whether the Japanese service multinationals were in the USA or Europe, the rationale was identical. The outlets were to provide an infrastructure for Japanese commercial (and informational) requirements. The central importance of the Japanese trading companies in the service group in both the USA and Europe seems evident. Japan was able to limit its trade deficits by handling its own commerce.[132] By the 1930s, much of Japan's external trade had come to be undertaken within Japanese trading companies, carried on Japanese ships, financed by Japanese banks (or by financing obtained through Japanese banks), and insured by Japanese insurers. We need to know much more about the role of these Japanese multinationals as conduits of technology sent from Europe to Japan.

In neither the USA nor Europe were the Japanese multinationals of any measurable consequence. At certain points, Japanese borrowing in London and the role of the Yokohama Specie Bank in aiding the process may have had importance. (The parallel in the USA was the borrowings in New York in the 1920s.) Mark suggests Japanese multinationals had an impact on Europe in connection with the silk trade. While silk production was vital for Lyons, Milan, and Krefeld, if we are studying French, Italian, or German, much less European, economic development, silk played a small part. In addition, it is not altogether clear how significant the Japanese were in the lengthy, overall history of the European silk industry.[133]

The global spread of Japan's service sector multinationals was interrupted by World War II and then once more resumed. As we consider the post-war years, once again the historical continuities (and discontinuities) between Japanese investments in Europe and the USA seem remarkable in their similarities, albeit there was some coincidental behaviour and,

[131] N. Tamaki, 'The Yokohama Specie Bank', in G. Jones, ed., *Banks as Multinationals* (London: Routledge, 1990), 212.

[132] For Japan's trade balances, see W. W. Lockwood, *The Economic Development of Japan* (Princeton: Princeton University Press, 1954), 401.

[133] The Instituto Internazionale di Storia Economica 'F. Datini' held a major conference (May 1992) on the European silk industry from the 13th to the 20th century. Two important insights emerge from the programme: (1) the European silk industry existed long before Japanese involvements, and (2) there was absolutely nothing in the programme that related specifically to Japan (!). Perhaps one can conclude from this that even in the silk industry, the Japanese role was peripheral, or maybe such a conclusion is not justified. This would seem to be a subject for future research. Questions I would like to see explored include: (1) how much of the European raw silk trade went through Japanese trading companies in the late 19th and 20th centuries (by the inter-war period, apparently a sizeable proportion of such trade); (2) were the Japanese participants in the Chinese and Indian silk trade (I have seen nothing at all on this subject); and (3) were the Japanese substantially more important in Lyons than in other silk centres (this seems to be the case); if so, why?

more often now, time-lags—with activities in the USA more often preceding those in Europe. In both the USA and Europe, the resumption of pre-war business took place in the 1950s. Synthetic fibres meant that silk would never have its historic importance. New products dominated the post-war world economy. In both host areas—the USA and Europe—some innovative Japanese manufacturing companies found that trading companies did not serve them adequately. These companies' differentiated products required a parent company-managed marketing organization. Elsewhere, I have pointed out that Japanese corporations with their new products behaved in a manner not unlike American companies in the late nineteenth and early twentieth century that bypassed independent wholesalers and export houses and integrated forward into handling their own sales.[134] These distribution networks then became available to American companies abroad when they embarked on manufacturing in foreign countries; so too, the Japanese sales outlets would provide the needed marketing structures, when later the Japanese decided to manufacture in the USA and Europe. The move to the USA and Europe of Japanese banks took place very rapidly. The story of Japanese banks as multinationals is a fascinating one and requires more attention.

Mason has a concluding section of this paper on 'cross-investments': European direct investments in Japan compared with Japanese FDI in Europe.[135] When I compared US direct investments in Japan with Japanese direct investments in the USA, I was astonished to find that while historically US direct investments in Japan had exceeded Japanese investments in the USA, by 1941 as US direct investments in Japan declined because of Japanese nationalistic policies, the dollar value of Japanese direct investments in the USA had come to exceed US direct investments in Japan ($35.1 m. versus $32.6 m.).[136] I think, however, that Mason's tentative

[134] Wilkins, 'Japanese Multinationals in the United States . . . 1879–1990', 603. One of Alfred Chandler's earliest contributions to American business history was to show how this was done domestically: in 1962, at Columbia Business School, he talked on forward vertical integration into sales to an attentive audience. Many American companies initially used independent export houses for trade, and then bypassed such trading-houses and set up their own selling organization abroad. This was true of the history of Ford Motor Company, for example. See M. Wilkins and F. E. Hill, *American Business Abroad: Ford on Six Continents* (Detroit: Wayne State University Press, 1964). See also M. Wilkins, *The Emergence of Multinational Enterprise: American Business Abroad from the Colonial Era to 1914* (Cambridge, Mass.: Harvard University Press, 1970) and id., *The Maturing of Multinational Enterprise: American Business Abroad from 1914 to 1970* (Cambridge, Mass.: Harvard University Press, 1974).

[135] This follows a long-standing interest in cross-investments by students of multinationals enterprise. See e.g. S. Hymer, *The International Operations of National Firms* (Cambridge, Mass.: MIT Press, 1976); M. Wilkins, 'American–Japanese Direct Foreign Investment Relationships, 1930–1952', *Business History Review*, 61 (Winter 1982), 497–518; and D. J. Encarnation, 'Cross-Investment: A Second Front of Economic Rivalry', in T. K. McCraw, ed., *America versus Japan* (Boston: Harvard Business School Press, 1986), ch. 4.

[136] Wilkins, 'American–Japanese Direct Foreign Investment Relationships', 505–6. This was contrary to what I would have predicted when I started to write that paper.

conclusion that there was not a comparable reversal in the Japanese–European direct investment positions is probably correct; regrettably the data to demonstrate this are lacking.

As pledged, my comments have not extended to the period after 1971. Obviously, in both the USA and Europe, dramatic developments occurred in the early 1970s that resulted in the subsequent rapid increase in Japanese direct investments in these host locales. Yet, before I conclude my comments, I do want to add a handful of thoughts related to the impact of the study of history on present-day Japanese FDI.

(1) When we consider Japanese multinationals of early years the trading companies stand out. They appear to continue to be significant in US–Japanese relations. Thus, Professor Robert Lawrence has indicated (February 1990) that 60 per cent of US exports to Japan are handled by affiliates of six major Japanese trading companies.[137] In recent years Japanese trading companies in the USA have made 'venture capital' investments in small firms, obtaining information, and then if the outlook was promising, notifying Japanese enterprises in the specialized industry.[138] But Mason suggests, by contrast, that the role of Japanese trading companies in Europe has diminished. Is this a real difference between Japanese direct investments in the USA and Europe?

(2) How important historically and contemporaneously is the co-operation between and among Japanese companies? Americans are very used to thinking about firms as distinct entities, yet recent research on the history of British business abroad has shown the early importance of clusters of companies.[139] As I reflect on Japanese business abroad, the cluster notion seems highly germane—especially in the *zaibatsu* and *keiretsu* context. Likewise, much of what we now identify as strategic alliances has a long history; the clusters seem worth studying.

(3) In my comments I have noted the parallels between Japanese investments in Europe and those in the USA. Where do the European investments by the Japanese fit into the more general picture of Japanese business abroad? As we study Japanese multinationals in Europe, we must never forget that these firms were and are making investments on a global basis. We must look at how their role in Europe is part of their broader expansion, their activities in third countries.[140]

(4) We need far more systematic research on the historical and contemporary role of Japanese multinationals in the transfer of technology from and to Europe.

(5) Mason places major emphasis on the continuing Japanese state

---

[137] Quoted in Wilkins, 'Japanese Multinationals in the United States . . . 1879–1990', 618.
[138] Ibid.
[139] See M. Wilkins, 'The Free-standing Company, 1870–1914', *Economic History Review*, 2nd ser. 61 (May 1988), 259–82.
[140] On this see Wilkins, 'Hosts to Transnational Investments'.

involvements, stressing the significance of the Japanese state in the early history of Japanese business overseas. Yet there was also historically a considerable amount of non-governmental initiative. As we study the history of Japanese multinationals, as well as their contemporary behaviour, we need to ponder the weight we want to give to the activities of Japanese firms and to the Japanese government. Obviously, the Japanese government was important in the evolution of Japanese international business (we can, I think, all agree on that); none the less, I am not fully convinced of the centrality of its role in the overall spread of Japanese multinational enterprise. Perhaps the ingenuity of the businessmen who ran these service sector activities has been understated.

In conclusion, Mark Mason has written an outstanding paper that breaks new ground and opens the way to many new avenues of research.

PART II
GENERAL CAUSES AND CONSEQUENCES

2

The Strategy of Japanese and US Manufacturing Investment in Europe

John Dunning

1. INTRODUCTION

This paper first examines the current patterns of Japanese- and US-owned economic activity in Western European manufacturing industry. Sections 3–5 suggest some hypotheses for the similarities and differences in these patterns, within the framework of one of the most generally accepted paradigms and some of the best-known theories of foreign direct investment (FDI) and the activities of multinational enterprises (MNEs). Section 6 offers some exploratory evidence on the significance of the variables identified in Sections 3–5. Section 7 concludes by considering whether or not the distinctive structure of Japanese MNE activity in Europe is likely to continue in the later 1990s.

2. SOME STATISTICAL DATA

We draw upon two sets of data. The first, set out in Table 2.1, compares and contrasts the industrial distribution of the stock of US and Japanese direct investment in European manufacturing industry at the end of 1991 (in the case of US investment) and 31 March 1992 (in the case of Japanese investment). The data reveal that while both Japanese and US investment in the European manufacturing sector is largely directed to high-value-added fabricating and processing industries, producing Schumpeterian-type goods (Hirsch and Meshulach 1992), Japanese investment is relatively more concentrated in the electrical and electronic equipment and motor vehicle industries. The final column of Table 2.1 calculates a Japanese concentration coefficient (JCC), which is obtained by dividing the share of the total Japanese capital stake accounted for by a particular sector by the corresponding US share.

Overall, the direct investment stake in European manufacturing industry of Japanese MNEs was about one-fifth of that of their American counterparts at the beginning of the 1990s. However, for all sectors, the

I am most grateful for the research assistance given by Rajneesh Narula in the preparation of this paper, and also for the comments by Dennis Encarnation on an earlier draft.

T AB L E 2.1. *Japanese and US direct investment in Europe, by industry, early 1990s*

	Japan (Mar. 1992)*		US (Dec. 1990)		JCC
	$ m.	%	$ m.	%	
1. MANUFACTURING INDUSTRIES					
Processing Industries					
Food products	573	3.8	9,437	10.6	0.36
Chemicals & allied products	1,640	10.9	19,262	21.6	0.50
Metals	693	4.5	4,131	4.6	0.98
Textiles & clothing	1,022	6.7	1,042[†]	1.2	5.58
Wood-related products	94	0.6	313[†]	0.4	1.50
Fabricating Industries					
Electrical & electronic equipment	4,823	31.7	6,013	6.7	4.73
Non-electrical machinery	2,362	15.5	19,105	21.4	0.72
Transportation	2,618	17.2	9,870	11.1	1.55
Other products	1,406	9.2	19,917	22.4	0.41
TOTAL MANUFACTURING	15,230	100.0	89,090	100.0	1.00
2. OTHER INDUSTRIES					
Services					
Wholesale trade & commerce[‡]	8329	15.6	2,4875	18.6	0.84
Banking, finance, insurance & real estate	35,415	66.3	74,370	55.7	1.19
Other services	5,583	10.5	6,159	4.6	2.28
Other Industry[§]	4,079	7.6	28,060	21.1	0.36
TOTAL OTHER INDUSTRIES	53,406	100.0	133,464	100.0	1.00
TOTAL ALL INDUSTRY	68,636	100.0	224,554	100.0	1.00

JCC = Japanese concentration coefficient ratio (% of Japanese investment in a particular sector divided by % of US investment in a particular sector).

  * Represents cumulative FDI, April 1951 to March 1992.
  [†] Estimated on basis of total asset data set out in Table 25 of US Department of Commerce 1991.
  [‡] Note that these investments may include investments in marketing and distribution by manufacturing companies.
  [§] Including that not classified.

Source: Japan: Ministry of Finance (based on investments approved by the Ministry); USA: US Department of Commerce 1991 (based on information provided by US MNEs).

value of the Japanese stake in March 1992 was $68.0 billion, some 25.4 per cent of the US stake of $224.6 billion in December 1991. This relatively higher Japanese participation reflects the fact that the Japanese stake in European service industries was $49.3 billion[1], 46.8 per cent of the US stake

  [1] The Japanese figure includes a small amount of agricultural and mining activities.

of $105.4 billion. In finance, insurance, and property alone, the Japanese investment was $35.4 billion, 47.6 per cent of the US investment of $74.4 billion, whereas in wholesale trade, the percentage of Japanese to US capital stock was nearly twice that in manufacturing industry, namely 33.5 per cent compared to 17.1 per cent.

More detailed data are available on the employment of Japanese manufacturing affiliates in 1990 and US manufacturing affiliates in 1989. Some of these are reproduced in Table 2.2. They broadly corroborate the data in Table 2.1, but suggest that within sectors, there may be quite significant differences in the JCC ratio. Other data (JETRO 1991) also reveal that in the general machinery sector and instruments sector, it was especially high in office and photographic equipment; while in the electrical and electronic sector, it was more marked in the production of consumer goods (notably colour TV sets, video recorders, microwave ovens) than in the production of electronic components.

The final column of Table 2.2 makes use of what we shall call the Japanese/US revealed employment advantage ratio (Japanese/US REA). This ratio is obtained by dividing the share of the total employment of US manufacturing subsidiaries accounted for by a particular sector by the share of the Japanese subsidiaries in that sector.[2] For the remainder of this paper, Japanese/US REA is the variable which—in the absence of more detailed data on capital stock or sales—we shall take as our own proxy for the relative significance of Japanese (cf. US) direct participation in European manufacturing industry.[3]

3. EXPLAINING THE DIFFERENT STRUCTURE OF JAPANESE MNE ACTIVITY IN EUROPEAN MANUFACTURING INDUSTRY

3.1. Some Alternative Theories

It is, perhaps, worth recalling that, in the early 1970s, when the first wave of Japanese manufacturing investment in Europe occurred, US foreign subsidiaries were already contributing between 12 and 15 per cent of the manufacturing output of the major European industrial powers. This investment had been initiated as market-seeking investment, and was primarily prompted by the world-wide shortage of US dollars. Later, as a result of the removal of the tariff barriers between member countries of a newly formed European Economic Community (EC), the European production by US MNEs was restructured to better exploit the economies of scope

---

[2] Namely, $E_{Ji}/E_{USi} - E_{Jt}/E_{USt}$ where i = a particular industrial sector and t = all manufacturing sectors.

[3] There is an implicit assumption in this procedure that sectoral capital/labour ratios for Japanese affiliates are broadly similar to those of their US affiliates. I am grateful to Dennis Encarnation for pointing this out to me.

TABLE 2.2. *Employment distribution of Japanese and US affiliates in European manufacturing*

	Japan 1990	%	US 1989 000s	%	J/US REA
Processing Industries					
1. Food & kindred products	453	0.50	119.7	7.95	0.06
2. Pharmaceuticals	1,823	2.01	79.5	5.28	0.38
3. Other chemical products*	4,800	5.29	177.7	11.81	0.45
4. Iron and steel[†]	450[‡]	0.49	36.5	2.43	0.20
5. Textiles & clothing	493	0.54	30.6	2.03	0.27
6. Wood-related products	14	0.02	6.9	0.46	0.04
7. Rubber products	18,778	20.72	40.8	2.71	7.65
8. Non-ferrous materials[§]	4,010[‡]	4.42	72.5	4.82	0.92
Fabricating Industries					
9. General machinery	8,384	9.25	158.5	10.53	0.88
10. Electronic & electronic equipment**	22,981	25.36	268.6	17.85	1.42
11. Transport equipment	21,061	23.24	309.1	20.54	1.13
12. Instruments	3,905	4.31	107.2	7.12	0.61
13. Other industries	3,459	3.82	97.5	6.48	0.59
All Industries	90,611	100.00	1505.1	100.00	1.00

J/US REA = Japanese/US revealed employment advantage. (For definition, see text.)

*   Includes plastics.
†   Includes metal products.
‡   MITI figures adjusted based on data from Yamawaki (1991).
§   Includes glass, stone and ceramics.
** Includes computers, office machinery and computers.

Source: MITI 1991; US Department of Commerce 1991; Yamawaki 1991.

and large-scale production (Cantwell 1992); and by 1977, not only were US affiliates in the EC exporting 39 per cent of their output to countries other than the US (and mainly to elsewhere in the EC), but 59 per cent of these exports were to sister affiliates (US Department of Commerce 1981).

From the start, however, Japanese investment in the EC has been aimed at exploiting the European market as a whole. Like its US counterpart, it was (and is) essentially market-seeking; and like the US MNEs in the 1950s, Japanese MNEs have been persuaded to invest in Europe earlier than they might have done by the inability of European consumers to purchase freely the imports they wanted.[4] Partly because of the moves towards regional integration, and partly because of their need to 'catch up' in the globalization process, Japanese firms have pursued a rationalized

---

[4] Except that in the 1980s, tariff barriers, import quotas and voluntary export restrictions limited Japanese exports to Europe in the way the high value and absolute US shortage of US dollars limited the import.

and asset-acquiring European investment strategy from the start. Especially in sectors in which there is (or was) surplus capacity, Japanese firms have entered the European market by acquiring existing producers, rather than setting up new greenfield ventures. The rubber tyre sector is a particularly good example of a sector which is strongly globalized in its orientation. Yet to serve the foreign transplants of their own motor vehicle firms, and indeed other auto producers, more efficiently, Japanese firms have chosen to acquire established—and for the most part ailing—European or US MNEs.[5]

In recent years, attempts by economists to explain the foreign activities of MNEs have mainly fallen into two groups. The first are those which seek to offer generic paradigms, within which it is possible to accommodate a variety of specific, and operationally testable, theories of FDI and the internationalization of production. The internalization and eclectic paradigms fall into this category. The second are those which identify and seek to assess the significance of a number of operationally testable variables in explaining particular kinds of aspects of MNE activity.

Our basic assertion is that the phenomenon of Japanese direct investment in Europe requires only minor modification to the existing paradigms of international production; but that the specific variables which economists have used to explain much of US direct investment in Europe in the 1960s and 1970s are not those which best explain much of current Japanese MNE activity in that area.

While we shall primarily use the framework of the eclectic paradigm of international production to support our argument, it may be helpful very briefly to review the applicability of some of the theories earlier put forward to explain outbound US FDI to our present discussion.

(*a*) *The product cycle thesis.* In many ways, Raymond Vernon's original product cycle theory (1966) is a better explanation for much of recent Japanese investment in Europe than it is for explaining the contemporary activities of US MNEs. Goods requiring resources and capabilities in which Japan had (or managed to create for herself) a comparative advantage were first exported by Japan to countries with similar income levels and tastes, e.g. much of Western Europe (Ozawa 1992). Then when, because of improved market prospects, it became more profitable to produce these goods (or part of their value added) in Europe, or barriers were placed on Japanese exports, Japanese firms set up (or acquired) production facilities in Europe. Between 1975 and 1990, for example, the ratio of cars exported from Japan to Europe relative to those produced by Japanese companies in Europe fell from near infinity to 6.0, and of CTV sets from 8.0 to 0.8.

---

[5] Examples include Bridgestone's acquisition of Firestone (US) and Sumitomo's acquisition of Dunlop (UK). Whether they be US or European companies, however, the acquired tyre makers had (and have) substantial European investments.

Year	1970–5	1976–80	1981–5	1986–91
CTVs	4	1	5	6
Photocopiers	1		1	8
Rubber products			6	4
Motor vehicles			2	3
Year	1970–5	1976–80	1981–5	1986–91

Note: Figures in circles represent number of firms established in 5-year period.

FIG. 2.1. Clustering of Japanese subsidiaries in Europe

The major differences between the thrust of US firms into Europe in the 1960s and that of their Japanese counterparts in the 1980s is that first, unlike their predecessors, Japanese MNEs have treated Europe as a single market and, in that light, have pursued a regionally integrated product and locational strategy; and second (as will be discussed later), the form and interaction between the competitive or ownership-specific advantages of Japanese (cf. US) firms and the competitive or location-specific advantages of Japan (cf. the USA) have led to a different industrial structure of such investment.

(*b*) *The 'follow my leader' thesis.* Working on data on the internationalization of US-based MNEs, Knickerbocker (1973) concluded that the timing of the entry of US firms into foreign markets was bunched. He asserted that this reflected the oligopolistic behaviour of such firms. This hypothesis is, again, broadly upheld by the data on the entry of Japanese foreign investors into Europe. Fig. 2.1 illustrates the kind of bunching revealed by Japanese MNEs entering into the consumer electronics industry

in the 1970s and the motor vehicle, rubber tyre, and photocopying industries in the 1980s.[6] Again however, it is worth noting that while Knickerbocker considered individual countries in Europe as separate (and largely
independent) locations, in the case of Japanese investors, it is more appropriate to consider them as regions of an integrated Europe.

(*c*) *The risk-diversification thesis.* The idea that the location of the foreign value-added activity of a company is a function of its propensity to
diversify country-specific risk was first analysed by Rugman (1979) based
upon some earlier work by Grubel (1968). We believe this has only limited
explanatory relevance as far as the current wave of Japanese investment
in Europe is concerned, chiefly because such investment is generally not
competitive with that which might have been directed to other countries,
and, apart from exchange rate fluctuations (now greatly modified by the
alignment of the currencies of the EC countries), the risk premium of
investing in Europe is little different from investing in Japan or the US.

However, as in the case of US investors in the 1960s, Japanese MNEs
are becoming increasingly sensitive about the distribution of their value-
added activities within Europe. Partly, this is for political reasons (e.g.
to pacify the French and Italians over the concentration of Japanese auto
investment in the UK, and the accusation of exporting Japanese cars to
France and Italy through a UK gateway!) and partly to ensure a reasonably
balanced portfolio of key European currencies.

(*d*) *The intangible assets thesis.* The idea that firms will invest abroad in
those sectors in which, relative to their foreign competitors, they possess
superior intangible assets, is associated with the work of many scholars,
including that of Hymer (1960, 1968), Caves (1971, 1974), Owen (1982),
Lall (1980), and Lall and Siddarthan (1982). One of the key components
of the thesis is that in order to produce in particular countries, foreign
firms need to possess a set of intangible assets (referred to by Hymer as
monopolistic advantages) which are sufficient to outweigh the specific costs
which they have to incur in undertaking the investment. Almost certainly,
these entry costs—and especially language problems and the unfamiliarity
with political, economic, and legal institutions, business customs, organizational structures, supplying facilities, industrial relations, and government regulations have been (and are) higher for Japanese than for US
firms; and to some extent at least, these differences explain the greater
preference of the former relative to the latter to supply the European
markets via exports.[7]

---

[6] Other examples are given by Micossi and Viesti 1991. Outside manufacturing industry,
there are examples of Japanese firms pursuing 'follow my leader' strategies in retail and
wholesale banking.

[7] In 1990, while 80% of manufactured products supplied by US firms and bought by
European consumers were made in Europe by US manufacturing subsidiaries, the equivalent
percentage for Japanese firms was 20%. These percentages have been calculated from various

However, as has been shown elsewhere (United Nations 1992), the nature of these intangible assets is likely to be both industry and country specific; hence those which might satisfactorily explain the industry structure of US direct investment in Europe may not be appropriate to explaining Japanese investment in Europe. Moreover, as Kogut (1983) has demonstrated, the kind of advantages which lead firms to initially forage abroad may be quite different from those likely to determine the sequential growth of such investments. In particular, the literature has distinguished between the ownership-specific advantages which stem from possession of specific assets (e.g. a particular technology or type of product market), and those which arise from the cross-border governance of a collection of assets. We shall consider this distinction in more detail in Section 4 of this paper.

(*e*) *The Kojima hypothesis.* In several contributions, both the present author (1958 and 1981) and Kijoshi Kojima (1978, 1990) have argued that FDI should follow the principle of comparative advantage, and that firms should only engage in foreign value-added activities which require an input of natural resources or created capabilities in which the host country is comparatively well endowed relative to the home country. In the past, Kojima has consistently alleged that the geographical distribution of Japanese MNE activity more nearly meets his criteria than that of US MNE activity. However, to explain the rapid growth of Japanese FDI in Europe, and its industrial distribution, Kojima would either have to abandon his earlier assertion that Japanese investment is more trade-oriented than its US counterpart, or to accept that there are other kinds of efficiency enhancing FDI (particularly of an intra-industry variety), or to acknowledge that the kind of market imperfections (e.g. tariff barriers) imposed on US exports, or oligopolistic tactics deployed by US MNEs, are now being imposed on Japanese exports or being practised by Japanese firms. Whatever the explanation, Kojima's thesis, as initially stated, is not very helpful in explaining much of the growth of Japanese MNE activity in European manufacturing industry, and particularly that which has occurred as a result of mergers and acquisitions (M&As) in recent years.

3.2. General Paradigms

Turning to the two general economic explanations of international production, we shall concentrate on the eclectic paradigm, as it also embraces the essential features of the internalization paradigm.[8] Essentially, the paradigm avers that the propensity of firms to engage in FDI will depend

---

trade and production data published by the Department of Commerce, MITI, and the Japanese Ministry of Finance.

[8] For a discussion of the distinction between the two paradigms see Dunning 1991.

on the interaction between their unique competitive and/or monopolistic (or ownership specific [O]) advantages and the locational [L] attractions of alternative sites for the creation or use of those advantages;[9] and also on the extent to which firms find it in their interests to internally [I] govern these resources and capabilities in preference to other organizational routes, e.g. the external market or co-operative arrangements.

The paradigm further suggests that the exact configuration of the *OLI* advantages facing firms and their strategic response to it will depend on (i) the countries of origin of the investing companies and the countries in which they are making the investment; (ii) the characteristics of the value activities financed by the FDI (usually considered as industry specific characteristics); and (iii) the economic and behavioural attributes of the investing firms themselves—that is, characteristics *apart* from their nationality of ownership, or degree of multinationality.

For example, since the competitive advantages of enterprises are, to some extent at least, likely to reflect the location-bound characteristics of their home countries, it may be reasonable to hypothesize that the *O* advantages which are most pertinent to explaining US MNE activity in Europe will be different from those explaining Japanese direct investment in that region. Similarly, the variables likely to influence the *L* advantages facing US firms in supplying the European market, from a USA relative to a European production facility, may not be the same as those facing Japanese MNEs; while the kinds of market failure most relevant to explaining why US firms may choose to engage in FDI in Europe, rather than conclude co-operative, but non-equity, agreements with European firms, may be different from those which Japanese firms consider most appropriate in their organizational strategies.

The task of the economist seeking to explain differences in the level and composition of Japanese and US investment in Europe by use of the eclectic paradigm is twofold. First, it is to identify and evaluate which of the many possible *OLI* variables[10] is, or are, more likely to influence the two kinds of investment and why. Second, it is to establish how far and why such variables, and/or their values, may be different between value-added activities (in this case, industrial sectors). In pursuing both these tasks, it may be necessary for the analyst to draw upon some of the more specific theories outlined above and/or others put forward by business strategists, plus marketing and organizational scholars. Indeed, as we have repeatedly emphasized elsewhere (e.g. Dunning 1988), the eclectic paradigm should not be considered as a competing theory to these explanations,

---

[9] In a sense all advantages of firms are monopolistic, but it is useful to distinguish between those designed to exploit or extend a monopolistic position, and those (e.g. of a Schumpterian) kind which are designed to improve the static or dynamic efficiency of resource allocation.

[10] Set out in various publications of the author, but most recently in Dunning 1990.

but rather as an integrating framework both analysing them and evaluating their validity.

To the extent that patterns of trade differ between countries, and reflect the structure of the resources and capabilities of the trading nations, it is hardly surprising that patterns of outward or inward direct investment—which are, to some extent, based on the same specific endowments—are also country specific. Raymond Vernon was one of the first economists to make use of both the neoclassical and neo-technology theories of trade to explain the characteristics of US FDI (Vernon 1966, 1970); and his seminal contributions have been followed by others which assert that the competitive advantages possessed by firms at time '*t*' strongly reflect the immobile resources and capabilities of the countries from which they emanate in time '*t*-1'. More recently, Michael Porter (1990) has offered a conceptual framework for identifying the determinants of the competitive advantages of nations; while many of the attempts to explain the economic renaissance of Japan have sought to pinpoint the unique (that is, Japanese specific) factors influencing the productivity and behaviour of Japanese firms.

4. THE OWNERSHIP ADVANTAGES OF JAPANESE AND US FIRMS IN
EUROPE

4.1. Asset-Specific Advantages

Casual empiricism takes us some way in pinpointing the symptoms of Japanese economic success. Ask any European consumer why he or she buys a motor vehicle made by a Japanese firm rather than one made by a European or American firm, and the answer usually comes down to a combination of quality, price, reliability, and the technical and other attributes of the vehicle. It is now widely acknowledged that in the 1960s and 1970s, the only way the Japanese auto producers could effectively compete with the established Western car producers was either to produce a similar car at a lower price and higher quality, or to produce a car (in size, technical quality, and 'complementary' features such as cruise control, electric windows, etc.) which the existing producers were not supplying, and which consumers were signalling they wanted to buy (see e.g. Abegglen and Stalk 1985). Had the European- and US-owned car firms been producing at optimal (or '*X*') efficiency, the entry of Japanese producers into their territories would have been much more difficult. As it is, over the last two decades, the Japanese have continuously upgraded their competitive advantages, and are now in the vanguard of product and process innovation.

It is possible to identify specific intangible assets which firms of different nationalities may possess at the same or different time periods, the origin of which, at least, partly reflects the location-bound resources of the countries which give rise to them.[11] We say partly, because some of the *O* advantages evolved by Japanese firms reflect those of a newcomer entering an industry in which there existed some kind of static or dynamic inefficiency—including a failure of existing producers to identify existing or future consumer needs.

The example of the auto industry can be replicated in other sectors. The point is that whereas in the 1950s and 1960s, the *O*-specific advantages of US firms were primarily based on their ability to innovate new products and production processes, devise more appropriate organizational structures and professionalize structures, their marketing and budgetary control techniques, the *O* advantages of Japanese firms in the 1970s and 1980s essentially comprised their capability to co-ordinate and manage the resources and capabilities within their jurisdiction—including those acquired from Western nations—so as to minimize their '*X*' production and transaction costs.[12]

However, these symptoms of success themselves need explaining. They also beg many questions. Why is the Japanese economic prowess limited to particular kinds of activities? And why these particular activities? Exactly how have the Japanese been able to make such inroads into markets traditionally served by North American or European producers?

4.2. Governance–Specific Advantages

To answer these questions we need to turn to a second kind of *O*-specific advantage which firms may possess. This may best be described as the ability systemically to organize resources and capabilities under their governance. We have described these, for instance in Dunning 1988, as transaction cost minimizing or common governance ownership advantage (*Ot*).[13] Here the essential proposition is that the country of origin of a MNE is relevant in explaining the modalities of which it organizes its value-added activities, and that different modalities are more suited for some kinds of production than others. It is also likely that the *L*-specific endowments of a home country will influence a MNE's response to different types of market failure.

The questions which now arise are threefold. First, what are the particular attributes of Japanese, compared with US, firms in their governance of both internal and external transactions? Second, how do they impact on

---

[11] Tying *O*-specific advantages to a particular country becomes difficult as a firm becomes multinational, and especially as it undertakes high value activities outside its home country. But as far as Japanese MNEs are concerned, the great majority of innovatory activity (which results in the upgrading of the specific *O* assets of firms) is still undertaken in Japan.

[12] The comparative competitive advantages of the Japanese and US economies is further explored in Dunning 1990.

[13] Distinguishing them from *O* advantages based upon the possession or more efficient use of a specific asset, which we have referred to as *Oa*.

their response to different kinds of market failure? Third, given the answer to these questions, to what extent are these attributes specific to particular kinds of transactions or industrial sectors?

In answer to the first question, scholars are generally agreed that the governance of Japanese, relative to US, MNEs tends to be best marked by the ability efficiently to generate and sustain a consensus among the stakeholders involved in the production of goods and services to provide these goods and services at highest possible quality at the lowest possible cost. Put another way, their form of governance seems to be especially successful in managing idiosyncratic human-intensive transnational relations, whether they be organized within or between hierarchies. By contrast, casual inspection of the organizational structures of US MNEs suggest they have a comparative advantage in the administration of formalized, but more technical and standardized transactional relations.

Second, it is possible to classify different kinds of market failure according to the extent to which they can be best organized through tacit or informal systems of human co-operation or by formal hierarchical control and/or inter-firm contractual relationships. Some suggestions are put forward in Table 2.3. In this table, we have attempted to rank some of the reasons why firms may wish directly to control transnational relationships (whether via the hierarchical or a non-equity mode), by our perception of importance of the human intensity content relative to the technical intensity content of these relationships. For example, transactions which involve substantial search and negotiating costs, which have a high opportunistic element attached to them, which require the fullest co-operation of workers to ensure that rigorous quality control procedures are maintained, and the success of which is strongly dependent on supplier reliability and the readiness of sales agents to behave in a way which advances the interests of their principals, are among those classified as (relatively) human-intensive. On the other hand, the ability of firms to engage in price discrimination, to capture the economies of interdependent activities, to compensate for the absence of futures markets, to control suppliers or market outlets, and to reduce the risks of exchange fluctuations, all are transaction-related activities which depend more on the technical characteristics of the firm and/or on the business acumen of its managers.

Third, the presence of at least some of these market failures is likely to vary between industrial sectors. Table 2.3 sets out our estimate on a ranking of 1 to 3 of the relevance of different kinds of market failure to particular sectors. As the table reveals, human-related market failure is relatively most pronounced in the fabricating sectors, while technical market failure, though no less significant in these sectors, tends to be more significant than human-related market failure in the processing sectors.

Most of the literature on market failure tends to take as given the transaction costs of using external markets, and considers the conditions under

TABLE 2.3. *Hypothetical variation of internal governance by industry*

	Processing sectors								Fabricating sectors			
	1	2	3	4	5	6	7	8	9	10	11	12
1. Relatively human-intensive												
Search & negotiating costs	2	2	1	1	2	2	1	2	3	3	3	3
Quality control (of labour-intensive production)	2	2	2	1	3	2	2	1	3	3	3	3
Supplier reliability	2	3	1	2	2	2	1	1	3	3	3	3
Agent reliability	1	3	1	1	2	1	1	1	2	3	3	3
Opportunism in labour market *et al.*	1	1	1	2	2	2	1	2	3	3	3	3
2. Relatively technical-intensive												
Protection of property rights	2	3	3	2	1	1	2	1	3	3	2	3
Protection of trademarks	3	3	2	1	2	1	3	3	1	2	2	2
Economies of scale or scope	3	2	2	2	1	2	2	3	3	3	3	1
Diversification of risks	2	3	3	2	1	1	2	1	2	2	2	2
Economies of joint supply	2	2	2	2	2	2	1	2	3	2	1	2
Arbitraging of markets	2	2	2	1	1	1	2	1	2	2	2	1
Price discrimination	3	3	2	1	2	2	2	2	2	2	2	2
Quality control (of machine-intensive production)	3	3	3	2	2	2	3	3	2	2	2	2

Key to sectors

1 Food and kindred products	7 Rubber products
2 Pharmaceuticals	8 Non-metallic materials
3 Other chemicals	9 General machinery
4 Iron and steel	10 Computers, electrical equipment & goods
5 Textiles and clothing	11 Transport equipment & parts
6 Wood-related products	12 Photographic and precision instruments

Note: The higher the figures in the table, the more important the reasons are perceived to be.

which firms can lower these costs by internalizing these markets.[14] But there are other alternatives open to firms. Moreover, the extent and pattern of the failure of a particular market or the market system *in toto* may vary over time. One option to administered hierarchies—often neglected by economists—is for a firm to try to improve the efficiency of external markets by tilting the terms of exchange and conditions of demand and/or supply in their favour. For example, it might be possible for an MNE to improve the quality of a product supplied by its subcontractor or the reliability with which it is supplied by providing advice to its suppliers as to how best to remedy these deficiencies. Also, by a restructuring of incentives, a sales agent may be persuaded to work more in his principal's interests than he is currently doing. Alternatively, firms may reduce the organizational costs of markets by engaging in co-operative ventures which are 'in between' arm's-length transactions and internal hierarchies.

The response of MNEs to both domestic and cross-border market failure is likely to be country-, industry-, and firm-specific. For example, the Japanese auto industry in Japan is considerably less vertically integrated than its US counterpart in the USA. There are various reasons for this, but, most surely, one of the most important is that the relationships which Japanese auto-assemblers have forged with their suppliers have helped lower the (inter-firm) transaction costs of using intermediate product markets (Okada 1991). In other words, by helping to reduce market failure, the Japanese auto-assemblers have had less incentive to internalize such markets. Secondly, the suitability of using a particular organizational route may vary according to the character of the products being supplied.

In our analysis of *O*-specific factors influencing the Japanese/US REA ratio, we shall assume that the costs and benefits of common governance economies will depend on the kind and complexity of transactions—and especially the human-intensity content of them—and also the number of particular kinds of benefits.

Let us sum up this part of our paper. The competitive or *O* advantages of MNEs fall into two groups. First the possession of specific income-generating assets; and second, the way in which a firm governs the organization of these assets, in response to its perceived costs and benefits of alternative modes. It is our contention that both kinds of *O* advantages are partly country specific, and reflect the structure of the location-based resources and capabilities of the countries of origin of MNEs, as well as those of countries in which their subsidiaries operate.[15]

In this section, we have suggested that there are reasons to suppose that differences in Japanese and US country-specific characteristics (e.g. as

---

[14] For a recent analysis of the costs and benefits of organizing transactions subject to different kinds of market failure see Kojima 1992.

[15] This paper does not consider this second influence on the *O*-specific advantage of firms.

identified by Porter 1990[16]) not only cause Japanese and US firms to possess (or seek to acquire) different kinds of O advantages, but that these, in turn, will affect their relative abilities to supply particular kinds of products. Thus for these reasons alone, we would expect the revealed employment advantage of Japanese and US manufacturing affiliates in Europe to be different.

More specifically, and set out as two hypotheses (0^1, 0^2), we are suggesting that:

0^1 The more Japanese firms, relative to US firms, possess (or utilize efficiently) specific asset advantages, the higher the Japanese/US employment ratio in Europe is likely to be.

0^2 The greater the common governance advantages of Japanese relative to US firms, the higher the Japanese/US employment ratio in Europe is likely to be.

We are also hypothesizing that both of these advantages are also likely to be of varying importance between industrial sectors.

5. THE COMPARATIVE LOCATIONAL ADVANTAGES OF EUROPE AS A PRODUCTION BASE TO JAPANESE AND US FIRMS

It is one thing to identify the country-specific, competitive, or O advantages of Japanese and US firms, but quite another to conclude that the FDI structures of the two groups of firms should necessarily be different. For, given the same O advantages, it may be profitable for Japanese firms to create or utilize these advantages from a home location rather than a European location, while US firms may find it profitable to create or utilize their O advantages from a European, rather than a home, location. The Japanese/US REA ratio could, then, reflect the different locational perceptions and preferences of the two groups of firms.

The literature is replete with explanations of the variables influencing the location of the activities by MNEs (United Nations 1992). Some are likely to be product or host country specific rather than home country (or home to host country) specific. Examples include products which need to be adapted to the needs of foreign purchasers, and non-discriminatory taxes, incentives, and import controls imposed by host country governments.

---

[16] In his 'diamond of competitive advantages' Porter distinguishes between four attributes: factor endowments, inter-firm rivalry, presence of related and supporting industries, and quality of consumer demand. Each of these, in turn, may be affected by government and by chance. In our review of Porter's work (Dunning 1992) we added another exogenous variable, namely, international business activity. It is not difficult to trace how each of these advantages may lead to Japanese and US firms developing a different structure of Oa and Ot advantages, which, in turn, will result in a different pattern of Japanese- and US-owned domestic and foreign activity.

But others which reflect differences in the resource capabilities and endowments of the home and host countries, physical or psychic distances between these countries, and discriminatory import and investment policies of a host government towards a particular foreign country or its firms, will affect the way in which a particular market is served, and hence the revealed employment ratio of foreign subsidiaries.

Table 2.4 identifies some of these variables and estimates their likely significance as factors influencing the locational determinants by Japanese and US MNEs selling to European markets. The impact of these variables is also most likely to be activity and sector specific, and some estimates—on a scale of 1 to 3[17]—of which sectors are likely to be affected by any particular factor are also given in the table.

Our reading of the literature on the motives for Japanese and US direct investment in European industry (e.g. JETRO 1991) suggests that, besides the real exchange rate, there are four locational variables, the value of which, or the response to which, is likely to be very different between the two home countries.

(1) *Productivity in the home country.* Here the hypothesis (L^1) is that the higher the productivity in Japan relative to that in the USA, the less the Japanese/US employment ratio in Europe is likely to be. (This hypothesis would be nullified if it could be shown that the differences in productivity were not country but firm specific, and that they are transferable across national borders.) For reasons set out in Section 3, these differences are also likely to be partly industry specific. While, ideally, one would like to include all factors of production in our productivity measure, in practice, one has to make do with a labour productivity measure (see Sect. 6 below).

(2) *Distance costs.* These are determined by the physical and psychic distance between the exporting and importing countries and the nature of the product being supplied. Casual observation would suggest that both kinds of distance costs are likely to be greater between Japan and Europe than the USA and Europe.[18] Clearly, too, these distance costs are likely to vary between products according to such variables as weight, bulkiness, fragility, or perishability of the products being transported. The hypothesis (L^2) here is that the greater the transport costs per unit of product produced the greater the Japanese/US employment ratio in Europe is likely to be, because Japanese firms would have a relatively greater incentive to supply the European market for a European location.

(3) *Tariff and non-tariff barriers.* Most government-imposed barriers to imports from Japan and the USA do not discriminate by country of origin, but some do; over the past decade, most discriminatory measures have

---

[17] In ascending order of significance as a locational variable.
[18] The sea distance from Tokyo to Southampton is approximately 15,000 miles and from New York approximately 3,000 miles.

TABLE 2.4. *Likely influences on the location of MNE activity, by industry*

	Processing sectors								Fabricating sectors			
	1	2	3	4	5	6	7	8	9	10	11	12
1. Tending to favour a home location												
Low transport costs of finished products	1	3	2	1	3	2	2	3	2	2	1	2
Substantial plant economies of scale	2	3	3	3	2	1	1	3	3	3	3	3
Low real input prices in home cf. host country	1	2	1	1	2	1	1	1	1	1	1	1
Large physical or cultural distance between home & host countries	2	1	1	1	3	2	1	1	1	1	1	1
Relatively high intra-firm communication costs												
High risk/commitment ratio costs of investing in a foreign location	2	3	3	3	2	1	2	2	2	2	2	1
Near location of important inputs	3	1	1	1	1	1	1	1	2	2	2	3
2. Tending to favour a foreign (European) location												
Need to adapt products to local consumer needs	3	2	1	3	3	2	1	1	1	2	2	1
High transport costs of finished products	2	1	2	3	1	2	2	3	2	1	2	1
High production costs of home cf. host country	3	1	2	1	1	1	1	1	2	2	2	1
Tariff or non-tariff barriers	1	2	1	3	2	1	1	1	2	3	3	1
Relatively low intra-firm communication costs	1	2	2	1	1	2	1	2	3	3	2	2
Investment incentives	1	2	2	1	3	2	2	1	2	3	2	2
Good local infrastructure and/or supplier networks	2	2	2	1	1	1	2	1	2	1	3	2
Near location of important inputs	2	1	2	3	2	3	2	2	2	2	2	2

Key to sectors

1 Food and kindred products
2 Pharmaceuticals
3 Other chemicals
4 Iron and steel
5 Textiles and clothing
6 Wood-related products

7 Rubber products
8 Non-metallic materials
9 General machinery
10 Computers, electrical equipment & goods
11 Transport equipment & parts
12 Photographic and precision instruments

Note: The higher the figures in the table, the more important the reasons are perceived to be.

arisen as a result either of the perceived dumping by Japanese producers of such products as cameras and photocopiers, or of the unacceptable (speed of the) penetration of European markets by Japanese exporters of such products as autos, CTV sets, VTRs, etc. Our hypothesis (L^3) here is that the greater the discriminatory import measures against Japanese firms in any one sector, the higher the Japanese/US employment ratio in Europe is likely to be.

(4) *Revealed comparative exporting advantage* (RCA). Finally, we consider a measure which encompasses revealed comparative advantage (RCA) in exports. This represents the extent to which exports from Japan to Europe, relative to exports from the US in particular sectors, are shown (on the basis of past data) to be higher or lower than the exports of all products from Japan to Europe, relative to exports from the US. Here there are two conflicting hypotheses. The first (L^{4a}) is that Japanese or US exports to Europe and the European production of their subsidiaries are substitutes for each other, and that the RCA of Japanese exports is likely to be negatively correlated with the Japanese/US REA ratio in Europe (i.e. the L advantage favours the home country). The other hypothesis (L^{4b}) is that exports and foreign production are alternative indices of the competitive advantage of the exporting and investing country, and that a high RCA of Japanese exports in Europe is likely to be positively correlated with a high Japanese/US REA ratio (i.e. the L advantage favours the host country).

6. DO JAPANESE MNES INTERNALIZE INTERMEDIATE PRODUCT MARKETS BETWEEN JAPAN AND EUROPE MORE THAN THEIR US COUNTERPARTS?

Ethier (1986) has referred to the internalization variable as being the 'Caesar' in the *OLI* triumvirate explaining MNE activity. In the current exercise, it plays a less significant role. Partly this is because we have subsumed the relative ability of US and Japanese hierarchies to govern the resources and capabilities within their jurisdiction under the second group of *O*-specific advantages. Partly it is because there are few reasons to suppose that the transactional costs[19] of engaging in trans-Atlantic or trans-Asian arm's-length transactions should be substantially different. Exceptions might include the costs of upgrading the quality of local inputs to a differential level of quality expected by Japanese (cf. US) firms, and the identification and nurturing of appropriate distribution channels and after-sales servicing facilities.

One area in which the opportunity and incentive (as opposed to the ability) of firms to internalize cross-border markets is likely to vary

---

[19] As opposed to the way in which Japanese or US firms might affect these costs by endogenizing them.

according to the nationality of the investing firm relates to the extent to which it is possible for it to exploit economies of scale or scope. Clearly this opportunity is related to the size and geographical distribution of MNEs in different parts of Europe. Since US direct investment in Europe is so much larger and geographically more dispersed than its Japanese counterpart, it is reasonable to assume that the opportunities for it to exploit the benefits of process and product specialization are that much greater. The literature, for example, strongly suggests that, irrespective of their nationalities, MNEs which pursue regional or globally integrated strategies tend to internalize their cross-border markets more than those which supply products wholly for domestic markets (Doz 1986, Cantwell 1992).

One index that might be used to demonstrate the validity or otherwise of this proposition is the proportion of intra-firm European trade by Japanese (cf. US) firms in Europe. Unfortunately we only have data for the latter. Since we know, however, that the volume of intra-European exports by Japanese firms is small and that most of them are intra-firm, we may hypothesize (as we do in I^1) that the Japanese/US employment ratio in Europe is likely to be positively related to the ratio between intra-European exports of Japanese subsidiaries and the intra-firm, intra-European exports of US subsidiaries.[20]

One other measure of the relative propensity of Japanese and US firms to internalize their trans-Asian and trans-Atlantic intermediate markets relates to their respective opportunities to forge vertical or horizontal networks in Europe. This networking propensity is extremely difficult to measure, but one such index could be the extent to which a particular industrial sector is dominated by firms belonging to the six leading *keiretsu*. Because some estimates are available, we have chosen to take as our independent variable the proportion of the output of a sector supplied by the six leading *keiretsu* (Gerlach 1992). The hypothesis here (I^2) is that the higher the networking of Japanese firms (in Japan) the greater the Japanese/US employment ratio—it being somewhat heroically assumed that the benefits of networking in Japan can be transferred to a European location.

7. SOME EXPLORATORY TESTING

Since Japanese direct investment in Europe is still a very recent phenomenon and much of the data we need to test the kind of hypotheses set out earlier in this paper is not disaggregated in sufficient industrial detail, we have had to abandon the kind of econometric exercise we had originally hoped to conduct. In later years, as the volume of Japanese investment

[20] For example, from surveys conducted by JETRO of manufacturing subsidiaries in Europe.

increases, and its pattern becomes more geographically and industrially diversified, it may be possible to undertake some pooled cross-sectional regression or logit analysis using data from the individual European countries. We experimented with such an exercise in the course of this paper, but, with the exception of a significant relationship between the Japanese/US employment ratio and the revealed comparative exporting advantage (L^4), it produced completely inconclusive results.

Instead, in Tables 2.5 and 2.6, we have set some data about the values of the independent variable and the seven independent variables identified in Sections 3–5 of our paper. In most cases, we have presented the actual values of the various data and then ranked these by sector. In two cases, we have compiled an estimated ranking from a composite of proxy variables.

While we would be the first to admit that this procedure leaves much to be desired, we none the less believe that the data set out in Tables 2.5 and 2.6 do tell an interesting and, for the most part, consistent story. First, it is possible to identify a number of unique characteristics associated with Japanese (cf. US) direct investment in Europe. Most certainly, some of these characteristics reflect the much more recent entry of Japanese MNEs into Europe, their relative lack of knowledge and experience of European markets, their smaller size, and their limited industrial and geographical diversification. But others, at least in the 1980s, reflect the different configuration of *OLI* variables facing Japanese cf. US firms, which specifically reflect the unique features of their respective home economies—and which, in turn, lead to distinctive production, marketing, and organizational strategies on the part of Japanese MNEs.

The data in Tables 2.5 and 2.6 confirm that the industrial structures of Japanese and US manufacturing affiliates in Europe are generally positively correlated with their respective revealed patenting and common governance advantages. The main exception is the relatively large investment by Japanese firms in the rubber industry, which mainly reflects the strategic purchases by Sumitomo and Bridgestone of the Dunlop and Firestone rubber tyre plants in Europe.[21] More particularly, the value of the independent variable is highest in those sectors in which the human-intensity market-related transaction costs are also higher.

The *L*-specific variables identified yield mixed results. The tables show that the Japanese/US employment ratio in electrical and transport equipment is positively related to the non-tariff barriers exerted on these products by European governments, while, excepting iron and steel products, there is some suggestion that Japanese and US exports are complementary with, rather than substitutable for, FDI. On the other hand, there seems to be little systematic relationship between the composition of Japanese

---

[21] Such investment would be regarded as auto-supporting investment. The Japanese preferred the A&M route to the greenfield route of entry because of surplus capacity in the European auto industry.

TABLE 2.5. *A list of variables explaining Japanese/US employment ratios, by industry*

	J/US (employment ratio)	O^1	O^2	L^1	L^2	$L^{3\dagger}$	L^4	I^1	I^2
Processing industries									
Food and kindred products	0.06	0.64	7	0.61	16.6	10.26	0.03	1.30	n.a.
Pharmaceuticals	0.38	0.89	12	1.11	0.7	(1.52)	0.16)	0.58	46.3
Other chemicals	0.45	0.88	8	1.15	38.0	(	0.36)	1.22	63.5
Iron and steel†	0.20	0.67	5	1.43	21.7	9.74	1.04	1.22	79.0
Textiles and clothing	0.27	0.52	6	0.85	35.7	7.26	0.79	0.24	40.3
Wood-related products	0.04	n.a.	11	0.92	n.a.	0.00	0.03	0.00	35.6
Rubber	7.65	1.08	9	0.90	39.4	0.52	2.49	n.a.	59.9
Non-ferrous materials†	0.92	1.10	10	1.02	42.6	0.38	0.37	1.06	82.5
Fabricating industries									
General machinery	0.88	0.69	3	1.00	10.1	1.60	0.57	2.10	77.1
Electrical equipment*	1.42	1.53	2	0.87	17.1	1.72†	1.40	1.13	70.8
Transport equipment	1.13	1.46	1	0.93	4.3	3.15†	1.26	1.25	87.1
Instruments	0.59	1.57	4	0.63	5.0	n.a.	0.85	0.14	30.8

O^1 = Ratio of revealed technological advantage of Japan and USA in overall innovation 1978–86 (Cantwell and Hodson 1991, table 5.10).

O^2 = Author's estimate based on an estimate of average number of transactions involved in production of goods.

L^1 = Ratio of labour productivity (value added divided by average employment) in Japan and USA (1986) (United Nations 1990).

L^2 = Estimated value of transportation costs per unit value in each industry based on average value of Japanese and US exports to Germany (1989) [defined as CIF value minus FOB value] (OECD 1990).

L^3 = Average estimated *ad valorem* equivalents of non-tariff barriers in European countries (%) (Saxonhouse and Stern 1989, table 9.4).

L^4 = Ratio between the revealed comparative advantage of Japan and US exports (1989) (United Nations *Commodity Trade Statistics*, 1990).

I^1 = Estimate of ratios between Japanese and US intra-firm, intra-European exports to total exports (1979) (US Department of Commerce 1991, MITI 1991).

I^2 = % of sales of Japanese firms accounted for by *keiretsu* (Dodwell Marketing Consultants 1986, Gerlach 1992).

* Includes computers and office machinery.

† The percentage *ad valorem* in those industries does not reflect the actions of individual EC countries in restricting imports of Japanese goods.

TABLE 2.6. *The ranking of variables explaining Japanese/US employment ratios, by industry*

	J/US (employment ratio)	O^1	O^2	L^1	L^2	$L^{3\dagger}$	L^4	I^1	I^2
Processing industries									
Food and kindred products	11	10	7	12	7	3	11	2	n.a.
Pharmaceuticals	8	6	12	3	11	7	10	7	8
Other chemicals	7	7	8	2	3	7	9	7	6
Iron and steel†	10	9	5	1	5	4	4	4	3
Textiles and clothing	9	11	6	10	4	5	6	9	9
Wood-related products	12	n.a.	11	7	n.a.	11	11	11	10
Rubber	1	5	10	8	2	9	1	n.a.	7
Non-ferrous materials	4	4	9	4	1	10	8	6	2
Average ranking	7.8	7.4	8.5	5.9	4.7	7	7.5	6.6	6.4
Fabricating industries									
General machinery	5	8	3	5	8	6	7	1	4
Electrical equipment*	2	2	2	9	6	1†	2	5	5
Transport equipment	3	3	1	6	10	1†	3	3	1
Instruments	6	1	4	11	9	n.a.	5	10	11
Average ranking	4.0	3.5	2.5	7.8	8.3	2.7	4.3	4.8	5.2
Rank coefficient of correlation (with J/US Emp)	n.a.	+0.737	+0.350	−0.014	+0.164	+0.137	+0.739	+0.305	+0.409

* Includes computers and office machinery.
† The percentage *ad valorem* in those industries does not reflect the actions of individual EC countries in restricting imports of Japanese goods.

and US MNE activities and that of domestic labour productivity or of the estimated transportation costs. Of the two proxies for internalization advantages, only the second—membership of one of the leading *keiretsu*—seems to be positively and closely ranked with the dependent variable.

It is also clear from Tables 2.5 and 2.6 that the factors influencing the Japanese/US employment ratio differ between sectors. For example, partly reflecting the distinctiveness of Japanese tastes and partly the comparatively low propensity of the Japanese to engage in foreign patenting, there is little Japanese FDI in the European food and beverage sector. This could change in the 1990s if and when the population of East Asians in Europe increases. By contrast, with the exception of transportation costs, the ranking of each of the explanatory variables for transport equipment and electronic products is either very or quite closely ranked with the Japanese/US employment ratio.

The case of rubber products is an interesting one. The Japanese do not appear to have strong *O*-specific advantages in this sector. Yet it is one which is dominated by large MNEs which, in the past, have tended to follow auto companies abroad. However, because of surplus capacity in rubber tyres and the relative unimportance of human-intensive transaction costs in their production, Japanese firms have preferred to invest in Europe (and the USA) by way of acquisition rather than greenfield investment. Hence their comparatively large volume of FDI and employment in this sector.

Despite relatively high transport costs and non-tariff barriers, there is little Japanese investment in the European iron and steel industry. This is a sector in which the Japanese firms enjoy relatively few *O*-specific advantages, *vis-à-vis* their US counterparts, but which, nevertheless, records higher labour productivity ratios in Japan. The relatively high Japanese/US employment ratio in non-ferrous materials is entirely due to a single large Japanese FDI in a Belgian glass-manufacturing company.

While Japanese firms record the highest revealed patenting advantage in instruments (including photographic equipment), their domestic productivity in this sector is the lowest. Transportation costs are relatively insignificant, as is the incentive to internalize cross-border markets. The relationships for general machinery and textiles and clothing also yield ambiguous results, although, in both cases, the mean ranking of the explanatory variables is broadly consistent with that of the Japanese/US employment ratio.

8. SOME UNRESOLVED QUESTIONS

There remain several interesting issues which only future events will resolve. We might identify just four of them; others may arise in the course of discussion. The first question concerns the extent to which the country-specific O advantages of Japanese firms are transferable to a European location. To what extent will the Japanese MNEs lose some of their competitive advantages as they are forced to engage in more international production? We are getting some hints from the experience of Japanese affiliates in both USA and Europe that many of them are, but it is early days yet. Most Japanese affiliates are still producing at the lower value-added part of their value chain and have yet to be fully integrated into the local economies of which they are a part.

Second, to what extent are the kind of O advantages, which are the basis of Japanese direct investment in Europe, capable of being copied by their foreign competitors (and especially US and European MNEs)? Again, we have strong suggestions that in some industries—especially the colour TV and photographic equipment sector—they have been, or are being. There is, for example, much less difference in the quality and reliability of the current generation of colour TVs and cameras now being marketed by firms of different nationalities than there was a decade or so ago.

Third, can one predict the kind of assets or forms of governance likely to determine the success of MNEs in the future? And even if one could—as some business scholars, such as Bartlett and Ghoshal (1989) and Doz and Prahalad (1987) have attempted—can one predict which country-specific characteristics are most likely to give rise to these advantages? In other words, is the present structure of Japanese investment in Europe a reflection of the past competitive advantages of Japan, which might be quite different from those which are likely to be the critical determinants of future outbound activity by Japanese MNEs?

Fourth, unlike its US counterpart, much of Japanese investment in Europe is initial rather than sequential; and the literature (e.g. Kogut 1983) suggests that as firms increase their degrees of multinationality, the structure of their OLI configuration changes; and that, in its turn, such change may affect particular sectors differently. For this reason, too, one might expect some realignment of the structure and significance of US and Japanese investment in Europe.

Much, of course, will depend on the form and pattern of growth of Japanese participation in Europe. Will growth occur along the value chain (e.g. via a deepening in the quality of such investment) or by product diversification? To what extent is Japanese investment, relative to US investment, likely to be directed to acquiring new competitive advantages (most noticeably through the joint venture and M&A route) rather than exploiting existing competitive advantages?

It would be a bold person who feels comfortable in predicting the comparative OLI configuration facing Japanese and US firms over the next decade. While the competitiveness convergence paradigm has much appeal, the idea of vicious and virtuous asset-generating circles (Cantwell

1989) suggests there could be considerable periods in which particular countries or firms can sustain, or even advance, their competitive positions. Certainly, the more one discerns about the commitment of the Japanese to the upgrading of human and physical capital, and their continued efforts to promote governance systems which are geared to advancing national and international competitiveness, the more one is led to infer that not only will the share of Japanese, relative to US, direct investment in European industry continue to increase, but, in those sectors which are most regionalized or globalized in their orientation, the share is likely to increase the fastest. Of course, macro-economic and other factors may completely negate this inference, but these are the subject of other papers in this Conference.

REFERENCES

ABEGGLEN, J., and STALK, G. (1985), *Kaisha: The Japanese Corporation* (New York: Basic Books).

BARTLETT, C., and GHOSHAL, S. (1989), *Managing Across Borders: The Transnational Solution* (Boston: Harvard Business School Press).

CANTWELL, J. (1989), *Technological Innovation and the Multinational Corporation* (Oxford: Basil Blackwell).

—— (1992), 'The Effect of Integration on the Structure of Multinational Corporation Activity in the EC', in M. Klein and P. Welfens, eds., *Multinationals in the New Europe and Global Trade* (Berlin and New York: Springer-Verlag).

—— and HODSON, C. (1991), 'Global R&D and UK Competitiveness', in M. Casson, ed., *Global Research Strategy and International Competitiveness* (Oxford: Basil Blackwell), 133–82.

CAVES, R. (1971), 'International Corporations: The Industrial Corporations of Foreign Investment', *Economica*, 38, 1–27.

—— (1974), 'Causes of Direct Investment: Foreign Firms Shares in Canadian and UK Manufacturing Industries', *Review of Economics and Statistics*, 56, 279–93.

Dodwell Marketing Consultants (1986), *Industrial Groupings in Japan* (7th edn. Tokyo: Dodwell Marketing Consultants).

DOZ, Y. (1986), *Strategic Management in Multinational Companies* (Oxford: Pergammon).

—— and PRAHALAD, C. (1987), *The Multinational Mission* (New York: The Free Press).

DUNNING, J. (1958), *American Investment in British Manufacturing Industry* (London: Allen and Unwin).

—— (1981), *International Production and the Multinational Enterprise* (London: Allen and Unwin).

—— (1988), *Explaining International Production* (London: Unwin Hyman).

—— (1989), 'The Theory of International Production', in K. Fatemi, ed., *The Theory of International Trade* (New York and London: Taylor and Francis).

—— (1990), *The Governance of Japanese and US Manufacturing Affiliates in the UK: Some Country Specific Differences* (Newark: University of Rutgers, GSM Working Paper 90–17, Aug.).

—— (1991), 'The Eclectic Paradigm of International Production: A Personal Note', in C. Pitelis and R. Sugden, eds., *The Nature of the Transnational Firm* (London and Boston: Routledge).

—— and CANTWELL, J. (1991), 'Japanese Direct Investment in Europe', in B. Bürgenmeier and J. Mucchielli, eds., *Multinationals and Europe (1992)* (London and New York: Routledge).

—— and GITTELMAN, M. (1992), 'Japanese Multinationals in Europe and the United States: Some Comparisons and Contrasts', in M. Klein and P. Welfens, eds., *Multinationals in the New Europe and Global Trade* (Berlin and New York: Springer-Verlag).

ETHIER, W. (1986), 'The Multinational Firm', *Quarterly Journal of Economics*, 101, 805–33.

GERLACH, M. (1992), *The Keiretsu: A Primer* (New York: Japan Society).

GRUBEL, H. (1968), 'International Diversified Portfolios: Welfare Gains and Capital Flows', *American Economic Review*, 58, 1299–314.

HENNART, J. (1991), 'The Transaction Cost Theory of Joint Ventures: An Empirical Study of Japanese Subsidiaries in the United States', *Management Science*, 37, 483–97.

HIRSCH, S., and MESHULACH, A. (1992), 'Towards a Unified Theory of Internationalization' (Tel Aviv and Hebrew Universities, mimeo).

HOOD, N., and TRUIJENS, T. (1992), 'European Locational Decisions of Japanese Manufacturers: Survey Evidence in the Case of the UK' (University of Strathclyde, mimeo).

HYMER, S. (1960), 'The International Operation of National Firms: A Study of Direct Investment' (Ph.D. dissertation, MIT; published by MIT Press, 1976).

—— (1968), 'La Grande Firme multinationale', *Revue économique*, 19, 943–73.

JETRO (1990), *Sixth Survey of Japanese Manufacturing Investment in Europe* (Tokyo: Japanese External Trade Organization, International Economic and Trade Information Center).

—— (1991), *Seventh Survey of European Operations of Japanese Companies in the Manufacturing Sector* (Tokyo: Japanese External Trade Organization, International Economic and Trade Information Center, Mar.).

Keizai Koho Center (1990), *Japan 1991: An International Comparison* (1st edn. Tokyo: Japan Institution for Social and Economic Affairs).

KNICKERBOCKER, F. (1973), *Oligopolistic Reaction of Multinational Enterprise* (Boston: Harvard University Press).

KOGUT, B. (1983), 'Foreign Direct Investment as a Sequential Process', in C. Kindleberger and D. Andretsch, eds., *Multinational Corporations in the 1980s* (Cambridge: MIT Press).

KOJIMA, K. (1978), *Direct Foreign Investment: A Japanese Model of Multinational Business* (London: Croom Helm).

—— (1990), *Japanese Investment Abroad* (Tokyo: International Christian University, Social Science Research Institute, Monograph Series, 1).

—— (1992), 'Internalization vs Cooperation of MNC's Business', *Hitutsubashi Journal of Economics*, 33/1 (June), 1–17.

LALL, S. (1980), 'Monopolistic Advantages and Foreign Investments by US Manufacturing Industry', *Oxford Economic Papers*, 32, 102–22.

—— and Siddarthan, N. (1982), 'The Monopolistic Advantages of Multinationals: Lessons from Foreign Investment in the US', *Economic Journal*, 92, 668–83.

LINCOLN, J. R. (1992), 'Work Organization in Japan and the United States', in B. Kogut, ed., *Comparative Work Practices of Multinational Firms* (Oxford: Oxford University Press).

MICOSSI, S., and VIESTI, G. (1991), 'Japanese Investment in Manufacturing in Europe', in L. A. Winters and A. Venables, eds., *European Integration, Trade and Industry* (Cambridge: Cambridge University Press).

Ministry of Finance (v.d.), *Japanese Direct Investment Abroad* (Tokyo).

MITI (1991), *Dai Yon Kai Kaigai Jigyo Katsudo Kihon Chosa Kaigai Toshi Tokei Soran* (Tokyo: MITI, International Policy Department, Sept.).

NARULA, R., and GUGLER, P. (1991), *Japanese Direct Investment in Europe: Structure and Trends in the Manufacturing Industry* (Newark: Rutgers University, GSM Working Paper 91–4).

OECD (1990), *Foreign Trade by Commodities, Series C* (Paris: Department of Economics and Statistics, OECD).

OKADA, Y. (1991), 'Cooperative Sectoral Governance Strategies of Japanese Automobile Multinationals in Asian Countries' (International University of Japan, mimeo).

OWEN, R. (1982), 'Inter-Industry Determinants of Foreign Direct Investments: A Canadian Perspective', in A. Rugman, ed., *New Theories of Multinational Enterprise* (London: Croom Helm).

OZAWA, T. (1992), 'Cross-Investments between Japan and the EC: Income Similarity, Product Variation and Economies of Scope', in J. Cantwell, ed., *Multinational Investment in Modern Europe: Strategic Interaction in the Integrated Community* (Cheltenham: Edward Elgar).

PORTER, M. (1990), *The Competitive Advantage of Nations* (New York: The Free Press).

RUGMAN, A. (1979), *International Diversification and the Multinational Enterprise* (Lexington, Ky.: Lexington Books).

SAXONHOUSE, G., and STERN, R. (1989), 'An Analytical Survey of Formal and Informal Barriers to International Trade and Investment in the United States, Canada and Japan', in R. Stern, ed., *Trade and Investment Relations among the United States, Canada and Japan* (Chicago: University of Chicago Press).

United Nations (v.d.), *Commodity Trade Statistics* (New York: United Nations).

—— (1990), *Industrial Statistics Yearbook, 1988* (New York: United Nations).

—— (1992), *The Determinants of Foreign Direct Investment: A Survey of the Evidence* (New York, UN Centre on Transnational Corporations, ST/CTC/121).

US Department of Commerce (1981), *US Direct Investment Abroad, 1977* (Washington, DC: US Government Printing Office).

—— (1990), 'US Direct Investment Abroad: Detail for Position and Balance of Payments Flows', *Survey of Current Business* (Aug.), 56–89.

—— (1991), 'Provisional Results of Survey on US Direct Investment Abroad, 1989' (Washington, DC: US Government Printing Office).

VERNON, R. (1966), 'International Investment and International Trade in the Product Cycle', *Quarterly Journal of Economics*, 80, 190–207.

—— ed. (1970), *The Technology Factor in International Trade* (New York: Columbia University Press).

WATANABE, S. (1988), 'Trends of Japan's Direct Investment in Europe: Mainly Investment in Manufacturing into EC', *Exim Review* (9 Oct.).

YAMAWAKI, H. (1991), 'Location Decisions of Japanese Multinational Firms in European Manufacturing Industries', in K. Hughes, ed., *European Competitiveness* (Cambridge: Cambridge University Press).

COMMENT

Kozo Yamamura

As expected of a doyen among scholars of FDI, Dunning provides us with a useful overview of Japanese FDI in Europe, a succinct survey of theories of FDI (including a judicious critique of Kojima's theory of FDI and a good discussion of the usefulness and limitations of his own eclectic theory), and suggestive results of testing (under the serious data constraints he carefully delineates) several hypotheses regarding the patterns and motivations of Japanese FDI *vis-à-vis* those of American FDI. His contributions, raising our understanding of patterns and motivations of Japanese investment in the EC by a distinct notch, serve as an important foundation on which to build further studies on the increasing Japanese economic presence in Europe.

Thus, my brief comment offers only the following reflection-*cum*-suggestion, which I hope will be useful to those who do not specialize in the Japanese economy but who wish to follow the path Dunning cleared, and to test analytic propositions and/or to make policy recommendations concerning Japanese FDI in Europe.

After presenting a useful discussion of the obvious reasons for differences in patterns and motivations between Japanese and American FDI in Europe (e.g. differences in productivity, timing, and rate of increase), much of Dunning's concern is focused on describing and testing hypotheses on the possible effects of the institutional characteristics of Japanese firms (i.e. their governance structure, management of human resources, and inter-firm relationships) on the patterns and motivations of their FDI in Europe. This is why, for example, in contrasting Japanese and American FDI, Dunning places emphasis on advantages specific to the organizations (governance structure) of firms that 'systematically organize resources and capabilities under their [firms'] governance', on how one form of governance 'seems to be especially successful in managing idiosyncratic human-intensive transnational relations', and on how market failures are dealt with 'through tacit or informal systems of human co-operation or by formal hierarchical control and/or inter-firm contractual relationships'. And this also is why most of the hypotheses he tested are either directly or indirectly related to the institutional characteristics of Japanese firms.

To be sure, Dunning's discussions and hypothesis-testing are valuable because they clearly indicate the importance of better understanding how the governance structure and behaviour of Japanese firms differs from those of US (and European) firms and how the differences shape the motivations and behaviour of Japanese firms in Europe. However, if

European scholars wish to test hypotheses concerning the effects of institutional characteristics of Japanese firms on the patterns and motivations of Japanese FDI and the behaviour of Japanese firms in their midst, I suggest that they be prepared to make more than 'only *minor* modifications to the existing paradigms of international production' (emphasis added). This is because, in analysing Japanese FDI and the behaviour of Japanese firms, hypotheses need to be formulated and the results of testing them must be interpreted with an awareness that the institutional characteristics and behaviour of Japanese firms, as well as Japanese economic policies and bureaucratic practices, still differ from those in the West in substantive ways. That is, despite the significant changes that have occurred in the Japanese economy during the past few decades, the institutions and behaviour of Japanese firms have changed very slowly and some of the institutional characteristics and practices of Japanese firms have changed little.

To list only the most salient among these slowly changing or non-changing institutional characteristics and behaviour (and to state them comparatively *vis-à-vis* their Western counterparts): (1) the power of shareholders remains significantly weaker, enabling the *de facto* coalition of management (promoted from within) and 'permanent' employees (who receive extensive on-the-job training and acquire multiple skills) to determine most substantive corporate strategies; (2) 'stable shareholders', consisting of firms belonging to the same *keiretsu* (enterprise group), hold a majority of shares; (3) inter-firm relations among *keiretsu* firms and between parent and subsidiaries (including distribution outlets) are significantly more intensive and longer term; and (4) subsidiaries supply substantially larger amounts of the total value added of parent firms, and much more extensive distribution networks are maintained by producers. Among the policies and bureaucratic practices that continue to shape the institutions and behaviour of Japanese firms, the most important include (again stated comparatively *vis-à-vis* the Western counterparts): (1) substantially closer government–business relations; (2) demonstrably weaker enforcement of anti-trust (anti-competition) statutes; (3) significantly weaker control of various practices by the largest financial institutions that benefit the largest clients at the cost of smaller clients; and (4) increasingly indirect but still more active government involvement in promoting the technological capabilities of high-technology industries.

These institutional characteristics of Japanese firms and Japan's policies and bureaucratic practices cannot but affect, directly and indirectly, the patterns and motivations of Japanese firms' investment and behaviour in Europe. A few examples of significant effects include: (1) relieved of shareholder pressure for short-term profit, Japanese firms exhibit a distinct tendency to increase market share aggressively in order to increase productivity and profits over a longer time horizon; (2) to maintain a level of employment and to minimize disruption in close inter-firm relations at home, Japanese firms attempt to increase the local content of their production in Europe slowly, and this tendency becomes more pronounced when subsidiaries of the firms making FDI also enter into Europe along with the parent firms; (3) the patterns and magnitudes of exports to Japan from Europe are inevitably affected by (2); and (4) Japanese firms in Europe are more likely to internalize the technological and managerial advantages among Japanese firms that maintain close inter-firm relations in Japan. And we should also note that along with the institutional characteristics and behaviour of Japanese firms, the Japanese policies and bureaucratic practices described above cannot but help to increase both the international competitiveness of Japanese firms and the difficulties of foreign firms in gaining market shares in Japan and acquiring Japanese firms.

I am not unaware that many economists today argue, drawing upon the analytic insights of 'new industrial organization', that the intensive and long-term inter-firms relations maintained among Japanese firms are efficiency-promoting (i.e. reduce transaction costs via close and effective inter-firm co-operation). The value and virtues of co-operation between government and business and between management and employees too are strongly defended. And I am not denying the essential validity of theoretical analysis that FDI in most cases increases the welfare of host nations.

Rather, what I suggest is that in analysing the patterns, motivations, and effects of Japanese FDI in Europe, we need to keep firmly in mind that the institutional characteristics, and thus the behaviour, of Japanese firms still differ from those of Western firms, and that policies and government–business relations in Japan also differ from their counterparts in European nations. This is why, as those familiar with Japan know, Akio Morita, Chairman of Sony, in a recent, by now well-known article, called for fundamental changes in the behaviour of Japanese firms in order for Japan to become an exporting nation that observes the rules followed by others.[23] And this is also why many Japanese pundits and scholars are today engaged in intensive debate on how Japan must change.[24] In short, many Japanese too are aware today that the sole explanation for the large trade surplus Japan earns against the USA and against the EC as a whole ($27.4 billion in 1991 and in excess of $30 billion in 1992) cannot be the lack of competitiveness of American and European firms.

Since I am unable to elaborate on the institutional characteristics and behaviour of Japanese firms and on Japanese policies and bureaucratic

---

[23] The original version in Japanese is A. Morita, 'Nihon-gata keiei ga abunai', *Bungei shunju* (Feb. 1992), 94–103.
[24] For a description of the debate, see my 'Four More Books on *Nichibei Keizai Massatsu*', *Journal of Japanese Studies*, 19/1 (Winter 1993), 189–201.

practices in this brief comment, let me conclude by suggesting the following reading list for European scholars who wish to undertake studies of Japanese FDI and the behaviour of Japanese firms in Europe. The list includes, in addition to those most useful recent books on the institutional characteristics of Japanese firms and on Japanese policies and bureaucratic practices, selected works on Japanese investment in the USA and Asia that contain descriptions, analyses, and insights that are useful in examining Japanese FDI in Europe.

ANCHORDOGUY, M., *Computers Inc.: Japan's Challenge to IBM* (Cambridge, Mass.: Council on East Asian Studies, Harvard University, 1989).

AOKI, M., *Information, Incentives, and Bargaining in the Japanese Economy* (Cambridge: Cambridge University Press, 1988).

ENCARNATION, D., *Rivals Beyond Trade: America versus Japan in Global Competition* (Ithaca, NY: Cornell University Press, 1992).

GERLACH, M., *Alliance Capitalism: The Social Organization of Japanese Business* (Berkeley: University of California Press, 1992).

KRUGMAN, P., ed., *Trade with Japan: Has the Door Opened Wider?* (Chicago: University of Chicago Press, 1991).

LAWRENCE, R., and SCHULTZE, C., eds., *An American Trade Strategy: Options for the 1990s* (Washington: Brookings Institution, 1990).

LINCOLN, E., *Japan's Unequal Trade* (Washington, DC: Brookings Institution, 1990).

MASON, M., *American Multinationals and Japan: The Political Economy of Japanese Capital Controls, 1899–1980* (Cambridge, Mass.: Council on East Asian Studies, Harvard University, 1992).

OKIMOTO, D., *Between MITI and the Market: Japanese Industrial Policy for High Technology* (Stanford: Stanford University Press, 1989).

SHEARD, P., ed., *International Adjustment and the Japanese Firm* (St Leonards, Australia: Allen & Unwin, 1992).

TOKUNAGA, S., ed., *Japan's Foreign Investment and Asian Economic Interdependence: Production, Trade, and Financial Systems* (Tokyo: University of Tokyo Press, 1992).

YAMAMURA, K., ed., *Japanese Investment in the United States: Should we be Concerned?* (Seattle: Society for Japanese Studies, 1989).

—— ed., *Japan's Economic Structure: Should it Change?* (Seattle: Society for Japanese Studies, 1990).

YAMASHITA, S., ed., *Transfer of Japanese Technology and Management to the ASEAN Countries* (Tokyo: University of Tokyo Press, 1991).

3

Entry Patterns of Japanese Multinationals in US and European Manufacturing*

Hideki Yamawaki

1. INTRODUCTION

Japanese firms, beginning in the mid-1980s, have vastly expanded their presence in the US manufacturing sector through foreign direct investment (FDI). The flow of Japanese manufacturing FDI in North America surged from US$1.2 billion in 1985 to US$4.8 billion in 1987, and peaked in 1989 with the amount of US$9.6 billion. Indeed, the investment flow during the 1985–90 period alone accounted for approximately 85 per cent of the cumulative flow of Japanese manufacturing FDI into North America between 1967 and 1990. Japanese firms entered into a broad range of US manufacturing industries not only by establishing greenfield plants but also by acquiring existing local firms. The presence of Japanese firms now extends from food-processing, chemical products, and steel products to general and electrical machinery and automobiles.

This growing presence of Japanese firms is not peculiar to the US markets. Japanese firms started investing extensively in European manufacturing industries as well during the 1980s. The flow of direct investment in manufacturing from Japan to Europe grew rapidly after 1987 and continues to grow beyond 1990. Japanese firms are now present in various member states of the European Community extending from the UK and Germany to Spain and Portugal.

The extent and pattern of such growing outflow of direct investments from Japan into the USA and Europe during the 1980s have been well documented by previous researchers (e.g. Dunning 1986; Graham and Krugman 1989; Froot 1991; Akimune 1991; Micossi and Viesti 1991; Jacquemin and Buigues 1991; and Sazanami 1991). However, surprisingly little attention has been paid to the questions of whether there exists a strategic link between Japanese FDI activity in the USA and Europe and whether Japanese FDI activity is similar or dissimilar between the USA and Europe. This paper attempts to address these questions by assembling evidence on the presence of Japanese manufacturing firms in the USA and Europe, the patterns of entry, product and diversification strategies, and

* I am grateful to Dennis Encarnation for helpful comments and suggestions.

the distribution of their subsidiaries and affiliates across industries and countries. To accomplish such goals this paper employs a new data set that is constructed from the individual subsidiary-level data for 1990. While this paper addresses the question of whether the behavioural pattern of Japanese multinational firms differs importantly between the US and European markets, the paper's principal goal is to provide a factual picture of the behavioural pattern of Japanese multinationals in the USA and Europe on which future theoretical and statistical work may be based.

This paper summarizes the empirical results that focus on three aspects of the direct investment activity of Japanese firms. First, the pattern of entry by Japanese firms into the US and European markets, the mode of entry, and the extent of ownership control of subsidiaries are identified. Second, the extent of diversifying direct investment is examined, and the pattern of diversification is identified by examining the principal activities of the parent firm and its subsidiary. Third, the distribution of Japanese firms' subsidiaries among industries is compared among types of firms and between the USA and Europe. The empirical results on these three aspects suggest that the patterns of entry, product policies, and diversification strategies of Japanese firms differ distinctively among types of firms and industries, and between the USA and Europe.

The next section explains the data set and provides an overview of the profile of firms in the sample. Section 3 shows the distribution of US and European subsidiaries by the year of entry, the method of entry, and the extent of ownership control. Section 4 examines the pattern of diversifying entry, and Section 5 assesses the distribution of subsidiaries across 2- and 3-digit manufacturing industries. Finally, Section 6 summarizes the results and provides some concluding remarks.

2. THE DATA

The data set for this study is constructed from the individual subsidiary level data collected in Toyo Keizai, *Kaigai shinshutsu kigyo soran: 1991* [Directory of Japanese Multinational Corporations: 1991]. This corporate directory lists 5,300 Japanese firms and their 12,500 subsidiaries and affiliates distributed among 130 countries for which Toyo Keizai conducted an annual survey, based on questionnaires, in December 1990. The sample in this survey comprises subsidiaries and affiliates that are more than 10 per cent owned by Japanese firms and that are distributed among manufacturing as well as non-manufacturing industries. The information provided for an individual subsidiary in this directory is naturally qualitative rather than quantitative and includes such items as percentage shares controlled by parent firms, the mode of entry, the year of entry, the amount of equity capital, the number of employees, sales,[1] and the line of business. While the Ministry of International Trade and Industry (MITI) conducts a more detailed survey on the behavioural pattern of Japanese firms abroad and publishes the summary of its results every three years,[2] information on individual firms and subsidiaries collected for this MITI survey is not easily accessible. For this reason, the Toyo Keizai survey data are used in this study.[3]

One weakness of these data is that some quantitative variables such as sales, employment, and total assets are occasionally missing for some companies. While it is desirable to use these variables for some analyses, this requires the size of sample to be significantly reduced. Therefore, given such data limitations and the nature of analysis in this paper, the present study resorts primarily to qualitative information.

Out of the 12,522 subsidiaries of Japanese firms listed in the Toyo Keizai survey, 3,282 subsidiaries are located in the USA and 2,549 subsidiaries are located in Europe. A further breakdown by sectors reveals that 1,054 US subsidiaries and 524 European subsidiaries of Japanese firms are in the manufacturing sector. From this sample of 1,054 US manufacturing subsidiaries and 524 European manufacturing subsidiaries, 631 US subsidiaries and 336 European subsidiaries, whose parents are also in manufacturing and for which data are available,[4] were further selected to construct the final data set for this study.

Table 3.1 presents a summary of the number of Japanese parent firms and their subsidiaries in the USA and Europe. In this sample, there are 631 subsidiaries in the USA that are controlled by 391 Japanese parent firms, while there are 336 European subsidiaries that are controlled by 193 Japanese parents. When these are disaggregated into firms that own subsidiaries in the USA but not in Europe,[5] firms that own subsidiaries in Europe but not in the USA, and firms which own subsidiaries both in the USA and Europe, the table shows that firms that own subsidiaries only in the USA account for 57.6 per cent of the total number of firms in the sample, but firms which own subsidiaries only in Europe account for 14.1 per cent of the total number of firms. Firms that own subsidiaries in the USA and Europe account for 28.4 per cent of the total number of firms. Firms that operate either in the USA or Europe own, on average, approximately one subsidiary, while firms that operate both in the USA and Europe own, on average, approximately two subsidiaries in the two regions combined.

---

[1] Sales figures are, however, incomplete and are not recorded for every subsidiary. For some subsidiaries total assets or value of output are recorded instead.

[2] MITI, *Kaigai jigyo katsudo kihon chosa: Kaigai toshi tokei soran*. [Basic Survey of Overseas Business Activities: Statistical Overview of Overseas Investment], various years.

[3] The Toyo Keizai data have been used by some previous researchers for statistical analysis; see, for example, Hennart 1991, Yamawaki 1991, and Belderbos 1992.

[4] This procedure eliminates the subsidiaries of general trading companies from the sample.

[5] Here, we consider only the subsidiaries in the USA and Europe and ignore those in Asia and other areas.

TABLE 3.1. *Ownership patterns for Japanese firms and their subsidiaries in the USA and Europe, 1990*

Type of parent firm	No. of parent firms	No. of subsidiaries			No. of subsidiaries per firm
		USA	Europe	Total	
Firms that own subsidiaries in the USA but not in Europe	262 (57.6%)	345 (54.7%)		345 (35.7%)	1.32
Firms that own subsidiaries in Europe but not in the USA	64 (14.1%)		74 (22.0%)	74 (7.3%)	1.11
Firms that own subsidiaries both in the USA and Europe	129 (28.4%)	286 (45.3%)	262 (78.0%)	548 (56.7%)	2.22 in the USA 2.03 in Europe
TOTAL	455 (100.0%)	631 (100.0%)	336 (100.0%)	967 (100.0%)	2.13

Note: Shares of total number of firms are in parentheses. Percentages may not add up to 100.0 due to rounding errors.

Reflecting this relative importance of multiplant activity for firms that operate both in the USA and Europe, the number of subsidiaries for these firms is larger than the numbers of subsidiaries owned by firms that operate either in the USA or Europe. The maximum number of subsidiaries owned by a firm is eleven in the USA (Kobe Steel), and fifteen in Europe (Yoshida Kogyo).

A marked difference between the USA and Europe that emerges from Table 3.1 is that only 22 per cent of the total number of subsidiaries in Europe are owned by firms that operate only in Europe, while approximately 50 per cent of the total number of subsidiaries in the USA are owned by firms that operate only in the USA. On the other hand, US subsidiaries are distributed among firms that operate exclusively in the USA and firms that operate both in the USA and Europe. Thus, Table 3.1 suggests that the type of parent firm differs between US and European subsidiaries.

3. PATTERNS OF ENTRY

In this section, patterns of entry by Japanese firms into the US and European manufacturing industries are described.

3.1. Year of Entry

Table 3.2 reports the distribution of parent firms by year of entry and types of sequential entry process. The first three types of entry process correspond to the type of parent firm described in the last section as the firms that own subsidiaries both in the USA and Europe. Seventy-one firms out of these 262 firms first entered the US market and subsequently entered the European market, while 52 firms first chose the European market and later entered the US market. The second row of Table 3.2 reports the number of firms by the year in which their first US subsidiary was established, and shows that eighteen firms entered before 1970, 24 firms entered during the 1970s, and 29 firms entered during the 1980s. The next three rows show the distribution of these 71 firms by first entry year in the US and by subsequent entry year in Europe. Thus the table shows that among the eighteen firms that entered the US market before 1970, four firms subsequently entered into the European market during the 1970s, and ten firms entered during the 1980s. The last several rows show the distribution of firms that first entered the European market and then the US market in the same manner as described above.

Several interesting observations emerge from Table 3.2. First, firms that own subsidiaries either in the USA or in Europe entered into the markets rather recently. More than 70 per cent of these firms established their first subsidiaries in these regions during the 1980s. Second, in contrast,

T ABLE 3.2. *Parent firms by year and sequence of entry in the USA and Europe*

	Total no. of firms	Year of first entry		
		before 1970	1970–9	1980–90
Entered the USA first				
then Europe	71			
First entry in the USA		18	24	29
Subsequent entry				
in Europe				
Before 1970		4	—	—
1970–9		4	8	—
1980–90		10	16	29
Entered Europe first	52			
then the USA				
First entry in Europe		3	22	27
Subsequent entry				
in the USA				
Before 1970		3	—	—
1970–9		0	5	—
1980–90		0	17	27
Entered the USA and				
Europe in the same year	6	0	2	4
Entered only the USA	262	11	43	208
Entered only Europe	64	2	14	48

approximately 50 per cent of the firms that entered both the USA and Europe had already established their first subsidiaries in these regions by the late 1970s. Third, more than 50 per cent of the firms that entered the US market before 1970 waited to establish their first European subsidiaries until the 1980s.

3.2. Method of Entry

Table 3.3 reports the distribution of US and European subsidiaries by method of entry and diversification strategy. A general pattern that emerges from this table is that Japanese firms prefer greenfield investments to acquisition and capital participation. Indeed, 77 per cent of the total number of subsidiaries in each area, or 489 out of 631 US subsidiaries and 258 out of 336 European subsidiaries, were established through greenfield investments, while the remaining 23 per cent of subsidiaries were established through acquisition and capital participation.[6] Of the 142 subsidiaries that entered the US market through acquisition and capital participation, 111

---

[6] For a similar result obtained for the pattern of method of entry by Japanese firms abroad, see Tsurumi 1976: 194–5.

TABLE 3.3. *Japanese subsidiaries by type of entry and degree of diversification in the USA and Europe*

Location of subsidiaries	Total no. of subsidiaries	Greenfield entry			Acquisition and capital participation		
		Total	Horizontal	Diversifying	Total	Horizontal	Diversifying
USA	631 (100%)	489 (77.4%) (100%)	430 (87.9%)	59 (12.1%)	142 (22.5%) (100.0%)	105 (73.9%)	37 (26.1%)
Europe	336 (100%)	258 (76.8%) (100.0%)	234 (90.7%)	24 (9.3%)	78 (23.2%) (100.0%)	74 (94.9%)	4 (5.1%)

Note: (1) Diversifying entry is identified if the subsidiary's principal product is classified into the 2-digit industry that does not contain the parent's principal product.

(2) Shares of total number of subsidiaries are in parentheses of rows 2 and 5; shares of total number of subsidiaries for each entry mode and in each location are in parentheses of rows 3 and 6.

(3) Percentages may not add up to 100.0 because of rounding errors.

of them are through acquisition, and 134 of these acquisitions and capital participations took place after 1980. In Europe, of the 78 entries through acquisition and capital participation, 47 entries are through acquisition, and 71 of these acquisitions and capital participations were carried out after 1980.

This similarity in the choice of method of entry between the USA and Europe is weaker when the breakdown is made between horizontal and diversifying entries. To examine this, Table 3.3 classifies the method of entry according to whether the subsidiary's product line differs from the parent's product line. In Table 3.3 a diversifying entry is identified if the subsidiary's principal product is classified into the 2-digit industry that does not contain the parent's principal product. All other types of entry are simply categorized here as 'horizontal' entry. The most remarkable observation that emerges from this is the fact that entry through acquisition and capital participation is more frequently associated with diversifying entry in the USA than in Europe. In fact, 26 per cent of the total number of entries into the USA through acquisition and capital participation is diversifying entry, while the corresponding figure for Europe is only 5 per cent. In other words, 95 per cent of entries through acquisition and capital participation in Europe are horizontal entries.

Another important finding from Table 3.3 is the difference in the importance of diversifying entry between acquisition and capital participation, and greenfield investments in the USA. Diversifying entry accounts for 26 per cent of the total number of entries through acquisition and capital participation, but it accounts for 12 per cent of entries through greenfield investments in the USA. Correspondingly, horizontal entry accounts for 88 per cent of the total number of entries through greenfield investments, while it accounts for 74 per cent of entries through acquisition and capital participation. Thus, diversifying entry appears to be more often associated with acquisition and capital participation than with greenfield investments in the USA[7]. By contrast, such differences in the relative importance of diversifying entry between acquisition and capital participation, and greenfield investments does not exist in Europe, where more than 90 per cent of entries through greenfield investments and acquisition and capital participation are accounted for by horizontal entry.

Table 3.4 shows how these data on the mode of entry vary over time by comparing the subsidiaries established before and after 1980. The most important finding from Table 3.4 is the increase in the number of entries through acquisition and capital participation in both the USA and Europe. Before 1980, less than 10 per cent of the entries were through acquisition and capital participation, both in the USA and Europe. By comparison,

---

[7] This finding is consistent with the previous statistical evidence on the choice of method of entry; see Caves and Mehra 1986, and Caves 1982: 83–4.

TABLE 3.4. *Japanese subsidiaries by type and year of entry in the USA and Europe*

Location of subsidiaries	Total no. of subsidiaries	Subsidiaries established before 1980			Subsidiaries established after 1980		
		Total	Greenfield	Acquisition and capital participation	Total	Greenfield	Acquisition and capital participation
USA	631 (100%)	114 (18.1%) (100.0%)	106 (93.0%)	8 (7.0%)	517 (81.9%) (100.0%)	383 (74.1%)	134 (25.9%)
Europe	336 (100%)	81 (24.1%) (100.0%)	74 (91.4%)	7 (8.6%)	255 (75.9%) (100.0%)	184 (72.2%)	71 (27.8%)

Note: see Table 3.3.

after 1980, the entries through acquisition and capital participation accounted for roughly a quarter of the total entries recorded for that period. This clearly indicates that acquisition and capital participation had become more popular among the Japanese multinationals during the 1980s.

The average statistics provided above do not provide information on the patterns of entry through acquisition and capital participation across industries. Table 3.5 reports the numbers for acquisition and capital participation in the USA and Europe across the 2-digit industries to which the parents' products are classified. A pattern observed commonly in the USA and Europe is that the number of acquisitions and capital participations originating in the chemical, non-electrical machinery, electrical machinery, and transportation equipment industries accounts for about 65 per cent of the total number in both areas. However, some distinctive differences exist between these areas in the ranking of industries. First, most remarkable is that Japanese parent firms in the food industry use acquisition and capital participation more often in the USA. In fact, seventeen acquisitions originated from the food industry (or 12.0 per cent of the total number), while only three acquiring firms came from the same industry in Europe (or 3.8 per cent of the total number). Second, acquisitions originating from chemicals and primary metals (iron and steel and non-ferrous metals) account for larger shares of the total number in the USA (23.9 and 8.5 per cent, respectively) than in Europe (14.1 and 2.6 per cent, respectively). Third, in contrast, acquisitions that originated from clothing and transportation equipment account for larger shares in Europe (6.4 and 17.9 per cent, respectively) than in the USA (0.7 and 8.5 per cent, respectively).

Table 3.5 also presents information on the number of diversifying acquisitions and capital participations. As discussed earlier in this section, diversifying entry accounts for 26 per cent of the total number of entry through acquisition and capital participation in the USA. When disaggregated by industries, it is evident from Table 3.5 that the chemical industry is primarily responsible for this figure. In fact, fifteen out of the 34 acquisitions and capital participations which originated from chemicals (or 44 per cent) are diversifying entries. Thus, the incidence of acquisition and capital participation which originated from the chemical industry appears to be related to the parent's strategy to diversify out of this industry into other US industries. By contrast, such a relation does not seem to exist for the food-processing industry, where only one out of the seventeen acquisitions and capital participations is a diversifying entry.

When these statistics are reclassified according to the subsidiary's principal industry, one can observe the pattern of choice on the method of entry across the industries entered. The list of industries entered where acquisition and capital participation are relatively commonly employed as the method of entry includes food, rubber products, stone, clay, and glass products for the USA, while it includes rubber products, stone, clay, and glass products, and clothing for Europe (See Tables 3.6 and 3.7).

TABLE 3.5. *Japanese acquisitions in the USA and Europe, by industry*

2-digit industry to which the parent's principal product is classified	USA		Europe	
	No. of acquisitions	No. of diversifying acquisitions	No. of acquisitions	No. of diversifying acquisitions
Food processing	17	1	3	0
Textiles	1	0	0	0
Clothing	1	0	5	0
Timber	0	0	0	0
Furniture	2	0	0	0
Paper	0	0	0	0
Printing	1	1	0	0
Chemicals	34	15	11	1
Rubber products	3	0	4	0
Plastic products	1	0	2	0
Stone, clay, glass products	4	1	6	1
Iron and steel	6	2	1	0
Non-ferrous metals	6	4	1	1
Fabricated metals	1	0	0	0
Non-electrical machinery	27	7	17	0
Electrical machinery	21	3	9	0
Transportation equipment	12	1	14	0
Instruments	2	1	2	1
Miscellaneous	3	1	3	0
TOTAL	142	37	78	4

While to identify the determinants of the observed pattern of the mode of entry across industries requires resort to rigorous statistical analysis, the findings above that Japanese firms in food processing and chemicals tend to use acquisition and capital participation more often than others seem to be explained to some extent by the fact that US and European producers in these industries have competitive advantages over their Japanese rivals (Porter 1990). The Japanese firms that intend to become internationally competitive within a short period of time must acquire local producers. This motivation of Japanese firms in the international markets, along with the general tendency of the Japanese firms in food processing and chemicals to use merger and acquisition more frequently than the firms in other industries even when they enter Japanese markets (Odagiri 1992), certainly explains their strong preference for merger and acquisition as a mode of entry.

3.3. Extent of Ownership Control

Table 3.8 shows the distribution of US and European subsidiaries of Japanese manufacturing firms by the extent of ownership control at the end

TABLE 3.6. *Japanese subsidiaries by type of entry in the USA, by industry*

Industry	No. of subsidiaries	Type of entry					
		Greenfield		Acquisition		Capital participation	
Food processing	40 (100.0%)	22	(55.0%)	13	(32.5%)	5	(12.5%)
Textiles	7	6	(85.7)	0	(0.0)	1	(14.3)
Clothing	3	2	(66.7)	1	(33.3)	0	(0.0)
Timber	1	1	(100.0)	0	(0.0)	0	(0.0)
Furniture	5	3	(60.0)	2	(40.0)	0	(0.0)
Paper	3	3	(100.0)	0	(0.0)	0	(0.0)
Printing	2	2	(100.0)	0	(0.0)	0	(0.0)
Chemicals	58	39	(67.2)	17	(29.3)	2	(3.4)
Rubber products	7	4	(57.1)	3	(42.9)	0	(0.0)
Plastic products	29	25	(86.2)	3	(10.3)	1	(3.4)
Stone, clay, and glass	19	11	(57.9)	8	(42.1)	0	(0.0)
Iron and steel	20	16	(80.0)	2	(10.0)	2	(10.0)
Non-ferrous metals	27	22	(81.5)	3	(11.1)	2	(7.4)
Fabricated metals	8	7	(87.5)	1	(12.5)	0	(0.0)
Non-electrical machinery	88	66	(75.0)	15	(17.0)	7	(8.0)
Electrical machinery	147	117	(79.6)	25	(17.0)	5	(3.4)
Transportation equipment	127	113	(89.0)	9	(7.1)	5	(3.9)
Instruments	13	9	(69.2)	3	(23.1)	1	(7.7)
Miscellaneous	27	21	(77.8)	6	(22.2)	0	(0.0)
TOTAL	631	489	(77.5)	111	(17.6)	31	(4.9)

Note: Shares of total number of subsidiaries in each industry are in parentheses. Percentages may not add up to 100.0 due to rounding errors.

of 1990. As found by MITI (1991), 80 per cent of subsidiaries in the USA and Europe are majority controlled, and more than 50 per cent of these subsidiaries are wholly controlled. The average pattern on the extent of ownership control is thus quite similar between US and European subsidiaries, but this differs from those in Asia and other regions (MITI 1991).

Table 3.9 shows how the extent of ownership control varies over time by breaking down the data in Table 3.8 into the periods before 1980 and after 1980. The most remarkable finding from Table 3.9 is the existence of some tendency toward minority-controlled ownership particularly in the USA. Of the 114 subsidiaries established before 1980, only fourteen were minority controlled, representing 12 per cent of the total in the USA. By contrast, of the 509 US subsidiaries established after 1980, 110 subsidiaries or 22 per cent were minority controlled. Thus the relative importance of minority-controlled subsidiaries increased after 1980, particularly in the

TABLE 3.7. *Japanese subsidiaries by type of entry in Europe, by industry*

Industry	No. of subsidiaries	Type of entry					
		Greenfield		Acquisition		Capital participation	
Food processing	6 (100.0%)	3	(50.0%)	3	(50.0%)	0	(0.0%)
Textiles	9	8	(88.9)	1	(11.1)	0	(0.0)
Clothing	9	4	(44.4)	3	(33.3)	2	(22.2)
Timber	0	0	(0.0)	0	(0.0)	0	(0.0)
Furniture	2	1	(50.0)	0	(0.0)	1	(50.0)
Paper	0	0	(0.0)	0	(0.0)	0	(0.0)
Printing	0	0	(0.0)	0	(0.0)	0	(0.0)
Chemicals	33	24	(72.7)	6	(18.2)	3	(9.1)
Rubber products	6	2	(33.3)	3	(50.0)	1	(16.7)
Plastic products	16	14	(87.5)	2	(12.5)	0	(0.0)
Stone, clay, and glass	8	3	(37.5)	2	(25.0)	3	(37.5)
Iron and steel	3	2	(66.7)	1	(33.3)	0	(0.0)
Non-ferrous metals	6	6	(100.0)	0	(0.0)	0	(0.0)
Fabricated metals	1	1	(100.0)	0	(0.0)	0	(0.0)
Non-electrical machinery	61	42	(68.9)	12	(19.7)	7	(11.5)
Electrical machinery	99	90	(90.9)	5	(5.1)	4	(4.0)
Transportation equipment	35	21	(60.0)	6	(17.1)	8	(22.9)
Instruments	13	12	(92.3)	1	(7.7)	0	(0.0)
Miscellaneous	29	25	(86.2)	2	(6.9)	2	(6.9)
TOTAL	336	258	(76.8)	47	(14.0)	31	(9.2)

Note: Shares of total number of subsidiaries in each industry are in parentheses. Percentages may not add up to 100.0 due to rounding errors.

TABLE 3.8. *The ownership of Japanese subsidiaries in the USA and Europe*

	Majority owned			Minority owned			Total
	Total	100%	99–51%	Total	50%	49–10%	
USA	499	363	136	124	51	73	623
	(80.1%)	(58.3%)	(21.8%)	(19.9%)	(8.2%)	(11.7%)	(100.0%)
Europe	267	181	86	68	26	42	335
	(79.7%)	(54.0%)	(25.7%)	(20.3%)	(7.8%)	(12.5%)	(100.0%)
TOTAL	766	544	222	192	77	115	958
	(80.0%)	(56.8%)	(23.2%)	(20.0%)	(8.0%)	(12.0%)	(100.0%)

Note: Shares of total number of subsidiaries are in parentheses. Total numbers of majority-controlled subsidiaries (col. 1) and minority-controlled subsidiaries (col. 4) add up to 100% (col. 7).

TABLE 3.9. *Ownership levels for Japanese subsidiaries in the USA and Europe, by year of entry*

Location	Total no. of subsidiaries	Subsidiaries established before 1980			Subsidiaries established after 1980		
		Total	Majority owned	Minority owned	Total	Majority owned	Minority owned
USA	623	114 (100.0%)	100 (87.7%)	14 (12.3%)	509 (100.0%)	399 (78.4%)	110 (21.6%)
Europe	335	81 (100.0%)	67 (82.7%)	14 (17.3%)	254 (100.0%)	200 (78.7%)	54 (21.3%)

TABLE 3.10. *Ownership levels for Japanese subsidiaries in the USA, by industry*

Industry	No. of Subsidiaries	Level of Japanese ownership					
		100–51%		50%		49–10%	
Food processing	40 (100%)	35	(87.5%)	3	(7.5%)	2	(5.0%)
Textiles	7	6	(85.7)	0	(0.0)	1	(14.3)
Clothing	3	3	(100.0)	0	(0.0)	0	(0.0)
Timber	1	1	(100.0)	0	(0.0)	0	(0.0)
Furniture	5	5	(100.0)	0	(0.0)	0	(0.0)
Paper	3	2	(66.7)	0	(0.0)	1	(33.3)
Printing	2	2	(100.0)	0	(0.0)	0	(0.0)
Chemicals	58	49	(84.5)	4	(6.9)	4	(6.9)
Rubber products	7	6	(85.7)	0	(0.0)	1	(14.3)
Plastic products	29	24	(82.8)	3	(10.3)	2	(6.9)
Stone, clay, and glass	19	15	(78.9)	2	(10.5)	2	(10.5)
Iron and steel	20	9	(45.0)	4	(20.0)	7	(35.0)
Non-ferrous metals	27	17	(63.0)	3	(11.1)	7	(25.9)
Fabricated metals	8	6	(75.0)	1	(12.5)	1	(12.5)
Non-electrical machinery	88	73	(83.0)	6	(6.8)	8	(9.1)
Electrical machinery	147	128	(87.1)	4	(2.7)	11	(7.5)
Transportation equipment	127	82	(64.6)	19	(15.0)	25	(19.7)
Instruments	13	12	(92.3)	0	(0.0)	0	(0.0)
Miscellaneous	27	24	(88.9)	2	(7.4)	1	(3.7)
TOTAL	631	499	(79.1)	51	(8.1)	73	(11.6)

Note: Shares of total number of subsidiaries in each industry are in parentheses. Percentages may not add up to 100.0 due to rounding errors and missing observations [in chemicals (4), non-electrical machinery (1), electrical machinery (1), transportation equipment (1), and instruments (1)].

USA. In Europe, there exists a similar but weaker tendency towards minority-controlled ownership.

The increase in the importance of minority-controlled subsidiaries after 1980 in the USA reflects somewhat the inter-industry pattern of entry of Japanese firms into the USA. Table 3.10 indicates that relatively large proportions of subsidiaries in iron and steel (55 per cent), non-ferrous metals (37 per cent), and transportation equipment (35 per cent) are minority controlled. A large proportion of these subsidiaries were established after 1980.

When disaggregated into industries, some differences emerge between US and European subsidiaries (Tables 3.10 and 3.11). First, most remarkable is that 55 per cent of US subsidiaries in iron and steel are minority

TABLE 3.11. *Ownership levels for Japanese subsidiaries in Europe, by industry*

Industry	No. of Subsidiaries	Level of Japanese Ownership					
		100–51%		50%		49–10%	
Food processing	6 (100.0%)	3	(50.0%)	2	(33.3%)	1	(16.7%)
Textiles	9	6	(66.7)	1	(11.1)	2	(22.2)
Clothing	9	6	(66.7)	1	(11.1)	2	(22.2)
Timber	0	0	(0.0)	0	(0.0)	0	(0.0)
Furniture	2	1	(50.0)	0	(0.0)	1	(50.0)
Paper	0	0	(0.0)	0	(0.0)	0	(0.0)
Printing	0	0	(0.0)	0	(0.0)	0	(0.0)
Chemicals	33	18	(54.5)	8	(24.2)	7	(21.2)
Rubber products	6	5	(83.3)	1	(16.7)	0	(0.0)
Plastic products	16	12	(75.0)	1	(6.3)	3	(18.8)
Stone, clay, and glass	8	6	(75.0)	0	(0.0)	2	(25.0)
Iron and steel	3	2	(66.7)	0	(0.0)	1	(33.3)
Non-ferrous metals	6	5	(83.3)	0	(0.0)	1	(16.7)
Fabricated metals	1	1	(100.0)	0	(0.0)	0	(0.0)
Non-electrical machinery	61	52	(85.2)	5	(8.2)	4	(6.6)
Electrical machinery	99	88	(88.9)	5	(5.1)	6	(6.1)
Transportation equipment	35	23	(65.7)	1	(2.9)	10	(28.6)
Instruments	13	11	(84.6)	1	(7.7)	1	(7.7)
Miscellaneous	29	28	((96.6)	0	(0.0)	1	(3.4)
TOTAL	336	267	(79.5)	26	(7.7)	42	(12.5)

Note: Shares of total number of subsidiaries in each industry are in parentheses. Percentages may not add up to 100.0 due to rounding errors and a missing observation in transportation equipment.

controlled, which is the highest share in the sample. To a lesser degree, approximately 40 per cent of US subsidiaries in non-ferrous metals are also minority controlled. Second, about 50 per cent of European subsidiaries in food and chemicals are minority controlled, while less than 20 per cent of US subsidiaries in these two industries are minority controlled. Third, a relatively high percentage (about 35 per cent) of US and European subsidiaries in transportation equipment are minority controlled.

4. INTERNATIONAL DIVERSIFICATION STRATEGY

While the international diversification activity of Japanese firms was briefly introduced in relation to acquisition activity in the last section, its pattern

TABLE 3.12. *Number of Japanese subsidiaries in the USA, parent's industry* v. *subsidiary's industry*

Subsidiary's industry \ Parent's industry	Food	Textile	Paper	Printing	Chemicals	Rubber and plastics	Stone, clay, glass	Iron and steel	Non-ferrous metal
Food					3				
Textile									
Paper									
Printing									
Chemicals	1		1				1		
Rubber and plastics					6			1	
Stone, clay, glass					4				1
Iron and steel									
Non-ferrous metal							2	1	
Fabricated metals								1	1
Non-electrical machinery					2			3	4
Eletrical machinery				2	6			7	3
Transportation equipment		1					1	4	4
Instruments					2				
Miscellaneous					1	1			2
TOTAL	1	1	1	2	24	1	4	17	15

Note: Clothing, timber, and furniture are suppressed from the table because no diversification into and out of these industries is observed.

will be examined in this section. The parent's diversification activity is defined by the same method as introduced in the last section. Diversification activity is identified if the subsidiary's principal product is classified into the 2-digit industry that does not contain the parent's principal product. In the USA, 96 out of the 631 subsidiaries in the sample, or 15 per cent of them, were found to produce goods that were different from their parents' principal products. In Europe where the extent of diversification activity is much lower, 28 out of the 336 subsidiaries, or 8 per cent of them, were classified as diversifying subsidiaries. When the sample includes the subsidiary whose principal product is classified in the 3-digit industry that is different from the parents' 3-digit industry but within the same 2-digit industry, the number of diversifying subsidiaries becomes 102 for the USA and 32 for Europe.

Table 3.12 presents the distribution of diversifying subsidiaries in the USA by the parent's 2-digit industry and the subsidiary's 2-digit industry.

TABLE 3.12 *(cont.)*.

Fabricated metals	Non-electrical machinery	Electrical machinery	Transportation equipment	Instruments	Miscellaneous	TOTAL
						3
						0
						0
						0
		1		2		6
						7
						5
						0
						3
						2
		1	1	2		13
	7			2	1	28
	7					17
		3				5
		3				7
0	14	8	1	6	1	96

Thus, the table shows the origin of outbound diversification and the destination of such diversification. Outbound diversification is most prominent in chemicals, iron and steel, non-ferrous metals, and non-electrical machinery. Indeed, 70 cases out of the 96 cases of diversification in the USA, or 73 per cent of them, originate from these four industries. Turning to inbound diversification, 60 per cent of the total number of inbound diversifications, 58 cases out of the total of 96, concentrate on three industries, non-electrical machinery, electrical machinery, and transportation equipment.

Comparing the origin of outbound diversification with its destination, one can find quickly that parents that produce chemicals, iron and steel, and non-ferrous metals are more likely to diversify into the US non-electrical machinery, electrical machinery, and transportation equipment industries. Indeed, 33 out of the 58 diversifying entries into these three US industries, or approximately 60 per cent of these entries, originate from the chemical, iron and steel, and non-ferrous metal industries. This pattern is more acute for firms in the iron and steel and non-ferrous metal industries, where approximately 80 per cent of diversifying entries are into the non-electrical machinery, electrical machinery, and transportation equipment industries. Thus, firms from these slow-growing industries tend to diversify into fast-growing industries that are more intensive in research and development (R&D). This tendency of Japanese firms in slow-growing industries to diversify into fast-growing industries is quite consistent with the empirical finding of the previous research on the diversification strategy of Japanese firms in their domestic markets (Yoshihara, Sakuma, Itami, and Kagono 1981).

While 30 per cent of diversifying entries from chemicals are into machinery, 25 per cent of them are into production of rubber and plastic products that are more related to the parent's original line of business. Firms from non-electrical machinery also tend to diversify into more related businesses within the electrical machinery and transportation equipment industries. In fact, all fourteen diversifying subsidiaries from non-electrical machinery are found in these two industries.

Turning to the pattern of diversification in Europe, the first observation that emerges from Table 3.13 is that the total number of diversifying entries is small compared to the case in the USA. When Japanese manufacturing firms diversify internationally, they seem to choose the USA rather than Europe to locate their diversifying subsidiaries. Second, the origins of outbound diversification are concentrated in four industries (chemicals, non-ferrous metals, electrical machinery, and transportation equipment), which account for 86 per cent of the total number of diversifying entries. Thus, as in the USA, chemicals and non-ferrous metals are the major suppliers of diversifying entry. Third, twelve out of the total of 28 diversifications, or 43 per cent of them, enter into the non-electrical machinery industry. This pattern of inbound diversification is different from the pattern observed for the USA, where entry into electrical machinery accounts for the largest share of the total number (29 per cent). The origin of inbound diversification into the European non-electrical machinery industry is equally distributed among non-ferrous metals, electrical machinery, and instruments.

The observations made in the last section on the choice of method of entry and the extent of ownership control and the observation in this section on the pattern of diversification throw some interesting light on the strategy of Japanese multinationals in the USA and Europe. First, as we have already discussed in the last section, Japanese firms in the chemical industry are more likely to use acquisition and capital participation when they diversify into other US industries. Fifteen out of the 24 US diversifying subsidiaries of Japanese chemical firms, or 63 per cent of them, were established through acquisition and capital participation. By contrast, 33 out of the 52 US horizontal subsidiaries of Japanese chemical firms, or 63 per cent of them, were established through greenfield investments. Second, by contrast, Japanese firms in the iron and steel industry use

TABLE 3.13. *Number of Japanese subsidiaries in Europe, parent's industry v. subsidiary's industry*

Subsidiary's industry \ Parent's industry	Food	Textile	Furniture	Chemicals	Rubber and plastics	Stone, clay, glass	Non-ferrous metal	Non-electrical machinery	Electrical machinery	Transportation equipment	Instruments	Miscellaneous	Total
Food				1									1
Textile				1									1
Furniture						1							1
Chemicals													0
Rubber and plastics		1		2									3
Stone, clay, glass													0
Non-ferrous metal				1									1
Non-electrical machinery				1			4		3		4		12
Electrical machinery				1			1				1	1	4
Transportation equipment								1					1
Instruments													0
Miscellaneous				1			1		2				4
TOTAL	0	1	0	8	0	1	6	1	5	0	5	1	28

Note: Clothing, paper, printing, iron & steel, and fabricated metals are suppressed from the table because no diversification into and out of these industries is observed.

predominantly greenfield investments when they diversify into US industries. In fact, only two out of the seventeen US diversifying subsidiaries which originated from this industry were established though acquisition. While Japanese manufacturers of iron and steel tend to use greenfield investments also to enter horizontally into the US iron and steel industry, they are more likely to establish their subsidiaries as minority controlled. As mentioned earlier in this paper, 55 per cent of such US horizontal subsidiaries in the iron and steel industry are minority controlled. This preference for minority controlled subsidiaries also seems to be present in the non-ferrous metal industry, where approximately 40 per cent of US horizontal subsidiaries are minority controlled. Third, acquisition and capital participation are used more often by Japanese firms in the food industry even when they enter horizontally into the US food industry. In fact, sixteen out of the 24 US horizontal subsidiaries of Japanese food producers, or 67 per cent of them, were established through acquisition and capital participation. And parents from this industry do not seem to diversify into other industries.

The most remarkable difference in the behaviour of Japanese firms in the USA and Europe is the fact that Japanese chemical firms do not use acquisition and capital participation when they diversify into European industries. This pattern can also be observed for other industries from which Japanese firms diversify. Thus, the general pattern for European subsidiaries is that Japanese firms use greenfield investments even when they diversify.

5. DISTRIBUTION OF SUBSIDIARIES ACROSS INDUSTRIES

This section examines the cross-sectional patterns of the presence of Japanese manufacturing subsidiaries in the USA and Europe. To assess the difference in the pattern of local production by Japanese multinationals between the USA and Europe, the distribution of subsidiaries across industries at the disaggregated level must be examined. Table 3.14 presents the distribution of US subsidiaries of Japanese firms across the 2-digit and 3-digit industries. As shown in the average statistics in Table 3.1, subsidiaries in this table are divided into two sub-groups according to whether their parents also own subsidiaries in Europe. Several interesting observations emerge from Table 3.14. First, not surprisingly, the electric and electronic equipment, and automobile industries receive more than 40 per cent of the total number of US subsidiaries of Japanese firms. Particularly noteworthy is the presence of large numbers of Japanese suppliers of motor vehicle parts and components (115 firms) and electronic components (66 firms). Among other industries that receive large numbers of Japanese firms are non-electrical machinery, chemicals, plastic products, food, and

TABLE 3.14. *Ownership patterns of Japanese subsidiaries in the USA, by industry*

Industry	No. of subsidiaries			% share of total no. of subsidiaries in the USA
	Parent owns subsidiaries only in the USA	Parent owns subsidiaries in the USA and Europe	Total	
Food products	24	3	27	4.3
Beverages	4	9	13	2.1
Textiles	6	1	7	1.1
Clothing	2	1	3	0.5
Timber and wood products	1	0	1	0.2
Furniture	4	1	5	0.8
Paper and paper products	3	0	3	0.5
Printing	2	0	2	0.3
Chemicals			58	9.2
Inorganic and organic	5	11		
Detergents, paints, and ink	11	0		
Drugs	2	5		
Miscellaneous	7	17		
Plastic products	19	10	29	4.6
Rubber products	3	4	7	1.1
Stone, clay, glass products			19	3.0
Glass	3	2		
Cement	3	0		
Pottery and clay products	1	5		
Miscellaneous	2	3		
Iron and steel	19	1	20	3.2
Non-ferrous metals			27	4.3
Non-ferrous metals	7	5		
Electric wire and cable	8	7		
Fabricated metal products	6	2	8	1.3
Non-electrical machinery			88	13.9
General machinery	12	6		
Metalworking machinery	12	6		
Construction machinery	8	4		
Special industry machinery	6	3		
Office machines	5	7		
Miscellaneous	9	10		
Electric and electronic equipment			147	23.3
Electrical industrial apparatus	11	17		
Household appliances	0	7		
Telecommunication and TV equipment	11	22		
Computing machines	1	6		
Electronic components	32	34		
Miscellaneous	1	5		

TABLE 3.14 *(cont.)*.

Industry	No. of subsidiaries			% share of total no. of subsidiaries in the USA
	Parent owns subsidiaries only in the USA	Parent owns subsidiaries in the USA and Europe	Total	
Transportation equipment			127	20.1
Motor vehicles	4	5		
Motor vehicle parts	76	39		
Others	0	3		
Instruments				
Measuring devices	2	4	13	2.1
Medical instruments	0	4		
Optical and photographic Instruments	2	1		
Other				
Miscellaneous	0	0		
Musical instruments			27	4.3
Toys	2	6		
Office supplies	1	0		
Other	1	0		
	7	10		
TOTAL	345	286	631	100%

Note: Percentages may not add up to 100.0 due to rounding errors.

iron and steel. Second, when the sample is divided into two groups according to the type of parent, a distinctive difference emerges between the two sub-groups for some industries. Most remarkable is the presence of a disproportionately large number of subsidiaries in motor vehicle parts, food, and iron and steel from the parents that do not own subsidiaries in Europe. Thus, more than 85 per cent of US subsidiaries in food and iron and steel, and approximately 70 per cent of US subsidiaries in motor vehicle parts are controlled by parents whose operations are confined to the USA. By contrast, US subsidiaries in electric and electronic equipment, except their parts and components, are more controlled by parents who operate both in the USA and Europe. Approximately 70 per cent of subsidiaries in this industry are owned by this type of parent.

While the distribution of subsidiaries across industries in Table 3.14 reveals the relative importance of the electric and electronic equipment, and automobile industries as the two major hosts of Japanese direct investment in US manufacturing, it may yet underestimate the extent of the importance of these two industries as magnets to attract direct investment from related industries. Examining the distribution of US subsidiaries across disaggregated product classes, one can find immediately that not a small number of subsidiaries in paints and ink, plastic products, and electric wire and cable are producing products that are related to office machines and electric and electronic equipment. Similarly, a large number of subsidiaries in electric wire and cable, iron and steel, glass, and general machinery are likely to supply their products as inputs to production of automobiles. However, it is not possible from the data source used to identify the extent to which these intermediate products produced by the US subsidiaries of Japanese firms are consumed by the US subsidiaries of Japanese automobile manufacturers.

Table 3.15 reports the distribution of European subsidiaries across industries in the same manner as Table 3.14. The most important general pattern emerging from this table is that in terms of the number of subsidiaries the electric and electronic equipment industry is the single largest recipient of Japanese direct investment in Europe. Among other industries that are important as hosts are non-electrical machinery, transportation equipment, chemicals, plastic products, and instruments. Second, as discussed already in Section 2, a large portion (approximately 80 per cent) of European subsidiaries is owned by Japanese parents who own subsidiaries also in the USA. In fact, only 74 out of the 336 European subsidiaries are owned by parents that do not own subsidiaries in the USA.

Turning our attention to comparison between the US and European subsidiaries of Japanese firms, we find again several distinctive differences between these subsidiaries. First, most importantly, the presence of Japanese suppliers of motor vehicle parts and components is far more extensive in the USA than in Europe. In the sample of the present study, 115 subsidiaries of auto parts suppliers are present in the USA, while only nineteen subsidiaries are recorded in Europe. It is not surprising to observe this pattern because local production of automobiles by Japanese manufacturers in the USA began much earlier and has become more extensive than in Europe. Of the eighteen Japanese manufacturers of motor vehicle parts that own subsidiaries in the USA and supply primarily to Nissan, only six of them have set up European subsidiaries by 1990. Similarly, only two out of the ten Japanese parts manufacturers that own subsidiaries in the USA and supply primarily to Toyota have established European subsidiaries.

Second, a similar observation can be made for the manufacturers of electronic components. Japanese manufacturers of electronic components, as in the case of the suppliers of motor vehicle parts, tend to enter the US market as a bunch. At the end of 1990, the present data records 66 subsidiaries in the USA, while it lists 23 subsidiaries in Europe.

Third, Japanese firms from some particular industries have set up their subsidiaries almost exclusively in the USA. These include food and beverage (40 subsidiaries in the USA, but six in Europe), iron and steel (20

TABLE 3.15. *Ownership patterns of Japanese subsidiaries in Europe, by industry*

Industry	No. of subsidiaries			% share of total no. of subsidiaries in Europe
	Parent owns subsidiaries only in Europe	Parent owns subsidiaries in the USA and Europe	Total	
Food products	0	2	2	0.6
Beverages	0	4	4	0.1
Textiles	5	4	9	2.7
Clothing	4	5	9	2.7
Timber and wood products	0	0	0	0.0
Furniture	1	1	2	0.6
Paper and paper products	0	0	0	0.0
Printing	0	0	0	0.0
Chemicals			33	9.8
Inorganic and organic	3	7		
Detergents, paints, and ink	0	1		
Drugs	4	5		
Miscellaneous	0	13		
Plastic products	6	10	16	4.8
Rubber products	1	5	6	1.8
Stone, clay, glass products			8	2.4
Glass	0	2		
Cement	0	0		
Pottery and clay products	4	2		
Miscellaneous	0	0		
Iron and steel	2	1	3	0.9
Non-ferrous metals			6	1.8
Non-ferrous metals	1	3		
Electric wire and cable	0	2		
Fabricated metal products	1	0	1	0.3
Non-electrical machinery			61	18.2
General machinery	0	8		
Metalworking machinery	4	6		
Construction machinery	2	9		
Special industry machinery	2	0		
Office machines	3	14		
Miscellaneous	1	12		
Electric and electronic equipment			99	29.5
Electrical industrial apparatus	6	13		
Household appliances	0	5		
Telecommunication and TV equipment	8	29		
Computing machines	4	6		
Electronic components	4	19		
Miscellaneous	0	5		
Transportation equipment			35	10.4

TABLE 3.15 *(cont.)*.

Industry	No. of subsidiaries			% share of total no. of subsidiaries in Europe
	Parent owns subsidiaries only in the Europe	Parent owns subsidiaries in the USA and Europe	Total	
Motor vehicles	0	12		
Motor vehicle parts	0	19		
Others	3	1		
Instruments			13	3.9
Measuring devices	0	5		
Medical instruments	0	1		
Optical and photographic Instruments	1	6		
Other	0	0		
Miscellaneous			29	8.6
Musical instruments	0	4		
Toys	3	0		
Office supplies	0	0		
Other	1	21		
TOTAL	74	262	336	100%

Note: Percentages may not add up to 100.0 due to rounding errors.

in the USA, but three in Europe), and non-ferrous metals (27 in the USA, but six in Europe).

Fourth, on the other hand, some industries in Europe receive more Japanese multinationals than in the USA. Particularly noteworthy among them are clothing, textiles, drugs, office machines, computing machines, and optical and photographic instruments. Among these industries, office machines and computing machines are cases of particular interest because the major products produced by Japanese manufacturers in these two industries are copiers, electric typewriters, and printers, which were under anti-dumping investigations by the EC Commission in the mid-1980s. Indeed, about 25 per cent of firms that have established subsidiaries in Europe but not in the USA engage in various manufacturing activities related to the production of copiers, printers, and other office machines.

To examine the difference in product policy implemented between US and European subsidiaries of the same parent, the US subsidiary's principal product line was compared with the European subsidiary's principal product line for the 129 Japanese multinationals that own subsidiaries both in the USA and Europe. Of these 129 firms, 36 firms were found to implement product policy that differs between the US and European markets. The US subsidiaries of these 36 firms have produced products that are different from the 3-digit industries in which their European subsidiaries' principal products are classified. Among the 36 firms are six major manufacturers of electric and electronic equipment whose European subsidiaries tend to focus more on copiers, printers, and other office machines.

The determinants of the inter-industry pattern of Japanese direct investment in the USA have been investigated by Drake and Caves (1990) and Kogut and Chang (1991). These statistical studies have found evidence supporting the hypothesis that the increasing importance of intangible assets possessed by Japanese firms and the use of these assets in global markets have enhanced the presence of Japanese firms in the USA. Indeed, Drake and Caves, and Kogut and Chang, have identified that Japanese industries intensive in R&D and sales promotion outlays are more likely to invest directly in the USA. Drake and Caves found particularly that the accumulation of intangible assets by Japanese firms during the 1980s has strongly promoted direct investment flows to the USA.

Another important economic factor that has been identified by previous research to explain the industry pattern of Japanese FDI in the USA and Europe is the presence of trade barriers in certain industries. The Japanese FDI-inducing effect of trade barriers such as tariffs and non-tariff barriers have been identified for the USA (Drake and Caves 1990; Mann 1990; Kogut and Chang 1991) as well as for Europe (Heitger and Stehn 1990; Jacquemin and Buigues 1991). The more specific influence of anti-dumping investigations by the EC Commission on the shift from exports to local production by Japanese firms producing electric typewriters, microwave ovens, semiconductors, copiers, printers, and CD players is well documented by Belderbos (1991).

6. SUMMARY AND CONCLUSIONS

This paper has examined the patterns of entry by Japanese multinationals into the US and European manufacturing industries, their international diversification policies, and the patterns of local production across industries, by using a newly constructed subsidiary-level data set. The principal goal of this paper was to provide stylized facts on these aspects while focusing on the differences between US and European subsidiaries. Since each section summarizes the specific results, this section only summarizes the most important general results concerning the difference between the US and European manufacturing subsidiaries of Japanese multinationals:

(1) A large majority of European subsidiaries are owned by Japanese parents who also own subsidiaries in the USA, and concentrated in non-electrical machinery and electrical machinery. In the USA, there exist two large clusters of Japanese firms, one represented by the suppliers of motor

vehicle parts and another by the suppliers of electronic parts, which have not yet emerged in Europe.

(2) There exists a marked difference in the distribution of subsidiaries across industries between the USA and Europe. Japanese firms that produce food and beverages, iron and steel, and non-ferrous metals tend to prefer with a great margin the USA over Europe. By contrast, firms producing clothing, textiles, office machines, computers and related products, and optical instruments are quite keen on local production in Europe.

(3) Acquisition and capital participation are more likely to be used as a method of entry in the USA than in Europe. Japanese firms that diversify into US industries are beginning to take acquisition into consideration as an effective way to enter. Meantime, by contrast, this tendency has not yet been observed in Europe.

(4) Japanese firms from some particular industries use acquisition and capital participation more frequently than others. Among these are firms in the chemical and food industries.

(5) Japanese firms are more likely to diversify into US manufacturing industries than into European manufacturing industries. In particular, Japanese firms in the primary metal sector (iron and steel and non-ferrous metals) are quite eager to diversify into the US industries such as non-electrical machinery, electrical machinery, and transportation equipment. When Japanese firms diversify into European manufacturing industries, they are more likely to enter into the office machine industry within the non-electrical machinery sector.

(6) While the average statistics on the extent of ownership control show a quite high degree of similarity between US and European subsidiaries, some difference seems to emerge when the statistics are broken down into industries.

In addition to these findings, this paper identified importantly that the data on the mode of entry and the extent of ownership control by Japanese firms vary between the periods before 1980 and after 1980. After 1980, Japanese firms tend more often to use acquisition and capital participation to enter the US and European markets. The paper also found that the merger and acquisition activity is associated with the diversification strategy of Japanese firms particularly in chemical industries. These findings imply that the Japanese firms that do not possess competitive advantages must buy local firms if they are to become internationally competitive.

This paper has provided the statistics that describe several aspects of FDI, including the choice of method of entry, the extent of ownership control, international diversification, and the location decision of multinational corporations. To provide theoretical explanations of the patterns found is beyond the scope of the present paper, because the present research design does not allow one to disentangle a multiplicity of underlying factors that are influencing the observed patterns. While to identify the determinants of the observed patterns of the behaviour of Japanese multinationals has to await a more rigorous statistical analysis which is currently being prepared by the author, the more recent statistical studies on Japanese and other foreign multinationals in the USA (e.g. Caves and Mehra 1986; Kogut and Sing 1988; Kogut and Chang 1991; Hennart 1991) have suggested that the choice of method of entry and the extent of ownership control of foreign subsidiaries are determined primarily by: (1) the characteristics of the parent firm; (2) the characteristics of products produced by the subsidiary and parent; (3) competitive conditions of the parent's domestic industry; (4) competitive conditions of the market entered; (5) the availability of going firms for local procurement and sourcing, acquisition, and joint venture.[8]

While this paper has examined the patterns of entry by Japanese multinationals into manufacturing industries, it is worth noting that Japanese manufacturing firms have invested heavily in distribution as well to support their local and exporting activities. Japanese direct investments in distribution are aimed at establishing distributional channels and service facilities and providing better customer services in the local markets. These distributional activities of US affiliates of Japanese manufacturers have been found to promote exports of goods produced in Japan (Yamawaki 1991*a*). In Europe, Japanese manufacturers have located their distributional subsidiaries to meet the emergence of the unified European Common Market in 1993 (Williamson and Yamawaki 1991). Thus the entry of Japanese firms into manufacturing must be interrelated in a certain way to their entry into distributional activities.

While these specific factors and the differences in some of these factors between the USA and Europe are expected to explain the observed patterns of the behaviour of Japanese multinationals in the USA and Europe, the historical difference in the development of these two areas to host Japanese multinationals (Yamawaki, Lee, and Fukasaku 1992) has certainly played an important role in determining particularly the cross-country difference in the distribution of subsidiaries across industries. The relatively large presence of Japanese manufacturers of automobiles and their parts in the USA and the presence of Japanese manufacturers of office machines such as copiers and printers in Europe must have been importantly influenced by the historical development of trade policies in the USA and Europe.[9] Future study should then identify the relative importance of these factors that give rise to cross-country differences in the behaviour of Japanese multinational firms.

---

[8] For a broader survey of the extensive literature on the theoretical aspects of multinational corporations, see Caves 1982.

[9] For a detailed account of the effect of anti-dumping investigations in the EC on Japanese FDI, see Belderbos 1991.

REFERENCES

AKIMUNE, I. (1991), 'Overview: Japan's Direct Investment in the E.C.', in Sumitomo Life Research Institute, *Japanese Direct Investment in the E.C.* (Aldershot: Avebury).

BELDERBOS, R. (1991), 'On the Advance of Japanese Electronics Multinationals in the E.C.: Companies, Trends, and Trade Policy' (paper presented at the 8th conference of the Euro-Asia Management Studies Association at INSEAD, Oct.).

—— (1992), 'Firm Determinants of Japanese Direct Foreign Investment in South-East Asia, Europe, and the United States' (Rotterdam: Tinbérgen Institute, Erasmus University, mimeo; Apr.).

CAVES, R. (1982), *Multinational Enterprise and Economic Analysis* (Cambridge: Cambridge University Press).

—— and MEHRA, S. (1986), 'Entry of Foreign Multinationals into U.S. Manufacturing Industries', in M. Porter, ed., *Competition in Global Industries* (Boston: Harvard Business School Press).

DRAKE, T., and CAVES, R. (1990), 'Changing Determinants of Japan's Foreign Direct Investment in the United States' (Cambridge, Mass.: Harvard Institute of Economic Research Discussion Paper 1483, May).

DUNNING, J. (1986), *Japanese Participation in British Industry* (London: Croom Helm).

FROOT, K. (1991), 'Japanese Foreign Direct Investment' (NBER Working Paper Series, 3737, June).

GRAHAM, E., and KRUGMAN, P. (1989), *Foreign Direct Investment in the United States* (Washington, DC: Institute for International Economics).

HEITGER, B., and STEHN, J. (1990), 'Japanese Direct Investments in the E.C.: Response to the Internal Market 1993?', *Journal of Common Market Studies*, 29 (Sept.), 1–15.

HENNART, J. (1991), 'The Transaction Costs Theory of Joint Ventures: An Empirical Study of Japanese Subsidiaries in the United States', *Management Science*, 37 (Apr.), 483–97.

JACQUEMIN, A., and BUIGUES, P. (1991), "Foreign Direct Investments and Exports in the Common Market: Theoretical, Empirical, and Policy Issues' (Brussels: Centre for European Policy Studies Working Documents, Oct.).

KOGUT, B., and SING, H. (1988), 'The Effect of National Culture on the Choice of Entry Mode', *Journal of International Business Studies* (Fall), 411–32.

KOGUT, B., and CHANG, S. (1991), 'Technological Capabilities and Japanese Foreign Direct Investment in the United States', *Review of Economics and Statistics*, 73 (Aug.), 401–13.

MANN, C. (1990), 'Determinants of Japanese Direct Investment in US Manufacturing Industries' (Washington, DC: Federal Reserve Board, mimeo; July).

MICOSSI, S., and VIESTI, G. (1991), 'Japanese Direct Manufacturing Investment in Europe', in L. A. Winters and A. Venables, eds., *European Integration: Trade and Industry* (Cambridge: Cambridge University Press).

MITI (1991), *Dai 4 kai kaigai jigyokatsudo kihonchosa no gaiyo* [Summary of the 4th Report on Foreign Activity of Japanese Firms] (Tokyo).

ODAGIRI, H. (1992), *Growth through Competition, Competition through Growth: Strategic Management and the Economy in Japan* (Oxford: Oxford University Press).

PORTER, M. (1990), *The Competitive Advantage of Nations* (London: MacMillan).

SAZANAMI, Y. (1991), 'Determinants of Japanese Foreign Direct Investment: Locational Attractiveness of European Countries to Japanese Multinationals' (Keio Economic Society Discussion Paper Series, 9102, Keio University, Sept.).

TSURUMI, Y. (1976), *The Japanese are Coming: A Multinational Interaction of Firms and Politics* (Cambridge, Mass.: Ballinger).

WILLIAMSON, P., and YAMAWAKI, H. (1991), 'The Japanese Distribution Network in Europe: Ready and Waiting for the Single Market' (London: London Business School, mimeo; Aug.).

YAMAWAKI, H. (1991a), 'Exports and Foreign Distributional Activities: Evidence on Japanese Firms in the United States', *Review of Economics and Statistics*, 73 (May), 294–300.

—— (1991b), 'Location Decisions of Japanese Multinational Firms in European Manufacturing Industries', in K. Hughes, ed., *European Competitiveness* (Cambridge: Cambridge University Press), forthcoming.

—— LEE, G., and FUKASAKU, K. (1992), 'EC 1992 and Japanese Direct Investment' (Report for the project on 'Globalization, Regionalization' by the Development Centre, OECD, Apr.).

YOSHIHARA, H., SAKUMA, A., ITAMI, H. and KAGONO, T. (1981), *Nihon Kigyo no Takakuka Senryaku* [*Diversification Strategies of Japanese Firms*] (Tokyo: Nihon Keizai Shimbun Sha).

COMMENT

Bruce Kogut

The chapter by Hideki Yamawaki compiles creatively unusual data on the growing expansion of Japanese investment in both Europe and the USA. He asks two questions. First, to what extent is the industrial distribution of investment, and the strategic behaviour of Japanese firms, the same in the two regions? Second, are investments co-ordinated by parents owning subsidiaries in Europe and the USA?

Even though the results of this endeavour more satisfactorily address the first question than the second, Yamawaki's comparison of the investment patterns in the two regions is unique. It points even at this stage, prior to more formal testing, to intriguing patterns. At the same time, as he notes, many of the reputed relationships may not hold up to a statistical scrutiny. A major influence on many of these patterns may be simply, as discussed below, that Japanese subsidiaries in the USA are on average older.

The most exciting contribution made by Yamawaki is the description not only of the simple distribution of investments, but also of what he calls the 'sequential entry process'. The straightforward analysis is that Japanese entry into manufacturing is about two times more numerous in the USA than in Europe, the target industries in the USA are transport equipment, electrical and electronic equipment, and non-electric machinery, and the primary industry recipient in Europe is the electrical and electronic equipment industry. These data conceal, however, a partial clue to the second question, as the electrical and electronic industry has the remarkable trait that 80 per cent of the European subsidiaries have a US counterpart owned by the same Japanese parent.

The results regarding sequential entry are especially provoking. Section 4 presents tersely the statistical facts regarding the pattern of diversification. (Diversification is measured by whether the subsidiary is outside the parent's 2-digit industry.) There is a much greater diversification by Japanese companies in the USA (15 per cent of all subsidiaries) than in Europe (8 per cent). A very engaging finding is that in both the USA and Europe, certain industries are more likely to serve as points of expansion into other industries; these common industries are chemicals and non-ferrous metals. However, the electrical and electronic industries tend to be more prominent in Europe, and the non-electrical machinery industry in the USA, as platforms from which Japanese firms have expanded into other industries. It is of importance that the target industries vary dramatically, with Japanese firms diversifying into non-electrical machinery, electrical, and transportation industries in the USA, and into largely non-electrical machinery in Europe.

The above are the presented facts. Their interpretation depends upon the questions we want to ask and the qualifications we should add. For example, one important qualification is the effect of time. It seems that Japanese investments have been longest concentrated in the electrical and electronic industries in Europe; hence, it may be guessed that many of the Japanese parents having already invested in this industry have expanded into others, since they have simply been longer in Europe.

What we do not know, in fact, is whether the industrial diversification patterns hold at the firm level: do Japanese firms already in the European electrical and electronics industry diversify into other industries? Is diversification influenced by previous investments, and if so, what is the effect of time in explaining the difference in investment patterns?

These issues are relevant for sorting out two different influences on FDI. The first is simply the conditions of the home market on outward investment; that is, does home rivalry 'push' investment to other foreign markets?[10] Traditionally, the literature on FDI has focused on this extension of home market advantages (e.g. brand labels, technology) to other countries. The second influence is how the technological strengths of the target country 'pull' foreign investment into particular industries. It is not hard to imagine, for example, that non-American companies would take equity stakes in US biotechnology firms in order to have access to the resident technology.[11] In fact, as Yamawaki (1991) has already shown, Japanese investment in Europe has flown to the high-wage German location in technologically sophisticated industries, reflecting the importance of a skilled work-force and resident technologies.[12]

These considerations are relevant to the current study in two respects: the initial distribution of investments and the pattern of expansion. It is possible that a firm invests in Germany for the sole purpose of accessing the resident technological strengths in chemicals. However, it is difficult to imagine that a firm would undertake such an investment unless it already had experience in chemicals. It is probable, therefore, that both influences are often at work: firms tend to exploit their home advantage overseas, but they are also drawn to locating operations in regions already strong in the relevant technologies.

The kind of story to which I think the data presented by Yamawaki alludes is the following. In both regions, Japanese investment is pushed outward due to home rivalry. The primary example is the electrical and electronics industry, where the push of home market rivalry explains why

[10] See Yamawaki 1986 for a study on the home market influence on export patterns.
[11] See Shan 1991 for evidence in this regard.
[12] See Cantwell 1989, for broad evidence, and Kogut and Chang 1991 for a discussion of Japanese sourcing of technology in the USA.

the same firms in this industry own subsidiaries in both regions. Competition in the USA and Europe is simply the extension of home market oligopolistic rivalry across borders. (The destruction of the American consumer electronics industry was very likely a secondary consequence of this fundamental rivalry.)

However, once these firms have established positions in the USA and Europe, they face the same opportunities as any domestic firm. In this regard, we would say that the initial investment has given the foreign firm a 'within-country' option to expand in the domestic market.[13] It would be especially attractive, as Yamawaki notes, for firms in slow-growing industries to be attracted to fast-growing ones. However, this trait does not seem especially Japanese. To the contrary, one of the most robust findings on entry is the positive influence of industry growth.[14] We should expect, then, that Japanese firms with established positions in the region, like any domestic firm, would to be drawn to growing industries. And in turn, these industries should reflect the technological advantages of the host country, as would appear to be the case for non-electrical machinery in Europe (or should we say Germany?).

It is instructive that similar industries (i.e. chemicals and non-ferrous) in the USA and Europe should also show greater likelihood to expand into other industries. Certain industries appear to set up assets in foreign countries which serve as platforms into other industries. What is different is that the target of expansion differs between the two regions because, we suspect, the opportunities for entry and growth are different across industries in Europe and the USA.

It remains to consider, however, the second question of across-region co-ordination which Yamawaki posed. A way to think about this element consistent with the above story is that the establishment of subsidiaries in different countries provides a set of 'across-country' options. These options could be to co-ordinate manufacturing production across countries or to transfer new practices and innovations across borders.

The data which Yamawaki has collected do not appear likely to cast much light on this question, outside one important pattern. Certain industries, such as electrical and increasingly auto production, are more characterized by parents owning assets in both regions. This pattern raises the puzzle: why should common ownership matter? As suggested above, one answer is that it does not; it only reflects the fact that investment is being pushed out from the home market into multiple regions of the world. The answer we suggest is that joint ownership does matter, because across-border co-ordination benefits a firm that has established subsidiaries in both regions.

---

[13] This notion of the sequential nature of FDI as a growth option is discussed in Kogut 1983, with a formalization given in Kogut and Kulatilaka, forthcoming.
[14] See the review in Kogut and Chang 1991.

Of course, amid this speculation is a more prosaic interpretation of the industrial pattern: government-imposed barriers to trade have led to tariff (or anti-dumping) hopping investment. The study by Chang and myself clearly found voluntary export restraints to promote Japanese investment in the USA. Yamawaki suggests a similar process is at work in Europe. This effect of government commercial policy on encouraging investment has long been recognized in historical and empirical studies.[15] To understand this effect in the regional context, however, requires a more thorough understanding of the similarity and differences between American and European commercial policies. What we can say is that commercial policy regarding exports unquestionably influences direct investment patterns. The interesting issue is whether policymakers know this, and would this knowledge affect their evaluation of the desirability of restraints on trade.

[15] See the summary given in Caves 1982.

REFERENCES

CANTWELL, J. (1989), *Technological Innovations and the Multinational Corporation* (London: Basil Blackwell).

CAVES, R. (1982), *Economic Analysis and the Multinational Enterprise* (Cambridge: Cambridge University Press).

KOGUT, B. (1983), 'Foreign Direct Investment as a Sequential Process', in C. Kindleberger and D. Audretsch, *The Multinational Corporation in the 1980s* (Cambridge, Mass.: MIT).

—— and KULATILAKA, N. (forthcoming), 'Operating Flexibility, Global Manufacturing, and the Option Value of a Multinational Network', *Management Science*.

—— and CHANG, S. (1991), 'Technological Capability and Japanese Foreign Direct Investment in the United States', *Review of Economics and Statistics*, 73, 401–13.

SHAN, W. (1991), 'Strategic Direct Investment in the Biotechnology Industry' (Wharton School, mimeo).

YAMAWAKI, H. (1986), 'Exports, Foreign Market Structure and Profitability in Japanese and US Manufacturing', *Review of Economics and Statistics*, 68, 618–27.

—— (1991), 'Location Decisions of Japanese Multinational Firms in European Manufacturing Industries', in K. Hughes, ed., *European Competitiveness* (Cambridge: Cambridge University Press).

4

The Performance and Structure of Japanese Affiliates in the European Community*

Michelle Gittelman and Edward Graham

INTRODUCTION

In this paper, we explore the economic performance and industrial structure of affiliates of Japanese firms operating in Europe. The exploration is largely data-driven; that is to say, to the extent allowed by the data, we are attempting to report primarily 'what is' rather than 'why it should be so'.

In the classic industrial organizational paradigm, one would address the issues in the following order: structure, conduct, and performance, on the assumption that structure largely determines conduct and that structure and conduct co-determine performance. In this paper, however, we focus on only structure and performance, reversing the normal order of these, to emphasize two points: first, we do not really have sufficient information at this point to do a full-blown analysis of structure, conduct, and performance of European affiliates of Japanese firms, and second, information specifically on conduct of these affiliates is almost completely lacking. Thus what we are able to present in the pages that follow is a preliminary and incomplete picture, one that leaves many important questions unanswered.

But while our picture is incomplete, we do not believe that it is altogether pointless to present it at this time. Japanese direct investment in Europe is by and large very new, and we believe that this study provides a point by which to calibrate future efforts embodying longer (and, with luck, more comprehensive) data sets to analyse this recent and complex phenomenon.

1. ECONOMIC PERFORMANCE OF AFFILIATES IN THE EUROPEAN COMMUNITY OF US- AND JAPAN-BASED FIRMS

More than anything, what policymakers need to undertand about Japanese FDI in the European Community is the economic performance of affiliates of Japanese-controlled affiliates. Is, for example, the marginal productivity of a worker employed by such an affiliate higher than of a worker employed by a comparable European- or US-owned operation? Is the rate of growth of this productivity higher for the Japanese-controlled

* Hiroshi Fukukawa provided invaluable research assistance in the preparation of this paper.

operation? Do Japanese-controlled operations contribute positively to Europe's research and development efforts? The answers to these questions bear importantly on what should be Europe's policy towards inward direct investment from Japan.

Non-availability of necessary data, alas, makes it impossible to answer these and related questions comprehensively or even in many cases directly. We have been able to assemble data to give an incomplete indication of the relative economic performance of Japanese-controlled operations in the European Community. Again, we do so more in order to set the stage for more comprehensive studies in the future than to claim a definitive analysis at this time.

What we have done is to compare data on EC affiliates of Japanese firms with comparable (but not identical) data on EC affiliates of US firms. The former data come from the Japanese Ministry of International Trade and Industry (MITI), *Survey on Overseas Business Activities*. The sample of firms from which data for this survey were compiled is known to be incomplete: completion of the survey questionnaire was voluntary, and not all firms having overseas business activities actually completed questionnaires. In particular, many small and medium-sized enterprises failed to respond to this survey, and this failure could lead (e.g.) to distortions in the sectoral distribution of reported FDI. Comparing FDI as reported on an approvals basis by the Japanese Ministry of Finance with the MITI survey data, the latter seems to cover about 44 per cent of all Japanese FDI in the European Community and about 61 per cent of such FDI in the manufacturing sector.[1]

The data on European affiliates of US firms come from the US Department of Commerce, Bureau of Economic Analysis, *Benchmark Survey of US Direct Investment Abroad*. Completion of the questionnaires for this survey is mandatory under US law for US firms with overseas operations, and therefore the data sample in this case is, in principle, the universal set. All data (for both affiliates of Japanese firms and US firms) presented in the tables that follow are for 1989. The MITI survey reports all monetary figures in yen; the corresponding figures reported here are in US$, translated at the rate of 158 yen to $1.00, the average rate of exchange for 1989.

Comparing the European subsidiaries of Japanese firms with European subsidiaries of US firms is not the ideal means for determining the economic

---

[1] Comparisons of the Ministry of Finance (MOF) and MITI data reveal possible problems with comparability of the data at a detailed industry level. For example, the MITI survey indicates FDI in the construction and transport sectors actually to be higher than reported by the MOF, whose data represent in principle the universe of all FDI approved. However, we are told that the MOF data themselves are incomplete, and in the case of these sectors, the MITI data may simply be more complete than the MOF data. But also, the MOF data include FDI projects that are approved but not transacted. This latter fact might explain why, for example, the MITI figures for the services sector are but a small fraction of the figures reported by the MOF.

performance of the latter (e.g. one would prefer to make similar comparisons between the Euro-affiliates of Japanese firms and comparable, European-owned operations), but available data makes this comparison feasible whereas the analysis one might ideally do is, as suggested above, not feasible due to data limitations. The Japanese firm/US firm comparison is not, however, totally without merit. It has been long acknowledged that the European operations of US firms perform at or above the levels of their purely domestic rivals. Indeed, much of the theory of the multinational enterprise rests on the notion that these firms possess some sort of ownership-specific advantage that enables them to outperform local rivals, although whether or not this advantage always works to the favour of the local economy is less clear. It is also doubtless true that in current times US firms have lost much of their advantages relative to their European rivals, and much of the remaining advantages of the former might be more in the order of 'incumbency advantages' than of advantages born of, say, superior technology or managerial prowess. None the less, it is probably safe to say that European affiliates of US firms, even today, do not significantly lag behind their European rivals in terms of economic performance characteristics. If this is indeed true, then if European affiliates of Japanese firms significantly outperform European affiliates of US firms, these former probably also outperform domestically owned operations.

European operations of Japanese firms seem to be more fragmented than US operations of the same firms; otherwise put, in Europe Japanese firms tend to establish more but smaller facilities than they do in the USA, doing so perhaps in response to pressures, real or perceived, to have a physical presence in all European countries. In some contrast, many US-based firms have been moving towards greater Europe-wide integration and rationalization of their European operations, whereby sub-optimally scaled operations in some countries have been shut down and local markets in these countries served by production from other affiliates (see e.g. Graham 1991). The fragmentation of Japanese operations in Europe stands in contrast to the operations of Japanese-controlled firms in North America or Asia, where the rule is towards integrated operations.

There are two possible explanations, apart for the political explanation suggested just above, for the apparently fragmented nature of Japanese-controlled operations in Europe. First, these operations tend to be of quite recent vintage, and the data may in some cases simply reflect undertakings that are not yet fully implemented. Second, in Europe Japanese-controlled firms have been under considerable pressure to source inputs from locally owned suppliers. This latter has been especially so in the automotive industry where, unlike the case in North America, locally owned auto parts suppliers are readily able to meet the technical and quality standards demanded by the major Japanese automotive firms (although apparently not always the delivery schedule requirements).

TABLE 4.1. *Summary data for EC affiliates of US and Japanese corporations, 1989*

	EC affiliates of Japanese firms	EC affiliates of US firms
Total no. of affiliates	1106	7391
Total employees of affiliates (thousands)	120.3	2539.7
Total assets of affiliates (US$ billion)	118.4	657.7
Employees per affiliate	108	344
Assets per affiliate (US$ million)	107.05	88.99
Assets per employee (US$ thousand)	932.3	242.8

Source: Calculated from data in MITI 1991 and US Department of Commerce 1992.

The apparent tendency towards fragmentation of Japanese FDI in Europe is supported by certain of the data presented below in Table 4.1, but not others. For example, the average number of employees per affiliate of US firms in Europe is over three times as great as the same figure per affiliate of Japanese firms. Unfortunately, these averages cannot be broken down by sector. Sectoral figures are available for the affiliates of Japanese firms, and *inter alia* the figures show that the average such affiliate operating in the manufacturing sector employs 263 persons, a figure roughly comparable to the 344 employees per affiliate of US firms in all industries.

Although the average European affiliate of a Japanese firm is smaller than the average European affiliate of a US firm when measured by number of employees, the opposite holds true when one measures by total assets. Thus, the average Japanese affiliate holds $107 million in total assets, as against only $89 million for the average affiliate of a US firm. This leads to wildly different figures for capital per employee, one measure of capital intensity: $932 thousand for the Japanese firm versus only $249 thousand for the US firm. A fair question is, what can account for these discrepancies?

A candidate answer to this last question is that the size distribution of affiliates is different for Japanese and US firms. If, for example, this distribution for Euro-affiliates of Japanese firms were to be bi-modal, such that the sample consisted of a few very large operations combined with a number of much smaller ones, the discrepancies noted above could occur. Table 4.2 examines total assets and assets per employee of Euro-affiliates of US and Japanese firms broken down by major sector. As can be seen, the size distribution of Euro-affiliates of Japanese firms is significantly skewed. Non-manufacturing affiliates figure relatively large in terms of

TABLE 4.2. *Assets per employee in EC affiliates of Japanese and US firms, by major sector, 1989* ($ thousand)

Sector	EC affiliates of Japanese firms	EC affiliates of US firms
All	932.3	242.8
Non-manufacturing	1,730.1	354.5
Manufacturing	580.3	205.2
Chemicals	222.9	337.6
Electrical and electronic	171.6	74.1
Transport	1889.7	207.2
Machinery	160.1	281.3

Source: Calculated from data in MITI 1991 and US Department of Commerce 1992.

assets per employee, as do affiliates in the transport sector. The non-manufacturing sector figure is probably accounted for by a heavy presence of asset-intensive subsectors such as finance, banking, insurance, and property in the non-manufacturing category. The transport sector almost surely reflects large subsidiaries of the Japanese auto manufacturers which had assets committed to them but had not yet been brought fully onto line at the time the MITI survey was conducted (and hence had not yet completed hiring their employees, thus accounting for the extraordinarily large reported assets per employee). Data from the MITI survey (MITI's table 2–6–9) indicate that 38 per cent of all Japanese direct investment projects in this sector were initiated in the last three years covered by the survey (1987–9), and press reports suggest that these investments included a number of very large-scale projects that might not have been completed at the time the survey was taken.

In the other sectors, the Euro-affiliates of Japanese firms reported neither particularly large assets per employee nor assets per affiliate. Indeed, in two out of three sectors (chemicals and machinery) the Euro-affiliates of US firms reported significantly higher assets per employee, whereas in the third (electrical and electronic machinery) the opposite was reported, although in this last sector the difference, while substantial, was not extraordinary. Table 4.3 below indicates the assets per affiliate of Euro-affiliates of Japanese firms in four manufacturing sectors. (Comparable data for US firms is, alas, not available.) Again, the extraordinarily large assets per affiliate of the transport sector stand out, tending to confirm the hypothesis of a highly skewed size distribution of affiliates by sector for Japanese firms.

In particular, the large investments in the auto sector do indeed (apparently) distort the all-industry assets per affiliate for Japanese firms' operations in Europe.

TABLE 4.3. *Assets per affiliate in EC affiliates of Japanese firms, 1989* ($ million)

Sector	Assets
Chemicals	44.58
Electrical and electronic	37.53
Transport	1,172.74
Machinery	28.62

Source: Calculated from data in MITI 1991.

TABLE 4.4. *Total sales by EC affiliates of Japanese and US firms, 1989* ($ billion)

Sector	EC affiliates of Japanese firms	EC affiliates of US firms
All industries	164.8	508.5
Manufacturing	18.8	280.1
Chemicals	1.2	59.1
Electrical and electronic	6.9	32.7
Transport	5.2	36.5
Machinery	1.8	61.0

Source: Calculated from data in MITI 1991 and US Department of Commerce 1992.

It is possible that some of the difference in assets per employee as between Euro-affiliates of Japanese and US firms is the result of sample bias. In particular, respondents to the MITI survey tended to be the larger firms, for which one might expect larger assets per employee than for smaller firms. Thus, to the extent that this bias is present, it would probably exaggerate the assets per employee of the Euro-affiliates of Japanese firms relative to their US-controlled counterparts.

Table 4.4 indicates total sales of EC affiliates of Japanese and US firms. Total sales of the latter are somewhat more than three times the former, as one might expect, but sales of Euro-affiliates of US firms in manufacturing are almost fifteen times those of their Japanese counterparts. Thus, the manufacturing presence of US firms in Europe is simply much, much greater than that of Japanese firms, or at least, it was in 1989.

The share of the Euro-affiliates of Japanese firms in the transport sector of sales (relative to the sales of all Euro-affiliates in the manufacturing sector) is about 28 per cent, whereas the share of the former in assets is 78 per cent, tending to confirm our earlier speculation that European operations of the Japanese auto manufacturers were not fully on-line at the time the MITI survey was conducted and that this distorts certain aggregate measures (e.g. assets per employee) in this sector.

TABLE 4.5. *Destination of sales by EC affiliates of Japanese and US firms, 1989* (%)

Sector	EC affiliates of Japanese firms			EC affiliates of US firms		
	Local	Home	Other	Local	Home	Other
All	45.4	12.6	42.0	69.0	4.6	26.4
Manufacturing	66.4	1.6	32.0	60.2	5.4	34.4
Chemical	51.8	0.8	48.1	56.8	2.7	40.4
Electrical and electronic	73.4	0.8	25.8	28.1	2.1	69.8
Transport	50.9	0.8	48.3	83.5	3.2	13.2
Machinery	59.2	3.4	40.5	53.5	15.8	30.7

Source: Calculated from data in MITI 1992 and US Department of Commerce 1992.

Table 4.5 examines the percentage breakdown of sales of Euro-affiliates of the two sets of firms by destination, that is, sales to the host country market and to export markets, divided into the home country (Japan for the Japanese firms, the USA for the US firms) and other. 'Other' for both sets of firms is overwhelmingly exports to other European Community countries.

These data show that within the manufacturing sector, on average the Euro-affiliates of Japanese and US firms ship close to the same percentage of output to regional markets (the sum of host and other markets), but that by sector there is substantial variation both by sector and by nationality of ownership of affiliate.

These data reveal some information about the extent of regional integration and rationalization of Euro-affiliates of both Japanese and US firms, in that if operations are integrated and rationalized across national boundaries, one might expect the ratio of host country sales to sales to other countries (except Japan; most of these sales are to the EC) to be lower than if these operations were not integrated and rationalized. (Table 4.6 indicates these ratios.) By this measure, one sees that, overall, the Euro-affiliates of US firms in the manufacturing sector are more integrated and rationalized than those of Japanese firms, but that this is not consistently true by subsector. Thus, data in the table show that Japanese firms are more integrated and rationalized in the chemical, transport, and machinery subsectors; but US firms are more integrated and rationalized in other manufacturing subsectors such as food-processing (not shown in the table). One should note that the bias in the MITI data towards larger firms in the universe of foreign direct investors might lead this measure to overstate the full extent of regional integration and rationalization of Euro-affiliates of Japanese firms relative to their US counterparts.

Non-manufacturing Euro-affiliates of Japanese firms ship a much higher

TABLE 4.6. *The ratio of host-country sales to sales in other countries (except home country), 1989*

Sector	EC affiliates of Japanese firms	EC affiliates of US firms
All	1.08	2.61
Manufacturing	2.07	1.75
Chemical	1.08	1.41
Electrical and electronic	2.85	0.40
Transport	1.05	6.32
Machinery	1.46	1.74

Source: Calculated from figures in Table 4.5.

TABLE 4.7. *Sales and compensation per employee by EC affiliates of Japanese and US firms, 1989* ($ thousand)

Sector	EC affiliates of Japanese firms		EC affiliates of US firms	
	Sales	Compensation	Sales	Compensation
Manufacturing	223.9	22.3	163.1	32.1
Chemicals	208.9	7.2	238.3	35.6
Electrical and electronic	281.1	14.7	128.7	25.4
Transport	257.0	13.3	112.6	31.5
Machinery	215.2	36.6	209.6	38.6

Note: EC affiliates of US firms include majority-owned affiliates only.

Source: Calculated from data in MITI 1992 and US Department of Commerce 1992.

percentage of their sales to the home market than do their US counterparts, but this is an expected result because the former include European subsidiaries of the large Japanese trading firms whose major business is export and import from and to Japan.

Table 4.7 indicates sales and compensation per employee for the two sets of Euro-affiliates. These must be taken as (rather poor) surrogates for productivity figures, as these latter are not available. These data, if they are to be believed, indicate that in every sector except chemicals the Euro-affiliates of Japanese firms achieve greater sales per employee than do their US-owned counterparts, but without exception they compensate their employees less. The latter in particular is suspect. The very low figure reported for compensation by Euro-affiliates of Japanese firms in the chemicals sector is almost surely the result of a misprint in the MITI data or some other source of error. Otherwise, the fact that the figures for the Euro-affiliates of Japanese firms are so consistently below those for the

Euro-affiliates of US firms also suggests systematic differences in the way the data are collected or aggregated (e.g. the US Commerce Department data reflect wage and non-wage compensation, whereas we are not sure if possibly the MITI data reflect wage data only).

Beyond suspecting data discrepancies, can we make any sense out of these numbers? Sales per employee is a poor proxy for value added per employee, and one possible reason why the Euro-affiliates of Japanese firms outperform their US counterparts on the basis of the former measure might very well be that the sales figures are not well correlated with the value-added figures for these sets of firms. This could be the case, for example, if sales included products not actually manufactured in Europe.

In this last regard, it is instructive to note that in the chemicals sector, where this last possibility probably does not hold to any great degree, the US firms outperform the Japanese ones. Also, this is a sector where it is widely agreed that US firms still hold significant competitive advantages over their Japanese rivals. In the electrical and electronics sector and in the transport sector (especially the automobile subsector), it is commonly held that the competitive edge is held by Japanese firms, and the figures in Table 4.6 are consistent with this. However, the discrepancies between the two sets of firms seem wildly high to be indicative of productivity differences: Euro-affiliates of Japanese firms sell over twice the value of product per employee as do their US counterparts in both sectors, and although most analysts would probably accept that the former firms are likely to be on average more productive than the latter in both sectors, few would accept that the difference would be over 100 per cent.

The apparent discrepancy in the transport sector might be in part accounted for by the apparent fact, noted earlier, that large-scale operations of European affiliates of the Japanese auto manufacturers were not fully on-line at the time the MITI survey was made. (For this to be true, however, these same affiliates would have had to be importing significant amounts of products at the time the survey was conducted.) These facilities would also be expected to employ younger workers for whom considerable on-the-job training was required (and hence would have less-well-compensated workers). Finally, the Japanese-owned facilities in this sector are heavily concentrated in the relatively low-wage UK, whereas many US-owned facilities are located in relatively high-wage Germany.

No explanations quite as easy as these are apparent for the electrical and electronic sector, however. By contrast, in the machinery sector, the Japanese Euro-affiliates do show higher sales per employee than do the US Euro-affiliates, but the difference is not large.

To the extent that the differences in compensation per employee are to be taken seriously, they imply conclusions opposite to those implied by the sales per employee differences. That is, whereas the latter data imply that in the manufacturing industries (with the exception of chemicals) the Euro-affiliates of Japanese firms are more productive than their US counterparts, the former data—assuming that wages reflect the value of the marginal product of labour, as economic theory would predict—imply the very opposite. Not only would these data show the Euro-affiliates of US firms to be more productive (at the margin and for all of the sectors considered) than their Japanese counterparts, again the implied differences are just too great to be taken too seriously. (Again, the difference for the machinery sector is not great, but the difference favours the US firms.) In a word, if sales per employee is a valid proxy for average product of workers, and compensation per employee is a valid proxy for marginal product of workers, then the data suggest that on average the Euro-affiliates of Japanese firms are much more productive than their US counterparts (except in chemicals), but that the US Euro-affiliates are at the margin much more productive than their Japanese counterparts.

These two statements are not likely to be true simultaneously. (Although it is not theoretically impossible that average productivity for one set of firms is higher whereas the ordering is reversed for marginal productivity, this is highly implausible in practice; it certainly would not be the case if, as is likely, marginal product of a worker is roughly constant in the range of optimal rate of output.) We might note that Graham and Krugman (1991) found weak evidence suggesting that the US affiliates of Japanese firms are on average more productive (in terms of value added per worker) than are domestic rivals or, indeed, US affiliates of European firms. Is this likely to be the case for European affiliates of Japanese firms? Are they more productive than either domestic European rivals or European affiliates of US firms? One supposes that this might indeed be the case, as we have suggested, but the data to test this hypothesis directly are not readily available and, as just discussed, the available surrogates simply neither strongly support nor strongly reject the hypothesis.

Whatever the case with respect to productivity, there is one dimension on which the European affiliates of Japanese firms significantly lag behind their US counterparts, and this is the amount of research and development currently performed in the European Community. In 1989, Euro-affiliates of US firms reported an aggregate total of $5.4 billion spent on research and development conducted in the Community, or almost $2,500 per employee. The Euro-affiliates of Japanese firms, in contrast, reported aggregate research and development expenditures in the Community of only $86.9 million, or about $725 per employee.

Are the Japanese to be faulted for such low expenditures? Any negative reaction surely for the moment would be premature. Japanese direct investment in Europe is on average of very recent vintage, whereas the largest US firms with European subsidiaries have typically been involved in Europe for decades. Research and development activities are typically undertaken by multinational firms in locations outside their home countries only after production and distribution operations are well established. In the USA, where most affiliates of Japanese firms are also of recent vintage, but not quite as recent vintage, on average, as in Europe, research and development expenditures of local affiliates of Japanese firms have grown spectacularly in recent years, although in the aggregate they still account for only a tiny fraction of all US industrial R&D (see Graham 1992). What will be the trajectory of R&D expenditures in the European Community in the future is simply not known, but it is not unreasonable to expect fairly healthy growth in these expenditures in coming years. But if this growth is not forthcoming, and given the significant positive externalities that typically are imputed to these activities, Europe would be justifiably disappointed.

3. ORGANIZATIONAL ASPECTS OF JAPANESE FDI IN THE EC

The discussion so far has concerned itself with a comparison of the performance of Japanese Euro-affiliates with the Euro-affiliates of US-owned firms. Even allowing for differences in timing, sectoral composition, and corporate strategic goals, such a comparison is a useful, albeit incomplete, indicator of the possible economic impact of Japanese FDI on the European economy. However, there is a mounting suspicion among policy-makers, researchers, and business leaders that Japanese investment needs to be viewed through a different prism than investment from other countries. This view stems from a growing awareness of the unique form of industrial organization prevalent in Japan, in which firms do not compete as independent entities but as members of large, loosely defined webs of inter-related companies, known as *keiretsu*. From an economic point of view, *keiretsu* have been identified as an important variable explaining the low levels of both Western imports and Western investment in Japan; in this sense they form an organizational barrier to entry to Japan's highly lucrative domestic markets.[2] From a business-organization point of view, the *keiretsu* are increasingly seen as conferring special competitive advantages on their members which Western firms can not match, enabling Japanese firms to wage protracted competitive battles and win large shares of overseas markets.[3] They also have been credited with allowing Japanese firms to gain critical techno-manufacturing skills which will enable them to gain control of strategic industries in the future.

These perceptions have led, at one extreme, to demands for the dissolving of *keiretsu* relationships in Japan and, at the other, to calls-to-arms for

[2] Encarnation 1992; Lawrence 1991 and 1992; but see also Sheard 1992.
[3] See e.g. Aoki 1991.

Western firms to form *keiretsu* of their own.[4] In between these two stances has been a rising recognition among policymakers as to the importance of *keiretsu* and the need to somehow deal with them; how this should be done, however, remains unclear. In the meantime, the issue of Japanese industrial organization is being placed squarely at the centre of high-level policy arenas, such as the Strategic Industries Initiative, that are likely to have a significant impact on bilateral economic relations with Japan.

One problem is that *keiretsu* remain a little-understood and at times maligned concept among Western observers. While there is no doubt that the impact of *keiretsu* on Japanese economic performance both at home and abroad is formidable, they are by no means the monolithic structures they are sometimes supposed to be, systematically organized to power the Japanese economy and steamroll over foreign markets. Rather, relationships within *keiretsu* can take on a variety of different forms, depending on such variables as the industry and firm in question, the particular point in the history of the Japanese economy, and even the behaviour of a single business leader. Indeed, it is plausible that *keiretsu* might actually, in some cases, retard the speed at which Japanese firms acquire competitive advantages. As one writer has stated, it is necessary to view the *keiretsu* not as a particular pattern but as an overall *process* which, in its essence, acts to replace arms-length transactions with a variety of forms of long-term, interfirm co-operation.[5] The *keiretsu* may thus be seen as occupying a novel position somewhere between the market and the hierarchy. Viewed in this way, the implications of *keiretsu* for international economic relations ought to be in the domain of theorists concerned with issues relating to industrial organization, trade and competition policy, before moving to the less-informed but more influential sphere of economic policymaking.

Now that Japanese outward FDI has reached some $311 billion,[6] Japanese FDI is joining trade as a central policy issue. The EC has recently defined the available market share available to Japanese automobile makers as including not only their exports from Japan, but also the sales of their European affiliates, and US policymakers are considering similar strategies while grappling with ways to limit Japanese acquisitions of high-technology firms.[7] Given this heightened attention to Japanese FDI, it is probable that the issue of whether *keiretsu* are a salient feature of that investment will quickly rise to the surface. At best, such concerns will be met with educated discussion about the implications of *keiretsu* for a wide range of policy areas; at worst, politically charged debates could give way to paranoia about 'Trojan horses' being delivered to overseas locations, where they

---

[4] Ferguson 1990.   [5] Gerlach 1992*b*, 5.

[6] Outward stock at the end of FY 1990, approvals basis, Ministry of Finance.

[7] The recent Gephardt–Dingell proposal to the US Congress would, if passed, define the Japanese share of the US auto industry as including both exports and direct sales through FDI.

might effectively finish off whatever was left over following the onslaught of Japanese exports.

This paper hopes to contribute to the former approach to the issue of Japanese FDI by examining the extent to which *keiretsu* organizations characterize Japanese investment in the EC and, for comparative purposes, the USA. It is not our purpose to present an overview of the evolution and nature of *keiretsu* themselves, an immensely complex topic in which the authors have few comparative advantages.[8] From the point of view of analysing Japan's outward FDI, the *keiretsu* relationships that matter are far less easily defined, much less analysed, than is commonly assumed. The *keiretsu* that Western observers are most familiar with are the so-called 'horizontal' *keiretsu*: six large, diversified families of companies, several of which have their roots in the early *zaibatsu* (conglomerates) that characterized the pre-war Japanese economy. These groups—Mitsui, Mitsubishi, Sumitomo, Fuyo, Sanwa, and Dai-Ichi Kangyo (DKB)—are comprised of a lead bank plus at least one company from each of Japan's leading industries. In addition to their close financial relationship with the lead bank, group members are interlinked through cross-holdings of each other's equity, which in some cases may exceed 50 per cent ownership. Members are typically among Japan's largest firms, and because of the preponderance of economic clout concentrated in these six groupings, they have attracted the most attention outside Japan.

Less well-known than horizontal *keiretsu*, but perhaps more important from the point of view of firm performance, are Japan's vertical *keiretsu*. In these groupings, member firms belong to the same industry, but perform different functions along that industry's value-added chain. Many members of the large horizontal *keiretsu* are themselves leaders of their own vertical *keiretsu*: Toshiba and Nissan, for instance, are each leaders of their own vertical *keiretsu* while also being members of the Mitsui and Fuyo groups, respectively. Other vertical leaders, such as industry newcomers Sony and Honda, operate more or less independently of the older horizontal groupings, although they may be non-core members of the latter (as Sony is in the Mitsui group). Unlike horizontal *keiretsu*, significant cross-ownership of equity is not always prevalent in the case of vertical *keiretsu*. Indeed, it is often difficult to identify a vertical *keiretsu* by looking at equity cross-holdings alone: on a financial reporting basis, Toyota claims to have only 23 firms in its vertical *keiretsu*; in addition, however, it maintains close relations with about 170 primary suppliers, which in turn are fed by some 4,000 smaller secondary suppliers and approximately 30,000 third-tier firms.[9] Rather than equity, the defining characteristic of vertical *keiretsu* is close co-operation in the production sphere, often within a tightly defined geographical space.

---

[8] For an excellent introduction to the topic, see Gerlach 1992*a*.   [9] Milelli 1991.

At the risk of over-simplification, it might be said that when a firm belongs to both a vertical and a horizontal *keiretsu*, its production linkages are likely to be more important within its vertical *keiretsu* rather than within its horizontal *keiretsu*, where relationships are primarily financial in nature.[10] Indeed, it is possible that these vertical inter-firm linkages are at the heart of Japanese competitiveness in manufacturing, particularly in the assembly-based automobile and electric and electronic equipment industries.[11] Furthermore, it is likely that such forms of organization yield qualitative differences in the behaviour and performance of Japanese firms *vis-à-vis* their US and European counterparts. For instance, Japanese automobile manufacturers source about 70 per cent of their value-added from outside suppliers, which are likely to be members of the manufacturer's vertical *keiretsu*, versus only about 30 per cent for American manufacturers, which typically engage in arm's-length transactions with independent suppliers.[12] The nature as well as the scope of manufacturer–supplier relationships in Japan is also markedly different from that practised in other countries; one defining characteristic is that such relationships are remarkably stable over time, extending well beyond the life of a given product or model. Suppliers are expected to keep pace with the rapid technological and product-development path of the lead company and to play a critical role in the latter's innovation process. Personnel and know-how are often shared. Given such tight and stable relationships that involve heavy intra-group product, technology, and information flows, the true boundaries of a large-scale Japanese manufacturer may be said to lie somewhere beyond the manufacturer itself, to include the network of quasi-independent firms belonging to its vertical *keiretsu*.

Given these observations, it is these vertical, transaction-based *keiretsu* relationships that merit the closest scrutiny when analysing the structure and performance of Japanese multinationals in overseas locations. In so far as such structures are important variables explaining Japanese firms' remarkable competitive performance in assembly-based industries, and in so far as a firm's unique competitive advantages may be transferred abroad through FDI, then as overseas Japanese manufacturing investment accumulates and matures, one might expect to see a build-up of similar networks

---

[10] Attention must be paid to the important exceptions to this rather broad generalization. Horizontal *keiretsu* members do sometimes act in concert on particular projects, to create large-scale, vertically integrated production structures; they may also engage in major technology-pooling efforts. The frequency with which such projects occur appears to depend on the nature of the industry in question and the particular relationships among members of a given *keiretsu*. Intra-group product flows may also be quite significant, depending again on the nature of the relationship (those between steel producers and trading houses tend to be particularly strong, for instance) and on the individual *keiretsu* in question. Finally, flows of information between members are also important (and institutionalized in the form of closed monthly meetings), but it is not clear that these result in co-ordinated strategic moves by members.   [11] Ozawa 1991; Gittelman and Dunning 1992.

[12] Womack, Jones, and Roos 1991.

outside Japan. This paper attempts to determine whether such an expectation can be confirmed by the available data on Japanese investment in Europe.

Keiretsu Formation in Europe

In order to evaluate the degree to which investments by *keiretsu* group members are being made in Europe, 590 separate investments by Japanese manufacturing firms in Europe were grouped according to their *keiretsu* affiliations.[13] As much as possible, primary affiliations within vertical *keiretsu* were used as the basis of identification, on the assumption that these would have greater implications than horizontal affiliations for inter-firm co-operation. Such an exercise is necessarily subjective, given the fluid nature of *keiretsu* affiliations, and alternative methods of assignment could easily have yielded different results, in particular if horizontal rather than vertical *keiretsu* affiliations were used as the unit of analysis.

The affiliates are categorized as either 'parent companies' or 'group companies' in a given vertical *keiretsu*. Group companies, all legally independent firms, are considered to belong to a *keiretsu* if they are related to the parent company in Japan; such a relationship may or may not involve significant equity holdings.[14]

By keeping to vertical linkages as the primary means of affiliation, the classification of parents does not necessarily lead back to the 'ultimate' parent of a horizontal *keiretsu*. For instance, Toshiba (electronics), Toyota (automobiles), and Toray (textiles), all members of the horizontal Mitsui group, are each leaders of important vertical *keiretsu*, and thus each is counted as a separate parent with its own cluster of group companies. The implicit assumption in this categorization is that the European affiliates of these parent firms operate independently of one another, despite their common membership in a horizontal *keiretsu*.[15] Analysing the data in this fashion counts parents rather heavily at the expense of group companies, and is thus a rather conservative means of delineating *keiretsu* relationships;

---

[13] 526 of the investments were from the sixth JETRO survey of Japanese manufacturing operations in Europe (JETRO 1990). An additional 57 were added from the 1991 survey (JETRO 1991). Nearly all the affiliates in the sample are located in the EC, although a handful are located in Austria and Finland. *Keiretsu* affiliations for the sample were determined from *Kigyo Keiretsu Soran* 1989.

[14] The source used to match group companies with their parents often identifies group affiliation even in the absence of an equity relationship.

[15] Such an assumption could, however, be persuasively challenged. Particularly with regard to Sumitomo and Mitsubishi, it is tempting to view the various parent companies as belonging to a single group, with a higher than average propensity to operate in a co-ordinated manner. For instance, there is evidence of intra-*keiretsu* co-operation taking place within the Mitsubishi company, where several of its members teamed up on a US automobile project (*Business Week* 1990), and in the Sumitomo *keiretsu*, where members have invested in 2 joint projects in Europe (JETRO 1991).

overall, however, one would expect to see low numbers of investments by parents in relation to group company investments, if the pyramidal production linkages that characterize vertical *keiretsu* structures in Japan were being transferred to Europe.

Out of the total 590 investments, 78 firms, which account for 90 discrete investments, are unlisted on any stock exchange, and could be not be traced back to any parent; they may or may not be linked to a *keiretsu* structure. The analysis focuses on the remaining 500 investments which could be traced back to a parent firm. Table 4.8 shows the *keiretsu* affiliations of those investments. 'Parent investments' are the Euro-affiliates of the parent itself (e.g. Canon Europe), while 'group company' investments represent the Euro-affiliates of companies that belong to that parent's *keiretsu* in Japan.

It should be stressed that just because European investments by a parent are matched by investments by its group companies, it cannot be assumed that parents and their group are in some way acting in concert in Europe. In the absence of more research into the conduct of these groups, one cannot know whether the inter-firm linkages which characterize their behaviour in Japan are indeed being transplanted to European soil. In several cases, investments by group companies were made before those of parents. Still, by looking at the distribution of parents versus group companies over a large number of companies, some broad organizational patterns emerge, indicating the extent to which the European investments of *keiretsu* parents have been matched by investments by their group companies.

Across all industries, the extent of such a pattern appears to be fairly weak. The 500 investments could be traced back to 173 parents; of those, 112 had only one or two investments in Europe, almost all of them by the parents themselves. The majority of Japanese investments in Europe, therefore, are single investments made by parent companies, without any accompanying investments by group members.

However, among the 61 companies that did have multiple investments in Europe (three or more, including investments by their group companies), a somewhat different picture emerges. Those 61 parents were linked to another 75 firms in Europe which could be classified as their *keiretsu* members. For those firms, then, there are more group companies in Europe than there are parents, a pattern one would broadly associate with *keiretsu* formation.

In terms of the total number of investments, however, parents still outnumber group companies. The 61 parent firms accounted for 246 separate investments, while their group companies had made only 108 investments, such that for every one group company investment, more than two were made by that company's *keiretsu* leader. Such a top-heavy structure would not appear to be reflective of *keiretsu* organization in Japan, where a parent

TABLE 4.8. *Structure of European investments by Japanese manufacturing companies, 1990–1991**

	No. of parent companies	No. of group companies associated with parents	No. of separate investments by parents	No. of separate investments by groups	Total investments (parent + group)
Companies with 1 or 2 investments in Europe[†]	112	5	141	5	146
Companies with 3 or more investments in Europe[†]	61	75	246	108	354
Total companies with identifiable parents	173	80	387	113	500

* Table includes only those companies with identifiable parents.
[†] Including investments by group companies.

Source: JETRO 1990, 1991; *Kigyo Keiretsu Soran* 1989.

can have tens if not hundreds of companies in its group; however, given the newness of Japanese investment in Europe, it might be expected that a period of several years would pass between the initial investments by parents and subsequent investments by their group members. In other words, these data may present only a snapshot of Japanese investment in Europe at a very early stage, with a possible deepening of *keiretsu* structures in the future.

Such an impression is strengthened by an industry-level analysis of firms with multiple investments in Europe, presented in Table 4.9. The horizontal *keiretsu* are shown separately from any industry, given the 'gray area' they seem to occupy between vertical and horizontal production linkages. However, each of the major horizontal group companies ('Sumitomo Rubber', 'Sumitomo Electric', etc.) has been counted as a separate parent in its own right. Across the entire sample of 500 investments, three industries—electric/electronic equipment, automobiles, and chemicals/pharmaceuticals—account for about 42 per cent (211) of all affiliates in the JETRO survey,[16] which roughly corresponds to those industries' combined share of 50 per cent of Japanese FDI stock in Europe at the end of 1990.

The industry breakdown reveals that the structural attributes of Japanese FDI in Europe differ markedly by industry and, furthermore, the organizational patterns that can be observed in Europe correspond broadly with those that prevail in Japan. Of the three predominant industries—electric/electronic equipment, automobiles, and chemicals/pharmaceuticals—only the chemical/pharmaceuticals industry shows minimal signs of *keiretsu* formation, with 54 separate investments by nine parents, against only eight investments by six group members. This flattened-out structure (high parent/group company ratio) is broadly consistent with what one would expect, given the organization of the chemical industry in Japan, and the relative advantages of Japanese *vis-à-vis* European chemical firms. Regarding the former, the *keiretsu* linkages of chemical firms in Japan are tightest with downstream distributors, rather than with suppliers and other manufacturers. In other words, *keiretsu* organizations geared towards co-ordinating production within a multi-firm network are of less importance to chemical companies than they are to assembly-based mass production industries. Regarding the second factor, the chemicals and pharmaceutical industry is somewhat unique in being one of the few in which European firms have, in the main, stronger competitive advantages than their Japanese counterparts. Given this configuration of advantages, the strategies of Japanese firms in this sector would presumably tend to focus more on acquiring new competitive advantages through acquisitions and tie-ups with local firms than on building up wholly owned overseas production structures to exert leverage on pre-existing advantages. One company in particular, DaiNippon

---

[16] These industries would account for an even higher share, if the 117 firms with only 1 or 2 investments in Europe had been allocated to industries, along with the subsidiaries of Sumitomo, Mitsubishi, and Mitsui involved in those industries.

TABLE 4.9. *Japanese firms with three or more investments in Europe, by industry and keiretsu*

Industry	No. of parent companies	No. of group companies associated with parents	No. of separate investments by parents	No. of separate investments by groups	Total investments (parent + group)
Horizontal *keiretsu*					
Sumitomo	5	4	15	4	19
Mitsubishi	7	4	15	8	23
Mitsui	4	1	8	1	9
Electric & electronic equipment	13	26	63	36	99
Transport equipment	3	20	18	32	50
Chemicals and pharmaceuticals	9	6	54	8	62
Industrial machinery	4	2	14	2	16
Precision machinery	5	5	14	8	22
Other, miscellaneous	11	7	45	9	54
TOTAL (companies with ≥ 3 investments)	61	75	246	108	354

Source: JETRO 1990, 1991; *Kigyo Keiretsu Soran* 1989.

Ink and Chemicals, is actively pursuing an aggressive market-seeking strategy in Europe through numerous acquisitions and, with 29 affiliates, has the single largest number of parent investments of any company in the JETRO survey, with no accompanying group company investments.[17]

In contrast to the chemicals/pharmaceuticals industry, Japanese firms in the automobile and electric/electronic equipment industries do enjoy substantial comparative advantages over European producers and, moreover, those advantages may be strongly bound up with the *keiretsu* form of industrial organization, as discussed briefly above. Such considerations would tend to encourage Japanese firms, once a given critical mass of investment had been reached, to shift the entire production structure to the overseas location, in order to maintain their multi-firm manufacturing networks.[18] In other words, in those industries in which *keiretsu* relationships are critical to competitive performance in Japan, one might expect to see a build-up of *keiretsu*-type structures in overseas locations. Such structures would presumably entail large numbers of investments by group companies against relatively fewer investments by parents (although the latter would tend to be much larger in size).

These predictions appear to be borne out by the data in Table 4.9. Of the 113 investments by all group companies in Europe, 37 per cent were in the electric/electronic equipment industry[19] and another 28 per cent in the automobile industry. These two industries thus accounted for two-thirds of total group-company investments in the sample, while they accounted for only 24 per cent of total investments by parents.[20] The low parent/group company ratio points rather persuasively to a possible formation of *keiretsu* organizations in both industries, which collectively account for about 50 per cent of the total investment stock of Japanese manufacturing firms in Europe (66 per cent in the UK). Weighted for the size of investments, then, *keiretsu* organizations in Europe might be more significant than initially meets the eye.

A key question regarding the implications of this pattern is how these clusters of related firms conduct themselves in the host country. It is also of interest to know whether, besides the industry-level differences observed in Table 4.9, firm-level differences in the degree of *keiretsu* formation also exist. A related issue in this regard is the extent to which clusters of *keiretsu* members strengthen the manufacturing capabilities of parent firms. Firm-level data sheds light on some of these issues, as well as revealing some interesting implications regarding the role of *keiretsu* in creating competitive advantages for Japanese firms.

[17] DaiNippon's presence in this sector is so strong that without its large constellation of European investments—many of them acquisitions—the share of the chemical industry in total affiliates in the sample would drop to under 10%.

[18] See Gittelman and Dunning 1992.

[19] This includes 6 group companies of Mitsubishi Electric.

[20] This includes 4 investments by Sumitomo Electric, 6 investments by Mitsubishi Electric, and 2 investments by Mitsubishi Motors.

2.1. Keiretsu in the Automobile and electric/electronic equipment (E&E) Industries: Comparisons with the USA

Table 4.10 compares investments by major Japanese automobile and E&E manufacturers in Europe and the USA at the beginning of the 1990s. Such a comparison is useful in order to analyse patterns in each of those industries, as well as differences regarding the two locations themselves.

Regarding industry differences, the extent of *keiretsu* formation appears to be deepest among automobile firms in both locations. In Europe, for every one investment by a parent there are nearly two investments by a group company; in the USA, *keiretsu* formation appears to be rather more advanced, with a ratio of parents to group companies of about 1 to 5.

Compared to the automobile industry, *keiretsu* appear to be shallower (more parents relative to group companies) in the E&E industry. A useful measure is the ratio of parent investments to total investments (parent + group companies) in the industry. In the automobile industry, this ratio is 36 per cent and 17 per cent in Europe and the USA, respectively. In the E&E industry, parents make up about 60 and 47 per cent of total investments in Europe and the USA, respectively. In both locations, then, pyramidal *keiretsu* structures appear to be most developed in the automobile industry.

The difference between the structure of investments in the two locations may be in part derived from differences in the role played by vertical *keiretsu* in those industries in Japan. The different role played by *keiretsu* is, in turn, often a function of structural differences in the industries themselves. Firms in the E&E industry tend to have more diversified product lines, their product cycles tend to be more rapid, and their supply lines shorter than in the automobile industry. These factors have led to a different evolutionary path of *keiretsu* in the two industries. Group companies of the large E&E firms are often spin-offs of the parent itself (and hence may bear the name of the parent company, e.g. 'Matsushita Communications Industry', 59 per cent owned by Matsushita) rather than independent, specialized small and medium-sized enterprises, as are prevalent in the automobile industry. Group members of E&E *keiretsu* often operate as large, specialized divisions, or 'responsibility centres', of the parent itself. Relationships with supplier companies tend to be looser, and transactions conducted in more of an arm's-length manner, than in the automobile industry. Relational networks between manufacturers and suppliers thus appear to be less critical in the E&E industry than in the case of automobiles. In this sense, the organizational structures of Japanese E&E firms appear to resemble more closely the structure of Western firms, with their specialized affiliates organized around business segments and short-term, market-based relationships with component suppliers, than they resemble Japanese automobile firms.

This difference in structure in Japan is likely to influence the extent of

TABLE 4.10. *Structure of Japanese investments in electric/electronic equipment and automobiles in the USA and Europe*

	Europe				USA			
	No. of investments by parent	No. of group companies	No. of investments by groups	Total investments (parents + groups)	No. of investments by parent	No. of group companies	No. of investments by groups	Total investments (parents + groups)
Electric/electronic equipment								
Matsushita	10	7	13	23	6	7	9	15
Toshiba	8	4	6	14	8	3	3	11
Hitachi	3	5	6	9	7	10	21	28
Fujitsu	6	3	3	9	3	3	4	7
Sony	7	1	1	8	4	1	1	5
Canon	4	1	1	5	3	0	0	3
NEC	3	1	1	4	3	1	1	4
TOTAL	42	22	28	72	34	25	39	73
Automobiles								
Nissan	4	8	15	19	2	16	21	23
Toyota	4	10	15	19	3	14	25	28
Honda	10	2	2	12	5	2	2	7
TOTAL	18	20	32	50	10	32	48	58

Source: JETRO 1990, 1991; *Kigyo Keiretsu Soran* 1989; *Kaigai Shinshutsu Kigyo Soran* 1991.

keiretsu formation through FDI and the nature of the parent/group company relationship in overseas locations. In the E&E industry, one might expect that the relationship is less of a vertical supply-based interaction than a joint undertaking in a specialized market-based activity. Indeed, many of the European investments by companies in the Matsushita *keiretsu* in Europe are 60 : 40 joint ventures with the parent (Matsushita Electric), engaged in the manufacture and sale of different final products (televisions, typewriters, car telephones). Hitachi exhibits a similar structure, with one European group company manufacturing power tools, another audio and video equipment, and a third colour televisions and microwave ovens. Such a structure would seem to indicate that what intra-group transactions did occur would primarily be more of a horizontal than a vertical nature, with a higher incidence of parent/group company joint ventures in a given product market. Across the *keiretsu*, core technologies and distribution and marketing channels might also be shared by group members.

Such a structure contrasts with the automobile manufacturers, where the critical inter-firm linkages are to suppliers of components and sub-systems for manufacture of final products by the car-makers (parents). For Toyota and (to a lesser extent) Nissan, an elaborate network of affiliated suppliers is a key element in their success as highly efficient manufacturers in Japan. Honda, in contrast, operates (in Japan) far more independently of a *keiretsu* than the other manufacturers, and its group is thinner and its members smaller than those of Toyota and Nissan.[21] Correspondingly, in both the USA and Europe, Toyota and Nissan exhibit the deepest *keiretsu* structures of all firms in Table 4.10, while Honda operates nearly independently of group companies.

A similar picture could be painted for Sony, a young company in the E&E industry. Like Honda, Sony is not a leader of an important *keiretsu* in Japan. If *keiretsu* organizations were important variables in explaining Japanese firms' competitive advantage in international markets, one might expect that Honda and Sony would be relatively disadvantaged relative to other Japanese firms (indeed, Honda lags behind other car-makers in its domestic market). Yet it is instructive to note that both Honda's and Sony were among the first in their industries to invest abroad, and both have become Japanese leaders in overseas markets. Indeed, it was Honda and Sony's relative weakness in the domestic market that pushed them to make early inroads in overseas markets before their more established competitors.

The absence of dense *keiretsu* organizations around the overseas operations of Sony and Honda does not immediately imply that they do not engage in *keiretsu*-type relationships. Their overseas affiliates may indeed conduct long-term inter-firm relationships with suppliers and related firms,

---

[21] While Toyota and Nissan are the top shareholders in 14 and 26 parts suppliers, respectively, in Japan, Honda holds that position in only 3 companies (Fujimoto 1992).

but those relationships are not necessarily codified into a formal *keiretsu* structure.[22] It is possible that by being able to transfer the practices of a vertical *keiretsu* from Japan, without actually having to transfer the *keiretsu* itself, Honda and Sony may enjoy options denied to their competitors in terms of choosing and managing their inter-firm affiliations. They may have more freedom to enter and exit the relationships as well have more of a margin to commit to local (European or US) firms without threatening commitments to Japanese suppliers. More intensive utilization of internal capabilities might also be advantageous in overseas, culturally distant locations where relationship-building is costlier and more time-consuming than in the home market.

Should such a line of reasoning prove correct, it would ironically lead to the conclusion that one of the key engines behind the remarkable success of Japanese automobile manufacturers in domestic and export markets— dense networks of geographically clustered firms—might actually act as a brake on Japanese companies when they invest abroad. Seen in this light, strong *keiretsu* groupings (at least vertical production *keiretsu*) may actually pose more of a threat to large-scale vertical *keiretsu* leaders such as Toyota and Nissan, facing pressures to establish overseas footholds, than to Japanese firms which operate independently of vertical *keiretsu* as well as firms from other countries, such as the USA. These latter firms may prove to be relatively more flexible in terms of their overseas manufacturing options.

2.2. Closed versus Open Keiretsu Networks

The impact on European industry of the build-up of *keiretsu* structures in Japan is as yet unclear. First, it would be necessary to determine whether manufacturers are indeed reproducing in Europe the inter-firm relationships they have in Japan, to the exclusion of other firms. Information concerning the exclusive nature of these relationships in Japan is instructive in this regard. In general, the larger the supplier firm, the more likely it is to sell to a large number of manufacturers; even so, over half the sales of *keiretsu*-affiliated suppliers will usually be accounted for by the *keiretsu* parent.[23] Since those parts suppliers that have invested in Europe are in the main the larger ones, it is plausible that they will not wholly restrict their sales to their *keiretsu* parent in the overseas location.

[22] Florida and Kenney (1991) report that Honda helped their Japanese suppliers finance and set up US operations, and that nearly half of Honda's suppliers in Japan operate in the USA. Only 12 of the 73 suppliers they surveyed, however, were partially owned by the assemblers they supply.
[23] In Japan, out of 400 members of the Japanese Automobile Parts Manufacturers Association, 40% sell parts to 1–4 manufacturers, 21% to 5–8 manufacturers, and 17% to 9–12 manufacturers. Those companies whose capital exceeded 5 billion yen (71 firms in total) sold parts to 9–12 car manufacturers (there are 13 car-makers in Japan). *Toyo Keizai Weekly*.

From a host country perspective, an issue of greater concern than the openness of *keiretsu* suppliers to multiple manufacturers is the openness of Japanese *keiretsu* manufacturers to non-*keiretsu* (and, in particular, indigenous) suppliers. Including local suppliers in Japanese production networks can occur in two ways: either they will be brought in by Japanese manufacturers directly, or else they may be partners in joint ventures with Japanese supplier firms that have invested in the host country. Regarding the latter, according to the firm-level data presented earlier, in the USA about one-quarter of the overseas investments of group companies in the Toyota and Nissan group are joint ventures with local firms. In Europe, however, the number of joint ventures is somewhat lower. Regarding independent entry into Japanese networks, research and anecdotal evidence suggest that, to some extent, Japanese manufacturers in the USA and Europe are utilizing indigenous supplier firms, and that the latter are being inducted into the Japanese system of inter-firm relations in the process.[24] Anecdotal evidence also points to the fact that European supplier firms in the automobile industry (such as Germany's Bosch) are more likely to possess the necessary technological and quality capabilities required by Japanese purchasers than their US counterparts. If so, European suppliers are thus more capable of assuming leading roles in the latter's European networks. These indicators, albeit highly incomplete and non-rigorous, therefore suggest that Japanese manufacturer–supplier networks do not remain completely closed to firms from the host country.

2.3. Europe versus the USA as Production Locations

The average vintage of US affiliates of Japanese firms is somewhat greater than that of their European affiliates, which would presumably allow more time for *keiretsu* structures, should they be important, to develop. This appears to be generally the case for both the automotive and electric/electronic equipment industries (although not necessarily for all firms): Table 4.10 shows that in the USA there have been high numbers of investments by group companies relative to fewer investments by parents. Such a structure mimics, on a miniature scale, the structure of firm organization in Japan itself, where a parent firm sits atop a pyramid of several tiers—each of them larger than the last—of group members.[25]

In Europe, by contrast, Japanese investments exhibit more of a horizontal structure, with a high number of investments by parents against relatively few investments by group companies. Indeed, a surprising feature of Table

---

[24] See Florida and Kenney 1991; *New York Times* 1990; *Financial Times* 1992; *Wall Street Journal* 1991.
[25] Florida and Kenney (1991) agree with this supposition, concluding (p. 392) that Japanese automobile investments in the USA are 'essentially "stretched out" versions of Japan's geographically concentrated just-in-time system of interorganizational linkages'.

4.10 is that every parent firm (with the exception of Hitachi) has made more manufacturing investments in Europe than it has in the USA. It is unlikely that this can be directly attributable to relative market size in the two locations, even though Europe—particularly since the broadening of the available market in the late 1980s to include both EFTA countries as well as Eastern Europe—is perceived to be potentially a larger market than the USA for Japanese firms.[26]

A major aim of the 1992 programme was to encourage the efficient rationalization of production in the EC region, with fewer, larger, more specialized plants. The high number of parent manufacturing firms located in Europe appears to belie this intention. Rather, it is plausible that the need to make primary investments in several European countries—motivated perhaps more by political than efficiency reasons—is behind the relatively high numbers of parent company investments in Europe as compared to the USA. In this regard, the 'singleness' of Europe appears not to have matched the 'singleness' of the USA in terms of locating major manufacturing investments. This possibility could have significant implications for the structure and performance of Japanese firms in both locations.

A look at the geographical distribution of the two most important overseas *keiretsu*—Toyota and Nissan and their respective group companies—adds to the impression that there may be fundamental differences in the way Japanese firms invest in the USA versus Europe (Figs. 4.1 and 4.2). In the USA, dense clusters of group companies surround the manufacturing plants of each parent, whose numbers are kept to a minimum: Nissan has only one manufacturing plant in the USA, while Toyota has two, one in Kentucky, and the other in California, some 3,000 km. away. In the UK, which accounts for 48 per cent of Japanese automobile FDI in Europe, Nissan and Toyota clusters have also emerged, but they are top-heavy as compared to the USA. Both firms have established two manufacturing plants each in that country. They have also spread more manufacturing operations to other locations in Europe, and a cluster of *keiretsu* suppliers appears to be forming in the Spain/Portugal region.[27]

The configuration in Europe, taken on its own, could reflect a rational allocation of resources, with production in low-wage areas linked to operations in the North. Indeed, it may explain the pattern observed in the first part of this paper, in which Japanese firms appeared to achieve higher productivity levels and pay lower wages relative to American firms.

---

[26] Our data set, showing all investments made by the end of 1990, is likely to reflect investor perceptions formed before the potential for the enlargement of the EC market became apparent.

[27] One major automobile supplier, Yazaki, has established a large operation in Portugal which supplies Nissan's UK factory, as well as other non-Japanese auto plants (Ozawa 1991). It has not been included as it is an independent parts supplier.

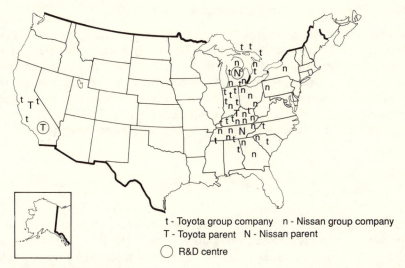

t - Toyota group company   n - Nissan group company
T - Toyota parent   N - Nissan parent
◯ R&D centre

Note: Affiliates are shown in the State in which they are located. Figure does not indicate exact location within that State.

Source: Prepared by authors from *Toyo Keizai* 1989 and 1991.

Fig. 4.1. US affiliates of Nissan and Toyota, and their *keiretsu*-related suppliers, 1991

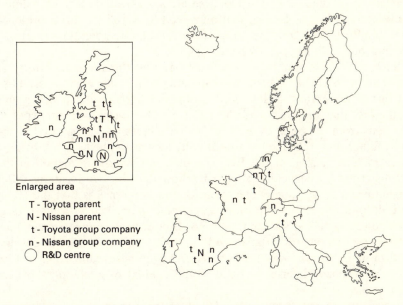

Enlarged area

T - Toyota parent
N - Nissan parent
t - Toyota group company
n - Nissan group company
◯ R&D centre

Note: Affiliates are shown in the country in which they are located. Figure does not indicate exact location within that country.

Source: Prepared by authors from JETRO 1990, JETRO 1991, and *Toyo Keizai* 1989.

Fig. 4.2. European affiliates of Nissan and Toyota, and their *keiretsu*-related suppliers, 1991

However, the configuration in Europe looks to be rather unwieldy when compared to the configuration in the USA, where fewer plants are spread over a much larger distance. This points to the fact that Japanese automobile manufacturers, given the uncertainty which prevails over the policies of the individual European countries *vis-à-vis* their operations, may have opted for second-best solutions from an efficiency viewpoint. Their *keiretsu* suppliers, in turn, have followed suit by investing near their parents.

3. CONCLUSIONS

It has been less than five years since Japanese firms began their rapid build-up of overseas manufacturing operations in the EC. Therefore, it is still too early to assess exactly what such investment means for the region's economy and for its indigenous industries. Based on the above analysis, however, some preliminary conclusions emerge. Both the macro-level data in Part 1 and the micro-level data in Part 2 of this paper point to the fact that Japanese manufacturing investment in Europe appears to be less regionally integrated, and for this reason perhaps less efficient, than comparable investment by US firms. This difference is probably a result of the perception on the part of the Japanese firms, motivated more by political rather than economic factors, that they need to establish a direct presence in several European countries rather than concentrate operations in a small number of locations, as they have in the USA.

Such a finding modifies the hypothesis that Japanese investors, as latecomers to the EC, have the advantage of being able to establish regionally integrated, rationalized production structures. It also points to the fact that the USA and the EC are in fact very different types of locations from the point of view of Japanese investors, as opposed to the (prevailing) idea that they are essentially similar, with the USA being a more mature version of the EC. The data on *keiretsu* formation in the two locations, in particular, appear to show that the two locations differ qualitatively. A possible explanation for the difference is that the EC is still, despite the 1992 unification programme, perceived as a more fragmented production space than the USA. If our supposition is correct, then future research regarding Japanese FDI in Europe would need to develop its own set of assumptions, predictions, and hypotheses rather than rely on those which have been developed in the context of analysing Japanese FDI in the USA.

Regarding the performance of Japanese firms in the EC, the data are mixed concerning their productivity *vis-à-vis* US firms, although the above finding might imply lower levels of efficiency of Japanese investment compared to their US counterparts. A key performance measurement, the amount of R&D performed in the host country, shows that Japanese firms significantly underperform US firms in the EC, although it is still too early to know whether this is a vintage effect—such that Japanese firms would eventually reach R&D levels achieved by US firms—or signifies a lower propensity of Japanese firms to perform R&D in overseas locations.

The analysis of the structure of Japanese investment in the EC reveals that in two key industries, *keiretsu* organizations do appear to be significant. Particularly in the automobile industry, many of the *keiretsu* members of Japanese manufacturers are making their own European investments, and geographically dense clusters of parents and groups can be observed. These incipient patterns—which currently are more pronounced in the USA than in Europe—raise a number of questions regarding the economic impact of Japanese investment on host countries. Some of the more important issues that are raised with respect to the EC include the following:

- Japanese manufacturing investment is moving beyond the 'screwdriver' stage to full-fledged production in the EC, with the possible introduction of Japanese production methods and new organizational forms to EC locations.
- The build-up of networks of Japanese firms is likely to raise local content levels, a key concern for European policy-makers. European suppliers might suffer, however, if Japanese production networks remain closed to them, that is, if Japanese manufacturers extend preferential treatment to the Euro-affiliates of their Japanese suppliers. Conversely, European suppliers could become strengthened if Japanese networks are opened to include them.
- The introduction of new production methods and organizational forms in the EC might be to the benefit of the EC economy if it improves upon the prevailing performance of domestic industry, particularly where EC firms are relatively strong *vis-à-vis* Japanese rivals.
- In industries in which EC countries have strong locational advantages, and in which EC firms are weak relative to Japanese competitors, the transfer of Japanese practices to the host country may enable Japanese firms to establish strong footholds in EC industries, to the possible long-term detriment of EC firms.
- Distortions could occur in European factor markets if *keiretsu* members extend preferential treatment to one another; challenges to European competition policy may also arise in the face of a large-scale build-up of *keiretsu* groupings.
- In so far as the European networks of Japanese firms are tied into two-way supply relationships with similar networks in Japan, they are likely to exert a structural influence on Japanese–European trade relations.

These points rest on a critical assumption: that the joint presence of Japanese *keiretsu* members in the EC means that those firms are transferring the special relationship they enjoy in Japan to Europe. Such an assumption is by no means trivial, and the data presented above are insufficient to address this fundamental question. Rather, they provide a basis from which to frame further research regarding the conduct of Japanese firms in the EC. Our analysis confirms that a significant proportion of Japanese investment in the EC can be characterized by groups of *keiretsu*-related companies. Should further research indicate that such groups bring with them their Japanese-style relationships, then it is clear that the overall impact of Japanese FDI in Europe is likely to be greater than the sum of its parts, and that the organization of Japanese firms abroad carries important implications for a broad range of policy-related issues.

REFERENCES

AOKI, M. (1991), 'The Japanese Firm as a System: Survey and Research Agenda' (paper presented at conference on 'Japan in a Global Economy: A European Perspective', held at Stockholm School of Economics, 2–6 Sept.).

Business Week (1990), 'Mighty Mitsubishi is on the Move' (24 Sept.), 98–107.

DUNNING, J., and CANTWELL, J. (1989), 'Japanese Manufacturing Direct Investment in the EEC, post 1992: Some Alternative Scenarios' (University of Reading, Dept. of Economics, Discussion Paper 132, Ser. B, vol. ii (Sept.)).

ENCARNATION, D. (1992), *Rivals beyond Trade* (Ithaca, NY: Cornell University Press).

Far Eastern Economic Review (1991), 'Double Standards' (8 Aug.), 54–5.

FERGUSON, C. (1990), 'Computers and the Coming of the U.S. Keiretsu', *Harvard Business Review* (July–Aug.).

Financial Times (1992), 'Nissan Flexes More of its Muscle' (17 Jan.).

FLORIDA, R., and KENNEY, M. (1991), 'Transplanted Organizations: The Transfer of Japanese Industrial Organization to the United States', *American Sociological Review*, 56 (June), 381–98.

Fortune (1991), 'Why Japan Keeps Winning' (15 July), 76–85.

FUJIMOTO, H. (1992), 'Japan's Automobile Keiretsu Changing for the Better', *Tokyo Business Today* (Feb.), 50–1.

GENTHER, P., and DALTON, D. (1990), 'Japanese Direct Investment in US Manufacturing' (US Dept. of Commerce, International Trade Administration, Economics, and Statistics Administration (Oct.)).

GERLACH, M. (1992a), 'The Keiretsu: A Primer' (The Japan Society, New York).

—— (1992b), 'Twilight of the Keiretsu? A Critical Assessment', *Journal of Japanese Studies* (Winter, forthcoming).

GITTELMAN, M., and DUNNING, J. (1992), 'Japanese Investment in the United States and the EC: Some Comparisons and Contrasts', in M. Klein and P. Welfens, eds., *Multinationals in the New Europe and Global Trade* (Berlin: Springer Verlag).

GRAHAM, E. (1991), 'Strategies of US Multinational Firms to the Emerging Internal Market of the EEC', in G. Yannopolous, ed., *Europe and America, 1992: US–EC Economic Relations and the Single European Market* (Manchester, UK: Manchester University Press).

—— (1992), 'Japanese Control of R&D Activities in the United States: Is this Cause for Concern?', In T. Arrison, C. Bergsten, E. Graham, and M. Harris, eds., *Japan's Growing Technological Capability: Implications for the US Economy* (Washington, DC: National Academies Press).

—— and KRUGMAN, P. (1991), *Foreign Direct Investment in the United States* (2nd edn. Washington, DC: Institute for International Economics).

Industry Week (1992), 'The Mighty Keiretsu' (20 Jan.), 52–4.

JETRO (1990), *Current Situation of Business Operations of Japanese Manufacturing Enterprises in Europe: Sixth Survey Report* (Mar.).

—— (1991), *Current Situation of Business Operations of Japanese Manufacturing Enterprises in Europe: Seventh Survey Report* (Mar.).

Kigyo Keiretsu Soran (1989) [Directory of *Keiretsu* of Japanese Companies] (Tokyo: Toyo Keizai).

Kaigai Shinshutsu Kigyo Soran (1991) [Directory of Overseas Affiliates of Japanese Companies] (Tokyo: Toyo Keizai).

LAWRENCE, R. (1991), 'Efficient or Exclusionist? The Import Behavior of Japanese Corporate Groups', in W. Brainard and G. Perry, *Brookings Papers on Economic Activity*, 1, 311–30.

—— (1992), 'Why is Foreign Direct Investment in Japan so Low?' (paper presented at NBER conference, 'Foreign Direct Investment Today', Boston, 15–16 May.

MICOSSI, S., and VIESTI, G. (1990), 'Japanese Direct Manufacturing Investment in Europe' (paper prepared for conference on 'The Impact of 1992 on European Trade and Industry', CEPR, Centro Studi Cofindustria and STEP, Urbino, 15–16 Mar.

MILELLI, C. (1991), 'Investissements industriels japonais en Europe: 1960–1989', in C. Dupuy, C. Milelli, and J. Savary, eds., *Atlas mondial des multinationales, ii. Strategies des multinationales* (Paris: Reclus).

MITI (1991), *Kaigai Toshi Tokei Soran* (Dai 4 Kai Kaigai Jigyo Katsudo Kihon Chosa) [4th Basic Survey of the Overseas Activities of Japanese Companies] (Tokyo: MITI).

New York Times (1990), 'Honda Blurs Line between American and Foreign' (14 Mar.).

OZAWA, T. (1991), 'Japanese Multinationals and 1992', in B. Burgenmeier and J. L. Mucchielli, eds., *Multinationals and Europe 1992: Strategies for the Future* (London: Routledge), 135–54.

Production (1991), 'Auto Suppliers: Trouble Ahead, Trouble Behind' (Oct.), 38–41.

SHEARD, P. (1992), 'Keiretsu and Closedness of the Japanese Market: An Economic Appraisal' (Discussion Paper 273, Institute of Social and Economic Research, Osaka University, June).

THOMSEN, S., and NICOLAIDES, P. (1991), *The Evolution of Japanese Direct Investment in Europe: Death of a Transistor Salesman* (Hertfordshire: Harvester Wheatsheaf).

Toyo Keizai Weekly, various issues.

US Department of Commence, Bureau of Economic Analysis (1992), 'US Direct Investment Abroad: 1989 Benchmark Survey, Final Results' (Washington, DC: US Government Prining Office).

Wall Street Journal (1991), 'Japanese Auto Makers Help US suppliers become More Efficient' (9 Sept.).

WOMACK, J., JONES, D., and ROOS, D. (1991), *The Machine that Changed the World: The Story of Lean Production* (New York: Harper Perennial).

COMMENT

Raymond Vernon

My sympathy was with the authors, as they struggled with their assignment to make something of the pitifully inadequate data purporting to describe Japanese FDI in Europe. What they have produced in the end is really two papers bundled into one, with only tenuous ties between the two parts. The first part tries to present a picture of the character and extent of such investment, with occasional speculative asides on what the data may indicate regarding performance. The second section concentrates on one feature of such investments, namely, the extend of their affiliations with *keiretsu* groups.

It is hard to be critical of the authors' efforts to milk the existing data for clues as to the character and extent of Japan's FDI. They themselves are painfully aware of how little their data have to offer. Essentially what we are told is what we already know: that Japan's FDI in Europe has expanded vigorously of late; and that Japan's manufacturing activities in Europe are bunched in the industries that typically have been associated with multinational enterprises in advanced industrialized countries—automobiles, electronics, chemicals, and machinery. The bunching of these enterprises in the familiar list of industries suggests that there are no big surprises likely to be found in the structure, function, and performance of these undertakings; but one cannot be certain.

The data also tell us that Japan's non-manufacturing investments are disproportionately high, at least by comparison with the FDI of US-based enterprises; and, as the authors point out, this familiar characteristic of Japanese FDI probably reflects the key role of Japan's giant trading companies, reinforced by the very strong preference of Japanese managers for dealing with other Japanese in the provision of services such as banking and wholesaling.

It would be wrong, however, to lay all of the blame for these skimpy findings at the feet of the government agencies that compiled the data. The authors had no right to expect that official figures purporting to report on the European subsidiaries of Japanese firms could shed much light on their function or their performance. One can never lose sight of the fact that such subsidiaries are units in a global network, and that their resources and their performance are functions of the resources and performance of the networks to which they belong. Drawing data from the European subsidiaries alone, therefore, is like studying the left hind leg of an elephant in order to assess its damage potential; the study is relevant but it is less than adequate.

To be sure, it is not altogether irrelevant to ask how many workers these subsidiaries employ in Europe and what assets they carry on their books; but gauging their resources and assessing their performance require data of a more inclusive and less static kind. Experience suggests that the authors might have gotten much closer to their objective by studying the annual reports of, say, the fifty leading Japanese firms with substantial facilities in Europe.

The authors, of course, thoroughly appreciate the fact that the performance of these European subsidiaries is a function of the global structure in which they operate; otherwise, it would be difficult to understand their interest in analysing the *keiretsu* affiliations of these firms. That their *keiretsu* affiliations are germane to their performance is clear enough from various pieces of research by others.[28] But in assessing the likely performance of these subsidiaries, it is easy to exaggerate the influence of *keiretsu* ties or to misinterpret their consequences. The authors themselves provide the likely explanation for their emphasis on this issue: they went where the data were. But the unwary reader needs a warning that the implications of the *keiretsu* affiliation must be handled with care.

In any case, it would have been helpful if the authors could have explored more fully the implications of a *keiretsu* tie in terms of likely performance. The obvious implication is that such ties will reduce the willingness of the *keiretsu* firms to look for the most efficient suppliers, including non-Japanese suppliers located in Europe. That possiblity cannot be shrugged off. But there is a series of questions to be answered before one can get a firm hold on the implications of a *keiretsu* tie.

One such question is whether the existence of *keiretsu* ties generates greater lumpiness in Japanese direct investment; that is, whether the decision of a *keiretsu* member to set up a plant in Europe generates a following wave of linked investments to an extent greater than would have occurred in the absence of the *keiretsu* link. And if the answer is affirmative, the obvious next question is whether the infusion of the added capital and technology associated with the incremental investment represents a net gain or net loss for the economy. The answer is not obvious, turning in part on whether the increment adds to productive European assets or displaces facilities that otherwise would be operating in Europe.

Another question of relevance is whether the disposition of a Japanese firm in Europe to favour a known source of inputs represents a source of inefficiency. That question plunges us into the familiar miasma of the virtues of markets versus hierarchies. Obviously, the internalization of some sources of supply is not always regarded as ineffcient. By the same token,

---

[28] See e.g. R. Lawrence, 'Efficient or Exclusionist? The Import Behavior of Japanese Corporate Groups', in *Brookings Papers on Economic Activity*, 1 (1991), 311–41. The paper includes a bibliography containing the principal analyses of *keiretsu* behaviour published in recent years.

keiretsu ties are not always a source of inefficiency; indeed, Western observers have often reached the opposite conclusion. And the disposition to favour known sources has commonly been remarked in the behaviour of US-owned manufacturing subsidiaries operating in unfamiliar environments, even where ownership ties have not existed between the subsidiaries and their suppliers; the Big Three US automobile producers, for example, commonly pull some of their major suppliers into foreign countries in which they have set up production facilities.

None of the answers necessary for an evaluation of the role of Japanese subsidiaries in Europe is likely to come easy. Researchers who consciously concentrated their search where the light was shining brightest could scarcely have been expected to provide the answers. But the reader should be on notice that the truth sometimes lurks in the darker corners.

5

Foreign Direct Investment and Exports to the European Community

Pierre Buigues and Alexis Jacquemin

1. INTRODUCTION

Although the extent of direct investment varies enormously across countries, it is well known that today every industrial nation has more of its economy under the control of foreign firms than a decade ago. One implication is that a country's trade balance becomes an ambiguous indicator of its economic health. As shown recently (D. Julius 1990), putting trade balance on to an ownership basis rather than geography can lead to quite new pictures. For example, in 1986, at a world-wide level, sales by American-owned companies to non-American-owned ones exceeded America's conventionally measured exports by a factor of five, while purchases from foreign companies were three times greater than America's imports.

Analysing the nature of a phenomenon such as direct investment requires more than a global approach. Indeed, direct investment is a special type of international capital flow, given that competitive conditions in the nation's markets as well as its stock of productive factors are affected (Caves and Jones 1977). Its distinctiveness lies in several traits. First, direct investment involves a capital that is entrepreneurial or risk-bearing, usually linked to the transfer of managerial skills and knowledge from one country to another.[1] Second, this type of capital is not perfectly flexible and the corresponding investment should be considered partially irreversible. One implication is the phenomenon of 'hysteresis': the effect of a temporary change may persist after the cause of this change has disappeared. For example, a temporary appreciation of the dollar with respect to the ecu could be an incentive to replace exports to Europe by direct investment. Once the investment in European real capital has been made,

* The views expressed are those of the authors, and are not attributable to the Commission of the European Communities, by which they are employed. The authors want to thanks J. Vinals, C. Wyplosz, C. Mathieu, M. Berges, F. Proud'homme, and J. Climent-Leal for their collaboration.

[1] This trait corresponds to a broad definition of FDI; i.e. any investment directed towards obtaining actual control over foreign productive capacity. In this sense, an international capital flow may not even be necessary. Local resources such as loans from local banks, or reinvested profits could be used. The balance of payments concept is more stringent: in addition to the actual control objective, it requires that the investment is financed by transfers from the domestic parent to the foreign subsidiary.

a relative fall of the dollar will not automatically lead to disinvestment.[2] Third, as a way of reallocating production internationally, FDI (foreign direct investment) is strongly industry-specific, which means that it is not so much a transfer of capital from country A to country B, as from A's x industry to B's x or y industry.

In this framework, the purpose of our paper is to examine some theoretical, empirical, and policy issues raised by the growing inward investment and exports to the EC.

The first section looks at the theory of FDI, the emphasis being on the distinction between efficiency considerations and strategic ones, and on the relationship between FDI and exports. The second section presents a statistical analysis of FDI and exports in the EC and focuses on US and Japanese operations in manufacturing. It examines their recent trends, at the global and sectoral level, the EC's attractiveness relative to the rest of the world, and the empirical links between exports and FDI. The last section considers some possible implications of a growth in FDI and exports for the process of economic integration in the Community and for policy orientations.

2. CAUSES OF DIRECT INVESTMENT

2.1. Necessary and Sufficient Conditions for FDI

Traditional models of international trade prove rather inadequate for explaining the causes of international direct investment, since in a world of perfect competition there is no place for multinational enterprises which are the result of FDI. It is only when imperfections are introduced into the organization of industry and the structure of markets that the multinational becomes a logical possibility. According to the argumentation proposed by Dunning (1982), a firm will engage in FDI if each of the following three conditions is satisfied:

(a) It possesses net ownership advantages *vis-à-vis* firms of other nationalities in serving particular markets. These ownership-specific advantages largely take the form of the possession of intangible assets which, at least for a period of time, are the exclusive right of the firm possessing them.

(b) Assuming condition (a) is satisfied, it must be more beneficial for the enterprise possessing these advantages to use them itself rather than to lease them for foreign firms to use; i.e. to internalize its

---

[2] This is already partially true for exports. There is a whole literature on the exchange rate impact on FDI. Among the important factors to take into account are the currency denomination of the subsidiary's costs and revenues, the use of real exchange rates, and the temporal framework. For a short survey, see Capel 1990.

TABLE 5.1. *Strategic options for supplying foreign markets*

Route of serving market	Ownership	Internalization	Foreign location
Foreign direct investment	Yes	Yes	Yes
Exports	Yes	Yes	No
Portfolio resource transfers	Yes	No	No

Source: Dunning 1982.

advantages through an extension of its own activities rather than externalize them through market transactions with independent firms.

(*c*) Assuming conditions (*a*) and (*b*) are satisfied, it must be beneficial for the enterprise to utilize these advantages in conjunction with at least some factor inputs (including natural resources) outside its home country; otherwise foreign markets would be served entirely by exports and domestic markets by domestic production.

The different options for servicing a market—FDI, exports, and portfolio resources transfers (financial transfer without ownership's control)—are illustrated by Dunning (1982) in the matrix above (see Table 5.1), which relates to the presence or absence of the three conditions already mentioned. He argues that a country's propensity to engage in foreign direct investment depends entirely on the extent and form of the ownership advantages of its enterprises, and how far these latter find it beneficial to exploit those advantages in a foreign rather than a domestic location. The nature and significance of these advantages will differ according to country-, industry-, or firm-specific characteristics.

Whereas the first two types of advantages are necessary conditions, only the last one (location advantage) is also sufficient for international direct investment to take place.

If we try to identify the advantages expected from ownership, internalization and location, a very long and diversified list appears.

Ownership advantages

(1) Size — less expensive inputs or exclusive access to inputs
better access to product markets
product or process diversification
economies of scale, both at the plant level and firm level

(2) Intangible assets — proprietary knowledge, technology, trademarks, product management, marketing, R&D, human capital

(3) Government — policies which favour business in the home country

Internalization advantages

(1) Market failure in market for final goods	reduce costs associated with market transactions
	compensate for absence of futures markets
(2) Market failure in market for inputs	avoid costs of enforcing property rights
	buyer uncertainty about nature and value of inputs
	control supplies and conditions of sale of inputs
(3) Monopoly power	where market does not permit price discrimination
	control market outlets
	engage in anti-competitive practices such as cross-subsidization and predatory pricing
(4) Product differentiation	need of seller to protect quality of product
(5) Government	avoid or exploit government intervention (quotas, tariffs, taxes, price controls)

Location advantages

(1) Inputs	spatial distribution of inputs and markets
	input prices, quality, and productivity
(2) Economies of scale	extent to which plant-level economies of scale make for centralization of production
(3) Government	government intervention
	control of imports (tariffs, etc.), tax rates, incentives, investment climate, political stability
(4) Other	transport and communications costs
	infrastructure (commercial, legal, transportation)
	psychic distance (language, culture, business customs)

Source: Thomsen and Nicolaides 1991.

One way of classifying them is to distinguish between efficiency and strategic considerations. Foreign location for those firms seeking efficiency gains will be influenced by favourable unit labour and social costs, the availability of efficient infrastructures, the presence of local suppliers who can provide competitively priced inputs. In this sense, direct investment is an alternative to factor mobility: FDI will be encouraged by the relative attractiveness of various immobile factors located in the foreign market. Similarly, a relatively dynamic demand could attract FDI with the necessity of responding quickly to the new opportunities. The second kind of explanation can be related to the strategic behaviour of the multinational intended to improve its market power or to defend it by overcoming existing or expected barriers to entry which protect foreign markets (Markusen 1984, Smith 1987, Jacquemin 1989, Acocella 1991, Motta 1992). The basic idea is that direct investment can be more profitable than arm's-length transactions such as exports if specific assets exist. Indeed, FDI can create a more highly credible commitment to a foreign market as a result of its extreme specificity and its sunk cost (irreversible) character.

Let us note that two (explicit or implicit) assumptions characterize most of these models. First, it is often assumed that a choice has to be made between explanations based on efficiency considerations and those relying on strategic behaviour. Second, FDI and exports are either not considered together or are viewed as substitutes. Both types of assumptions can be challenged and tested.[3]

2.2. Simultaneous Incentives to Invest in the EC

It can be argued (Jacquemin 1989) that the search for reducing transactions costs and the search for market power are not two independent motivations of FDI corresponding to two independent theories. Direct investment can be more profitable than arm's-length transactions such as exports and portfolio resource transfers because the firm possesses specific attributes that can be exploited strategically in different countries and because it is cheaper to internalize the transfer of these attributes between countries than to do so through markets. So FDI allows simultaneously an efficient exploitation of these assets through internalization and through their strategic utilization for controlling the market.[4]

In the absence of such asset specificity, no cost has to be sunk, so that all capital is perfectly transferable through the market mechanism and direct investment is unnecessary. On the contrary, once there are sunk costs, even small ones, the opportunity for exerting market power, horizontally

---

[3] Indeed, from the efficiency point of view, asset specificity is required for explaining FDI because in its absence, all capital is perfectly transferable through the market mechanism. But once there is asset specificity, there are sunk costs giving rise to market imperfections and strategic FDI. See Jacquemin 1989.

[4] In his review of Williamson's book on *The Economic Institutions of Capitalism*, Baumol (1986) rightly underlines that the transaction cost analysis requires three necessary conditions: asset specificity, limits on information and calculation ability, willingness to profit at the expense of others. Hence, 'the Williamson world, characterized as it is by heavy sunk costs, is vulnerable to well-known problems of market imperfections such as monopolization and strategic behaviour' (p. 282).

and vertically, is also strongly enlarged. Hence the organizational structure stemming from FDI can simultaneously be seen both as an efficient adaptation to characteristics of given assets, and as the outcome of a deliberate strategy for market power. It is used to minimize transaction costs, but also to create highly credible threats as a result of the extreme specificity and the often sunk-cost character of such an investment (a formal treatment of investment as an entry deterrent is in Dixit 1980). In this case, FDI can complement or replace exports, even in the absence of, say, tariff barriers, because it simultaneously reduces transaction cost such as contractual costs, and increases market power through a commitment of sunk assets, exploiting an irreversible location advantage in a foreign market. Even more, a direct investment can be a more costly option than exports in terms of managerial diseconomies and transaction costs, including the cost of international communication and co-ordination, but the corresponding additional costs could still enable the multinational firm rapidly to gain control of a local market and credibly defer to future foreign or domestic entries, so that a net profit is obtained over a longer term. This type of situation is probably frequent in markets characterized by strategic barriers created by firms and governments.[5] The literature on first-mover advantage, learning process, and action for increasing rival costs is especially relevant here (Jacquemin 1989a). A very simple illustration is the following. Assume a two-stage game where, first, the foreign firm decides whether to export or to invest, while a potential domestic entrant has to decide whether to enter into its domestic market. At the second stage, if both have entered, the firms compete as Cournot duopolists and output levels are determined. If the foreign firm exports its output to the host country, transport and tariff costs must be incurred as well as a domestic (constant) average variable cost. In Fig. 5.1, representing the sales in the host market, reaction line RA–RA of the foreign firm corresponds to this case.

But if the foreign firm chooses direct investment, it must incur only local variable unit costs. Let us assume, however, that these local costs are higher than the average variable costs incurred by the foreign firm in its home country plus the transport and tariff costs. This leads to a new reaction the RB-RB of the foreign firm at the left of RA–RA. The Cournot–Nash equilibrium shifts from CNA to CNB, corresponding to a less advantageous situation for the multinational. Even in this case, where transaction costs theory would exclude direct investment, such a strategy could still be rewarding. Indeed, let the foreign firm move first through direct investment implying a more or less irreversible commitment linked to specific sunk costs. This investment could then deter the entry of the domestic firm in its own market as long as this firm could make a positive

---

[5] An important example of a credible strategy where multinational corporation and government interact is when there are contracts with the local government committing FDI to minimum production levels over a period of time.

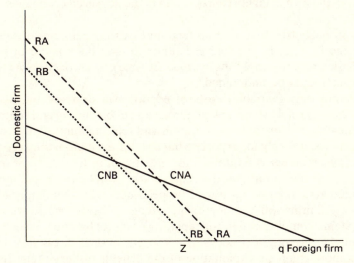

Fig. 5.1. Theoretical perspectives on sales in host markets: domestic *v.* foreign firms

profit from entering only if the foreign firm is an exporter. The equilibrium will be Z where the foreign firm controls the whole domestic market, and its gross profit is higher than in the Cournot–Nash equilibrium CNA.[6]

These general considerations can be applied to international direct investments in the European Community, in the 1992 perspective. We have seen that two major determinants of direct investment can be distinguished: the search for increased efficiency linked to transaction and production cost reductions, and a strategic goal linked to the pursuance of market power and control over prices. *A priori*, it is evident that the completion of the single internal market might influence both types of incentives.

And, indeed, at the level of the Community as a whole, some authors (see e.g. Itaki and Waterson 1990) argue that the level of new FDI in the internal market will decrease after 1992. Due to the fact that country resource endowments will become less idiosyncratic and the legal framework more homogeneous, firms will have fewer reasons for multinationalization after completion of the internal market. In particular, 'completion of the internal market will accelerate the free movement of labour forces across national boundaries and thereby destroy the basis of the comparative advantage, turning it into an absolute advantage. As cheap labour is attracted by the central high-wage economies, domestic markets of the peripheral economies will shrink and, taking the Community as a whole, sales

---

[6] Its profit net of the specific sunk costs of direct investment could be higher than the one obtained in CNA. Fig. 5.1 is only one element of a multi-stage game that has to be constructed. This type of analysis has been made by Smith (1987).

markets will become highly concentrated in the advanced economies' (Itaki and Waterson 1990: 19).

It is probably true that once protectionist barriers fall, firms outside and within the EC may have strong incentives to limit the number of foreign subsidiaries and to supply the various EC markets through exports. But two aspects must be underlined.

First, not only (variable) costs of exports will decrease but also the (fixed) costs of establishing a plant abroad and of organizing and controlling its production activities. Transportation and telecommunication costs will also decrease, not only for exporters but also for the multinational corporations. This argument is reinforced for investment in the EC from outside of the EC, to the extent that the single market will be more and more an integrated system based on trans-European networks. One implication is that non-EC firms will have a growing interest in being located within the 'EC system', complementing (or replacing) exports by direct investments, even in the absence of trade barriers, because such direct investments allow a more complete exploitation of the benefits of the system. Indeed, if lower costs compared to the home country were the only criterion for US and Japanese firms, other locations such as South-East Asia would be more attractive. However, once the decision to invest in the Community has been taken, the precise location within the EC could still be based on cost considerations. Contrary to the previous argument, Southern European countries could then still be attractive, given their lower wages and the limited labour mobility in Europe, caused by the natural heterogeneity of European populations that will not disappear with the suppression of non-tariff barriers.

From a strategic point of view, it can be argued that the main forces explaining multinational behaviour are not exogenous, as assumed by traditional trade theory. The prospect of increased competition resulting from the completion of the internal market will induce strategies to create or safeguard various forms of market power. Indeed, even after the promised liberalization in Europe, intra-EC trade will still be affected by extensive product differentiation, non-convexities in production, and incomplete information. Collusive and non-collusive oligopolistic behaviour will then be able to exploit and reinforce these imperfections. Among them, transnational mergers and acquisitions, as well as greenfield direct investments, could play a growing role.

In terms of the location aspects, we have argued that certain productions at the mature stages of product development, with standardized technology, could be shifted through FDI towards countries where labour costs are comparatively lower. However, some direct investment in countries like Spain and Portugal can also be motivated by a strategy of pre-empting high-technology industries (computers, telecommunications . . .) or more mature sectors (motor vehicles) where domestic or foreign competitors are not yet (firmly) established. For the original six Member States, plus the UK and Denmark, all characterized by more or less similar levels of productivity, wages, and capital–labour ratios, the multinationalization process is probably mainly motivated by strategic rather than factor-cost type considerations. This situation is also mirrored in the overwhelming role of intra-industry trade in the growth of intra-Community trade.

In all these situations there is, then, a related danger of a monopolization of certain markets based on multinational oligopolies that could exploit dominant positions and behave strategically against governments. Furthermore, since some industries yield sustainable higher returns than others, national public authorities have themselves an incentive to engage in beggar-thy-neighbour policies, taking unilateral measures to secure a larger share of these sectors by attracting the establishment of the corresponding oligopolists on their territory. *A priori*, the sole abolition of non-tariff barriers and liberalization of direct investments cannot guarantee optimum outcomes.

2.3. Direct Investment and Exports: Complements or Substitutes?

From the previous discussion, it is implicit that FDI and exports, be they motivated by efficiency or by strategic considerations, are not necessarily substitute ways to go abroad. On the contrary they can be two forms of penetration reinforcing each other. One example, sustained by numerous empirical studies (see esp. Glesjer, Jacquemin, and Petit 1980) have shown that multinational subsidiaries tend to import from the parent firm's country a large proportion of their capital, intermediate, and associated goods.

The various possible combinations can be illustrated with respect to the Community, in the case of US and Japanese operations. Four basic situations are possible (Fig. 5.2). Some sectors are characterized by relatively low foreign involvement in terms of both exports and direct investment. At the other extreme, both means of market penetration are used in some sectors to a higher degree than the industrial average. Between the two, foreign companies might show clear preferences for exports or direct investment. This taxonomy corresponds to various types of investment and trade responses to economic integration.

There could, then, be situations where both FDI and exports are strategically motivated, or are both induced by efficiency considerations, as well as situations where, for example, exports based on a search for efficiency are complemented by FDI made necessary to control the foreign market.[7]

---

[7] Along this line, Yannopoulos (1990) shows that a distinction between 'investment creation' and 'investment diversion' is to use terms which do not capture the full complexity of these relations. Instead he suggests four types of investment response: defensive import-substituting investment, offensive import-substituting investment, reorganization investment, and relationalized investment.

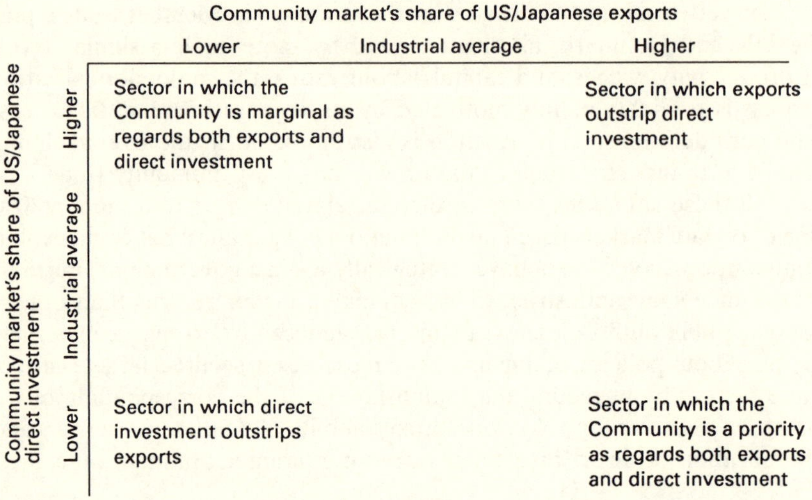

Community market's share of US/Japanese exports

	Lower	Industrial average	Higher
Higher	Sector in which the Community is marginal as regards both exports and direct investment		Sector in which exports outstrip direct investment
Industrial average			
Lower	Sector in which direct investment outstrips exports		Sector in which the Community is a priority as regards both exports and direct investment

(Vertical axis label: Community market's share of US/Japanese direct investment)

FIG. 5.2. The hypothesized relationship between exports and FDI, by sector (EC market as % of world total)

3. EMPIRICAL INVESTIGATION

The imperfections of the statistical data on FDI are well known. Firstly, statistical data, especially those expressed in absolute amounts, must be treated with caution. For example, Japanese exports to the Community cannot be equated with exports by Japanese companies to Europe, since some Japanese companies located in the USA also export to Europe. An initial difficulty is thus encountered in using export flows for which no breakdown is available by type of company involved.

Likewise, the information on direct investment provided by statistics may cover acquisitions and holdings, or physical investment in the setting up of a new subsidiary. In addition, an increase in the production capacity of a subsidiary already established in the Community may not be caught by direct investment statistics at all if it is financed by reinvested profits.

Finally, the subsidiary of a US or Japanese group may itself buy up a European company without this showing up in direct investment flows. A great deal of caution must therefore be exercised when using the available statistics, particularly since the statistical definition of direct investment may itself vary from one country to another (Hager 1989). Thus the US Department of Commerce applies a 10 per cent threshold in respect of holdings to distinguish between direct investment and financial investment. In contrast, MITI in Japan applies a 30 per cent threshold, and the German authorities one of 25 per cent. These differences therefore make it difficult to compare levels. Finally, the treatment of reinvested profits varies from one country to another.

The following empirical investigation does not escape from this constraint.

3.1. The Triad

Flows of FDI at the world level have continued to grow during the 1980s, reaching the level of nearly $200 billion in 1989. The Triad (USA, EC, and Japan) represents 80 per cent of world stocks and flows of FDI compared to 50 per cent of total world trade (UNCTC 1991). Table 5.2 presents the FDI to and from the Triad for 1980 to 1989. The main conclusions that can be drawn from this table are the following:

- At the beginning of the 1980s, the USA dominated the global pattern of FDI in terms of stock (46 per cent against 33 per cent for the EC and 4 per cent for Japan). However, this share has decreased significantly in favour of Japan, which in terms of flows surpassed the USA at the end of the 1980s (23 per cent against 17 per cent).
- The EC has increased its share in the Triad (37 per cent of total world outward stock against 33 per cent in 1980) and is now the world leader above the USA (37 per cent against 35 per cent).[8]

At the same time, as the UNCTC reports states, 'The 1992 programme to unify the regional market has provoked an unprecedented level of intra-regional foreign direct investment within the EC.'

The intra-EC FDI has increased at about 15 per cent a year, surpassing the growth of intra-EC trade of 9 per cent a year over the 1980s. It is therefore interesting to examine to what extent this buoyancy of intra-Community industrial trade has been assisted by export flows and direct investment from the USA and Japan.

---

[8] Most FDI by the EC is located in the USA, Japan accounting for less than 1% of the EC's stock of intra-Triad investment. As stated in the United Nations' *World Investment Report* (1991) 'From a strategy point of view, many of those investments (done by the EC in the US market) are aimed at gaining the critical mass which will propel EC companies to the status of global competitors, able to compete effectively with large United States and Japanese transnational corporations.'

For 1990, the FDI position of Europe in the USA on a historical-cost basis was $125.6 billion for manufacturing: 17% in food and related products, 27.5% in chemicals and allied products, 10% in primary and fabricated metals, 18% in machinery, and 27.5% in other manufacturing. In the case of Japan, the total amount in 1990 is $1.5 billion, mainly in chemicals and machinery.

TABLE 5.2. *FDI to/from the EC, USA, and Japan, 1980–1989*

	Stock				Flow (annual average)			
	Outward		Inward		Outward		Inward	
	1980	1987	1980	1987	1980–4	1985–9	1980–4	1985–9
EC (excludes intra-EC FDI)*								
$ billion	153	343	143	244	18	39	10	19
% of world total	33	37	31	26	41	37	23	19
USA								
$ billion	220	322	83	272	14	18	19	46
% of world total	46	35	18	28	31	17	41	46
Japan								
$ billion	20	99	3	9	4	24	0	0
% of world total	4	11	1	1	10	23	1	0
Triad								
$ billion	398	765	230	525	36	81	29	65
% of world total	84	83	50	55	82	77	64	65
World								
$ billion	474	925	464	957	44	105	45	100

* Concerning intra-EC direct investment for the same period of time (1980–90), Morsink (1991) showed a strong growth in total intra-EC direct investment between 1980–4 and 1984–8 of 55.9%. 'It can be argued that the increasing direct investment flows testify to an increasing interaction between the economies of the European Community. Consequently the growing import-ance of intra-EC direct investment flows show an increasing integration of the European economy' (ibid.).

Note: The data on outward stock for Japan for 1987 include reinvested profits. The data for the EC do not include Ireland, Greece, and Luxembourg.

Source: UNCTC, *Handbook on Transnational Corporations* (New York, UNCTC: forthcoming).

3.2. The Case of the USA

How economically important is the EC, seen from the USA?[9] The answer is that the Community is its largest trading partner, taking in 1990, 25 per cent of total exports of goods in terms of value. Over the period 1974–90, this share remained relatively stable in terms of value, a pattern which

[9] When taking account of the EC market as a percentage of the world total, both for exports and direct investment, there is no direct valuation effect on the index used here. However, if the exchange rate of the EC is seen differently from that of the rest of the world as viewed from the USA or Japan, it could have an indirect effect. Measuring this distortion could be useful but complex. As the impact will affect industry generally, and not one sector specifically, our analysis, which is sectoral, will probably be distorted only in a minor way.

could incorporate a certain change in the mix of product categories exported by the USA to the Community (Table 5.3).

Taking manufactured products alone, an increase in the Community's share of total exports of such products by the USA can be observed (+4.3 percentage points between 1985 and 1990). Overall, the Community's share of US exports has remained relatively stable throughout the period under review, except perhaps that of manufactured products, which increased between 1985 and 1989.

The lessons that can be drawn from an analysis of the Community's share of US direct investment abroad are different, however (Table 5.4). The EC accounts for a substantial share of total US foreign investment (around 40 per cent), whilst as we have seen, this share of US exports is some 24 per cent.

Between 1980 and 1984, however, the Community's share fell from 37.4 per cent to 34.0 per cent. It was from 1985 onwards that a spectacular recovery occurred. In 1990, at 40.7 per cent of total US direct investment abroad, the Community's share was larger than at any other time in the 1980s.

For manufacturing industry, the share of US FDI going to Europe increased in almost every year from 1950 to 1980. The European share of US FDI was around 25 per cent at the beginning of the 1950s, 35 per cent in the early 1960s, and about 40 per cent in the early 1970s.

In the 1980s, US direct investment in manufacturing industry alone shows a similar trend to exports. There too, a rapid decline occurred in the Community's share between 1980 and 1984 (a drop of 6.8 percentage points in four years). The recovery was again spectacular from 1985 onwards, with the share rising to 50.9 per cent in 1987, then a slight decline to 48.3 in 1990.

Consequently, while it was not possible to identify any systematic pull of the internal market as far as exports were concerned, except perhaps for manufactured products, the direct investment trend was very clear. It should also be stressed that the proportion of investment made up of reinvested profits is increasing very significantly, and is becoming a major source of investment growth, in contrast to the pattern of European investment in the USA (Table 5.5).

In contrast with the first wave of US industrial settlement in Europe around the beginning of the 1970s, US direct investment in Europe has therefore been self-sustaining in recent years, with no assistance from the parent companies. Moreover, it reflects a structural shift which, over the long term, shows relatively little vulnerability to swings in the business cycle (Lanteri 1989). This phenomenon of US multinationals becoming ever more firmly anchored in the Community reflects, as in the case of companies such as IBM and Ford, a high level of commitment to the European economy and a growing degree of autonomy *vis-à-vis* the United States. This can only intensify as 1992 approaches.

TABLE 5.3. *The EC's share of US exports* (%)

Share of EUR 12 exports	1980	1981	1982	1983	1984	1985	1986	1987	1988	1989	1990
All goods combined	26.7	24.4	24.7	24.2	23.2	23.0	24.4	23.3	23.9	23.7	25.0
Manufactured products	26.3	22.6	23.1	23.8	23.0	22.9	24.7	24.7	25.1	25.8	27.2

Source: Eurostat.

TABLE 5.4. *The EC's share of total US FDI*

	1980	1981	1982	1983	1984	1985	1986	1987	1988	1989	1990
Stocks*											
Total											
in $ billion	80.7	83.8	84.3	72.7	71.8	83.9	98.6	120.1	131.1	149.5	172.9
in % of world	37.4	37.0	35.8	35.1	34.0	36.4	38.0	39.0	39.1	40.4	40.7
Manufacturing Industry											
in US$ billion	43.4	43.2	36.0	36.2	35.9	43.4	50.1	64.7	67.7	70.9	81.2
in % of world	48.6	45.8	43.2	43.7	41.8	45.8	47.7	50.9	48.9	47.5	48.3
Flows†											
Total ($ billion)	11.2	3.4	0.8	-0.8	-0.1	12.1	12.8	18.9	9.7	17.1	9.1
Manufacturing industry ($ billion)	5.5	0.1	1.1	0.2	-0.7	7.2	6.7	13.8	3.3	3.5	3.1

* US direct investment abroad.
† Capital outflows.

Source: Survey of Current Business.

TABLE 5.5. *Reinvested earnings as a percentage of US–EC FDI flows*

	1961–9	1970–3	1974–7	1978–82	1983–7
US investment in Europe	39	56	62	94	99.6
European investment in the USA	—	—	32	2	8.7

Source: Survey of Current Business and Lanteri 1989.

3.3. The Case of Japan

How economically important is the EC for Japan? To begin with, the Community has taken an ever growing share of Japanese exports. Whereas in 1982, 13 per cent of Japanese exports went to the Community market, the proportion increased to 18.8 per cent of the total value of exports in 1990 (Table 5.6).

Turning to Japanese direct investment in Europe, a very sharp increase in value can be observed (from $10 billion in 1985 up to $55.3 billion in 1990). For manufacturing only, the Community's overall share increased sharply from 8.3 per cent in 1985 to 15 per cent in 1990 (Table 5.7).

There was a large change during the 1980s in Japanese FDI. Figure 5.3 presents the share of Japanese FDI flowing into the USA, the EC, and the rest of the world (mainly developing countries) over the 1980s. The importance of developing countries has declined sharply, while the shares to the EC and the USA have grown at the same rate. However, the US share was twice as high as the European one.

Total Japanese direct investment in industry is well below their total stock in the EC. This is because half of Japanese direct investment in Europe is in banking and insurance, with the stock of industrial investment accounting for only 22 per cent of the total in 1990. By way of comparison, more than 53 per cent of US direct investment in Europe is concentrated in industry. Here again, we can see a significant difference in the respective structure of US and Japanese direct investment in Europe. This suggests that, overall, Japanese direct investment has little impact at present on European industry, in contrast to direct investment by the USA, but that an important upward trend appears. However, the turbulent experiences of the dollar in the period could have influenced this evolution in value, although not the percentage of the flows of FDI to the EC compared to the total for the world.

Moreover, concerning Japanese firms' strategies in the EC and US markets, it appears that cumulative Japanese manufacturing investments in the US are still four times as high as in the EC while exports are only twice as high. In other words, even if we adjust for the fact that the US market is more important for Japanese firms than the European one, we are still left with the conclusion that Japanese manufacturing FDI in

TABLE 5.6. *The EC's share of Japanese exports*

Share of EUR 12 exports	1980	1981	1982	1983	1984	1985	1986	1987	1988	1989	1990
Manufactured products (%)	13.9	13.1	13.0	13.2	11.9	12.0	14.8	16.6	17.8	17.5	18.8

Source: Eurostat.

TABLE 5.7. *The EC's share of Japanese FDI*

	1980	1981	1982	1983	1984	1985	1986	1987	1988	1989	1990
Stocks											
Total											
in $ billion	4.0	4.8	5.6	6.5	8.2	10.0	13.4	19.6	28.0	38.0	55.3
in % of world	11.1	10.5	10.4	10.6	11.5	12.0	12.6	14.1	15.0	16.4	17.7
Manufacturing industry											
in $ billion	0.8	1.0	1.2	1.4	1.7	2.0	2.4	3.2	4.6	7.7	12.2
in % of world	6.5	6.8	6.8	7.1	7.8	8.3	8.4	8.8	9.3	11.6	15.0
Flows											
Total ($ billion)	0.5	0.7	0.8	0.9	1.7	1.9	3.3	6.3	8.3	14.0	13.3
Manufacturing industry ($ billion)	0.2	0.2	0.1	0.2	-0.7	0.3	0.3	0.8	1.5	3.0	4.5

Source: Ministry of Finances, Tokyo (fiscal year).

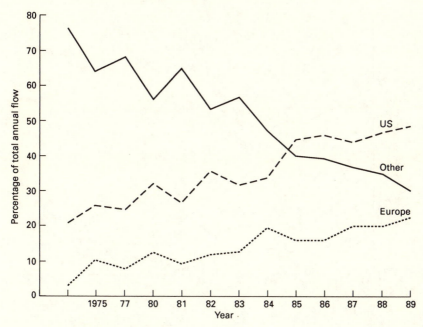

Source: Thomsen and Nicolaides 1991.

Fig. 5.3. Japanese FDI by region, percentage of annual flows, 1973–89

Europe is much less important than in the US (Thomsen and Nicolaides 1991).

3.4. Relationship between Trade and FDI

At this stage, it is important to consider the various possible methods by which European industry has been infiltrated by foreign entry; in this respect the relationship between direct investment and exports is critical. As the literature shows (see Sect. 2.3), recourse to direct investment does not imply that exports need to be substituted. Sometimes direct investments, particularly in the distribution trades, are even aimed at facilitating export.

Figures 5.4 and 5.5 present the evolution of trade and FDI of the USA and Japan to the EC for manufacturing products, during the 1980s.[10] For

---

[10] The stock of FDI is preferred to annual flows and we compare it with exports, which are a flow. In fact, to get an idea of the possible supply availability of American and Japanese and firms in the EC, we have to combine the annual exports to the EC of those firms with the production capacity of their stock of cumulated capital in Europe. Taking the case of Japanese involvement in the European car market, we should add together total Japanese car exports from Japan to Europe in one year with the total production capacity of Japanese-owned car plants inside the EC that same year.

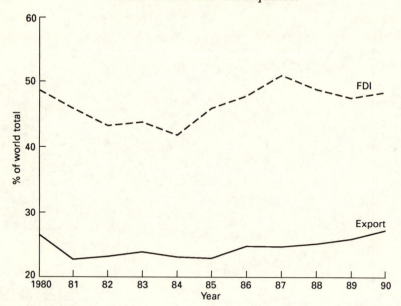

Source: Eurostat.

FIG. 5.4. US FDI and exports to the EC, 1980–90

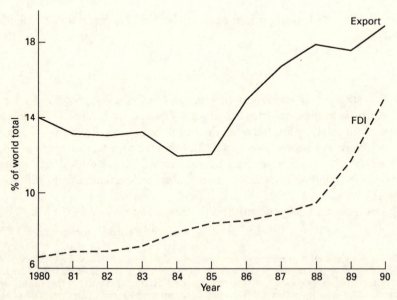

Source: Eurostat.

FIG. 5.5. Japanese FDI and exports to the EC, 1980–90

both exports and the stock of FDI, we take the percentage of world total devoted to the EC market. Roughly speaking, the general patterns of FDI and exports are similar, which could be explained by the fact that both foreign direct investment and trade are explained by the same general factor: a common response to an increase in EC demand. However, the differences between the mix of FDI/exports in relation to the EC market are quite important. In the case of the US in 1990, the Community's share of US manufacturing exports was 27.2 per cent and its share of US FDI was 48.3 per cent. In the case of Japan, the opposite was true with the Community's share of Japanese manufacturing exports being 18.8 per cent, which was more important than the Community's share of their FDI (15 per cent).

The relative position of Japanese FDI compared to exports was even worse in 1980 (6.5 per cent versus 14 per cent), and the catching up of FDI in ten years has been striking. The differences between the presence of the USA and Japan in the EC market could reflect differences in maturity and be explained by Vernon's theory (1968). According to this scenario, the product is initially produced at home for the domestic market, then an export market develops, and finally production begins abroad. In the 1990s, we could then expect a catching up by Japanese FDI.

3.5. The Main Sectors in which the Single Market is Exerting a Pull

It is obvious that US and Japanese exports and direct investment are not distributed evenly among the various sectors of activity of the European economy. As we have seen in Section 2, several factors can influence their distribution which are strongly industry-specific.

It is possible from this point of view to show the sectoral position of US and Japanese companies in the Community market by identifying the activities in which they aim for exports rather than direct investment, and vice versa.

We shall first examine the situation which existed in 1989, and then consider the trend which emerged between 1984 and 1989. 1984 corresponds for the US and Japan to their inflexion point both for exports and FDI.

3.6. The Sectoral Penetration of the USA in the EC

A sectoral comparison of the relative importance of US exports and direct investments is presented in Table 5.8. This table shows the following: first, in the machinery/data-processing equipment sector and chemical products, the Community market is a prime target for both exports and direct investment. Second, in the areas of metal products and electrical/electronic

TABLE 5.8. *The EC's share of US exports and FDI, 1990 (%)*

	US exports	Stock of US FDI
1. Food products	21.9	50.3
2. Chemical and related products	28.2	49.3
3. Metal products	22.3	39.3
4. Machinery/data-processing equipment	32.9	62.0
5. Electrical/electronic equipment	19.9	33.3
6. Transport equipment*	22.4	36.4
7. Other manufactured products	25.1	51.4
Manufactured products combined	25.8	48.3

* 'Transport equipment' includes motor vehicles and aeronautics.

Source: Direct investment, Survey of Current Business; exports, Eurostat.

equipment there is a relatively low degree of penetration by either approach. Applying the general Figure 5.2 presented above, Figure 5.6 illustrates the corresponding relations between exports and FDI.

Against the background of the process of completion of the internal market, it is useful to examine whether the various positions are the result of a trend over recent years. This is because, although no causal relationship can be established, this process may reasonably be expected to lead to either a strengthening of existing sectoral positions, withdrawals, or a switch to other sectors.

Table 5.9 indicates some trends for the period 1984–90. It can be seen from this table that, over the period 1984–90, the average degree of US industrial penetration in the Community, as compared to its penetration elsewhere in the world, increased by +2.8 per cent for exports and by +6.5 per cent for direct investment.

The following trends also emerge:

- there was a relative contraction of the US presence in sectors in which the initial relative position was already weak in terms of both exports and direct investment. This is the case for electrical and electronic equipment and, to a lesser extent, metal products.
- on the other hand, those areas of activity in which exports were relatively high saw a relative consolidation based on exports but mostly on direct investment (chemicals and machinery).

It may be concluded that the sectoral pull exerted on US producers by the European market has resulted in a reinforcement of existing strong positions, such as chemicals, machinery, and transport equipment, and a withdrawal in areas in which penetration of the European market was relatively low. In the light of what we will see in the case of Japan, such a trend might suggest a growing division of labour in the world.

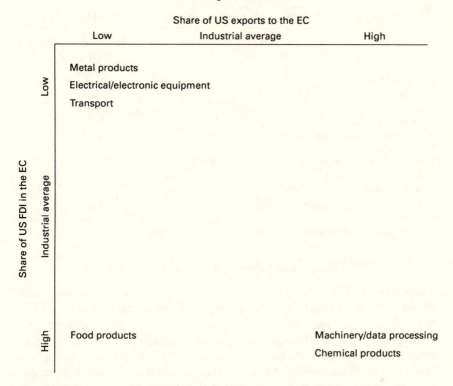

FIG. 5.6. The relationship between US exports and US FDI to the EC, by industry, 1989

TABLE 5.9. *Changes in the EC's share of US exports and FDI, 1984–1990* (%)

	US Exports	Stock of US FDI
1. Food products	− 2.2	+ 5.7
2. Chemical and related products	+ 2.2	+ 13.3
3. Metal products	+ 4.4	+ 4.1
4. Machinery/data-processing equipment	+ 4.3	+ 7.0
5. Electrical/electronic equipment	− 3.9	− 4.9
6. Transport equipment*	+ 9.5	+ 1.3
7. Other manufactured products	+ 2.0	+ 8.3
Manufactured products combined	+ 2.8	+ 6.5

* 'Transport equipment' includes motor vehicles and aeronautics.

Source: Direct investment, Survey of Current Business; exports, Eurostat.

TABLE 5.10. *The EC's share of Japanese exports and FDI, 1990 (%)*

	Japanese exports	Stock of Japanese FDI
Food products	9.6	12.3
Textiles	14.2	20.8
Paper	14.8	0.4
Chemical products	17.6	12.9
Non-ferrous metal products	6.4	5.4
Machinery	15.7	22.3
Electrical/electronic equipment	24.9	20.9
Transport equipment	16.9	17.4
Other manufactured products	26.4	9.9
All manufactured products combined	18.9	15.0

Source: Direct investment, Ministry of Finance, Tokyo; exports, Eurostat.

3.7. *The Sectoral Penetration of Japan in the EC*

Table 5.10 and Fig. 5.7 compare the relative importance of Japanese direct investment and export flows. The electrical and electronic sector plays a dominant role for Japanese industry, as regards both exports and direct investment. In transport equipment and machinery, areas in which Japanese industry excels, direct investment in Europe is also important. However, the food industry, the non-ferrous metal industries, and the paper industry are relatively minor players, whether in terms of exports or direct investment.

The changes in Japanese industrial positions between 1984 and 1990 are shown in Table 5.11. The following features over the period 1984–90 are apparent from this table:

(*a*) the average degree of Japanese industrial penetration in the Community, compared to its penetration elsewhere in the world, increased by 5.8 per cent for exports, and 7.2 per cent for direct investment;

(*b*) compared to this industrial average, an already strong position in the electrical/electronic equipment and machinery industries, including data-processing equipment sectors, was further strengthened;

(*c*) there was a relative contraction of the Japanese presence, in terms of both exports and direct investment, in the non-ferrous metals and food industries, where the Japanese positions were rather weak.

In conclusion, three aspects must be stressed in comparing Japanese and US trends:

1. Whereas the pull exerted by the Community market on Japanese companies is powerful in the electrical/electronic industry, where they maintain their leadership, US companies are clearly withdrawing from this industry.

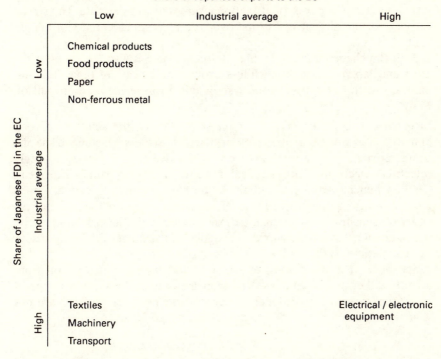

Fɪɢ. 5.7. The relationship between Japanese exports and Japanese FDI to the EC, by industry, 1989

Tᴀʙʟᴇ 5.11. *Changes in the EC's share of Japanese exports and FDI, 1984–1990*

	Japanese exports (%)	Stock of Japanese FDI (%)
Food products	− 2.3	+ 7.0
Textiles	+ 7.4	+ 12.2
Paper	+ 6.5	+ 0.4
Chemical products	+ 6.1	+ 7.6
Non-ferrous metal products	+ 3.2	− 0.8
Machinery	+ 7.1	+ 10.9
Electrical/electronic equipment	+ 7.5	+ 10.0
Transport equipment	+ 5.7	+ 6.6
Other manufactured products	+ 5.4	− 5.0
All manufactured products combined	+ 7.0	+ 7.2

Source: Eurostat.

2. Conversely, in the machinery (capital goods) sectors, the Community displays a stronger power of attraction *vis-à-vis* its two partners. The strong recovery of investment in Europe over recent years has no doubt been a central factor.

3. In the chemical industry, this attractive force is also felt by both the USA and Japan, although much less strongly in the case of Japanese companies, but this attractive force was mainly focused in a strong pull on FDI.

In general, two points may be emphasized. Firstly, the single European market's power of attraction is felt primarily in sectors which have specific characteristics. They are those where world demand is growing strongly (electrical/electronic and chemical industries), and in which European demand benefits from particularly favourable conditions (capital goods and transport equipment). Moreover, all these sectors belong to the category of 'sensitive' industries, i.e. those which are particularly affected by the removal of non-tariff barriers (Buigues and Ilzkovitz 1988) and where the competitive stakes will be high.

Secondly, it is interesting to observe that in many sectors one can identify either a simultaneous decline or increase in the shares of exports and direct investment, although American and Japanese patterns are not similar.

3.8. Determinants of the Relative Pull Exerted by the Single Market on US and Japanese Direct Investments

Now that the main sectoral features of the US and Japanese direct investments and exports in the EC have been described, the purpose of this section is to test whether these US and Japanese operations are influenced by different determinants, corresponding more or less to efficiency and strategic considerations (see Sect. 2.1).

Our dependent variable is the Community's share of total US or Japanese direct investments in manufactured activities, for the years 1980 to 1989.

Given the difficulties in obtaining relevant disaggregated statistics, a very limited number of variables are associated with this dependent variable, so that it is not possible, at this stage, to disentangle the respective roles of efficiency and strategic considerations. One central question that is tackled by our regression analysis is based on the view that Japanese investments in the EC could be mainly motivated by defensive strategic considerations: the fear of a 'fortress Europe' and the will to protect or to enhance their local market share in a more irreversible way than through exports. On the contrary, US companies have been dominant players within the common market for a long time, whether in terms of exports or of direct investments. The increased power of attraction of the internal market is then expected to lead principally to an overall consolidation, especially in sectors where there are location advantages revealed by the relatively strong EC position at the world level.[11]

Four variables are used. The first variable is the Community's share of total US or Japanese exports, which is expected to exercise a positive or a negative influence, according to the complementarity or the substitutability nature of the relations between trade and investment. Complementarity suggests that investment and trade flows reinforce each other; it could correspond to offensive investments whose strategic motivation is to consolidate in a more irreversible way a position in the common market. By contrast, substitutability corresponds more to a response to possible trade diversion effects of integration.

A second variable is intra-EC non-tariff barriers. These barriers affect mainly trade with the rest of the world. This applies especially in activities in which trade is subject to Article 115 of the Treaty of Rome. In such cases, national barriers to intra-EC trade have been erected in order to limit extra-EC imports, and it cannot be excluded that, for some of them, EC industrial and commercial measures could replace national measures after 1992. Such pessimistic expectations could encourage FDI as a strategy for overcoming existing or anticipated barriers to entry. The source to measure intra-EC non-tariff barriers is Buigues and Ilzkovitz (1988).

The third variable is the rate of growth of demand defined as apparent consumption (production + imports − exports) in each sector in the EC with respect to US/Japanese apparent consumption in the same sector. This variable, corresponding to a search for efficient location, is expected to exert a positive influence on investments where sectoral demand in Europe is growing faster than in the USA or Japan. The variable is calculated as being the sectoral growth of demand in the EC divided by the growth of demand in the same sectors in the USA and Japan during the last four years.

A fourth variable is the Community's sectoral specialization, which is expected to exercise a positive influence on FDI as the EC has a 'location advantage' in sectors where it is specialized. The variable is the 'Balassa index' of specialization, calculated as the EC's exports for sector i in total EC exports of manufactured products, divided by the same index for OECD.

The available observations correspond to the seven sectors presented

---

[11] A survey carried out amongst the major Japanese and US industrial companies (Ernst and Whinney 1989) asked for comments on the anticipated impact of the internal market on the activities of multinationals in Europe. Two-thirds of the Japanese industrial companies stated that they were expecting increased protectionism in the Europe of 1992, as compared with 44% in the case of US companies. This information is confirmed by the fifth JETRO report (1989) on the management situations of Japanese manufacturing enterprises in Europe; according to the 216 companies which replied to that survey, the acceleration in direct investment in Europe is due more to Japan–EC trade friction than to the prospects opened up by the 1992 programme.

in section 3.6 for the USA and to the nine sectors presented in section 3.7 for Japan. The period is 1980–90 for the USA and for Japan.

The results of the two linear regressions for the USA and Japan appear in Table 5.12.[12] The estimates of the coefficients are generally consistent with our expectations. The adjusted R^2 and F statistics are relatively high.

Comparison between the US and Japanese equations leads to the following conclusions:

In both cases, there is a strong and significant complementarity between direct investment and exports: at the sectoral level, the relative strengthening or withdrawal of US and Japanese firms in the EC occurs in tandem.[13] Given the level of aggregation, this evolution does not prejudge the substitutability or complementarity of the products concerned.[14]

In the Japanese case, strong non-tariff barriers to trade are a major determinant of direct investments, confirming the role of the fear of a fortress Europe and the importance of strategic considerations. In the USA, non-tariff barriers have no significant impact.

For EC sectoral demand growth and EC sectoral specialization which are based on the 'location efficiency advantages' of the EC, the picture is different for US and Japanese investors. In the Japanese case, there is a statistically significant positive impact of both variables, while for the USA only sectoral specialization variable has a significant impact.

Although encouraging, these results are very preliminary. Further analysis will require a less aggregated approach, including case studies. Besides, distinguishing between efficiency and strategic objectives demands the introduction of supplementary variables to capture this distinction. Finally, a model based on simultaneous equations could be used to take into account the endogeneity of FDI and exports.

4. FDI, EC INTEGRATION, AND POLICY ISSUES

The previous sections have described the nature of the pull which the large internal market is exerting on exports and direct investment from the United States and Japan.

The question which now arises is whether these international operations assist the necessary restructuring, the emergence of an integrated productive system, and growing economic cohesion and efficiency—or whether they

[12] Similar results are obtained by a double logarithmic specification.

[13] This result implies that the EC 92 liberalization yields trade-promoting rather than trade-substituting investment.

[14] For some sectors such as electrical equipment, the complementary is predominant for the USA and Japan, although in a reverse way. In other cases, such as transport equipment, this is not clear.

TABLE 5.12. *Determinants of US and Japanese FDI in the EC*

	Constant term	Share of total exports devoted to the EC	Growth of demand in EC divided by growth of demand in US/Japan market	Non-tariff barriers in EC	EC sectoral specialization	R^2	F
US	11 (1.04)	0.72 (3.29)	0.03 (1.21)	0.50 (0.36)	0.20 (1.80)	0.37	10.18
Japan	−14.19 (6.18)	0.26 (5.68)	0.05 (2.84)	1.41 (3.02)	0.10 (8.04)	0.73	60.70

are likely to lead to instability of trade, to increased uncertainty, to the creation of dominant positions, or even to the structural disintegration of the system.

4.1. Exports, FDI, and Competitiveness

In general, the non-EC export flows to the Community have a favourable competitive effect on domestic producers and are consistent with the world division of labour, which is mainly based on the principle of comparative advantage. Furthermore, the new Community dynamism makes it possible to view these foreign exports with greater equanimity: the dynamism tends to reduce their relative scale, with the abolition of internal non-tariff barriers boosting the competitiveness of European firms in their own market independently of any increase in external protection (an intra-Community trade creation effect and not a deflection effect).[15]

It should be pointed out, however, that econometric studies (Neven and Roller 1989, Jacquemin and Sapir 1991), have shown that these non-tariff barriers currently provide on average more protection against extra-Community imports than against intra-Community imports, and also that disciplinary pressure on European industrial mark-ups is principally exerted by the former imports. Finally, recent statistics (*European Economy*, 42 (1989)) indicate that in high technology industries, extra-Community imports, primarily from Japan and the USA, were tending during the period 1986–8 to grow more rapidly than intra-Community imports, reflecting increased dependence on third country suppliers. Still, it can be argued that extra-Community imports could always be controlled by various indirect devices such as voluntary export restraints (VERs).

Conversely, FDI, given its stronger and more visible implementation within the host country, evokes stronger sentiments. It has often been seen as an attempt to control the host country's economy or certain industries, compromising its sovereignty. This political viewpoint is counterbalanced by the opinion of most economists. According to their arguments, FDI raises the host nation's productive capacity through transnational geographic and industrial reallocation of resources; it reduces production costs and prices and increases the degree of competition.

Unlike exports, direct investment also creates employment and transfers specific assets from the parent company in the form of production techniques, managerial capacity, and technology. Such investment can contribute to the European restructuring process by giving it greater depth and

---

[15] According to simulations carried out by the Commission, a reduction of between 7.7 per cent and 10.3 per cent in extra-Community imports can be expected. However, this reduction may be offset partially by a favourable impact of a higher rate of growth pof Community GNP on the level of extra-Community imports.

speed and can improve European competitiveness in foreign markets, to which Community subsidiaries of foreign multinationals can export.

FDI generates a net income in the EC even if we take into account profits accruing to the foreign owners. Indeed, the bulk of that income goes mainly to employees in the form of wages and salaries.

However, the first section has suggested that FDI is not only motivated by efficiency considerations; it also corresponds to strategic moves intended to create or to safeguard various forms of economic power. These could include the establishment of dominant positions on certain markets, the transfer of centres of strategic decision-making, preferential reliance on imports from the country of the parent company, and poor integration into the European system and its values.

It is not possible, on the basis of the information provided by the preceding sections, to offer a full answer to these questions. Nevertheless, a number of essential aspects have been identified.

4.2. US versus Japanese Operations

Overall, the USA continues to be a dominant player in the Community's internal market, whether in terms of exports or in terms of direct investment. In the case of the latter, the power of attraction of the internal market is clear and seems to be leading to growing integration, in that profits earned on the Community market are automatically being reinvested here. In the case of Japan, the proportion of Japanese exports going to the Community has grown sharply, in both value and volume terms; however, until recently, the general growth in direct investment in manufacturing industry, although high, has not been particularly oriented towards the Community. In March 1989, 48 per cent of Japanese investment in manufacturing industry went to North America, 25 per cent to Asia, 10.9 per cent to Latin America, and only 9.7 per cent to Europe.

At the sectoral level, it is clear that the Community's power of attraction has led principally to the consolidation of strong positions by both US and Japanese companies. However, there are differences between the two in respect of certain areas of emphasis. While Japanese firms are particularly well represented in the electrical and electronics industry, US companies are reinforcing their positions in the agri-foodstuffs and chemical industries. In sectors such as capital goods, however, the Community is exerting a pull on both countries.

All of these sectors are high-growth strategic activity sectors and are sensitive to the removal of non-tariff barriers. It follows that in the post-1992 *grand marché* these subsidiaries of foreign multinationals will be particularly powerful competitors.

Finally, at the level of corporate strategies, the subsidiaries of US multinationals have, up to now, integrated to a greater extent into the European industrial system than those of Japanese groups: US subsidiaries enjoy greater autonomy, their management is more 'Europeanized' (as is their management training), there is greater concern to adapt products to the Community market and to develop pan-European brands, they do not hesitate to transfer R&D facilities to Europe, and their organizational structure cuts across European borders. The Japanese companies seem less sensitive to the need to incorporate a specific European dimension into their strategies.[16]

These differences will not necessarily last, since they partly reflect the fact that US companies have been established in the Community for a long time. A climate of trust has been built up *vis-à-vis* US companies, which are regarded as observing the 'rules of the game' in the Community (including those in the social field). Japanese operations may well evolve along similar lines, in the not so distant future.

4.3. EC Policy Issues

With regard to Community policies, two levels of discussion can be distinguished: first, what are the existing tools; second, what could be required?

(*a*) At present, the EC has no Community-wide restrictions on the establishment of foreign companies, through greenfield investment or acquisition. On the contrary, according to Article 52 of the Treaty of Rome, the subsidiaries of foreign multinationals should enjoy identical conditions of access to the Community market, even if their countries of origin do not accord the same treatment to Community firms.

In contrast, the so-called Exon–Florio amendment (from the names of its sponsors) provides that the President of the USA (or his nominee) may investigate the effects on US national security of any mergers, acquisitions, and takeovers which could result in foreign control of persons engaged in interstate commerce in the USA. Should the President decide that any such transactions threaten national security, he may take action to suspend or prohibit them. This could include the forced divestment of assets. It is important to highlight the lack of a definition of national security and the uncertainty as to which transactions are notifiable. These uncertainties, coupled with the fear of potential forced divestment, have meant in practice that many foreign investors have felt compelled to give prior notification of their proposed investments. Indeed the Treasury itself has estimated that 350 of an expected 700 foreign acquisitions of $1 million or more will seek prior notification in 1990.

Concerning Japan, there are relatively few formal, explicit, legal, and regulatory barriers to merger and acquisition activity. Those that do exist relate primarily to takeovers by foreign investors. In 1980, with the enactment of

---

[16] See e.g. the report by Ernst and Whinney (1989).

a new Foreign Exchange and Foreign Trade Control Law, direct foreign investment in the equity of Japanese companies became permissible in principle. Investments that would elevate total foreign ownership of a Japanese company to a level in excess of 25 per cent required review by the Bank of Japan, but only prior notification of the investment was needed rather than prior approval on a case-by-case basis. By 1984, even this prior notification was relaxed to the extent of requiring notice only when a single foreign investor intended to acquire more than 10 per cent of a listed company's stock. Although liberalization of the Foreign Exchange and Foreign Trade Control Law was associated with a sharp upturn in acquisitions by foreigners (nearly as many occurred between 1980 and 1984 as in the prior 25 years), the 'deal flow' into Japan has remained remarkably low and slow. Factors which inhibit foreigners creating subsidiaries in Japan or targeting Japanese firms for M&A are not therefore primarily legal, but reflect other constraints: the cost of doing business in Japan, the difficulty in finding high-quality Japanese staff in one of the world's tightest labour markets, the prevalent tendency for Japanese firms to maintain very close business relationships, the difficulty of access by foreigners to company data in Japan.

Confronted with such an asymmetric situation within the Triad, two extreme views can be adopted for the EC. On the one hand, it can be argued that a policy of reciprocity must be implemented, and foreign investments have to be impeded if investment by home firms in foreign countries are obstructed. At the other extreme, another view is to consider that FDI is systematically beneficial for the host countries, and a policy which actively promotes investments from abroad should be pursued, even if this policy is unilateral.

Our own approach is based on two dimensions, internal and external.

(*b*) At the internal level, three principles are suggested:

- Firstly, general protective measures against US and Japanese direct investment cannot in any way be justified, both because of the limited overall share of these operations and because of the generally positive role they can be expected to play. In any case, given the tendency for production to be located all over the world and the confusion over the origin of products, selective commercial policies can only get bogged down in increasingly unwieldy and complicated implementing measures based on more or less arbitrary criteria.

  But these statements leave open several questions. What is the real intensity of technology transfer when R&D is mainly conducted in the home country? What is the net effect of FDI on overall employment once the crowding out of domestic producers is taken into account? What are the implications of asymmetric degrees of openness between the EC and the home country of the multinationals because of domestic practices discriminating against foreign firms and products?

- Secondly, it is necessary to obtain precise and regular information on Community-scale operations of direct investment and future possible trends. A policy of openness is perfectly compatible with a policy of transparency. One aim should be to prevent a competitive escalation of national or regional aid for such investments which, in some cases, could be undertaken under conditions which are unfair to European competitors who are already present in the markets concerned or who also wish to enter them. Another aim of a better overall view of inward investment in the EC is to allow the European authorities to examine in a systematic way the implications of such investments for their common trade, regional, and R&D policies.

  Among the various possible legal bases, Article 213 of the Treaty of Rome states that the Commission may collect any information required for the performance of the tasks entrusted to it. Decisions based on this article can be taken following a simple majority.

- Thirdly, in some sectors, US and Japanese companies could acquire dominant positions at world level and have the means of abusing these dominant positions in the Community market. From that point of view, it is ambiguous to state that a company will acquire another one only if it can make a better use of it. This use could correspond to higher monopoly rents, but not necessarily to higher social surplus. The question is especially important in sectors in which the Community is losing market share both within and outside the Community, namely advanced, high-tech products. Non-discriminatory but firm application of Community competition policy is essential here (Jacquemin 1989*b*).

(*c*) At the external level, the globalization of markets and the rising interdependence of private and government actions highlight the market access problems. The OECD informal understanding on investment could then be useful, but unhappily it is unenforceable. During the Uruguay Round, proposals concerning restrictive practices have been made with respect to the so-called trade-related investment measures (TRIMs). The possibility of initiating negotiations within the GATT framework would also be a useful multilateral approach. But actually, a country with a grievance has to resort to unilateral approaches extending domestic rules and enforcement mechanisms to the control of restrictive practices involving foreign elements, as well as to bilateral agreements leading to co-operation among anti-trust authorities. The recent EC regulation on mergers and acquisitions deals with this issue. According to its Article 24,

1. The Member States shall inform the Commission of any general difficulties encountered by their undertakings with concentrations . . . in a non-member country.
2. Initially not more than one year after the entry into force of this Regulation and thereafter periodically the Commission shall draw up a report examining

the treatment accorded to Community undertakings, . . . as regards concentrations in non-member countries. The Commission shall submit those reports to the Council, together with any recommendations.

3. Whenever it appears to the Commission, either on the basis of the reports referred to in paragraph 2 or on the basis of other information, that a non-member country does not grant Community undertakings treatment comparable to that granted by the Community to undertakings from that non-member country, the Commission may submit proposals to the Council for the appropriate mandate for negotiation with a view to obtaining comparable treatment for Community undertakings.

This article dealing with concentrations in non-member countries requires information and actions intended to give Community corporations participating in such operations a 'competition policy' treatment comparable to that granted to foreign corporations acting in the EC. Given that the regulation states that effective competition is the only reference for accepting or prohibiting a merger in the EC, Article 24 implies that the use of alternative criteria (of an industrial policy type) by a foreign country for blocking an acquisition by an EC firm would lead to an international negotiation.

All these evolutions suggest that the growing overlap between internal and external competition will lead to a multiplication of international conflicts. To sustain the efficiency gains from FDI and to control its impact on market power, there is an urgent need to implement a transnational co-ordination and integration of competition policies.

REFERENCES

ACOCELLA, N. (1991), 'Strategic Foreign Direct Investment in the EC' (University of Rome, mimeo.).

BAUMOL, W. (1986), Review of Williamson's *The Economic Institutions of Capitalism*, *Rand Journal of Economics*, 7.

BUIGUES, P., and ILZKOVITZ, F. (1988), 'Les Enjeux sectoriels du marché intérieur', *Revue d'Économie Industrielle*, 45.

CAPEL, J. (1990), 'The Exchange Rate Impact on Foreign Direct Investment', *Tinbergen Institute Research Bulletin* (University of Amsterdam), 1.

CAVES, R., and JONES, R. (1977), *World Trade and Payments*, (Boston: Little Brown).

Commission of the European Communities (1989), 'The Community Economy at the Turn of the Decade', *European Economy* (Brussels), 42.

DIXIT, A. (1980), 'The Role of Investment in Entry-Deterrence', *Economic Journal*, 90.

DONNENFELD, S., and PRUSA, T. (1990), 'Monitoring and Co-ordination in Multinational Corporations', WPN 90–14, Department of Economics, York University, Canada.

DUNNING, J. (1982), 'Multinational Enterprises in the 1970's', in K. Hopt, *European Merger Control*, i (Berlin: de Gruyter).

—— and CANTWELL, J. (1989), 'Japanese Manufacturing Direct Investment in the EEC, post 1992. Some Alternative Scenarios' (London, mimeo.).

ERNST and WHITNEY (1989), 'Business Responses to the 1992 European Initiative' (mimeo.).

ETHIER, W. (1986), 'The Multinational Corporation', *Quarterly Journal of Economics*, 101.

GLESJER, H., JACQUEMIN, A., and PETIT, M. (1980), 'Exports in an Imperfect Competition Framework: An Analysis of 1,466 Small Country Exporters', *Quarterly Journal of Economics* (May).

GRAHAM, E. (1978), 'Transatlantic Investment by Multinational Firms: A Rivalistic Phenomenon', *Journal of Post-Keynesian Economics*, 1/1.

—— (1990), 'Exchange of Threat between Multinational Firms as an Infinitely Repeated Non-Cooperative Game', *International Trade Journal*, 3.

HAGER, W. (1989), 'Inward Investment', *Panorama of EC Industry* (Brussels: Commission of the European Community).

HELPMAN, E., and KRUGMAN, P. (1985), *Market Structure and Foreign Trade* (Cambridge, Mass.: MIT Press).

HYMER, S., and ROWTHORN, R. (1970) 'Multinational Corporations and International Oligopoly: The Non-American Challenge', in C. Kindleberger, *The International Corporation: A Symposium* (Cambridge, Mass.: MIT Press).

ITAKI, M., and WATERSON, M. (1990), 'European Multinationals and 1992' (International Investment and Business Studies, University of Reading).

JACQUEMIN, A. (1988*a*), 'International and Multinational Strategic Behaviour', *Kyklos*, 4.

—— (1989*b*) 'Horizontal Concentration and European Merger Policy', *European Economic Review*, 34.

—— and SAPIR, A. (1991), 'Competition and Imports in the European Market', in A. Winters and A. Venables, eds., *European Integration: Trade and Industry* (Cambridge: Cambridge University Press).

JETRO (1989), 'Current Management Situations of Japanese Manufacturing Enterprises in Europe' (Tokyo; Mar.).

JULIUS, D. (1990), *Global Companies and Public Policy: The Growing Challenge of Foreign Direct Investment* (London: Royal Institute & International Studies).

—— and THOMSEN, S. (1989), 'Inward Investment and Foreign-Owned Firms in the 65' (London: Royal Institute of International Affairs).

KPMG (1989), 'International Mergers and Acquisitions', *Deal Watch* (June).

LANTERI, M. (1989), 'Les Investissements directs États-Unis/Europe: Analyse des évolutions récentes', *Revue d'Économie Industrielle*, 48.

LAWRENCE, R. (1991), 'Political and Economic Aspects of Japanese Market Behaviour' (mimeo., The Brookings Institution; May).

MARKUSEN, J. (1984), 'Multinationals, Multi-Market Economies and the Gains from Trade', *Journal of International Economics*, 16.

MORSINK, R. (1991), 'Direct Investments within the European Community, Main Trends and the Factors Behind' (paper presented at the Euro-Invest Conference, Paris, Oct. 1991).

MOTTA, M. (1992), 'Multinational Firms and the Tariff-Jumping Argument', *European Economic Review*.

NEVEN, D., and ROLLER, L. (1989), 'European Integration and Trade Flows' (mimeo., INSEAD).

REICH, R. (1988), 'Corporation and Nation', *Atlantic*, 1.

SMITH, A. (1987), 'Strategic Investments, Multinational Corporations and Trade Policy', *European Economic Review*, 31.

TEECE, D. (1985), 'Multinational Enterprise, Internal Governance and Industrial Organization', *American Economic Review*, 75.

THOMSEN, S., and NICOLAIDES, P. (1991), 'The Evolution of Japanese Direct Investment in Europe: Death of a Transistor Salesman' (London: Royal Institute of International Affairs).

United Nations (1991), 'World Investment Report, 1991: The Triad in Foreign Direct Investment' (New York).

UNCTC (1991), 'The Triad in Foreign Direct Investment', Commission of Transindustrial Corporations, UN document no. E/C10/1991/2.

VERNON, R. (1966), 'International Investment and International Trade in the Product Cycle', *Quarterly Journal of Economics*, 2.

YANNOPOULOS, G. (1990), 'Foreign Direct Investment and European Integration', *Journal of Common Market Studies*, 3.

COMMENT

Stephen Thomsen

The authors begin with a discussion of FDI as either a cost-minimizing or profit-maximizing strategy of multinational enterprises (MNEs). This efficiency versus market power argument harks back to Hymer and Rowthorn (1970) and was raised more recently in Pitelis (1991). The strategic argument follows Dixit (1980) in arguing that investment might be undertaken to deter other potential entrants into that market. While it is an intriguing possibility, the literature on FDI suggests that, rather than deterring investment, actions by one firm will stimulate competitors at home to follow suit (Knickerbocker 1973) and, eventually, host-country firms will respond by investing in the other country (Graham 1978). In other words, the actions by one MNE do not deter others; they force them to respond aggressively. As a result, while Buigues and Jacquemin envisage the possibility of a decrease in competition, Erdilek (1985) and others working on intra-industry direct investment have emphasized the pro-competitive effects. While this important difference does not dramatically alter their conclusions, it does suggest other areas for policy initiatives, as we shall see later.

One of the strengths of the paper is that it draws an explicit link between trade and FDI, recognizing that they are two forms of market access. This is a point stressed in Thomsen and Woolcock (1993) with respect to intra-European investment. But it must also be recognized that there are a good many other possible motives for FDI, such as the acquisition of technology or the need for abundant labour, which have nothing to do with existing trade patterns or levels.

Furthermore, although comparisons of Japanese FDI in the US and Europe may be fruitful, comparing the Community's share of total Japanese exports and FDI may be less relevant. The rising share of Europe in total Japanese FDI is as much a result of the sectoral shift in Japanese investment as it is any interest in the European market. While early Japanese investments were characterized by heavy involvement in the resource industries of neighbouring developing countries, as manufacturing and services have become more important, so too have the markets of Europe and North America. Both of these markets have seen rising shares of Japanese investment, and it is important to note that increases in Europe have not come at the expense of investment in North America, which is still twice as high on a flows basis.

Taking the European share of total Japanese outflows thus does not strictly speaking compare like with like. The increase for Europe is partly the result of the slow growth of investments in developing countries (with the exception of a handful of Asian countries) in the 1980s. This situation characterized almost all home countries during that period, as FDI in developing countries was discouraged by low commodity prices and slow growth as a result of the debt crisis. Thus, what may appear as an irreversible trend towards ever more Japanese investment in Europe in Table 5.7 may reverse itself in the 1990s. Indeed, Japanese manufacturing investment in Europe fell by more than that in the rest of the world in the most recent figures for 1991, with Asia the principal beneficiary. A recent survey by the Japanese Export-Import Bank (Tejima 1992) showed this trend back towards Asia is likely to continue in the near future.

Nevertheless, ignoring these shortcomings, the approach adopted by the authors of looking at trade and investment jointly is a useful one. It is an interesting point that the 1980s witnessed a consolidation of both exports and FDI from the USA in Europe in certain sectors and a retrenchment in others. The authors suggest that the process of completion of the internal market was behind these shifts. It seems more likely, however, that the retrenchment by US firms in the electronics sector has more to do with the joint increase in Japanese exports and investment in Europe in that sector, which the authors also document, than it does with any putative increase in European competitiveness as a result of 1992.

To bring out more clearly the possible effects from the internal market, the authors regress the Community's share of total US or Japanese direct investment for a number of manufacturing sectors from 1980 to 1989 against four variables related to the Community's internal market programme. While the regressions do provide some idea about potential correlations between the FDI share and the explanatory variables, they also suffer from a number of shortcomings. First, the strong positive relationship between trade and investment shares which suggests that the two are complementary overall is an interesting finding, but are we to understand that growth in the export share to Europe from the USA and Japan encourages FDI? One could argue that at the present stage of the product cycle where Japanese firms find themselves, exports are likely to precede FDI, but the authors use contemporaneous exports. Furthermore, what possible relationship could US exports have with American investment, almost all of which occurs through retained earnings of existing affiliates, as the authors themselves demonstrate? Another problem with the regression for US FDI is the fact that 38 per cent of US exports to Europe are shipped by US MNEs to their European affiliates. Rather than explaining FDI, exports are likely to be determined by the same factors as FDI, that is, the three remaining exogenous variables, particularly the growth in demand. For this reason, it is possible that the equations suffer from multicollinearity. In addition, it is not clear why the authors include a variable for non-tariff barriers within the EC to explain direct investment from the USA and Japan. If there is any particular EC trade policy to which Japanese firms are responding then it is surely anti-dumping duties and national quotas such as in the automotive sector.

In the policy discussion, the authors return to the question of strategic versus efficiency motives for FDI. The three general principles suggested by the authors are eminently sensible and could have been made without even including the theoretical and empirical sections. The thrust of the principles is essentially liberal, arguing against general protective measures against US and Japanese direct investment. The call for more precise and regular information on direct investment to help anticipate trends is one that most researchers on FDI would welcome. It seems slightly misplaced, however, to suggest that more is needed with respect to US and Japanese investment. These two countries, particularly the USA, already provide more data on the operations of US-owned firms in Europe than do European countries of their own firms. The lacunas in the data are on the European side.

The need to prevent a competitive escalation of national and regional aid to lure investors is another recommendation that has been endorsed by a number of authors such as Balasubramanyam and Greenaway (1992). The same competition occurs among states in the USA and, to a lesser extent, at a global level. Thomsen and Woolcock (1993) suggest that competition among governments within Europe may have less effect on investors' behaviour than is commonly believed. The potential harm of such competition therefore comes more from rent-snatching by investing firms than from any distortion in the allocation of resources within the Community.

The third principle enunciated by the authors is that of non-discriminatory but firm application of Community competition policy. Mr Bangemann notwithstanding, such a policy is clearly the aim of Sir Leon Brittan at the European Commission. The question is whether there is any scope for transnational co-ordination and integration of competition policies. There are already procedures for consultation and exchange of information, but it remains to be seen how the example of supra-national competition policy in the EC can incorporate the USA without some institution comparable to the European Court of Justice. Nevertheless, it appears to be a policy objective well worth pursuing in a world where corporations' actions encompass several jurisdictions.

The thrust of the authors' policy recommendations is essentially open and liberal. They do nevertheless suggest that EC firms are not given as favourable treatment in the USA and Japan as firms from those countries receive in the Community. To arrive at this conclusion, the authors mix statutory and structural barriers together and fail to mention that non-EC firms face national restrictions within the Community even though the EC has no Community-wide restrictions on the establishment of foreign companies through greenfield investment or acquisition. To suggest that the absence of restrictive Community policies makes the EC more open than the USA is clearly far-fetched. Each and every Member State in the Community has potentially more restrictive policies towards inward investors than does the USA under the Exon–Florio amendment. The amendment was only applied once under President Bush, against a Chinese company where national security was clearly a valid consideration.

Furthermore, the authors are comparing only statutory barriers, whereas the debate is increasingly focusing on structural impediments to investment. In that respect, it is difficult to argue that the USA, with its actions in the 1980s to break up monopolies and to deregulate industries, lags behind much of Europe. The authors do recognize that in the case of Japan, it is these structural barriers rather than anything on the books that deters investors. It is unclear whether they would recommend following the US example in the form of an EC Structural Impediments Initiative (SII) with respect to Japan. It is by no means clear that the Commission will be in the role of *demandeur* given the structural barriers that exist within Member States with respect to inward investment. Indeed, many of the arguments concerning strategic moves by investors and the need for an active competition policy may be more relevant with respect to intra-EC flows, which far exceed inflows from Japan and the USA over the past few years.

In spite of some of these somewhat niggling criticisms, the authors should be congratulated for their ambitious attempt to draw together theoretical, empirical, and policy issues on a subject that no country can afford to ignore.

REFERENCES

BALASUBRAMANYAM, S., and GREENAWAY, D. (1992), 'Economic Integration and Foreign Direct Investment: Japanese Investment in the EC', *Journal of Common Market Studies*, 30. 2 (June), 175–93.

DIXIT, A. (1980), 'The Role of Investment in Entry-Deterrence', *Economic Journal*, 90, 95–106.

ERDILEK, A., ed. (1985), *Multinationals as Mutual Invaders: Intra-Industry Direct Foreign Investment* (London: Croom Helm).

GRAHAM, E. (1978), 'Transatlantic Investment by Multinational Firms: A Rivalistic Phenomenon?', *Journal of Post-Keynesian Economics*, 1/1, 82–99.

HYMER, S., and ROWTHORNE, R. (1970), 'Multinational Corporations and International Oligopoly: The Non-American Challenge', in C. Kindleberger, ed., *The International Corporation* (Cambridge, Mass.: MIT Press), 57–95.

KNICKERBOCKER, F. (1973), *Oligopolistic Reaction and the Multinational Enterprise* (Cambridge, Mass.: Harvard University Press).

PITELIS, C. (1991), 'The Transnational Corporation: Demand-Side Issues and a Synthesis', in C. Pitelis and R. Sugden, eds., *The Nature of the Transnational Firm* (London: Routledge), 194–212.

TEJIMA, S. (1992), 'Japanese Foreign Direct Investment in the 1980s and its Prospect for the 1990s', *EXIM Review* (Tokyo: Export-Import Bank of Japan; July), 25–51.

THOMSEN, S., and WOOLCOCK, S. (1993), *Direct Investment and European Integration: Competition among Firms and Governments* (London: Pinter/RIIA).

6

Investment and Trade by American, European, and Japanese Multinationals across the Triad

Dennis Encarnation

Multinational corporations have fundamentally transformed the international political economy.[1] Today, through FDI, they exercise a powerful influence on international trade, largely through intra-company shipments linking multinational parents with their majority-owned subsidiaries. These subsidiaries, moreover, actually record more foreign sales through offshore production and overseas distribution than is now generated through *all* international trade. Multinationals combine this production and distribution to supply those local markets expressly hosting their foreign subsidiaries, and then ship what remains to export markets in nearby countries or back to their parent's home base. As a result, FDI has emerged as the principal means for US, European, and Japanese corporations to secure access to overseas markets. Especially when these markets are located in the advanced economies of the Triad formed by East Asia, the USA, and Western Europe, multinationals have surely carried global competition well beyond simple trade rivalries.

Majority foreign-owned subsidiaries lie at the centre of these several transformations, as multinational corporations seek to create and sustain their competitive advantage through the skilful management of tangible and intangible assets in technology, marketing, and organization.[2] Such assets are specific to each individual firm, and seem best exploited when foreign multinationals own a majority of the equity shareholdings in their overseas subsidiaries. Compared to minority shareholdings, a majority position grants the multinational parent a higher degree of managerial control over the foreign use of their firm-specific assets. Such managerial control, in turn, helps to reduce the high costs that plague more 'arm's-length' transactions between foreign suppliers of firm-specific assets and unaffiliated buyers overseas.[3] So instead of using such arm's-length

---

[1] For an earlier analysis of these transformations, see my *Rivals beyond Trade: America versus Japan in Global Competition* (Cornell: Cornell University Press, 1992), esp. 1–31, 183–202.

[2] For a survey of these assets, see R. Caves, *Multinational Enterprise and Economic Analysis* (Cambridge: Cambridge University Press, 1982), esp. 1–30, 195–211.

[3] For a description of the infirmities afflicting the efficient allocation of intangible assets through conventional markets, see O. Williamson, 'Markets and Hierarchies: Some Elementary Considerations', *American Economic Review* (May 1973), 316–25.

transactions, these foreign suppliers transfer their tangible and intangible assets internally—directly to their majority subsidiaries abroad. Later, such transfers reverse, as foreign subsidiaries also begin to ship goods and services back to their multinational parent (as well as to other related affiliates overseas). In the end, this circular flow enhances the total pool of technological, marketing, and organizational assets available to both the multinational parent and its majority subsidiaries.

Even for less firm-specific goods and services, intra-company transactions have also come to account for much of the trade conducted by multinational corporations, a fact which has important implications not only for these corporations, but also for national economies.[4] For multinationals, intra-company trade once again ensures greater control over both upstream supplies and downstream markets than do more arm's-length transactions among unaffiliated buyers and suppliers. But for multinational parents to exercise a sizeable impact on international trade, majority subsidiaries—rather than minority affiliates—must represent the principal class of buyers abroad. For only with majority ownership do multinationals exercise sufficient managerial control to dictate their subsidiaries' decisions to import supplies from their parents. Such control does not exist in minority affiliates, which more frequently serve as offshore suppliers rather than foreign buyers when trading with their multinational parents. Majority ownership, it seems, is simply not necessary to convince these foreign suppliers to export to their US parents. Thus, relationships resulting from equity ownership and managerial control—rather than only those transactions based principally on relative prices—can be expected to determine patterns of intra-company trade. By this same logic, intra-company trade may prove far less responsive to short-term swings in foreign-exchange rates, thereby blunting national policies designed to alter currency movements. And just such an impact on national policy can be sizeable, because intra-company transactions have now grown to dominate international trade among industrialized countries.

After securing majority ownership and managerial control over a broad range of intra-company transfers, multinationals typically employ their overseas subsidiaries to sell in foreign markets far more than they and other exporters back home ship to these same markets. In general, foreign sales come from three sources: the host-country market of the overseas subsidiary, the home-country market of that subsidiary's parent, and third-country markets that are typically in close geographic proximity to the host country. To supply these several markets, multinationals may decide to invest in overseas distribution channels consisting of dedicated sales and service networks; or they may decide to invest directly in offshore

---

[4] For a review of these implications, see Encarnation, *Rivals beyond Trade*, esp. 26–31, 190–7; also see D. Julius, *Global Companies and Public Policy: The Growing Challenge of Foreign Direct Investment* (London: Royal Institute of International Studies, 1990), esp. 71–92.

production. Here, pressures to increase such offshore production greatly increase when *any* of four conditions arise: when national governments severely constrain, or credibly threaten to limit, imports;[5] when global competitors derive significant advantage from their location;[6] when indigenous buyers demand closer relations with their suppliers;[7] and when foreign exporters fear the increased risks of exchange-rate fluctuations.[8] Thus, each source of foreign sales by multinational corporations reflects a different foreign investment and related trade strategy.

Understanding such persistent differences, while also accounting for the emerging similarities evidenced across multinational corporations, are the subjects of this paper. Specifically, do the foreign investment and related trade strategies implemented by US, European, and Japanese multinationals systematically differ? Or have these multinationals in roughly equal measure contributed to the historical transformation of the international political economy? In sum, then, this paper seeks to add to an ongoing debate relevant to both public policy and corporate strategy, a debate focusing on a single overarching question: does ownership matter?[9]

MAJORITY SUBSIDIARIES *V.* MINORITY AFFILIATES

Multinational corporations have consistently evidenced a strong preference to invest in majority foreign-owned subsidiaries, rather than in minority affiliates of equal-partnership joint ventures. American multinationals, for example, have long reported this preference to the US Commerce Department, beginning with the first post-war census of US FDI abroad. According to that 1957 census, these multinationals owned upwards of three-quarters of the equity invested in their subsidiaries abroad.[10] Such shareholdings were highest across Western Europe and other industrialized countries, and considerably lower across a wide range of developing

---

[5] For an early analysis of the relationship between trade policies and FDI, see G. Reuber *et al.*, *Foreign Private Investment in Development* (Oxford: Oxford University Press for the Organization of Economic Cooperation and Development, 1973), especially pp. 120–32; for a more recent analysis, see S. Guisinger *et al.*, *Investment Incentives and Performance Requirements: Patterns of International Trade, Production and Investment* (New York: Praeger, 1985), esp. 48–54.

[6] For a recent study of location-specific advantages, see M. Porter, *The Competitive Advantage of Nations* (New York: Free Press, 1990).

[7] For the impact of such 'buyer power', see M. Porter, *Competitive Strategy: Techniques for Analyzing Industries and Competitors* (New York: Free Press, 1980).

[8] Julius, *Global Companies and Public Policy*, 88–91.

[9] This question has most recently been raised (and then answered, in part) by R. Reich, 'Who Is Us?', *Harvard Business Review*, 68 (Jan.–Feb. 1990), 53–64; and 'Who Is They?', *Harvard Business Review*, 69 (Mar.–Apr. 1991), 77–88.

[10] US Commerce Dept., Office of Business Economics, *U.S. Business Investments in Foreign Countries: A Supplement to the Survey of Current Business* (Washington: USGPO, 1960), table 20, p. 108; hereafter cited as Commerce Dept., *US FDI, 1957 Survey*.

countries. For the Americans, this strong preference for majority share-holdings remained phenomenally stable over the next three decades,[11] even as fresh outflows of US FDI reached their post-war high (during the late 1960s and early 1970s) and then subsequently fell off, to be replaced by reinvested earnings in existing subsidiaries.[12] As a result of these investments, American multinationals consistently reported that their majority-owned subsidiaries contributed between three-quarters (during 1966, in the Commerce Department's first 'benchmark' survey of US FDI[13]) and four-fifths (by 1990, in the Department's most recent annual survey[14]) of total foreign sales recorded by all US affiliates abroad. Thus today, for American multinationals, majority ownership of foreign subsidiaries remains a prominent characteristic of their foreign-investment strategies.

Similarly, majority ownership has become central to the investment strategies of Japanese multinationals. Indeed, for 1990 (again, the most recent year for which data are available), Japanese multinationals reported to Japan's Ministry of International Trade and Industry (MITI) that majority-owned subsidiaries contributed over 85 per cent of their foreign sales.[15] That share—roughly comparable to sales reported by the majority subsidiaries of American multinationals—may possibly be of more recent origin. Indeed, a long-standing consensus among Japanese scholars (all reporting data gathered during the mid-1970s) argues that Japanese investors have been more likely than the Americans to establish abroad minority-owned and equal-partnership joint ventures, occasionally with multiple Japanese partners.[16] These earlier findings, however, may well represent a

---

[11] For example, during 1977, US multinationals reported to the Commerce Department that over 80% of their 'owners' equity' resided in majority US-owned subsidiaries; see US Commerce Dept., Bureau of Economic Analysis, *U.S. Direct Investment Abroad, 1977* (Washington: USGPO, 1981), table II.A.18, p. 123 and Table III.A.18, p. 242; hereafter cited as Commerce Dept., *US FDI, 1977 Benchmark*.

[12] R. Lipsey, 'Changing Patterns of International Investment in and by the United States', in M. Feldstein, ed., *The United States in the World Economy* (Chicago: University of Chicago Press for the National Bureau of Economic Research, 1988), 488–92; D. Goldsbrough, 'Investment Trends and Prospects: The Link with Bank Lending', in T. Moran, ed., *Investing in Development: New Roles for Private Capital?* (Washington, DC: Overseas Development Council, 1986).

[13] US Commerce Dept., Bureau of Economic Analysis, *U.S. Direct Investment Abroad, 1966: Final Data* (Washington: USGPO, 1975), esp. table J-4, p. 167, and table L-1, p. 197; hereafter cited as Commerce Dept., *US FDI, 1966 Benchmark*.

[14] US Commerce Dept., Bureau of Economic Analysis, *U.S. Direct Investment Abroad: Operations of U.S. Parent Companies and their Foreign Affiliates, Preliminary 1990 Estimates* (Washington: USGPO, Nov. 1992), tables II.E.3 and III.E.3, n.p.; hereafter cited as Commerce Dept., *US FDI, 1990 Survey*.

[15] Japan, Ministry of International Trade and Industry, Industrial Policy Bureau, International Business Affairs Division, *The 21st Survey of the Overseas Business Activities of Japanese Enterprises* [*Dai nijyuichi-kai wagakuni kigyo no kaigai jigyo katsudo*] (Tokyo: Ministry of Finance Printing Bureau, 1992), table 9, p. 12; hereafter cited as MITI, *Japanese FDI, 21st Survey*.

[16] This conclusion permeates both the English and Japanese literature on Japanese multinationals; see e.g. R. Wakasugi, *International Trade, Foreign Direct Investment, and Japanese Industrial Organization* [*Boeki-Chokusetsu toshi to nihon no sangyo soshiki*] (Tokyo: Toyo

simple artefact of the specific indicator that scholars examined: the actual number of joint ventures and majority subsidiaries established by Japanese multinationals. Such a measure may overestimate the relative importance of small investments in a large number of minority-owned and equal-partnership joint ventures.[17] However, even by this peculiar measure, at least during 1990, majority Japanese-owned subsidiaries accounted for well over nine out of every ten Japanese affiliates established in either the EC or the USA[18]—and, correlatively, comparable proportions of total sales (see Fig. 6.1). It therefore seems accurate to claim that during the late 1970s, and throughout the 1980s, any earlier differences in patterns of ownership that distinguished US from Japanese subsidiaries abroad had surely withered away.

Yet no similar convergence of ownership patterns in favour of majority subsidiaries is apparent in bilateral investment flows either between Japan and the USA, or between Japan and the EC—in marked contrast to comparable bilateral flows between the USA and EC (see Fig. 6.1). In fact, as a proportion of all sales recorded during 1990 by American multinationals with foreign investments in the EC, majority US subsidiaries accounted for nearly 90 per cent—roughly the same proportion recorded by the majority subsidiaries of EC multinationals operating in the USA. Similarly, in both the USA and Europe, Japanese multinationals also generated nearly 90 per cent of their investment-related sales from majority-owned subsidiaries. But back in Japan, neither the Americans nor the Europeans have ever seen majority subsidiaries generate a comparable global share of foreign sales. On the contrary, as late as 1990, majority US-owned subsidiaries in Japan still generated less than 40 per cent of the sales recorded by all US multinationals there. The remainder, accounting for the bulk of multinational sales in Japan, still came during 1990 from minority US affiliates, even though the relative position of these minority affiliates had actually declined over the previous decade. With such a great preponderance of minority affiliates, in fact, Japan actually has as much in

Keizai Shimposha, 1989), esp. 119–27; R. Komiya, *The Contemporary Japanese Economy* [*Gendai nihon Keizai*] (Tokyo: University of Tokyo Press, 1988), esp. 221–95; S. Sekiguchi, *New Developments in Foreign Investment* [*Kaigai toshi no shintenkai*] (Tokyo: Nihon Keizai Shinbun-sha, 1979); T. Ozawa, *Multinationalism, Japanese Style: The Political Economy of Outward Dependency* (Princeton, NJ: Princeton University Press, 1979), esp. 227–8; K. Kojima, *Direct Foreign Investment: A Japanese Model of Multinational Business Operations* (London: Croom Helm, 1978); M. Yoshino, *Japan's Multinational Enterprises* (Cambridge, Mass.: Harvard University Press, 1976), esp. ch. 5; Y. Tsurumi, *The Japanese are Coming: A Multinational Spread of Japanese Firms* (Cambridge, Mass.: Ballinger, 1976); S. Sekiguchi and M. Matsuba, *Japan's Direct Investment* [*Nihon no chokusetsu toshi*] (Tokyo: Nihon Keizai Shinbun-sha, 1974).

[17] Indeed, by this measure, US multinationals during 1977 (the same year examined in many of the earlier Japanese studies) proved as likely to establish minority US-owned affiliates as they did to invest in majority subsidiaries. Specifically, that year, US multinationals reported direct investments in 11,900 majority US-owned subsidiaries and 11,800 minority US-owned affiliates; see Commerce Dept., *US FDI, 1977 Benchmark*, table D, p. 20.

[18] MITI, *Japanese FDI, 21st Survey*, table 8, p. 11.

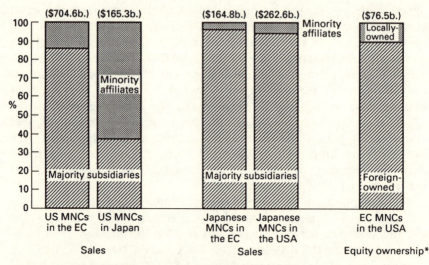

* Equity ownership defined as owners' equity less reinvested earnings; data available only for France, Germany, the Netherlands, and the UK.

Sources: US Commerce Dept., Bureau of Economic Analysis, *U.S. Direct Investment Abroad: Operations of U.S. Parent Companies and their Foreign Affiliates, Preliminary 1990 Estimates* (Washington: USGPO, Sept. 1992), tables II.E.3 and III.E.3, n.p.; and *Foreign Direct Investment in the United States: 1987 Benchmark Survey, Final Results* (Washington, DC: USGPO, Aug. 1990), tables C-3, C-4, C-5, C-7, and C-9, pp. 34–40. Japan, MITI, Industrial Policy Bureau, International Business Affairs Division, *The 21st Survey of the Overseas Business Activities of Japanese Enterprises* [*Dai nijyuichi-kai wagakuni kigyo no kaigai jigyo katsudou*] (Tokyo: Ministry of Finance Printing Bureau, 1992), tables III-2-5-(2) and III-2-5-(9), pp. 66, 70; and *The Fourth Comprehensive Survey of Foreign Investment Statistics* [*Kaigai toshi tokei soran*] (Tokyo: Ministry of Finance Printing Bureau, 1991), table IV-2-22, p. 192, and table IV-4-3, p. 506.

Fig. 6.1. Foreign ownership by US, European, and Japanese multinationals abroad, late 1980s/early 1990s. Data on Japanese MNCs in the USA and EC are for 1989, data on EC MNCs in the USA are for 1987

common with developing India,[19] where the dislodging of multinationals long represented the national strategy,[20] as with industrialized North America or the several countries of the EC. For in no other *advanced* economy do majority foreign-owned subsidiaries continue to occupy such a lowly position as they do in Japan.[21] In sum, this lower incidence of majority foreign subsidiaries in Japan worked to deny US (and, by inference, European)

[19] Commerce Dept., *US FDI, 1990 Survey*, table II.E.3 and table III.E.3, n.p.; in India, majority US-owned subsidiaries accounted for less than 20 per cent of all foreign sales by US multinationals.

[20] See D. Encarnation, *Dislodging Multinationals: India's Strategy in Comparative Perspective* (Ithaca, NY: Cornell University Press, Cornell Series in Political Economy, 1989).

[21] To illustrate: in Germany, as well as in Canada, the UK, and France—each with economies less than half Japan's size—majority US subsidiaries recorded larger dollar sales than they did in Japan; see *US FDI, 1990 Survey*, table III.E.3, n.p.

multinationals the same access that they enjoyed in each other's market—and that the Japanese came to enjoy in both the USA and Europe.

FOREIGN SALES V. INTERNATIONAL TRADE

After securing majority ownership and managerial control, multinational corporations typically use their overseas subsidiaries to sell in foreign markets far more than they and other exporters back home ship to these same markets. For the Americans, at least, the predominance of foreign sales over international trade is *not new*, although some analysts have only recently discovered it.[22] Indeed, as early as 1957, the overseas (largely majority US-owned) subsidiaries of American multinationals reported foreign sales at twice the value of US exports.[23] A decade later, by 1966, the foreign sales of these majority US-owned subsidiaries had risen to represent three times the value of all US exports.[24] Subsequently, that 3 : 1 ratio of foreign sales to international trade has remained largely unaltered. In fact, during 1990, American multinationals continued to sell just over three times as much overseas through their majority subsidiaries than the USA exported to the world[25]—further testimony to the fact that US FDI continues to carry international competition well beyond cross-border trade.

For the Americans, however, the relative mix of overseas sales generated either by foreign investment or international trade varies widely across regions. Here, Europe and Japan offer sharply contrasting examples (see Fig. 6.2). At one extreme lies the EC Community, where majority US-owned subsidiaries during 1990 sold well over six times more than did US-based exporters; at the other extreme lies Japan, where US-owned subsidiaries suffered from roughly the same, limited market access afforded to US-based exporters. Indeed, in both regions, the ratio of foreign sales to international trade—6 : 1 in the EC, 1 : 1 in Japan—has remained quite stable over time, dating back at least to the mid-1960s.[26] By then, at least in Europe, several factors combined to attract the foreign investments of US multinationals: the erection of common barriers to EC imports from

[22] For example, S. Strange asserts that in the 'evolution of international business...the mid-1980s were a milestone as the volume of international production for the *first time* exceeded the volume of international trade' (italics added). See ead., 'The Name of the Game', in N. Rizopoulos, ed., *Sea-Changes: American Foreign Policy in a World Transformed* (New York: Council on Foreign Relations Press, 1991), 242.

[23] For sales data, see Commerce Dept., *US FDI, 1957 Survey*, table 22, p. 110; for trade data, see US Commerce Dept., Bureau of International Commerce, 'United States Trade with Major World Areas, 1955 and 1956', *Overseas Business Reports* (May 1957), 2, 8.

[24] For sales data, see Commerce Dept., *US FDI, 1966 Benchmark*, table L-2, p. 198; for trade data, see US Commerce Dept., Bureau of International Commerce, 'United States Trade with Major World Areas, 1965 and 1966', *Overseas Business Reports* (May 1967), 3, 12.

[25] For sales data, see Commerce Dept., *US FDI, 1990 Survey*, table III.E.3, n.p.; for trade data, see US Commerce Dept., International Trade Administration, *US Foreign Trade Highlights: 1991* (Washington, DC: USGPO, May 1992), table 2, p. 11.

[26] For data, see n. 24 above.

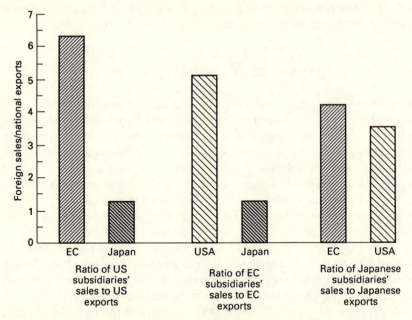

Sources: US Commerce Dept., Bureau of Economic Analysis, *U.S. Direct Investment Abroad: Operations of U.S. Parent Companies and their Foreign Affiliates, Preliminary 1990 Estimates* (Washington: USGPO, Sept. 1992), table III.E.3, n.p.; and *Foreign Direct Investment in the United States: Operations of US Affiliates of Foreign Companies, Preliminary 1990 Estimates* (Washington: USGPO, Aug. 1992), table E-4, n.p.; and International Trade Administration, Office of Trade and Investment Analysis, *US Foreign Trade Highlights: 1991* (Washington, DC: USGPO, May 1992), table 2, p. 11; Japan, MITI, Industrial Policy Bureau, International Business Affairs Division, *The 21st Survey of the Overseas Business Activities of Japanese Enterprises* [*Dai nijyuichi-kai wagakuni kigyo no kaigai jigyo katsudou*] (Tokyo: Ministry of Finance Printing Bureau, 1992), table III.2.12, pp. 78–9, 86–7; and *The 25th Survey of Business Activities of Foreign Enterprises in Japan* [*Dai nijyugo-kai gaishikei kigyo no dookoo*] (Tokyo: Ministry of Finance Printing Bureau, 1992), table 24-4, pp. 77–87; International Monetary Fund, *Direction of Trade Statistics Yearbook: 1992* (Washington, DC: IMF, 1992), table 158, p. 240.

Fig. 6.2. The ratio of foreign sales by majority subsidiaries to national exports: USA, EC, and Japan, 1990

the USA, the reduction of comparable barriers to internal EC trade, and the exertion of formidable pressures by both strong EC buyers and powerful EC competitors. By contrast, in Japan, import protection combined with capital controls both to limit overall FDI inflows and to concentrate those inflows in minority foreign-owned affiliates. This legacy changed little with trade and capital liberalization: by then, as US FDI flows worldwide began to taper off, Japanese industrial organization replaced Japanese government policies as the principal barriers to market access in Japan.[27] Consequently,

---

[27] D. Encarnation and M. Mason, 'Neither MITI nor America: The Political Economy of Capital Liberalization in Japan', *International Organization* (Winter 1990), 29–54.

the same foreign-investment and related trade strategies implemented successfully by the Americans in Europe continued to flounder in Japan.

By comparison, the evolution of European multinationals eventually mirrored that of their US counterparts (see Fig. 6.2). In Japan, the Europeans encountered the same entry barriers already experienced by the Americans, and thus also reported during 1990 low levels of foreign sales to match their limited exports. By contrast, in the USA, European subsidiaries recorded nearly the same level of foreign sales enjoyed by US subsidiaries in Europe. But their success would lag behind that of the Americans. By 1974, for example, European subsidiaries sold three times more in the USA than did European-based exporters; this 3 : 1 ratio for the Europeans fell far short of the 6 : 1 ratio of foreign sales to international trade enjoyed at that time by the Americans in Europe.[28] However, over the next two decades, the Europeans erased this difference, so that by 1990 EC subsidiaries in the USA actually reported US sales five times larger than US imports from Europe (see Fig. 6.2). Thus, quite recently, the Europeans in the USA and the Americans in the European Community have achieved a rough parity in the strategic mix of both foreign investment and international trade they employ to secure access to each other's market.

Similarly, Japanese corporations have also come to generate more of their overseas sales through foreign investment rather than through international trade. But for the Japanese, this evolution is of very recent origin, reflecting their prolonged status as traders rather than investors. In fact, as late as 1977, Japanese subsidiaries reported total foreign sales to be roughly equivalent to Japanese exports worldwide.[29] But by 1990, following a decade of rapid growth in Japanese FDI abroad, Japanese subsidiaries (most of which were majority Japanese-owned) reported foreign sales two-and-a-half times larger than all Japanese exports worldwide.[30] This ratio proved even larger in both the USA and the EC where during 1990 Japanese subsidiaries sold four times more than did Japanese exporters (see Fig. 6.2). Thus, in both the USA and the EC, the Japanese have come to pursue the same foreign-investment strategies that have continued to elude the Americans and Europeans in Japan—strategies which elsewhere

[28] For sales data, see US Commerce Dept., Bureau of Economic Analysis, *Foreign Direct Investment in the United States, ii. Report of the Secretary of Commerce, Benchmark Survey, 1974* (Washington, DC: USGPO, April 1976), table K-5, p. 139; for trade data, see US Dept. of Commerce, International Trade Administration, Office of Trade and Investment Analysis, *US Foreign Trade Highlights* (Washington, DC: USGPO, various years).

[29] During 1977, when Japanese exports to the world totalled $85 billion, Japanese affiliates abroad reported foreign sales of roughly $85 billion (or 22.8 trillion yen). For sales data, see Japan, MITI, Industrial Policy Bureau, *The 8th Survey of the Overseas Business Activities of Japanese Enterprises [Dai hachi-kai wagakuni kigyo no kaigai jigyo katsudo]* (Tokyo: MITI, 1979), table 51, p. 54; hereafter cited as MITI, *Japanese FDI, 8th Survey*. For trade data, see International Monetary Fund, *International Trade Statistics Yearbook: 1980* (Washington, DC: IMF, 1981), 243.

[30] For sales data, see MITI, *Japanese FDI, 21st Survey*, table 2-12, pp. 88–9; for trade data, see International Monetary Fund, *Direction of Trade Statistics Yearbook: 1992* (Washington, DC: IMF, 1992), 158.

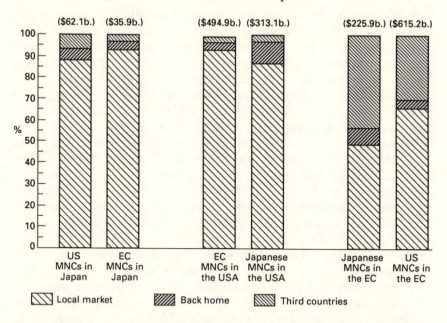

Sources: US Commerce Dept., Bureau of Economic Analysis, *U.S. Direct Investment Abroad: Operations of U.S. Parent Companies and their Foreign Affiliates, Preliminary 1990 Estimates* (Washington: USGPO, Sept. 1992), table III.F.2, n.p.; and *Foreign Direct Investment in the United States: Operations of US Affiliates of Foreign Companies, Preliminary 1990 Estimates* (Washington: USGPO, Aug. 1992), tables E-4 and G-2, n.p.; and *Foreign Direct Investment in the United States: 1987 Benchmark Survey, Final Results* (Washington, DC: USGPO, Aug. 1990), tables G-2 and G-24, pp. 120, 142. Japan, MITI, Industrial Policy Bureau, International Business Affairs Division, *The 21st Survey of the Overseas Business Activities of Japanese Enterprises* [*Dai nijyuichi-kai wagakuni kigyo no kaigai jigyo katsudou*] (Tokyo: Ministry of Finance Printing Bureau, 1992), table III.2.12, pp. 86–7; and *The 25th Survey of Business Activities of Foreign Enterprises in Japan* [*Dai nijyugo-kai gaishikei kigyo no dookoo*] (Tokyo: Ministry of Finance Printing Bureau, 1992), tables 24-4 and 29-1, pp. 80, 99.

Fig. 6.3. Destination of sales by US, European, and Japanese subsidiaries abroad, 1990. Exports back home and to third countries by both EC and Japanese MNCs operating in the USA are estimated for 1990 using 1987 data

in the world have proved so successful first for US, then for European, and now for Japanese multinationals.

LOCAL *V.* EXPORT MARKETS

Multinational corporations continue to generate most foreign sales in those local markets hosting their majority subsidiaries (see Fig. 6.3). What has changed over time, however, is the relative importance of that host-country market. Let us compare the evolution of US and Japanese multinationals. For the Americans, beginning as early as 1957 (in the first post-war survey of US FDI) and continuing for at least another decade, local markets in host countries accounted for three-quarters of all foreign sales generated by majority US subsidiaries.[31] However, beginning by the late 1970s and through the 1980s, the contribution of host markets to the worldwide revenues of majority US subsidiaries gradually declined, so that by 1990 that contribution reaches two-thirds of total foreign sales.[32] Japanese subsidiaries evidenced a similar reduction between the early 1970s (when local markets also contributed three-quarters of total foreign sales) and the early 1990s (when that sales share dropped to three-fifths).[33] While moving at different paces, then, both US and Japanese multinationals again evolved in a common direction, by pursuing similar global strategies.

Leading that decline in local sales were US and Japanese subsidiaries operating in the EC (see Fig. 6.3). There, exports to third countries, mostly other EC members, contributed nearly 30 per cent of the total sales recorded by US subsidiaries; for Japanese subsidiaries, that share was even higher, exceeding 40 per cent of their total EC sales. Worldwide, by comparison, both US and Japanese subsidiaries sold just over 20 per cent of total foreign sales in third-country markets.[34] Smaller still were third-country exports (roughly 6 per cent of all foreign sales) recorded both by American subsidiaries in Japan and Japanese subsidiaries in America.[35] In short, when American and Japanese multinationals invested in each other's home markets, their subsidiaries concentrated principally on local sales. These accounted for nearly 90 per cent of US subsidiaries' sales in Japan, and nearly 80 per cent of Japanese subsidiaries' sales in the USA (see Fig. 6.3). Similarly, EC subsidiaries in both Japan and the USA report that these local markets generate over 90 per cent of their total sales. Like the Americans in Japan and the Japanese in America, then, European multinationals operating in the world's two most advanced economies have also come to pursue comparable global strategies.

What remains of foreign sales, after subtracting those destined for host- and third-country markets, are largely shipped back home. Over the post-war period, exports back to the home market have either doubled (for the Americans) or tripled (for the Japanese) their relative contribution to total sales by foreign subsidiaries.[36] More generally, worldwide, exports back home account for anywhere between one-tenth (for the Americans) and one-sixth (for the Japanese) of total foreign sales by multinationals based

[31] Commerce Dept., *US FDI, 1957 Survey*, table 22, p. 110; Commerce Dept., *US FDI, 1966 Benchmark*, table L-1, p. 197.

[32] Commerce Dept., *US FDI, 1977 Benchmark*, table II.H.1, p. 318; Commerce Dept., *US FDI, 1988 Survey*, table 34, n.p.; Commerce Dept., *US FDI, 1990 Survey*, table III.F.2, n.p.

[33] For 1971, see Japan, MITI, Industrial Policy Bureau, *Overseas Business Activities of Japanese Enterprises: Current Situation and Problems* [*Wagakuni kigyo no kaigai jigyo katsudo: sono gendai to mondaiten*] (Tokyo: MITI, 1973), table 4-2-2, pp. 86–7. For 1988, see MITI, *Japanese FDI, 19th Survey*, 82–3. For 1990, see MITI, *Japanese FDI, 21st Survey*, 88–9.

[34] MITI, *21st Overseas Survey*, 78–9, 88–9; Commerce Dept., *US FDI: 1990 Annual Survey*, table III.F.2, n.p.   [35] Ibid.

[36] For the Americans, see nn. 31 and 32 above; for the Japanese, see n. 33 above.

in these two countries.[37] Such differences in export performance have led at least one important school of Japanese scholars to argue that Japanese multinationals pursue investment strategies that are far more trade-enhancing than those favoured by US multinationals.[38] But this conclusion ignores some equally strong commonalities: when confronted with political and economic pressures toward ever-more regional integration (as in the EC), or with the escalating demands of a burgeoning local market (as in the USA and Japan), US, European, and Japanese multinationals respond in strikingly similar fashion.

OFFSHORE PRODUCTION *V.* OVERSEAS DISTRIBUTION

Multinational corporations often invest in majority subsidiaries that produce offshore many of the goods and services that are then supplied to markets abroad and back home. Quick to respond to the pressures for offshore production have been the Americans: at least as early as 1957, and continuing beyond the next three decades, US subsidiaries engaged in overseas manufacturing reported foreign sales to be double the value of US-manufactured exports.[39] The Americans concentrated most of this foreign production in advanced markets, especially the EC, where during 1990 majority US-owned manufacturing subsidiaries generated sales nearly five times larger than US-based manufacturers exported to the EC (see Fig. 6.4). By contrast, Japan actually invites comparisons not with other industrialized countries, but with developing economies: for in these economies, as in Japan, the ratio of offshore production by foreign subsidiaries to international trade barely approaches 1 : 1.[40] In Japan, then, US multinationals failed to implement a strategy of offshore production that has served them well in the EC and other industrialized countries.

---

[37] For the Japanese, see MITI, *Japanese FDI, 21st Overseas Survey*, 88–9; for the Americans, see Commerce Dept., *US FDI, 1990 Survey*, table III.F.2, n.p.

[38] This school of thought owes its origins to the work of K. Kojima; see his 'Japanese Direct Investment Abroad' (Monograph Series 1, Social Science Research Institute, International Christian University, Tokyo, 1990); (with T. Ozawa), 'Japanese-Style Direct Foreign Investment', *Japanese Economic Studies* (Spring 1986), 52–82; 'Japanese and American Direct Investment in Asia: A Comparative Analysis', *Hitotsubashi Journal of Economics* (June 1985), 1–35; *Japan's Foreign Direct Investment* [*Nihon no kaigai chokusetsu toshi*] (Tokyo: Bunshindo, 1985), esp. 6–14; *Foreign Direct Investment* [*Kaigai chokusetsu toshi ron*] (Tokyo: Daiyamondo-sha, 1979); *Direct Foreign Investment: A Japanese Model of Multinational Business Operations* (London: Croom Helm, 1978); 'Transfer of Technology to Developing Countries: Japanese Type Versus American Type', *Hitotsubashi Journal of Economics* (Feb. 1977), 1–14; 'A Macroeconomic Approach to Foreign Direct Investment', *Hitotsubashi Journal of Economics* (June 1973), 1–21.

[39] For sales data, see the following Commerce Department publications: *1957 Survey*, table 22, p. 110; *US FDI, 1966 Benchmark*, table L-3, p. 199; *1977 Benchmark*, table II.H.1, p. 318; *US FDI, 1988 Survey*, table 34, n.p.; *US FDI, 1990 Survey*, table III.F.2, n.p. For trade data, see Commerce Dept., 'International Business Indicators', *Overseas Business Reports* (Jan. 1973), table 5, p. 14; *US Foreign Trade Highlights* (various years).

[40] For Japan, see Fig. 6.2 above. For economically less developed countries, see Commerce Dept., *US FDI, 1990 Survey*, tables II.E.3 and III.E.3, n.p.; and *US Foreign Trade Highlights: 1991*, table 10, p. 28.

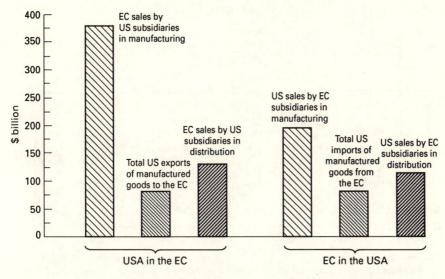

Sources: US Commerce Dept., Bureau of Economic analysis, *U.S. Direct Investment Abroad: Operations of U.S. Parent Companies and their Foreign Affiliates, Preliminary 1990 Estimates* (Washington: USGPO, Sept. 1990), table II.E.3, n.p.; and *Foreign Direct Investment in the United States: Operations of US Affiliates of Foreign Companies, Preliminary 1990 Estimates* (Washington: USGPO, Aug. 1992), table E-4, n.p.; and International Trade Administration, Office of Trade and Investment Analysis, *US Foreign Trade Highlights: 1991* (Washington, DC: USGPO, May 1992), tables 10 and 11, pp. 28, 32.

Fig. 6.4. Bilateral production, trade, and distribution: USA *v.* EC, 1990

By comparison, offshore production by European multinationals has slowly evolved to mirror that of the Americans. In Japan, for example, the Europeans evidenced the same low level of local production to match their limited exports there (see Fig. 6.2). Such low levels also characterize European multinationals operating in the USA for much of the post-war period: in fact, as recently as 1974, those European subsidiaries engaged specifically in US manufacturing recorded sales roughly equal to US imports of European manufactured goods.[41] When we add to this figure the estimated value of additional assembly operations by European subsidiaries engaged principally in US wholesaling, the total value of local production probably does exceed all US imports from Europe. Still, such offshore manufacturing remained well below comparable production by US subsidiaries in Europe. However, over the next two decades, the Europeans moved to cut this difference in half, so that by 1990 their manufacturing subsidiaries in the USA actually reported US sales nearly three times

[41] US Commerce Dept., Bureau of Economic Analysis, *Foreign Direct Investment in the United States, ii. Report of the Secretary of Commerce, Benchmark Survey, 1974* (Washington, DC: USGPO, Apr. 1976), table K-5, p. 139; US Dept. of Commerce, International Trade Administration, Office of Trade and Investment Analysis, *US Foreign Trade Highlights* (Washington, DC: USGPO, various years).

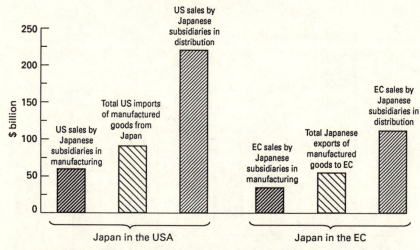

Sources: US Commerce Dept., Bureau of Economic Analysis, *Foreign Direct Investment in the United States: Operations of US Affiliates of Foreign Companies, Preliminary 1990 Estimates* (Washington: USGPO, Aug. 1992), table E-4, n.p.; and International Trade Administration, Office of Trade and Investment Analysis, *US Foreign Trade Highlights: 1991* (Washington, DC: USGPO, May 1992), table 11, p. 32. Japan, MITI, Industrial Policy Bureau, International Business Affairs Division, *The 21st Survey of the Overseas Business Activities of Japanese Enterprises* [*Dai nijyuichi-kai wagakuni kigyo no kaigai jigyo katsudou*] (Tokyo: Ministry of Finance Printing Bureau, 1992), table III.2.12, pp. 86–7; International Monetary Fund, *Direction of Trade Statistics Yearbook: 1992* (Washington, DC: IMF, 1992), table 158, p. 240.

Fig. 6.5. Japanese production, trade, and distribution in the USA and the EC, 1990

larger than US imports of European manufactured goods (see Fig. 6.4). As a result, both US and European multinationals have generally managed to produce and sell many more manufactured goods in each other's home market than they and other national exporters shipped across the Atlantic.

From across the Pacific, however, the Japanese have continued to pursue a very different offshore-manufacturing strategy, one that still lags behind Japanese exports of manufactured goods. As recently as 1990, for example, foreign sales resulting from offshore production by Japanese subsidiaries worldwide were two-thirds the total value of Japanese manufactured exports.[42] Such a ratio of local production to foreign trade remained quite consistent across Japan's two largest export markets, the USA and Europe (see Fig. 6.5). Even when we add to these local sales the assembly operations of Japanese subsidiaries engaged principally in overseas distribution, the total value of Japanese production in the USA and Europe still barely equals US and European imports of manufactured goods from Japan.

[42] MITI, *Japanese FDI, 21th Survey*, table III-2-12, pp. 88–9; IMF, *Direction of Trade Statistics: 1992*, table 158, p. 240.

For the Japanese, however, this low ratio of foreign production to international trade actually represented a significant increase in offshore manufacturing. Indeed, just over a decade earlier (in 1977), Japanese manufacturers had reported exports from home four times larger than the worldwide production recorded by Japanese subsidiaries abroad.[43] Yet, even after such growth, these Japanese subsidiaries still shared much in common with US and European multinationals operating in Japan and in a wide range of developing countries—but not in other industrialized countries. That is, for the Japanese, offshore production competed almost evenly with international trade as a source of foreign sales.

Far more central to the foreign-investment strategies of Japanese multinationals has been the establishment of majority subsidiaries engaged in overseas distribution (see Fig. 6.5). These subsidiaries establish dedicated sales and service networks for shipments between their parents back home and affiliated subsidiaries abroad.[44] During 1990, such intra-company shipments accounted for over 40 per cent of all Japanese exports worldwide.[45] That contribution is higher still for Japanese exports to both the USA and Europe, where over 60 per cent of all such trade enters through Japanese subsidiaries principally engaged in either US or EC wholesaling.[46] For the Japanese, then, wholesaling subsidiaries have become a foreign extension of their own national industrial organization—for back home, the parents of Japanese multinationals also tightly control their own proprietary distribution systems.[47]

Moreover, in Japan, local control over distribution channels severely constrains a foreigner's market access.[48] Seeking to overcome such entry

---

[43] For sales data, see MITI, *Japanese FDI, 8th Survey*, table 51, p. 54; for trade data, see IMF, *Direction of Trade Statistics Yearbook: 1980*, p. 242. Specifically, in the USA, 1974 estimates of Japanese manufactured exports ranged as high as ten times the value of local production.

[44] For evidence, see D. Encarnation, 'Cross-Investment', in T. McCraw, *America versus Japan* (Boston: Harvard Business School Press, 1986), table 4-2 and 4-3, pp. 120, 126; and 'American–Japanese Cross-Investment', in S. Haggard and C. Moon, eds., *Pacific Dynamics: The International Politics of Industrial Change* (Boulder: Westview Press, 1989), tables 8.2 and 8.4, pp. 212, 232. Also see H. Yamawaki, 'Exports and Direct Investment in Distribution: Evidence on Japanese Firms in the United States' (Discussion Paper FS 111, Wissenschaftszentrum, Berlin, n.d.).

[45] For sales data, see MITI, *Japanese FDI, 21st Survey*, pp. 104–5; for trade data, see IMF, *Direction of Trade Statistics Yearbook: 1992*, table 158, p. 240.

[46] For sales data, see US Commerce Dept., Bureau of Economic Analysis, *Foreign Direct Investment in the United States: Operations of US Affiliates of Foreign Companies, Preliminary 1990 Estimates* (Washington: USGPO, Aug. 1992), tables E-4, G-2, n.p.; for trade data, see Commerce Dept., *US Foreign Trade Highlights: 1991*, table 11, p. 32.

[47] For an early survey of these barriers see M. Yoshino, *The Japanese Marketing System: Adaptations and Innovations* (Cambridge, Mass.: MIT Press, 1971); for more recent surveys, see the following chapters in P. Krugman, ed., *The US and Japan: Trade and Investment* (Cambridge, Mass.: MIT Press for the National Bureau of Economic Research, 1992): M. Itoh, 'The Japanese Distribution System and Access to the Japanese Market', and T. Ito and M. Maruyama, 'Is the Japanese Distribution System Really Inefficient?'.

[48] This subject has attracted much recent attention among scholars and policymakers; see e.g. R. Lawrence, 'Efficient or Exclusionist? The Import Behavior of Japanese Corporate Groups' (paper prepared for the Brookings Panel on Economic Activity, 4–5 Apr. 1991).

barriers, US and European multinationals have aggressively invested in majority subsidiaries engaged principally in Japanese distribution; in this way, they have pursued an unusual strategy, one without parallel for either Americans or Europeans operating in other industrialized countries. Through their marketing subsidiaries, for example, US multinationals during 1990 sold roughly 10 per cent of all US exports to Japan, twice the trade contribution of those US subsidiaries manufacturing in Japan.[49] EC subsidiaries in Japanese wholesaling have also reported a similar share.[50] Outside Japan, however, majority US subsidiaries engaged principally in foreign manufacturing—and not marketing—actually serve as more important final markets and intermediary channels for US and EC exports. To illustrate: during 1990, these manufacturing subsidiaries bought roughly 15 per cent of all US exports, twice the global share sold through US marketing subsidiaries.[51] By comparison, then, the establishment of wholesaling subsidiaries in Japan by US and European multinationals represents a significant adaptation to the peculiarities of the local Japanese market.

In addition to downstream marketing of home-country exports, wholesaling subsidiaries also increase foreign sales, by serving as upstream sources of overseas supplies. Specifically, these subsidiaries often serve as purchasing agents, both for their parents back home and for affiliated subsidiaries in third countries. Of particular significance to American multinationals have been those US wholesaling subsidiaries which supply third-country markets—especially those in Europe, where affiliated subsidiaries were among their major buyers.[52] Otherwise, for the Americans, wholesaling subsidiaries have proved to be of little value as purchasing agents for shipments back home, supplying less than 2 per cent of all US imports during 1990.[53] However, for the Japanese, wholesaling subsidiaries represent much more important sources of shipments back home. These Japanese subsidiaries reported to MITI during 1990 that they had supplied nearly 50 per cent of all Japanese imports worldwide—and the figure was higher still (roughly 80 per cent) for Japanese imports from America.[54]

[49] For sales data, see Commerce Dept., *US FDI: 1990 Annual Survey*, table III.H.5, n.p.; for trade data, Commerce Dept., *US Foreign Trade Highlights: 1991*, table 2, p. 11.

[50] For trade data, see IMF, *Direction of Trade Statistics: 1992*, table 158, p. 240. For sales data, see Japan, MITI, Industrial Policy Bureau, International Business Affairs Division, *The 25th Survey of Business Activities of Foreign Enterprises in Japan* [*Dai nijyugo-kai gaishikei kigyo no doko*] (Tokyo: Ministry of Finance Printing Bureau, 1992), table 24-4, p. 80; hereafter cited as MITI, *FDI in Japan, 25th Survey*.

[51] For sales data, see Commerce Dept., *US FDI, 1990 Survey*, III.H.5, n.p.; for trade data, see Commerce Dept., *US Foreign Trade Highlights: 1991*, table 2, p. 11.

[52] For intra-company trade within Europe, the most recent data are for 1989; see US Commerce Dept., Bureau of Economic Analysis, *U.S. Direct Investment Abroad: 1989 Benchmark Survey, Final Results* (Washington, DC: USGPO, Oct. 1992), Tables III.F.10 and III.F.11, pp. 198–9. For third-country sales during 1990, see Commerce Dept., *US FDI: 1990 Annual Survey*, tables III.F.8, n.p.

[53] For sales data, see Commerce Dept., *US FDI, 1990 Survey*, table II.H.22, n.p.; for trade data, see Commerce Dept., *US Foreign Trade Highlights: 1991*, table 3, p. 15.

[54] For sales date, see MITI, *21st Overseas Survey*, table 2-12, pp. 78–9, 88–9; for trade data, see IMF, *Direction of Trade Statistics: 1992*, table 158, p. 240.

These imports consisted largely of agricultural products, metals, and other raw materials—all of which remained in short supply in Japan but were plentiful in the USA. So, in marked contrast to the Americans, the Japanese (especially trading companies) invested far more aggressively in wholesaling subsidiaries in order to ensure the security of imported supplies.

INTRA-COMPANY SHIPMENTS *V*. ARM'S-LENGTH TRADE

Much of the trade conducted by multinational corporations is shipped intra-company, among and between parents and their subsidiaries—a fact only recently recognized by academic scholars.[55] During 1990, for example, majority US subsidiaries operating in either Europe of Japan purchased over 85 per cent of their US inputs from their American parents who, in turn, bought comparable shares of their subsidiaries' shipments back to the USA.[56] Similarly, in the USA, Japanese subsidiaries followed a parallel strategy of intra-company trade: during 1990, they purchased over 80 per cent of their US imports from their parents back home, to whom they shipped nearly 60 per cent of their US exports.[57] By comparison, European subsidiaries remained somewhat less dependent on intra-company trade, which accounted for over 60 per cent of their US imports from the EC, but only one-quarter of their US exports to the EC.[58] What limited data exists outside the USA only confirms the singular importance of shipments between multinational parents and their overseas subsidiaries.[59] So it seems that US, European, and Japanese multinationals have all come to pursue markedly similar global strategies; this time the results are measured in terms of the intra-company trade resulting from foreign investment.

Largely because of such intra-company trade, foreign investment exerts an impressive influence on international trade. Nowhere is this more apparent than in Japan's bilateral relations with both the EC and the USA (see Figs. 6.6 and 6.7). In both markets, at least 60 per cent of all national imports from Japan (nearly all manufactured goods) are shipped intra-company, largely from the parents of Japanese multinationals to their (principally majority) subsidiaries in the USA and Europe. These same Japanese subsidiaries are also the principal buyers of what little remains

---

[55] See e.g. Encarnation, *Rivals beyond Trade*, esp. 26–31, 190–7; L. Sleuwaegen and H. Yamawaki, 'Foreign Direct Investment and Intra-Firm Trade: Evidence from Japan' (Discussion Paper No. 9002/G, Institute for Economic Research, Erasmus University (Rotterdam), n.d.).

[56] Commerce Dept., *US FDI, 1990 Survey*, tables III.H.5, III.H.9, III.H.22, III.H.26, n.p.

[57] Commerce Dept., *FDI in the US, 1990 Survey*, table G-2, n.p.

[58] Ibid.

[59] For 1989 (the most recent year for which data are available), Japanese affiliates abroad reported that they purchased over 70% of their Japanese inputs from their Japanese parents who, in turn, bought at least 40% of their affiliates' shipments back to Japan; see Japan, MITI, International Business Affairs Division, *The Fourth Comprehensive Survey of Foreign Investment Statistics* [*Kaigai toshi tokei soran*] (Tokyo: Ministry of Finance Printing Bureau, 1991), table IV-2-27-(12), p. 229, and table IV-2-28-(12), p. 235.

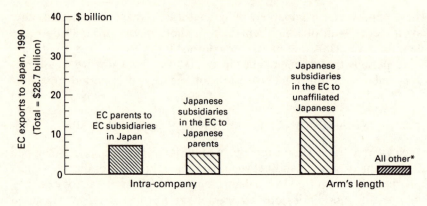

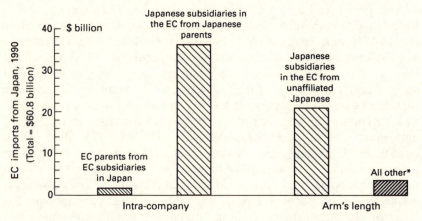

* Includes negligible sums shipped between EC subsidiaries in Japan and unaffiliated EC companies.

Sources: Japan, MITI, Industrial Policy Bureau, International Business Affairs Division, *The 21st Survey of the Overseas Business Activities of Japanese Enterprises* [*Dai nijyuichi-kai wagakuni kigyo no kaigai jigyo katsudou*] (Tokyo: Ministry of Finance Printing Bureau, 1992), table III.2.12 and III.2.14, pp. 86–7, 102–3; and *The Fourth Comprehensive Survey of Foreign Investment Statistics* [*Kaigai toshi tokei soran*] (Tokyo: Ministry of Finance Printing Bureau, 1991), table IV-2-27-(9), p. 228, and table IV-2-28-(9), p. 234; and *The 25th Survey of Business Activities of Foreign Enterprises in Japan* [*Dai nijyugo-kai gaishikei kigyo no dookoo*] (Tokyo: Ministry of Finance Printing Bureau, 1992), tables 24-(4), 29-(1), 37-(4), and 42-(1), pp. 80, 99, 114, 133; International Monetary Fund, *Direction of Trade Statistics Yearbook: 1992* (Washington, DC: IMF, 1992), table 998, p. 56.

FIG. 6.6. EC trade with Japan: intra-company *v.* arm's-length shipments, 1990. Intra-company trade for Japanese multinationals is estimated for 1990 using 1989 data

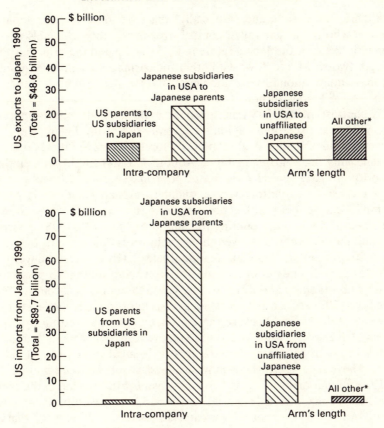

* Includes negligible sums shipped between US subsidiaries in Japan and unaffiliated US companies.

Sources: US Commerce Dept., Bureau of Economic Analysis, *U.S. Direct Investment Abroad: Operations of U.S. Parent Companies and their Foreign Affiliates, Preliminary 1990 Estimates* (Washington: USGPO, Sept. 1992), table III.H.1, n.p.; and *Foreign Direct Investment in the United States: Operations of US Affiliates of Foreign Companies, Preliminary 1990 Estimates* (Washington: USGPO, Aug. 1992), table G-2, n.p.; and International Trade Administration, Office of Trade and Investment Analysis, *US Foreign Trade Highlights: 1991* (Washington, DC: USGPO, May 1992), tables 2 and 3, pp. 11, 15.

Fig. 6.7. US trade with Japan: intra-company *v.* arm's-length shipments, 1990

of both EC and US imports from Japan, largely arm's-length shipments by Japanese suppliers unaffiliated to their overseas buyers. Looking now at trade in the opposite direction, Japanese subsidiaries again play a pivotal role, accounting for roughly 65 per cent of all US exports to Japan (principally raw materials and agricultural products) and roughly 60 per cent of all EC exports to Japan (a mixture of intermediate and industrial products). Once again, much of this trade is shipped intra-company, from Japanese subsidiaries in Europe and (especially) the USA back to their Japanese parents, who retain unrivalled control over distribution channels in their home market. For the Japanese, then, FDI has created the principal channels for two-way trade flows with other industrialized economies, granting Japanese multinationals unrivalled control over their country's trade with both the USA and Europe.

By contrast, neither US nor European multinationals exercise appreciable influence over their region's bilateral trade with Japan. Here, the concentration of limited FDI in minority foreign-owned affiliates serves as an especially high barrier in Japan to both US and EC exports. Indeed, minority affiliates typically represent poor markets for national exports, even in those host countries where affiliates' sales are relatively large. For example, during 1990, US exports to minority US affiliates worldwide remained negligible—accounting for only 6 per cent of all US exports to US multinationals abroad—even though minority affiliates contributed just under 20 per cent of all US multinational sales.[60] (By contrast, minority US affiliates prove to be better sources of supply, contributing 13 per cent of all US imports shipped during 1990 by US multinationals abroad.[61]) More specifically, Japan has long hosted a disproportionately large share of minority affiliates, and because these affiliates generally refrain from purchasing US exports (while contributing more to US imports), US multinationals in Japan have contributed a relatively small share of this bilateral trade. These same conclusions may also be drawn from more limited data on EC multinationals in Japan.[62] By contrast, for the Japanese, the higher incidence of majority subsidiaries in the USA and Europe has actually granted to Japanese exports far greater access to the US and EC markets than the Americans and Europeans, through their limited investments in minority affiliates, have been able to secure in Japan.

Outside Japan, however, in other industrialized countries, the higher level of FDI and the higher incidence of majority foreign subsidiaries has granted to US and European multinationals much greater access to export markets and to sources of imported supplies. Consider, for example, USA–EC trade (see Fig. 6.8). During 1990, intra-company trade contributed over 50 per cent of all US imports from the EC, and over one-third of total US exports there. Among these US exports, shipments from US parents to their majority subsidiaries in Europe contributed much more than did shipments from EC subsidiaries in the USA back to their parents. Conversely, these EC parents contributed much more to US imports from Europe through shipments to their subsidiaries in the USA than did US multinationals engaged in comparable intra-company trade. What remains of USA–EC trade is shipped at arm's-length, between unaffiliated exporters

---

[60] For US exports to US affiliates abroad, and overall sales data, see Commerce Dept., *US FDI, 1990 Survey*, tables II.E.3, II.H.5, II.H.22, III.E.3, III.H.2, n.p.; for overall US exports, see Commerce Dept., *US Foreign Trade Highlights: 1991*, table 2, p. 11.

[61] Ibid.   [62] MITI, *25th Survey of FDI in Japan*, table 41 (3), p. 133.

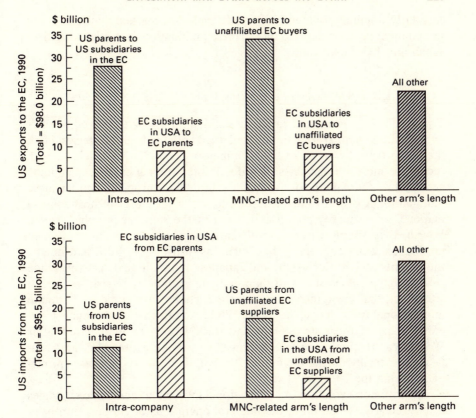

Sources: US Commerce Dept., Bureau of Economic Analysis, *U.S. Direct Investment Abroad: Operations of U.S. Parent Companies and their Foreign Affiliates, Preliminary 1990 Estimates* (Washington: USGPO, Sept. 1992), table III.H.1, n.p.; and *Foreign Direct Investment in the United States: Operations of US Affiliates of Foreign Companies, Preliminary 1990 Estimates* (Washington: USGPO, Aug. 1992), table G-2, n.p.; and *U.S. Direct Investment Abroad: 1989 Benchmark Survey, Final Results* (Washington, DC: USGPO, Oct. 1992), tables II.Q.2 and II.Q.5, pp. 113, 116; and *Foreign Direct Investment in the United States: 1987 Benchmark Survey, Final Results* (Washington, DC: USGPO, Aug. 1990), tables G-24, G-28, G-30, G-34, pp. 142–52; and International Trade Administration, Office of Trade and Investment Analysis, *US Foreign Trade Highlights: 1991* (Washington, DC: USGPO, May 1992), tables 2 and 3, pp. 11, 15.

Fig. 6.8. US trade with the EC: intra-company *v.* arm's-length shipments, 1990. MNC-related arm's-length trade is estimated for 1990 using data from 1989 (for US MNCs) and 1987 (for EC MNCs)

and importers. Here again, FDI plays a major role, with the US parents of US multinationals serving both as major exporters to unaffiliated EC buyers, and as major importers from unaffiliated EC suppliers. This has left all other US-owned enterprises to ship, again through arm's-length trade, roughly 20 per cent of the USA's exports to the EC, and roughly 35 per cent of US imports from the EC. Thus, neither US nor European multinationals singularly dominate bilateral USA–EC trade—in marked contrast to the pre-eminent position enjoyed by Japanese multinationals in bilateral USA–Japan and EC–Japan trade.

CONCLUSIONS: EMERGING SIMILARITIES AND PERSISTENT DIFFERENCES

Today, US, European, and Japanese multinationals have evolved to evidence markedly similar foreign investment and related trade strategies. First, they each typically invest overseas in majority subsidiaries which, second, record far more foreign sales than do all international exporters shipping across either the Atlantic or the Pacific. Third, US, European, and Japanese multinationals concentrate their subsidiaries' sales either in host-country markets, or in nearby countries located in the same geographic region. Fourth, they supply these several markets by increasing their offshore production while deepening their overseas distribution. Fifth and finally, the parents of US, European, and Japanese multinationals actively trade with their manufacturing and marketing subsidiaries overseas—so much so, in fact, that these intra-company transactions have come to dominate international trade across the Triad. While American multinationals pioneered many of these investment and trade strategies immediately after World War II, they were later followed to varying degrees by the Europeans (especially during the mid-1970s) and then by the Japanese (principally during the late 1980s).

This common evolution of multinational investment and trade strategies is most clearly evidenced in the bilateral operations of US and European multinationals. Specifically, in the USA, EC multinationals have finally begun to operate much like US multinationals in the EC. With their bilateral investments concentrated in majority subsidiaries, both US and European multinationals have significantly expanded offshore production in each other's home market. But these US and EC expansions did not occur simultaneously: for the Americans, the value of that production greatly exceeded the value of US exports at least by the 1950s; while for the Europeans, it would take another two decades (into the 1970s) before local US production even exceeded EC exports to the USA. And it would still take two more decades (into the 1990s) before US and European multinationals would approach parity: today, US and EC subsidiaries each sell in the other's home market five times more than either EC or US exporters ship across the Atlantic. Much of this trans-Atlantic trade, moreover, is controlled by US and European multinationals, principally through intra-company shipments between multinational parents and their majority subsidiaries. For US exports to the EC, US parents are the largest suppliers, with US subsidiaries across the Atlantic their largest buyers; conversely, for EC exports to the USA, EC parents are the largest EC-based suppliers, with EC subsidiaries in America their largest US-based buyers. In short, the same foreign investment and related trade strategies implemented successfully by the Americans in Europe have also come to be implemented successfully by the Europeans in the USA.

Moreover, when US and European multinationals do operate outside each other's home market, their investment and trade strategies again evolve in markedly similar ways. In Japan, for example, limited US and EC investments remain concentrated in minority affiliates. What few majority subsidiaries do exist generate just about the same paltry level of Japanese sales as that generated by EC- and US-based exporters. Moreover, many of these US and EC exporters, seeking to overcome high entry to the local Japanese market, have invested aggressively in majority foreign-owned subsidiaries engaged in Japanese distribution. While uncommon elsewhere, such US and EC investments in overseas distribution represent a significant adaptation to the peculiarities of the Japanese market. With that adaptation, US and European multinationals again evidence a strikingly similar response to common host-country conditions.

By comparison with the Americans and Europeans, the historical evolution of Japanese multinationals does evidence some striking similarities, even though important differences do remain. For sure, Japanese multinationals operating in either the US or EC markets have come to pursue many of the same foreign investment and trade strategies denied to both the Americans and the Europeans in Japan, but actively implemented by these foreigners elsewhere in the Triad. Namely, Japanese multinationals have concentrated their investments in majority subsidiaries, which go on to generate far more foreign sales in both the US and EC markets than do Japanese exporters. However, in marked contrast to either the Europeans in the USA or the Americans in Europe, Japanese multinationals still sell in each of those two markets far more manufactured goods through international trade than they do through offshore production. Even after the rapid growth in such production over the past decade, Japanese production in the EC during the early 1990s still lags by at least four decades behind comparable manufacturing by the well-established Americans; while in the USA offshore production by Japanese multinationals continues to lag by at least two decades behind that of their European counterparts.

Rather than relying on offshore production, Japanese multinationals generate most of their US and EC sales from their substantial investments in local distribution. These investments remain much larger than those recorded either by Americans in the EC or Europeans in the USA. Through their proprietary distribution channels, Japanese multinationals go on to exercise unparalleled control over both USA–Japan and EC–Japan trade. Most of this trade is shipped intra-company, between Japanese parents and their majority subsidiaries. Just such asymmetric control over bilateral trade adds credence to the argument that, in the creation and distribution of wealth, ownership can and does matter.[63]

---

[63] For further analysis of both the causes and consequences of persistent asymmetries in foreign investment and related trade, see Encarnation, *Rivals beyond Trade.*

COMMENT

Peter J. Buckley

Encarnation's meticulous study of intra Triad relations (between the USA, Japan, and Europe) has many virtues. One of these virtues is to show the centrality of FDI in cementing international economic relations. FDI is more than just a strategic weapon in a multinational firm's armoury or a choice of a particular foreign market servicing strategy (Buckley and Casson 1976; Buckley and Prescott 1989); it is a manifestation of a serious competitive commitment in an increasingly interdependent global economy. Indeed, in many markets, it is not possible to gain a sizeable market share without commiting investment funds. Increasingly, arm's-length exports to major markets are futile. Selling through agents or distributors does not allow control of the operation nor effective flow-back of information to the principal. In markets such as Japan, the complexity of the distribution system demands a presence, and the necessity for investment increases the costs of effective entry (Buckley, Mirza, and Sparkes 1987). The centrality of direct investment in penetrating foreign markets is illustrated by Fig. 6.9. The growth in outflows of direct investment have outpaced both GDP and domestic investment since the middle of the 1980s.

In itself, presence in a foreign market is not sufficient to ensure success. Achieving the correct form of initial entry to a foreign market is essential, but so is development. Various models of entry and development have been suggested and one such is illustrated as Fig. 6.10, which shows a 'switch' in foreign market servicing strategy at an achieved market size q. The institutional form is also important. Multinational firms have crucial choices to make in terms of ownership strategy (wholly owned subsidiary, majority ownership or minority ownership in joint ventures) and in entry mode (take-over versus greenfield venture). The difficulties of the take-over route in certain host countries, notably Japan but also some Continental European states, increases the difficulty of market penetration by outsiders, particularly in circumstances where the entrant firm is looking for rapid entry.

Ownership strategies, as Encarnation shows, differ across the Triad members. Joint ventures are the most common means of entry into the Japanese market, and there is a lively dispute as to the efficacy of using Japanese joint venture partners, both at home and in Japan. In essence, new entrants to Japan are unlikely to gain a foothold without a local partner. However, such an arrangement is not fixed for all time, and many US and European investors in Japan later increase their ownership share

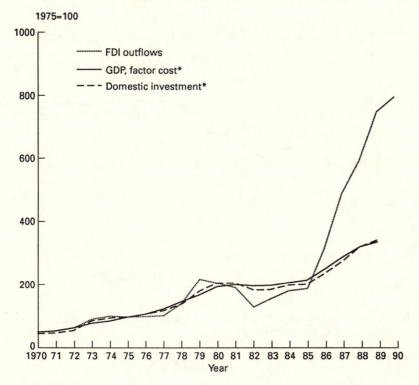

1975=100

* Data for 1989 are preliminary.

Source: Transnational Corporations and Management Division, *World Investment Report 1992: Transnational Corporations as Engines of Growth* (UN publication, sales no. E.92.II.A.19).

Fig. 6.9. FDI, gross domestic product, and domestic investment, 1970–90

of an existing joint venture or add a parallel wholly owned operation, utilizing the accumulated experience gained by the joint venture.

The centrality of FDI is further reinforced by Encarnation's treatment of intra-company transactions. Control over both ends of the trading relationship allows multinationals to set internal transfer prices which can differ from 'arms-length' or market prices. Control of such prices allows the multinational to cross-subsidize units facing high levels of competition, using funds from units which face low levels of competition (including those in markets protected by restricted entry or government restrictions such as tariffs). Consequently, transfer prices are a formidable strategic weapon. In addition, the careful use of transfer prices can reduce a firm's overall tax bill, enabling it to accrue further investable resources. Again

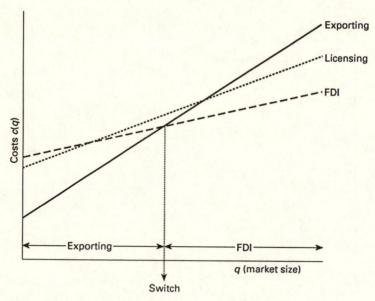

Note that in this example, licensing is never the preferred alternative.
Source: Buckley and Casson 1981: 80.

FIG. 6.10. The timing of FDI: theoretical perspectives

the centrality of FDI as a competitive weapon is apparent. It should further be noted that joint-venture partners may represent a constraint on transfer pricing practices, as they will not wish to lose out from an unfavourable internal pricing regime.

In addition to securing market penetration, FDI is utilized by multinationals to reduce costs. Production might take place in the host country market in which the foreign multinational wishes to sell its output, or it may take place in a third country. There is considerable evidence that such indirect targeting of markets through third country bases is increasing. The use of Canada and Mexico to penetrate the USA, and the use of North Africa, or peripheral European locations (Ireland, Portugal) to penetrate the EC market is growing. Such a strategy is less well suited to the Japanese market, where proximity to the market does not confer easier access. In Japan, presence is everything. However, Japanese multinationals themselves use neighbouring cheaper-labour countries of Asia to reduce costs of production aimed for the Japanese market as well as for the USA and Europe. Japanese multinationals, however, do have an advantage in accessing the Japanese distribution system. Encarnation is right in distinguishing manufacturing from distribution in FDI. It is not always the case that a manufacturing presence is necessary in FDI. Indeed, an optimal global location strategy will often dictate the locational separation of production from distribution. Co-ordination costs then become important and the superior management of co-ordination can confer competitive benefits (Buckley, Pass, and Prescott 1990).

Encarnation's basic thesis is that the Triad members are converging on broadly similar foreign investment and trade strategies. This needs qualification, in terms of the different strategies dictated by the differences in the requirements for success in the key markets as outlined above, in the variances in the institutional arrangements in the major source countries (e.g. the importance of *sogo shosha* in Japanese trade), and in the time dimension of FDI (the recency of Japanese manufacturing entry into the EC compared to the longstanding US involvement, for instance). Overall ownership does matter, and the instrument of that ownership, FDI, is the central feature both of the strategy of the multinational firm and of international economic relations.

REFERENCES

BUCKLEY, P., and CASSON, M. (1976), *The Future of the Multinational Enterprise* (London: Macmillan).

—— and —— (1981), 'The Optimal Timing of a Foreign Direct Investment', *Economic Journal*, 92/361 (Mar.), 70–87.

—— MIRZA, H. and SPARKES, J. (1987), 'Direct Foreign Investment in Japan as a Means of Market Entry: The Case of European Firms', *Journal of Marketing Management*, 2/3 (Mar.), 241–58.

—— PASS, C., and PRESCOTT, K. (1990), 'Foreign Market Servicing by Multinationals: An Integrated Approach', *International Marketing Review*, 7/4, 25–40.

—— and PRESCOTT, K. (1989), 'The Structure of British Industry's Sales in Foreign Markets', *Managerial and Decision Economics*, 10/1 (Sept.), 189–208.

PART III
INDUSTRY STUDIES

7

The Japanese Presence in the European Financial Services Sector

Gabriel Hawawini and
Michael Schill

1. INTRODUCTION

From the mid-1980s onwards, Japanese financial institutions have emerged as a dominant force in the global economy and have assumed a decisive leadership role in the world financial sector. The shift from the West to Japan as the most important global centre for financial service intermediaries has occurred for both banking and investment services. For example, during the period 1987 to 1991 Nomura Securities, the largest Japanese securities house, has led the world in international bond underwriting, ahead of Deutsche Bank and Crédit Suisse, the two Western leaders. And in the 1991 list of the world's largest commercial banks, Japan boasted six banks with more assets than the Western leader, Crédit Agricole.

The displacement of Western banks as total volume leaders in the provision of financial services has generated considerable concern in both North American and European countries. With the tide of Japanese cheap capital inundating Western markets during the latter half of the 1980s, such traditional banking powerhouses as Citibank and Barclays Bank have long dropped out of the list of the world's top ten largest banks in terms of asset size.

In the late 1960s, Japan's largest banks were only marginal players in the international banking arena, while Japanese investment houses were only active domestically. Table 7.1 tracks the rise of the Japanese banks up through the world rankings since 1969. During the 1980s, Japanese banks steadily displaced their Western counterparts as the world's largest banking institutions. By 1991, Crédit Agricole, which led the rankings in 1979, had fallen to seventh place, while Citibank, the leader in the mid-1980s, had fallen to twentieth place. Eleven Japanese banks ranked in the top twenty in 1991, whereas France had four, the UK two, and Germany, the Netherlands, and the USA only one bank each.

As for the securities houses, Table 7.2 logs the rankings of international bond underwriting leadership since 1984. Most striking is Nomura's consistent number 1 position, beginning in 1987.[1] The Japanese presence was

---

[1] Preliminary results for 1992 seem to indicate that Nomura will drop to second place for that year.

TABLE 7.1. Rankings of the world's largest banks, 1969–1991 (by dollar-denominated assets)

		1969	1979	1981	1982	1985	1988	1990	1991
Dai-Ichi Kangyo Bank	Japan	17	10	8	8	2	1	1	1
Sumitomo Bank	Japan	16	16	11	13	4	2	3	2
Mitsubishi Bank	Japan	29	17	14	12	5	4	2	3
Mitsui (Sakura) Bank	Japan		36	24	23	18	13	4	4
Taiyo Kobe*	Japan		42	37	40	26	20	—	—
Fuji Bank	Japan	13	14	13	10	3	3	6	5
Sanwa Bank	Japan	18	18	17	16	7	5	5	6
Crédit Agricole	France		1	4	4	8	8	7	7
Norinchukin Bank	Japan		19	20	25	11	7	14	8
Crédit Lyonnais	France	21	6	5	5	10	16	10	9
Industrial Bank of Japan	Japan	28	22	25	21	13	6	9	10
Deutsche Bank	Germany	24	5	9	11	15	19	11	11
Banque Nationale de Paris	France	15	4	3	3	6	12	8	12
Barclays Bank	UK	4	9	6	6	16	14	12	13
Tokai Bank	Japan	36	35	27	29	17	9	13	14
ABN (ABN-Amro) Bank	Netherlands	63	33	33	36	48		16	15
Amro Bank*	Netherlands	68	27	42	43	50		—	—
National Westminster Bank	UK	7	11	10	7	12	17	15	16
Société Générale	France	34	7	7	9	14		19	17
Long-Term Credit Bank	Japan	55	39	36	35	23	18	20	18
Bank of Tokyo	Japan	26	43	22	18	24	18	17	19
Citicorp	USA	2	3	2	1	1	11	18	20

* Merged with above bank.

Source: various issues of The Banker.

TABLE 7.2. *Rankings of international bond underwriting activity, 1984–1991 (denominated in US$)*

		1984	1985	1986	1987	1988	1989	1990	1991
Nomura International Group	Japan	6	5	4	1	1	1	1	1
Crédit Suisse/CSFB Group	Switz./USA	5	3	7	2	2	6	2	2
Daiwa Securities	Japan	8	10	8	3	4	2	5	3
Deutsche Bank	Germany	4	6	3	5	3	5	4	4
Goldman Sachs	USA	17	19	16	18	16	15	13	5
Paribas	France	14	16	11	12	9	11	11	6
Merrill Lynch	USA	9	7	5	22	8	9	12	7
Union Bank of Switzerland	Switzerland	3	2	1	7	5	14	3	8
Morgan Stanley	USA	7	8	6	9	17	10	20	9
Swiss Bank Corp.	Switzerland	2	1	2	10	14	22	7	10
Yamaichi Securities	Japan	16	17	17	6	7	3	10	11
Nikko Securities	Japan	15	18	12	4	6	4	9	12
Salomon Brothers	USA	1	4	9	13	15	12	8	13
J. P. Morgan	USA	7	9	10	8	11	7	6	14
S. G. Warburg Group	UK	10	11	13	11	10	17	16	15
Crédit Lyonnais	France	27	21	23	48	30	16	19	16
Industrial Bank of Japan	Japan	33	24	21	14	13	13	14	17
Crédit Commercial de France	France	50	32	39	34	28	24	15	18
Dresdner Bank	Germany	13	15	18	17	18	21	31	19
Hambros Bank	UK	—	—	—	25	20	19	22	20

Source: various issues of *Institutional Investor Magazine.*

felt most profoundly in 1989, when the Big Four Japanese houses held the top four world positions. As underwriters, the other countries are more evenly represented, with Switzerland, the USA, France, Germany, and the UK holding between two and five of the top twenty positions since 1984.

The paper begins with a review of the motives which may explain the presence of Japanese institutions in Europe since the early 1950s, and follows with an examination of the factors which have contributed to their rise to the top of the list of the world's largest financial institutions by the late 1980s. Given the dynamics of the Japanese and European financial services industries in the early 1990s, the paper moves on to evaluate the relative strength of Japanese financial institutions (banks and securities houses) in a rapidly changing domestic and European environment.

The paper is divided into four parts. Section 2 provides a historical perspective on the Japanese penetration of the European financial services industry since the end of World War II. Section 3 analyses the reasons behind the strong Japanese growth and identifies the bases upon which Japanese financial institutions have built their competitive advantage. Section 4 discusses the sustainability of Japanese financial institutions' competitive advantage in light of (1) a number of important developments which occurred in the early 1990s in Japan's financial sector which may partly erode the competitive advantage enjoyed by Japanese financial institutions during the latter half of the 1980s, and (2) the structural changes occurring within the European financial services industry. Given the new European market dynamics and the shifts taking place in the historical competitive advantage of Japanese financial institutions, Section 5 concludes with the implications of these developments for the future of the Japanese presence in the European financial services industry.

2. HISTORICAL PERSPECTIVE ON JAPANESE FINANCIAL INSTITUTIONS' PRESENCE IN EUROPE

Although Japanese banks have long held very large asset bases, it was only during the 1980s that these assets have become a dominant world force. The Japanese presence in the European financial services industry has been apparent in both the rush of assets and the increase in European offices. Between December 1980 and March 1992, the total number of Japanese branches and subsidiaries tripled from 63 (41 subsidiaries and 22 branches) to 187 (79 subsidiaries and 108 branches).[2]

In Europe, as in the USA, this process of strengthening Japanese banking power has evolved through three distinct stages: (1) service to Japanese manufacturing firms operating abroad, (2) access to European capital markets, and (3) participation in host-country financial activities.

[2] Guyot 1992: 900.

TABLE 7.3. *Japanese manufacturing enterprises in Europe by country and industry, end 1989*

	No.	Major Industry
UK	132	Electronics; transportation equipment
France	95	Electronics; food products
Germany	89	Electronics; electrical equipment; machinery
Spain	55	Transportation equipment; chemicals
Netherlands	34	Chemicals
Italy	28	Chemicals; electronics
Belgium	25	Chemicals
Ireland	22	Electronics
Portugal	13	Textiles
Denmark	3	Chemicals; electronics
Greece	3	Iron & steel
Luxemburg	2	Electronics; machinery
TOTAL	501	

Source: JETRO Survey.

2.1. Servicing Japanese Industrial Expansion Abroad

From the 1960s to the 1970s, the European branching of Japanese banks most naturally accompanied foreign penetration of Japanese manufacturing companies. Japan's massive overseas direct investment by its highly successful manufacturing giants required a proportionate level of financial support from their respective Japanese 'main bank'.

Beginning with YKK's entry into Britain in 1966,[3] Europe has experienced a steady growth in Japanese manufacturing capacity. The Japanese familiarity with the English language, as well as lower labour costs in the UK compared to most developed countries on the Continent, were the major determinants in the relative attraction of Japanese companies to the UK, as shown in Table 7.3. As of January 1990, the UK was home to 132 Japanese manufacturing enterprises, 60 per cent of which operated in the electronic or transportation equipment industries.

Recent investment has been made to establish many of the 95 and 55 enterprises in France and Spain, respectively. Germany, with 89 Japanese enterprises—55 per cent of which are in electronics, electrical equipment, and machinery—maintains a longer history of welcoming Japanese manufacturing investment. Japan's manufacturing presence in Europe reached 157 companies by 1983, 501 in 1990, and 676 in 1991.[4]

Japanese banks followed this large-scale emigration of manufacturing capacity to provide advisory services, working capital, or project finance. Not surprisingly, the European branches of Japanese banks in the 1960s

---

[3] YKK is the world's largest producer of zip fasteners.   [4] JETRO Survey 1992.

and 1970s were located close to the Japanese manufacturing centres of the time, in London and Düsseldorf. The later Japanese industrial investment in France in the late 1980s, most notably by Nissan and Hitachi, was accompanied by the first penetration of French borders by such banks as Dai-Ichi Kangyo Bank (1987), Sumitomo Bank (1988), Sanwa Bank (1988), and Mitsubishi Bank (1989).[5]

2.2. Access to European Financial Markets: Liquidity-Seeking and Learning

As of 31 March 1991, Japanese financial services investment in North America represented 14 per cent of the $136 billion of total Japanese foreign investment. In Asia, financial services accounted for 9 per cent of the $48 billion of Japanese investment. In Europe, however, financial services represented a solid 42 per cent of the total $59 billion of total direct investment.[6] Although the aggregation methodology of foreign direct investment (FDI) data makes generalizations of industry trends somewhat unfair, the fact that such a relatively large proportion of total Japanese investment in Europe is in financial services indicates a strong interest in that sector on the part of Japanese investment. Moreover, it suggests that the need for Japanese institutions to service domestic clients operating in Europe does not entirely explain the level of investment undertaken by Japanese financial institutions in Europe.[7]

The emergence of the Euromarkets in London in the early 1960s stimulated immediate interest from the Japanese Ministry of Finance (MOF) for a Japanese presence in the European capital markets. Participation in the market gave both banks and securities houses the opportunity to develop investment banking skills not available at the time in Japan.[8] Japan's largest securities houses soon opened subsidiaries in London. In turn, Japan's large commercial banks in the City gained access to Eurobond market syndications via a consortium bank sponsored by the MOF. The attractive opportunity for Japanese banks to participate in bond underwriting had previously been prohibited under Section 34 of the Securities and Exchange Law set up after the end of World War II.

From the mid-1970s to the early 1980s, Japanese banks began to look increasingly to Europe as the centre for securities trading and capital market

---

[5] Guyot 1992: 901–2.   [6] Japan, Ministry of Finance 1992: 56.

[7] If we assume that the primary motive for the migration of Japanese financial institutions abroad is to service their overseas clients, then we should expect financial services as a proportion of total FDI to be of the same order of magnitude across the three regions (North America, Asia, and Europe). A significantly higher ratio in Europe indicates that other reasons may have induced Japanese financial institutions to locate in Europe.

[8] Note that Japanese banks could not have acquired these skills in the USA because of the Glass–Steagall Act which prohibits banks operating in the USA from investment banking services.

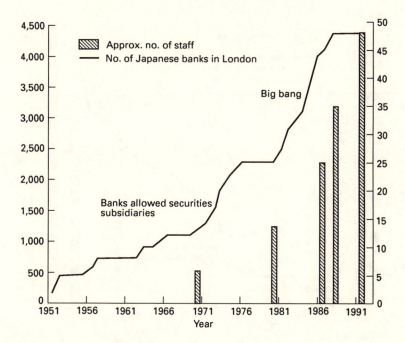

Source: Various issues of the *Banker*.

Fig. 7.1. Japanese banking activity in London, 1951–91

access. Further attraction to European financial markets was stimulated by the MOF's decision to allow major Japanese banks *direct* access to securities trading in overseas markets. The emergence of separate trading subsidiaries in Europe slowly phased out the previous consortium bank approach.

Factors such as London's market sophistication and its pool of talented professionals, as well as its large share of the Eurocurrency market, were important reasons for the development of the City as a major financial centre. Moreover, throughout the Thatcher years (1979–90), the City's accelerated deregulation, culminating in the Big Bang of October 1986, solidified London's pre-eminence as the most attractive foreign market to fund Japanese industrial expansion and international trade surplus. Fig. 7.1 charts the penetration of Japanese banks in London. From the post-war entry of the Bank of Tokyo in 1952, the presence of Japan's commercial banks has grown to nearly 50 banks with a staff of over 4,300. For the brokerage houses, Fig. 7.2 shows a similar dramatic increase in their presence in London during the 1970s and 1980s. Original entrants into the London securities market were the Big Four Japanese brokerage firms—firstly Daiwa, then Nikko, Nomura, and Yamaichi—in the early 1960s, at

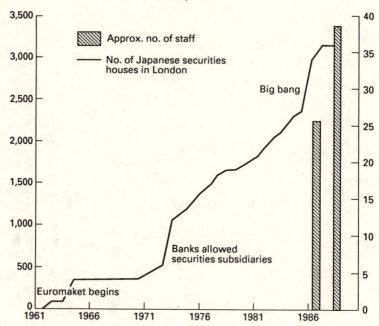

Source: Various issues of the *Banker*.

FIG. 7.2. Japanese security house activity in London, 1961–86

the invitation of the MOF. Both charts show strong increases in the early 1970s, again due to the lifting of MOF regulations. The 1980s witnessed an additional large surge in Japanese entry due to London's 'Big Bang', as well as the general increasing strength of Japanese financial institutions.

London provided a highly liquid market without the heavy regulation of the Japanese domestic system. Japanese corporations found that the less restrictive offshore markets provided significantly cheaper debt and equity funding. To exploit these opportunities, London was used as a net source of funding for Japanese banks' home operations. The move towards off-shore financing, combined with the impact of Japan's rising stock market, culminated in the extremely high-volume, convertible bond and warrant bond issues of the late 1980s, illustrated in Fig. 7.3. While Japanese straight-bond issues for corporations remained at about 1 trillion yen through the 1980s, Japanese corporate convertible bonds and warrant bond issues surged to a combined amount of nearly 15 trillion yen. Japanese bank and securities houses participated both as issuers of their own paper and as advisers and underwriters of their Japanese clients. The trend contributed substantially to establishing the Japanese presence in the European financial sector.

In 1970, Japan was already the world's second-largest economy based

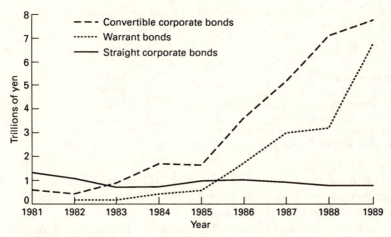

Note: 1989 warrant bond issuance includes only the first eight months.

Source: Data obtained from Downes and Elven 1990 and Bond Underwriters Association of Japan 1990.

Fig. 7.3. Japanese bond issuance, 1981–9

on GNP. In order for Japan to take its new place as a leading world economy, international recognition of its financial power was deemed essential by the Japanese. Joining international loan syndicates in London provided one opportunity effectively to establish the presence of the Japanese banking industry in the international financial community. In addition, participation in the relatively sophisticated London market allowed Japanese institutions to learn Western wholesale banking techniques.

Due to the importance of the Swiss financial market, creating a Japanese presence in the major Swiss financial centres was an additional important step to developing the Japanese financial services franchise in Europe. Luxemburg subsidiaries were later established for much the same reasons.

2.3. The Challenge of Building up a European Client Base

Gaining access to the local client base proved the most difficult stage of Japanese penetration of the European market. Japanese encroachment into the financial services sector was strongly resisted by most European governments, with barriers such as inordinately high equity capital ratios (in France), and with fiercely protective local financial institutions, such as Deutsche Bank in Germany. Again, the UK proved to be the most hospitable beach-head.

To steer clients away from their well-established relationships with European or US banks, Japanese banks relied primarily on a very aggressive pricing strategy. The undercutting of local competition helped Japan

T ABLE 7.4. *Domestic sterling business by foreign banks in the UK, 1987 and 1990* (£ million)

	1987	1990
Japanese bank market loans	3,927	10,940
US bank market loans	3,025	4,233
Japanese bank private sector deposits	4,042	9,209
US bank private sector deposits	4,409	6,823

Source: *Bank of England Quarterly Bulletin* (May 1988; Aug. 1991).

to double its share of the UK lending market between 1977 and 1983.[9] Moreover, as shown in Table 7.4, UK private sector deposits from 1987 to 1990 have more than doubled—twice the penetration which US banks were able to achieve over the same time-frame. In terms of market loans, by 1990 Japan had dwarfed the US loan business, with over 2.5 times its volume.

The success of Japan's local penetration is even more impressive, given that their European strategy relied heavily on internally generated growth, rather than on gaining local expertise and client networks with a series of local bank acquisitions. The level of Japanese acquisition activity in the European financial services industry totalled $510 million in 1990 but fell to only $191 million in 1991.[10]

Part of Japanese banks' success can be explained by their commitment to concentrate on selected target industry sectors. Table 7.5 identifies the market share of Japanese lending in each of ten UK industries. Government services (30 per cent), water supplies (34 per cent), and energy companies (13 per cent) have been targeted, possibly because of their high profile, yet low-risk nature. The UK wholesale distribution sector used Japanese banks to account for 31 per cent of its lending in 1983 and 37 per cent in 1987. The non-bank financial services industry—building societies (34 per cent) and securities dealers (27 per cent)—was an area highly targeted by Japanese banks in the late 1980s. The backing of Eurotunnel and EuroDisney further exemplifies the importance of high-profile project finance for Japanese banks. The majority of European airlines, moreover, have become regular clients for Japanese financing.

Although the total market share gains in Europe paint a very successful picture, bank profitability on these loans was very low. In the late 1980s average spreads were as low as five to ten basis points, or ten times lower than the spreads prevailing in 1992.

Moreover, Japanese banks have relied heavily on co-operation with local UK firms to build their presence in Britain. The agreement between Fuji Bank and the Northern Development Company is an example. The

---

[9] Fairlamb 1983; Duser 1990: 121.   [10] M&A Japan 1992: 11.

TABLE 7.5. *Lending to UK Residents by Japanese banks, 1983 and 1987* (sterling plus foreign currency lending)

Borrower	Share, Nov. 1983 (%)	Share, Aug. 1987 (%)	Outstanding in Aug. 1987 (£ billion)
Securities dealers*	—	27	4.4
Building societies	14	34	1.3
Other financial services	6	11	3.3
Wholesale distribution[†]	31	37	3.9
Manufacturing	3	4	1.1
Construction	1	6	0.4
Property companies	—	4	0.5
Water supply	—	34	0.2
Energy companies	13	13	0.6
Government services	18	30	0.4
TOTAL[‡]	5	8	19.1

* Includes Japanese-owned securities houses and merchant banks.
† Includes UK offices of Japanese trading companies and wholesale distribution arms of Japanese exporters, including electronics and automobiles.
‡ Japanese banks' market share in Aug. 1987 for solely sterling lending was 3%.

Source: *Bank of England Quarterly Bulletin* (Nov. 1987: 523).

willingness of both companies to work together to improve Japan–Northern Britain trade proved an enlightening example for many other banks. Other alliances playing a part in the Japanese effort to penetrate the UK market include:[11]

Bank of Tokyo	Touche Remnant	1984
Sumitomo T&B	Ivory & Sime	1986
LTCB	Foreign & Colonial	1988

Although Germany is Japan's largest European trading partner, and the only example of true universal banking, Japanese banks have been much less successful here than in the UK at penetrating the domestic lending market. Much of this difficulty is due to the highly protective nature of large German banks with regard to their home market. In 1988, Japanese banks maintained asset levels roughly on a par with those of American banks in Germany. Less than 40 per cent of Japanese bank business was with local companies, and only 5 per cent of the largest German companies maintained relationships with Japanese banks.[12] Fig. 7.4 portrays the 1984 balance sheet structure of Germany's leading foreign bankers: the USA and Japan. As in much of Europe, most of the business done by both

[11] Duser 1990: 121–2.   [12] Duser 1990: 126.

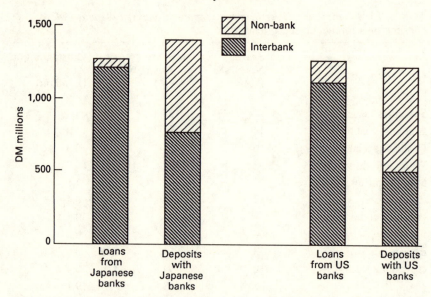

Source: Based on estimates in Banco di Napoli, in Duser 1990: 127.

FIG. 7.4. Balance-sheet structure of Japanese and US banks in Germany, 1984

TABLE 7.6. *Foreign banks operating in France, 1985 and 1991*

Home	Jan. 1985	Jan. 1991
Total EC	22	33
Other Europe	1	2
Japan	3	10
North America	12	8
Middle East	9	9
India & Pakistan	4	4
Other	7	12

Source: Banque de France, 1992.

countries' banks is purely thin-margin inter-bank lending and borrowing. An inability to penetrate the German lending market is evidenced by the small portion of both US and Japanese lending to non-banks.

In other European financial centres the Japanese presence is much more recent. The regulation of the French market with policies such as credit ceilings or capital requirements kept all but the Bank of Tokyo out of Paris until the early 1980s. The entry of Japanese banks into Paris again followed the increased interest on the part of Japanese manufacturing firms in locating in France. As shown in Table 7.6, the number of Japanese

TABLE 7.7. *Japanese banking in France, 1991*

	Total assets	Interbank assets	Local loan assets	Local loan (%)
Bank of Tokyo	24,977	18,209	3,803	15
Fuji Bank	77,863	70,440	2,917	4
Mitsubishi Bank	70,647	65,771	1,954	3
Dai-Ichi Kangyo Bank	56,891	52,976	1,259	2
Sanwa Bank	72,906	69,117	1,137	2
Sumitomo Bank	94,334	90,949	1,317	1

Source: Nikkei Kinyu Shinbun, 14 Apr. 1992.

banks opening offices in France has outpaced the rate of any other world region, with representation there more than tripling. Although increased Japanese manufacturing activity in France provides one explanation for this increase, the high level of rivalry among Japanese banks is another. The City banks' obsession with keeping up with their peers has led to something of a 'me too' strategy for office openings.

One factor in the delay of Japanese entry into the French market is the handicapping effect of French government regulation on foreign banks. In 1991, lending to French companies was still quite low, as can be seen in Table 7.7. Except for the per cent local loan structure achieved by the Bank of Tokyo's relatively small investment, the activity of French branches in the early 1990s was almost entirely based on inter-bank lending. Almost 94 per cent of the combined assets of Fuji, Mitsubishi, Dai-Ichi Kangyo, Sanwa, and Sumitomo Bank are invested in low-margin inter-bank lending. The high value perceived by the banks in maintaining beach-heads for future expansion opportunities is evidenced by their ongoing determination to be present in Europe despite the low returns they have achieved in the early 1990s.

Branches eventually opened for most Japanese institutions in France, Italy, the Netherlands, Spain, and Sweden following the Japanese manufacturing success on the Continent. Table 7.8 traces the development of the network of European offices of Japan's largest commercial bank, Dai-Ichi Kangyo (DKB). Creating its first European office in 1971, DKB has since expanded from London into nine European countries. In addition to traditional commercial banking, DKB now conducts securities activities in London, Zurich, Amsterdam, and Frankfurt.

2.4. Investment Services

In terms of office networks, the large Japanese securities houses have been even more aggressive than banks in developing their presence in Europe. Table 7.9 contrasts Nomura Securities' European office development to

TABLE 7.8. *European offices of Dai-Ichi Kangyo Bank, by country, 1983–1990*

	1983	1984	1985	1986	1987	1988	1989	1990
UK	S/B	S/B	S/B	S/B	S/B	S/B	S/B	S/B
Germany	B/RO	B/RO	B/RO	B/RO	B/RO	2B/RO	S/2B/RO	S/2B/RO
Switzerland	S	S	S	S	S	S	S	S
Netherlands	S	S	S	S	S	S	S	S
France	RO	RO	RO	RO	B	B	B	B
Spain	RO	RO	RO	RO	RO	RO	RO	RO
Sweden			RO	RO	RO	RO	RO	RO
Luxemburg				S	S	S	S	S
Italy				RO	RO	RO	RO	B

Key: S = subsidiary; B = branch; RO = representative office.
Source: Annual Reports.

TABLE 7.9. *European offices of Nomura Securities, by country, 1983–1991*

	1983	1984	1985	1986	1987	1988	1989	1990	1991
UK	2S	2S	2S	2S	2S	2S	2S	2S	2S
Switzerland	2S	3S	3S	3S	3S	3S	3S	4S	4S
Germany	1S	1S	1S	1S	1S	1S	2S	2S/RO	2S/RO
Netherlands	S	S	S	S	S	S	S	S	S
France	S	S	S	S	S	S	S	S	S
Italy				RO	RO	S			S/RO
Sweden				RO	RO	RO	RO	RO	RO
Spain					RO	RO	RO	RO	S
Luxemburg							RO	S	S
Austria							RO	RO	RO
Hungary									S

Key: S = subsidiary; B = branch; RO = representative office.
Source: Annual Reports.

that of DKB. Nomura's network is much larger with offices spread over eighteen European locations, including a recent entry into Eastern Europe. Nomura Securities invested in locating securities subsidiaries at each of the European financial centres, necessitating in the case of Switzerland the opening of offices in Zurich, Geneva, Basle, and Lugano.

Throughout the late 1980s, Japanese financial institutions have also played a very important role in the European investment services industry. Table 7.10 presents the significant share of international underwriting volume acquired in the Euromarket. As lead managers, the Big Four Japanese securities houses (Nomura, Daiwa, Yamaichi, and Nikko) were credited with over $80 billion of underwriting activity, representing 39 per cent of the entire market volume in 1989 and 24 per cent of total number of issues. In more specific areas, the position of the Big Four was even more pronounced. In Eurodollar bonds they accounted for 61 per cent of volume, and in yen bonds, 67 per cent of volume. The Big Four's $66 billion of equity warrant bond underwriting represented 88 per cent of that market, and in straight international equity issues, they held a 23 per cent share. Table 7.10 also indicates the strong down-turn in the underwriting volume of the Big Four in 1991.

2.5. Retail Banking

The financing of loans made by Japanese banks in Europe has been raised primarily through the issue of local certificates of deposit, as well as extensive inter-bank borrowing. In contrast to the US strategy, the decision not to open a European retail channel may have resulted from lessons learned from the California experience.

The localization (*dochaku-ka*) of Japanese banks in California has been quite effective in penetrating the local retail banking market. Banks were initially established to cater to the needs of Japanese-Americans and the subsidiaries of Japanese companies located in California. Later acquisitions of retail networks greatly increased the size of the Japanese presence in the retail sector. The Bank of Tokyo acquired Union Bank, Mitsubishi bought the Bank of California, and Sanwa Bank took over Lloyds Bank of California. By June 1991 the three banks held positions five, six, and seven, respectively, in California's banking market.[13]

Yet these subsidiaries have suffered considerable losses in the early 1990s. The Bank of California wrote off $250 million in loan losses in 1991, and all have started, or were likely to start, laying off employees in the early 1990s.[14] Even though the whole of the California banking market was suffering in the early 1990s, Japanese banks have been relatively more vulnerable throughout the 1980s. Such factors as over-ambitious management, limited communication of a clear strategy, lack of critical mass, heavy concentration in risky lending and real-estate investment, and an inability to attract talented local professionals or manage local employees have been cited as reasons for Japan's limited success in Californian retail banking.

Given the difficulty experienced by Japanese banks in California, it is not surprising that entry into the more difficult European retail market has not been pursued. The existence of dominant domestic banks and strongly country-segmented markets made the prospects of establishing a successful beach-head for pan-European retail banking appear limited.

---

[13] Sender 1991: 105.   [14] Unger 1992.

TABLE 7.10. *International underwriting activity of the Big Four Japanese securities firms in the Euromarket, 1989 and 1991*

	1989				1991			
	$ volume (millions)	Share of market (%)	No. of issues	Share of issues (%)	$ volume (millions)	Share of market (%)	No. of issues	Share of issues (%)
Eurobonds								
Nomura	32,014		147		21,328		121	
Daiwa	16,692		93		16,093		99	
Yamaichi	16,332		78		10,168		74	
Nikko	15,294		54		9,757		73	
Big Four	80,332	39	372	24	57,346	25	367	28
Eurodollar bonds								
Nomura	27,841		95		8,614		51	
Daiwa	13,980		58		4,900		33	
Yamaichi	15,250		63		4,550		25	
Nikko	14,690		44		3,701		29	
Big Four	71,761	61	260	47	21,765	32	138	36
Yen bonds								
Nomura	4,953		54		13,488		72	
Daiwa	3,458		38		11,460		56	
Yamaichi	2,054		22		5,361		39	
Nikko	1,340		12		5,006		26	
Big Four	11,805	67	126	58	35,316	86	193	84

Equity warrant bonds							
Nomura	23,461		76		7,047		50
Daiwa	11,308		40		5,424		43
Yamaichi	13,730		51		5,377		36
Nikko	14,086		39		4,221		42
Big Four	62,585	88	206	76	22,069	83	171	86
International equity							
Nomura	1,113		11		541		3
Daiwa	1,034		3		354		3
Yamaichi	517		2		—		—
Nikko	118		2		—		—
Big Four	2,782	23	18	9	895	5	6	2

Note: 1987: 138 yen = 1 US dollar; 1991: 125 yen = 1 US dollar. Book runner receives full credit. *Eurobonds*: underwritings of international syndicates with significant portions sold in two or more countries other than the country of currency in which the issue is denominated; *Eurodollar bonds*: US dollar underwritings, excluding foreign deals done in the USA; *Yen bonds*: yen-denominated underwritings, including Euromarket, *samurai*, and *daimyo* issues; *Equity warrant bonds*: underwritings of international deals offering equity warrants; *International equity*: equity issues placed or syndicated outside the domestic market of the issuer.

Source: Institutional Investor (Feb. 1990, Feb. 1992).

3. SOURCES OF COMPETITIVE ADVANTAGE FOR JAPANESE FINANCIAL INSTITUTIONS

Historically, banking has tended to be a strongly domestic industry. In general, foreign banks find it difficult to achieve the economic advantage necessary to remain competitive given the additional costs of operating abroad.[15] To be successful abroad, Japanese institutions must possess a superior competitive advantage which compensates them for the costliness of operating outside their home market. This section will more carefully analyse the sources of competitive advantage used by Japanese financial institutions to build a financial-services franchise in Europe. The discussion is based on the standard categorization of the sources of competitive advantage: those based on 'differentiation' (an advantage that allows the bank to sell a service or a product at a relative premium) and those based on cost and operational efficiency. Section 4 follows with a description of the events which may, particularly in the 1990s, be challenging the Japanese advantage.

3.1. Differentiation Advantage Linked to the Domestic Market

For a financial intermediary, market differentiation advantage may be gained across a range of dimensions. The following dimensions are deemed salient in the context of this discussion and are evaluated as to their importance as factors contributing to the growth of Japanese financial institutions in Europe in the 1980s: product innovation, technical sophistication, ability to attract high-quality local professional staff, breadth of line of services, affiliation with or knowledge of home market, and capability to service home clients' operations in Europe.

- *Product innovation and technical sophistication*: Although Japanese institutions have secured a large share of the world banking market, it is difficult to argue that such share is based on market differentiation characterized by superior product innovation or technical sophistication. The use of many financial innovations and operating techniques, which have become standard activities in some Western institutions, are more slowly adopted in Japanese institutions.[16] Except in some key niche areas such as aircraft finance, potential banking clients looking to deal with the overall most technically sophisticated partner would rarely be drawn to a Japanese financial institution as opposed to another major Western firm.

---

[15] Grubel 1977 and Tschoegl 1987.

[16] For example, one can cite the case of the American head of Nomura Securities' New York office who has encountered considerable resistance from Tokyo against initiating computerized trading schemes (program trading) in New York.

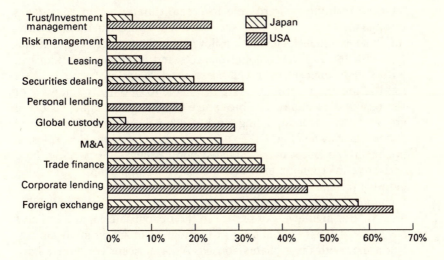

Source: The *Banker* (Nov. 1991).

Fig. 7.5. Japanese and US banks in London, by activity

- *Ability to attract high-quality local professional staff*: Japanese financial institutions experience difficulty in differentiating themselves on the basis of the quality of their local professional staff, meaning those with the best skills, most experience, or greatest number of meaningful client contacts. It seems that the brightest and best of host European financial circles are often discouraged from joining Japanese institutions due to their perceived limited career potential and difficult integration process.
- *Breadth of line of services*: Furthermore, in differentiating themselves Japanese banks do not rely on providing a distinctive, broad line of banking services. Due to both regulatory requirements and strategic choice, Japanese banks rarely offer the supermarket of services found in many European universal banks or even the more regulated American institutions. Some evidence of their restricted range of services, as well as the lower level of sophistication, can be observed in Fig. 7.5. The chart presents the number of foreign banks in London participating in selected banking activities. The data have been aggregated to give a breakdown of participation rates for each of the activities for both US and Japanese banks. The evidence highlights that in all cases, except corporate lending, the US banks appear to participate more predominantly than the Japanese banks, particularly in such sophisticated services as global custody or risk management.
- *Affiliation with or knowledge of home market*: Despite the apparent lack of differentiation capability across the above dimensions, Japanese

financial institutions were able to create differentiation advantages through their knowledge and experience in their home market.[17] Firstly, the Japanese financial institutions leveraged their expertise and affiliation with the Japanese capital markets and economic conditions to differentiate themselves in yen-based services and instruments. As a result, Japanese institutions have been able to ride the recent wave of yen-based transactions. The brokerage houses, for example, benefited greatly from a steadily rising stock market during the 1985 to 1989 period. As shown in Fig. 7.3, Tokyo's bull market triggered an explosion in convertible and warrant-attached bond issues. Underwriting these derivative instruments provided a substantial opportunity for strong industry profits.

- *Capability to service home clients' operations in Europe*: The willingness to offer high levels of service to their expatriate Japanese clients has allowed Japanese financial institutions to maintain important relationships with these clients abroad. As Americans consumers have switched to Toyotas, and Europeans to Sonys, the large banks and securities houses have quickly reacted to the changing needs of their clients and have maintained the mutual trust, personal contacts, and cultural familiarity inherent in the important main bank relationship with these companies even on the opposite side of the globe. Maintaining this relationship has required an expansion of their office networks in order to be near both the client and the sources of financing required by the client, as discussed in Section 2. It has been suggested that successfully servicing the needs of domestic clients operating abroad is not only a differentiation advantage but also a cost advantage: the long-standing relationship between the two firms at home allows the bank to respond more quickly and efficiently to loan demands made abroad.[18]

3.2. Cost and Operational Advantages

Although differentiation advantages have been important factors for Japanese institutions, the most striking explanation for Japanese financial success is on the cost side. As is well documented for manufacturing companies, Japanese financial institutions appear similarly to have built their world position through superior cost and operational advantages at home. The following discussion of the Japanese cost and efficiency advantages will consider both macro-economic and micro-economic factors. The former are home-country advantages resulting from favourable economic conditions in Japan, while the latter are factors resulting from an industry-wide commitment to building more efficient operations.

[17] Hirtle 1991: 48.   [18] Grubel 1977.

3.2.1. Macro-economic Factors

The tremendous growth of the Japanese financial sector has been greatly aided by a number of favourable macro-economic factors prevailing during the second half of the 1980s. Such macro-economic advantages include the appreciation of the yen, advantageous sources of funding, and gains in both the equity and the property markets. Each of these effects, which are not unrelated, will now be discussed in turn.

(*a*) *Appreciation of the yen*. The rise in the international importance of Japanese banks can in part be traced to the impact of decisions made in New York City in September 1985. During a meeting of the Group of Seven (G-7) finance ministers, an agreement (the so-called Plaza Accord) was made collectively to reduce the value of the US dollar in foreign exchange markets. The result of this action vaulted the yen from an average dollar exchange rate of 239 yen in 1985 to 128 yen in 1988. This appreciation of the yen was an important factor in the ability of Japanese companies to make large dollar-denominated investments in foreign property and to acquire foreign companies. To finance the strong growth of their clients' direct investment in the USA, Japanese banks increased their lending activity significantly.

It is unlikely, however, that a similar *direct* currency effect has been at work in the case of Japanese investment in Europe. Indeed, looking over the same time-frame, the value of the yen remained fairly constant against European currencies, as charted in Fig. 7.6. The difference in the behaviour of the yen/US dollar and the yen/ECU exchange rates shown in Fig. 7.6 may partly explain the significantly larger direct investment made by Japanese firms between 1985 and 1990 in the USA ($111 billion) in comparison to that made in Europe ($50 billion).[19] The strengthening of the yen relative to the US dollar during the latter part of the 1980s certainly contributed to the growth of Japanese financial institutions both at home and abroad, but can provide only a partial explanation of the increased activity by Japanese financial institutions in Europe during that period of time, since the exchange rate between the yen and the ECU during the latter part of the 1980s remained fairly stable in comparison to the yen/US dollar rate.

(*b*) *Advantageous cost of capital*. As shown in Fig. 7.7, the Bank of Japan (BOJ) promoted Japanese capital investment from 1986 to 1989 with a policy of lower interest rates, the official discount rate dropping to a low of 2.5 per cent in February 1987, until May 1989, when the BOJ raised it by 0.75 per cent. This expansionary monetary policy provided easy financing to both banks and non-banking firms.[20] Moreover, another low-cost

---

[19] Ministry of Finance.

[20] The BOJ adopted an expansionary monetary policy following the Plaza Accord in order to prevent the yen from strengthening further *vis-à-vis* the US dollar, as well as to increase domestic consumption and help export-oriented Japanese companies to restructure themselves to meet rising domestic demand.

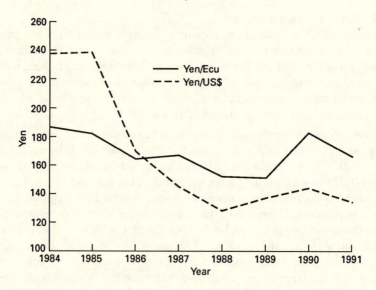

Source: IMF, *International Financial Statistics*.

FIG. 7.6. Yen exchange rate, 1984–91

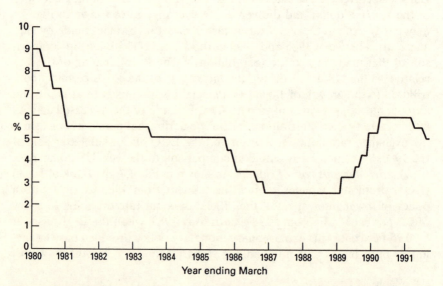

Source: Ministry of Finance Institute of Fiscal and Monetary Policy, *Monthly Finance Review* (Dec. 1992), 16.

FIG. 7.7. Official Japanese discount rate, 1980–91

financing opportunity, used by both banks and industrial companies, was accessible via the Eurobond market. Companies typically issued Eurodollar convertible bonds or bonds with attached warrants in London. Given the steady rise in equity prices, investors were willing to accept very low coupon rates on these bonds because of the spectacular returns they expected to realize when the bonds would be converted into equity. The payment exposure could then be swapped from a fixed-rate liability to floating-rate liability and from dollars into yen, often resulting in close to zero cost of funds at the time of issue.

In addition, Japanese banks in the latter part of the 1980s, like most of their European counterparts, were still facing regulated interest rates on most deposits. This system protected banks from competing against one another for funds by bidding up the interest rate offered on deposits. The interest rate ceiling on deposits, combined with the high Japanese savings rate, created a substantial pool of cheap deposits available for Japanese banks.[21]

(*c*) *Rising stock market.* A steadily rising equity market is generally beneficial to a country's financial services industry. In the case of Japan, two structural factors provide a strong link between changes in stock market value and the lending capacity of Japanese banks.

Firstly, due to the significant cross-ownership of company shares within Japanese corporate relationships, banks maintain a large investment in the equity securities of other firms. Table 7.11 provides evidence of the relatively larger equity holdings of Japanese banks compared to both US and German banks. The market value of equity securities held as a share of total assets for Japanese banks is 11 per cent versus 3.8 per cent for Germany (5.4 per cent including book value of equity participation) and 0.6 per cent for the USA.

The second factor is the Bank for International Settlements (BIS) agreement allowing Japanese banks to recognize 45 per cent of the unrealized gains on their stockholdings as part of their capital base.

Consequently, as the market rises, a bank's capital base expands, allowing it to fund more loans. The existing cross-ownership structure and BIS allowance created the opportunity for Japanese banks to use the rising stock market to fuel their growth during the latter part of the 1980s. The net effect was to allow banks to create loans over their capital gains at the ratio of over 12 to 1, yet maintain the same 'on-paper' financial strength. The relative advantage of the Japanese banks in benefiting from such a market is shown below. The dramatic 31 per cent compound annual growth rate of the Tokyo stock market during the four-year period from December 1985 to December 1989 (when the Tokyo market reached its peak)

---

[21] Section 4.2 and Table 7.16 provide further data and discussion on the level of unregulated interest rates on bank funds.

TABLE 7.11. *Equity held by banks in Germany, Japan, and the USA (%)*

	Book value of equity securities held as a share of bank's book shareholder equity	Market value of equity securities held as a share of bank's shareholder equity adjusted for unrealized gains on equities	Market value of equity securities held as a share of total assets
Japan	125.2	107.0	11.0
USA	11.7	11.7*	0.6
Germany	35.1	57.9	3.8
(including book value of equity participations)	75.1	83.5	5.4

* Book value of equity securities held is taken as a proxy for market value because of existing acquisition and high turnover.

Note: Data cover sample banks for Japan and Germany; data for US average cover six sample banks in the Second Federal Reserve District. Data for Japan are for Mar. 1990.

Source: Zimmer and McCauley 1991: 53.

TABLE 7.12. *Ratio of average market price to year-end book value for selected banks, 1985–1989*

	1985	1986	1987	1988	1989
Industrial Bank of Japan	4.4	7.0	8.6	9.0	8.7
Mitsubishi Bank	4.7	6.4	7.4	7.4	6.6
Fuji Bank	4.4	6.0	7.1	7.3	6.6
Sumitomo Bank	4.7	6.6	7.9	8.1	6.9
Dai-Ichi Kangyo Bank	5.0	7.0	7.9	7.8	6.6
Deutsche Bank		2.0	2.0	2.0	2.2
Barclays Bank		0.8	0.8	0.9	0.9
Citicorp	0.9	0.9	0.9	0.9	1.0
Banque Nationale de Paris	0.2	0.3	0.3	0.4	0.6

Source: Disclosure/Worldscope Global Database.

exceeded the 4 to 20 per cent growth rates experienced in the other major equity markets during the same period.

	Market indices (end of year)		Compound annual growth rate (%)
	1985	1989	
Japan (Nikkei 225)	13,083	38,916	31
USA (Dow Jones 30)	1,541	2,732	15
UK (FT 100)	1,414	2,399	14
Germany (FAZ)	626	741	4
France (CAC 40)	264	552	20

Moreover, as the stock market rose higher, Japanese banks issued new equity to strengthen their capital further. From 1985 to 1989 Japanese banks issued a combined 12.3 trillion yen ($91 billion) in equity financing, seven times the amount issued by their US counterparts ($13 billion) over the same period.[22]

The effect of the rise in the market value of Japanese banks can be seen in the market-to-book ratios of Western banks relative to that of their Japanese counterparts, shown in Table 7.12. The data shows distinctly higher ratios for selected Japanese banks than for leading Western banks: Deutsche Bank, Barclays Bank, Citicorp, and Banque Nationale de Paris. The proportion of market value to book equity investment in the Industrial Bank of Japan, for example, exceeded that of the listed Western banks from four to nearly 30 times in the late 1980s. Such high market multiples on Japanese bank equity created attractive opportunities to fund on-going growth through new equity issues. In effect, by leveraging on the rising equity market, Japanese institutions were able to fund the capitalization

---

[22] Daquil 1991: 39.

bases required to support asset growth in a fashion not available to their Western competitors.[23]

(*d*) *Appreciating property value.* The traditional belief in the value of land had long convinced most Japanese that land ownership provides a nearly riskless asset. The post-war Japanese view was that the price of property would never decline. Moreover, in step with the cash generated during the prosperous 1980s, and an expansionary monetary policy accompanied by low interest rates, the price of land soared. Banks lent against increasing land value (rather than the borrower's capacity to generate future operating cash flow). Borrowers used the cash to invest further in the rising equity and property markets. The increase in land value provided more backing for further lending, thus refuelling the cycle. In effect, via the banking sector, valuable but illiquid property was transformed into a liquid stock market investment. What was happening could be described as a 'pseudo-securitization' of property through the banking sector.

Fig. 7.8 illustrates the level of the speculative property market. In the 1980s, total Japanese land value rose to five times GNP, far above the steady US level of less than GNP. Furthermore, although the USA is 25 times larger than Japan, the Japanese total land value of 20 trillion yen at the end of the 1980s was four times the total US land value.

As the speculative cycle soared even higher, Japanese banks became highly dependent on property lending. By 1990 Japanese property-backed loans had increased to 23 per cent of the City banks' total loans.[24]

The dramatic increase in the price of land had similar impacts on corporate balance sheets. With the strong appreciation of collaterable assets, Japanese corporations took advantage of their ability to obtain inexpensive land-backed loans. From 1983 to 1989, bank lending more than tripled, in part due to the tremendous appreciation in the value of land.[25]

3.2.2. *Micro-economic Factors*

In addition to the favourable macro-economic climate which contributed so strongly to the advantageous competitive position of Japanese financial institutions in international markets, these firms have also built some strong operating cost advantages of their own.

Table 7.13 displays a cross-country comparison of profitability ratios based on aggregated financial statements for the large commercial banks in each country from 1988 to 1990. In effect, the table decomposes pre-tax

---

[23] It should be pointed out that bank loans were made mostly to individuals and to small and medium-sized companies that could not access the stock market. As pointed out earlier in the paper, large quoted companies had less need for bank borrowing because they were able to issue convertible bonds at a yen cost which was close to zero.

[24] Lake 1992: 39.

[25] These were mostly companies not listed on the stock exchange and hence unable to issue convertible bonds (see n. 20 above).

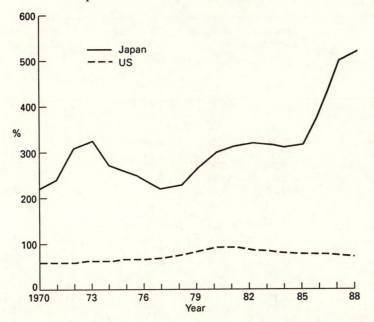

Source: Economic Planning Agency, Annual Reports on the National Economy; Federal Reserve Board, Balance Sheets for the US Economy; *Tokyo Business Today* (1991).

Fig. 7.8. Japanese and US land values as a percentage of GNP, 1970–88

return on equity (ROE)[26] into four factors: yield on assets (YOA); operating costs as percent of assets (XOA); interest-rate spread, and balance-sheet leverage (financial leverage). Appendix 7A provides a proof of the equation noted at the foot of Table 7.13, according to which ROE can be broken down as follows:

$$ROE = (YOA - XOA) + (Spread - XOA) (Leverage)$$

Banks may achieve similar levels of overall profitability (ROE) through different combinations of the four factors. It should be noted, however, that given the differing cost of capital across countries, straight comparisons may be misleading. Nevertheless, rough cross-country comparisons, and examination of the relative contribution of each factor (YOA, XOA, Spread, and Leverage) within each country, provide insightful clues on the approach and success of the respective strategies.

From 1988 to 1990, Japanese banks were able to achieve on average the highest pre-tax ROE of any of the eight selected countries. Such a level of profitability is striking given the relative low cost of capital required in

[26] Pre-tax return on equity (ROE) is equal to pre-tax profit divided by the book value of equity. All other definitions are given at the bottom of Table 7.13.

TABLE 7.13. *Cross-national comparisons of commercial bank financial ratios, 1988–1990*

	Pre-tax ROE* (%) (1)	Yield on assets (%) (2)	Oper. costs per assets (%) (3)	Interest spread (%) (4)	Financial leverage (5)
1988					
France	15.29	7.42	1.64	1.85	45.3
Germany	17.93	6.89	2.36	3.02	20.3
Italy	10.60	7.69	2.77	3.13	15.8
Japan	**25.18**	**5.28**	**0.68**	**1.20**	**39.1**
Spain	13.82	9.61	3.25	4.20	7.8
Switzerland	10.24	5.99	1.45	1.83	15.3
UK	24.77	11.04	3.29	4.33	16.3
USA	21.28	9.94	3.23	4.09	16.9
1989					
France	15.05	8.08	1.56	1.75	44.6
Germany	16.88	7.66	2.22	2.84	18.4
Italy	12.49	7.01	2.16	2.60	17.3
Japan	**15.69**	**5.65**	**0.54**	**0.83**	**36.1**
Spain	16.84	10.53	3.11	4.16	9.0
Switzerland	10.21	7.39	1.54	1.84	14.4
UK	2.10	11.65	3.19	2.87	19.4
USA	11.00	10.49	3.28	3.50	17.4
1990					
France	11.48	8.21	1.47	1.60	38.0
Germany	14.92	7.93	2.09	2.59	18.3
Italy	13.59	8.31	2.57	3.10	15.0
Japan	**11.40**	**6.90**	**0.60**	**0.75**	**33.1**
Spain	16.33	11.38	3.12	4.02	9.0
Switzerland	8.26	8.06	1.54	1.66	14.8
UK	13.76	13.20	3.32	3.51	20.4
USA	10.09	10.47	3.48	3.67	16.4
3-year Average					
France	13.94	7.90	1.56	1.73	42.6
Germany	16.58	7.49	2.22	2.82	19.0
Italy	12.23	7.67	2.50	2.94	16.0
Japan	**17.42**	**5.94**	**0.60**	**0.93**	**36.1**
Spain	15.66	10.51	3.16	4.13	8.6
Switzerland	9.57	7.15	1.51	1.78	14.8
UK	13.54	11.96	3.27	3.57	18.7
USA	14.12	10.30	3.33	3.75	16.9
Average of non-Japanese	**13.66**	**9.00**	**2.51**	**2.96**	**19.5**

Note: The ratios presented in this table are based on aggregated financial statements for the large commercial banks in each country. The number of banks included (by year when necessary) is as follows: France (8), Germany (6), Italy (7), Japan (13/13/12), Spain (6), Switzerland (5/5/4), UK (50/47/45), USA (360/373/370).

*(1) Pre-tax return on equity (ROE) = (2) – (3) + (4) – (3) × (5) (see Appendix 7A for a proof)

(2) Yield on assets (YOA) = (interest and non-interest revenue – bad debt provisions/assets

(3) Operating costs per assets (XOA) = operating expenses/assets

(4) Interest spread = YOA – (interest expense/liabilities)

(5) Financial leverage = liabilities/equity

Source: OECD 1992a.

Japan. From a 1988 pre-tax ROE of more than 25 per cent, Japanese banks slipped to a 1990 return of 11.4 per cent. Yet, over the three years, the Japanese bank average of 17.4 per cent was well above that of the other European aggregates: Germany (16.6 per cent), Spain (15.7 per cent), France (13.9 per cent), the UK (13.5 per cent), Italy (12.2 per cent), and Switzerland (9.6 per cent).

The Japanese ability to achieve such a high pre-tax ROE is the result of an effective strategy of offsetting weak yields on assets (YOA) and interest-rate spreads with strong operating efficiency (XOA) and high financial leverage. In all three years, Japanese banks had the lowest asset yields and interest-rate spreads. Relative to Japanese banks, the Anglophone countries produce twice the revenue for each asset quantity and four times the interest-rate spread; the three-year average YOA is 5.9 per cent for Japan versus 12.0 per cent for the UK and 10.3 per cent for the USA, with a Japanese interest-rate spread of 0.9 per cent *vis-à-vis* 3.6 per cent in the Uk and 3.8 per cent in the USA. However, Japanese bank operating costs of 0.7 per cent, 0.5 per cent, and 0.6 per cent of assets were consistently less than half the level of the most efficient European countries—France and Switzerland—during 1988, 1989, and 1990, respectively. Leverage for the Japanese banks is also relatively high, the average deposit-to-equity ratio being 36.1 times, which may be more easily interpreted as an equity-to-asset ratio of 2.7 per cent.[27]

Superior operating cost efficiency ratios can be attributed to several dominant factors in the Japanese banking industry, including:

(1) *Product mix*: a relatively larger proportion of loan-based revenues in comparison to fee-generating activities (the former requiring relatively lower operating costs).

(2) *Focused product portfolio*: a relatively limited product line that produces large economies of scale which in turn reduce operating cost.

(3) *Demographic distribution*: concentration of people in Japan around and within large urban centres facilitates more revenue activities and deposit-taking with less operating expense.

(4) *Effective internal communication*: the substitution of effective informal communication over misleading and constraining paper-reporting procedures.[28]

(5) *Balance-sheet values*: growth of bank assets during booms in equity and property markets created Japanese balance sheets which have been more recently repriced to high market levels and hence yield lower operating costs per unit of assets.

In the typical bank operating cost structure, employee-related expenses account for the largest portion of total operating expenses. By significantly

---

[27] This ratio should not be confused with the BIS capital ratios which are based on risk-adjusted assets.   [28] Dufey 1990.

limiting the number of employees required to sustain a level of assets, Japanese banks gain strong operating cost advantages over their Western peers.

Tables 7.14 and 7.15 present asset-to-employee ratios for a selection of the largest banks in Japan, Europe, and the USA. From the data, Japanese banks appear systematically to sustain higher levels of total assets per employee. According to this measure, the most efficient bank in 1991, Long-Term Credit Bank of Japan, managed to sustain nearly $67 million of assets per full-time employee, whereas the Western leader, J. P. Morgan, achieved under $8 million.

As mentioned above, focused product portfolio and product mix are two factors important to Japanese bank operating efficiency. The effect of these factors can be seen in the relative ranking of the Japanese banks in Table 7.14. Note that the three long-term credit banks decisively lead the other institutions, with $54 to $67 million of assets per employee versus $31 million for Sanwa Bank. Post-war legislation gave the long-term credit banks responsibility over long-term lending. Rather than rely on deposits for funding, those banks are permitted to issue bank debentures. The highly focused nature of their banking activity reduces their interest-spread earnings but dramatically improves their operating efficiency, partly via the impact of a lower staffing requirement.

In the lower tier of the listed operating efficiency rankings of Japanese banks are the regional banks, of which the three largest had asset levels of $11 to $16 million per employee. Lending by regional banks tends to be focused on small- to medium-sized firms. Most of the bank funding comes from individual deposits through the banks' retail operations. Maintenance of these operations requires, in turn, relatively larger staff levels. The City banks (for which the data in Table 7.13 were calculated) and trust banks fall somewhat between the two extremes in terms of staffing needs. The Bank of Tokyo's greater fee-based business lowers its asset-carrying capability to that of commercial banks.

It is not surprising to see the same effect among Western banks. J. P. Morgan's exclusively wholesale operations allow it to maintain relatively low employee levels, whereas the heavy retail nature of the American regional banks requires much higher levels of staff.

One additional factor not mentioned above is the greater efficiency created through the collaborative nature of the Japanese cross-ownership structure (*keiretsu*). As *keiretsu* banks maintain deeply-rooted relationships with their *keiretsu* member companies, these banks may face reduced operating costs in attracting and maintaining loans from these clients. Although Table 7.14 shows some indication of lower asset-to-employee ratios in *keiretsu* banks compared to non-*keiretsu* banks, the ranking order may be merely a function of size.

It should also be understood that the comparability of asset-to-employee

TABLE 7.14. *Employee productivity in Japanese financial institutions, 1991*

Institution	Type	Keiretsu	Assets ($ million)	Employees	Assets per employee ($ million)
Long-Term Credit Bank of Japan	Long-term credit	—	230,775	3,448	66.9
Industrial Bank of Japan	Long-term credit	IBJ	320,498	4,900	65.4
Nippon Credit Bank	Long-term credit	—	131,337	2,449	53.6
Sanwa Bank	City	Sanwa	436,750	13,913	31.4
Mitsubishi Bank	City	Mitsubishi	423,243	13,899	30.5
Fuji Bank	City	Fuyo	436,970	15,200	28.7
Sumitomo Bank	City	Sumitomo	446,472	16,669	26.8
Dai-Ichi Kangyo Bank	City	DKB	458,962	18,640	24.6
Tokai Bank	City	Tokai	269,523	11,748	22.9
Mitsubishi T&B	Trust	Mitsubishi	139,950	6,667	21.0
Sakura Bank	City	Mitsui	435,846	22,919	19.0
Sumitomo T&B	Trust	Sumitomo	126,856	7,451	17.0
Mitsui T&B	Trust	Mitsui	109,395	6,582	16.6
Bank of Yokohama	Regional	—	98,378	6,143	16.0
Yasuda T&B	Trust	Fuyo	94,431	6,002	15.7
Kyowa Saitama Bank	City	—	120,192	7,970	15.1
Bank of Tokyo	City/Foreign exchange	—	252,262	17,081	14.8
Daiwa Bank	City	—	129,815	9,338	13.9
Chiba Bank	Regional	—	63,919	4,613	13.9
Hokkaido Takushoku Bank	City	—	81,849	6,282	13.0
Toyo T&B	Trust	Sanwa	68,670	5,377	12.8
Shizuoka Bank	Regional	—	54,730	5,131	10.7

Note: Foreign exchange rate: 1 US dollar = 140.6 yen. Database includes the largest twenty banks based on capital.

Source: Morningstar Japan; Bank of Tokyo Annual Report.

TABLE 7.15. *Employee productivity in Western financial institutions, 1991*

Institution	Country	Type	Assets ($ million)	Employees	Assets per employee ($ million)
JP Morgan	USA	Commercial[†]	102.416	13,323	7.7
Bankers Trust	USA	Commercial	63,684	12,171	5.2
Banque Nationale de Paris	France	Commercial	289,747	59,676	4.9*
Société Générale	France	Commercial	204,485	45,776	4.5*
Crédit Lyonnais	France	Commercial	285,238	68,486	4.2*
ABN–Amro Bank	Netherlands	Commercial	242,686	58,329	4.2
Deutsche Bank	Germany	Commercial	296,226	71,400	4.1
Crédit Agricole	France	Commercial	302,983	74,450	4.1*
Chemical Banking	USA	Commercial	137,623	41,951	3.3
Chase Manhattan	USA	Commercial	97,275	35,760	2.7
PNC Financial	USA	Regional	45,111	18,000	2.5
Citicorp	USA	Commercial	215,355	86,000	2.5
Barclays Bank	UK	Commercial	258,339	111,400	2.3
Bank America	USA	Commercial	114,004	54,400	2.1
Nations Bank	USA	Regional	109,944	57,177	1.9
Fleet/Norstar Financial	USA	Regional	45,578	27,000	1.7

* Data for 1990.

[†] All commercial banks listed above are large size.

Source: Disclosure/Worldscope Global Database; Value Line.

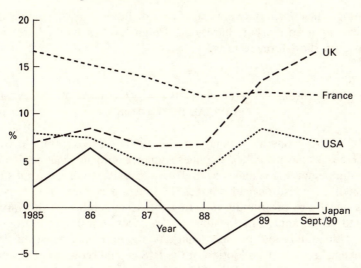

Note: The real lending rate equals the prime rate minus the producer's price index.
Source: IMF, *International Financial Statistics*.

Fig. 7.9. Real lending rate across countries, 1985–90

ratios may not be completely fair across countries. Rules used for adding up the number of employees may differ, and accounting standards are not identical. For example, management of bank assets by employees of bank subsidiaries, which are not counted by the parent company (for example, consumer finance companies) would overstate operating efficiency. However, although the ratios may not be wholly comparable, available data still seem to support the existence of Japanese operating cost efficiency achieved partly through employee cost control.

The decomposition of bank profitability reaffirms the strong emphasis of Japanese banks on operating efficiency. The data show that Japanese banks are able to support from two to six times the level of assets with the same level of operating expense as their Western counterparts. From 1988 to 1990, this advantageous operating cost position allowed Japanese banks to offset their unfavourable yield on assets and interest-rate spread positions.

The effect of such cost advantages can be seen in the ability of Japanese banks to price loans far below the rates required by Western banks. Charging significantly below market rates allowed Japanese banks quickly to expand their loan volume. Fig. 7.9 approximates the real lending rate and shows the trend in the rate for Japan, France, the UK, and the USA. The negative real lending rate experienced by Japanese banks during the latter part of the 1980s highlights the effect of such factors as strong operating efficiency, relatively lower cost of funds, a management desire to gain long-term market share, and a high level of bank shareholders' patience on short-term returns.

4. SUSTAINABILITY OF COMPETITIVE ADVANTAGE FOR JAPANESE FINANCIAL INSTITUTIONS

As the macro-economic climate of the 1980s created competitive cost advantages which propelled Japanese finance into international market leadership, emerging changes in the 1990s threaten to erode a substantial portion of these historical advantages. This section examines four important trends which are profoundly affecting the sustainability of the Japanese competitive advantage in the financial services industry in Europe: the crash of the equity and property markets, the deregulation of the Japanese financial sector, the adoption of the BIS capital requirements, and the growing competitiveness of the European financial market.

4.1. Stock Market and Property Market Crashes

As the Nikkei average was approaching 40,000 in late 1989, underlying macro-economic factors were undermining the future direction of the market. The BOJ had already demonstrated its concern over rising inflation through back-to-back hikes in the discount rate from 2.50 per cent to 3.75 per cent in May and October 1989 (see Fig. 7.7). The rise in market interest rates was particularly damaging to banks due to the above-mentioned deregulation of interest rates on deposits. Even though banks were consistently being required to pay higher market rates on deposits, they nevertheless maintained their relatively low lending rates to hold or gain market share, even at near-zero spreads (see Table 7.13).

In December 1989, Yasushi Mieno, the newly-appointed Governor of the BOJ, communicated his determination to shrink the speculative bubble in the stock and property markets. Within one week of his appointment, he had announced the third increase in the discount rate to a level of 4.25 per cent. Fig 7.7 summarizes the timing of discount rate changes.

Interest rate instability was accompanied by political uncertainty created by worry that the long-ruling Liberal Democratic Party (LDP) would lose its majority in the February 1990 elections. In the early months of 1990 the market remained jittery in anticipation of the election and further expected hikes in the discount rate.

When the election votes were counted on 18 February, the LDP had achieved a landslide victory in the House of Representatives and managed better than expected in the lower house. Analysts expected the results to send the yen and the Nikkei up. The appreciation of the yen never materialized, and when the Tokyo stock market closed on 19 February, the Nikkei was down. Within one week the Nikkei dropped 5,000 points, a 14 per cent decline from its peak level. A month later, the BOJ raised the discount rate another full percentage point. The market continued in a downward spiral through April. A rebound in the early summer brought the Nikkei back to a steady 32,000.

Hopes that the market would make a quick recovery were dashed in August with the invasion of Kuwait by Iraq. The resulting global bear market had a doubling impact in Tokyo as the BOJ raised the discount rate again on 30 August 1990, to 6.0 per cent.

To make matters worse, Daiwa Securities was found guilty of compensating losses incurred by preferred clients. And Sumitomo Bank Chairman Ichiro Isoda announced his resignation, accepting responsibility for illegal, speculative lending activities both by a local branch and through direct support of a speculative property client.

By 1 October 1990, the Nikkei dropped below 20,000—48 per cent lower than its peak only nine months earlier. The drop represented a paper value loss of 300 trillion yen,[29] or 70 per cent of Japan's 1990 GDP.[30]

At the resolution of the Gulf War in the spring of 1991, the Nikkei, unlike other major world exchanges, did not rebound. Through early 1992 the Nikkei appeared stable at 23,000. However, as the fiscal year reached its end, the large Japanese manufacturing firms began to report significant downturns in their expected earnings. The world had assumed that the Japanese economy would continue to grow despite the global recession. The Japanese had hoped that the recession would end quickly and that their economy would be unaffected. But as purchases of Japanese products in foreign markets continued to weaken, the world's recession finally caught up with Japan.

In March 1992 the market plunged again below the 20,000 level. Governor Mieno, hoping to boost the 31 March end-of-fiscal-year financial statements with a last-minute stock market surge, lowered the discount rate 100 basis points. But as 31 March ticked away, stock prices did not increase. Investors, for the most part, had believed that in the final event, the BOJ would have the power to support the market. The realization of this fallacy sent the market into a panic. Gloomy economic reports for Japan further reduced investor confidence, and by mid-August 1992 the Nikkei had dropped to 14,309—its lowest level in six years, and 63 per cent off its all-time high. In order to prevent a free fall in the Nikkei, and to boost investors' confidence in the market, the government announced on 18 August an 'emergency economic support package' which was successful in temporarily lifting the Nikkei index back to the 18,000 range. The market, however, quickly realized that the government would not be able to

---

[29] Wood 1990.   [30] OECD 1992*b*.

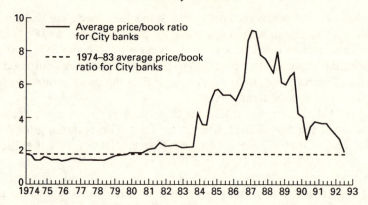

Note: All data until Jan. 1992 on a quarterly basis; data thereafter on a monthly basis.
Source: Salomon Brothers, 'Japan Equity Research' (14 Apr. 1992), 3.

FIG. 7.10. The ratio of average market value to book value, 1974–92

continue to 'talk the Nikkei up' as long as underlying economic conditions remained weak.

As shown in Fig. 7.10, the reduced level of City bank market-to-book ratios in 1992 suggests an adjustment of share prices to 'pre-bubble' levels. Should these prove to be, in fact, the long-term equilibrium level of share prices, banks must adjust their financial strategies to conform better to such a reality. The reality of a stock market stabilizing in the 15,000 to 20,000 range has strong implications for Japanese financial institutions. After the stock market crash, Japanese underwriters experienced a virtual disappearance of the market for equity-linked instruments. The tremendous demand created by the convertible bond issues (see Fig. 7.5) or the warrant issues came to an abrupt halt. Financial institutions which had built a large underwriting potential, especially in Europe, were left with large over-capacity. Moreover, Japanese financing costs increased significantly for both industrial and financial institutions. In May 1992, for example, Toyota Motor issued $1.0 billion worth of bonds with a coupon rate of 6.88 per cent, far above the 1.14 per cent paid on its $0.8 billion of bonds issued five years earlier.

Furthermore, the sharp decline in the property market raised considerable concern over the strength of the loan portfolios of Japanese banks. Since banks held large amounts of loans which were backed by artificially high land values, the fall in the property market had an especially strong effect on the Japanese banking industry.

By mid-1992, industry analysts had estimated the value of Japanese banks' bad debt to be from 5 to 50 trillion yen, most of which was linked to the collapse of the property market. The MOF tried to calm fears of an industry-wide financial crisis by announcing the total amount of bad debt of City, Long-Term Credit, and Trust banks to be only 2 to 3 trillion yen. Ironically, rather than assure the public of the industry's financial health, widespread disbelief in the MOF estimates further deteriorated common trust in Japan's financial sector.

4.2. Japanese Financial System Deregulation

One of the major business phenomena of the 1980s, and that most likely to continue into the 1990s, is deregulation. As with the deregulation of any industry, the direct result of such a structural change is increased competition. In Japan, government-imposed deposit rate ceilings, and functional segregation of financial activities, should disappear during the latter part of the 1990s.

During the early 1990s, the MOF has also studied reforms to abolish the barriers between commercial banks, Trust banks, Long-Term Credit banks, and securities houses. The existing system in Japan, defined by Article 65 of the Securities and Exchange Law, which is even more restrictive than the Glass–Steagall Act in the USA, compartmentalizes Japanese financial institutions by operating function and transaction maturity. During the early 1990s, the MOF was studying reforms to abolish the barriers between commercial banks, Trust banks, Long-Term Credit banks, and securities houses.

The proposed reforms would allow some merger or ownership of subsidiaries of functionally different banking entities. Banks could own more than 50 per cent of a securities subsidiary and securities houses could own over 50 per cent of a banking subsidiary. The restriction on maturity of deposits and lending would also be eased, allowing City banks to participate in long-term credit, and Long-Term Credit banks to accept short-term transactions. Acceptance of the bill by the Diet (expected in 1993) is forecast to benefit primarily the City banks. With an already strong branch network and the close relationships with clients as 'main bank', the City banks should rapidly gain full universal bank status by the end of the century.

However, in addition to the increased competition among financial institutions resulting from the breaking-down of walls between functional compartments, deregulation also opens the door for the entry of Japanese manufacturing companies into the financial services sector. The creation of the Toyota Bank, for example, is becoming a more disconcerting reality for Japanese banks. Toyota already operates a finance corporation for its dealers, and in March 1991 it acquired 40 per cent of Merrill Lynch's Japanese fund management subsidiary. Toyota is expected to target the consumer finance segment through banking offices in its 5,000 sales outlets.

TABLE 7.16. *City bank unregulated funds, 1986–1990* (data for end of fiscal years)

	1986	1987	1988	1989	1990
Ratio of unregulated rates on deposits (%)	24	37	47	61	70
Ratio of unregulated rates on funds (%)	36	46	55	67	73

Note: ratio of unregulated rates on deposits = (foreign currency deposits + non-resident yen deposits + MMCs + large denominated time deposits) / total funds. Ratio of unregulated funds = (call money + bills sold + non-BOJ borrowings + foreign currency deposits + non-resident yen deposits + MMCs + large denominated time deposits + CDs) / total funds.
Source: Bank of Japan, *Annual Review, 1991.*

The largest City bank office network in Japan, Sakura Bank, maintains less than 600 offices. Much like the US experience, Japanese banks fear that Toyota will exploit its funding potential as it holds a higher bond rating than any of the City banks.[31]

Unlike the US authorities, who have slowed the process of deregulation in the face of increased financial market volatility, Japanese bankers expect the MOF to accelerate the process of deregulation even if the market continues to deteriorate. Deregulation is seen as a way to help the ailing securities firms by increasing consolidation and establishing a more globally competitive financial industry. The MOF expects that the creation of such financial giants will strengthen large banks rather than make them more financially risky. Nevertheless, a post-Article 65 Japanese financial system is bound to be characterized in the 1990s by wide instability and large market consolidation.

Over the late 1980s and early 1990s, the deregulation of interest rate ceilings on deposits has been progressively implemented. Without the artificial ceiling, banks are required to pay significantly higher market rates on their accepted deposits. Table 7.16 traces the rise in the ratios of unregulated deposits and funds, to total deposits and total funds, respectively. From 1986 to 1990 the ratio of unregulated rates on deposits to total deposits had grown from 24 to 70 per cent, and that of unregulated funds to total funds expanded from 24 to 73 per cent. Until the mid-1980s not only had regulation held interest rates at an attractive level, but the prohibition of advertising also kept operating expenses down. The ongoing liberalization of interest rates creates a major challenge for Japanese banks, which are expected to continue to face significantly higher costs of funds.

[31] Shale 1991: 28–32.

4.3. The BIS Capital Requirement

In July of 1988 the Banking Regulations and Supervisory Practices Committee of the Bank for International Settlements in Basel adopted a set of capital adequacy guidelines to reduce the sources of competitive inequality in the international banking industry. The original framework was devised jointly by the banking authorities in the UK and USA in Jaunary 1987. Banking regulators from each of the Group of Ten (G-10) as well as Luxemburg and Switzerland, having reviewed and approved the proposal, had the measure ratified within their home country.

The BIS regulation required banks to meet two standards.[32] Both hurdles were subject to a two-year phase-in period begining on 31 March 1991, followed by a permanent hurdle, post-31 March 1993:[33]

	Temporary (Mar. 1991)	Permanent (Mar. 1993)
Tier 1 capital ratio:		
$\dfrac{\text{Tier 1 capital}}{\text{Risk-adjusted assets}}$	3.25%	4%
Tier 2 capital ratio:		
$\dfrac{\text{Tier 1 \& 2 capital}}{\text{Risk-adjusted assets}}$	7.25%	8%

Although the regulation has no formal enforcement mechanism, the banks were strongly pressured to maintain the requisite ratio in order to keep their good standing among other international banks.

In 1987, as the proposal was first being considered, Japanese banks were struck by the impact the BIS regulations would have on their balance sheets. Based on the prior year financials, the average capital ratio of Japanese banks was at 2.7 per cent, far below the required rate of 7.25 per cent. Japanese banks argued that they were as stable as Western banks because of the additional stability received from Japanese inter-bank support and BOJ protection. The MOF refused Japanese bank arguments and demanded full adherence to the BIS guideline. One adjustment to the international guidelines conceded to Japanese banks was the recognition of 45 per cent of unrealized gains on securities holdings as Tier 2 capital. By December 1988 the MOF had set a new capital ratio requirement in line with BIS regulations.[34] It should be noted that Japan was in fact the only country to include the 45 per cent capital gain recognition allowance by the BIS within its own legislation.

---

[32] For a more complete discussion of the BIS capital ratio calculation, refer to Appendix 7B. See also Hawawini and Swary 1990: ch. 6.

[33] These dates reflect the ends of Japanese fiscal years. Western banks were required to meet the requirement by 31 Dec. 1990 and 31 Dec. 1992, respectively.

[34] Smith and Walter 1990: 742–3.

The BIS felt that the regulation created much more equitable competition in the international banking industry. And the existence of an international standard for capital allowed national regulatory authorities to further banking deregulation. The emphasis on Tier 1 capital required banking operations to focus on profitability rather than on volume-oriented business. And the risk-adjustment calculation discouraged excessive high-risk lending and off-balance-sheet exposure.

To meet BIS capital ratio standards, Japanese banks faced two alternatives. First, they could reduce their asset base by either slowing their lending activities or selling part of their large equity investments in their client companies (traditional *keiretsu* ownership structure involves considerable cross-ownership of partner companies). Secondly, the banks could raise their Tier 1 capital through common equity issues or Tier 2 capital through preferred stock or subordinated debt issues.

The near-trebling of the Nikkei 225 from 13,083 (end of 1985) to 38,916 (end of 1989) provided Japanese banks with the ability to raise the required capital easily, either via new equity issues or through the recognition of their unrealized capital gains. From 1986 to 1988 the thirteen City banks actually issued 6 trillion yen in equity and equity-related financing.[35] In addition, Tier 2 capital was automatically increased through the ballooning of unrealized capital gains on the security holdings of banks. By March 1990 almost all banks were well above the 7.25 per cent requirement one year ahead of schedule.

The collapse of the Tokyo Stock Market reversed both effects; unrealized gains were shrinking and new issues were no longer possible. In April 1990 the MOF froze all new issues of both equity and debt in order to alleviate the downward pressure on prices on the Tokyo Stock Exchange. The Ministry was particularly worried that large life insurance companies, preferring to shift their portfolio to higher-coupon new debt issues (offering higher current income), would dump their equity holdings and further undermine the support of the stock market.

By June the ban on subordinated issues was eased. Over the summer, Japanese banks issued 2 trillion yen of subordinated debt at an uncomfortable 8.4 per cent coupon rate. Yet contrary to the spirit of the BIS regulations, much of these new issues were placed through dual agreements between the bank and the buyer: banks would lend the necessary funds to their clients to allow them to purchase the banks' debt issue. At the close of the fiscal year in March 1992, Sakura was the only bank below the 8 per cent hurdle, at 7.92 per cent as shown in Table 7.17. Loan growth for the banks with the lowest ratios, Sakura Bank and the Bank of Tokyo, actually fell in the fiscal year ending March 1992 by 0.9 per cent and 1.2 per cent, respectively.

[35] Wood 1990.

TABLE 7.17. *City bank capital adequacy ratios and required stock market levels*

City banks	Capital ratio, 31 Mar. 1992 (%)	Nikkei level to meet BIS ratio (%)
Dai-Ichi Kangyo Bank	8.24	16,000
Sakura Bank	7.92	18,900
Sumitomo Bank	8.43	11,600
Fuji Bank	8.04	16,000
Mitsubishi Bank	8.20	16,000
Sanwa Bank	8.10	15,100
Tokai Bank	8.38	17,000
Kyowa Saitama Bank	8.30	13,500
Daiwa Bank	8.27	13,900
Bank of Tokyo	8.10	18.500

Source: 'Major Banks', Japan Equity Research, Salomon Brothers, 26 Mar. 1992; *Financial Times* (29 May 1992).

Given the March 1992 balance-sheet structure, Table 7.17 presents the level of the Nikkei average necessary to provide sufficient securities gains to meet the 8.0 per cent capital ratio requirement. Sumitomo Bank was by far the most secure of the City banks with an 8.43 per cent capital ratio and a requirement that the Nikkei stay above 11,600.

As the March 1993 deadline approached, Japanese banks were highly concerned about the effect of further decreases in their capital bases. A profound result of both the BIS requirement and the stock market crash has been a marked shift in the orientation of Japanese banks from an emphasis on asset growth to a reliance on profitability. Interest-rate spreads had risen from 50 to 100 basis points, which improved profitability and eventually increased Tier 1 capital through earnings retention. The on-going deep concern of Japanese bankers for meeting BIS requirements should continue to fuel the trend towards higher profitability rather than greater volume.

4.4. Structural Changes in the European Financial-Services Industry

The European financial services industry has been undergoing a turbulent structural overhaul.[36] As the emerging European market promises to be a more competitive, efficient financial arena, the ability of Japanese institutions to sustain their cost advantage may be questioned.

The growing effect of financial market globalization, technology adoption, EC integration, and a desire to resist the penetration of foreign competitors has resulted in a number of important structural changes in

[36] For a detailed discussion on the transformation of the European financial services industry, see Hawawini and Rajendra 1989.

the European financial market. The growing structural movements in Europe include the on-going privatization of state-owned financial institutions, consolidation of both large and small firms in order to build 'critical mass' at a pan-European level, and increasing acceptance of the 'universal bank' model in Continental Europe. Other changes are the integration of European markets and systems, and an 'equalization' of individual country markets through the harmonization of regulation and the convergence of economic structures.

These factors are having, and will continue to have, a significant effect on the structure of the European financial-services industry. Two obvious implications for the industry are improved market efficiency and fierce near-term competition.

4.4.1. Improved Market Efficiency

The strong shift toward a more competitive and 'harmonized' European financial services industry will produce significant improvement in market efficiency. As in most other industries, the trends in the 1990s towards greater efficiency in Europe's financial sectors should create major market improvements for customers through superior service and lower prices.

The oft-quoted Price Waterhouse study (see Table 7.18) estimates the cost of not having a financially integrated Europe. The study assumes that integration will cause prices to decrease to the level of Europe's most competitive markets. Potential price reductions were established by comparing prevailing prices to the average price for selected services in the four least expensive countries. In aggregate, the study established potential price reductions for financial products and services in every member country (ranging from 9 per cent in the Netherlands to 34 per cent in Spain). Adjusted for the possibility that the European markets may not soon become perfectly competitive and integrated, more realistic price reductions in the range of 4 to 21 per cent were estimated as shown in the indicative price reductions row.

These estimations are most revealing when we examine each product line. The resulting checkerboard picture of efficiency across European financial services confirms that the benefits of market integration will be found in different product categories and different countries. For example, the UK is listed as highly inefficient in private equity transactions, yet quite competitively priced in institutional equity trading. In commercial loans, the French market is highly efficient whereas Dutch loans are relatively highly priced.

This environment may provide a number of profitable opportunities to financial institutions operating across European markets if they are able quickly to identify pockets of inefficiency and exploit them rapidly to their advantage. Although it may be possible for some well-placed non-European financial institutions to follow this strategy successfully, the approach requires a comparatively high degree of technical sophistication, a pan-European market knowledge and presence, and rapid decision-making. Given the relatively weak advantage possessed by Japanese institutions across these dimensions as discussed in Section 3, they appear ill-placed to capitalize on this opportunity.

4.4.2. Fierce Near-Term Competition

Until the European financial services industry can reach a structural equilibrium, the desire to establish a favourable position in the evolving industry will generate intense competition among European institutions. Firms will strive to improve their competitive standing and countries will attempt to preserve the position of their financial services industry. As the challenge to establish a favourable competitive posture intensifies, foreign firms will find it increasingly difficult to maintain a profitable European operation.

The champion European firms which will emerge from this structural adjustment will be positioned to become dominant forces in the international markets as well. Non-European institutions will consequently face a growing threat in their domestic markets as more formidable European competitors attempt to gain stronger footholds abroad.

4.5. Expectations

As the 1990s unfold, the Japanese financial services industry faces a challenging future. Historically abnormal interest-rate spreads will eventually disappear as deposit and lending rates rise to market levels, and competition among financial institutions intensifies. With the evaporation of the market for new equity-linked securities due to the stock market crash, financing costs are expected to climb during the 1990s. Downturns in both securities and property markets have triggered strong concern over the strength of bank loan portfolios. Moreover, the decrease in securities issues has created large over-capacities among Japanese underwriters, particularly in Europe.

But the deregulation of Japan's financial system and the crisis affecting financial institutions in that country in the early 1990s opens the door for significant industry consolidation before the end of the century. The resulting banking overhaul, coupled with the strong pressure on Japanese banks to meet BIS capital ratio standards and alter their strategy from growth to profitability, create the likely necessity for Japanese institutions to gain control of their domestic market at the expense of the foreign business. Moreover, the growing efficiency and inter-institution rivalry present in the European market raises further doubt about the sustainability of Japanese competitive advantages in Europe.

Given this background, the next section examines the prospects for the continued presence of Japanese financial institutions in Europe.

TABLE 7.18. *Estimated price reduction in financial products resulting from complete European financial integration, by country*

	Belgium	Germany	Spain	France	Italy	Lux.	Neth.	UK
1. Percentage difference in prices of financial products compared with the average of the four lowest observations								
Banking								
Consumer cards	-41	136	39	105		-26	31	121
Credit cards	79	60	26	-30	89	-12	43	16
Mortgages	31	57	118	78	-4		-6	-20
Letters of credit	22	-10	59	-7	9	27	17	8
Foreign exchange	6	31	196	56	23	33	-46	16
Travellers cheques	35	-7	30	39	22	-7	33	-7
Commercial loans	-5	6	19	-7	9	6	43	46
Insurance								
Life	78	5	37	33	83	66	-9	-30
Home	-16	3	-4	39	81	57	17	90
Motor	30	15	100	9	148	77	-7	-17
Commercial fire, theft	-9	43	24	153	245	-15	-1	27
Public liability	13	47	60	117	77	9	-16	-7
Securities								
Private equity	36	7	65	-13	-3	7	114	123
Private gilts	14	90	217	21	-63	27	161	36
Institutional equity	26	69	153	-5	47	68	26	-47
Institutional gilts	284	-4	60	57	92	-36	21	—

2. Theoretical potential price reductions

Banking	15	33	34	18	16	10	18
Insurance	31	10	32	51	37	1	4
Securities	52	11	44	33	9	18	12
Total	23	25	34	29	17	9	13

3. Indicative price reductions

All financial services							
Range	6–16	5–15	16–26	9–19	7–17	3–13	0–9	2–12
Centre of range	11	10	21	14	12	8	4	7

Note: The figures in part 1 of the table show the extent to which financial product prices, in each country, are above a low reference level. Each of these price differences implies a theoretical potential price fall from existing price levels to the low reference level. Part 2 sets down the weighted averages of the theoretical potential price falls for each sub-sector. Indicative price falls in part 3 are based on scaling down the theoretical potential price reductions, taking into account the extent to which perfectly competitive and integrated conditions will not be attained plus information for each financial services sub-sector, such as gross margins and administrative cost as a proportion of total costs.

Source: Commission of the European Communities, based on study by Price Waterhouse.

TABLE 7.19. *Summary of the competitive advantages of Japanese banks, 1980s v. 1990s*

Differentiation Advantage	1980s	1990s
Product innovation	Limited	Limited
Technical sophistication	Limited	Limited
Ability to attract high-quality local professional staff	Limited	Limited
Breadth of line of services	Limited	Limited
Affiliation with/knowledge of home market	Strong	Strong, but less salient
Capability to service home clients' operations in Europe	Strong	Strong
Macro-economic factors		
Appreciation of yen	Strong *v.* dollar Limited *v.* ECU	Strong *v.* dollar Limited *v.* ECU
Advantageous cost of capital	Strong	Weakened
Rising stock market	Strong	Limited
Appreciating property value	Strong	Limited
Micro-economic cost advantage		
Operating efficiency	Strong	Weakened

5. IMPLICATIONS FOR JAPANESE FINANCIAL INSTITUTIONS

Through the 1980s, Europe attracted significant investment by Japanese financial institutions wishing to serve the needs of a growing Japanese industrial presence, access the world's most liquid capital markets, and penetrate local markets abroad by leveraging their unique strengths. As the goal of a single market Europe becomes an increasing reality, Japanese financial institutions will continue to be attracted by the potential to establish the beach-head needed to take part in the potential upside of European unification. Given both the dynamics of the European market and the competitive position of Japanese financial institutions in the 1990s, this section considers the role that Japanese institutions can be expected to occupy in the future Europe.

5.1. Deterioration of Japanese Competitive Advantage

The level of future Japanese participation in the European financial services industry is dependent upon the competitive advantage possessed by Japanese institutions. Table 7.19 summarizes the competitive advantage profile of Japanese financial institutions as developed in this paper. The '1980s' column presents the factors which contributed to Japanese financial institutions success in the 1980s, as outlined in Section 3. The '1990s' column alters the competitive advantage profile of Japanese financial institutions to reflect the adverse changes which challenge the sustainability of their advantage, as presented in Section 4. The following discussion highlights the impact of these changes.

5.1.1. Differentiation Advantage
In the 1980s, European-based Japanese financial institutions used their differentiated affiliation with Japan to exploit the rapid growth of the capital and property markets. But in the 1990s, the ability of Japanese financial institutions to exert pressure through their affiliation with their home financial market disappeared abruptly with the crash of the Japanese financial markets. As described, the market downturn essentially dried up the interest in Japanese financial-market-based instruments.

As further outlined in Table 7.19, the other more firm-specific dimensions of competitive advantage—i.e. product innovation, technical sophistication, ability to attract high-quality local professional staff, and breadth of line of services—are expected to continue to remain relatively weak areas for Japanese financial institutions.

5.1.2. Macro-economic Factors
The financial market readjustment, combined with the trend towards greater deregulation of the Japanese financial sector, significantly reduces the importance of the macro-economic factors—i.e. yen appreciation, cost-of-capital advantage, and stock market and property market effects. The reduction of the Japanese advantage in these areas is evident in a number of key trends. The question of potentially bad property-backed debt on the books of Japanese banks has raised strong doubts as to the solvency of the Japanese financial system. Funding costs now approach Western levels as Japanese institutions are no longer sheltered from paying market interest rates on deposits, and must refinance staggering sums of warrant and convertible bonds originally floated when Japanese derivative issues provided near zero-rate capital costs. However, a high savings rate in Japan, as well as patient investors, will continue to offer some relief for Japanese financial institutions.

The limited value of the listed macro-economic factors in the 1990s is also evident in the disappearance of the heavy underwriting activity enjoyed by Japanese financial institutions in the 1980s. During the early 1990s, the European operations of Japanese banks and securities firms have experienced (and will continue to experience) a significant drop-off in business. With the volume of international security underwriting significantly reduced (see Table 7.10), Japanese institutions have recognized the value of rationalizing their large European operations. For example, in February 1992, Nikko Securities reduced its staff from 59 to 49 in London, while the smaller New Japan Securities and Kankaku Securities closed their respective Paris and Milan offices in 1992. Expectations for the Japanese securities business fall into three categories: the Big Four securities firms, which will maintain a strong yet somewhat scaled-back presence in Europe; the smaller securities firms, which will encounter significant down-sizing, if not closing, of operations; and bank subsidiaries, whose *raison d'être* will depend heavily on the degree of liberalization offered them by the financial system reform.

The Japanese banks are also being deeply affected by the necessity to transform their business from a focus on volume to a focus on profitability. The impact of less favourable macro-economic factors, coupled with international regulations and domestic deregulations, have strongly curbed the rampant loan portfolio growth of the 1980s. As Japanese banks are still very hesitant to begin new operations in Europe, such as retail banking, the future emphasis should remain in the wholesale market.

5.1.3. Micro-economic Cost and Operational Advantage

The micro-economic cost advantage also appears to be in question due to the impact of BIS regulation on capital adequacy and the increased efficiency and competition in the European financial services industry. The BIS regulation has created a need for Japanese banks to shift their focus from a high-volume, cost-based strategy to a high-margin, differentiation-based strategy. Due to the aforementioned factors, one must remain dubious as to the ability of Japanese banks successfully to pursue a differentiation-based strategy.

Furthermore, the increased efficiency and competitiveness of the European players, resulting from the structural changes described earlier, will most likely erode the relative historical cost advantages enjoyed by Japanese financial institutions in Europe. As European market prices adjust downward, these firms' European offices will find it more difficult to compete effectively based on price. Also, due to the necessity in Japan of providing reciprocal treatment for European firms operating in that country, the potential for Japanese banks to be adversely affected by a European presence on their home turf cannot be dismissed as unlikely. Under established and pending EC legislation, non-EC countries must provide a 'level playing-field' between domestic and EC banks operating within their country, in order for those countries' banks to benefit from the EC 'single passport' in Europe. Given the success of US investment banks in profitably penetrating the Japanese market in the late 1980s, the successful entry of the strongest of European banks into the Japanese market cannot be ruled out.

5.2. What Future for Japanese Financial Institutions in the 1990s?

Had Japanese banks and securities houses taken advantage of the 'window of opportunity' in the late 1980s to build more differentiating advantages, their position might not appear so tenuous today. Although some innovative advantages were exploited by Japanese firms (such as in aircraft finance), the sector as a whole has developed relatively few areas of valued expertise. This lack of investment in sustainable advantages will become ever more apparent as Europe becomes increasingly market-driven.

This bleak picture, however, does not forecast the utter extinction of Japanese financial institutions from the European scene. Some factors still exist which will prove highly valuable in maintaining a Japanese presence. The primary factor is the on-going global success of Japanese manufacturing firms in Europe. As presented in Table 7.19, this competitive advantage remains the sole factor likely to continue at full strength into the 1990s. The erosion of Japan's macro-economic advantages and the increasing competitiveness of European institutions will not alter the deep-seated relationships that exist between Japanese financial institutions and their domestic clients operating in Europe. As industrial firms are expected to continue to enjoy an important presence in the future Europe, so will banks continue to service these companies.

Although Japanese financial institutions clearly have several formidable challenges to overcome, they still remain potentially very strong competitors. Two possible scenarios can be put forward regarding the future presence of Japanese financial institutions in Europe.

The first scenario assumes a continuation of the trends of the early 1990s, including down-sizing of operations in Europe and retrenchment into Japan for an extended period of time.

The second scenario is patterned after the surprising turnaround capabilities which some Japanese manufacturing firms have shown in the past. Although a return to the 'Golden Age' of their European presence may be beyond reach in the foreseeable future, Japanese institutions still have considerable potential for a successful comeback. This second scenario predicts a galvanization of the Japanese financial sector, brought on by the hardships of the early 1990s. The temporary retrenchment of the industry will be followed by the emergence of a leaner, more competitive, more innovative Japanese financial power led by a few world-class, truly universal financial institutions which will be the outcome of mergers between banks and securities companies. The realization of this scenario depends on (1) the ability of Japanese institutions quickly to mimic, adapt, and improve upon the ways of the best Western firms, and (2) the capacity of the MOF to orchestrate a few successful mergers between banks and securities companies. As seen in many other world industries, the Japanese capacity to recognize their weaknesses and implement an improvement upon Western methods suggests that the potential for a future resurgence of Japanese financial institutions in a more competitive European market cannot be ruled out.

APPENDIX 7A:
ROE DECOMPOSITION FORMULA

Consider the following notations:

E = Equity
D = Deposits and other liabilities
A = Assets = E + D
R = Revenues form assets
B = Bad debt expense
X = Operating expense
i = Average interest rate paid on deposits and liabilities
iD = Interest expense
YOA = Yield on assets = (R–B)/A
XOA = Operating expense per unit of assets = X/A
ROE = Pre-tax return on equity

$$ROE = \frac{R - B - X - iD}{E}$$

$$= \left\{ \frac{R - B}{A} - \frac{X}{A} \right\} \frac{A}{E} - i \left\{ \frac{D}{E} \right\}$$

$$= (YOA - XOA)\left\{ \frac{E + D}{E} \right\} - i\left\{ \frac{D}{E} \right\}$$

$$\boxed{ROE = (YOA - XOA) + (YOA - i) - XOA\left\{ \frac{D}{E} \right\}}$$

where—

$$YOA - i = \text{Spread}$$

$$\left\{ \frac{D}{E} \right\} = \text{Leverage}$$

APPENDIX 7B: DEFINITIONS OF **BIS** CAPITAL ADEQUACY RATIOS

This regulation requires all banks involved in international transactions to adhere to a limit on capital-to-asset ratios based on common capital and risk-adjusted asset calculations. The BIS capital ratio requires calculating three numbers: Tier 1 capital, Tier 2 capital, and risk-adjusted assets.

Tier 1 ('core') capital: defined as retained earnings, common stock, qualifying non-cumulative perpetual preferred stock, minority interests, *less* goodwill.

Tier 2 ('supplementary') capital: includes preferred stock, hybrid capital instruments, subordinated debt, and 45 per cent of unrealized gains on marketable securities.

Risk-adjusted assets: rather than require banks to maintain a specific capital base for all assets on the balance sheet, the BIS requires capital to back assets only in proportion to their relative risk. Moreover, off-balance-sheet items which also increased claims on the bank's capital are added to the BIS asset calculation.

The framework is designed to be rather simple in order to facilitate international application. Each asset or off-balance-sheet exposure is designated to one of four risk categories. Then, the sum of each category is multiplied by a risk weighting. For example, cash is assigned to the least risky category and receives a risk weighting of 0 per cent, meaning that none of the cash balance is required to be backed by capital. However, all loans other than residential mortgages are assigned to the most risky category and receive a 100 per cent risk weighting. Thus the full value of the loans must be accounted for in the risk-adjusted asset figure. A simplified categorization of the weighting system is as follows:

Cash, government securities	0%
Interbank lending	20%
Mortgages	50%
Commercial lending	100%

REFERENCES

Bank of England Quarterly Bulletin (Nov. 1987).
—— (May 1988).
—— (Aug. 1991).
Bank of Japan, *Annual Review, 1991*.
Bond Underwriters Association of Japan (1990), *Bond Market in Japan, 1990* (Tokyo).
DAQUIL, L. (1991), *Winners in the Japanese Banking Industry* (Tokyo: UBS Phillips & Drew, Mar.).
DOWNES, R., and ELVEN, C. (1990), *Japanese Equity Warrants* (London: Eurostudy Publishing Co. Ltd.).
DUFEY, G. (1990), 'The Role of Japanese Financial Institutions Abroad', in *Japanese Financial Growth*, ed. Charles Goodhart and George Sutija (London: Macmillan).
DUSER, J. (1990), *International Strategies of Japanese Banks: The European Perspective* (London: Macmillan).
FAIRLAMB, D. (1983), 'International Banking in London Holds its Sway', *Banking World* (Aug.), 11–13.
FRANKEL, A., and MORGAN, P. (1992), 'Deregulation and Competition in Japanese Banking', *Federal Reserve Bulletin* (Aug.).
GRUBEL, H. (1977), 'A Theory of Multinational Banking', *Banca Nazionale de Lavoro Quarterly Review* (Dec.).
GUYOT, N. (1992), 'Les Banques japonaises en Europe et en France: La Nouvelle Donne' (Japanese Banks in Europe and in France: The New Given), *La Revue Banque*, 531 (Oct.), 900–2.
HAWAWINI, G., and RAJENDRA, E. (1989), 'The Transformation of the European Financial Services Industry: From Fragmentation to Integration' (Monograph Series in Finance and Economics, 4; New York: Salomon Brothers Center for the Study of Financial Institutions).
—— and SWARY, I. (1990), *Mergers and Acquisitions in the U.S. Banking Industry: Evidence from the Capital Markets* (Amsterdam: North Holland).
HIRTLE, B. (1991), 'Factors Affecting the Competitiveness of Internationally Active Financial Institutions', *Federal Reserve Bank of New York Quarterly Review* (Spring), 38–51.
Japan, Ministry of Finance (Institute of Fiscal and Monetary Policy) (1992), *Monthly Finance Review* (Dec.).
Japan 1992: An International Comparison (Tokyo: Keizai Koho Centre, 1991).
LAKE D. (1992), *Japanese Capital: How Corporations Tap the World's Largest Liquidity Pool* (Business International Ltd., Special Report P 333; London: The Economist Intelligence Unit, Feb.).
M&A Japan (Feb. 1992), 11.
National Westminster Bank (1991), *Quarterly Review* (Nov.).
OECD (1992a), *Bank Profitability, Statistical Supplement: Financial Statements of Banks, 1981–1990* (Paris).
OECD (1992b), *National Accounts: Main Aggregates, 1960–1990* (Paris).

OKABE, S. and TAKIZAWA, Y. (1992), 'L'Avenir du secteur bancaire japonais', *La Revue Banque*, 531 (Oct.), 874–7.

Salomon Brothers (1992), *International Bank Weekly* (International Equity Research, 5 Mar.).

SENDER, H. (1991), 'Japan's California Come-uppance', *Institutional Investor* (Dec.), 105–10.

SHALE, T. (1991), 'Toyota Aims to Earn its Bank Tag', *Euromoney* (Nov. 1991), 28–32.

SMITH, R., and WALTER, I. (1990), *Global Financial Services* (New York: Harper & Row).

SUZUKI, Y. (1987), *The Japanese Financial System* (Oxford: Clarendon Press).

The Economist (1992), 'Italian Banking: Half a Renaissance' (21 Mar.), 88–9.

Tokyo Business Today (1991), 'Curbing Land Prices in Tokyo: Causes and Effects of the New Land Tax' (Jan. 1991), 10–16.

TSCHOEGL, A. (1987), 'International Retail Banking as a Strategy: An Assessment', *Journal of International Business Studies*, 19, 67–88.

UNGER, B. (1992), 'World Banking', *The Economist* (2 May).

WOOD, C. (1990), 'A Survey of Japanese Finance', *The Economist* (8 Dec.).

ZIMMER, S., and McCAULEY, R. (1991), 'Bank Cost of Capital and International Competitiveness', *Federal Reserve Bank of New York Quarterly Review* (Winter).

COMMENT

Gunter Dufey

Anyone who takes on, courageously or foolishly, the job of assessing a phenomenon as complex as the international expansion pattern of Japanese financial institutions has a difficult time identifying any meaningful long-term trend: to distinguish between factors that are associated with the very rapid expansion in the 1980s in an environment that many observers with the benefit of hindsight have labelled a 'bubble', and the equally rapid contraction in the deflation that characterizes Japanese financial markets in the early 1990s, is truly a challenge. The paper presented by Hawawini and Schill contributes significantly to the analysis of the issues by diligently assembling a large amount of data and by offering a balanced assessment in terms of a historical perspective and future outlook for Japanese financial institutions outside Japan, and especially in Europe. I have few quibbles with the authors' guarded conclusions; however, instead of trying to find fault with minor points, this comment develops some alternative interpretations and broader themes in an effort to provide additional insights into this complex phenomenon.

There is no doubt that Japan's financial institutions have expanded dramatically the scope and volume of their activities outside Japan during the 1980s. In order to assess the contribution of various factors to this growth path, one might begin by establishing a baseline: that is, what would one expect the role of Japanese institutions to be?

In this respect, it seems obvious that a large part of Japanese institutions' growth must be labelled 'catching-up'. While much has been written on the relationship between the financial sector of the economy and 'real' business, there is no doubt that in terms of economic output of goods and services, international trade, and foreign investment, Japan represents clearly the second most important economy in the world. It is, therefore, not surprising that Japanese financial institutions in the aggregate should play a role second only to those based in the USA.

It is also quite apparent that simple rankings of the competitive role of the size of institutions neglect to account for both differences in the structure of industry among different countries and variances in the nature of the business in which they engage. Concentration ratios in financial institutions between the USA and Japan are clearly different. There is nothing equivalent in the USA to the dominance of the City banks in Japan's corporate credit markets. Likewise, there is nothing in the USA that resembles the power of the 'Big Four' securities houses (Daiwa, Nikko, Nomura, and Yamaichi) relative to the many small securities firms. The number of competitors in every bracket of business in the USA is a multiple of Japan; a multiple that is more than two times, were one naïvely to relate concentration ratios to GNP.

As far as the nature of the business is concerned, this is a major problem in the comparison of the performance among financial institutions, since financial services comprise such a wide variety of products with very different cost, revenue, and risk profiles. One factor is evident, however, and has been flagged by the authors very clearly: the Japanese have dominated in their international business primarily through low margin, asset-intensive lending operations to corporates and governments. Obviously, if asset size is the criterion for performance, the Japanese banks have done amazingly well internationally. However, such comparisons leave out another factor, namely, risk. Indeed, if one reads the strategy statements of many financial institutions in the West, risky balance-sheet lending is being spurred in favour of off-balance-sheet fee income. In this context, productivity-per-employee calculations are extremely misleading, since the quality of earnings is so different, not only among institutions headquartered in different countries, but even among institutions within countries.

There is no doubt that real economic growth in Japan has exceeded that of virtually all Western industrialized countries, but to what extent that growth has been catch-up and to what extent it is driven by internal efficiencies of its institutions and systems requires more than simply straight-line extrapolation of growth rates taken from the past. This methodological point applies also for financial institutions. For example, the real appreciation of the Japanese currency *vis-à-vis* the dollar contributed to the growth of Japanese institutions even in Europe, since much of their activity in the European theatre, particularly out of London, is based on the US dollar. Therefore, a very large proportion of all off-shore transactions are still based on US currency; the European currencies, even in the aggregate, are less important, and the yen plays a negligible role.

There is a related additional factor that has received very little attention in the analysis of the growth of Japanese institutions outside Japan: repression of financial market development inside Japan. For the past 30 years, or even longer, discussions of Japan's financial markets in general have been dominated by two themes: liberalization and internationalization. Accordingly, every major and not-so-major publication dealing with the analysis of Japanese financial markets contains an appendix with an extensive timetable of various liberalization measures.[37] A fundamental facet of the Japanese political economy is that financial markets are considered too important to be left to the free play of market forces. In Japan, deeply

---

[37] For an example, see M. Takeda and P. Turner, 'The Liberalisation of Japan's Financial Markets: Some Major Themes' (BIS Economic Papers, 34; Basle: Bank for International Settlements, Nov. 1992), 99–121.

ingrained beliefs based on the scarcity of resources, together with high population density and a long history of frequent man-made and natural calamities, have convinced the Japanese that society has to be well regulated in order to avoid chaos and destruction. Based on Confucian values, wise leaders set policy, implemented by an all-knowing and pervasive bureau-cracy, which is usually honest and, at times, even efficient.

At the same time, destructive conflicts among major interest groups are to be avoided by all means; consensus is achieved through lengthy negotiations, and various factions are persuaded and bribed to agree to compromise. Often, the compromise consists of the status quo being pre-served with only minor cosmetic changes.

Foreign pressure wields a special influence in the Japanese negotiation process. It would be wrong to credit outside forces with being at the source of all significant changes in Japanese financial markets; however, when outside pressures coincide with those of significant domestic groups, change usually does occur.[38] The crux of it all is that there has to be so much liberalization and even more talk about liberalization because so many aspects of Japan's financial markets have been tightly controlled.

Interestingly, one significant strategy for financial institutions to escape domestic market controls has been to go abroad. Indeed, not only Japan-ese financial institutions go abroad, but their corporate customers as well; they use the external markets, primarily the Eurodollar and Eurobond markets, extensively as safety valves to escape the constraints and costs of funding in domestic markets. Much of the data that the authors present about the rapid rise of Japanese institutions in the Euromarkets reflect merely the shifting of funding as well as investment activities of Japanese corporations and investors into the offshore markets, because there they were able to do what was either against the rules at home, or at least subject to high transactions costs. A careful analysis of the role of Jap-anese securities houses' growth in Europe shows that transactions either involved a Japanese issuer or, when non-Japanese issuers were brought to the market, an overwhelming part of the paper issued wound up with Japanese investors.

In a way, the Japanese role internationally, from the earliest ventures of banks abroad, was not only to follow their customers, but also to get access to US dollars, which were used to finance Japanese trade since short-term credit markets for yen were either non-existent or so hemmed in by regulations that interest rates were 'off market' and quantitative limits came into play. This phenomenon persists even today where a dis-proportionately small amount of Japan's imports or exports are financed not in yen, but rather in third currencies. This practice, by the way, is

---

[38] See A. Prindl, *Japanese Finance: A Guide to Banking in Japan* (New York: John Wiley & Sons, 1981); and F. Rosenbluth, *Financial Politics in Contemporary Japan* (Ithaca, NY: Cornell University Press, 1989).

in marked contrast to the use of the Deutschmark for intra-European trade.

Regulation also plays a role in shaping the pattern of Japanese financial institutions, since money flows across borders with relative ease. A closer look at Japanese accounting rules, which make it possible for bad assets to be hidden in unconsolidated foreign subsidiaries (i.e. in Luxemburg or Switzerland), shows that these have much more power to explain the existence of Japanese subsidiaries in those countries than any grand market penetration strategies intended to conquer the world of finance. The same is true for special-purpose financing such as aircraft financing. It is doubtful whether the Japanese have developed any special expertise in that business to a sufficient extent, especially since most of the contracts are drawn up by London- or New York-based lawyers. Instead, Japanese leadership in that business is rather founded on the special tax environment, that is, largely a combination of high marginal tax rates plus fast depreciation schedules, in combination with the Japanese government's policies to promote imports. In this context, it is worth remembering that US planes leased by Japanese leasing companies to, say, Air France count fully as Japanese imports when the lease transaction is put on the books.

When one assesses in the end the unique conditions for Japanese organizations internationally, one has to note that those institutions definitely have a very strong competitive advantage in the business relationship with companies from their home country. Much has been written about the importance of relationships in Japan, and that aspect is even more important for Japanese institutions in the hostile world for Japanese corporations outside Japan. Thus, as long as one expects Japanese manufacturers to play a role abroad commensurate with the technical capabilities of Japan's industry, it is safe to conclude that most of those entities' banking business will be done by Japanese financial institutions, in Europe or elsewhere. It is also true that as long as the yen plays an international role as a currency that is lower than second place because of remaining restrictions and institutional constraints in Japan, Japanese institutions will have to engage in various activities that provide access to secure and diverse sources of funds. A large part of the motivation for venturing into the retail business in the USA by Japanese can only be understood because of that rationale.

These advantages must be balanced against disadvantages in hiring, motivating, and integrating non-Japanese professional work forces into Japanese organizations and into the decision processes that drive those organizations. Major changes in the Japanese corporate culture will be necessary before this disadvantage is to be conquered. But such a change would also take away one of the more important advantages of Japanese financial institutions: the effective and efficient communication among Japanese managers in large and far-flung organizations.

Last, but not least, a final point of caution: one has to be careful when attempting to apply lessons learned from one sector of the economy (i.e. manufacturing) to another sector (i.e. the financial services industry). In drawing such comparisons one has to account diligently for the different firm economics, since the resulting outcomes may be quite different. The contribution of Hawawini and Schill has furthered our understanding of this complex issue, but at the same time raises many new questions.[39]

[39] G. Dufey, 'The Role of Japanese Financial Institutions Abroad', in C. Goodhart and G. Sutija, eds., *Japanese Financial Growth* (London: Macmillan, 1990).

8

Japanese Direct Investment in the European Semiconductor Industry

Yui Kimura

1. INTRODUCTION

Today Japan is at the forefront of global competition in a select group of high technology industries. These industries include computers, telecommunications equipment, automobiles, office equipment, home electronics entertainment, and robotics. The semiconductor industry is an industry that must also be included in such a list.

In 1991 Japan accounted for a 50 per cent share of world semiconductor production, and six Japanese semiconductor firms were among the world's ten largest semiconductor firms, with the top three positions being occupied by the three largest Japanese semiconductor firms. Also, they were ranked among the top in patent awards in semiconductor technologies. A few of these simple statistics are sufficient to tell us the significance of the presence of the Japanese semiconductor industry in the world.

In contrast to Japan, Europe as a whole accounted for about 18 per cent of world production in 1990. Within Europe, the European firms supplied about 40 per cent of the demand, while US and Japanese firms filled the remaining 40 and 20 per cent of the demand, respectively. Among the top ten semiconductor firms in sales in Europe, five were American and two were Japanese in 1990. Among them were only three Community-based firms, though they occupied the top three ranks in semiconductor sales. The position of the European firms has been slipping in the world semiconductor industry, and the users of microelectronic components in Europe have been increasingly dependent on supplies from firms based outside the Community.

This alarming state of the semiconductor industry in the Community raises a number of questions: Can the unification in 1992 arrest the decline of the European semiconductor industry? Or does it offer opportunities for further market penetration by US and Japanese semiconductor firms? Indeed, there has been a surge of interest among Japanese semiconductor

The author thanks Thomas A. Pugel, Mark Mason, Dennis Encarnation, John Dunning, Hellmut Schütte, Gabriel Hawawini, and Henri-Claude de Bettignies for their useful comments. He also gratefully acknowledges the editorial assistance of Marc W. Modica and the research assistance of Naoya Takezawa.

firms in Europe—particularly the EC countries—as a location for their production and marketing activities. What factors, then, are motivating the Japanese semiconductor firms to undertake foreign direct investment (FDI) in the Community? What strategies are they adopting, and what impact are they likely to have on the industry itself and the adjacent industries?

The purpose of this paper is an attempt to provide answers to some of these questions. In this paper we examine FDI by Japanese semiconductor firms in the EC.

In Section 2, we place the FDI activities of Japanese semiconductor firms in a global perspective, drawing contrasts between FDI in Europe and that in the USA and Asia. In doing so, we examine various motivating factors stemming from the technological capabilities of Japanese firms, the structure of the industry, and the competitive conditions they confronted.

In Section 3, we discuss Japanese semiconductor FDI in the EC and analyse the factors that motivated those FDI activities. Diverse incentives give rise to different competitive strategies.

In Section 4, we provide an analysis of competitive strategies of Japanese firms in the industry in Europe, including the strategic alliances that are emerging between Japanese and European firms. These competitive strategies involve not only the semiconductor industry itself but also adjacent industries through varied horizontal and vertical linkages, inside and outside the firm. We examine these linkages, trying to assess the impact of the competitive strategies of the Japanese firms on the adjacent industries in the EC.

From our analysis of FDI activities of the Japanese semiconductor firms, we hope to develop some assessment of the impact of the Japanese presence in the Community through direct investment. In our assessment, we focus on the impacts of the industrial organization of Japanese FDI on the Community. We conclude the paper with implications for the European and Japanese electronics firms and the industry. We also suggest some implications for Community and Japanese policymakers.

2. FDI BY JAPANESE SEMICONDUCTOR FIRMS

We begin with an overview of the FDI activities of Japanese semiconductor firms. First, we discuss the Japanese semiconductor manufacturers, and examine how their semiconductor operations relate to their corporate structure. We then describe Japanese FDI activities in the semiconductor industry in a global perspective, and examine the incentives of the Japanese semiconductor firms to undertake FDI. The analysis encompasses the influences on Japanese global competitiveness of their technological leadership and the dynamic structural change of the semiconductor industry.

TABLE 8.1. *World's top twenty semiconductor firms, 1991*

Firms	Sales ($ million)	World market share (%)
NEC (JPN)	5,547	8.5
Toshiba (JPN)	5,337	8.2
Hitachi (JPN)	4,351	6.7
Intel	4,059	6.3
Motorola	3,915	6.0
Fujitsu (JPN)	3,111	4.8
Texas Instruments	2,753	4.2
Mitsubishi (JPN)	2,421	3.7
Matsushita (JPN)	2,568	4.0
Philips	2,072	3.2
National Semiconductors	1,697	2.6
Sanyo (JPN)	1,612	2.5
Samsung	1,592	2.5
Sharp (JPN)	1,562	2.4
SGS-Thomson	1,490	2.3
Sony (JPN)	1,426	2.2
Siemens	1,250	1.9
AMD	1,185	1.8
Oki (JPN)	1,157	1.8
Rohm (JPN)	1,029	1.6

Source: Dataquest, 1992.

This section is intended to provide a context in which to examine Japanese semiconductor FDI in the EC.

2.1. Japanese Semiconductor Firms

There are about 30 to 35 firms that are engaged in production of integrated circuit devices in Japan, and of these 30 to 35 firms, about a dozen are large semiconductor producers, and they maintain significant production of semiconductor devices abroad. These firms achieve multi-billion dollar sales figures, and are highly diversified multinational electric/electronics firms. Table 8.1 lists these firms and their semiconductor sales in 1991, relative to other semiconductor firms in the world.

Among the firms in the table, Hitachi, Toshiba, and Mitsubishi operate in a broad array of industries, ranging from nuclear power generators to computers to home appliances. Fujitsu, NEC, and Oki are manufacturers of telecommunications equipment and computers, while Matsushita, Sanyo, and Sony are consumer electric/electronics manufacturers. Some other firms, like Sharp and Ricoh, focus on office equipment businesses.

These firms manufacture semiconductors for merchant sales as well as

for internal captive consumption. Within the large semiconductor manufacturers the proportion of captive consumption is limited, but their
semiconductor production is directed in varying degrees to the captive
consumption in their own equipment manufacturing. As we will discuss in
a later section, the diversified operations of these firms and the partially
internalized vertical linkages of semiconductor operations with downstream
activities seem to influence their competitive strategies and positions in a
number of ways, including their FDI activities and competitive strategies
in overseas markets.

2.2. *Japanese Semiconductor FDI in Global Perspective*

FDI by these Japanese semiconductor firms began in 1969, first by Toshiba
in Mexico. It increased slowly in the 1970s. A rapid expansion of Japanese
semiconductor firms in international production locations took place in
the late 1970s to mid-1980s. FDI by Japanese semiconductor firms has
increased again in the early 1990s. Table 8.2 summarizes manufacturing
FDI undertaken by Japanese semiconductor firms as of 1990.

It seems that there is a pattern in the FDI activities of Japanese semiconductor firms, and it differs across regions at different times. The FDI
activities by these firms may be classified into three rather distinct phases.
The first international move by Japanese firms of production sites from
Japan took place in the late 1960s and early 1970s. It focused on Asia
(except Toshiba's FDI in Mexico in 1969), and the size and scope of the
FDI activities were very limited. The second wave, significantly larger in
scale than the first, came in the late 1970s and early 1980s, and targeted
advanced countries, particularly the USA. The Japanese firms were more
committed than before, so much so that many of them included the upstream stage of production (i.e. wafer processing) in their activities abroad.
The early 1990s is witnessing the third wave of FDI by Japanese semiconductor firms. It has focused on the EC as a location of production sites,
and the Japanese firms seem fully committed to integrated production
in the Community. This paper focuses on this phase of Japanese FDI
activities.

In the study of the Japanese semiconductor industry, Kimura (1988,
1989) shows that the observed pattern is largely due to the differences in
motivating factors that drove their FDI activities in those different regions
at different times. These motivations reflected the technological capabilities
of Japanese firms relative to US firms, the structure of the industry,
the trade policies of the host-country governments, and the competitive
circumstances they faced at these times.

(*a*) *The early FDI activities in South-East Asia.* In the late 1960s and early
1970s, the Japanese semiconductor industry was still in its infancy, struggling
to catch up with the technological lead of the US industry in integrated

TABLE 8.2. *Japanese semiconductor production abroad, by country and year*

Firm	Country	Year established
NEC	Singapore	1976
	Malaysia	1976
	USA	1978
	UK	1982
	Ireland	1976
	China	1991
Hitachi	Malaysia	1973
	USA	1979
	Germany	1980
Toshiba	Malaysia	1975
	Korea	1969
	Mexico	1966
	USA	1980
	Germany	1984
Mitsubishi	USA	1985
	Germany	1989
Fujitsu	USA	1979
	UK	1983
	Ireland	1981
	Singapore	1986
Matsushita	Singapore	1979
	USA	1990
Sanyo	Korea	1973
	Taiwan	1974
	China	1985
Sony	USA	1990
	Thailand	1988
Oki	USA	1980
	Thailand	1991
Rohm	USA	1990
	Brazil	1972
	Korea	1972

Sources: Shimura 1992, and *Toyo Keizai Shimposha*, 1991.

circuits (ICs). At that time Japan was an importer of IC devices, trying hard to defend its own infant industry from US imports. The dominant technology was bipolar technology, and it was dominated by the US firms. Metal-oxide semiconductor (MOS) technology, which was later to become a dominant technology, was yet to appear on the industry scene. The production process was highly labour-intensive, requiring significantly less capital compared to the capital requirements of today's production facilities.

One significant strategic move that the US semiconductor firms made

during this period was to move offshore the assembly operations of the IC
devices, a later stage of semiconductor production, to save on high labour
costs in the USA. This was indeed a great threat to the infant Japanese
semiconductor industry: this meant that lower-priced advanced ICs would
be readily available from these off-shore plants to Japanese end-users.
Some Japanese firms thus responded to the move of the US firms by
setting up their own assembly operations in South-East Asia. They engaged in assembly of bipolar linear ICs and discrete semiconductor devices
in the region. At this stage, FDI by the Japanese semiconductor firms was
defensive *vis-à-vis* the US multinational semiconductor firms.

(*b*) *The second wave: FDI in the USA.* The second wave of FDI by
Japanese firms was motivated by different incentives. By the early 1980s,
the leading Japanese semiconductor firms had established their technological leadership in MOS memory technology, and they were running at
the forefront of its development. Although Japanese government support
for semiconductor firms for technological development was limited, in the
late 1970s and early 1980s they very rapidly built their technological capabilities, particularly in MOS process technologies. The rapid technological
upgrading and catch-up also involved technological upgrading of the
supplier industries, such as production of silicon wafers and equipment,
like steppers and aligners.

Japanese firms exported 16K DRAMs to the USA and attained a small
share of the market in the 1970s. Japanese penetration into the US market
increased to 70 per cent for 64K DRAMs in 1981, and to 90 per cent
for 256K DRAMs in 1985 (Kimura 1988). The US market was supplied
by Japanese firms through export from their Japanese plants, and Japan
became a net exporter of integrated circuit devices *vis-à-vis* the rest of the
world in 1980. US computer manufacturers were the major customers for
these exports.

US firms and policymakers became increasingly concerned with the
rapidly increasing penetration by the Japanese industry in the US and
world semiconductor markets. Japanese firms felt threatened by the imminent protectionism arising in the USA, and in response to such a threat
undertook FDI there. Of course, there were other factors that also motivated them to undertake FDI in the USA, such as operating within the
market and avoidance of foreign exchange risks, but this was the predominant consideration.

Without the threat of protectionism, it might have been less costly
and risky for the Japanese firms to service the US market through export,
given the presence of significant economies of scale and learning economies in the industry. Clearly, the choice of the Japanese firms to begin
production in the USA was based on political considerations, and their
objective was to sidestep the controls of the US government over market
access through exports. Despite the US government's intention to ward off

market penetration by the Japanese semiconductor industry, Japanese firms took deep root in US soil with a firm commitment to the market. Some firms also made direct investments in Europe during this period.

Unlike investments in South-East Asia, many of these direct investments involved integrated production of advanced high volume standard MOS memory chips in the USA. Assembly alone was not considered sufficient to avoid imminent import controls. Such controls were actually brought into effect in 1986. The USA and Japan concluded a bilateral agreement to administer Japanese import prices based on the concept of Fair Market Value (FMV). As a result, import prices of Japanese ICs increased, but this did not help stem the market penetration of the Japanese semiconductor firms into the USA, but rather raised the cost of key components to US end-users, and negatively affected their international competitiveness.

As the technological capabilities of the Japanese firms improved, and as the domestic market in the newly industrializing economies of Asia expanded, the nature of FDI activities of Japanese firms in the region also changed. Increasingly, semiconductor production was upgraded to include advanced MOS memory chips, and was directed more toward the local operations of Japanese and other multinational systems manufacturers and indigenous firms in the region. These production locations were also used as sourcing points for their export to the USA to moderate the rapidly increasing Japanese trade surpluses in semiconductors *vis-à-vis* the USA.

(c) *The third wave: FDI in Europe.* The recent move of Japanese semiconductor firms to undertake full-scale FDI in the EC constitutes the third phase of the global expansion of Japanese semiconductor firms. They have built large-scale, state-of-the-art plants to manufacture largely the most advanced MOS memory devices and ASICs (application-specific ICs). Simultaneously, the depth of production activities of the Japanese semiconductor firms has increased in the USA, focusing more on specialized chips such as ASICs (Shimura 1992). In addition, the second-tier firms like Sony and Matsushita made inroads into the USA by purchasing the assets of AMD and National Semiconductors respectively.

Japanese FDI activities in the Community share some similarities with those in the USA in motivation, strategy, and modes of deployment, but the context in which they took place may be somewhat different. Thus, understanding the Japanese FDI activities in the Community requires closer examination, which we will turn to in a later section.

2.3. Technological Leadership as a Driving Force of Japanese FDI

As the above overview of Japanese semiconductor FDI shows, it is clear that the global expansion of Japanese semiconductor firms has been propelled by the rapid catch-up and upgrading of their technological base in semiconductor technology. Our observation is highly consistent with the explanations advanced by various theories of FDI.

The technology gap theory of international trade (Linder 1961), industry cycle theory (MaGee 1977), and eclectic theory of FDI (Dunning 1977; Rugman 1980; Hennart 1985) suggest that international expansion of a country's industry through exports and FDI is triggered by the competitive advantage of the firm, based on intangible assets such as technology and marketing know-how that more than compensates for the disadvantages of operating in unfamiliar business environments from a distance. The firm's choice of foreign locations over domestic locations in the use of *internalized* intangible assets generates FDI and multinational firms. Furthermore, as Porter (1990) argues, creation of such intangible assets does not take place in a vacuum. Their creation requires broad industrial infrastructure and support industries in a home country, conducive to such development.[1]

Indeed, the global expansion of the Japanese semiconductor industry has been driven by the rapid accumulation of intangible assets—technology, strongly supported by the rapid technological upgrading of the supplier industries. The beginning of the rapid international expansion of Japanese firms through exports and FDI coincides with the time when they attained at least a technological parity with US firms in some key technology areas.

As to the determinants of the Japanese semiconductor FDI, Kimura (1988, 1989) provides empirical evidence. In his statistical study of major Japanese semiconductor firms for 1978–82, he shows that the size of the FDI activities of Japanese semiconductor firms rests on their technological leadership in semiconductor technologies, after controlling for the influence of the size of the firm. His findings suggest that Japanese semiconductor FDI activities were propelled largely by the firms' leadership in MOS memory and bipolar logic technologies, and that the size of FDI activities of individual firms depends to a larger extent on the degree of its technological leadership in those relevant technological areas. These findings were particularly true of the FDI activities in the advanced countries. FDI in developing countries, mostly in South-East Asia, was motivated by other considerations, such as the vertical linkages with the firms' own downstream equipment manufacturing operations in those locations.

2.4. Vertical Linkages within Japanese Semiconductor Firms

Another factor that characterizes Japanese semiconductor firms and that may influence their global competitiveness is the vertical linkages of semiconductor manufacturing with the downstream equipment or systems manufacturing. As we pointed out earlier, unlike many US semiconductor

---

[1] Teece 1992 also emphasizes the strategic significance of the horizontal and vertical intra-firm and inter-firm linkages of innovative activities. For a detailed discussion, see Teece 1992.

firms, that is, the firms that are not diversified, Japanese semiconductor manufacturers are large, highly diversified multinational electric/electronics firms. In the semiconductor industry, they sell IC devices as a merchant vendor to end-users and also supply their own systems equipment manufacturing divisions.

The well-diversified operations of these firms and these vertical linkages within the firm may offer a number of competitive advantages relative to the firms that are not vertically integrated. Diversified operations offer them opportunities to cross-subsidize semiconductor operations in hard times. Also, vertical linkages influence the product mix of the firm's semiconductor business, forcing it to focus, at least to the extent of its captive consumption, on the devices its downstream divisions consume. In the relevant product areas, those linkages may facilitate smoother co-ordination in R&D and production between the semiconductor and downstream divisions within the firm. They may also provide production volumes that would enable them to move down the learning curve in production more quickly.

In the above study, Kimura (1988, 1989) confirms such influences on the firm's competitive positions, including the influence on location and size of FDI activities in the late 1970s and early 1980s. The results of his study suggest that the semiconductor firms that focused on telecommunications equipment and computers in their downstream operations tended to focus on the devices for these applications, and to undertake FDI for production of these devices in the USA and Europe so that they would have ready access to the market. On the other hand, the firms that concentrated on consumer electronics tended to focus on bipolar analog devices, and located their production in Asia, close to their own consumer electronics operations and indigenous customers in the region. In the early 1990s, these distinctions in strategy between these two groups of firms (strategic groups) are somewhat blurred, but it seems that the vertical linkages still have some influence on the firms' strategies in FDI activities.

The global expansion of Japanese semiconductor firms has thus been based on their competitive advantage in continuously renewed technological leadership in the semiconductor technologies, which was further boosted by their diversified electronics businesses and vertical linkages with the downstream businesses. An implication is that the firms that lag behind in R&D may find it very difficult to continue to compete on a global basis. They may be forced to operate in geographical or product niche markets.

Japanese semiconductor firms served markets abroad through export, and their FDI activities were often in strategic response to the threats of their exclusion from foreign markets by importing countries. An implication for policymakers here is that policy efforts to exclude or ward off imports may accelerate rather than decelerate market penetration by the Japanese. It would be attained through FDI in place of exports. With FDI, the degree of the firm's commitment to local production in the country would increase rather than decrease.

2.5. Changing Industry Structure

Coupled with the increased technological capabilities of the Japanese semiconductor firms, some aspects of the structural conditions of this industry have dynamically changed since the time when Japanese semiconductor firms rushed to commence FDI activities in the USA.[2] Those dynamically changing aspects of structure may have helped entrench the competitive positions of Japanese firms relative to those firms based elsewhere, and this may have contributed to the larger presence of the Japanese in the global semiconductor industry. Thus it should be noted that the context in which current Japanese FDI activities are taking place in the Community may differ significantly from that in which they took place in the USA in the early 1980s. The competitive position of the Japanese firms has risen significantly and become stronger than that of firms in other countries in broad product areas. As a result, they have begun to take a global view of their FDI activities. It seems that these changes in structural conditions have important implications for global competition in this industry and the Japanese penetration of the EC.

The elements of structure that have undergone significant changes include increasing complexities of technology and increasing capital requirements for R&D and production facilities. These dynamic structural changes have been triggered by the continuously advancing technologies and the associated capital requirements in the industry, but simultaneously the strategic thrust in R&D and capital investment of firms, particularly those Japanese firms, may also have accelerated the pace of these changes.

(*a*) *Increasing technological complexities and R&D expenditure.* The density and complexity of semiconductor chips increased with the arrival of every new generation of chips. Along with an increase in design complexities, corporate resource requirements for R&D dramatically increased. The top twelve Japanese semiconductor firms spent 21.5 billion yen on R&D in 1975. The R&D expenditures of these firms increased to 254.9 billion yen in 1985, and to 446.2 billion yen in 1990. They increased at an annual rate of 22 per cent in these fifteen years. The firms have spent about 15 per cent of total semiconductor sales on R&D, a level higher than the R&D efforts maintained by US firms, which on average spent 11.0 per cent of sales. This suggests that US and European firms are falling behind the Japanese in R&D in the semiconductor industry.

---

[2] For a detailed analysis of the overall structure of the Japanese semiconductor industry in the early 1980s, see Kimura 1988.

The rapid increase of required R&D expenditures stems from the increasing complexities of new generation integrated circuits as well as the facilities, equipment, and manpower that the development of new generation devices requires. Shimura (1992) suggests that development of 64K DRAM memory devices, the most advanced memory chips now in the very early developmental stage, requires five to six times larger R&D staff than were needed for the development of 4K DRAM chips. Clearly, during the time period between these generations of DRAM, the design methods have changed drastically, due to the introduction and fast advancement of computer-aided design technologies.

The industry engineers and scientists believe that there are still abundant opportunities for further technological development and for a good return on investment in R&D in the industry. It seems that industry experts generally agree that the increasing trend of R&D expenditure will continue into the future (Shimura 1992).

(*b*) *Increasing capital requirements for production facilities*. As in the case of R&D expenditures, the capital requirements for production facilities have also rapidly increased in the past fifteen years. In 1990, the top ten Japanese semiconductor firms invested 820 billion yen in production facilities, about twice the level of capital investment in 1983, showing an average of a 10 per cent annual increase between these years (Shimura 1992). Here, too, US and European firms are lagging behind.

The rapid increase in capital investment has been attributable to the increasing prices of production equipment stemming from the increasing complexities of semiconductor devices, increasing size of silicon wafers, increasing needs for automation, and increasing cost of design and testing equipment. Also, investment costs have increased due to the longer production process.

(*c*) *Continued decline in capacity for investment to generate sales*. If the increased capital investment results in a more-than-proportionate increase in sales and/or the economic life of such investment is long, it may not be a source of serious concern to new entrants to the industry or the incumbents. In the semiconductor industry, however, this has not been the case.

The marginal ratio of the previous year's capital investment to the current year's incremental increase in sales had been declining and finally went below 1.0 in 1989 (Shimura 1992). This means that it takes more than one dollar of investment this year to generate an incremental sale of a dollar next year. If the income-generating capacity of these assets is small at the margin in the short-run, then assets must have a long economic life so as to generate a satisfactory return on the investment over that life. However, the economic life of such assets is only a few years in this industry. Production facilities and equipment become obsolete very quickly due to rapid technological advancement. Investment in production facilities and equipment must thus be well timed so that production comes on stream to hit the rapid growth stage of a product cycle of a new generation of ICs.

These dynamic structural changes have led to significant heightening of risk of entry and staying in the business, and hence the barriers to entry and mobility in the industry. Higher risk and costs in R&D and higher capital requirements have made entry and survival in the industry more difficult. The going is getting rough for everyone. Even the largest firms are finding it difficult to do everything in-house.[3] This is particularly true for firms that lack a strong technological and financial resource base, and also for firms whose time horizon for decision-making is short, and whose objective is short-run profit maximization.

In the midst of severe global competition and dynamic structural changes, it seems that many Japanese semiconductor firms are better positioned in terms of technological leadership, production capacity, and firm structure (how their semiconductor business relates to other parts of the firm) than those firms based in the USA and Europe. Such well-positioned firms are now trying to penetrate into the EC. What are the incentives for these firms to launch FDI activities in the Community? What strategies are they adopting there? What impact do they have on competitors and end-users based in the Community? The foregoing analysis of FDI activities by Japanese semiconductor firms and the changing aspects of industry structure provides the background for our analysis of their FDI activities in the EC.

3. JAPANESE SEMICONDUCTOR FDI IN THE EC

FDI by Japanese semiconductor firms in Europe dates back to 1976. In that year NEC began assembly operations of memory ICs in Ireland, and in 1982, in the UK. Fujitsu undertook FDI to assemble memory chips in Ireland in 1980, and Hitachi in Germany in the same year. Since then no other semiconductor firms, except NEC and Toshiba, have committed significant FDI to Europe, and Japanese firms have continued to serve the market largely through exports. It is only since the end of the 1980s that Japanese semiconductor FDI in Europe has gained momentum. There was a sudden surge of interest by Japanese semiconductor firms in Europe as a location of *integrated* production, as well as of other key activities, such as development of customer-specific products (see Table 8.3).

3.1. The Semiconductor Industry in the Community

The market for semiconductor devices is large in the Community. The market in Europe totalled $10.7 billion, and it accounted for 18 per cent

---

[3] The recent announcement of the formation of an R&D alliance between Toshiba, IBM, and Siemens for the development of the next generation of memory chips (July 1992) is a case in point.

TABLE 8.3. *Japanese semiconductor production in Europe, by year and level of activity*

Firm	Location	Date established	Date of integrated production	Nature of FDI activities
NEC	UK	1981	1987	Integrated production. 1M, 4M DRAMs and other ICs. 18,000 wafers/ month
Hitachi	Germany	1980	1992	Integrated production. 1M, 4M DRAMs, ASICs. 500 4M DRAMs/ month
Fujitsu	UK	1983	1992	Integrated production. 4M DRAMs, MOS logic ICs. 12,000– 13,000 wafers/ month
Mitsubishi	Germany	1989	1992	Integrated production. 1M, 4M DRAMs, microprocessors
Toshiba	Germany	1984	NA	Assembly and testing of VLSI ICs. Integrated production is being planned

Sources: Nikkei Microdevices 1990*d* and Shimura 1992.

of the world market, in 1990. The relative share of Europe has been slipping in the past decade from the level of 26 per cent in 1980. Nevertheless, the market is large, having a strong potential for growth significantly greater than within markets in other parts of the world (Nikkei Microdevices 1990*d*). Fast growth is anticipated in all types of integrated circuits, but very rapid growth is expected particularly in MOS logic ICs (including

TABLE 8.4. *European sales by the top ten semiconductor firms, 1990*

Firms	Sales ($ million)
Philips	1,104
Siemens	965
SGS-Thomson	908
Motorola	771
Texas Instruments	637
Intel	620
Toshiba (JPN)	524
NEC (JPN)	436
National Semiconductors	389
AMD	280

Source: Dataquest, 1991.

microprocessors), DRAMs, and SRAMs. The unification of the Community is the strong driving force of this market growth.

However, despite the large size and the significant market potential, the supply capability of EC-based semiconductor firms is very limited. Of the $10.7 billion demand in Europe, EC-based firms supplied only 40 per cent, while US and Japanese firms supplied 40 and 20 per cent, respectively (*Dataquest*, as quoted in Shimura 1992). Table 8.4 lists the ten largest semiconductor firms in sales in Europe in 1990. It shows that of all these ten largest firms only three are EC-based, while the other seven are US and Japanese. Most of these US and Japanese firms have located their production activities in the EC, and supply some part of the demand from their plants there. The strong presence of US firms in the Community reflects their early entry in the market and their strong technological capabilities *vis-à-vis* Community-based firms. The relatively small size of Japanese firms' sales in the market is due to their recent entry into Europe.

In contrast to the expanding activities of US and Japanese semiconductor firms in the EC, the positions of EC-based firms have been slipping within Europe and the world. EC-based firms have mostly specialized in ICs for telecommunications and military applications, and they have been weak in general-purpose, high volume, standard ICs (Sumitomo–Life Research Institute 1990). They have been outdistanced by the US and Japanese firms in those standard product areas, and they needed to license technologies from them in these product areas (Shimura 1992; Bowen 1991). The weakness of the EC-based firms in those product categories may be underscored by the recent departure of Philips from this area. In 1990, Philips decided to withdraw from the technological race for development of mega-bit class SRAM. Given the significance of MOS memory

ICs as the 'technological driver', the withdrawal of Philips from the memory race suggests that it is leaving the mainstream of semiconductor technologies.

The decline of the industry in the Community triggered the efforts of EC-based firms and policymakers to stem the decline. These efforts include a Community-wide effort called the EUREKA project and other alliances in R&D among EC-based firms, such as Siemens, Philips, and SGS-Thomson, and other, smaller, firms (Bowen 1991). Along with these efforts to upgrade their technological capabilities, the Community instituted local content requirements and administered minimum prices of semiconductors imported from Japan in 1989 and 1990, respectively, to protect EC-based semiconductor firms.

3.2. FDI Activities in the Community

Japanese firms undertook production FDI in such a market environment. Obviously, their interest in Europe as a location for FDI was spurred by the unification of the Community scheduled for 1992. For the firms based outside the Community, the unification in 1992 both offers significant opportunities and poses potential threats.

It offers great opportunities for multinational firms, based either in or outside the EC, to take advantage of potential economies that may stem from the integration of national markets hitherto compartmentalized by national trade policies and controls. More efficient resource allocation resulting from unification may accelerate the growth of the economy, driving the demand for electronic systems products and hence the demand for semiconductors. Also, unification may enhance the dynamic economic efficiency activating entrepreneurship and innovation in the Community. The threat to these firms based outside the Community is the threat of exclusion from the larger and more efficient markets, as typified by the concept of 'Fortress Europe'. To take advantage of these opportunities and cope with the potential threats of exclusion, Japanese semiconductor firms have become very active in undertaking FDI in the EC in the late 1980s and early 1990s.

Table 8.3 describes the Japanese FDI activities in the EC. The table suggests that of ten large Japanese semiconductor firms only the leading Japanese semiconductor firms are engaged in fully integrated production of state-of-the-art memory devices as well as specialized ICs such as ASICs, logic ICs, and microprocessors. Other firms are now trying to develop strategic alliances with EC-based semiconductor firms.

Leading firms, notably NEC, Fujitsu, and Hitachi, have started or are starting fully integrated production of state-of-the-art memory chips. NEC's FDI activities are located in the UK and Ireland, while those of Toshiba and Hitachi are in Germany. Fujitsu bases its FDI activities in the UK and

Ireland. Their production activities are fully integrated with wafer processing and assembly of these state-of-the-art ICs (except Toshiba). The IC devices produced locally include the most advanced MOS DRAMs, SRAMs, MOS logic devices, microprocessors, and ASICs. Of these four firms, Hitachi and Fujitsu have also established R&D facilities in Germany and the UK respectively, widening the scope of their value-added activities in those foreign locations.

The second-tier semiconductor firms, like Matsushita, Oki, and Sanyo, are pursuing opportunities for strategic alliances, rather than undertaking wholly-owned FDI activities in the EC. Clearly, those firms lack the technological leadership and/or financial resources that the leader firms have. Also, their product line, as we shall see later, may not fit the demand pattern in the EC. These firms are producers of chips largely for consumer electronics applications, and it is believed that the demand for these types of products is still limited.

Local production activities of Japanese semiconductor firms thus involve highly advanced MOS IC devices in large-scale, fully integrated, state-of-the-art plants. Another characteristic is the proliferation of strategic alliances. These kinds of behaviour by Japanese firms in the Community contrast with their behaviour in Asian countries and the early phases of their FDI in the USA.

3.3. Incentives for Japanese Semiconductor FDI in the Community

The FDI activities of Japanese semiconductor firms as described above have been motivated by a number of different, but often interrelated incentives. These incentives include: exploitation of their technological leadership; establishment of a foothold for market access in the EC; expectation of demand growth both within the Community and neighbouring countries; and inducement by the systems manufacturer end-users. We now examine these incentives that have driven the FDI activities of Japanese firms in the Community.

(a) *Exploiting technological leadership.* As we pointed out in the earlier part of this paper, the leading Japanese semiconductor firms are advancing the technological frontier in a broad spectrum of semiconductor technologies. For those firms that are heavily engaged in R&D in broad semiconductor technologies, the market is global. Their technological leadership allows them to exploit the technological gaps that exist between Japan and Europe. As we have seen earlier, leading Japanese firms clearly have a significant technological edge in broad technology areas *vis-à-vis* European semiconductor firms, and this offers substantial opportunities to penetrate the European market. Furthermore, to amortize the large amount of investment in R&D in a very short period of time, they need a volume that goes far beyond that of a single national market.

Clearly there are several ways to exploit technological leadership. The methods of appropriation of rents arising from technological leadership include export, FDI, and other modes of strategic alliance such as joint ventures and licensing. Given the high value-to-volume ratio and the presence of economies of scale and learning economies, concentration of production in a few locations in the world and servicing the global market through exports from these locations may be the most logical approach in this industry. Full-scale integrated production FDI makes economic sense only when the volume of production in one location reaches minimum efficient scale. This suggests that the strategic approach that the Japanese semiconductor firms (or firms of any nationality for that matter) should adopt is to concentrate production in the home country and service the foreign markets through export until their sales in the foreign markets reach minimum economic scale, and that they should consider undertaking FDI when this level of sales is attained. Indeed, as we have seen earlier, this is the strategic pattern that Japanese semiconductor firms have followed until recent years. This strategic approach may be more compelling when economies of scale and capital requirements for production plants are increasing.

Today, in Europe as elsewhere, it seems that many Japanese technological leader firms prefer FDI over other modes. The choice of FDI over other modes of entry also involves some other strategic considerations. One of these considerations is their expectation of future demand growth and market size in both the Community and neighbouring countries in Europe. Another is their concern about their potential exclusion from the future growth market. They are also undertaking FDI to maintain the buyer–supplier relationships with current multinational systems of end-user customers by servicing on-site in the Community countries.

(*b*) *Expectation for expanding demand for semiconductors, both within the EC and neighbouring areas.* It seems that many Japanese semiconductor firms have a strong expectation of growth of semiconductor markets to be unleashed by unification. Nikkei Microdevices (1990*d*) suggests that the size of the market for integrated circuits will expand rapidly in a unified Europe, exceeding the average rate of growth of the world market.

In particular, it is expected that market growth will be rapid for MOS memory and logic ICs in the Community. Also, some Japanese firms see that there will be a large opportunity for market growth for gate arrays and standard cells. The impetus for expansion in memory ICs comes largely from the expected increase in market penetration in personal computers, engineering work stations, and mini-computers.

The growth in demand for logic ICs will probably be propelled by the expansion of the market for telecommunications equipment. The European IC demand for telecommunications equipment applications is relatively greater than in the USA or Japan. Some Japanese firms expect that there will probably be a significant market for ASICs for applications in high volume fast digital transmissions of information. Another application area that will probably grow is microprocessors for exhaust control systems in automobiles. The demand for ICs for consumer electronics applications is still small and may be slow to take off, but some Japanese firms foresee a growth potential for ASICs for HDTVs after 1995 when broadcasting is scheduled to be in full operation.

Furthermore, Japanese firms are looking beyond the current boundaries of the Community. They see a potential that in Europe the Eastern European countries will play a role *vis-à-vis* Western Europe similar to that of South-East Asia *vis-à-vis* Japan, engaging in assembly operations of electronic equipment in the early stage of their economic development. They expect, then, that the ICs and other components will probably be sourced from their European plants.

The Japanese semiconductor firms thus hold high expectations for fast market growth in Europe. They see a unified Europe as a large market in which they can exploit their technological leadership, and this is an important factor that motivated them to locate in the Community. Clearly, it seems that Japanese semiconductor firms expect that they will be able to attain sales volumes in Europe significantly above rapidly increasing minimum economic scale.

(c) *Market access*. This has been perhaps the most important concern of Japanese firms that motivated them to undertake FDI in the EC.

Generally, creation of a common market leads to an application of unified tariffs to imports from non-member countries. This tends to divert trade with efficient non-member countries to less efficient member countries. The efficient exporters in non-member countries are excluded from or disadvantaged in the common market due to such unified tariffs. This provides an incentive for the firms based in non-member countries to locate production within the member countries and to service the market inside the tariff walls. Moreover, local content requirements tend to reduce further the extent of possible market access to the exporters based in non-member countries.

This was one major concern that Japanese firms had about unification. As unification approached, and as the concept of 'Fortress Europe' became a subject of public debate, they sensed the risk of being excluded from this large market with a potential for further expansion. They thus accelerated FDI in Europe in the late 1980s.

Their worry became a reality when the Community issued in 1989 a local content requirement for ICs. It identified the diffusion process as the 'last substantial process' and required that the diffusion process must be carried out in the Community in order to qualify as 'made in the Community'. This requirement forced the leading Japanese semiconductor firms to locate fully integrated production of ICs in the EC (Nikkei Microdevices 1990*d*).

Furthermore, the Community instituted in 1990 an administered minimum price for DRAM imports that were diffusion-processed in Japan. The scope of the restriction expanded to include other devices. This made market access more difficult for the DRAMs that were diffusion-processed in Japan. It seems that the objective for such a restriction was to divert the DRAM import from Japan to other sources, hopefully those in the Community (*Nihon Keizai Shimbun* 1989).

The second-tier firms that lacked the resources to engage in fully integrated production in the Community sought strategic alliances with local firms in order to avoid exclusion from the market. To qualify as 'EC-made', these strategic alliances must involve production, particularly the diffusion process, in the Community (Nikkei Microdevices 1990*d*). In these cases, development work is still kept in Japan. Some firms thus show a concern that the Community may require that more high value-added activities should be carried out in the Community in the future, and they started R&D operations, though still on a very limited scale, in the EC.

(*d*) *Inducement by multinational systems manufacturers.* As a merchant vendor, the Japanese semiconductor firms supply multinational systems manufacturer end-users based in Japan and elsewhere on a global basis, and they were induced by those end-users to commence local production in Europe (Nikkei Microdevices 1990*d*). Some firms were compelled to do so in order to maintain the on-going business with their end-user customers around the world.

Like semiconductor firms, those multinational system manufacturer end-users also see potential market growth resulting from unification, but they are also confronted with potential or real market-access barriers, such as protectionist administered prices and local content requirements. They thus locate their production activities in the EC and try to increase the proportion of local content as much as possible. This requires them to use componets that qualify as 'made in the Community'. Indeed, it is reported that IBM, for instance, had attained a 70–80 per cent level of local contents in production of ICs by 1989. US systems manufacturers, like IBM and Digital Equipment Corporation, have been trying hard to induce Japanese semiconductor firms to produce and supply them with locally made ICs. Japanese systems manufacturers that are engaged in production in Europe have also been attempting to encourage integrated local production of ICs by Japanese firms. Such pressure on Japanese semiconductor firms from those multinational systems manufacturers has intensified since the late 1980s.

These are the major incentives that motivated Japanese semiconductor firms to undertake FDI in the EC. These motivations are varied, but interrelated. It seems difficult to separate them in analysing a specific case of FDI by a Japanese firm. They interacted with each other and as a whole motivated Japanese firms to undertake FDI in this industry in Europe.

4. STRATEGIES OF JAPANESE SEMICONDUCTOR FIRMS IN THE COMMUNITY

Although the same or similar factors may have motivated Japanese firms to undertake FDI or to engage in market activities in different modes in the Community, the strategies they have adopted differ from firm to firm. These differences arise from the differences in their competitive position, corporate resources available, technological leadership, and firm structure (Kimura 1989). Depending on the positions of individual firms in these strategic dimensions, their strategic responses to the opportunities and threats in a unifying Europe differ significantly.

We examine their strategies with respect to some key strategic dimensions, such as product mix and production process, and vertical linkages with suppliers. We discuss specific cases of strategic alliances between Japanese and EC-based firms. We also look at how FDI activities fit in their broader multinational strategies in this industry.

(*a*) *Product mix and dynamic changes in product mix*. To take full advantage of the technological leadership *vis-à-vis* lagging Community-based semiconductor firms, the leading Japanese firms, as we have seen earlier, are focusing largely on advanced state-of-the-art high volume MOS products, such as dynamic random access memory ICs and logic chips for computers, in their production activities in Europe.

NEC, Hitachi, Fujitsu, and Mitsubishi are and will be engaged in fully integrated production of 1M and 4M DRAMs in their plants in Europe. They focus on the memory chips at least at the early stage of start-ups of the diffusion process in Europe for several reasons. For one, these are the products for which there is a large potential demand derived from the increasing demand for electronics equipment in the Community. Also this is the area in which Japanese firms have strong technological leadership.

Furthermore, these memory chips serve as a vehicle for debugging new production processes in new plants (Nikkei Microdevices 1990*b*). Of the various types of advanced MOS VLSI and ULSI chips of the same generation, DRAM is simplest in structural design and wafer process, and hence provides a base for clearing technological hurdles before mastering the technology. Without mastering the production process with the structurally simplest products, one cannot proceed to the production of structurally more complex products. Thus, DRAM technology is often called the 'technology driver'. All these leading Japanese firms are using these 1M DRAMs to debug the MOS process in their European plants and plan to proceed to production of more complex products. They also expect to amortize the large amount of investment in facilities in the shortest period of time on these high volume standard products.

After bringing their plants on stream with 1M and 4M DRAMs in the initial phase, they have expanded, or plan to expand, their product line to include more complex products such as ASICs and microprocessors at a later stage. Fujitsu has, for instance, set up in the same facility a separate production line specifically designed for ASICs. It has started fully integrated operations to include the development and fully integrated processing of ICs in the UK (Nikkei Microdevices 1990*b*).

The FDI activities of leading Japanese semiconductor firms are not limited to the MOS DRAMs alone, and the nature of these activities seems to differ from those of off-shore plants only to supplement the export from Japan. The ranges of product lines are broader so that they are able to service a broad array of customers in the Community.

(*b*) *Production processes and vertical linkages with suppliers.* Since the late 1980s, these leading firms have begun building new plants for the new generations of integrated circuits. The basic strategy for production facilities common to all these firms is that they have more or less copied the state-of-the-art plants that went into operation recently or were under construction in Japan. Maintaining the commonality between the plants located overseas and those in Japan is believed to make it easier to solve production problems encountered in plants overseas. The scale of plants is to process 1.2–1.5 million wafers per month, as in the case of plants located in Japan. This scale attains the production level of minimum economic scale.

These firms differ in the extent to which they adopted automated lines in those plants located in the Community. NEC, for instance, believes that adoption of automation to the greatest extent possible is necessary because of the increased complexity of the production process and the increased number of steps in the process. Mitsubishi's production line handles high volumes of a limited variety of products and almost entirely automates its plant operations. Fujitsu is more cautious in automating its European (i.e. UK) plant because it sees the difficulty in operating an automated plant with a less adequately trained maintenance crew. The new plants of these Japanese firms are built as pollution free as possible with the currently available technologies. They believe that they must be accepted by the EC as good corporate citizens, and they are therefore trying to meet environmental concerns in the Community.

These production activities by the Japanese in the Community involve supporting industries for acquisition of equipment and supply of materials. To maintain compatibility, the process equipment used in these brand new facilities is essentially the same as in their newest parent plants in Japan. At least at an early stage of the start-up of FDI activities, equipment is sourced from the same vendors that the parent companies use at home. These leading Japanese firms feel obliged to source equipment from within the Community, but they are unable to do so, at least for the moment, because there exist no local vendors that can supply the equipment that meets their technological requirements (Nikkei Microdevices 1990*a*).

This suggests that those vendors are mostly Japanese and, to a lesser extent, US equipment manufacturers. Efficient operation of production facilities demands 24-hour availability of maintenance and repair services, and this would require that vendors build service centres in the buyers' plant locations to meet customer needs. This has been inducing the equipment vendors to locate at least their service functions in the Community. Equipment vendors, such as Nikon, Canon, NEC Anelba, and Applied Materials, Japan, have been strengthening and extending service networks in the EC.

As with process equipment, supply of materials is also an issue. The most critical materials in semiconductor production are silicon wafers and photo-resist. Those Japanese firms locating in the Community consider it almost impossible to switch vendors of these materials from those firms they have continued to work with to new vendors. Only established vendors are able to supply the materials prepared to the exact specifications of the buyers and to make any delicate adjustment in the materials they deliver to them when required. This is critical to increasing yields in production, and the knowledge and know-how concerning the buyers' technical needs have been developed through close interaction over a long period of time. Switching from those vendors that they have long used in Japan to new ones in new locations involves significant switching costs. This, again, would induce those suppliers to bring at least a part of their production process to a location in the EC. Some multinational vendors based in the Community that have on-going business relationships with Japanese semiconductor firms in Japan see such a move as an opportunity to expand their business with them in the Community as well as in Japan (Nikkei Microdevices 1990*c*).

For the materials that require less close interaction between buyers and suppliers, such switching of vendors can more readily occur. Such materials include various chemicals for cleansing wafers and gases. Many Japanese vendors of these materials seem reluctant to go to Europe with their clients. Supplying these materials to the plants in Europe through export is difficult, and thus it requires local production. However, switching can more readily occur.

(*c*) *Strategic alliances with EC multinational firms.* The second-tier firms, notably Oki, Matsushita, and Sanyo, developed strategic alliances with EC-based firms. As we discussed earlier, the incentives for these second-tier firms to enter into strategic alliances with local firms were: (1) to maintain market access while compensating through these alliances for their

TABLE 8.5. *Strategic alliances between semiconductor firms in Europe*

Japanese firms	European partners	Nature of alliance
Matsushita	Philips	Contract or co-production of Matsushita-designed ICs. Possible formation of a joint venture
Oki	SGS-Thomson	Contract assembly of Oki-produced 1M and 4M DRAMs
Sanyo	SGS-Thomson	Marketing of Sanyo-produced ICs
Sony	Texas Instruments (Europe)	Contract production of Sony-designed specialized ICs
Toshiba	Siemens	Contract production of standard cells, DRAMs, and ICs for telecommunications
	SGS-Thomson	Contract production of standard cells, DRAMs, and ICs for telecommunications

Note: This list does not include technology licensing agreements.
Sources: Nikkei Microdevices 1990*d* and *Nikkei Sangyo Shimbun* 1990.

lack of the resources needed for undertaking FDI in Europe, or (2) to save resources for other activities as the market in the Community is not important enough for them to undertake FDI. Table 8.5 lists strategic alliances between Japanese and European firms.

These strategic alliances include joint ventures, contract production, and original equipment manufacturing (OEM) relationships. One of those firms was considering establishing a fully integrated production facility in Europe through a joint venture to produce ICs using photo-masks brought in from Japan. Another typical approach was to contract local firms to produce ICs using the Japan-made photo-masks (*Nikkei Microdevices* 1990*d*).

Matsushita, for instance, entered into an agreement in 1990 with Philips to establish a joint venture to produce Matsushita-designed and perhaps also Philips-designed products. Given the recent withdrawal of Philips from the semiconductor business, we are not able to see what might have resulted from this agreement, although Matsushita may consider undertaking FDI on its own in the EC. Oki has an agreement with SGS-Thomson to assemble Oki-designed 1M and 4M DRAM chips under contract (*Nikkei Sangyo*

Shimbun 1990). Sanyo's alliance with SGS-Thomson involves marketing Sanyo's products through the latter's marketing channel in the EC. Among the second-tier firms, Sony plans to undertake FDI on its own, although it currently has a co-operative arrangement with Texas Instruments to produce some types of Sony-designed specialized ICs under contract in Germany.

More specifically, the leading firms seem to position their semiconductor business within the company structure as an important, but more or less independent business, though partially linked with downstream operations. This positioning of the semiconductor business motivates them as a merchant vendor to continue to remain a global technological and market leader. These firms, then, try to advance technological frontiers in a broad spectrum of semiconductor technologies, cover a wide range of product lines, and locate production activities close to key markets around the world.

The current FDI activities of these firms in Europe, as elsewhere, seem to reflect this goal. Compared with their FDI activities undertaken earlier in Asia and the USA, they seem increasingly to position their European FDI within a broader global strategic framework. An implication of this for their global strategies in the semiconductor business in the future is that their FDI activities in Europe will be a part of their global sourcing–marketing system once their production activities in Europe come on stream. Thus we may see in the future a significant rise in cross-hauling of technologies and finished products among their foreign subsidiaries in Asia, the USA, and Europe. A potential impediment to such a strategy is the formation of a regional economic bloc by the EC, that is, the emergence of 'Fortress Europe'. If this happens, their integrated global strategy may degenerate into a regionally integrated multinational strategy.

The second-tier firms (consumer electronics firms), on the other hand, tend to subordinate the semiconductor business to other consumer electronics final systems businesses in their systems of goals and company structure, though they sell today a significant part of their output in the merchant market. It thus seems that their strategies in the semiconductor business are much influenced by those in their downstream businesses. This is true of their focus on technologies and product line. Their technological and product focus is limited to narrower segments of the market that are more closely related to consumer electronics. Their FDI activities are thus greatly influenced by their FDI activities in the downstream businesses.

Furthermore, although those leading firms have chosen to service the market through wholly owned production subsidiaries, Toshiba has developed an alliance with Siemens and SGS-Thomson to produce standard cells, DRAM memories, and ICs for telecommunications equipment. Toshiba may have needed such an alliance because it does not have an integrated production facility in Europe. Such behaviour by Toshiba in Europe may also be considered an attempt to signal to the local firms that it is willing to co-operate with them on their own territory.

(*d*) *FDI in Europe as a part of broader firm strategies*. From the above analysis of strategies of the Japanese semiconductor firms in the EC, it seems that their strategic positioning in Europe differs largely between two groups of firms. Clearly, one of these is a group of leading firms that includes NEC, Mitsubishi, Hitachi, Fujitsu, and to a lesser extent Toshiba. This group of firms is very active in FDI activities in the Community, as well as in other parts of the world. Oki, Matsushita, Sanyo, and Sony constitute the other group. These firms are trying to maintain market access to the Community through alliances with local firms, without making substantive commitments to the market through FDI.

These observed differences between firms in their strategies in Europe are consistent with the strategic groups Kimura identified from their domestic strategies (1988, 1990) and FDI activities elsewhere (1989). His findings suggest that those strategic differences in their home territory and other foreign markets reflect the differences in their goals in this industry and their sustainable competitive advantage based on such factors as technological leadership, market scope, and company structure. These differences seem to have been sustained over the past ten years and to have extended to their activities in Europe.

These differences in their FDI behaviour in Europe, as well as in their overall strategy, may be explained by differences in their competitive advantages, but it seems that these differences may be traced ultimately to differences in their strategic positioning of the semiconductor business in their systems of goals and company structures.

These firms may be content with strategic alliances with local firms in Europe as long as they serve their own downstream operations and their end-user customers in the Community. At this time, they do not seem to be much interested in developing a global sourcing–marketing network. They may seriously consider undertaking FDI when their downstream businesses grow large, and when they come under strong pressure for higher local content in the Community.

5. IMPACTS OF JAPANESE FDI ON THE EC

The increasing and more committed presence of Japanese semiconductor firms through FDI will probably have an impact on the EC in a number of ways. In this section we provide an assessment of these impacts on the Community. Some of these impacts are direct and others are more indirect. The Japanese FDI activities directly affect competitive conditions in the semiconductor industry in the Community. They also affect competition in adjacent industries through supplier–buyer relationships. These influences eventually pervade the entire economy of the EC. Through this assessment of these potential impacts of Japanese FDI activities, we suggest implications for competitors, suppliers, end-users, and policy-makers. Given the fact that these FDI activities are now being undertaken, and that Japanese company strategies vary significantly among different firms, it is extremely difficult to develop an overall assessment of these impacts in quantitative terms *ex ante*. Our assessment is thus more qualitative in nature.

5.1. Effects of the Semiconductor Industry

The increased penetration of Japanese semiconductor firms directly affects competition in the industry within Europe. The European market has traditionally been served by EC-based firms and those from the USA, while Japanese firms have held only about 20 per cent of the market, mostly through exports from Japan. Now with production facilities in place, they are to remain in the Community for the long haul and are more committed to the market. This will probably affect concentration and competition. This will in turn influence performance in terms of allocative and technical efficiency of the industry and technological progressiveness of the EC-based firms.

(*a*) *Concentration and competitive structure.* Through FDI, Japanese firms have added significant production capacity in the Community. In the early phase of their FDI activities, locally produced output at those plants may simply replace import from Japan. However, as those plants come on stream and begin to produce in large volume, they may cause a significant shake-up in market shares, affecting overall market concentration. The added production capacity may reduce market concentration and intensify competition in the industry.

The degree of market concentration and competition is also affected by some other factors. One such factor is the growth of demand for semiconductor devices. If unification accelerates the growth of the electronics equipment industry in the Community and neighbouring countries leading to a substantial increase in demand for semiconductor devices, the growth may simply absorb the output from the Japanese firms' added capacity. The capacity expansion by Japanese firms, then, may not have a significant influence on market concentration and competition. On the other hand, if the growth of downstream industries turns out to be slow, a decline in concentration and an increase in competition will be highly likely. Due to the short economic life of production facilities and equipment, semiconductor firms are under strong pressure to amortize the capital investment in three to four years with a subsequent need for large volumes of output. Furthermore, firms' profitability in this industry hinges strongly on yields in production, and they need to accumulate production volume very quickly ahead of competitors. Thus, they may be motivated to increase rather than to reduce output, despite the slow demand growth. This would increase competition, leading to lower prices and lower market concentration.

Another factor to consider is market interdependence between local and Japanese firms in the EC. Market interdependence refers to the extent to which firms compete for the same customers in the market. Even if overall market concentration may decline due to new entry, it does not necessarily mean that market competition increases if new entrants do not compete directly with incumbent firms for the same customers or for the same customer needs.

All the Japanese semiconductor firms are focusing on MOS-based DRAM and SRAM memory chip production in Europe. The EC-based firms do produce these products, but these are the products in which they are not particularly strong. Although there may be some market interdependence in memory chips between the EC-based and Japanese firms, it may be limited. As the Japanese firms broaden their scope of product line to include various ASICs and ICs for telecommunications applications, their market interdependence with the local firms may increase.

In the area of memory chips, the market interdependence between local firms and Japanese firms may be limited, but it is very high among Japanese firms themselves, particularly among the firms that are leaders in their home market as well as in foreign markets. Thus, these leading Japanese firms may enter into fierce competition among themselves for market share in the European market as they do at home, reducing the market price and profitability in these product lines. If the market growth in memory devices is slow, we may expect a protracted rivalry. Depending on market interdependence for these products, the rivalry among Japanese firms may draw in local firms, and this may further affect prices and profitability in these product areas.

As for the second-tier firms, at least for the moment they seem to be trying to avoid market interdependence with the Japanese leader firms and also with local firms. They are trying to hive off from the leader firms in their segment focus, and to complement the local firms in their product lines through strategic alliances.

Ultimately, how the semiconductor industry will be organized in the future in the EC and in the world is yet to be seen. One scenario is that the industry may develop into a tight oligopoly dominated by five or six large, diversified, vertically integrated Japanese firms and three or four US firms that produce a wide range of large-volume standard products such as memories and microprocessors. (Other smaller firms may be driven out of business, or driven to the fringe of the industry and forced to focus on specific product segments or niches that those large firms tend to ignore.) Protected by the heightened mobility barriers, those few firms may be able collectively to set prices above competitive levels.

Given the rapidly heightening entry and mobility barriers in technological and capital requirements, and given the recent exit of Philips from this
industry, this scenario cannot readily be set aside as unlikely. If it turns out
to be the case, all those EC-based semiconductor firms may fall into the
group of fringe firms. Their survival as leader firms in the industry in the
Community seems to rest on their ability to strengthen their technological
capability and to alter the company structure in such a way as to take full
advantage of the linkages of various value-added activities between semiconductor operations and diverse downstream final systems equipment
businesses.

Another scenario may be based on the gradual market shift from large-
volume, general-purpose, standard products to smaller volume customer-
specific or application-specific products. Proponents of this scenario (e.g.
Bowen 1991) argue that customer requirements are becoming very diverse
and application-specific, and what counts in this market environment are
the technological capabilities of firms to develop chips that meet customers'
needs, not their capacity to build large plants and produce standard items
at low cost. If this scenario turns out to be true, we may not need to be
much concerned about the market dominance by a small number of firms.
The market needs are too diverse for only that small number of firms
to cater to them. The structure of the industry would, in that case, tend to
be more fragmented around diverse product segments, leaving ample room
for smaller firms, including European firms, to concentrate on diverse
specialized market segments.

Perhaps the truth may lie somewhere between these two scenarios.
However, it seems that the truth may lie closer to the first, given the dynamically heightening mobility barriers in this industry.

(*b*) *Allocative and technical efficiency.* To the extent that the FDI activities of Japanese semiconductor firms reduce market prices and any above-
competitive profitability of firms in the industry, increased competition
resulting from Japanese FDI improves the allocative efficiency of this industry in the EC. As we have seen above, a number of factors influence
market concentration and intra-industry rivalry, and it is almost impossible
to assess the degree to which Japanese FDI improves overall allocative
efficiency. In any case, to the extent that competition reduces prices of
microdevices, the cost to end-users would be lower, and this would reduce
unrealized demand and increase consumer surpluses. End-users' low cost
would potentially lead to lower prices of electronic equipment to consumers,
which would in turn achieve unrealized consumer demand and increase
their surpluses in electronic systems equipment. If the rivalry between the
local and Japanese firms and also among the Japanese firms themselves
turns out to be intense, and given the high technical efficiency of Japanese
firms, end-users may expect ready availability of low-cost component devices
in the Community.

Technical efficiency refers to cost efficiency of producers. Leading Japanese semiconductor firms are known as low-cost producers of high-volume, standard microdevices. Through an intense rivalry at home and abroad, they have attained the low-cost position using state-of-the-art production technologies. With FDI in the EC, leading Japanese firms have taken those most advanced production technologies to Europe, and built plants at scales above minimum economic scale. Thus, their cost position may be comparable to that in Japan. NEC, for instance, reports that its plant in Ireland has cost parity with its plants in Japan (Nikkei Microdevices 1990*b*). This would force local firms to attain the level of technical efficiency comparable to that of the Japanese firms.

(*c*) *Technological progressiveness.* Technological progressiveness concerns the impact of competition in stimulating technological innovations among the players in an industry. New entry, particularly by those firms with strong technological capabilities, provokes responses from incumbent firms to accelerate their innovative activities, improving the technological progressiveness of the industry. How, then, is the competition from the FDI activities of Japanese firms likely to affect technological innovations in the semiconductor industry in the EC? Does the Japanese challenge on their own ground serve to vitalize the innovative activities of the EC-based semiconductor firms? Given the fact that technological innovations are driving this industry, how local firms respond to the challenge will determine not only the technological progressiveness of the industry in the Community, but perhaps more importantly the market positions of its firms in their home market as well as in the world market.

Policymakers and firms in the EC had a sense of crisis about the alarming state of its semiconductor industry well before Japanese firms began to make serious inroads into the Community. An increasing Japanese share in the world market gave rise to their concern. Indeed, there is a clear sign that the Japanese challenge has stimulated innovative activities by EC-based firms. Community-wide efforts, such as the Eureka project, have been made to arrest the decline of the Community-based firms due to global competition. The technological efforts under the Eureka project (JESSI) involve six Community member countries, over 30 firms, 20,000 man-years of R&D staff per year, and a total spending of ECU 3.8 billion over the 1989–96 period. The project is targeted at establishing the sub-micron level technology necessary for the development of 64M DRAM and EPROM and 16M SRAM ICs through basic research and development of specific technologies in semiconductor materials, processes, production equipment, and automation (Shimura 1992).

These efforts are now under way, and it is too early to evaluate their effective impact on technological and market competition among EC-based firms and firms based elsewhere. However, we are at least able to point to the factors that may lead the technological efforts to success. Those factors include the attitude of the EC-based firms toward technological innovations in this industry, their ability to link those innovations with downstream applications, and their willingness to work with US and Japanese firms.

Some industry observers argue that the declining significance of Europe in this industry may be traced back to its late start in integrated circuits, and that this may have been due to over-confidence in traditional technologies and reluctance to innovate in new, uncertain technologies on the part of its firms. Another weakness of these firms may be the lack of capabilities in terms of company structure to link the semiconductor technologies effectively with downstream applications. Indeed, Porter (1985) points out that these effective intra-firm linkages provide a basis for strong competitive advantage. Kimura (1989, 1990) confirms their strategic significance for the Japanese semiconductor firms. It may be interesting to ask why the EC-based semiconductor firms with a company structure similar to that of Japanese firms were not very effective in exploiting these linkages. They may now need to consider altering their company structure to tap the potential of these linkages of value-added activities within the firm. The effective European response to the Japanese challenge thus rests on whether EC-based firms are able to overcome these setbacks in the course of the project. Perhaps strategic alliances in R&D with US and Japanese firms may also be an effective approach alternative to, or complementary with, the independent EC-based development project.

All this suggests some implications for competitive policies for this industry in the Community. It seems that Japanese FDI activities have positive influences on competition in this industry that would lead to desirable market performance. Thus, policy should be directed at enhancing competition in the industry in the EC. For the Community to benefit most from unification, it should not be aimed at excluding firms and countries with strong competitiveness from a unified Europe to protect EC-based firms from global competition. Rather it should focus on development of the competitiveness of EC-based firms so that they are able to compete effectively with highly competitive firms based outside the Community. Offence is the best defence, and co-operative R&D projects like the Eureka project may be a very effective way to improve the competitiveness of the industry. Protection of a domestic industry from global competition tends to weaken rather than strengthen the industry in the Community. It reduces allocative efficiency, technical efficiency, and dynamic efficiency.

5.2. Influence on Adjacent Industries and the Economy

The Japanese FDI activities also affect adjacent industries in the EC through supplier–buyer relationships. Global competitiveness of a country in an industry does not develop in a vacuum. Highly competitive electronic systems industries require a strong semiconductor industry, and a strong semiconductor industry needs strong process equipment and material industries.

The strong presence of leading Japanese semiconductor firms may thus provide a solid infrastructural base for systems equipment manufacturers in Europe. To be competitive in the market, the systems manufacturers require advanced semiconductor chips that optimize the design objectives. Development and selection of desired devices demand close interaction between the systems manufacturers and the semiconductor firms. The FDI activities in production and product development by Japanese firms in the Community are likely to help end-user systems manufacturers improve their international competitiveness in the EC.

The production activities of these Japanese firms may also stimulate local supplier industries to upgrade their technological base to a level sufficient to support their production in the Community. As we have seen, Japanese semiconductor firms still rely heavily on Japanese rather than local suppliers for sourcing equipment and materials for technological reasons. However, for some materials they may be forced to source from local suppliers because of the absence of Japanese suppliers in those production locations. Then, they may need to help local suppliers elevate their technological competence so that they can serve as a source of supply. This will probably happen first in the areas of materials where switching of suppliers is easiest. Process equipment and strategic materials, such as silicon wafers and photo-resist, may be the last industries in which switching will take place. In those industries, the presence of Japanese suppliers may stimulate technological catch-up of local suppliers. If switching to local suppliers fails to take place due to their slow technological upgrading, the local supplier industries may eventually be populated by multinational suppliers. The Community may need a policy to help local supplier industries elevate their technological capabilities.

Japanese FDI activities in the EC seem thus to have a number of positive impacts. The presence of strong semiconductor firms is likely to elevate the competitiveness of both downstream and upstream industries in the Community. The expansion of this and adjacent industries will likely create employment opportunities for high-income professionals, reduce the import of microdevices and final systems equipment, increase their export and affect positively the balance of payments, and stimulate the growth of the overall economy.

To end this section, we would like to note that it seems very important that Japanese FDI activities should be effectively linked and integrated with the activities of local firms, horizontally and vertically, to maximize the potential benefits the presence of the Japanese semiconductor industry offers the Community. This would set the industry in a 'virtuous cycle of increasing technological capability' in Europe (Dunning and Cantwell 1991). Policymakers may need to develop a policy framework to induce the development of such linkages between Japanese semiconductor firms and EC-based firms. This may require encouragement of both Japanese and EC-based firms to develop these linkages. These linkages help integrate non-EC-based firms into the economy, and the presence of these non-EC-based firms will contribute to the Community's growth and development.

If such linkages fail to develop between EC-based firms and multinational firms based elsewhere, the non-EC multinational firms may tend to develop linkages with other non-EC firms operating in the Community, and the EC-based firms may be left out of these linkages. This would eliminate potential opportunities that may offer significant benefits to the local firms and to the local economy. This outcome may result if policymakers are concerned only with protecting 'domestic' firms from global competition, and if EC-based firms and non-EC-based firms are not willing to co-operate. The extreme aggressiveness of Japanese firms in competition may also drive the Community to the verge of retreating behind the wall of 'Fortress Europe'. A unified Europe might then revert to regionalism. However, we also see signs contrary to this possibility in the semiconductor industry in Europe.

6. CONCLUSIONS

In this paper, we have examined Japanese FDI in the semiconductor industry in the EC. We contrasted FDI in Europe with that undertaken earlier in Asia and the USA. We identified the incentives underlying Japanese FDI, and examined related strategies for Europe. Then, we evaluated the impacts of Japanese FDI on the semiconductor and adjacent industries and the overall economy in the Community.

This study shows that the FDI activities of Japanese semiconductor firms differ significantly from their earlier FDI activities in Asia and the USA. The FDI activities in the Community involve fully integrated production in state-of-the-art facilities, with a broader product line that includes the most advanced memories, logic ICs, and ASIC chips. The incentives that drove these FDI activities are the Japanese firms' high expectation for market growth in the EC and neighbouring countries, their concerns with market access, and the inducement by multinational systems manufacturer end-users located in the EC to undertake FDI. The second-tier firms that lack resources for FDI developed strategic alliances with local firms to maintain market access to a unified Europe. In contrast to these earlier FDI in Asia and the USA, FDI in Europe is part of Japanese firms' broader global strategies. This reflects their current strong technological and market leadership based on the dynamic structural changes that have taken place in the industry over the past decade.

These FDI activities of Japanese semiconductor firms are likely to have positive effects on the industry in Europe, improving allocative and technical efficiency and technological progressiveness. Due to the Japanese presence, there is likely to be intensified competition, and this is likely to provoke EC firms to revitalize their innovative efforts. The competitive semiconductor industry improves the global competitiveness of downstream industries. The FDI activities of the Japanese may also influence the supplier industries, although the degree of impact seems to depend on whether the Japanese firms are motivated to switch to local suppliers. Their impacts will eventually permeate the entire economy, influencing employment, international trade, and economic growth.

Thus, the FDI activities of Japanese semiconductor firms are likely to have a number of potentially positive effects on the EC. However, a note of caution is in order. To exploit these potential benefits of Japanese FDI activities, the Community must attempt effectively to integrate those activities with its adjacent industries and the overall economy of the EC. To attain this goal, we need an open technology, trade, and industrial policy and a policy framework in the Community to develop these linkages between EC-based firms and those based elsewhere but operating in Europe. A retreat from an open policy to a 'Fortress Europe' would significantly reduce the opportunities for further development of the semiconductor industry itself as well as of adjacent industries and the overall economy of Europe. We must note that a closed regionalism would work to nobody's advantage.

REFERENCES

BOWEN, H. (1991), 'Electronic Components and Semiconductors', in D. Mayes, ed., *The European Challenge: Industry's Response to the 1992 Programme* (Hertfordshire: Harvester Wheatsheaf) 209–54.

DUNNING, J. (1977), 'Trade, Location of Economic Activity and MNE: A Search for an Eclectic Approach', in B. Ohlin, P.-O. Hesselborn, and P. Wilkman, eds., *The International Allocation of Economic Activity* (London: Macmillan), 395–418.

—— and CANTWELL, J. (1991), 'MNEs, Technology, and the Competitiveness of European Industries', in G. Faulhaber and G. Tamburini, eds., *European Economic Integration: The Role of Technology* (Boston: Kluwer Academic Publishers), 117–48.

HENNERT, J.-F. (1985), *A Theory of Multinational Enterprise* (Ann Arbor: University of Michigan Press).

KIMURA, Y. (1988), *The Japanese Semiconductor Industry: Structure, Competitive Strategies and Performance* (Greenwich, Conn.: JAI Press).

—— (1989), 'Firm-Specific Strategic Advantages and Foreign Direct Investment Behavior: The Case of Japanese Semiconductor Firms', *Journal of International Business Studies*, 20/2, 296–314.

—— (1990), 'Sustainable Competitive Advantages and Market Share Performance of Firms: The Case of Japanese Semiconductor Industry', *International Journal of Industrial Organization*, 8/1, 73–92.

LINDER, S. (1961), *An Essay on Trade and Transformation* (Stockholm: Almqvist and Wiksell).

MAGEE, S. (1977), 'Information and the Multinational Corporation: An Appropriability Theory of Direct Foreign Investment', in J. N. Bhagwati, ed., *The New International Economic Order: The North–South Debate* (Cambridge, Mass.: MIT Press), 317–40.

Nihon Keizai Shimbun (1989), 'EC Saitei Hanbai-kakaku-sei donyu wo hashira-tosuru Kakaku yakusoku o Ryosho' [The Japanese Agree to the EC Minimum Sales Price Scheme], 6 Dec.

Nikkei Microdevices (1990a), 'User to Micchaku: Service taisei Totonou' [Working Closely with Users: Setup for Providing Services], July, 74–8.

—— (1990b), 'DRAM de Soki Tachiage' [Quick Start in DRAMs], July, 55–63.

—— (1990c), 'Sekkyokuha to Shokyokuha ni Nibun: Shinshutsu-jiki wo Saguru' [Aggressive Firms and Cautious Firms: Exploring the Timing for Direct Investment], July, 64–73.

—— (1990d), 'Shinshutsu Rush, 92-nen ni Kokunai 4-sha no Zen-Kotei Kado' [Rush to Europe: Four Japanese Firms Commence Operations of Wafer Processing in 1992], July, 44–55.

Nikkei Sangyo Shimbun (1990), 'Oki Denki Kogyo to SGS-Thomson, 4M DRAM o Kyodo Seisan' [Oki and SGS-Thomson Agree to Co-produce 4M DRAM ICs], 26 Feb.

PORTER, M. E. (1985), *Competitive Advantage: Creating and Sustaining Superior Performance* (New York: Free Press).

—— (1990), *The Competitive Advantage of Nations* (New York: Free Press).

RUGMAN, A. (1980), 'Internalization as a General Theory of Foreign Direct Investment', *Weltwirtschaftliches Archiv*, 166 (June), 365–79.

SHIMURA, Y. (1992), *2000-nen no Handotai Sangyo: Nihon ga Hiraku Gijutsu Frontier* [The Semiconductor Industry in the Year 2000: Japan Opens the Technological Frontier] (Tokyo: Nihon Noristu Kyokai Management Centre).

Sumitomo–Life Research Institute, with YOSHITOMI, M. (1991), *Japanese Direct Investment in Europe: Motives, Impact and Policy Implications* (Avebury).

TEECE, D. (1992), 'Competition, Cooperation, and Innovation: Organizational Arrangements for Regimes of Rapid Technological Progress', *Journal of Economic Behavior and Organization*, 18/1, 1–25.

COMMENT

Arnoud De Meyer

The present paper by Yui Kimura is an excellent though somewhat optimistic description of the growth of the Japanese semiconductor industry, and the current FDI by Japanese companies in Europe. Optimistic, because it seems to start with the premise that Japanese semiconductor companies have nothing but a bright future and that Japanese investment in Europe can only be good for Europe. The underlying hypothesis seems to be that the growth of the Japanese presence in semiconductors in Europe can only create more competition and competition is ultimately good for the world. Though I do subscribe to the ultimate benefit of competition, I am somewhat less optimistic about the future of Japanese semiconductor companies and their investments in Europe.

The author explains the growth of the Japanese semiconductor industry by three elements. The technological advantage built up by these companies over their European and US competitors combined with the vertical integration for some of them with the users of semiconductor-based components are the drive for the growth in FDI. These two favourable factors are reinforced by the influence exerted by the fast pace of change in the industry, which favours the companies that have the resources to invest in both product and process development. Though this seems to be a plausible economic analysis, it does neglect the influence of the favourable investment climate created by the Japanese government in the 1970s as well as the direct help and protection from which the Japanese semiconductor industry has benefited during the 1970s. The development of the first VLSI chip technology in Japan has often been described as one of the few very successful collaborative research ventures. This type of government guidance and support has made a difference for the Japanese semiconductor industry. One could argue that FDI is independent of these types of influence. But expansion overseas has obviously benefited from the stability derived from a combination of internal competition in Japan with protection from outside competition. Any analysis of FDI should indeed include the relationship between the evolution in the home market and foreign markets.

The success of the Japanese semiconductor industry is undeniable. Yet treating semiconductor-based components as one market, as the author seems to do, is perhaps somewhat simplistic. It is clear that Japanese companies have built up an extremely strong position in memories, but that in more sophisticated ICs such as microprocessors or ASICs their position is far less strong. The study of the effect of investment in Europe would in my opinion benefit greatly from a discussion that keeps that differentiation in mind.

In the paper we learn that Japanese companies have followed two different strategies in their development. Both strategies have been successful until now. Will these strategies be as successful in the future as they were in the past? Some Japanese firms have benefited in their development from the fact that the production of semiconductor components was integrated with the production of (consumer) electronics. The author argues that this provides a focus to the development and ties the component development in a more effective way to real market needs. He does not indicate whether he has observed cross-subsidization between the consumer business and the design and production of components, but his argument seems to suggest this. If this is the case, we are left with at least two unanswered questions. First, the same policy was indeed applied by Philips, where a similar integration with consumer products existed. The gradual withdrawal of Philips from the production of the most sophisticated components suggests that simple integration is not necessarily beneficial. The real question is how to organize that integration in order to improve the development performance upstream from the market. Secondly, in a booming market for consumer electronics it seems not so difficult to cross-subsidize the development of components. However, the current market conditions are far from favourable for these companies. The results for 1992 for Matsushita, Sony, Oki, and others seem to confirm this. Combined with a glut in the market for memories, the vertical integration between component design and consumer goods production may become a liability rather than an asset.

The case for the second group of players is not obvious either. These seem to be companies which pursue a global strategy, that is, become a fully integrated producer of state-of-the-art memory devices as well as specialized ICs in all relevant industrialized regions of the world. For these companies the paper seems to argue that large full-scale producers have a better chance of playing the 'timing game'. Kimura argues correctly that in an industry where the marginal ratio of the previous year's capital investment to current year's incremental increase in sales goes below 1.0, one of the major competitive challenges is to time the introduction of new production facilities and equipment correctly. The implicit suggestion seems to be that these large producers would be better at responding to this challenge than others. The history of other maturing industries, such as the steel industry, for example, indicates that nothing guarantees that this is a correct assumption. The current demise of some of the largest computer companies seems to indicate the opposite.

Furthermore, the success of the global strategy is dependent on the extent to which these companies can combine a global strategy with local responsiveness. The paper very clearly indicates the difficulty that these companies have in building up a technological network in which they can embed themselves in Europe. I am fully convinced that, as in other maturing industries, the close interaction between product and process development is a key to competitive success. Such a close interaction assumes that equipment vendors and suppliers of key materials work in close collaboration with the semiconductor firms. Though we do not have enough data to verify to what extent the vendors and suppliers of Japanese semiconductor firms are setting up factories in Europe, we get the impression that their willingness to do so is limited. If this is the case, the strategy to make the European factories an equal partner in the global development and production network may well be doomed. The paper makes an interesting observation about the unwillingness of Japanese semiconductor companies to go into partnership with European suppliers, except for some minor and non-essential raw materials. Again this requires further study, but, if the hypothesis is confirmed, this situation would not easily lead to a successful strategy of local responsiveness.

Finally, the paper suggests that investments in Europe by the Japanese would be beneficial for the EC. The core argument is based on the assumption that these investments would lead to more competition, which would force local firms to become more competitive, and which would lead to better-performing upstream and downstream industries. This requires the EC to implement policies in order to preserve the competition. The only suggestion which is made by the paper is to develop the competitiveness of local European firms through co-operative R&D projects. I am not convinced that this is a correct vision. Co-operative R&D projects may be very effective in the case of emerging or new technologies. The semiconductor industry is not an emerging industry but has many of the characteristics of a mature industry. In mature industries other measures to preserve competition, such as the application of anti-trust and anti-monopoly legislation, seem to be much more appropriate.

9

Can Japanese Direct Investment Sustain European Development in Electronics?

John Zysman

European governments, and the European Commission, sought through the 1980s to help their corporations establish or improve their position in global markets for advanced electronics. As Japan's industrial power surged and America seemed to stumble, Europe reconsidered its options.[1] Programmes for promoting the electronics industry, including Esprit and Eureka, were aimed not only at revitalizing the industry, but also at helping recast the European bargain.[2] The programmes did not meet their central objectives, however, and recent evaluations have concluded that they did not help bolster the market position of Europe's electronics firms.[3] On the contrary, in the most visible sectors European electronics firms remained weak. Indeed there were several dramatic competitive collapses, including the downsizing of Philips, the several crises at Bull, and the purchase of ICL by Fujitsu.

The competitive vacuum in electronics has been filled by foreign firms, principally US but increasingly Japanese, with the result that competition within the Community will intensify over the next few years. Until the mid-1980s the Japanese firms supplied these markets principally through imports. But now, in the fear of being closed out of Europe as the EC market solidifies, they are making heavy direct investments to establish production, distribution, and even R&D. At the same time, there has been substantial new US investment in recent years as many US firms expand their production and others open facilities for the first time.

The basic parameters of Japanese investment in European electronics are clear. European competitive weakness created a market opening first captured by imports; political threats to close the market and policies that discouraged imports but tolerated investment induced a Japanese surge. The meaning and future of that investment—the place of Japanese firms in the European industrial fabric—will depend on the competitive position of European firms and the terms of the policy debate.

[1] W. Sandholtz and J. Zysman, 'Europe's Emergence as a Global Protagonist', in W. Sandholtz et al., The Highest Stakes: The Economic Foundations of the Next Security System (New York: Oxford University Press, 1992), 81–113.

[2] W. Sandholtz, High-Tech Europe: The Politics of International Cooperation (Berkeley, Calif.: University of California, 1991).

[3] 'The Report of the Information and Communications Technologies Review Board', June 1992. This review board, chaired by Wisse Dekker of Philips, was invited by the EC to review the progress of the major programmes in information and communications technologies.

1. EUROPEAN POLICY FOR ELECTRONICS

European national governments and the European Commission have made electronics a focus of industry policy. The reasons for the focus are clear. The electronics industry now approaches automobiles in output and employment, and continues to grow rapidly. And as a symbol of the foundations of advanced industry in the late twentieth century, the sector has taken on a significance beyond the employment, production, and trade that the sector generates. In fact, there is an element of truth in the symbol. Information technology is a transformative technology that touches a broad range of economic activities; indeed, its effective use is central to the competitive position of firms in most industries.[4]

The difficulty is that the policy, at best, was not a success. Consequently, European corporate leaders and policymakers now wonder whether they can succeed at the task at which they failed in the 1980s, that is, create a competitive electronics industry. The character of the policy problems in the past decades suggests the nature of the choices today.

1.1. Protection and Producer Promotion

European policy governing foreign direct investment (FDI), though 'largely ad hoc and poorly coordinated', powerfully affected the industry throughout the 1980s.[5] Over this decade the weight of European FDI policy was reversed, essentially because there was little else Europe could do. US investment notwithstanding, European governments had previously discouraged 'excessive' or 'inappropriate investment.' The new policy, created in small steps without a coherent vision, amounted to trading imports for FDI; that is, discouraging imports but tolerating and often 'directing' FDI. The first element of the policy was dumping duties. For example, as Asian electronics imports poured into the Community in the 1980s, the EC began to implement anti-dumping policies that would 'prevent foreign manufacturers from putting European firms out of business by flooding the market with goods at below-cost prices'.[6] Then, to limit the use of final assembly of imported components ('screwdriver' factories) as a means of stepping around trade barriers and dumping duties, the Community began to implement tight rules of origin. Access to public markets for imports was restricted by rules that permitted a bid to be rejected if less than half

---

[4] M. Catinat, 'L'Informatique et les automatismes' (paper presented at international seminar on 'Le Devenir industriel de la France: Coopérer', Paris, 7–9 Sept. 1992), 11.

[5] See L. Tyson, *Who's Bashing Whom: Trade Conflicts in High-Technology Industries* (Washington, DC: Institute for International Economics, 1992), ch. 6. See also the excellent article by Robin Gaster that discusses European FDI policies, 'Protectionism with Purpose: Guiding Foreign Investment', *Foreign Policy* (Fall 1992). I find myself in full agreement with his interpretation of the European case, and indeed sympathetic to his interpretation of its implications for the USA.   [6] R. Gaster, 'Protectionism', 97.

of its value would be created outside the Community. Not surprisingly, 'importers got the protectionist message . . . Japanese investment flows grew from \$549 million in 1980 to \$8.9 billion by 1988.'[7] To prevent the various national, regional, and local authorities from competing for investment and creating a bidding war that would transfer Community resources to the foreign investors, restrictions on subsidies were implemented. Firms were encouraged to conduct the higher value-added segments of their work in Europe. As Robin Gaster has argued, the success of the programme seems clear, particularly in contrast with similar investments in the USA.[8]

Three interconnected problems plagued European policies in the 1980s. First, government policies often tended to channel firms into established and highly competitive market segments. The core objectives of European policy have been industrial stability, technological virtuosity, and employment. The policies of promotion therefore focused on and spent the largest sums of money on existing producers (often national symbols) making identifiable groups of known or anticipated products. There were a variety of national programmes to support diffusion, to encourage smaller companies, and to encourage new producers and products, but on balance policies favoured producers over not just consumers, but industrial users as well. Most spending supported existing producers along identifiable trajectories. Yet this funding of the large, national firms tended to push them into established and highly competitive market segments.[9] Little wonder the firms found it hard to establish defensible market positions; indeed, it could be argued that their governments pushed them into strategically impossible situations.

Second, favouring producers over low prices and easy access for consumers and industrial users discouraged widespread diffusion of advanced technologies among sophisticated users—the essential ingredient for creating launch markets for innovative products and entrepreneurial firms. As a consequence, the use of advanced electronics in Europe is generally lower than in Japan or the USA (as measured by the consumption of microelectronics per capita).[10] This is not surprising, since the prices of advanced electronics were pushed up by policies seeking to support European producers and encourage local production rather than imports. That slowed the diffusion and use of new products. In turn, a slowly expanding market dampened the demand for related and innovative products. This is certainly most visible in consumer electronics—a segment increasingly critical, since it is consumer digital electronics products that are now advancing the technology frontier. Many of these advanced

---

[7] Ibid.   [8] Ibid.   [9] Ibid.

[10] The *per capita* figures for personal computer installed base illustrate this fact: Europe: 1 personal computer for every 10 people; USA: 1 personal computer for every 4 people. *Source*: Dataquest, Inc., 'PC Europe' (San Jose, Calif., 1993).

electronic products are intermediary goods; that is, they are used to design, make, and service goods actually used by consumers. Telecommunication networks constitute the electronic highways of the next century. Higher prices that slow the use of applications technology thus affect the entire economy. Some sectors of European industry (in Germany and Sweden in particular) are certainly leading users of new production equipment. Some European companies such as Bosch are distinctly effective at applications in anti-lock braking and engine control systems. These are areas where the competitive position is least sensitive to the price of inputs. The penalty or handicap can be buried in the overall system costs. So where European markets create leading-edge demand for advanced products, European producers of advanced electronics are often competitive; where those leading-edge markets have not emerged, the producers are usually not competitive. The price of promotion for existing producers is often paid in the slowed market demand. The price is paid another way, since the policies have rarely succeeded in their overt purpose of establishing the sustained competitive position of major firms.

Third, European policy sought to locate production of key technologies in Europe. One objective was to maintain employment and trade balances. A second objective was to force technology transfer by establishing production. The French government and some in Brussels believed that the Japanese advantage would be blunted if they had to produce in Europe with European labour practices and wage/overhead costs. Or Japanese firms could at least be controlled and channelled to force technology transfer. If the European governments were right and could buy time for adjustment, European-owned production could be sustained; if they were wrong, at least jobs would be retained and technology transferred. Local suppliers would learn from working with Japanese firms; local R&D would build up fonts of knowledge and technology. But corresponding policies to encourage widespread diffusion of advanced technologies among sophisticated users were never implemented in the 1980s. Such policies could have served not only to support the competitive position of user industries but to create conditions for innovation in producer companies.

Policy that discouraged imports but accepted investment constituted an invitation. In the case of England, the invitation tendered by policy actively encouraged investment as an element of re-industrialization. (And, in fact, Japanese firms have been able to reorganize production, particularly in Britain, to step around established lines of industrial fracture and conflict.) But it is not evident that things will work out quite as planned. In the USA, for example, Japanese firms have tended to bring their own suppliers with them. If the same happens in Europe, this will limit the extent of technology transfer to European management.

The lesson of the past decade is that neither policies of promotion (such as the HDTV undertaking) or of protection (that encouraged FDI) have served to preserve the position of established European producers in their own markets, let alone improve their overall position in global markets.

1.2. Reframing the European Choices in Electronics

The Community's policy for information and communications technology industries (ICT industries) is being reconsidered.[11] That is essential, because to date the terms of this policy debate are often misphrased. The focus of European policy in the last decade has been to correct weaknesses rather than building on strengths. Rather than encouraging innovation from positions of European strength toward new breakthrough technologies, the policy encouraged European firms to compete directly in markets where their competitors had greatest advantage. It is little surprise that the policy failed. More than patience and money is called for. The terms of debate have hidden real European strengths in electronics, particularly in industrial applications. The policy approach to Japanese FDI in electronics will be set by how the basic European position is viewed.

The nature of the policy debate will have to be re-framed. That requires two things: first, rethinking the character of the policy problem itself; and second, re-evaluating the competitive position of the several segments of the electronics industry. We address these matters in turn.

Policy choices about programmes to support the industry's development, encourage technological diffusion, and either promote or restrict FDI should not rest on the sector's aggregate importance or symbolic significance. Rather, they must turn on a judgement about how the development of electronics influences the competitive position of firms in other industries, and particularly about how electronics technology flows from producer to user. There are two extreme views about these matters that suggest two different approaches to policy formulation.

The first view centres on applications expertise. Its proponents would argue that while production and employment in a growing sector is important, the critical factor is the capacity to apply the new technologies. In their view, Europe must first and foremost be able effectively to absorb, diffuse, and apply these technologies. The capacities required to absorb, diffuse, and apply technology are not only broader and deeper than the capacities required to produce the technology, but they are also more difficult to create and maintain. Gerd Junne writes, for example, that:

More important for the international competitiveness of a country than its share of new sectors in production and exports would, from this perspective, be its ability

---

[11] Various EC documents emphasize the opening debate. See the 'Report of the Information and Communications Technologies Review Board', June 1992, and Cowhey and Zysman, 'European Telecommunications at the Crossroads' (BRIE Research Note, 1992).

continually to generate new technologies and to diffuse and apply them in virtually all sectors of the economy.[12]

Or, even more explicitly:

More important to the overall competitiveness of the West German economy than its actual trade position in microelectronics, telecommunications, or biotechnology is the ability of West German firms to apply and diffuse these technologies throughout the economy.[13]

But if we adopt this vantage point, evaluating the precise technology position of a nation becomes very difficult. How does one measure, evaluate, and quantify the mechanisms that allow timely and efficient application of innovative technology, for example?

In this first view, a country (or a region) need not be a major producer of electronic or other advanced technologies to sustain a competitive position; new technologies will always be readily available in the market and can be bought, albeit at a somewhat higher price under some circumstances.[14] A country or a region must only be able to apply these technologies quickly and effectively to remain in a strong position. Thus, producers of Danish hearing-aids and Italian music boxes can compete effectively based on their sophisticated applications know-how if they are assured access to microelectronics technology.

The competing view, and really the dominant view in most European discussions, argues that only an intimate knowledge of the most advanced products permits timely flow of technology and intermediate product into final product. That intimate knowledge would depend on local production and local R&D, and perhaps even on local development and production, and ownership. For example, the argument suggests that a strength in consumer electronics or computer aided design (CAD) tools would require early command of advanced component technologies. In turn, advanced electronic products will increasingly turn on CAD tools and the components that go into consumer products.

Advocates of this second view argue that the types of technology readily available to companies often shape the choices firms make about which markets to address and what products to make. That is to say, broadly, their sources of technology shape the types of strategies available to them. Indeed, when the supply of advanced technology (in terms of access as well as price) dictates the strategies and development possibilities of firms critical to the welfare of the general economy, governments will be

---

[12] G. Junne, 'Competitiveness and the Impact of Change: Applications of High Technologies', in P. Katzenstein, ed., *Industry and Politics in West Germany* (Ithaca, NY: Cornell University Press, 1989), 250.   [13] Ibid. 25.

[14] This strategy of course is not always effective; see Junne, 'Competitiveness and the Impact of Change'.

concerned that those technology supplies are available. Europe's dilemma is that US and Japanese firms, not indigenous European producers, are the primary source of advanced electronics technology. That dependence raises concerns about both political autonomy and constraints on economic development.

European governments continually ask themselves how they should manage this dependence. Should Europe willingly accept imports to maintain lower prices, or should it restrain imports to encourage local producers—even if that involves penalties for the users who would employ the products? Or instead, should foreign producers be encouraged to develop and make products in Europe to assure closer links between foreign producers and European suppliers and to encourage technology transfer? If the foreign firm only wholesales commodity products or produces standard products largely from imported components in automated factories, then there will be limited technology transfer or learning within the home industry. The same would be true, of course, if a national firm merely assembled imported technological parts. Even local R&D may not be sufficient to assure technology transfer if the projects undertaken are so narrow and specific to particular products that the host country's broader technology competence is not nurtured.

Theoretical arguments alone cannot resolve this matter. In practice, the country's composition of electronics production, the types of final products and firms' market strategies, determine what access to emerging technology is required for them to be competitive. Governments of countries with very different industrial structures will reach sharply different conclusions about what they want made at home and what they are comfortable importing. The difference in the French and Danish position does not, for example, simply reflect differences in the traditions of debate about industrial policy. On balance, European governments have reluctantly and nervously accepted foreign substitutes for local production when there is no alternative, but have paid very high prices to support the market entry or re-entry of local producers.

The two viewpoints outlined above, one emphasizing applications know-how while downplaying concerns about foreign supplies of technology, and the other emphasizing the need for intimate access to rapidly evolving cutting-edge technology, represent two dimensions of the problem. Both are right, given particular kinds of circumstances. Consequently, the appropriate policy is very difficult to specify and will be even harder to implement.

Michael Borrus provides powerful tools, developed to debate US choices in the face of Japanese technological success, that can help clarify European choices. Let us consider the notions of an industrial and technological 'supply base' and the 'architecture' of that supply base. He defines the supply base as:

the parts, components, subsystems, materials and equipment technologies available for new products and process development, as well as the structure of relations among the firms that supply and use these elements. The supply base shapes the possibilities confronting users by enabling or deterring access to appropriate technologies in a timely fashion at a reasonable price.[15]

Logically, supply bases act as a structural constraint on individual company choices. In this sense, a supply base can be understood as an element of industrial structure or organization.[16] The notion has intuitive appeal, but applying it would seem problematic since it is very difficult to define which technologies are linked to which activities or in what way. But we really do not need such a precise measure for our purposes. As we shall see, most of the elements of the new electronics supply base are emerging in Asia, whichever measures and definitions we might use. Even without any sophisticated mapping of the industry, what can be systematically depicted is the 'architecture' of the supply base; that is, the structure of markets and communities through which the elements cited above reach producers. A market consisting of many 'flexibly specialized' small firms all in shifting horizontal relations, each supplying components and know-how to one another, has a very different architecture from a market in which concentrated suppliers compete with their customers (the latter describes the vertically arranged Japanese *keiretsu* in which component suppliers also produce the final product). Borrus is very clear and provides a useful tool for considering Europe's situation:

The architecture of the supply base matters to the extent that it influences access, timeliness and cost. Domestic industry that is significantly dependent on a foreign supply base (i.e. on imports of key inputs) will not be overly constrained wherever markets are open and competitive and suppliers are numerous, geographically dispersed, and not in the same lines of business as their customers.[17]

For Europe, the question is whether the architecture of its supply base is changing. There have long been concerns about dependence on American suppliers, but those suppliers were usually not in competition with their European customers, and product technology was relatively accessible. Now the supply base is increasingly Asian (usually Japanese) and the suppliers do compete with their customers in a wide range of products.

---

[15] M. Borrus, 'Re-organizing Asia: Japan's New Development Trajectory and the Regional Division of Labor' (BRIE Working Paper 53; 1992).

[16] P. Guerrieri, 'Technology and International Trade Performance of the Most Advanced Countries' (BRIE Working Paper 49; 1991). Seen from this vantage of a supply base that underpins final production, it is not surprising that Guerrieri finds that export competitiveness in production equipment is linked to the competitive position of firms in the final goods sector for which the equipment is used. Success in final goods and in production equipment that supports them are intertwined. Production equipment is an element of the supply base that is created by and makes possible competitive advantage in the final goods.

[17] M. Borrus and J. Zysman, 'Industrial Competitiveness and American National Security', in Sandholtz *et al.*, *The Highest Stakes*.

Increasingly, companies in one country or region are dependent on suppliers in another country or region. They should be concerned, Borrus argues, when:

The architecture of supply is characterized by closed markets, oligopolistic and geographic concentration, and, especially, wherever such concentrated suppliers compete directly with their customers. When suppliers have the ability to exercise market power or to act in concert to control technology flows, or when markets and technologies are not accessible because of trade (and investment) protection, then the architecture of supply can significantly constrain competitive adjustment to the disadvantage of domestic industry. Such an architecture is emerging today. . . . A small number of foreign suppliers, principally Japanese, are more and more driving the development costs, quality, and manufacture of the technological inputs critical to all manufacturers. Most of these suppliers of electronic components, manufacturing equipment, and sub-systems are also competitors in a range of electronics systems from TVs and portables phones to computers. These competitors are then increasingly in a position to dictate the degree of access [US and European] producers have to essential technologies, the speed at which they can bring new products incorporating them to market, and the price they pay for the privilege.[18]

The supply base is structured both by the composition of production (an industrial economics notion) and by the institutional arrangements of government and business organization (a political economy notion). Domestic institutions arrange the way technology flows internally, how it diffuses through the economy.[19] Analytically, we need to distinguish between the character of the *source* country, Japan or the USA, and the *host* country, the European region and the several political economies within it. When we consider the source country, we must be concerned with the kind of access available to European firms, not just the kinds of technology. The degree of access to technologies in Japan and the USA is very different, for example. America's technology pool is much more open than the Japanese technology pool. When we consider the host country structure, we must consider the institutional capacity to absorb and apply technology. Here we would find substantial differences between France and Germany, for example, and indeed substantial differences between very similar regions on opposite sides of borders.[20]

---

[18] Ibid. 26.

[19] See J. Zysman (with assistance from L. Tyson, G. Dosi, and S. Cohen), 'Trade, Technology and National Competition', in E. Deiaco, E. Hornell, and G. Vickery, eds., *Technology and Investment* (London: Printed for the Royal Swedish Academy of Engineering Sciences, 1990); and J. Zysman, *Political Strategies for Industrial Order: State, Market and Industry in France* (Berkeley, Calif.: UC Press, 1977).

[20] See M. Borrus, 'Chips of State: An Emergency Plan to Help the U.S. Semiconductor Industry Help Itself', *Issues in Science and Technology* (Fall 1990); and M. Borrus and J. Zysman, 'Industrial Competitiveness and American National Security', in W. Sandholtz *et al.*, *The Highest Stakes*.

To better pose the European problem, let us take as a stylized fact the existence of three distinct and distinctly organized economic and trade groups in Europe, North America, and a Japan-centered Asia.[21] For now the groups are mostly organized around the trade attraction of their neighbours. Whether these trade groups become economic blocs or political rivals is a separate matter. But each has, in fact, its own regional supply base with different capacities and dependencies on other regions. For example, it is very clear that in the electronics sector each of these regions is developing a distinct electronics supply base with particular strengths and vulnerabilities. A design-centred supply base is resident in North America and a components/sub-system-based supply base is entrenched in Asia. Accessability is the critical issue. Note that this analytic viewpoint suggests that company strategies and organizational norms are centrally a function of the national/regional environment in which they are developed.[22] This position also postulates that the flow of technological and industrial know-how is denser within a region than across regions, that there is no single global market for technology, but rather three distinct supply bases. Despite international markets for goods, technology still pools in localities.

A critical issue for corporate strategy and government policy then becomes how these three supply bases are linked together; that is, how technology flows among the regions. We must, of course, distinguish between scientific knowledge, formal and more specifiable, and technological knowledge, more implicit and less easily specified, noting that flows of scientific knowledge are much more open and much more international. To begin, let us specify three mechanisms of technology flow. First, industry technology flows through communities of company engineers. Such technological communities are inherently more local and national than international. Second, technology can flow through markets, but industrial structure and ordinary facts of distance and language can create a local bias. Moreover, national markets are often protected, the flows of technology distorted by trade protection. Not all buyers have equal access; local buyers are likely to have some initial advantage. This is particularly important when production and design supply bases are in the same region as launch markets for innovative products, as is now the case in Asia for electronics. Launch markets are where innovative products are first sold. There, not only is demand greatest, but firms also find the technology required to design and make advanced products. Outsiders have to launch products in markets away from home and will have to develop them with technologies sourced away from home. Third, though multinational corporations may act as bees sampling pollen in each of the three regions,

[21] M. Borrus and J. Zysman, 'Industrial Competitiveness'.
[22] See P. Guerrieri, 'Technology and International Trade Performance'.

they are likely to make honey in their home base, and keep the real expertise and markets at home.[23]

There are two significant implications for Europe. One implication, the emphasis in this paper, is that the character and sophistication of the market for final products is critical. A highly sophisticated market will induce producers to respond innovatively. The second implication for Europe is that the position of national or regional producers of particular final products is not necessarily the central question. The crucial issues are the character of the regional supply base, the access to supply bases outside Europe, and the ability to apply technology and combine components into systems whether those technologies are initially developed in Europe or not.

2. EVALUATING THE POSITION OF EUROPEAN ELECTRONICS

The next step in evaluating what policies European governments ought to adopt for their electronics sectors is a review of the competitive position of the European electronics industry. In my view—a position argued for many years—the visible problems hide less evident strengths; those real strengths can be used to offset and even repair weaknesses.[24] But to do so requires a change in policy and focus.

Clarifying the possibilities and the significance of the shift in policy requires an overview of the industry as a whole, not just a discussion of one or two sectors. In this we move from areas of clear European weakness that have been the focus of policy debate to areas of evident strength which must be the basis of any rebuilding strategy. Common to all the sectors, with very few exceptions, is the virtual absence of a European presence in the Japanese market. This is both a product of competitive weakness in areas such as semiconductors and a source of strategic weakness in the years that lie ahead.

2.1. Semiconductors

Semiconductors is the most evident area of European industrial weakness. Europe represents only 20 per cent of the world market for semiconductors, compared to 26.6 per cent for the USA and 36 per cent for Japan. In part, that difference in use of semiconductors reflects Japanese and US

---

[23] For a discussion of the social basis of technological trajectories and the regional problems of managing technology see J. Zysman in E. Deiaco, E. Hornell, and G. Vickery, eds., *Technology and Investment* and Zysman, *Political Strategies of Industrial Order*.

[24] See e.g. Zysman, *Political Strategies for Industrial Order* and id. (rapporteur and examiner), *Innovation Policy: France* (OECD, 1986).

exports of equipment embedding components to Europe, but more importantly it reflects very low overall use of electronics by Europe. As a consequence, European producers in 1991 held only 10 per cent of world semiconductor production compared to 38.4 per cent for the USA and 46.4 per cent for Japan. The European producers hold less than 40 per cent of their own market. More than 30 per cent of European use is supplied by foreign companies in Europe, with Americans providing 24 per cent and Japanese 7 per cent (though they are rapidly expanding their facilities). The trade deficit in active components was $4.15 billion in 1990.

The European market weakness is even deeper than these aggregate figures suggest. There are no robust European producers, and Europe does not have an entrenched position in any segment of the sector. Consider commodity memories, which are standard and depend on production skill. In the DRAM memory products that drive the advancing edge of process technology, only Siemens remains in the game at all, albeit through junior partner alliances with Toshiba and IBM—alliances from which it shows no signs of ever graduating to full partnership. Moreover, the equipment which underlies production is dominated by Japan and the USA.[25] (The positions shifted in favour of Japan in the 1980s and have shifted back somewhat toward the USA in the last few years.)

Microprocessors are dominated by American producers. The Europeans have no independent position either in traditional all-purpose processors or in the new RISC (reduced instruction set computing) processors. These tiny computers entail different proprietary hardware standards that represent powerful barriers to entry because software is adapted to them. Once a user base is created, the investment of these customers entrenches the market position of the standard processors. That customer base adapts to particular standards, and software operating systems in turn induce further development of software fitted to that standard.

One area of European semiconductor strength is in application-specific (ASIC) and customized chips that are adapted to particular market needs and usually made with processes that are not state of the art. But the Americans, and now the Japanese, have established extensive and substantial production facilities in Europe. Both have expanded their operations in anticipation of political restrictions that would close the market to them.[26]

European policy has sought to remedy the situation, but if anything it has made it much worse. The policy focus and debate have been on process technology rather than design technology. The assumption has been that only with a strong position in the commodity DRAMs could Europe establish a broad microelectronics position. Support has gone to those activities that would permit European firms to compete directly with US and Japanese firms in the main industry segment, but not to those that would underwrite and develop European market strengths. Policy has sought to correct the greatest weaknesses of European industry, but by pushing European firms into market competition with their most powerful competitors in their competitors' areas of greatest strength. The consequence of the policy has been that rather than repairing the structural weakness that policymakers perceived, the firms themselves have been undermined and their capacities reduced. This policy strategy has pushed European semiconductor producers away from building market positions that would play to their own real applications strengths and toward competition in the area in which they are weakest. Subsidies, protection, and privileged procurement could not rescue their position.

Two alternative policies that complement each other were available to the Europeans in the 1980s. First, support could have focused on application-specific and customer-specific application and design technologies. Support for rapid adoption of best-practice process technology rather than for leading-edge processes could have created distinctive capacities. Flexible production technology could have been considered. Second, creation of a leading-edge market for applications would have indirectly assisted producers. Many countries, including Germany and Switzerland, made a real effort to diffuse the use of microelectronics technology throughout industry. A heavy emphasis on diffusion would have helped both the user industries and the producers by encouraging the creation of a sophisticated domestic market. The producers would have faced increased demand for application-specific and custom circuits from sophisticated users, for example. In sum, given the extremely weak position, European companies and governments need to focus on the areas that are at once of critical importance to them and where firms can establish defensible market positions.

2.2. From Consumer Electronics to High-Volume High Technology

The Japanese control more than half of the world market in consumer electronics. The two leading companies are Japanese, but Philips and Thomson are none the less in the third and fourth positions, and Nokia, Grundig, and Bosch have strong positions both in Europe and the USA.[27] European-owned producers control 34 per cent of the European market— significantly more than US-owned producers control of the US market.[28] And European firms can be innovative. Philips has introduced significant new products to the market from the VCR through digital tape in 1992. The governments, moreover, are committed to maintaining a European

[27] T. Triomphe, 'Électronique Grand Public' (paper presented at international seminar on 'Les Nouvelles Armes du défi industriel').
[28] *Panorama of EC Industry* (1990), sects. 10–17 ff.

position in this sector. For example, there is a major policy commitment to establishing a single European system of High Definition Television as a means of recreating, or perhaps better creating, a powerful European presence in consumer electronics and the components that underlie those products.

European industry has seemingly withstood the Japanese challenge in consumer electronics better than the US industry. The question is whether the European position is in fact defensible. Vulnerabilities persist. They take several forms. First, the European market for consumer electronics is $28.4 billion, but European producers provide only $15.8 billion—a trade deficit of $12.6 billion. In other words, Europe is a huge importer, but exports almost nothing to the rest of the world. The deficit is in fact growing at least as fast as the market itself.[29] Moreover, Japanese factories in Europe provide 28 per cent of European production.[30] Of course, the Japanese market has been effectively closed—first by policy, and then by a mix of business practice and distribution arrangements. And the Japanese have often employed determined low-cost pricing strategies that sometimes drift into dumping. But the Japanese product strengths and production advantages are real. Without protection of the European market, it is our judgement that Asian producers would capture a much higher share of the European market. Overall, the European producers do not appear cost-competitive, are generally slower and less effective at establishing new product niches, and spend less on R&D than their Japanese competitors. And, in any case, evidence shows that the Japanese firms are more profitable.[31]

The impending round of competition in consumer electronics will be of massive significance for the European electronics industry in general. Very simply, many of the components and sub-systems that are the core of the new consumer electronics are cutting-edge products that define the new category of high-volume advanced digital technology.[32] Michael Borrus puts the case very well when he argues that the 'development and application of a broad range of subsystem, component and machinery and materials technologies are increasingly being driven by high-volume producers that boast leading edge sophistication and extremely high quality at remarkably low costs'.[33] The product set that uses these products include: lap-top, note-book and hand-held computers, optical disk mass storage systems, smart-cards, portable faxes, copiers, printers and electronic datebooks, portable and cellular telephones and pagers, camcorders, electronic still cameras, compact disc players, hand-held televisions, controllers for machine tools, robots and other industrial machinery, and embedded automotive systems like those for anti-skid braking, engine, transmission, and suspension control,

---

[29] Triomphe, 'Électronique Grand Public'.
[30] Ibid.; indeed, 32 per cent is by Asia as a whole.   [31] Ibid.
[32] M. Borrus and J. Hart, 'Display's the Thing: The Real Stakes in the Conflict Over High-Resolution Display' (BRIE Working Paper 52; 1992).   [33] Ibid.

and navigation. These products have a number of features in common. As Borrus argues:

These fastest growing products are miniaturized systems built around embedded, often dedicated microprocessors (or microcontrollers) with embedded software for control and applications. They are multi-functional, combining computing functionality with communications, consumer with office, etc. By virtue of their size, such products are increasingly portable. They are also networkable, that is, their capabilities are significantly enhanced by being networked together into larger information systems.

The most distinguishing characteristic of these products, however, is that they comprise sophisticated, industrially significant technologies, that are manufactured in volumes and at costs traditionally associated with consumer demand. Taken together, these products define a new electronics industry segment, being generated in Japan with only limited participation by firms outside Japanese industry— high volume digital electronics. Because of the push to produce high performance at the lowest possible price points, this high-volume electronics industry is . . . beginning to drive the development, costs, quality and manufacture of technological inputs critical to all electronics, and to industries like automotive being transformed by the application of electronics. At stake is a breathtaking range of essential technologies from semiconductors and storage devices to packaging, optics, interfaces, machinery and materials.[34]

The European companies will certainly face a ferocious competitive battle to maintain their position in the European home market and the US market in the next few years. Policy at either the European or national level is not likely to provide much support or protection. European standards and trade protection will not suffice in themselves to maintain the market for European producers. The Europeans refused the Japanese standard, and correctly so, since that standard would have required the immediate replacement of all televisions or the creation of parallel transmission systems. That refusal also served to prevent the Japanese, who had designed professional and consumer electronics equipment to their own standard, from immediately entering and dominating the European market for HDTV. The creation of a European standard means a delay that creates or maintains an opportunity for European producers. (Of course, the USA may choose a third and even more advanced digital standard.) But the Japanese firms will eventually adapt themselves to whatever standards for video or audio are selected by the Europeans. Once the standard is set, the Japanese will produce to it. Trade protection—whether in the form of domestic value-added rules, anti-dumping procedures, or outright quotas on imports—will simply encourage even more rapid investment by the

---

[34] M. Borrus, 'The Regional Architecture of Global Electronics: Trajectories, Linkages and Access to Technology', in P. Gourevitch, ed., *New Challenges to International Co-operation: Adjustments of Firms, Policies and Organizations to Global Competition* (San Diego: University of California, San Diego, forthcoming, 1993).

Japanese in Europe. As noted, Asians already control about one-third of European production. That proportion could rise.

It will be very difficult for European firms to build positions of long-term advantage in consumer electronics. Equally important, it will be hard for them to use this sector as a foundation on which to build broader competitive advantage. Arguably, the points of leverage and advantage in new product lines are dominated by the Americans and Japanese. The Americans have used skills in product definition and design to maintain market position. Amazingly, after having ceded the television and related product markets to Japanese and some European companies, new US firms are beginning to redefine the character of consumer electronics. These relative strengths suggest the pattern of deals between Japanese and US firms. The Americans create distinct product definitions which are often produced for them by the Japanese. The Japanese often then produce next generation design improvements which the Americans often then distribute under their own labels. There is seemingly little room for European companies unless they are able to find new and innovative product strategies.

Consider the two problems Europe must face if it is to create a defensible market advantage in consumer electronics. First, the Japanese advantage and points of leverage are in their control of components and sub-systems that allow them to differentiate their products and production systems; such control not only creates cost advantages but also allows flexible, quick responses to marketing. Their strong position rests on intense technology development and on the control of the flow of technology to suppliers and potential competitors; that is, the control of their supply base. Japanese FDI in Asia over the last decade, for example, has guaranteed a Japan-centred industrial economy and electronics supply base. Japan is the region's technology leader, its primary supplier of capital goods, its dominant exporter, its largest annual foreign direct investor and foreign aid supplier, and, increasingly, a vital market for imports (though the USA remains the largest single import market for Asian manufactures). Put differently, the region's production network appears to be a hierarchy dominated by Japan.[35] Advanced products and most of the underlying technologies are

[35] Japanese technology lies at the heart of an increasingly complementary relationship between Japan and its major Asian trading partners. Japanese companies supply technology-intensive components, sub-systems, parts, materials, and capital equipment to their affiliates, subcontractors, and independent producers in other Asian countries for assembly into products that are sold via export in third-country markets (primarily in the USA and other Asian countries). Conversely, non-affiliated labour-intensive manufactures and affiliated low-tech parts and components flow back into Japan from other Asian producers. Summarizing these trends, MITI noted in 1987 the 'growing tendency for Japanese industry, especially the electrical machinery industry, to view the Pacific region as a single market from which to pursue a global corporate strategy'. There are two key elements to this strategy which has been pursued not only in electronics but also in automobiles. One is to spread sub-system assembly throughout Asia while persuading each government to treat sub-systems originating in other Asian countries as being of 'domestic origin'.

controlled by Japanese companies, with labour-intensive and standard technology production in the periphery of the region and often under the control of Japanese industry.

The second problem Europe must face is that existing component and production dependencies in consumer electronics appear to be creating a cumulative knowledge gap which may be very difficult to eliminate. For example, Japanese producers have painstakingly acquired, iteratively over several product generations, the precision mechanical design expertise embedded in products such as VCRs, or the precision machining know-how in auto-focus camcorders. A leading US industrial laboratory recently reverse-engineered such products and concluded that the embedded precision mechanical skills probably no longer existed anywhere in the USA. Japanese firms intelligently and carefully manage their technology position to maximize what they control and to minimize their dependence for critical technology on outside sources. This component dependency is critical. The vertically integrated character of major Japanese firms means that firms selling components and equipment are often competing with their clients in the final product markets. Given this industrial structure, Japanese firms behave as we might expect, and as firms such as IBM or Boeing behave. Their goals are (1) to keep tight control over the underlying component, machinery, and materials technologies by regulating their availability to independent Asian producers, and (2) to keep advanced production at home. Together, these tend to deter too rapid a catch-up by independent producers to the competitive level of leading Japanese producers, while simultaneously developing Asia as a production base for Japanese exports to the USA and Europe.

As high-volume electronics production begins to use the sophisticated technological inputs that industrial systems share, it begins to drive common technological development. By spreading the huge development costs across many more sales, high-volume markets can support the development of advanced technologies previously initiated only by public spending. Consumer markets demand much lower costs—costs which are achieved through rapid attainment of economies of scale, learning, and the other attributes of the new manufacturing. The associated product development and process skills permit the technology to be cycled much more rapidly. Cost savings and rapid cycle times permit expanded R&D, broader experimentation, and the capturing of new opportunities for additional technological learning. The final result is a new technological development trajectory—new generations of cheaper but sophisticated technologies emerging from high-volume consumer applications, but applicable across the board in professional and military products, and therefore essential to the success of all other industries that produce or use electronics.

The importance of high-volume digital technologies to all segments of the electronics sector makes the success of European consumer electronics producers critical to the sector as a whole. At the firm level, the Europeans will have to solve the internal problems that have slowed market response and limited their ability to capture market position.

The supply base problem, described above, will not be resolved by wishing the re-creation of the entire electronics *filière* in Europe. First and foremost, Europe must secure access to the Asian supply base and work with US producers to maintain an open international supply base for producers from all regions.

2.3. Does the European Computer Industry Compute?

The weakness of the European computer industry is legendary; the measures of its weakness are extensive.[36] Europe imports roughly one-third of its computer and information technology needs.[37] European firms control only 34 per cent of their market, the rest—whether by import or local production—is controlled by foreign firms. By contrast, US firms control 92 per cent of the US market, while Japanese firms control 84 per cent of the Japanese market.[38]

But the weakness is even deeper when we look beyond these general figures. The microcomputer segment of the industry is controlled by US firms, with the largest European firm being Olivetti, with 5.5 per cent of the market in 1991.[39] Bull has become a player by buying Zenith. The mini-computer segment is dominated by IBM and DEC, while Bull and Siemens hold only 10 per cent each of the market. In mainframe systems the European position is a bit stronger, but each of the main European companies is substantially dependent on Japanese or US suppliers for major parts of their product line. Fujitsu now owns ICL, which has 7 per cent of the European market. Bull depends on NEC; Hitachi supplies Olivetti, Fujitsu provides for Siemens.[40]

If anything, the European position has deteriorated over the past ten years. The Japanese have come to challenge the Americans, increasing their share of the world market in the period 1984 to 1990 from 6.5 per cent to 18 per cent as the US share descended from 62.7 per cent to 47.4 per cent.[41] The Europeans might comfort themselves with explanations that American success rested on military spending (except that this was only the case in the very early years), and that Japanese successes rested on a large, coherent, and highly protected domestic market. However,

---

[36] The European computer market is much smaller than the US market; computers are simply not as widely used. The per capita figures for personal computer installed base illustrate this fact (source is Dataquest, 'PC Europe' [San Jose, Calif., 1993]):
  Europe   1 personal computer for every 10 people
  USA   1 personal computer for every 4 people.
[37] M. Catinat, 'L'Informatique et les automatismes', 11.   [38] Ibid.
[39] Dataquest, 'PC Europe'.   [40] Ibid.   [41] Ibid. 7–8.

the fact is that the Europeans largely missed the commercial-based work-station and microcomputing revolutions that are transforming the very character of the computer industry. European firms, often badly organized and insensitive to market requirements, coped very poorly with a difficult situation.

Government policy did not help. If anything it made matters worse, as I have argued for many years.[42] National policies created a fragmented European market that was slow to adopt new technologies. Policymakers sought to imitate the product mix and industrial structure they saw in the USA. They reasoned from the structures they wanted to the strategies they wanted the firms to adopt. The policies then pushed European firms directly into market segments dominated by the US giants. Bureaucrats could only, by the nature of the situation, play catch-up; they could not play the entrepreneurial role of imagining and inventing new industrial futures. And the catch-up game was difficult in the fragmented European market. Firms were discouraged from finding their own distinctive tech-nological avenues and consequently the possibility of innovative break-throughs that could permit European firms to become leaders. These views are beginning to find expression in Europe:

R&D policies targeted toward national champions and justified by the will to become technologically independent for national defense reasons had the result of encouraging corporate strategies that followed their strongest and most competi-tive rivals. This resulted in a delay in the introduction and commercialization of new innovative products. No European firm adopted innovative strategy concepts.[43]

In sum, the result has been a deep and enduring technological dependence in virtually all segments of the industry.

Europe made its first mistake by never even debating the notion that a sophisticated market could be the best possible assistance to producers. Policies for diffusion and use of advanced technology never received the same attention and weight as did producer-oriented support.[44] The sym-bolic consequence of producing particular products, not the broad economic gain from widespread adoption of new technologies, was the emphasis of policy debates. This is particularly significant now because the European position in systems integration—the development of large-scale networks of computers to apply to specific problems—is much stronger than in the hardware included.[45] European companies have a strong position in their own market. Equally important, the customized and skill-intensive nature of systems integration means that the fundamental technological know-how can grow up in Europe even if the company selling the service is American. Systems integration can create the sophisticated market. But

---

[42] J. Zysman, *Political Strategies* and id., *Innovation Policy.*
[43] M. Catinat, 'L'Informatique et les automatismes', 8.   [44] Ibid.
[45] Ibid.

there is, in any case, no vision in the policy community about how a solid position in systems integration can be used to rebuild a base in computer hardware.

2.4. Why Defence Electronics Cannot Defend the European Position in Commercial Markets

Defence electronics cannot defend the broader European position in electronics. As in the USA, the emerging high-volume digital technology industry described above is likely to make the military electronics industry ever more dependent on advances in the commercial industry. At BRIE we have explored this issue in both the US and the Japanese economies.[46] Borrus and I have argued that:

... a completely alternative military technology development trajectory is emerging from the innovations in production and consequent reshuffling of markets examined earlier ... This alternative drives technological advance from commercial rather than military applications. Technology diffuses from civilian to defense use rather than vice versa, a trajectory characterized as 'spin-on' in contrast to its predecessor. The new alternative is prospering most fully in Japan, where an increasing range of commercially developed technologies are directly, or with minor modification, finding their way into advanced military systems. In particular, militarily relevant sub-system, component, machinery, and materials technologies are increasingly driven by high-volume commercial applications that produce leading-edge sophistication, with extremely high reliability but remarkably low costs.[47]

As argued above, the high-volume electronics industry is beginning to drive the development, costs, quality, and manufacture of technological inputs critical to computing, communications, the military, and industrial electronics. I have argued the details elsewhere and here simply outline the conclusion.[48] The basic technological requirements of new consumer products now approach, equal, or at times surpass those needed for sophisticated military applications. They have also begun to share a common underlying base of components, machinery, and materials technologies. There are several significant implications. First, by spreading the huge development costs across many more units, high-volume markets can

---

[46] See esp. S. Vogel, 'The Power behind "Spin-Ons" ', and J. Stowsky, 'From Spin-Off to Spin-On: Redefining the Military's Role in American Technology Development', both in Sandholtz *et al.*, *The Highest Stakes*.

[47] See Borrus and Zysman, 'Industrial Competitiveness', 31. We argue there that: 'The case is clearest in electronics, where a new industry segment is being defined in Asia. Its distinguishing characteristic is the manufacture of products containing sophisticated, industrially significant technologies, in volumes and at costs traditionally associated with consumer demand. Such products include the latest consumer items, such as camcorders, electronic still cameras, compact disc players, and hand-held TVs, and new micro-systems, such as portable faxes, copiers and printers, electronic datebooks, laptop computers, optical disk mass storage systems, smartcards, and portable telephones.' [48] See ibid. 32.

support the development of advanced technologies previously initiated only by military spending. Second, price-sensitive consumer applications demand that the unit cost of the underlying technology components be very low.[49] The necessary low costs can be achieved only by the scale, scope, and learning economies of revolutionary production approaches. The end result is that new, militarily relevant generations of cheaper but sophisticated and reliable technologies emerge from high-volume commercial markets.[50]

2.5. Will Networks be the Link to European Success?

Telecommunications is the most evident European electronics strength and the major firms have been very successful. At least until the late 1980s the European equipment makers held on to the bulk of the European telecommunications market. The share of European telecommunications equipment provided by European suppliers has likewise remained high (see Table 9.1). Of course, national ministries or their agents served as monopoly buyers, a situation not different from the recognized monopoly of ATT, but many of the European firms have established themselves as major global competitors with substantial strengths. Some of the companies have been important innovators. Alcatel led the way to digital switching in France, which was the first country to take this significant step. Ericsson helped the rapid diffusion of cellular telephony in Sweden; indeed, Ericsson has been remarkably successful in international markets by carefully identifying market possibilities, understanding the needs of potential

---

[49] Ibid. For example, auto producers will pay an order of magnitude less for semiconductor component technologies than would contractors applying the same or similar products to military systems. Low consumer product costs cannot be achieved by reduced functionality or reduced reliability, since, for example, a real-time processor for engine or brake control on an automobile is a very sophisticated element incorporated in systems that must not fail in operation.

[50] There are real implications for the military, as argued in W. Sandholtz *et al.*, *The Highest Stakes*. Moreover, the new production model's emphasis on speed of product development and rapid cycling of technology introduction has additional, critical military consequences. Using the strategies and production capabilities of the new manufacturing, Honda and Toyota can now take an automobile from design to showroom in less than three and a half years. This is twice as fast as traditional mass production, even though, with the incorporation of electronics and other new technologies, automobiles pose highly complex systems development problems akin to military product development (albeit with different performance parameters). Imagine the implications for military system development, plagued as it is with cycle times that incorporate technologies often two generations old, technologies that are advanced as design begins but old by the time production starts.

It is a plausible hypothesis that civilian developers who have mastered the new manufacturing can move complex systems from design to battlefield faster than traditional military suppliers. They are better organized to do so. The very concept of the fastest route to the most advanced but reliable military systems in the field may have to change. The quickest route may no longer be to jump to the extreme limits of the technically feasible at the moment a system is conceived. Rather, the most effective route may well be the iterative innovation that Japanese firms have mastered.

TABLE 9.1. *Market shares of European cable transmission systems, by supplier company, 1990*

Supplier	Market Share (%)	US$ (millions)
Alcatel/Telettra	30	713
Siemens/GPT	25	594
Ericsson	5	119
Philips	5	119
Bosch	5	119
AT&T	5	119
Northern Telecom	5	119
Italtel	4	95
Nokia	3	71
Others	13	309
TOTAL	100	2,377

Source: Dataquest, 'Telecom, Europe' (San Jose, Calif., 1991).

customers, and pursuing them carefully for years. Siemens, a $7.3 billion company, remains entrenched in the German market while already establishing a real presence in the USA. Given this strength in the telecommunications sector, there are two major issues: first, can the Europeans maintain their position of strength in Europe and extend that into world markets? And second, can telecommunications be the foundation from which to rebuild the rest of the European electronics sector?

Foreign firms are not poised to capture a major piece of the telecommunications equipment markets in Europe. The Japanese firms are not distinctively strong in this sector and are unlikely to represent a powerful challenge in the next few years. Similarly, US equipment firms are not likely to displace their European rivals in the near future. The Europeans are not only quite competitive, but also benefit from intimate relationships with their users. Client markets, particularly the switching market, depend on close and careful interaction with the buyer, because the systems are inherently customized. The sales and the work require a sophisticated and permanent commitment to the customer. The US firms are only now beginning to establish those liaisons.

None the less, as the telecommunication service markets are deregulated and at least some competition in services is introduced, the European equipment companies and network providers must confront two problems if they are to hold their position.

First, there has been a burst of new peripheral equipment such as cellular telephones and palm computers, many with communications capacity. The new consumer electronics, high-volume high-technology digital equipment, is invading telecommunications. That of course opens up the market to firms other than established telecommunications companies, to consumer firms with whom the Europeans have had trouble competing.

Second, and more importantly, telecommunications policy in the Community has reached the end of a phase, as Peter Cowhey and I have argued.[51] This now-completed phase involved changes that separated regulation from operation, a round of marginal liberalization that did not alter the dominant position of the telecom operators, and efforts, mostly timid, at European harmonization. That period of re-regulation overlaps the move toward a single market. Together, the result was a dissolution of purely national supplier cartels linked to national public service providers. Those national cartels have not been replaced by an open and competitive European market. Rather, a European-wide oligopoly of equipment suppliers, albeit with room left for some US companies, has been established. The continued privileges of the now privatized and semi-autonomous telephone companies are essential to that oligopoly. The European experience is not unique. One might note that the break-up of the Bell system in the USA has not eliminated the purchasing biases in favour of US companies, though those biases have eroded. The Commission now finds itself in a stalemate. The Commission initiated the policy with support from large users and built a complex support base from the national governments. That support base, however, has not been strong enough to push forward to a next round of policy. Those in the Commission who created the first round would clearly like a second and more ambitious second phase. That next round of policy would involve some European-level regulation, efforts at liberalization that cut into the basic monopoly rate base, and the implementation of innovative services. If those regulatory changes come, they will involve not only a shift of position among European producers, but also entry for US and Japanese firms. For now, the debate appears as a struggle with established producers and network suppliers on one side and telecom users concerned with capturing the competitive advantages that early implementation of new network-based strategies can provide on the other. However, there is a distinct possibility that the debate will become more urgent.

Revolutionary changes in telecommunications networks use are taking a new form to which European users, equipment suppliers, and network providers will be compelled to adapt. The early signs are clear, the implications dramatic.[52] A broadband network future is arriving much faster than anticipated. The new broadband networks open dramatic service possibilities that are enormously attractive, and, indeed, in the few settings where the new networks are being fully implemented without serious

---

[51] P. Cowhey and J. Zysman, 'European Telecommunications at the Crossroads' (unpublished research note, 2 Apr. 1992).

[52] F. Bar and M. Borrus, 'The Future of Networking in the US' (BRIE Research Paper 4; Sept. 1992).

constraint, the network traffic is expanding as rapidly as 20 per cent a month, and the rate of increase is accelerating.[53] In just a decade, the telecommunications system of suppliers and providers could look very different than it does today. The notion of ISDN with a single integrated digital network may give way to a system with multiple networks linked together— not just because competition creates fragmentation (as some fear), but because each of the networks will have quite distinct characteristics. Each network may be optimized for particular use. Flexible networks may not just be adapted to shifting needs, but re-adapted continually as firms learn from using them and producers get feedback.[54] The established telecommunications operators may have trouble adapting without substantial pressure and real regulatory change. Yet for the equipment makers those new networks are essential, since they represent the innovative market of tomorrow. In sum, the Europeans have a strong foundation in telecommunications, but their position in the next generation of competition will rely on well-formulated and forward-thinking network policy and firm strategy.

The European telecommunications system from equipment suppliers to network providers—present and potential—seems well positioned to maintain control of European markets. But can success in telecommunications be the foundation from which to rebuild the rest of the European electronics sector? Here I have my doubts. The hope is that telecommunications companies can create demand for European suppliers of components and sub-systems. This will not be automatic by any means. Consider the components sector. Telecom equipment suppliers in Europe generate a huge demand for semiconductors. That demand is still largely filled by foreign-owned companies, whether they produce in Europe or not. One analysis prepared by Jean-Phillipe Dauvin of SGS-Thomson suggests that less than 30 per cent of the semiconductors in European telecom equipment are supplied by European-owned firms.[55] Similarly, there is a hope that as computing and telecommunications converge toward distributed computing, telecommunication networking skills and experience with digital switches would provide an opportunity for Europeans to establish a competitive position in computers. However, neither ATT nor Siemens have managed to switch over from a telecom base to a major computer position. Nor has IBM been able to move from its dominant position in computers to a strong position in telecom. The reason seems to be that the business problems and user requirements are distinct in each sector, so that business organizations and technologies generated in one segment cannot be directly

---

[53] F. Bar and M. Borrus, 'The Future of Networking in the US'.

[54] F. Bar and M. Borrus, *Information Networks and Competitive Advantage* (OECD–BRIE Telecom Project, 1; Paris: OECD, 1989).

[55] 'Le Future de l'industrie europeenne des semiconductors' (Paris, May 1991), prepared by the Communications Direction of Thomson Groupe under the direction of J.-P. Dauvin.

TABLE 9.2. *Employment and companies in the machine tool industry, by country, 1989*

Country	No. of employees	No. of companies
Belgium	2,100	28
Germany	95,000	380
Spain	7,874	143
France	9,475	150
Italy	32,100	450
Netherlands	960	20
Portugal	1,100	20
UK	23,700	200
Total EC	172,309	1,391
Switzerland	13,915	115
USA	46,258	269
Japan	50,097	213

Source: Panorama of EC Industry, 1991.

applied to another. Telecommunications may continue to be a bastion of European electronics strength, but it is not evident that it can nurture a rebirth of the industry as a whole.

2.6. Professional and Industrial Electronics

Industrial and professional electronics is a second area of real European strength. In this sector, the applications know-how rooted in the fundamental and deep scientific, technological, and industrial traditions of Europe matter the most. In a range of areas—including machine tools, hearing-aids, and automobile electronics—European producers are in fact quite strong. Consider automobiles, for example. The largest automobile electronics firm in the world is Bosch; three of the five leading companies are European, and four of the leading ten. Or consider machine tools, which is an industry made up of a myriad of smaller producers. Here Italy and Germany rank among the world's largest exporting nations (see Table 9.2). Indeed, when we look at production equipment in general, we find that the European position in global markets is very strong. These are all sectors in which creative application of electronics has been and will increasingly be critical. They are sectors which depend on access to advanced electronics, but which also represent a market for innovative producers.

The same two questions as in telecommunications confront us. First, can the Europeans maintain their market position? There are a number of competitive risks. The most serious is that the bulk of this sector—automobile electronics and production equipment such as machine tools—depends on demand from the rest of the industrial economy. If imports of automobiles displace European production there is a problem for equipment producers as well. Imports, by definition, dampen the domestic demand for equipment from European-owned producers. But FDI that maintains European final assembly may not maintain demand for production equipment, either. If foreign-owned producers import production equipment or bring their suppliers of equipment or components with them, then demand for European producers is dampened in the same way. As evidenced in the US case, Japanese companies (the principal new investors) do have a propensity to create an enclave economy inside the host country.

Second, the Japanese production innovations that have proved critical in a range of consumer durable sectors can also challenge the Europeans by the introduction of innovative production equipment. The US machine tool and robotics companies specializing in standard equipment were unable to respond to the more specialized and differently conceived Japanese products, for example. In that case, the Europeans defended their positions more effectively. They held market niches based on more specialized equipment in the first place. But now a new challenge looms. Let us return to the example of machine tools. The Japanese attempt to implement functions in electronics that the Germans implement mechanically. If there is long-term inherent advantage in electronic approaches, the Japanese will be well positioned. But it is not even that microelectronics underpins Japanese automation equipment. Rather, there is a different approach to the production line and the place of tools in the line. The difference in our view is driven by the primary final goods in the two countries: volume consumer durables in Japan, and capital equipment in Germany. The result is that the functions and design of tools are different. There is likely to be a serious challenge.

Assume that the European producers do retain their competitive edge in production equipment and professional electronics. Can this be a foundation from which to rebuild the rest of the sector? Automobile electronics will comprise an increasing portion of the electronics market as the use of electronically controlled active chassis, engine operations, safety systems, and entertainment and comfort systems expands and grows in value. Factory automation will become increasingly rooted in electronics. The demand for electronic components will thus expand, creating new opportunities. The question is whether the European companies can seize them. The risk and concern must be that the weakness in the broader electronics sectors will endanger the European competitive position in these segments where European companies hold defensible positions. Recall that in automobile electronics the European semiconductor industry provides only about a quarter of the European demand.[56] However, the

---

[56] Ibid.

one real strength of the European semiconductor industry is, as we noted, application-specific or custom circuits. These are the types of circuits critical to differentiating industrial products. Consequently, Europeans here can easily import commodity memory and even standard microprocessors if they can differentiate their electronic functions. The question—will strength underpin weakness or will weakness drown strength?—remains open.

THE PLACE OF JAPANESE INVESTMENT IN THE EUROPEAN ELECTRONICS INDUSTRY

The surge in Japanese FDI, the huge subsidies demanded by many producers, and the outright take-over and failure of others are together contributing to a re-formulation of European policy. Past policy of support for weak producers has failed to regenerate industrial position in those sectors defined as critical. Yet the fact of European and US investment has become so much a part of the industrial and policy landscape that continuation of that investment is not at issue. Since support is a given, the debate focuses on the character of policies to induce the competitive regeneration of European electronics and the character of research and industrial alliances needed to accomplish that goal. The future of Japanese investment will depend on the outcomes of these debates, to which we now turn.

Because funding of most European programmes is up for renewal, the EC is seeking to define a new 'framework', in this case the fourth framework, for situating and orienting European technology policy. The new policy orientation must address three areas of policy consideration, areas that each of the national governments must themselves address:

(*a*) First, should policy support weak producers in their efforts to entrench their market position? Or, alternatively, should it try to foster the diffusion and spread of advanced electronic applications? Put somewhat differently, should European policy try to bolster position in weak sectors thought to be critical or try to build from strength in those areas with a defensible position? It would be congenial to argue that government policy should do both. This seems to make market sense: help buyers to expand the market and producers to supply it. However, the policies conflict when support for producers results in higher prices or reduced supply, as is the case with the semiconductor tariff. It is important to remember that Japanese policy protected final producers, but generally allowed imports of intermediate goods required for production. Of course, FDI by importers who might entrench market position in Japan with local production was blocked so local Japanese producers could later attempt entry into these sectors.[57]

---

[57] A. Jacquemin has shown how FDI can discourage domestic entry in several unpublished papers.

Policies to support the diffusion of advanced technology are important to support general economic development, to speed applications, and to enhance the competitive position of user industries. However, a deep, diverse, and sophisticated user base is a means to induce supply from local sources, a means to create competitive producers, a mechanism to incite innovation. Powerful general-purpose suppliers of chips or computers might be attractive symbols, but they are not likely to be built simply by European policy. A network of sophisticated suppliers to users is needed to create the foundation of skills and equipment from which breakthrough innovations might emerge. A web of advanced users would mean that there was pressure on suppliers to generate sophisticated responses. Just as important, a sufficient European demand would allow innovative products to establish a sufficient home base for them to be able to set a global standard.

Computers and semiconductors were often thought to be the core technologies of the information era. Without them, it was argued, position in all other electronics sectors would be blocked. This takes us back to the dilemma posed at the beginning of the paper: for effective application of technology, will arms-length market access of advanced technology suffice, or is intimate involvement with the producers required? Yet the reality is that Bosch, an auto-electronics and communications company, is certainly one of the most sophisticated semiconductor producers in Europe. A strong applications position can *create* a foundation for strength in the production of underlying components. World-wide, this trend is evident: strength in semiconductors (and apparently in opto-electronics) reflects the final products and market position of the customers (internal or external to the firm). While the situation is obviously reciprocal and some draw the conclusion that semiconductor technology permits final product strength, we would argue that final market position in fact begets semiconductor strength. Final market strengths should therefore be the basis for formulating a strategy to induce innovation in supplier or intermediate industries, of which advanced electronics is one.

European policy, or at least the policy debate about Community policy, has at last begun to shift away from justifications of simple producer subsidy toward a 'user' orientation. Of course, the old programmes and biases toward producer subsidy do not disappear. The French have had to support Bull in the face of staggering losses, for example. But the hope that these programmes and subsidies will produce a commercial technology renaissance have diminished. The Commission Green Paper of 1987 that argued for a shift in emphasis was one of the first signs of a new debate.[58]

---

[58] Commission of the European Communities, 'Green Paper on the Development of the Common Market for Telecommunications Services and Equipment' (Brussels: Commission of the European Communities; Directorate-General for Telecommunications, Information Industries, and Innovation, 1987).

But the document contained at least two clear notions of a 'user' orientation. The first notion circles around public projects, 'grands projets', in which the state is the animator if not the buyer. The HDTV project and the European telecom highways strategy are examples. Here the risk is that very sophisticated technology will be developed, but that it will not generate firms or products adaptable to the broader commercial markets. The technological skills would certainly be generated and maintained, but not necessarily the competitive companies. The result could once again be a 'high technology commercial arsenal', but relatively weak firms that would not be able to take the next competitive step.[59] The second notion is of a diverse 'client' base creating a deep and sophisticated market. This is a strategy built on a broad diffusion of technology which requires both broad training of potential users and a supporting infrastructure to assure that support to the users is available. Semiconductor design centres are an instance of infrastructure. They often do not emerge from the competition of the semiconductor firms because the firms are focused on the largest and most obvious clients. They may not emerge as a service industry if a heavy investment and extensive early training of clients is required. In those cases, such centres often need to be created through public action whether they are run by the public or not. One might wonder whether heavy expenditure on design technology, user-friendly design technology to assure diffusion, application of distinct product knowledge in components such as those for low-power use to create market niches, and breakthrough R&D in areas without existing leaders would be the key to a European strategy. But the diffusion of electronics is not just about companies, but also about worker training and the arrangements of union/management relations that make possible flexible work organization that permits early adaptation of and experimentation with new technologies.

The possibility of a shift in the orientation of the policy debate is also suggested by the recent Dekkers Committee Review of DGXIII technology programmes.[60] Here the argument is explicit and supports a proposal to change quite profoundly the organization of European programmes. A technology push strategy, which in fact was always a producer subsidy, has not worked. Technology development strategies in telecom were useful, but the critical problem now is to assure competition in services so that technologies are implemented. Let Europe support programmes where market demand for technology is clear. Let Europe support the diffusion of technology as a means to advance growth and create markets. Some basic technology should be supported, but precisely because a scientific technological foundation is required, not because it will directly translate into product.

---

[59] The logic of the problem is certainly similar to that of the French efforts to support technology in the 1960s and 1970s. See Zysman, *Political Strategies for Industrial Order*, and also id., *Innovation Policy*.

[60] 'The Report of the Information and Communications Technologies Review Board'.

Setting aside critiques of the particulars in the Dekkers report, let us focus instead on how the terms of European discussion have shifted. That shift in posture and vocabulary is toward a technology development programme based on user strengths. Consider the programmes, particularly the heavily funded German one, in micro-systems technology.[61] The goal of such a programme is to establish a fundamental position in a new unfolding technology. That position will be rooted in the applications capacities and needs of the users of the technology. Micro-systems technology is part of an effort to embed entire control systems in single microchips; those control systems would include sensors (which determine the state of the system and its relation to its environment), actuators (which trigger a reaction by the system), and intelligence in the form of computer logic. We must not exaggerate the potential because there is no clear evidence of a broad early launch market for the actuated part of the product. The point, though, is that because the technology is emerging, corporate market positions are not yet created let alone entrenched, though existing semiconductor CAD and production tools and equipment may prove important. The hope is that these technologies would directly support the shifting requirements of professional and production equipment industries. Indeed, for that reason Germany has the sophisticated user base toward which new product innovation can be directed. Success in this sector could support many of the design and production technologies in which Europe is quite weak. Building from user strength could heal producer weakness. In such a case, an indirect policy might be the most effective.

(*b*) The second main policy choice is how policy should assure a strong supply base for sustained development. The choice to shift the balance of policy to support users means that, at least in the short term, policy will not be aimed at re-creating, under European control, all the elements of an electronics supply base. In that case, how should governments proceed to assure access to the technology and products needed by sophisticated users to make their product? And given that no one nation, nor even Europe as a whole, can construct an entirely independent supply base, how can policy secure access to other regions' supply bases?

It is essential to ensure that critical products and components are available in the open market; that is, to ensure that domestic producers have equal access to all supply bases of components, sub-systems, production equipment, and skills.[62] Since many of those elements are available in the electronics industry only in the USA, or Japan, it is essential that European

---

[61] See e.g. J. Gabriel and W. Gessner, eds., 'Government Promotion of Microsystem Technology in Europe' (VDI/VDE Technologiezentrum Informationstechnik, International Working Papers, 1; Oct. 1992).

[62] R. Crandall and K. Flamm, eds., *Changing the Rules: Technological Change, International Competition, and Regulation in Communications* (Washington, DC: Brookings Institution, 1989); and Borrus, 'Re-organizing Asia'.

producers maintain access to both. Ultimately, diversity of supply is essential—several suppliers in at least two global economic regions. Ideally, of course, it would be best to have evolving new technology close at home to profit from any spillovers or early usage that may result. But for the moment this is not a realistic possibility for Europe, or the USA for that matter, in many segments of the electronics industry. For now, Europe may have to settle for maintaining alternatives to Japanese sources; that is, to maintain a healthy US–Japanese competition in which because Europe is a critical test-ground much of the technology is transferred early.

(*c*) Maintaining competition between the three regions as a means of sustaining open access to technology leads to the third area of policy consideration. In many cases, alliances—both industrial and governmental—are needed. In semiconductors, the effort to maintain a non-Japanese source of advanced processing technology has led to JESSI in Europe and to Sematech in the USA. In fact, since the real challenge is a third party, there would be every reason to have hoped for earlier US–European alliances in process and equipment. Alliances such as Siemens–Toshiba can only be temporary palliatives. Because this alliance involved transferring the more advanced Toshiba know-how to Siemens, it was not a means of ending dependency, just a different form of it. The IBM/Siemens/Toshiba venture which is aimed at establishing a source of next generation production technology for each company may be more satisfactory. Note that for both IBM and Siemens their national/European support programmes may have been critical to maintaining their capacity to join the venture at all, in the case of Siemens, or to join as a dominant partner in development, in the case of IBM. Of course Toshiba is the strongest in actual production, and the way the three translate their development work into actual product will prove the key to who wins most from this deal.

For Europe, the US alliance in DRAMs would seem sensible. In that case Japanese producers threaten a lock on the market. However, in microprocessors, alliances with the Japanese would be appropriate. US firms dominate the world market in microprocessors, holding a virtual monopoly. Siemens joined in a failed attempt to develop the MIPS product as an alternative standard. In this case, though, the question of whether access to the Japanese technology supply base is as easy as to the US supply base would need to be faced. Our answer, biased by our involvement in the American discussions, is that—dramatic instances to the contrary—the US technology is widely open to Europe and will be increasingly open in the years to come.

The range of interesting alliances to offset weakness and exploit strength open to European companies is long. The simple point is that a purely regional European technology strategy probably will not be sufficient. However, a strategy that simply announces global markets and interdependence is likely to entrench dependency. More generally, the fact of regionally structured supply bases changes the problem of technology management for both governments and corporations.[63] It forces firms and governments to be concerned with the architecture of supply in the home regions of their rivals. At issue is not simply access to export markets in general, but access to technology and to markets that may be critical to the launch of new products. The surge of Japanese investment forces that question on the European directly.

[63] J. Zysman, 'Regional Blocs, Corporate Strategies, and the End of Free Trade', in M. Humbert, ed., *European Industry and Globalization* (Paris: Frances Pinter, 1993).

COMMENT

Susan Strange

Had I read this paper without knowing John Zysman, I might have imag-
ined him a West Point graduate, risen to high rank in the army general
staff—straight back, short haircut, tersed speech, jutting jaw, and all. For
his analysis of Europe's dilemma in the face of US and Japanese competition in the electronics industry reads for all the world like a report to
the general staff, a military guide to strategy for a forthcoming battle.

The language is all military, referring to 'defensible' and 'indefensible'
positions, to enemy penetration, to command of the higher ground, and to
the strength and weakness of allies in the field. As such, knowing much
less than he does about the electronics industry, its technology, and its
changing markets, I find his advice to the Europeans both plausible and
persuasive. It seems obvious, after reading what he says, that it is strategically better to fight back from positions of strength even if the base is
small than to attack the entrenched enemy, where he has all the advantages of numbers, terrain, and weapons. While the detail of different sectors—properly disaggregated in his analysis—reveals important differences
of relative strength and weakness within the broad field of electronics (as
it might be between the cavalry, the infantry, and the artillery), the common
theme comes over more strongly than the variations on it.

The strategic advice is also timely. It is true, as Zysman says, that the
EC is coming up to a point where some hard choices have to be made. The
1970s notion of building first of all national, then European, champions
has been tried. It has failed. And it is now widely discredited even in
France where it lingered longest. Nor is it only in Europe that national
champions have sometimes themselves been irked by such policies and
have sought to break away from the guardianship of the state. The time
has come to decide the direction of future industrial policy in Europe. In
the past, that policy was singularly ineffectual, so that in 1991, European
firms had only 10 per cent of world output compared with over 46 per cent
for Japanese and over 38 per cent for US firms. The question now is
whether the EC should seek to help European producers to compete against
the strong competition, especially in chips and consumer electronics, with
a mix of subsidy and protection, or whether it should concentrate policy
on expanding consumer demand in those niche areas where the EC firms
already have some competitive strength.

All the old excuses for Europe's comparative weakness have already
worn thin and are getting thinner by the day. It used to be said by European industrialists that US firms—IBM especially—had enjoyed the

tremendous initial advantage of a massive state-funded procurement programme associated with Western defence against the Soviet Union. Divided
European governments, it was said, had no comparable resources to give
their firms such a no-downside-risk assurance for technical innovation and
design. Nor could the European failures be attributed to Japan's invisible
barriers both to foreign imports and to production by foreign-owned firms
(FOFs), since US firms faced exactly the same barriers and still got a far
greater market share. Zysman rightly dismisses such excuses as no longer
valid. And with the run-down of US defence spending and slow but sure
opening up of the Japanese economy to FOFs, it will be still less valid in
future. He is right therefore to stress the point that the deficiencies of
European firms in competition with the Americans and the Japanese are
mostly self-inflicted not only by the firms themselves, but also by their
governments.

In such a situation, the advice is timely and welcome that the attention
of policymakers should be directed more at the users of electronics and
less at the producers. Notably he says, 'building from user strength can
heal producer weakness. An indirect policy may be most effective.'

The implicit assumption, however, is still that strategy will in the end
strengthen European-based producer firms against their US and Japanese
rivals. The focus of writers as different as Michael Porter, Gerd Junne and
Zysman himself is on the international competitiveness of *countries*. Their
implicit assumption is that the competition is between states more than
between firms. Therefore what is problematic is what strategies will in the
end strengthen producer firms run by Europeans against their US and
Japanese rivals.

But must that necessarily be the goal of industrial policy? Much American thinking—Robert Reich and a few others excepted—is not so sure.
Nor am I. If Japanese firms produce—as even without fears of 'Fortress
Europe', they will—on European soil, does it really matter if their European
factories are run by Japanese managers? This, in the last resort, is a question
of security, not so much of industrial policy and corporate strategy. In
short, we are back to a military more than an industrial question.

In order to think clearly about this issue, it seems to me necessary to go
back to fundamental assumptions of national security policy.

In the nineteenth century and even during World War I, the security of
the modern state demanded two things: a dependable supply of war material—warships, weapons and the explosives to go with them, and a large
reserve of soldiers and sailors to deploy these weapons in defence of the
territory of the state against its enemies. Great powers had to have a
supply of conscripts for the army and a reserve merchant marine for the
navy, but also the scientifically educated technicians to run a modern steel
industry, with its requisite resources of energy and skilled manpower, and
an advanced chemical industry. (Lack of the latter was a major weakness

of Britain in fighting the Germans in 1914–18, one which industrial policy remedied in the 1920s with the creation of ICI as Britain's national champion.) One of France's chief worries even in the 1930s concerned the shrinking cohorts of 18-year-olds for the army.

A number of big changes occurred in World War II: the growing significance of technological superiority (e.g. in aircraft, in radar, and in sonar); the triumph of speed, surprise, and mobility over numbers in the early part of the war; and in the latter part, of a technologically superior weapon, the atomic bomb. But this was forged for the USA in the Manhattan Project not by national scientists but by a multinational team of scientists. Numbers were immaterial in the end; technical superiority could no longer be achieved with the unaided resources of the nation.

By the time President Reagan in the 1980s conceived his Strategic Defence Initiative, the dependence of US national security in the future on the technology and skills to be found in foreign-owned firms had become evident even to the US Congress. American security advisers dreamt up formulas—like Theodore Moran's four firms, four countries, 50 per cent imports—to limit and control such dependence. But the writing is surely on the wall. National defensive security even for superpowers—and certainly for middle and small powers—rests on supplies beyond the sole control of the state, on transnational networks of enterprises in which 'security checks' cannot possibly be used. And the technological dependence on foreign firms must surely increase in the future.

(I am making the heroic assumption here that military security will still be a concern of American policymakers for at least another two generations, even though I personally think that the danger of major war between industrial powers is slight, to say the least. John Mueller may be exaggerating when he claims that the whole notion of major war has become *passé*, as obsolete as the notion of duelling or slavery.[64] But his intuition goes, I believe, in the right direction. There are other threats to the security of persons and property, but their requirements for defence programmes are different. Generals and governments, however, will be slow to drop their perception that the national security requires national defence forces.)

So how will these forces be supplied? Here we come to the key assumption underlying the argument for and against national champions: that the state cannot safely trust a foreign-owned firm to continue to co-operate in military production, even though the production takes place within the territory of the host state. That is, a Japanese firm producing in the USA for the US government is still a potential 'enemy' enterprise.

But a good deal of recent research especially in developing countries

---

[64] J. Muller, *Retreat from Doomsday: The Obsolescence of Major Wars* (New York: Basic Books, 1989).

suggests that the foreign-owned firm is rather more conscious of the need to be a good citizen, to make itself agreeable, to be a welcome guest, not a suspected intruder, than it ever was before.[65] Whether we look at oil companies in the Caribbean or the Pacific or construction companies in Africa and the Middle East, we find them falling over backwards to make themselves welcome in the host country. In many cases it would be difficult to find the local firms going to the same amount of trouble to comply with government aspirations and wishes.

The truth of this behavioural phenomenon in the case of Japanese firms is obscured, however, by another phenomenon which repeatedly crops up in such discussions of industrial policy as this: the phenomenon of Japanese xenophobia. As perceived by everyone in the USA, the UK, Brazil, South Africa, and other counties, the Japanese have a particular attitude to the *gaijin* which seldom allows foreigners even a fairly lowly place in the managerial structure of the enterprise. Foreign directors on the companies' main board are still much rarer in Japan than elsewhere. And when they are appointed, they are chosen more for any foreign government contacts they may have than for their industrial savvy. The exclusiveness of Japanese national psychology—even worse than the mystical but persistent German notion of *blut* as the basis for nationality and therefore for rights of asylum—is a potent source of foreign distrust of Japanese firms. And so long as this perception that the Japanese believe in the purity of their managers from foreign contamination persists, Japanese firms will continue to be regarded with suspicion and fear by foreign governments.

The problem, it seems to me, therefore, is more irrational on both sides than rational. The globalization of the Japanese corporate enterprise will eventually modify their xenophobia and reduce resistance. And such change will be in the interests of both the EC and of the Japanese themselves. This is all the more so since, as John Zysman argues, military production now depends, for its technological superiority, on developments in civilian industry and not the other way round. What it adds up to, I think, is that his analysis is relevant not only to the makers of industrial policy in the EC, to whom it is directly addressed, but also to a much broader audience of scholars in international relations, including strategic and defence studies.

---

[65] J. Stopford and S. Strange, *Rival States, Rival Firms: Competition for World Market Shares* (Cambridge: Cambridge University Press, 1991), D. Julius, *Global Companies and Public Policy: The Growing Challenge of Foreign Direct Investment* (London: Pinter for the Royal Institute of International Affairs).

10

The Strategy and Structure of Japanese Automobile Manufacturers in Europe

Takahiro Fujimoto, Toshihiro Nishiguchi,
and Shoichiro Sei

1. INTRODUCTION

This paper tries to describe and analyse patterns of direct investment in Europe by the Japanese automobile and auto parts industries. Our perspective is somewhat broad for three reasons. First, we are interested not only in the decision-making process concerning direct investments (e.g. whether or not to invest, how to deal with local governments, and where to locate) but also in operational consequences themselves. In other words, the study discusses how the direct investments by Japanese firms have been implemented, as well as who made such investment decisions when, where, and why. Now that many European investments by the Japanese automobile and auto parts makers are near completion, we claim that the issue of post-investment operations is as important as the investment decisions to both European economies and the investing firms.

Second, given the global nature of this industry, we are concerned not only with the bilateral relationships between Japanese and the European facilities but also trilateral interactions among Japanese, European, and American facilities. As almost all the Japanese automobile and auto parts makers that have established European operations had prior investment experience in America, it would be reasonable to assume that they transferred certain knowledge and experience from the USA to Europe.

Third, although the paper mainly analyses manufacturing investments, it also examines other important functional areas such as research and development (R&D) and sales, as well as the interrelationships among these functions. Thus, we consider the issues of direct investment by Japanese automobile manufacturers in Europe in broad contexts encompassing post-investment operations in multiple regions and functions.

In what follows, we will first review the historical and on-going developments of direct investments in the automobile industry (Sect. 2). After presenting some data on direct investment decisions, our focus will turn to issues of implementation and operations. We will first present a range of organizational typologies (or conceptual models) that help us understand certain aspects of these operational issues (Sect. 3). Using these typologies as our framework, we will then examine some empirical evidence on patterns of operations and technology transfers to show that implementation of direct investments is a multifaceted phenomenon to be best explained by multiple models (Sect. 4). Next, based on this observation, preliminary results of our questionnaire survey will be presented and analysed (Sect. 5). The results will re-confirm that different kinds of activities are best interpreted by different conceptual models of direct overseas investments. Although our study is still exploratory at this point, we will suggest that studying implementation stages of direct investments needs further detailed analyses of an individual firm's multidimensional activities.

2. OVERVIEW OF JAPANESE DIRECT INVESTMENTS IN EUROPE

2.1. A Brief History of Japanese Automobile Companies in Europe

(*a*) *The pattern of investments in all industries.* As a starting-point, let us look at the historical patterns of Japanese direct investments in Europe. A survey conducted by the Mitsubishi Research Institute in 1991 (sponsored by the Ministry of International Trade and Industry [MITI]; 572 samples, all industries) shows a clear pattern that direct investments by Japanese firms in Europe started in sales, followed gradually in the manufacturing area. That is, the number of newly-established sales facilities peaked in the early 1960s but gradually decreased after the late 1970s, whereas direct investments in manufacturing started in the early 1960s and then accelerated in the 1980s. Investments in R&D facilities started in the late 1970s, but the number has so far remained negligible.

This sequence (sales—manufacturing—R&D) is essentially the same as the one observed in direct investments in the USA, although the timing is somewhat different: sales investment in the USA apparently preceded that in Europe by about five years and the pace of new sales investments remained more stable (see Fig. 10.1). The timing of manufacturing investments has been similar in the USA and Europe: the investments accelerated in the late 1980s in both regions. The pace in the USA was about twice as high as that in Europe, however.

Incidentally, the sequence and timing of Japanese direct investments were quite different in Asia, where manufacturing investments tended slightly to precede sales investments.

(*b*) *The pattern in the automobile industry.* The general pattern noted above holds true also in the automobile industry. To examine this, we now review a brief history of Europe–Japan direct investments after World War II.

(1) *1950s*: This decade brought a transfer of European technologies to Japanese automobile manufacturers and auto parts suppliers. In 1952, MITI

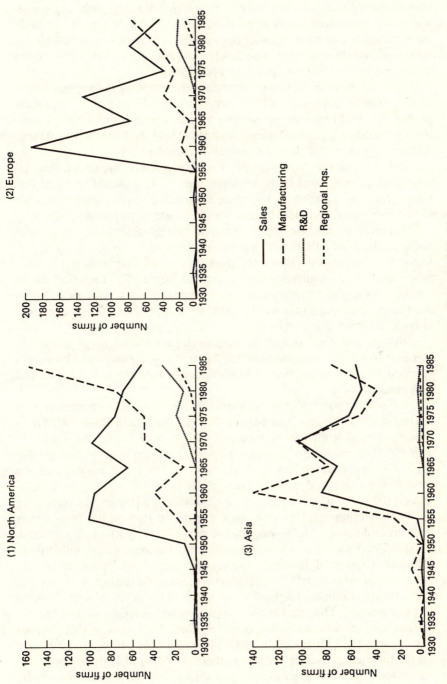

Fig. 10.1. Newly established facilities by Japanese firms, by region and type, 1930–85

issued the following policy on importing technologies for developing and manufacturing cars: the import of technologies through licensing agreements was promoted, while capital participation by foreign automobile manufacturers was prohibited as before; the import of complete vehicles was restricted through quotas on foreign currency (until 1965; $610,000 in 1955) and tariffs (35 to 40 per cent until 1968).

Based on these conditions, six technical tie-ups made application to MITI between 1952 and 1953. Fearing the disadvantage of small-scale production, MITI screened them into four groups: Nissan–Austin, Isuzu–Rootes (Hillman), Hino–Renault, and Mitsubishi–Willys (Jeep). Interestingly enough, three of the four projects involved European producers. By contrast, none of the American Big Three (apparently insisting on capital acquisition) participated in the arrangements. Also, it should be noted that there were some companies, including Toyota and Prince, which chose not to rely on formal technical tie-ups for passenger car technologies.

The period of Europe–Japan technical tie-ups did not last long. Due partly to the production/development experiences in trucks since the pre-war era, as well as the substantial development of basic material sectors, most parts were localized within five years (by 1957). Technical tie-up contracts were also terminated as the European models were replaced by local models, although they were derived from their European predecessors in basic design and concepts.

Although technical relations between Japanese and some European automobile manufacturers were at most temporary, the impact of European concepts on the basic design of Japanese passenger cars was decisive and long-standing.

(2) *1960s*: Exports of Japanese automobiles to the European market started in the 1960s (e.g. the Toyota Corona, the Nissan Bluebird). These exports started from the bottom end of the price range. As shown in Table 10.1, the number of Japanese passenger cars exported to Europe was negligible in the early 1960s: 14,008 units in 1965. The majority of the exports were directed outside Europe. In 1970, car exports to Europe totaled 100,000 units, about half of which were to the European Community (EC). The volume of Japanese truck exports to Europe has consistently been around one-quarter to one-fifth of that of car exports since that time.

(3) *1970s*: This was an era of expansion for Japanese automobile manufacturers. Exports of Japanese automobiles grew rapidly, and so did investments in sales outlets. Exports increased tenfold during the 1970s and reached one million in 1980, of which about three quarters were directed to EC countries. The market share of Japanese passenger cars in the EC market also grew dramatically: from less than 1 per cent in 1970 to over 9 per cent in 1980. By the early 1980s, eight of the nine Japanese passenger car manufacturers (except Isuzu, a General Motors [GM] group company) had entered the European market and established dealer networks there.

TABLE 10.1. *The market for Japanese automobiles in Europe*

Year	Exports to Europe (units)	Exports to EC (units)	European market (units)	EC market (units)	No. of dealers
1960					
1961					
1962					
1963					
1964					
1965	14,008	1,263			
1966					
1967					
1968					
1969					
1970	101,516	44,530			
1971					3,500
1972					
1973	359,469				
1974	340,842				
1975	482,002	368,264			
1976	663,889				7,300
1977	663,529				
1978	649,650				
1979	808,792		10,700,457	8,962,857	
1980	1,007,532	744,082	10,020,834	8,424,137	
1981	950,012		9,938,120	8,453,465	
1982	903,952		10,253,606	8,662,746	
1983	1,045,255	762,156	10,459,055	8,781,839	12,900
1984	1,043,306	790,361	10,198,876	8,629,414	
1985	1,093,500	791,365	10,750,857	8,922,934	13,700
1986	1,319,535	932,971	11,697,600	10,531,072	
1987	1,408,906	1,006,459	12,409,789	11,269,747	14,000
1988	1,456,959	1,037,924	12,953,056	11,780,574	
1989	1,449,182	1,057,438			15,500
1990					

Source: Nissan Motor Company, MRI.

(4) *1980s*: Japanese automobile manufacturers started direct investments in manufacturing facilities, as the sales/growth ratio decreased and trade friction with EC countries escalated. Unit sales of Japanese passenger cars in the European market remained around one million throughout the first half of the 1980s. Japanese exports then grew to 1.4 million units by the end of the decade, reflecting market expansion in the latter half of the 1980s, but the market share of Japanese cars remained between 9 and 10 per cent during the 1980s. Within EC countries, however, market shares of Japanese cars ranged widely from country to country. In 1989, for example, the market share in Spain and Portugal, where Japanese imports were

formally restricted by quotas, was about 1 per cent; in France and Italy, the share was informally restricted to about 3 and 1 per cent respectively. By contrast, Japanese market shares in such countries as Holland, Belgium, Denmark, Ireland and Greece, where large European automobile companies did not exist, were 20 to 40 per cent. Germany and the UK, with a Japanese share of 10 to 15 per cent, were in the middle range. At EC level, Japanese imports have been voluntarily restricted since 1986, due to guidelines set by MITI.

Trade friction and export restrictions in the EC markets triggered direct investments by Japanese companies in both automobile assembly and parts manufacturing in the late 1980s. The production facilities tended to be located in the UK for the following reasons: government incentives, language familiarity (English), lower wages, Anglo-American business atmosphere (experiences in the USA can be directly transferred), and access to the entire EC market. Bandwagon effects among Japanese parts suppliers in European direct investments were also observed.

2.2. Summary of Japanese Automobile Direct Investments in Manufacturing

Let us now take a brief look at the current data on direct investments by the Japanese auto and auto parts companies in Europe.

(1) *Assemblers*: The major direct manufacturing investments by Japanese automobile assemblers are summarized in Table 10.2. In the UK, Nissan and Honda have had assembly plants in operation since 1986 and 1989, respectively. Toyota also has an assembly plant and an engine plant under construction, to be opened in 1992. All of these plants are so-called greenfield plants, each of which is 100 per cent owned by a single company. They are, however, the only solo entry operations by Japanese assemblers.

The other Japanese manufacturing investments are mostly joint ventures with European or US automobile companies: Isuzu–GM truck assembly in the UK (1989); Toyota–Volkswagen (VW) joint production of trucks in Germany (1989); capital participation in Nissan Motor Ibérica in Spain (1987); Mazda's joint production with Ford in Germany (the early 1990s); and Suzuki's capital participation in Land Rover Santana in Spain for assembly of Jeep-type vehicles (1984). In Portugal, Toyota and Mitsubishi, respectively, have established joint ventures with local capital for truck/wagon production. In addition, Mitsubishi has announced a joint venture with Volvo for passenger car assembly in Holland (1995), and Daihatsu plans to assemble micromini trucks/vans jointly with Piaggio, a Fiat group motorcycle maker (1992). Another type of inter-firm cooperation is contract assembly: Honda consigned production of small passenger cars to the Rover group (1984), and Suzuki asked the GM–Isuzu joint venture mentioned above to assemble its micromini vans (1987).

TABLE 10.2. *European manufacturing investments by Japanese automobile manufacturers*

	UK					Germany	Spain	Portugal
	Nissan	Honda	Isuzu	Toyota		Toyota	Nissan	Toyota
Type of entry	Sole entry	Sole entry	Joint venture with GM	Sole entry		Joint production	Capital participation	Joint venture with Salvador Caetano
Name of Company	Nissan Motor Manufacturing (UK) Ltd.	Honda of the UK Mfg. Ltd.	IBC Vehicles Ltd.	Toyota Motor Manufacturing (UK) Ltd.		Volkswagen AG	Nissan Motor Ibérica, SA	Salvador Caetano IMVT, SA
Established	Apr. 1984	Feb. 1985	Sept. 1987	Dec. 1989		—	June 1987	1946
Share of equity	Nissan: 100%	Honda: 4.1%; Honda Motor Europe: 75.9%; Rover Group: 20%	GM: 60%; Isuzu: 40%	Toyota: 100%		—	Nissan: 67.6%; local: 32.4%	Toyota: 27%; local: 73%
Location	Tyne and Wear, England	Swindon, England	Luton, England	Burnaston, England	Deeside, Wales	Hanover	Barcelona	Ovar
Vehicles parts produced	Primera	Mid-size car, engines	Fargo, Carry, RV	1.8-litre passenger car	Engines	Toyota-Hilux, VW Taro	Safari, Vannette, trade, trucks, parts, engines, and transmissions	Dyna, Hiace, Hilux, Land Cruiser, Coaster
Start-up	July 1986	Oct. 1989	Sept. 1987	Late 1992	Mid-1992	Jan. 1989	Jan. 1983	Oct. 1968
Annual production capacity	100,000 units (200,000 in 1992)	100,000 cars, 70,000 engines	60,000–70,000 units	200,000 units (100,000 units in first phase)	200,000 units (100,000 units in first phase)	15,000 units	67,200 units	12,000 units

Table 10.2 (cont.).

	UK				Germany	Spain	Portugal
	Nissan	Honda	Isuzu	Toyota	Toyota	Nissan	Toyota
Employees	2,500	Cars: 1,500; engines: 300	2,000	3,000 (1,700 in first phase) 300 (200 in first phase)	—	6,870	2,360
Total investment	£600 m.	5 billion yen	£34 million	£700 million £149 million	n.a.	n.a.	n.a.
Affiliated technical design centres	Nissan European Technology Centre Ltd.; Nissan European Technology Centre (Brussels) N.V.	Honda R&D; Europe GmbH	—	Toyota Technical Center of Europe Toyota Europe Office of Creation	—	Nissan Motor Ibérica, S.A.	—
Local content	80%	n.a.	80%	1993: 60%; 1995: 80%	n.a.	n.a.	n.a.

Source: JAMA, 1991.

Thus, compared with direct investments in the USA, Japanese automobile manufacturers tend to rely more on joint ventures and other forms of inter-firm co-operation in their European assembly operations.

(2) *Parts suppliers*: Table 10.3 shows a list of direct investments in manufacturing by Japanese parts suppliers. Although it is rather difficult to develop a complete list, about 50 cases of direct manufacturing investments by the Japanese automobile parts suppliers were identified as of early 1992 (in North America there are about 200 cases). About twenty technical tie-up agreements, which did not involve capital participation, were also listed.

Although these investments and agreements included a variety of parts, there were certain patterns. A majority of them, for example, were found to be joint ventures with European or US partners: 27 were joint ventures, six were 100-per-cent-owned acquisitions, and only thirteen were 100-per-cent-owned greenfield operations. With eighteen technical tie-up agreements included, 70 per cent of the projects involved inter-firm co-operation with European companies. This contrasts with direct investments by Japanese suppliers in North America, who relied more on sole entry.

Geographically, nearly half the manufacturing facilities (22) are found in the UK, followed in number by those in Spain (9). Thus the UK and Spain together accounted for about 60 per cent of the manufacturing investments in Europe by auto parts suppliers. There were also four instances in Germany and five in France. A majority of them started production after the 1980s.

The size of the factories ranged widely. Of 36 cases of direct investment in which the numbers of employees were known, nine were plants with less than 100 employees; ten had 100 to 200; five had between 200 and 300, and eleven had 500 employees or more. Thus, most Japanese parts suppliers' facilities in Europe were small or medium-sized with less than 300 employees, but there were also fairly large factories with over 500 people.

Having explored basic patterns of investment by the Japanese automobile and auto parts manufacturers, let us now turn to the issue of implementation and operation of manufacturing facilities in Japan, Europe, and North America.

3. CONCEPTUAL MODELS OF TRILATERAL OVERSEAS OPERATIONS

As a groundwork for the implementation analysis, this section presents some conceptual models which may be consistent with observed patterns of operations and technology/knowledge transfers associated with direct investment.[1]

---

[1] Note that by model we simply mean a conceptual framework for summarizing and classifying data, rather than a hypothetical system of causal relations.

TABLE 10.3. *European direct investments by Japanese auto parts companies*

Company	Location	Start of production	Mode of operation	Product
Ikeda Hoover	UK	1986 (production)	J.V.: Ikeda (Japan) 51% Hoover (U.S.) 49%	seat, roof liner, door panel, head rest
Reydel Ltd.	UK	1989 (Kasai joined)	Capital Participation; Kasal 30%, Reydel (France) 70%	door trim
Calsonic Exhaust Systems	UK	1989 (acquisition)	100% Acquisition by Calsonic (Japan)	muffler, exhaust system
Lianelli Radiators	UK	1989 (acquisition)	100% Acquisition by Caisonic (Japan)	radiator, hoses, seat frame
Marley-Kanto	UK	1990 (established)	J.V.: Kansel (Japan) 50% Marley (U.K.) 50%	instrument panel, radiator grilles
Koyo Bearing Europe	UK	1991 (production)	100% by Koyo Seiko (Japan) green field	ball-bearing, taper roller bearing
Lucas SEI Wiring Systems	UK	n.a.	JV: Sumitomo Denki/Denso 30%; Lucas (U.K.) 70%	wire harness
European Components	UK	1988 (established)	Takata (Japan)	seat belt, door latch
Dunlop-Topy Wheels	UK	1987 (Topy joined)	J.V.: Topy (Japan) 15%; Dunlop (U.S.A.) 85%	steel wheel
Elta Plastics	UK	1990 (acquisition)	J.V.: Nifce (Japan) 80%; Marubeni (Japan) 15%	plastic parts
Bowden Controls	UK	1989 (NCS joined)	Capital Participation; Nihon Cable System (Japan), 35%	control cable
UK-NSI	UK	1987 (est.); 1988 (prod.)	100% by Nihon Seiko (Japan)	combination meter
NSK Bearing Europe	UK	1974 (est.); 1976 (prod.)	100% by Nihon Seiko (Japan)	bearing
NSK-AKS Precision Ball Europe	UK	1990 (production)	J.V.: Nihon Seiko (Japan) 60%; Amatsuji (Japan) 40%	ball for bearing
United Precision Industries	UK	1990 (acquisition)	100% by Nihon Seiko (Japan) Acquisition	bearing
ND Marston	UK	1989 (acquisition)	100% by Nippon Denso (Japan) Acquisition	radiator, oil cooler, intercooler, etc.
(Nippo Denso)	UK	1991 (production)	J.V.: Nippon Denso (Japan) 75% Magneti Marelli (Italy) 25%	air conditioner, heater
Hashimoto Ltd.	UK	1989 (est.); 1990 (prod.)	100% by Hashimoto Foaming (Japan)	exterior parts
Nissen Yamato Engineering	UK	1987 (est.); 1990 (prod.)	J.V.: Yamato Kogyo (Japan) 20%; Nissan (Japan) 80%	small stamping parts

No. of employees	Market/customer					Remarks
	OEM (Euro)	repair (Euro)	OEM (Japan)	repair (Japan)	others	
270	GM		NMUK			Local content ratio = 60–70% No. 2 plant is complete in 1992
255			NMUK			
63			NMUK			
1,052			NMUK			
n.a.			NMUK			Production starts in 1992
250 (plan)						
n.a.						
975						Northern Ireland
600						
n.a.	Ford		NMUK, Honda, Toyota			
250						
114	Rover					Plan for plant expansion in 1992, supplying to Audi, Fiat, Honda
n.a.			NMUK, etc.			Vertically integrated with casting and heat treatment
62						
n.a.						
960						
n.a.						No. 2 plant is complete in 1992
120			NMUK			
190			NMUK			

T ABLE 10.3 *(cont.).*

Company	Location	Start of production	Mode of operation	Product
Yuasa Battery Ltd.	UK	1981 (est.)	100% by Yuasa Battery (Japan)	battery
Lucas Yuasa Batteries	UK		J.V.: Yuasa (Japan) 50%; Lucas (U.K.) 50%	battery
Ryobi Aluminum Casting	UK	1990 (est.); 1992 (prod.)	100% by Ryobi (Japan)	transmission case, clutch case
Esteban Ikeda	Spain	1990 (est.); 1990 (prod.)	J.V.: Ikeda (Japan) 49% Esteban (Spain) 51%	seat
AP Amortiguadores, S.A.	Spain	1983 (Kayabs joined)	Capital Participation: Kayaba (Japan) 25%; TI (UK) 75%	shock absorber
Pacific Notario	Spain	1988 (acquisition)	99% by Taiheiyo Kogyo (Japan) Acquisition	tire valve, core
VND S.A.	Spain	1989 (est.); 1991 (prod.)	J.V.: Nippon Denso (Japan) 50%; Valeo 50%	DLI coil
Eguzkia-NHK S.A.	Spain	1980 (NHK joined)	J.V.: NHK/Nissho (Japan) 50%; MBHA (Spain) 50%	coil spring, stabilizer
Iberica de Suspensiones	Spain	1989 (est.); 1992 (prod.)	J.V.: NHK/Nissho (Japan) 50%; MBHA (Spain) 50%	coil spring
Nachi Industrial	Spain	1976 (established)	100% by Fujikeshi since '89 (originally J.V. with local)	ball bearing, roller bearing
Yazaki Monel	Spain	1988 (Yazaki joined)	J.V.: Yazaki Sangyo (Japan) 51%; local (Spain) 49%	wire harness
Durco Espana	Spain	1989 (established)		
Benoac Fertigteil	Germany	1986 (established)		
Simrax	Germany	1976 (est.); 1977 (prod.)	J.V.: NOK (Japan) 40% Froudenberg (Germany) 60%	mechanical seal
NTN Kugellagerfabrik	Germany	1971 (est.); 1972 (prod.)	100% by NTN (Japan)	ball bearing
Matsushita Communication Deutschland	Germany	1985 (est.) 1985 (prod.)	100% by Matsushita (Japan)	automobile telephone
PU S.A.	France	1990 (est.); 1990 (prod.)	J.V.: Uchiyama Kogyo (Japan) 40%; Procal (France) 60%	cylinder head cover, gasket, washer seal
Clarion France	France	1983 (est.); 1984 (prod.)	J.V.: Clarion (Japan) 95%; Group Bassis (France) 5%	car stereo set
Trio-Kenwood Bretagne	France	1984 (est.); 1985 (prod.)	J.V.: Kenwood (Japan) 50%; SOFREL, etc. (France) 50%	car stereo set, CD player

No. of employees	Market /customer					Remarks
	OEM (Euro)	repair (Euro)	OEM (Japan)	repair (Japan)	others	
479						
654						
plan	Ford					Northern Ireland; plan to get more customers
107			Motor Iberica			
740						
103						
n.a.						
63						
30						
170						
612						
26						
144						
140						
n.a.						
290						
49						

TABLE 10.3 *(cont.).*

Company	Location	Start of production	Mode of operation	Product
Stanley-Idess	France	1984 (est.); 1989 (prod.)	J.V.: Stanley (Japan) 83%; Idess, etc. (France) 17%	LED lamp
NOK Spark Plug Industries Europe	France	1990 (est.); 1991 (prod.)		spark plug
Calsonic Exhaust Systems B.V.	Holland	1989 (acquisition)	100% by Calsenic (Japan) Acquisition	muffler, exhaust pipe
Hokushin Europe B.V.	Holland	1987 (established)		
Flamm-GS S.P.A.	Italy	1988 (GS joined)	J.V.: Nihon Denki (65. Japan) 49%; FIAMM (Italy) 51%	battery
Yazaki Saltano	Portugal	1987 (established)	J.V.: Yazaki (Japan) 86%; Saltano (Portugal) 14%	wire harness
Semperit-MBL	Austria	1982 (established)	J.V.: Yazaki (Japan) 50%; Semperit (Austria) 50%	synthetic rubber belt
AW Europe	Belgium Belgium	1990 (established)	100% by Aishin AW (Japan)	automatic transmission
Zexel Gleason Europe		1989 (established)	J.V.: Zexel (Japan) 44%; Zexel Glesson USA 56%	n.a.
Glaverbel	Belgium	1981 (acquisition)	J.V.: Asahi Glass (Japan) 72%; local (Belgium) 28%	front glass, mirror
Massglass B.V.	Holland	1981 (acquisition)	J.V.: Asahi Glass (Japan) 40%; Glaverbel (Belgium) 60%	automobile glass
Sharp Precision	UK	1988 (established)	100% by Sharp Precision (Japan)	engineering plastic parts

Source: Japan Auto Parts Industries Association (JAPIA) data, FOURIN reports, Toyo Keizai directory.

For simplicity let us focus on trilateral relations, including facilities in Japan (home country), North America (mostly the USA), and Europe (mostly Western Europe), the three main regions of automobile production, ignoring the rest of the world. Also, since Japanese investments in manufacturing were the most significant in Europe during the 1980s, let us focus on manufacturing operations for now.

There are a series of criteria by which we can classify actual patterns of the trilateral operations into certain types: difference or similarity between patterns of operations; configuration; direction of flow; single versus multi-layer patterns of networks (Fig. 10.2).

| No. of employees | Market/customer | | | | others | Remarks |
	OEM (Euro)	repair (Euro)	OEM (Japan)	repair (Japan)		
n.a.						
37						
30						
2,071						
127 500 (plan)	Opel					Plan: start of production—1993; local content ratio + 60% (1996)
125						
3,600						
620						
59						

(1) *Difference or similarity between the Japanese and overseas operations*: Are manufacturing practices in the operational systems in Europe (or the USA) similar to those in the Japanese factories? Based on the assumption that in many operational aspects 'traditional' manufacturing practices, at least, were quite different between Western and Japanese producers,[2] Abo, Itagaki, *et al.* (1991) argue that application of the Japanese manufacturing practices to overseas direct investments suggests, by

[2] This assumption may itself have to be carefully examined with systematic empirical evidence. For example, the conceptual contrast between mass production and lean production (Womack, Jones, and Roos 1990) should provide a useful guide to such an examination. Focus on Western–Japanese differences and similarities in 'labour process' alone would lead to informative research results (e.g. Dohse, Juergens, and Malsch, 1985). However, such tasks go beyond the scope of this paper.

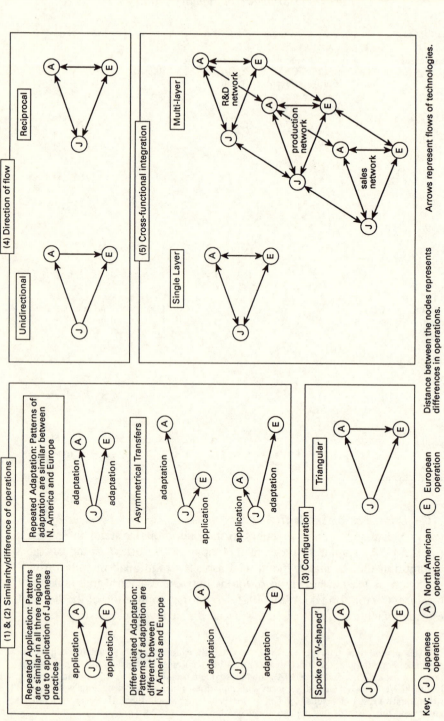

FIG. 10.2. Conceptual patterns of Japanese investment, by region

definition, similarity or few practical differences between the two operations. On the other hand, they argue that adaptation indicates substantial
modification of Japanese practices in response to foreign environments
in which direct investments are located. The notions of application and
adaptation may be usefully adopted and measured in our research in terms
of cognitive distance between Japanese and overseas operations—that is,
the extent to which various activities of the two operations are perceived
by the managers concerned as different or similar.

(2) *Difference or similarity between the European and American
operations*: In this case, similarity means either direct application of the
Japanese manufacturing systems (repeated application), or similarity of
local practices in Europe and the USA to which the Japanese firms adapted
themselves (repeated adaptation). The difference, on the other hand, means
either that the environments and local practices to which they adapted
themselves were very different (differentiated adaptation), or that the
Japanese system was applied in one region but not in the other region
(asymmetrical transfers).

(3) *Configuration*: Is there any direct exchange of managerial resources
between North American and European operations? If there is no significant flow of managerial resources across the Atlantic Ocean, we may
call the configuration 'spoke' or V-shaped. If there is, the configuration is
regarded as triangular.

(4) *Direction of flow*: Is the direction of technology transfers associated
with the direct investments unidirectional or reciprocal? Traditional theories
of multinational corporations tended to assume unidirectional transfer of
technologies and know-how (e.g. Vernon 1971). There may be exchanges
of such knowledge through the international networks of headquarters
and foreign subsidiaries, as the 'transnational' model by Bartlett and
Ghoshal (1989) predicts.

(5) *Cross-functional integration of the networks*: So far we have assumed
a single layer (i.e. single function) network of the trilateral operations
in manufacturing. However, a company may also have such networks in
marketing, R&D, and other functions. These networks may be managed
separately as single-layer networks, or they may be integrated into a multi-
layer international network.

By combining the above classifications, we can construct certain conceptual models or ideal types which may be consistent with the actual patterns
of the trilateral direct investments by the Japanese automobile and auto
parts manufacturers (Fig. 10.3). For example, a single-layer V-shaped model
with unidirectional and repeated application of the Japanese manufacturing practices may effectively explain certain behaviour of some Japanese
automobile and parts manufacturers. A question may arise, however: can
one single model explain their post-investment operations in Europe? The

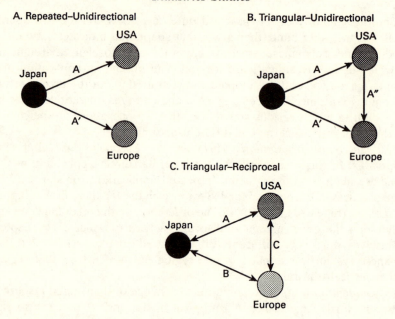

FIG. 10.3. Empirical patterns of overseas investment by Japanese automobile manufacturers

next section will examine some historical and anecdotal evidence which may support different models.

4. OPERATIONS OF THE EUROPEAN TRANSPLANTS: SOME ANECDOTAL EVIDENCE

In this section, we apply the conceptual models proposed in Section 3 to some anecdotal and historical evidence to indicate that alternative models may reasonably explain certain different aspects of direct investments in Europe. This makes us suspect that the Japanese direct investment in Europe is generally a multifaceted phenomenon, in which the model that can best explain readily may depend on the companies, countries, functional areas, and timing. To clarify our arguments, we will focus on four questions:

(1) Are patterns of investments in the USA and those in Europe different, or do they share common characteristics? (Sects. 4.1 and 4.2)

(2) Are the patterns of management transfers V-shaped (without any US–European linkage) or triangular (with transfers between the USA and Europe)? (Sect. 4.2)

(3) Are the managerial transfers unidirectional (from Japan to the USA and Europe only), or is there reciprocal flow of managerial resources? (Sect. 4.3)

(4) Are the patterns of the flow multi-layer, with sales, manufacturing, and R&D forming international-interfunctional networks? (Sect. 4.4)

4.1. Arguments Supporting the Repeated Application Model

We start with two basic facts widely observed during the 1980s:

(1) Recent studies are in general agreement about higher competitiveness of Japanese automobile manufacturers in production and product development compared with their US and European counterparts (e.g. lean production, which MIT's International Motor Vehicle Programme advocated).

(2) Based on the above competitive advantages back in their home country, and partly because of trade friction in the USA and Europe, the Japanese automobile manufacturers established their assembly plants mainly in North America during the 1980s. They were relatively successful in transferring management skills and production technologies from their home plants to their US plants. As mentioned, approximately 200 parts suppliers also set up their US plants in response to local content requirements imposed on assembly 'transplants.' In Europe, a similar, though smaller, boom of direct investments in manufacturing by the Japanese automobile and auto parts manufacturers was observed during the latter half of the 1980s.

A simple conceptual model that seems to be consistent with the above two facts is the 'unidirectional, V-shaped, repeated application model' (Fig. 10.3), in which Japanese producers merely repeat their home-grown successful patterns of management and technology in the USA and Europe. In this model, therefore, the difference between US and European direct investments is a matter of timing.

A story behind this repeated application model may go as follows: One thing that has been common in Japanese direct manufacturing investments in North America and Europe is the transfer of the 'best practice'. Japanese producers apply the same principle of paying management attention to the details of volume production and supplying high-quality, market-oriented products to the consumer at a low price. Thus, Japanese automobile manufacturers have developed a new manufacturing paradigm which synthesized many features of existing management methods during the post-war and high-growth periods, which they are now 'transplanting' to various localities outside Japan.

Across the Pacific, US manufacturing industry, including motor vehicles, had for long been at its peak, armed with mass production since the beginning of the century. Since the 1960s, however, 'hollowing out' has taken place because of long-term shortage of capital investment, the collapse of skilled labour development, resulting from recession and manufacturing cutbacks, and the weakening of related areas of industry, such as processed materials, auto parts, and electronic parts.

European manufacturing systems (sustained by skilled labour, advanced mechanical systems, and luxury car models) can be perceived as the foundations of the European automobile industry's competitiveness. The European market, however, has traditionally been segmented and compounded by political complications and import restrictions. In the mass market segment, moreover, its average competitiveness in terms of cost, productivity, and manufacturing quality has been significantly lower than that of the Japanese, and even lower on average than the US producers in productivity, according to MIT's International Motor Vehicle Programme (1990). Against this background, certain elements of lean production have recently been studied and adopted by an increasing number of European automobile companies through their own learning efforts, joint ventures with Japanese firms, and co-operation from American-owned firms with just-in-time experiences (for instance, Saab obtained technical assistance on manufacturing and sourcing systems from GM Europe). Given this situation, it would be reasonable to assume that the Japanese manufacturing activities in Europe can be well explained by the 'repeated-unidirectional' model.

Incidentally, the pattern of repeated applications may occur with or without direct flow of managerial resources from North America to Europe. In the former case, a relevant model is the 'triangular unidirectional model' (see Fig. 10.3) with repeated and successive application of the Japanese practices from Japan to North America and then to Europe. Although we will not discuss this version in detail, a typical example of the triangular configuration involves transferring know-how from Nissan's US plant in Smyrna, Tennessee, to its UK facility in Washington, Sunderland. A second example involves Nippondenso America transferring know-how to Nippondenso Europe.

4.2. Arguments Supporting the Differentiated Adaptation Model

An assumption behind the foregoing model of repeating was that Japanese firms tended toward application of their manufacturing systems in Japan, rather than adaptation of their systems to the local environments of the host countries. Thus, the same system in the home country was applied to different countries in a repeated manner. However, this simple model may not always apply. For example, the patterns of operations in the American and European transplants may differ significantly when transfer of certain technologies or managerial resources from the Japanese 'mother plant' is difficult for some reason, and when business environments are very different between North America and Europe.

(1) *The limits of technology transfer*: Although management and technology transfer to US production facilities has been generally successful during the 1980s, recent overseas experience indicates that international co-operation and management transfer in the R&D and white-collar sectors are more difficult than they had been. Even in manufacturing operations, there are certain activities (e.g. labour relations, wage systems, recruitment, just-in-time delivery) in which unilateral application of Japanese practices tended to create friction against local practices and stakeholders, which may result in erosion of competitiveness. In this case, firms may choose adaptation of the transplants' operations to local environments and practices in disregard of application of the Japanese practices.

(2) *Asymmetrical transfers between North America and Europe*: The adaptation model alone does not necessarily create the Euro-American differences in operational patterns if the environments in the two regions are similar to each other. In such a case, the repeated adaptation model in Section 3 would fit reality.

However, there are other cases which may create significant differences between the American and European operations. One possibility is that the Japanese system is applied to the North American operations, whereas the operating system is adapted more to local environments in Europe: the case of 'asymmetrical transfers' (see Fig. 10.2).

This seems to be particularly the case in the auto parts industry. As we have seen in Section 2, joint ventures between Japanese and local auto parts makers tend to be found more in Europe than in North America, where sole investment by the Japanese is the dominant mode of investment. It would be reasonable to predict more adaptation and less application in Europe due to this capital structure. Besides, after heavy investments in North American plant construction, and with severe labour shortage and declining profit performance in the early 1990s, many Japanese parts suppliers have found it difficult to make additional direct investments in Europe.

(3) *Differences between North America and Europe*: When the adaptation mode is chosen in both North American and European operations, the patterns of adaptation may still differ significantly when product markets, labour markets, supplier systems, government policies, and other business environments are very different between America and Europe (i.e. the 'differentiated adaptation model' in Fig. 10.2). This situation may happen more often in Continental Europe than in the UK, and in market environments in particular.

Traditionally, market characteristics in the USA and Europe have been different, and certain patterns of Japanese direct investments apparently corresponded to this difference. The US situation, for example, may be summarized as follows:

(i) The US market has historically been large-car-oriented within a single nation. In the 1960s, Japanese automobile manufacturers began to export small motor vehicles which did not directly compete against large American automobiles. After the oil crises of the 1970s, however, the US manufacturers started to downsize their products, which resulted in direct and intensifying competition between the US and the Japanese manufacturers in the same small-car segment of the North American market. The Japanese generally increased market shares, which triggered trade friction from the late 1970s. As the US manufacturers had to invest huge amounts of money throughout the 1980s on conversion of their entire product line to smaller vehicles (mostly with front-wheel-drive configuration and unit body structure, which they were not accustomed to), the Japanese manufacturers, with small car technologies and know-how on hand, could enjoy natural advantages in product choice in addition to productivity and quality. Such advantages for the Japanese did not exist *vis-à-vis* European competitors.

(ii) In the 1980s, Japanese manufacturers moved toward local production in North America to avoid intensifying trade friction (e.g. the voluntary restraint agreement in 1981). Either on their own or through joint ventures, Japanese automobile manufacturers started mostly greenfield-site operations. Taking into account American consumers' tastes, Japanese automobile manufacturers switched some of their popular cars from export to local production (e.g. the Nissan Sentra, Honda Accord, and Toyota Camry).

(iii) Japanese automobile manufacturers' R&D in the USA focused on increasing local content and testing local materials and parts. New, scaled-up models targeted at the US market were developed based on these studies. Simultaneously, the average size and product content of the Japanese automobiles sold in North America increased significantly as the Japanese manufacturers tried to maximize added value and profits from export models, thus getting around the constraints of export volume.

(iv) In the USA, the Big Three's components divisions have occupied a large fraction of the auto parts market. In recent years, the Big Three have been restructuring these divisions to improve the quality and competitiveness of their own products. Japanese automobile manufacturers needed to increase the local content of their products under political and regulatory pressures, which made way for many Japanese components manufacturers to localize their own production. As a result, many Japanese suppliers started North American manufacturing operations, mostly on greenfield-sites in response to the local demand for OEM parts by both Japanese and US automobile manufacturers.

In the European market, by contrast, small cars have long been the mainstream products. A wide variety of models from economy class to luxury have been offered. The European market has been divided into many countries, each of which has been relatively small and fragmented. Consequently, the models offered by Japanese manufacturers in Europe found themselves to be competing directly with the incumbent European offerings. Unlike in the USA, where Japanese direct investments were generally straightforward, their investments in Europe were thus compelled to take complicated 'detours'.

(i) The existence of many competitive small-car manufacturers, coupled with politically imposed volume restrictions, made it more difficult for Japanese automobile manufacturers to choose the right models and ascertain adequate sales volume. With the exception of Spain and the UK, Japanese car producers had to get started by way of project-oriented, 'licensed production' approaches, which produced mixed results. For example, Nissan/Alfa Romeo failed in model selection; Nissan/Motor Iberica in Spain, by introducing the basic model Micra, divided the work with Nissan's UK operation; Mazda and Ford spent years in speculating on model selection; VW/Toyota produced small vans through licensing, but their sales were slow; and Mitsubishi/Daimler-Benz abandoned a plan to develop a new 4WD model.

(ii) Direct investments have been mainly limited to the UK and Spain (see Sect. 2), where national champions are absent and there are fewer barriers to Japanese participation. In the UK, the Rover Group's market share is small, and Ford, GM, and imports from other countries divide the remaining market into small shares—market access has not been so difficult for Japanese car producers (e.g. Nissan, Toyota, and Honda). The Spanish market has also become an 'easy cropping' place for Japanese automobile manufacturers (e.g. Nissan).

(iii) The European automobile industry has had a long tradition of car-making and has entertained certain peculiarities in each local market. In order to accommodate diversity as well as reasonable economies of scale, product development activities for choosing the right products play a particularly important role there. In this context, Japanese automobile manufacturers have built their R&D centres on the Continent, prioritizing market and styling research over other issues (e.g. Honda, Toyota, and Mazda).

(iv) Two parallel patterns of Japanese participation are likely to continue. On the one hand, 100-per-cent Japanese-owned investments in greenfield-site European transplants are taking place (e.g. Nissan, Honda, and Toyota in the UK). On the other hand, there will continue to be heterogeneous forms of enterprise: project-based collaboration, licensed manufacturing, joint ventures, or acquisition of existing ones.

(v) The auto parts market in Europe has historically been different from that of the USA in that a small number of giant component suppliers coexisted with numerous small parts makers (see Tables 10.4 and 10.5). In order to avoid friction with the local supplier group, the dominant investment style of Japanese parts manufacturers has been either licensed manufacturing or acquisition of existing operations.

In summary, the pattern of Japanese direct investments in Europe differed from that in North America in many respects, reflecting the differences in history, geography, market conditions, incumbent products, industrial practices, and government policies. Thus, a simple repeated model of direct investments does not seem fully to explain the actual behaviour of the firms. A differentiated adaptation model would be more appropriate here.

4.3. The Reciprocal Model: Learning from the West

At the earlier stages of direct investments, the flow of technologies tended to be dominantly unidirectional from the Japanese parent plants to the overseas facilities. Recently, however, there are signs that reciprocal transfer of know-how and technology has been taking place between Europe, North America, and Japan. That is, situations which may be better explained by the 'triangular-reciprocal model' (see Fig. 10.2) seem to be beginning to take shape. For example, under the same specifications across Europe, Japan, and the USA, Mazda's regional R&D centres develop car models for each market, and Mazda's headquarters in Hiroshima integrate the best ideas to establish the concept of a new world car. This type of reciprocal model may be regarded as a version of what Bartlett and Ghoshal call 'transnational' operations. Another example is Honda. Certain experiences of Honda's Anna Engine plant in the USA, including in-house production of pistons and other engine components, and clean foundry which eliminates '3-D' (dirty, dangerous, demanding) work conditions, are unique at the US plant and have been effectively fed back to Honda's engine plant in Japan. Also, there are some indications that in the future the experiences of US–European operations (e.g. lean, flexible, and multi-skilled operations using a heterogeneous work-force) will be transferred back to Japan. Thus, on a limited scale at the level of assemblers at least, the transfer of know-how from offshore manufacturing sites back to Japan has already begun, and this aspect of the Japanese operations is likely to be better explained by the triangular-reciprocal model, rather than the unidirectional ones.

Behind the new developments described above seem to be the following larger trends.

(1) *Lean production facing internal problems*: Emerging problems of domestic labour shortage and excessive work hours, as well as slow down

TABLE 10.4. *The European auto component industry, by largest producer*

Country	Production ($ million)	No. of employees	Large company	Sales ($ million)
Germany	39,000	329,100	Bosch	7,611
			ZF	1,942
			Continental	1,772
			BASF	1,667
			Teves	1,306
			Mahle	861
			VDO	859
			Uni-Carden	795
			Behr	770
			Freudenberg	607
			Fichel & Sachs	602
			Hella	600
			Siemens	600
			Du Pont	600
			SWF Electric	483
France	21,500	168,700	Michelin	8,070
			Valeo	2,063
			GM Component	1,997
			Bendix France	779
			Saint Gobain	771
			Epeda Bertrand	655
			ECIA	550
			Motorola	530
			Huchinson	342
Italy	14,100	138,500	Pirelli	2,900
			Magneti Mareli	2,038
			Gilardini	394
Spain	11,200	147,100	Bendix Spain	150
UK	10,500	132,600	Lucas	1,989
			GKN	1,803
			T&N	1,080
			Pilkington	956
			BBA	928
			BTR	820
			Rockwell	770
			Eaton	241
Others	3,500	20,200	Philips	3,786
			SKF	1,779
			Goodyear	1,673
TOTAL	100,000	950,000		

Note: The market share of the seventeen largest companies (over $1,000 million) = 40.7%. Figures for totals columns rounded to the nearest 50,000.

Source: FOURIN 1991.

TABLE 10.5. *The European auto component industry, by country*

	Share (%) of European production	Export/ import	No. of employees	No. of companies	Market share of: (%)		
					Big 2	Big 5	Big 10
Germany	39.0	+9.05	329,100	600	24.5	36.7	46.6
France	21.5	+2.17	168,700	400	47.1	63.6	
Italy	14.1	+2.42	138,500	1,000	35.0	40.5	
Spain	11.2	−0.64	147,100	450	16.8		
UK	10.5	−1.15	132,600	350	36.1	64.3	
Others	3.7	−2.17	20,200	230+			
Europe	100.0	+9.68	950,000	3,030			

Source: FOURIN 1991.

of production in the 1990s, may jointly trigger in Japan a chain reaction which jeopardizes the effectiveness of the Japanese lean production as it is now. To avoid gradual destruction of the current manufacturing organizations from inside, the Japanese companies may have to overhaul the existing production systems so that they can respond even more flexibly to the changes in both product and labour markets.

In transforming the Japanese system to some kind of a 'post-lean' mode, it is quite likely that the Japanese manufacturers have to learn more from the experiences of European and American manufacturers, particularly in regard to how to maintain competitiveness and attractiveness of the workplace in the middle of labour shortage and reduction in hours of work. This kind of direct mutual learning between Japanese and Western automobile and parts companies may somewhat go beyond our primary concern of Japanese direct investments *per se*. But it is worth considering this issue here, as such interaction will be observed more often in the 1990s.

(2) *Partial catch-up of the Western automobile industries*: Although production and development systems of the Japanese automobile industry have shown significant international competitiveness during the 1980s, the performance gaps between the Japanese and the Western automobile companies have narrowed in many, if not all, aspects, including manufacturing costs, assembly productivity, manufacturing quality, and development lead time. The main reasons for this catch-up are: appreciation of the yen after 1985; learning efforts by the Western manufacturers; transfer of Japanese practices through inter-firm co-operation and Japanese direct investments; and slow-down of productivity improvements by the Japanese manufacturers during the 1980s. Under the circumstances, there seems to be less reason to believe in unilateral transfer of 'superior' manufacturing practices from Japan.

A sign of direct mutual learning has already been observed between Japan and Germany. In Europe, especially in Germany, fundamental manufacturing technology and workers' skills are generally perceived to be richer than in the USA. But Germany also has high wages and specific industrial relations. In the beginning, Japanese firms investing in Europe avoided this situation; their transplant operations tended to be located in the non-industrial areas of Wales, England, France, Spain, and Portugal.

Recently, however, Japanese investments in Europe have expanded to the heartland of Europe, including Germany. Increasingly, Japanese manufacturers are required to clarify their know-how and logically explain Japanese manufacturing methods to workers and suppliers of various nationalities, modifying traditional Japanese methods to fit various Western customs and labour relations.

To cope with the recent labour shortage in Japan, moreover, Japanese producers are developing new concepts of labour-saving production lines and management expertise. They are conducting experiments in an effort to determine know-how about short working hours, high skill levels, and automation based on information from Europe, especially Germany. For example, in preparation for building Toyota's newest production lines at its Tahara No. 4 assembly plant, over 1,000 staff—including union members—visited the assembly lines of Volkswagen, Toyota's collaboration partner, to study the labour and mechanical systems in Germany. The new concept, 'More Human, Easy-to-Work Production Lines' was born under the influence of such activities. There are reasons to believe that this type of interaction and learning will increasingly be observed as the traditional demarcation between domestic and multinational operations becomes blurred in the age of transnational corporations.

4.4. Toward the Multi-layer Reciprocal Network

As discussed, the pattern of Japanese investment in Europe was developed in line with the characteristics of each market, supported by the transference of the best practice. In this situation, the unidirectional transfer from Japan's know-how (whether or not it was repeated, triangular, or differentiated) was recognized. Given the increasing reciprocal influences among the Japanese, European and North American operations, however, Japanese producers are now reviewing the existing systems of overseas businesses and trying to link more strategically the three locations at multilayer levels, i.e. R&D, production, and marketing. Evidence suggests that networks are emerging in the direction which is consistent with the 'multilayer model' (see Fig. 10.2), although whether there will be a full-scale development remains to be seen.

Examples of such networks are vehicle exports from US plants to European markets based on local R&D activities. In 1991, Honda started selling its Accord Wagon, which was developed by Honda Research of America (HRA) and manufactured by Honda of America Manufacturing (HAM), in six European countries, including the UK, France and Germany, through Honda Motor Europe (HME). Mitsubishi also started exporting its Eclipse, made in the USA by Diamond-Star Motors Corporation, to Austria, Switzerland, and Sweden in 1991. Toyota will be exporting its Camry Wagon, assembled at Toyota Motor Manufacturing USA (TMM), to Europe some time in 1992. The above three models have also been exported to Japan.

Although the exports of complete vehicles originating from European plants to US and Japanese markets have not yet begun, it is likely that some European plants owned by Japanese automobile manufacturers will start exporting to those regions sooner or later, as they expand manufacturing operations in Europe. Thus, we may see a mutual and triangular pattern of vehicle exports through 'transnational' manufacturing–sales networks of Japanese automobile manufacturers in the foreseeable future.

R&D operations of Japanese automobile manufacturers in Europe are also emerging, although their pace is rather slow. Honda, for example, established Honda R&D Europe in Germany in 1988. Its main activities include emission-control testing and industrial design, as well as market research and product planning. Honda also established Honda Engineering Europe in the UK (on the Swindon plant site) to support manufacturing engineering in its European operations. Nissan set up three facilities, two in the UK in 1988 and one in Belgium in 1989, under the Nissan European Technology Center (NETC). With a staff of 350 as of 1991, the two UK facilities are taking charge of product planning, testing, prototype assembly, and support activities for localization of parts procurements. The Brussels facility, with a staff of 50, was established mainly for emission-control testing and will be expanded by 1994. Toyota, on the other hand, established a design centre (Europe Office of Creation, EPOC) in Belgium in 1989, and plans to set up another such centre in Italy. Toyota also has a technical centre in Belgium called Toyota Motor Europe Marketing and Engineering. Mazda has had an R&D office in Germany since 1990 for design (with a clay model room), product planning, and emission testing, with a staff of 50. Mitsubishi plans to create a design centre in Germany as part of Mitsubishi Motors Europe (MME).

Thus, we have seen a start-up boom of European R&D facilities by Japanese automobile manufacturers since the end of the 1980s. The size of the operations is generally small, however, and the tasks assigned to them so far tend to be limited to emission testing and product planning/design of the European version, and thus exclude large-scale operations for full-fledged component/vehicle engineering, which usually require at least a few hundred engineers and technicians per project.

Although we should not be too optimistic about quick development of the triangular, reciprocal, and multi-layer networks by major Japanese automobile manufacturers, it is obvious that the building blocks of such networks are gradually emerging. Whether current trends evolve into full-scale multi-layer networks depends partly upon product line-up policies of the companies; that is, allowing European operations to develop and manufacture a few models mainly for European markets (e.g. a five-door hatchback model) may justify investments in full-scale R&D operations in Europe, and will facilitate a significant amount of vehicle exports to the USA and/or Japan from Europe. This, in turn, will help these companies establish triangular, multi-layer, and reciprocal networks involving European operations in sales, engineering, R&D and manufacturing.

In summary, the foregoing discussion has generally demonstrated that implementation of Japanese direct investments in Europe and North America is a multifaceted phenomenon in that no single organizational model can explain the entire picture of the trilateral operations. In the next section, we will present some preliminary results of our survey, which systematically support our arguments at a more detailed level of analysis.

5. SURVEY RESULTS ON JAPANESE AUTOMOBILE PARTS SUPPLIERS

As discussed, it is not an easy task to describe and analyse implementation of trilateral direct investments. Which model in Section 3 would best fit the reality, for example, may depend upon company strategies, timing, and types of activities. Although it is beyond the scope of this paper to examine all aspects of this issue, it is at least possible to explore the relationship between types of activities and the proposed organizational models.

5.1. Outline of the Survey

In order to analyse the relationship between types of manufacturing activities and the conceptual models which is consistent with observable patterns of operations, we conducted a mail survey in 1992 in the Japanese auto parts industry. The questionnaire asked those Japanese parts suppliers which have made direct investments in manufacturing (including technical tie-ups) both in North America and Europe about patterns of operations and technology transfers by types of activities. Thus, our unit of analysis was chosen to be activities rather than companies. Specifically, 29 main activities in manufacturing operations (covering human resource management, production technology, facility management, supplier management, production and inventory control, quality control, and improvement programmes) were selected for the survey.

Sixty auto parts suppliers that had manufacturing experience in both North America and Europe were identified through our research, and to these we mailed a questionnaire. Most of them were relatively large first-tier suppliers. Nineteen companies (31.7 per cent response rate) returned usable responses, from which we calculated simple averages for our analytical purposes. Although we could analyse how patterns of direct investments differed across different types of companies based on the same survey data, this paper focuses on types of activities as a unit of analysis. That is, only aggregated data by activities are used for the analyses.

For example, a 'distance index' was calculated for each activity and each pair of regions (Japan–North America, Japan–Europe, and Europe–North America) by taking the ratio of those respondents who said that the operational pattern in the activity in question was somewhat or very different between the pair of regions. The indices were then used for subsequent analyses.

Also, the questionnaire results were supplemented by our clinical evidence from interviews and direct observations of the sample companies. Since we have visited a majority of the facilities in Europe and North America at first hand, field notes from our extensive visits were used for interpreting the quantitative data.

5.2. Summary of the Preliminary Results

Let us summarize the tentative results of the survey along the line of the models proposed in Section 3 (Fig. 10.2).

(1) *Similarity or difference between Japan and Europe/North America*: Figs. 10.4 and 10.5 summarize the results on the 'distance' index defined above between Japan and Europe and between Japan and North America, respectively. The larger the number, the larger the fraction of the respondents who think that the patterns of operations are different between the two regions in question. Assuming that the traditional practices have been significantly different between Japan and the West in all activities, a high score of the index is associated with a high degree of adaptation, while a low score would indicate a high degree of application.

As is clear in the figures, the profiles of the distances in 29 activities are very similar between the two pairs of regions. The activities with relatively high scores (i.e. cross-regional difference) include recruitment (no. 1), training (no. 2), union relations (no. 4), wage systems (no. 7), age of employees (no. 9), and work-in-process inventory policies (no. 24). The results were generally consistent with previous academic studies (e.g. Abo, Itagaki, *et al.* 1991) and consensus among practitioners. The activities which showed low scores (i.e. cross-regional similarity) include automation policy (no. 11), automation ratio (no. 12), requirements imposed on suppliers (no. 19), levels of inspection criteria (no. 26), and revisions process of standard operating procedures (no. 27). Thus, the data indicated a tendency

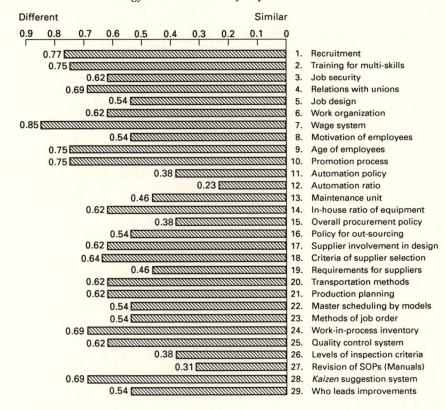

Different									Similar	
0.9	0.8	0.7	0.6	0.5	0.4	0.3	0.2	0.1	0	

Value	No.	Label
0.77	1.	Recruitment
0.75	2.	Training for multi-skills
0.62	3.	Job security
0.69	4.	Relations with unions
0.54	5.	Job design
0.62	6.	Work organization
0.85	7.	Wage system
0.54	8.	Motivation of employees
0.75	9.	Age of employees
0.75	10.	Promotion process
0.38	11.	Automation policy
0.23	12.	Automation ratio
0.46	13.	Maintenance unit
0.62	14.	In-house ratio of equipment
0.38	15.	Overall procurement policy
0.54	16.	Policy for out-sourcing
0.62	17.	Supplier involvement in design
0.64	18.	Criteria of supplier selection
0.46	19.	Requirements for suppliers
0.62	20.	Transportation methods
0.62	21.	Production planning
0.54	22.	Master scheduling by models
0.54	23.	Methods of job order
0.69	24.	Work-in-process inventory
0.62	25.	Quality control system
0.38	26.	Levels of inspection criteria
0.31	27.	Revision of SOPs (Manuals)
0.69	28.	*Kaizen* suggestion system
0.54	29.	Who leads improvements

Fig. 10.4. Japan–Europe distance index

toward application in certain production technologies and quality control standards, while adaptation to local environments was observed in activities associated with the external labour market.

Fig. 10.6, a scatter diagram between the Europe–Japan distance index and the USA–Japan index by activities, basically shows a high correlation between the two (correlation coefficient = 0.84). Since the points off the diagonal in Fig. 10.6 indicate the 'asymmetrical transfers' discussed in Sections 3 and 4, the high positive correlation means the lack of significant cases for the asymmetrical transfers, despite our prediction in Section 4. Also, the average score of the Europe–Japan distance index was 0.58, which was almost the same as that of the North America–Japan distance index (0.57). Thus, on average, the European operations and the North American operations were almost equally different from the Japanese operations.

(2) *Similarity or difference between Europe and North America*: The second basic question is whether the operational patterns of the European

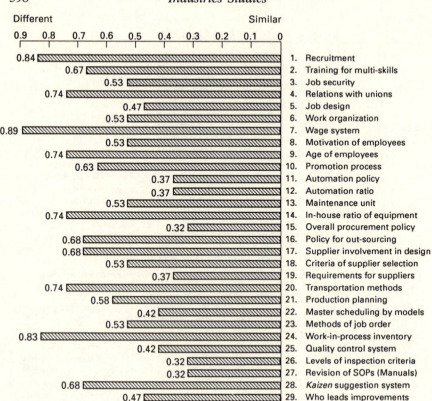

FIG. 10.5. Japan–USA distance index

and US facilities are similar (i.e. consistent with the repeated model) or different (i.e. consistent with the differentiated model). To answer this question, we made distance indices that measure the perceived differences between Europe and North America at the plant construction stage and the production stage. First we asked about the perceived difference in policies and technology transfers at plant construction stage. As shown in Fig. 10.7, the respondents saying that their experiences in American plants and European plants were different turned out to be a minority group. Although equipment procurement policy was significantly different between North America and Europe, the data did not indicate a large difference between the two regions at the construction stage.

Second, as a measure of the post-investment (i.e. production) stage, the distance index was measured between Europe and North America for the 29 activities. The result, shown in Fig. 10.8, is somewhat different from the result in Fig. 10.7. Particularly high scores of the Euro–American difference were observed in such activities as union relations (no. 4), job

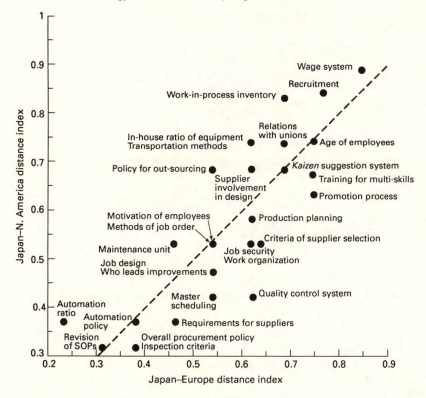

Fig. 10.6. Scattergram for distance indices (1)

design (no. 5), age of employees (no. 9), criteria for supplier selection (no. 18), transportation methods (no. 20), and quality control system (no. 25). Although detailed analysis of this pattern is beyond the scope of this paper, the data indicated that the absolute level of the Euro–American difference was significantly high (average distance = 0.43), although relatively low compared with the average Europe–Japan and North America–Japan differences.

Figs. 10.9 and 10.10 show scatter diagrams between the Euro–American distance index and the Euro–Japanese index, and between the Euro–American index and the American–Japanese index, respectively. Our models proposed in Section 3 predict a triangular distribution of data points in each diagram, with the 'repeated application' type in the lower left area, the 'repeated adaptation' in the lower right area of the diagonal, and the 'differentiated adaptation' in the upper right area. The distribution of the data points in the figures is generally consistent with this prediction. For example, a typical activity that fits the repeated application model is automation policy; promotion and recruitment policies are among the ones

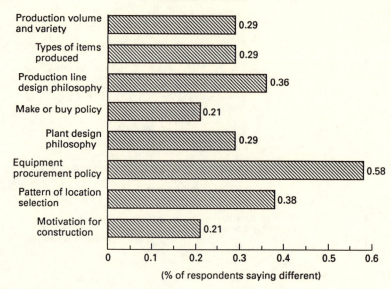

FIG. 10.7. Distance index in plant construction patterns, the USA *v.* Europe

that would fit the repeated adaptation model; relations with unions is a typical activity consistent with the differentiated adaptation model. Thus, the result generally confirms our idea that implementation of direct investments is a multifaceted phenomenon and that *different models would fit different types of activities.*

Finally, we examined a statistical model by which the Europe–Japan distance index for the 29 activities was regressed by the Japan–North America and North America–Europe indices, assuming that the decisions on direct investments in North America preceded those in Europe. The result was as follows (JE, JA, AE are Japan–Europe, Japan–North America, and North America–Europe distance index, respectively):

$$JE = 0.05 + 0.61 \ JA + 0.43 \ AE$$
$$(0.09) \qquad (0.15)$$

($R^2 = 0.78$. Standard errors in parenthesis. Degrees of freedom = 26)

Thus, the regression result was consistent with our idea that the perceived difference or similarity in operational patterns between Japan and Europe can be explained partly by the preceding experiences of application/ adaptation in the North American operations, and partly by the perceived difference between the North American and European patterns of operations.

(3) *Spoke versus triangle*: As for transferring managerial resources and technologies between the North American and the European facilities, about one-third said that they transferred at least part of the managerial

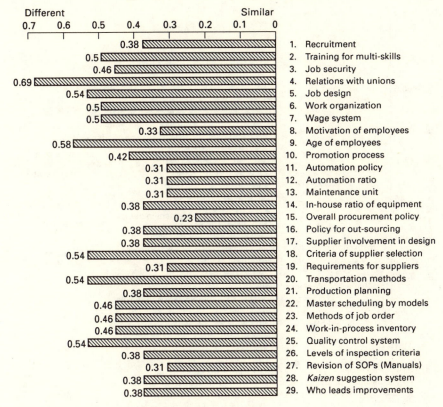

0.38	1. Recruitment
0.5	2. Training for multi-skills
0.46	3. Job security
0.69	4. Relations with unions
0.54	5. Job design
0.5	6. Work organization
0.5	7. Wage system
0.33	8. Motivation of employees
0.58	9. Age of employees
0.42	10. Promotion process
0.31	11. Automation policy
0.31	12. Automation ratio
0.31	13. Maintenance unit
0.38	14. In-house ratio of equipment
0.23	15. Overall procurement policy
0.38	16. Policy for out-sourcing
0.38	17. Supplier involvement in design
0.54	18. Criteria of supplier selection
0.31	19. Requirements for suppliers
0.54	20. Transportation methods
0.38	21. Production planning
0.46	22. Master scheduling by models
0.46	23. Methods of job order
0.46	24. Work-in-process inventory
0.54	25. Quality control system
0.38	26. Levels of inspection criteria
0.31	27. Revision of SOPs (Manuals)
0.38	28. *Kaizen* suggestion system
0.38	29. Who leads improvements

FIG. 10.8. Europe–North America distance index

resources between them (Fig. 10.11). Relatively high scores were observed in hardware and formal systems (e.g. organization design, cost control, and production technology), which are generally regarded as transferable. The score was somewhat lower in more 'soft' management practices such as personnel and suppliers.

Overall, the transfer of technologies and managerial resources was not active in a majority of the firms. Thus, in the auto parts industry, spoke or V-shaped configuration, rather than the triangular pattern, was a dominant mode.

(4) *Direction of flow*: In the case of the auto parts industry, very few cases of flow back to the Japanese plants were reported: only two companies out of nineteen respondents said that they had some experiences in the reverse technology transfers (negative = 11; no answer = 7). Thus, as far as this industry was concerned, the cases which fit the reciprocal model were very limited. Unidirectional mode was still dominant. In a way, this result contrasts with early anecdotal evidence of reverse technology

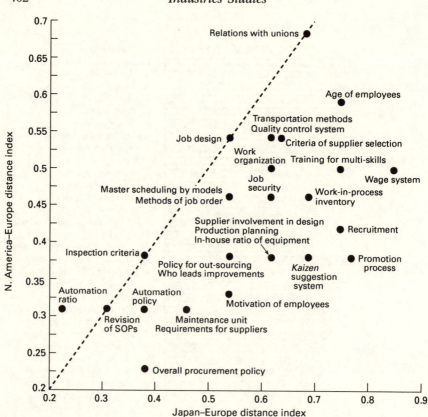

Fig. 10.9. Scattergram for distance indices (2)

transfer at the level of assemblers' international operations as discussed earlier, although more systematic and comparable evidence is yet to be produced.

The survey did not ask whether the manufacturers' network of operations was single-layered or multi-layered. Based on our interviews, direct observations, and literature surveys, however, we can assume that the cases of multi-layer management are as yet limited, except for certain larger assembly manufacturers, as indicated in Section 4.

In summary, the survey on the implementation of manufacturing direct investments by the Japanese auto parts industry has indicated that one configurational model that is consistent with the currently dominant practice is the unidirectional, spoke, and single layer model, although there are some indications that triangular and reciprocal models may become more relevant in future. Also, the survey has shown that the repeated application, repeated adaptation, or differentiated adaptation models are consistent

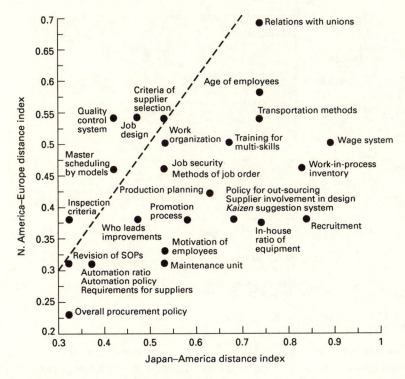

FIG. 10.10. Scattergram for distance indices (3)

with parts of the data, depending on the types of activities, apparently reflecting the multifaceted nature of direct investments.

6. CONCLUSION

This paper has described and analysed certain aspects of FDI in Europe by Japanese automobile and auto parts companies, with a particular focus on the implementation stage. After briefly discussing historical and current developments of the firms' investment decisions (Sect. 2), we turned to the issue of implementation and presented a series of conceptual models that may explain parts of the reality in the trilateral operations between Japan, Europe, and North America (Sect. 3). The subsequent discussions based on observable evidence (Sect. 4) made us assume that post-investment management of foreign operations is a multifaceted phenomenon, in that multiple models are required to explain the behaviour of the firms. The results of the survey conducted in the auto parts industry were generally consistent with our view that no single model can fully explain this complex

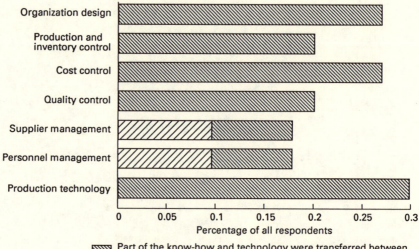

Fig. 10.11. USA–Europe management transfer index

phenomenon (Sect. 5). Furthermore, it was claimed that the configurational models (V-shaped or triangular) which take into account patterns of transfer (repeated or differentiated), operational modes (application or adaptation), and information flow (unidirectional or reciprocal) provide a more relevant framework to our subject. It was also indicated that a full-fledged system of triangular, reciprocal, and multi-layer configuration has not yet been developed in this industry, although early evidence in that direction was identified in some automobile manufacturers' transnational operations. Overall, the survey suggested that detailed empirical research at the operational level is essential for a deeper understanding of the complex reality.

Now that most major investment decisions by the Japanese automobile and auto parts companies have been made as of 1992, the issue of implementation and post-investment management of the global operational network will become increasingly important. In pursuing this area of research, we believe that we need to develop a broad perspective covering multiple regions (not only Europe but also other geographic areas), multiple functions, and detailed analyses at multidimensional operational levels. This paper has addressed the issue of transnational investments by Japanese firms with this motivation in mind.

Post-investment management on a global scale is a new challenge to many Japanese manufacturing firms. Although we could not as yet systematically present a strong case of trilateral, reciprocal, and multi-layer management of global operations, our interviews and other observable evidence indicated the budding of such a system. More detailed case studies as well as statistical surveys to capture the emergent patterns of management practices will be necessary. Whichever methods may be used, further research should integrate clinical and quantitative, as well as macroscopic and microscopic, aspects of this complex phenomenon.

REFERENCES

ABO, T., ITAGAKI, H., KAMIYAMA, K., KAWAMURA, T., and KUMON, H. (1991), *America ni Ikiru Nihonteki Seisan System* [The Japanese Production Systems in America] (Tokyo: Toyo Keizai Shinpo-sha).

BARTLETT, C., and GHOSHAL, S. (1989), *Managing Across Borders: The Transnational Solution* (Boston: Harvard Business School Press).

DOHSE, K., JUERGENS, U., and MALSCH, T. (1985), 'From "Fordism" to "Toyotism"? The Social Organization of the Labor Process in the Japanese Automobile Industry', *Politics and Society*, 14/2.

FLAHERTY, M. (1986), 'Coordinating International Manufacturing and Technology', in M. Porter, ed., *Competition in Global Industries* (Boston: Harvard Business School Press).

FOURIN (1991), *1991 Oshu Jidosha Buhin Sangyo: Shijo, Shuyo Kigyo Hen* [1991 European Auto Parts Industry: Market and Main Parts Companies] (Nagoya: FOURIN).

Japan Automobile Manufacturers Association, (JAMA) (1991), *1992: The Motor Industry of Japan* (Tokyo: JAMA).

Japan Auto Parts Industries Association (JAPIA) (1991), *Jidosha Buhin Kogyo Kaigai Jigyo Gaikyo Chosa* [A Study on Overseas Operations by the Auto Parts Industry] (Tokyo: JAPIA).

Mitsubishi Research Institute (MRI) (1991), *Globalization no Shinten to Sangyo Gijutsu ni kansuru Chosa Hokokusho* [Research Report on the Progress of Globalization and Industrial Technologies] (Tokyo: MRI).

Nissan Motor Company (1991), *Jidosha Sangyo Hand Book* [Automobile Industry Hand Book] (Tokyo: Nissan).

SHIMADA, H. (1988), *Humanware no Keizaigaku* [The Economics of Humanware] (Tokyo: Iwanami Shoten).

SUZUKI, N. (1991), *America Shakai no Naka no Nikkei Kigyo* [Japanese Companies in American Society] (Tokyo: Toyo Keizai Shinpo-sha).

VERNON, R. (1971), *Sovereignty at Bay* (New York: Basic Books).

WICKENS, P. (1987), *The Road to Nissan: Flexibility, Quality, Teamwork* (London: Macmillan).

WOMACK, J., JONES, D., and ROOS, D. (1990), *The Machine That Changed the World* (New York: Rawson Associates).

COMMENT

H. Landis Gabel

Professors Fujimoto, Nishiguchi, and Sei have presented a paper rich in detail regarding the post-investment operations of Japanese automobile sector plants in the USA and Europe. Rather than looking just at direct investments, they have chosen to focus their attention on the management of those investments. Furthermore, their paper is as much concerned with the USA as with Europe—in particular with the comparisons between those two markets—and as much with the auto parts businesses as with the automobile manufacturers themselves. Indeed, in their empirical survey, reported in Section 5 of the paper, they look exclusively at the parts suppliers. Rather than rework already well-ploughed land, their paper actually tills land both fertile and neglected.

After an Introduction, in Section 2 the authors give an overview of the patterns of Japanese FDI generally and with respect to the automobile industry, specifically. It is a nice descriptive summary, with an interesting chronology and supporting tables of data, but it will not offer much new to those generally familiar with the story except perhaps for some information on the less known auto parts business.

It is in Section 3 on 'Conceptual Models of Trilateral Overseas Operations' that the authors begin to engage the issues central to the paper. But the reader should be forewarned that what the authors mean when they use the term 'model' is not a causal relationship but simply a descriptive one. There is no subterfuge—they acknowledge the point explicitly, albeit in a footnote. But the distinction deserves emphasis, especially to those who instinctively look to models for explanations. And even the authors themselves, having acknowledged what they mean by the term, slip repeatedly into claims in Sections 3 and 4 and again in the Conclusion that their models 'explain' rather than just describe.

If I were to seek a weakness in the paper, it would be this neglect of explanation. The authors present several pictorial models varying in terms of the direction of flows of managerial and technological manufacturing resources and the similarity or difference in the pattern of operations at the end of the flows. The models illustrate as well the possibility that there might be differences in these directions and patterns across the multiple layers of, for example, sales, manufacturing, and R&D. Their next step is to try to determine which of the pictures best represents what is observed in Japanese FDI. It is in so doing that the authors present us with the rich detail alluded to above.

But the reader is left asking the question: what is the purpose of this matching of pictorial model to observation? That is, what is the utility of the exercise? A purist would insist on causal linkages, supported by a theoretical foundation, and then tested with data from the survey presented in Section 5. Only at that point could one confidently claim some understanding of the phenomena under study. That is not what is offered, as the authors admit. But even those tolerant of softer science will be left asking why certain 'models' might be more likely in one situation than another, and why we might expect to see the evolution that the authors anticipate.

A formal structural model is not the only recourse for answers. There is, in fact, an enormous literature that can be turned to. Yet the paper is surprisingly thin on references to principles of international trade (either inter-industry or intra-industry) or FDI. Even though the paper is not about why Japanese FDI has taken place, one might suspect that motives would influence how the foreign plants were operated. For example, a motive to avoid protectionist trade barriers (and the presence or absence of local content rules) would surely influence the geography of parts sourcing. I suspect that at least a portion of the observed differences between patterns in the USA and the UK were motivated by the need to ensure that cars made in the UK could be exported to the Continent despite certain French and Italian opposition.

Similarly, I found the paper thin on references to the theoretical and empirical literature of recent years on the management of multinational enterprises. There is a reference to Bartlett and Ghoshal, *Managing Across Borders*, but even if one were to accept that as a definitive work, it is not used in this paper as a basis for explaining observations.

Perhaps it is unfair to criticize a paper for doing what it claimed to do and not doing what it made no pretence to attempt. Certainly, the paper makes a contribution by describing much of the managerial detail formerly neglected. The empirical section reporting on the survey of the Japanese auto parts suppliers offers some fascinating information summarized in a 'distance index' of various activities between Europe, Japan, and the USA. The information is difficult to summarize, and this reader was left unclear precisely what model was most descriptive of what, but there is grist, none the less, for further work.

And yet the frequency with which I wrote the word 'why?' in the paper's margins suggests to me that the paper could have made a stronger contribution by beginning—and that is what it would do—to suggest answers to all the 'whys'. Why, for example, did the Japanese rely more on joint ventures or other forms of inter-firm co-operation in Europe than in the USA? Does this influence the difference observed between 'application' and 'adaption' that is described in the paper? Only when one knows answers to these and many other questions can one move on to tackle the important lessons that this case of Japanese FDI in this industry must hold.

What would some of those lessons be? I can suggest a few. In retrospect, was the Thatcher government strategy in the 1980s to use this investment to transfer manufacturing know-how to the UK for a trade advantage *vis-à-vis* Continental rivals successful? That is, did the 'Trojan Horse' strategy work? How would success be measured? If successful in terms of traditional trade figures, did it matter in retrospect that the name over the automobile plant door was Japanese? A search for the answer to this question leads directly to an inquiry into how those plants were managed. That is, it leads one to appreciate, as the authors write in their first paragraph, that 'the issue of post-investment operation is as important as the investment decision to both European economies and the investing firms.'

Another question that is important to fashioning trade policy in the 1990s is whether there was any welfare loss from supplanting cars exported from Japan to the USA or the EC with domestically produced 'Japanese' cars. Traditional models of international trade would predict such a loss arising from protectionism. But models of intra-industry trade might not. If the Japanese transplants were equally efficient as those in Japan, protectionsim might have had no net welfare cost and might only have redistributed income from Japan to its trade partners. Again, to answer these questions requires that we know both how *and why* those transplants worked, at the level of managerial detail this paper reveals.

11

The Political Economy of Japanese Automobile Investment in Europe

Mark Mason

The swift rise of Japanese automobile investment in the unifying European Community provoked powerful fears within many EC member states. Confronted with aggressive new challenges to home automotive markets, these states prompted the European Commission to negotiate a landmark agreement with the Japanese government. This agreement, the 1991 'Elements of Consensus', effectively placed numerical limits on Japanese motor vehicle exports to the Community as a whole and to specified member countries until the year 2000.[1] Moreover, complex and protracted negotiations also produced an arrangement which apparently placed implicit controls on Japan's European transplant factories.[2]

Yet the significance of the EC–Japan auto accord carries even wider implications, for this agreement represents Europe's principal policy response to a major external challenge in a critical industrial sector. In economic terms, for example, by 1990 the EC auto industry directly employed some 1.5 million and indirectly employed some 8.8 million European workers in manufacturing and related services, and accounted for roughly 9 per cent of industrial value added throughout the Community.[3]

Research for this paper was supported by a grant from the Alex C. Walker Educational and Charitable Foundation. An earlier draft was presented at the 1992 Annual Meeting of the Academy of International Business, Brussels, Belgium, Nov. 1992.

The author gratefully acknowledges the contributions of numerous participants who agreed to discuss candidly the process and outcome of these automobile negotiations, and to provide documentary materials relating to these events. These participants represented the European Commission, MITI, the economic ministries of certain individual European governments, the European Automobile Manufacturers Association, the Japanese Automobile Manufacturers Association, and certain individual European and Japanese automobile manufacturers. Prior agreements with these participants require that their names remain confidential.

In addition, the author wishes to thank in particular Dennis Encarnation, Chalmers Johnson, Hugh Patrick, Michael Smitka, Jonathan Story, and Louis Wells for their comments during the preparation of earlier drafts of this paper.

[1] Stated limits in the accord refer to 1999, although in practice those limits also apparently refer to intervening years. See below. Although the 1991 accord also deals with certain categories of trucks, this paper will focus exclusively on the automobile industry.

[2] This analysis of the 1991 EC–Japan automobile accord and related arrangements is based in part on copies of the original agreements made available to the author.

[3] Commission of the European Communities, *Panorama of EC Industry, 1991–1992* (Luxemburg: Office of Publications of the European Communities), 13–19.

In addition, for Europeans in many countries the automotive industry constituted nothing less than a symbol of national industrial strength and technological prowess.[4] Forging a response to this central Japanese challenge therefore represents a critical test case of EC foreign economic policymaking.[5]

To examine these and related issues, this paper analyses the creation and significance of the 1991 EC–Japan motor vehicle accord. First, this essay briefly describes the context in which the negotiations took place. Critical elements in this context included the competitive positions of the major firms in the region's automobile industry, as well as the development of Japanese auto strategies in Europe and the evolving responses of certain EC member governments towards this development. Second, this article examines in some detail the process of creating the 1991 accord, together with the outcomes and denouements which flowed from this process. Finally, the paper considers some of the larger implications and questions which stem from this crucial event.

1. CONTEXT

1.1. The European Automobile Industry

Six firms or groups of firms accounted for the great majority of Western European car production in 1990.[6] These firms, in descending order of output, were: the Volkswagen group (Audi, Seat, and VW), PSA (Peugeot, Citroen), the Fiat Group (Alfa, Ferrari, Fiat, Innocenti, and Lancia), the General Motors Group (GM/Opel, Saab), the Ford Group (Ford, Jaguar), and Renault (see Table 11.1). The size of these and other carmakers in Western Europe varied considerably, and included not only European-owned producers but also subsidiaries of American companies and, more recently, the local operations of Japanese auto firms as well. Despite the variety of companies and the diversity of their national origins, however,

---

[4] On the substantive but also symbolic importance of the automobile industry to France, for example, see J.-P. Lehmann, 'France, Japan, Europe and Industrial Competition: The Automotive Case', *International Affairs*, 68: 1 (1992), 44.

[5] For further discussion of the critical nature of the automobile case, see e.g. T. Tanaka, 'The European Community and Japan: Countdown to 1992', *Japan Review of International Affairs*, 3: 2 (Fall/Winter 1989), 221; and the *Financial Times*, various issues, 1991.

[6] For background on the development of the European automobile industry, see esp. D. Jones, *Maturity and Crisis in the European Car Industry: Structural Change and Public Policy* (Sussex, UK: Sussex European Research Centre, 1981); and S. Young, 'European Car Industry', in K. Macharzina and W. Staehle, eds., *European Approaches to International Management* (New York: Walter de Gruyter, 1986), 147–62.

TABLE 11.1. *Western European car production, by company, 1990*

Company	No. of units
VW Group	2,397,488
Audi	421,378
Seat	323,900
Volkswagen	1,652,210
PSA	2,349,372
Citroen	803,506
Peugeot	1,545,866
Fiat Group	1,870,736
Alfa	223,643
Ferrari	4,292
Fiat	1,325,414
Innocenti	4,221
Lancia	313,166
GM Group	1,750,918
GM/Opel	1,663,562
Saab	87,356
Ford Group	1,603,549
Ford	1,561,658
Jaguar	41,891
Renault	1,570,796
Mercedes	574,191
BMW	499,823
Rover	464,612
Volvo	369,840
Nissan	76,190
Porsche	32,162
Others	14,416
TOTAL	13,574,093

Source: Automotive Industry Data, Ltd., as cited in Automotive News, *Market Data Book, 1992*, 2–3.

in their local markets domestically owned firms generally outsold foreign-owned competitors by substantial margins (see Table 11.2).

By the late 1980s, many European-owned carmakers lagged considerably behind their foreign, and especially Japanese, counterparts. Studies conducted by the International Motor Vehicle Program (IMVP) of the Massachusetts Institute of Technology, for example, indicated that the assembly plant productivity of European-owned volume producers in Europe substantially trailed productivity levels achieved by Japanese- (and

TABLE 11.2. *Percentage shares of EC automobile markets by company, 1989*

Company	France	Germany	Italy	UK	Spain & Portugal	Rest of EC
VW Group	9.2	28.3	12.3	6.0	18.9	13.2
Fiat Group	7.3	4.8	57.2	3.4	9.0	6.2
PSA	32.8	3.6	7.7	8.9	17.4	13.1
Renault	29.0	3.4	7.1	3.8	19.3	7.1
Ford	7.1	10.1	4.8	26.4	13.1	10.1
GM	5.1	16.1	3.9	15.2	13.6	12.2
'Specialists'*	3.5	17.1	3.5	8.2	4.4	8.0
Japanese	2.8	15.1	1.4	11.1	1.8	24.8
Rover	1.7	0.2	0.9	13.6	1.3	1.0
Others	1.4	1.1	1.0	3.2	0.8	4.3
TOTAL	100.0	100.0	100.0	100.0	100.0	100.0

* 'Specialists' refers to the (principally German) luxury carmakers.

Source: Automobile Industry Data Ltd., *Market Data Book, 1990*, as adapted by S. Tolliday in 'Globalization or Regionalization: The European Automobile Industry Faces 1992' (Harvard Business School, Case no. 9–391–207).

often American-) owned assembly plants in Japan, North America, and even Europe.[7] In addition, studies by the IMVP and other groups suggested that, as compared with their Japanese counterparts in particular, Europe's volume manufacturers generally produced a smaller range of older and lower-quality automobiles, and failed to measure up to Japanese competition in other ways as well.[8]

Growing concerns over their international competitiveness led many European carmakers from the late 1980s to press for arrangements to secure public protection from greater Japanese competition through the 1990s. Most vocal in their calls for protection were, of course, those firms whose competitive positions were weakest and who therefore felt most vulnerable to the challenge from Japan. More than any other figure, PSA (hereafter, Peugeot) Chairman Jacques Calvet—the Lee Iacocca of the

[7] IMVP World Assembly Plant Survey, as cited in S. Tolliday, 'Globalization or Regionalization: The European Automobile Industry Faces 1992' (Harvard Business School, case no. 9–391–207).

[8] D. Jones, 'The Competitive Outlook for the European Motor Vehicle Industry', *International Journal of Vehicle Design*, 11: 3 (1990), 222–33; id., 'A Second Look at the European Motor Industry' (working paper, IMVP International Policy Forum, May 1989); J. Krafcik, 'European Manufacturing Practice in a World Perspective' (working paper, IMVP International Policy Forum, May 1988); IMVP World Assembly Plant Survey, as cited in Tolliday, 'Globalization or Regionalization'; and J. Womack, 'The European Motor Industry in a World Context: Some Strategic Dilemmas' (working paper, IMVP International Policy Forum, May 1988).

European automobile industry—openly and vigorously lobbied for such protection.[9] Pointing to the potentially severe consequences of increased Japanese market penetration for Europe's large auto companies—and convinced that European carmakers faced enormous obstacles to entry into the Japanese market—Calvet called for strict limits on Japanese auto firms' participation in the European Community after the projected completion of the internal market at the end of 1992. Joining Calvet in calling for substantial protection against the Japanese from the late 1980s were, among others, Fiat Chairman Giovanni Agnelli and Renault CEO Raymond Levy.[10]

Not all carmakers in Europe lobbied for protection from Japanese competition during the late 1980s, however. Perhaps most notably, the German luxury car specialists Mercedes, BMW, and Porsche believed they could effectively compete against Japanese makers even in a unified EC market, and worried about the implications of protectionist moves in Europe for their own vehicle sales in Japan and, especially, America. In addition, they were joined by fellow German producer VW, whose Chairman Carl Hahn hesitated at this point to seek protection from Japanese competitors. Hahn understood that Japan's producers represented a major challenge to VW, but opposed restrictions in part because he believed that the rigours of the open market ultimately would strengthen VW and the rest of the European auto industry. And finally, the British Rover Group had previously entered into a strategic alliance with Honda, and later sold 20 per cent of its equity to that Japanese producer. With this relationship in place, Rover declined to join those pressing for protection. During the course of the negotiations, however, the perceptions (and positions) of some of these European firms would change substantially.

1.2. Japanese Strategies, European Policies

Japanese automobile exports to Europe generally remained insignificant through the 1960s. Within the European Community, Japanese market share (supplied almost entirely through exports) by 1970 had exceeded a mere 1 per cent only in a few smaller EC markets such as those of Portugal, Belgium, Denmark, and the Netherlands. In the larger auto markets of the EC, by contrast, Japanese market share data suggest that by that same year exports from Japan were extremely small. Japanese auto firms

---

[9] For further explication of Calvet's views see esp. J. Calvet, 'Thank God for Quotas' (interview) in *European Affairs* (1 Dec. 1991), 68–71; and 'Preparing for the 1990s: PSA Aims to be Number One in the EC', *JAMA Forum*, 8: 1 (Sept. 1989), 8–13.

[10] Leading managers at the European subsidiaries of Ford and General Motors, motivated in part by their interpretations of the American experience with Japanese automotive competition in the USA, generally supported the positions of those calling for greater European protection.

in 1970 together held just 0.4 per cent of the British market, for example, 0.2 per cent of the French market, and negligible shares of the German and Italian markets.[11]

During the 1970s, however, Japan's exports and market shares rose considerably in virtually all the markets of the Community. Indeed, by 1980 Japanese auto firms had attained enormous shares in EC markets such as Belgium (24.7 per cent), the Netherlands (26.4 per cent), Denmark (30.9 per cent), Ireland (30.8 per cent) and Greece (42.9 per cent). In addition, by that year Japan's carmakers had attained sizeable shares of the British (11.9 per cent), French (2.9 per cent) and German (10.4 per cent) markets, although long-standing restrictions, described below, had kept Japan's share in Italy to just 0.14 per cent.[12] From a minor position in 1970, Japanese auto companies together had thus managed to attain, almost entirely through exports, major positions in most of the Community's automobile markets just ten years later.

Rising Japanese exports to Europe encouraged many host governments to implement (or extend) policies designed to limit the numbers of imported Japanese cars.[13] In 1975, for example, Britain obliged Japan to limit Japanese auto imports to 11 per cent of the UK automobile market. Two years later, the French government effectively placed a ceiling on Japanese car imports of just 3 per cent.[14] Spain and Portugal later restricted Japanese market shares to 1 per cent and 14 per cent, respectively. And an official bilateral accord dating from 1954 effectively enabled the Italian government to continue limiting Japanese imports to small (always less than 2 per cent) shares of Italy's automobile market in subsequent years.[15] These five EC nations—together with West Germany, which in 1981 forged an informal agreement to limit Japanese auto imports to no

---

[11] Nissan Jidosha, *Jidosha sangyo handobukku* [Automobile Industry Handbook] (Tokyo: Nissan Motor Company, 1990 edn.), 12–13.

[12] Ibid.

[13] These new, quantitative restrictions supplemented operative tariffs in the Community. Indeed, major European countries such as France, West Germany, the UK, and Italy all maintained separate (and high) tariffs on auto imports throughout the 1950s and early 1960s. By 1967, the six initial members of the European Economic Community had agreed to a common external automotive tariff of 17.6%, a rate which would fall in subsequent years (and which additional countries would eventually adopt after they had joined the Community). On the development of European public policies towards the automobile industry see esp. D. Jones, *Maturity and Crisis in the European Car Industry*; and É. de Banville and J.-J. Chanaron, *Vers un système automobile européen* [Towards a European Automobile System] (Paris: Economica, 1991).

[14] On the workings of the French system, which limited import penetration by placing percentage caps on annual Japanese car registrations, see D. Salvadori, 'The Automobile Industry', in H. Bowen *et. al.*, *The European Challenge: Industry's Response to the 1992 Programme* (London: Harvester Wheatsheaf, 1991), 62–3.

[15] This treaty was imposed on the Italians by the Japanese government, which feared the consequences of large numbers of small, competitive Italian automobiles imported into Japan. In exchange for agreeing to limit Italian car exports to Japan, Italy obtained the right to limit Japanese car imports to Italy. See Salvadori, 'The Automobile Industry', 63.

TABLE 11.3. *Japanese shares of European automobile markets, by company, 1989*

Company	Market share (%)
Nissan	2.9
Toyota	2.5
Mazda	1.8
Mitsubishi	1.2
Honda	1.0
Suzuki	0.6
Subaru	0.4
Daihatsu	0.3
Isuzu	0.1
TOTAL	10.8

Source: Automobile Industry Data Ltd., *Market Data Book, 1990*, as adapted by S. Tolliday in 'Globalization or Regionalization: The European Automobile Industry Faces 1992' (Harvard Business School, Case no. 9–391–207).

more than roughly 15 per cent of the local market—would continue to impose quantitative restrictions on Japanese auto imports throughout the 1980s.[16] In addition, Japan's penetration of numerous European markets was further limited by member-state-sanctioned exclusive dealership systems.[17]

Japanese firms continued to ship substantial numbers of automobiles to Europe in the 1980s, but the imposition of European restrictions effectively braked or sharply restrained Japanese market share growth in many Community markets during this decade. Although Japan's market share in Germany increased from 10.4 per cent to 15.2 per cent and in Italy increased from 0.14 per cent to 1.41 per cent during the years 1980 to 1989, for example, it actually *declined* in Britain from 11.9 per cent to 11.3 per cent and in France from 2.9 per cent to 2.8 per cent in this same period. Despite these restrictions, however, Japanese automobile firms together maintained important shares of the total European market at the end of the 1980s (see Table 11.3). Indeed, in 1989 Japan held roughly one-tenth

[16] The precise nature of the German arrangement with Japan remains controversial. The most commonly accepted version of that arrangement holds that the two sides came to a gentleman's agreement during a visit by Otto Lamsdorf to Tokyo in 1981—the same year as the USA and Japan settled on an auto restraint arrangement. The German–Japanese agreement, according to this telling of events, specified a 15% Japanese auto import ceiling. Other versions suggest that Japan agreed to limit increases of its auto exports to Germany to no more than 1% per year, or that the understanding began in 1985 rather than 1981.

[17] This system operated throughout the 1980s under a special DG IV announcement. During subsequent bargaining, the Commission at times sought to use the threat of discontinuing this derogation when disagreements arose with certain member states.

of the overall EC market, supplied almost entirely by exports numbering some 1.23 million vehicles.[18]

The postwar development of Japan's motor vehicle exports to the Community encouraged Japanese FDI in the EC first to support, and later to complement, this trade. Japanese carmakers began to directly invest in the region from the 1960s.[19] Toyota, for example, established marketing organizations in some of its principal European markets starting early in that decade. The first such organization Toyota set up in Denmark (1963), followed by the creation of similar operations in the Netherlands (1964), Finland (1964), the UK (1965), Belgium (1966), Switzerland (1966), Portugal (1968), and Sweden (1968). Nissan established similar operations in Europe during these same years, followed by the company's first European assembly arrangement—the establishment of Entreposto Comercial Veiculos e Macquinas, SA, a Nissan-created and wholly owned importer of knocked-down commercial vehicle kits, with assembly entrusted to the locally owned Entreposto Comercial de Automoveis—in Portugal in July 1968. Toyota set up a similar importing and assembly operation to produce commercial vehicles in Portugal—in Toyota's case, in concert with the local firm Salvador Caetano IMVT, SA—just three months later. Both of these Japanese motor vehicle producers had been preceded in Europe, however, by Honda, which in 1961 had created a European regional sales office in Hamburg, West Germany (European Honda Motor GmbH), followed by a British sales branch in London in 1962, both principally to support its burgeoning motorcycle sales.

Japanese producers began to establish their own motor vehicle assembly operations in Europe from the early 1970s. In 1972, for example, Toyota acquired a 27 per cent stake in Salvador Caetano, the Portuguese company to which it had heretofore consigned assembly of vehicles imported by a wholly Toyota-owned subsidiary. Indeed, Hino, Honda, Isuzu, Mitsubishi Motors, Nissan, and Toyo Kogyo (now Mazda) as well as Toyota all had established assembly operations in Europe by 1977—yet by that date not one had begun full-scale manufacturing in the region. These assembly operations were all located in Greece, Portugal, and Ireland in order to take advantage of low labour costs within the unifying European Community. This pattern contrasted with that of the American 'Big Three', which by this time had established comprehensive manufacturing plants as well as assembly operations in a number of the higher-wage Community markets.

The threat of increased EC protectionism and other factors motivated Japanese automobile manufacturers to expand their direct investments

[18] European Commission data, as cited in the *Financial Times*, 26 Sept. 1991.

[19] The following historical discussion is based largely on M. Mason, 'The Origins and Evolution of Japanese Direct Investment in Europe', *Business History Review*, 66: 1 (Autumn 1992), 435–74. See also, Ch. 1.

into local manufacturing in the Community starting in the 1980s. Although some EC member states remained leery of the prospects of major Japanese auto plants operating within their borders, the advent of the Thatcher government led the British authorities aggressively to encourage Japanese FDI in the UK through a variety of state incentives beginning in the early 1980s.[20] Nissan was the first Japanese firm to respond to Britain's overtures when, in 1984, Japan's second largest automobile manufacturer concluded an agreement with the British government to establish a major production facility in England.[21] Honda followed Nissan's lead by launching its own project to set up a British plant (with Rover) in 1985, followed by an Isuzu initiative (with GM) and a Toyota direct investment in the UK in 1987 and 1989, respectively.[22] This British FDI policy, as we shall see, would carry important implications for Community negotiations with the Japanese in the early 1990s over future automobile trade and investment restrictions. Nissan also directly invested in Spain (with local capital) and Toyota in Germany (with VW) during the 1980s, but well before the end of the decade it had become clear that Japan's major automobile manufacturers had chosen the UK as the principal site of their European manufacturing activities (see Table 10.2).

Approval of the EC's Single European Act (SEA) in 1986 thrust new challenges before member states determined to continue protecting their domestic automobile companies from Japanese competition. Under the terms of the Act, all EC member states were obliged to remove restrictions on the movement of goods within the Community by the end of 1992.[23] Since numerous EC governments did not limit auto imports from Japan, this obligation would enable Japanese firms to export vehicles to erstwhile protected EC countries via non-restricted Community markets. In addition, of course, completion of the internal market raised the possibility that Japanese transplant factories would produce autos in one EC

---

[20] The French government, on the other hand, once again demonstrated its long-standing ambivalence towards FDI in France's auto industry. This attitude led the French to reject, among other Japanese FDI proposals, Subaru's plan to establish a motor vehicle plant in Tours in 1988.

[21] On the Nissan entry into the UK see esp. P. Dicken, 'Japanese Penetration of the European Automobile Industry: The Arrival of Nissan in the United Kingdom', *Tijdschrift voor Econ. en Soc. Geografie*, 78: 2 (1987), 94–107.

[22] Toyota, the last of the major Japanese carmakers to establish a UK manufacturing plant, raced to produce its first automobile in that plant before completion of the internal market. This Toyota accomplished on 16 Dec. 1992—just 16 days before the formal opening of the new EC market! On Toyota's initial run, see the *Financial Times* (17 Dec. 1992).

[23] Member states effectively blocked imports of Japanese cars from other EC states by invoking Art. 115 of the Treaty of Rome. Art. 115 generally allows the Commission, in the event of certain economic difficulties, to authorize member states to enact protective measures against foreign competitors. However, in case of 'urgency' during the 'transitional period', member states *themselves* retain the sovereign right to implement such measures. After 1992, however, member states in all probability would lose the right unilaterally to invoke Art. 115 against Japanese auto imports from other EC countries.

country (the UK, for example) and then freely ship them to other EC countries (France and Italy, for instance).[24] The approaching changes in Community policy together with the lagging competitive positions of many European automobile manufacturers therefore placed increasing pressure on certain EC states to find new ways to support their domestic auto firms.[25]

2. ACCORD

2.1. Process

The Japanese automobile challenge to the unifying European Community led to long, complex, and often bitter negotiations involving numerous players from the EC and Japan. Officials of the Ministry of International Trade and Industry (MITI) represented the Japanese side in bilateral talks, though among government agencies the Ministry of Foreign Affairs also sought to influence the process. In addition, Japan's major carmakers consulted with government negotiators both individually and through the Japanese Automobile Manufacturers' Association (JAMA), the industry group then under the rotating presidency of Nissan's outspoken President Yutaka Kume. Recommended tactics and issue emphases occasionally differed among these players, yet on the whole they had established a general consensus on the major questions in the talks.

If the Japanese actors were relatively few and in general agreement on the central issues, however, the European side represented diverse players with varying interests. Bilateral negotiations on the European side were led by the Commission's Directorate General for External Relations (DG I), yet the Internal Market and Industry (DG III) and, to a lesser extent, the Competition (DG IV) Directorates General also played important roles in the bargaining process. Behind Commission negotiators, moreover, stood officials from the twelve Community governments. These governments each sent representatives to the Council of Ministers, the Community body which held formal power over the actions of the Commission. And finally, some of the major European carmakers also figured prominently in the bargaining process. These various Community players

---

[24] A preliminary (and highly publicized) skirmish took place in 1988, when French authorities threatened to block imports of Nissan Bluebirds assembled and partially manufactured in the UK. See e.g. *The Economist* (8 Oct. 1988). The French finally relented, but the affair underlined the extraordinary sensitivity of the issue.

[25] For an early attempt to assess EC policy options in the auto industry as unification approached, see G. Viesti and L. Zanzottera, 'Japanese Multinationals and EEC: The Case of [the] Car Industry' (Working Paper 30, Centro Studi sui Processi de Internazionalizzazione, Università Bocconi, Milan, Italy, Nov. 1989).

at times stood in general agreement, but more often pursued differing (and, at times, shifting) interests and goals.[26]

The process which culminated in the EC–Japan auto accord took more than three years to complete, and passed through four more or less distinct phases.[27] The first and longest phase ran from early 1988 through the end of 1989, and chiefly involved representatives of the European Commission together with officials from EC member states. The initiative to revise Community policy towards Japanese automobiles came principally from the Commission. Aware that completion of the internal market would require major changes in the auto policies of numerous member states, in early 1988 DG III began to study the position and likely development of the region's car industry. This work led to completion of an internal report entitled 'The Future of the EC Auto Industry', which was subsequently circulated within the Commission. DG III then combined this and other internal reports with externally commissioned research to provide a basis for future policy discussions.

Despite the central role of the Commission in initiating this first stage of the process, however, the critical direct and indirect roles of member states soon became apparent. With research in hand, Commissioner Martin Bangemann and DG III officials embarked upon an intensive consultation process with individual member states.[28] The positions of these states initially divided into four principal groups. Least influential in (and least directly affected by) this process were the six states without significant domestic auto industries: Belgium, Denmark, Greece, Ireland, Luxembourg, and the Netherlands.[29] These states naturally stood to gain little, if anything, by limiting Japanese cars in the EC after 1992, but chose to remain largely silent throughout the long process. This they did largely to appease their more concerned (and generally more powerful) fellow Community members, and to earn political capital useful in future EC inter-state bargaining. The UK staked out a second position. Although it no longer was home to a major auto industry controlled by domestic interests, the UK hosted not only the local subsidiaries of the American firms Ford and General Motors, but also the newly arrived and growing Japanese

[26] Resolutions approved by the EC Parliament regularly urged adoption of a tough policy line against the Japanese car industry in Europe, but the Parliament apparently had little direct impact on the negotiations.

[27] The following account necessarily simplifies an extraordinarily complex process. Within the Community itself, for example, a multiplicity of interactions took place between the Commission, member states, and firms. On the general nature of such interactions see e.g. S. Strange, *States and Markets* (London: Pinter, 1988).

[28] The Commission also consulted with MITI. However, the Japanese remained largely peripheral during these initial consultations, and did not become directly involved until the start of intensive Commission–MITI talks in Jan. 1990.

[29] Some of these states did, however, host limited foreign-controlled assembly operations, or were home to certain automobile parts suppliers.

operations of Nissan, Honda, and Toyota. In their talks with the Commission, UK representatives favoured complete freedom for Japanese transplants to produce and ship their goods throughout the Community, but quietly signalled their willingness to support continued controls over Japanese auto imports.

Two other groups of member states maintained still different views. The 'Latin 4' of France, Italy, Spain, and Portugal were home to domestic auto companies which felt most threatened by Japanese competition. Led by the French government, this 'Club Med' of the Community pressed for strong controls over Japanese participation in the EC auto industry after 1992. The (West) German government represented a fourth position during this early stage of the process. Though concerned about the future role of Japan in Community auto markets, German officials initially opposed controls on Japanese cars in part because, as previously suggested, many of their own automobile manufacturers remained confident and feared retaliation.

Following talks with member states, in mid-1989 the Commission began a process of inter-service consultations which finally produced an official EC position on the Japanese automobile question. Representatives of DG I, III, and IV all took part in the consultations. Moreover, the Commission in July 1989 formed a special *ad hoc* committee on automobiles composed of seven Cabinet members to facilitate and co-ordinate internal discussions. These various Commission players worked through that autumn to define a common position which generally met the requirements of the SEA as well as the special interests of vitally affected member states. Finally, in December 1989, the Commission settled on a list of broad principles designed to meet most of these various (though partially conflicting) demands. These principles reflected, among other factors, the determination to limit Japanese auto exports to the Community during a finite period of time and to seek Community assistance for domestic automobile manufacturers to help in their restructuring process. Less clear, however, was policy towards Japan's local transplants.

The process entered a second critical stage in January, 1990, when representatives of the European Commission and MITI began officially to consider how to modify and implement the general principles worked out the previous month. Following the issuance by the EC Council of Ministers of what amounted to an 'oral mandate'—remaining differences between member states, worries that an official (and therefore publicly announced) position would weaken the EC's bargaining position, and fears that any official agreement limiting Japanese autos in the Community resulting from these talks might violate GATT rules discouraged the issuance of a formal, written Council mandate to negotiate—the Commission contacted MITI to hammer out a draft bilateral accord. This round of talks dealt not only with Japanese auto imports into the Community as a whole, but also with imports into certain specific EC markets as well as the highly sensitive issue of Japanese transplant production and other matters.[30] MITI negotiators indicated flexibility in entertaining a number of possible restrictions in the proposed EC–Japan accord, but insisted in particular that no transplant restrictions of any kind be incorporated in such an agreement. On the basis of these discussions, Commission and MITI negotiators settled on a draft accord in August 1990 dubbed (by a DG I official) the 'Elements of Consensus'.

The draft 'Elements' set forth a number of more or less defined positions. For example, the Commission and MITI agreed on a transition period of between five and seven years from the projected completion of the internal market in January 1993 during which time Japanese auto imports would be restricted. This draft document also specified overall limits on cars which could be imported into the Community as a whole from Japan by the end of the transition period, although no estimates were offered for interim years and actual numbers would depend on the development of the local market. On the basis of these figures, the Commission anticipated that, including transplant production within the Community, Japan would be able to increase its share of the total EC car market from roughly 10 per cent in 1989 to about 21 per cent between 1997 and 1999. The draft also set fixed future ceilings on Japanese imports into the five countries with explicit Japanese quota arrangements, a 'no targeting' clause to prevent concentrated Japanese transplant sales in countries with such quantitative restrictions, and a semi-annual monitoring mechanism to insure that the terms of the accord would be faithfully executed.

Community states and carmakers then deliberated the merits of the proposed 'Elements' during a critical third phase of the process which lasted from roughly September 1990 through early April 1991. Shortly after the Commission and MITI had completed their draft 'Elements', DG III Commissioner Martin Bangemann set off a lively and protracted debate within the European automobile industry when he convened a meeting of the heads of three of the four EC mass auto producers (Fiat, Renault, and VW, but not Peugeot) to try to 'sell' them the proposed accord.[31] Bangemann understood that the EC's major volume carmakers felt most vulnerable to increased Japanese competition in the Community, and that their reactions to the draft 'Elements' would affect critically the positions of their governments and, therefore, the ultimate success of the proposed accord.

---

[30] The following account is drawn largely from the author's interviews with principals and others involved in this process, together with the account provided by T. Gandillot in his *La Dernière Bataille de l'automobile européene* [The Last Battle of the European Automobile] (Paris: Fayard, 1992).

[31] Bangemann apparently excluded Peugeot chairman Jacques Calvet because the French car manager proved exceptionally severe in his stance towards the Japanese. In his place, BMW management was invited to attend.

Much to Bangemann's (and the Commission's) dismay, however, these three European volume carmakers (together with the fourth, Peugeot, after it had learned of the discussions) rejected the draft 'Elements' as too favourable towards Japan, and resolved instead to forge a common industry position which met their requirements. Having reviewed voluminous and mounting evidence pointing to their acute vulnerability to Japanese competition, these carmakers had concluded that they would need far more protection than outlined in the draft 'Elements' successfully to meet the competition from Japan. Significantly, Fiat, Peugeot, and Renault were here joined by erstwhile free trader Carl Hahn, the chairman of VW, who would soon proclaim publicly what he had already concluded privately— that 'All Europeans are now vulnerable' to unfettered Japanese automobile participation in the Community.[32]

On 1 October 1990, the heads of the four mass producers—Agnelli (Fiat), Calvet (Peugeot), Levy (Renault), and Hahn (VW)—met to forge a common position which they intended to communicate to the Commission. Agnelli, Levy, and Hahn first drafted a letter setting out their joint position, which called for a longer transition period—of up to ten years in length—before Japanese auto exports could gain unrestricted access to the Community, together with limits on Japanese transplant production during this period. Peugeot's Calvet, however, refused to sign the common letter when presented with it. Instead, he called for even tougher measures against the Japanese, including in particular a halt to the development of Japanese transplant projects throughout the Community. Unable to convince Calvet to back down from his demands, the three authors of the joint position abandoned their idea to send the draft letter to the Commission. The meeting then broke up.

Unsuccessful in their efforts to forge a common position in this October meeting, the Fiat, Renault, and VW chiefs chose to craft a common stance through a reconstituted European automobile industry association. These three understood that the original association, the Comité des constructeurs du marché commun (the Committee of Common Market Manufacturers, or CCMC), made all decisions by unanimous vote—which meant that Calvet could derail any future efforts to create a position acceptable to all (14) CCMC members. In February 1991 they therefore created a new organization—the Association des constructeurs européens d'automobiles (the Association of European Automobile Manufacturers, or ACEA)—and wrote into the new organization's by-laws a provision which enabled

---

[32] On Hahn's revised thinking, see e.g. B. Avishai, 'A European Platform for Global Competition: An Interview with VW's Carl Hahn', *Harvard Business Review* (July–Aug. 1991), 103–13. Indeed, the growing success of Japan's luxury car lines, such as the Acura (Honda), the Infiniti (Nissan), and the Lexus (Toyota), soon would encourage even Germany's specialist makers to shift quietly towards this harder line.

members to make decisions by majority rather than unanimous vote.[33] Calvet was then invited to join this new association, but declined the offer when he realized that, alone, he could no longer block the will of the other industry members.

In its reconstituted form, the association quickly managed to agree on a common position with specific recommendations for an accord with the Japanese. This position, like the industry document prepared the previous October, advocated a transition period longer than that contained in the 'Elements', together with clear limits on Japanese transplant production. In addition, the ACEA called for a division of market growth between Japanese and European producers, a decrease in Japanese volume if the market contracted, and a Japanese market share cap of roughly 15 per cent—including transplant production—by the end of the transition period. Following completion and approval of this platform by member companies in March 1991, ACEA member firms were assigned the task of convincing their respective home governments to support the common industry stance. In addition, the Association sent a 4-page memorandum to the Commission setting forth its position.

Based in part on the reactions of their domestic carmakers, key EC member governments refined their own positions and instructed the Commission to modify its negotiating stance accordingly. Perhaps most importantly, the 'Latin 4' had by now solidified their views and constituted what one Commission official termed a 'blocking coalition' at the Community level to prevent any accord which they deemed too 'soft' on the Japanese. Specifically, these member states, largely following the wishes of their domestic auto firms, demanded among other things a minimum seven-year transition period from 1 January 1993, together with added clauses in the draft specifying changes in Japanese import levels if development of the Community market exceeded or fell short of anticipated levels during the life of the accord. They also pressed for some means explicitly to include Japanese transplant production in any final accord. Yet the 'Latin 4' chose not to press for a full ten-year transition period and other maximum demands expressed by their domestic firms, for these states generally believed that vigorous Japanese competition would speed desirable restructuring by their firms.

Greatly influenced by increasing concerns over Japanese competition even among its former free trader specialist carmakers, the German government in a critical development quietly tilted in favour of most of the demands set forth by the common Latin front. The Germans apparently refused, however, to back explicit limits on the Japanese transplants. The

---

[33] The European subsidiaries of Ford and General Motors also were granted full membership in the ACEA, a position denied them in the CCMC.

British government, for its part, publicly stressed strong opposition to any controls over Japanese transplants in the Community, but again expressed privately its willingness to support restrictions on Japanese auto imports. Based essentially on the positions of these six key governments, Commission representatives by the end of April had adopted a tougher position which they then presented to their MITI counterparts.[34]

MITI, however, refused to accept all of the new EC proposals—which led to a fourth, and final, phase requiring some three months of negotiation from April 1991. Although MITI representatives now professed a willingness to accept among other EC proposals a full seven-year transition period, together with the British they remained firmly opposed in particular to any clause formally limiting the number of cars which could be produced by the Japanese transplants. Japanese officials apparently were concerned, above all, that any such clause might create a precedent which would tempt the USA to imitate European practice.

This impasse was broken only by the Cabinet of EC Commission President Jacques Delors, which proposed that the Commission merely issue a unilateral oral declaration at the conclusion of the talks suggesting a link between the levels of transplant production and Japanese imports to the Community. In exchange, the Commission agreed to drop a number of other outstanding issues.[35] Before finalizing these arrangements, however, the Commission had to convince the French, in particular, to drop their concerns that the accord still was not tough enough on the Japanese. To persuade the French to go along, the Commission discreetly held out the carrot of significant future Community assistance for the restructuring of France's auto industry, and the stick of tougher enforcement of EC competition rules against French quotas on Japanese imports by local car distributors. French European Affairs Minister Elizabeth Guigou, charged with representing her government at the Council of Ministers, found herself caught between the liberal-leaning Minister of Industry Roger Farroux and the hardline inclinations of Prime Minister Edith Cresson.[36] Minister Guigou appealed directly to President François Mitterand, who apparently judged that the imperative of Community consensus together with the promises and implied threats of the Commission outweighed any remaining

[34] On 8 May 1991, the Permanent Representatives of the twelve EC members met to consider the revised Commission proposals. Even in its revised form, however, the proposed agreement remained too controversial for the adoption of a formal negotiating mandate. Therefore, by the time the Council of Ministers met on 13 May the automobile question had been removed from the agenda. Gandillot, *La Dernière Bataille*, 136.

[35] Chief among these outstanding issues was any mention in the accord of reciprocal European access to the Japanese automobile market, a measure advocated from time to time by EC hardliners.

[36] This internal French discord was also played out within the nation's auto industry: the impasse between Industry Minister Farroux and Prime Minister Cresson mirrored the split between Renault's Levy and Peugeot's Calvet. In the end, the authorities tilted towards the more conciliatory line of (state-owned) Renault.

concerns about the accord. These last disagreements resolved, the European Commission and MITI struck a final deal.

2.2. Outcome

The negotiations between Japan and the Community produced one of the most unusual understandings in modern international economic diplomacy. At the heart of these understandings, announced on 31 July 1991, was a substantially revised 'Elements of Consensus', a bilateral document which set forth a series of goals and measures concerning Japanese motor vehicles in the EC through the end of the decade. The Commission and the Japanese government adopted three common goals: first, the 'progressive' and, ultimately, 'full liberalization' of the EC motor vehicle market; second, 'avoidance' of EC market 'disruption' by Japanese vehicle exports; and third, a (Japanese) 'contribut[ion]' to enable EC manufacturers to attain 'adequate levels' of 'international competitiveness' by the granting of a 'transitional period' during which Community markets would remain regulated.

To attain these various goals, the parties agreed on a series of measures pertaining to Japanese participation in the EC motor vehicle market through 31 December 1999. First, the Commission promised that Community members immediately would begin to ease relevant national restrictions and measures taken under Article 115 of the Treaty of Rome, and would abolish such restrictions and measures no later than 1 January 1993.[37]

Second, the two sides agreed that Japan would 'monitor' through semi-annual consultations vehicle exports to the EC as a whole and to each 'restricted' EC market—what Bangemann called the 'double lock' on Japanese auto shipments to the Community—during a transition period to end on 31 December 1999. Specific export levels were provisionally set for the 1999 calendar year. These levels, however, were based on market forecasts, and both sides agreed that changes in actual market conditions would require revisions in Japanese export limits. The 1999 'forecast level' of Japanese vehicle exports to the EC as a whole was set at 1.23 million vehicles—virtually the same level as the 1989 figure—or roughly 8.1 per cent of the estimated EC market of 15.1 million vehicles in 1999. In addition, the 'Elements' set forth 'forecast levels' of Japanese vehicle exports to each of the five 'restricted' EC markets. Based on total anticipated demand in each of these markets, these 'forecast levels' indicated that Japanese producers would supply through exports roughly 5.3 per cent of the French, Italian, and Spanish markets, 7.0 per cent of the UK market, and 8.4 per cent of the Portuguese market in 1999 (see Table 11.4).

Third, the 'Elements' addressed the issue of the Japanese transplants in

---

[37] On the significance of Art. 115 for the EC automobile industry, see n. 23.

TABLE 11.4. *Japanese automobile exports to select EC countries in 1999: levels as agreed in the 'Elements of Consensus'*

Country	Anticipated total EC market demand (units)	Anticipated Japanese market share through exports (units)	Anticipated Japanese market share through exports (%)
France	2,850,000	150,000	5.3
Italy	2,600,000	138,000	5.3
Spain	1,475,000	79,000	5.3
UK	2,700,000	190,000	7.0
Portugal	275,000	23,000	8.4

Source: 'Elements of Consensus'.

the Community. In one part of the document, the Commission pledged that the EC would impose neither 'restrictions on Japanese investment' nor controls on 'the free circulation of its products in the Community'. At the same time, however, the Japanese side agreed to 'convey' to Japanese vehicle makers the Commission's 'repeatedly expressed concern' that concentrated sales in certain specific national markets of motor vehicles *produced by these makers in the Community* would create serious 'market disruption' and significantly frustrate the efforts of EC makers to attain international levels of competitiveness.

In addition to the Elements of Consensus, the EC and Japan simultaneously circulated to certain interested parties a number of unilateral interpretations and clarifications which touched on various points contained in the bilateral agreement. EC Vice-President Frans Andriessen (in Brussels) and MITI Vice-Minister Eiichi Nakao (in Tokyo), the nominal heads of the two negotiating teams, appended to the 'Elements', for example, individual statements largely reiterating various points in the 'Elements'. Further, the EC side issued an 'Internal Declaration' which specified the Commission's interpretation of two items set forth in the accord: first, the Commission held that Community manufacturers should enjoy at least one-third of any EC market growth beyond estimated levels throughout the transitional period; and second, the Commission expected that Japanese manufacturers would reduce their exports by 75 per cent of the proportionate drop in any overall EC market decline.

Finally, and most significantly, issued together with the 'Elements' were written versions of a carefully scripted and co-ordinated 'conclusive' oral declaration made by Andriessen to Nakao, together with Nakao's oral response to Andriessen. Andriessen stated in his declaration that, in its negotiations with Japan, the Commission adopted the 'working assumption' that 'Japanese owned factories located in the EC' would produce for sale in the Community roughly 1.2 million motor vehicles by the end of the

TABLE 11.5. *Japanese automobile market shares in select EC countries in 1999: Commission estimates based on internal working assumptions*

Country	Anticipated Japanese market share through exports (%)	Anticipated Japanese market share through transplants (%)	Total anticipated Japanese market share (%)
France	5.3	1.7–5.7	7–11
Italy	5.3	1.7–5.7	7–11
Spain	5.3	6.8–10.8	12.1–16.1
UK	7.0	13.9–19.9	20.9–26.9
Portugal	8.4	8.1–13.1	16.5–21.5

Source: Internal Commission documents.

transition period. Significantly, Nakao did not directly challenge this assumption, but rather 'called' Andriessen's 'attention' to the Commission's promise in the 'Elements' not to restrict 'Japanese investment or sales of its products' in the Community. The Commission's working assumption on total Japanese transplant sales in the Community, together with estimates of total Japanese exports to the region contained in the 'Elements', suggested that Japan would capture roughly 16.1 per cent of the total EC automobile market by 1999. In addition, internal EC estimates of transplant sales in each of the five restricted markets, together with projected Japanese exports to each of these markets as set forth in the 'Elements', also enabled the Commission to generate estimates of total Japanese market shares in these five countries for 1999 (see Table 11.5).

2.3. Denouements

Conclusion of this historic accord did not, of course, put an end to disputes over Japanese motor vehicle penetration of Community markets. To the contrary, conflicting interpretations of that accord provoked new disagreements beginning virtually the day of its announcement. These disagreements at times pitted Japan against the Community as a whole, but at other times caused deep divisions within the EC itself.

The proper interpretation of the accord's limits on Japanese exports has produced a number of controversies between Japan and the Community. Beginning in the autumn of 1992 and lasting more than six months, for example, the two sides disagreed over prospects for total 1993 EC new car demand—and, therefore, over allowable limits on Japanese auto imports during the first year of the accord's operation. On 1 April 1993, MITI and the Commission apparently reached an accord based on a bilateral consensus of estimated 1993 Community demand, yet future controversy is sure to arise in subsequent consultations.[38] In addition, the Community and Japan are still pondering the implications of the accord for exports to the EC of Japanese-badged motor vehicles produced in third countries—what the French sometimes call 'diverted exports'. Though such exports are nowhere mentioned in the 'Elements' or related statements, Japanese pursuit of this third-country strategy may well intensify relevant debates left unsettled in the 1991 arrangements.[39] Indeed, Honda already has begun to export the Accord model from its Ohio plant to the EC, and Toyota and Nissan also are reportedly ready to ship US-assembled and partially manufactured cars to the Community in the near future.[40] In addition, Mitsubishi Motors—the only major Japanese motor vehicle manufacturer without a manufacturing plant in the EC—has started or will soon start to export to the EC its automobiles and pick-up trucks produced in Australia, Malaysia, and Turkey.[41]

The issue of controls over Japanese transplant production in the Community has provoked at least equally great controversy, although here the arguments cause division within the EC as well as between the Community and Japan. On one side stand some of the Latin hardliners, who insist that the accord places a strict upper limit of 1.2 million vehicles produced at Japanese transplants through the 1990s. Not surprisingly, Peugeot's Calvet is among the most vociferous proponents of this view.[42] Somewhat more surprisingly, however, even such widely quoted Japanese sources as *Nihon keizai shimbun (Nikkei)*—the closest Japanese equivalent of the *Financial Times* or the *Wall Street Journal*—also have suggested that Japan in fact agreed to observe limits on transplant production by failing directly to contradict Andriessen's oral declaration in the carefully prepared exchange with Nakao. 'It will be difficult to expand local production beyond the number . . . forecast by the EC, since Japan did not forthrightly oppose it,' *Nikkei* stated, for example, in its lead editorial shortly after announcement

[38] Under the final terms, this bilateral consensus—which forecast a significant *contraction* of the 1993 EC auto market—reportedly led MITI to agree to *reduce* Japanese motor vehicle exports to the Community by 9.3% during the 1993 calendar year. See the *Financial Times* (2 Apr. 1993).

[39] Representatives of Toyota and Nissan reportedly told Commissioner Andriessen during the course of the negotiations that it was the practice of their companies to sell in local markets those cars they produced in local subsidiaries. Commission officials interpreted this statement as a subtle form of assurance that Japan's two major carmakers would not export to the EC cars produced in their US transplant factories. However, no written understanding about this issue was ever produced.

[40] Experience to date suggests that the Commission will classify as 'American' imports into the Community those Japanese-badged cars produced in the USA which the American authorities assert are 'American'. *Automotive News*, various issues; interview with Joseph Massey, formerly of the Office of the United States Trade Representative.

[41] *Nikkei Weekly* (14 Dec. 1992); *Ward's Automotive International* (Aug. 1992). The EC–Japan agreement also leaves open the tantalizing question of how the Community will handle auto imports from other rising Asian competitors such as Hyundai of South Korea.

[42] See e.g. Calvet interview in *Nihon keizai shimbun* (25 Oct. 1991).

of the accord.[43] Indeed, Japan's 'implicit acceptance' of the transplant number, *Nikkei* went on, 'set the limit for the expansion of transplant production'.[44]

Opposed to this viewpoint are the British and Japanese governments in particular, who maintain that the accord in no way restricts either the operation of Japanese motor vehicle factories in the Community nor the movement of products within the EC made at these plants. 'I am pleased,' stressed, for example, then UK Trade and Industry Secretary Peter Lilley at the announcement of the accord, 'that the Community has accepted there shall be no restriction on Japanese motor car manufacturing investment in the EC or on the freedom to sell the vehicles produced throughout the EC.'[45] MITI officials publicly have offered similar views, as has Nissan President Kume, who stated unequivocally: 'Whether [Japanese transplant production in the EC during the life of the accord] will be 1.2 million or not, this is what the EC Commission said unilaterally. This is not something that will bind the Japanese side.'[46]

Although these two viewpoints stand in contradiction, the text of the accord together with commentary by those who drafted it and other considerations suggest that the EC–Japan arrangement does indeed place implicit (though somewhat vague and ambiguous) limits on the Japanese transplants. First, the 'Elements' themselves include language warning Japanese carmakers against concentrating sales from their European transplant factories in the five restricted markets during the life of the agreement. Second, the fact that the chief Commission negotiator, following intensive consultations with the French and other member governments, clearly articulated to his MITI counterpart—and was not directly challenged by this counterpart—that the Community assumed Japanese transplant factories would produce for sale in the EC 1.2 million units by 1999, certainly suggests the possibility of an informal arrangement limiting Japanese firms to that level during the life of the accord. And third, interviews with Commission representatives and others suggest that, in interpreting the accord and related arrangements, the Commission might well compensate for any Japanese transplant production above negotiated levels by adjusting downward permissible levels of Japanese auto imports into the Community.[47] Therefore, although some of the precise implications of the accord for the operation of Japan's Community transplants remain controversial, through the 1991 bilateral understanding the European Community has apparently managed to institute implicit controls on Japanese foreign direct

[43] *Nihon keizai shimbun* (2 Aug. 1991).
[44] Ibid. (1 Aug. 1991).
[45] As quoted in *The Times* (London) (28 July 1991).
[46] As quoted in the *New York Times* (12 Aug. 1991).
[47] Indeed, the Commission reportedly stated that it had in fact 'taken into account' expected 1993 EC sales from Japanese transplant factories in calculating 1993 limits on Japan's auto exports to the Community. See the *Financial Times* (2 Apr. 1993).

investment in the EC automobile industry. Yet the (surely deliberate) ambiguities of interpreting and implementing measures relating to these transplants virtually assure that this issue will remain a point of great contention for years to come.

These and other ongoing disputes surrounding the 1991 accord point to continued conflict over Japanese penetration of the European Community's automobile markets. 'The agreement is politically fragile both within the EC and between the EC and Japan,' as one observer has rightly noted. 'There are big questions that won't go away.'[48] Indeed, official EC and Japanese statements notwithstanding, many experts believe that the Community will erect still new protections from Japanese competition even after the termination of the accord.[49]

3. CONCLUSIONS

What does this critical test case tell us about EC foreign economic policymaking? Analysis of the negotiation process and outcome suggests that, at least in this key example, individual state interests clearly dominate the Community's foreign economic policymaking process. Specifically, in the auto case it was the timing and substance of decisions rendered by critically affected EC member governments that largely dictated the course of the negotiations. It is certainly true that the Commission at times managed to influence certain aspects of member state positions. This the Commission accomplished largely through implicit and explicit rewards and threats. In addition, the Commission derived power from its privileged, intermediary position between the Japanese government and EC member states.

Yet the record indicates that, in general, member governments retained enormous powers to influence the policymaking process. Not all governments, of course, chose to exercise their influence: indeed, those governments without significant domestic auto industries chose to allow critically affected EC states to determine the course of the negotiations. This former group of governments calculated that such acquiescence would enable them to build precious political capital to use in future inter-state bargaining. Left in control were those (six) EC states with direct and vital interests at stake in the talks with Japan. Through implicit and explicit means, these

---

[48] H. Herke, GM Europe Vice-President for EC Relations, as cited in *Ward's Automotive International* (May 1992).

[49] See e.g. J. Womack and D. Jones, 'European Automotive Policy: Past, Present, and Future', in Committee on Foreign Affairs, US House of Representatives, *Europe and the United States: Competition and Cooperation in the 1990s* (June 1992), 209. A renewal of EC protections from 2000 would be consistent with what Fiat Chairman Agnelli predicted in 1989 would probably turn into 'a kind of permanent negotiation' between the Community and Japan. See 'Agnelli on Cars, Greens, and Japan', *Fortune* (31 July 1989), 133, 136.

states critically influenced the evolving positions of the Commission.[50] Where such states could reach fundamental agreement on a particular policy, the position of the Commission reflected this agreement; where states could not come to such agreement, the Commission crafted ambiguous terms which attempted to address most of the concerns of individual members. This state-dominated process finds clear reflection in the final accord and related understandings, which contain deliberately vague formulations concerning the transplant issue, together with detailed Community-wide, but also state-specific, regulations relating to imports—regulations which mock the notion of a truly 'common' EC external commercial policy.

This process created a highly unusual set of policy arrangements to meet the growing Japanese automotive challenge. These arrangements are distinctive in part because of their deliberately vague and ambiguous terms. In addition, the accord is unusual because it places limits not only on Japanese exports to the Community as whole, but on (five) individual EC markets as well. Moreover, this agreement is extraordinary because it constitutes one of the very first major accords between advanced industrialized countries which apparently restricts both exports and foreign direct investments.[51] And finally, the 'Elements' and related understandings may well represent the first major example among such countries in which restrictions are based on the nationality of the producer rather than the location of production.

These policy outcomes stand in marked contrast to the results of the automobile negotiations between the USA and Japan. In 1981, the USA negotiated its own automobile accord with the Japanese. This voluntary restraint agreement (VRA) placed limits on the number of imported Japanese automobiles and certain other motor vehicles for three years, but in no way linked Japanese transplants in the USA with Japanese imports, nor placed any other limits on Japanese automobile FDI in America. Following a temporary, one-year extension, in 1985 the Reagan Administration terminated the bilateral restraint agreement. For essentially political reasons,

[50] In addition to the expressed wishes of concerned EC states in talks with the Commission, member governments also wielded subtle but powerful influences over the Commission through other means as well. Indeed, even when not explicitly instructed to do so by these governments, the Commission tried to 'read' the thinking of member states and then to incorporate measures which reflected this thinking into arrangements with the Japanese. In addition, at least some states (such as Italy) derived effective power over the Commission because the Commission feared that the public controls such states had enacted to limit Japanese auto imports might well be GATT-conforming. If this proved to be the case, Commission officials worried, these states could veto the draft accord and continue to restrict Japanese car imports without fear of extra-Community legal sanctions even after completion of the Single Market.

[51] This policy initiative to link trade and investment *in practice* reflects in part the increasingly blurred distinctions between trade and FDI *in theory* as well. On the dissolution of conceptual distinctions see e.g. D. Encarnation, *Rivals Beyond Trade: America versus Japan in Global Competition* (Ithaca: Cornell University Press, 1992), ch. 1; and D. Julius, *Global Companies and Public Policy: The Growing Challenge of Foreign Direct Investment* (London: Pinter for the Royal Institute of International Affairs, 1990), ch. 4.

however, the Japanese government opted to continue to place limits on the number of motor vehicles it exported to the US market on a unilateral basis. Japan has renewed this voluntary export restraint (VER) in every subsequent year.[52]

This American approach contrasts with the European response in a number of important ways. Unlike the Americans, the Europeans, as we have seen, crafted arrangements implicitly to restrict Japanese transplants in the Community. This policy the Europeans chose because certain recipient countries in the Community insisted that total Japanese market shares in addition to the proportions of local markets supplied by Japanese exports would prove critical to long-term host country interests. In addition, the Community obtained at the outset a longer transitional period of protection than in the American case, hammered out specific numerical limits over Japanese auto exports throughout this period, and insisted on specific adjustments of these exports to take into account growth or decline in EC markets during these years. European authorities also have taken a far more activist approach towards other aspects of Japanese FDI in the EC automobile industry. Again in contrast to the USA, the British government, for example, has imposed specific local content requirements on Japanese auto transplants located within its borders, and the European Commission has set strict limits on state aid for automobile (and other) FDI projects in the Community.[53]

The net effect of these European policies on overall EC interests remains uncertain, but it is clear that such policies will create significant economic costs as well as benefits to the Community. European-based auto producers clearly stand to realize significant short-term advantages from the 1991 EC–Japan arrangements, for example, including protected local markets during a lengthy (seven-year) transition period.[54] At the same time, however, these producer advantages may well come at the expense of European consumers, who will face restricted supplies and presumably higher prices for Japanese (and possibly non-Japanese) automobiles. In addition, local content requirements surely will promote the interests of auto parts suppliers operating in Europe, but may lower the efficiency of Japanese transplants denied greater access to parts sourced from abroad. At this stage, however, it is not clear whether the benefits of these European initiatives will outweigh the costs for the Community as a whole.

[52] *New York Times* (30 Mar., 1 May, and 2 May 1981; 2 Mar., and 28 Mar. 1985; 13 Feb., and 14 Feb. 1986; 19 Mar. 1992).

[53] On British local content requirements see e.g. 'Local Content Arrangements in the United Kingdom' (unpublished report, UK Department of Trade and Industry, Jan. 1993); and Dicken, 'Japanese Penetration of the European Automobile Industry', 98. On Community controls over state aid to inward FDI projects, see e.g. J. Womack and D. Jones, 'European Automobile Policy', 203.

[54] Similar to European-based auto producers but in marked contrast to their Japanese counterparts, the European subsidiaries of Ford and GM also stand to benefit significantly from the 1991 arrangements.

COMMENT

Jonathan Story

Two key points stand out in Mark Mason's account of the EC–Japan automobile agreements of July 1991: (1) state interests dominate in EC foreign economic policymaking as regards the deal, and (2) there is an implicit restraint on Japanese EC market shares contained in what M. Lévy, chairman of the state-owned French producer Renault, has called 'le non-dit' of the accords. Two further remarks may be added: (3) the July 1991 agreements clearly fall into a grey area, tokened by the commitment of both sides to notify the GATT; (4) states and corporations compete for markets from differing institutional and political contexts.

Take the last statement first. There was little to suggest that the European governments and manufacturers would ever be able to agree on a common policy. The histories, contexts, and markets had developed in too divergent a way for the evidence to suggest any clear convergence of interests. Germany's automobile industry accounted for about 4 million jobs, directly or indirectly, and was embedded in the country's corporate culture, with the emphasis on close co-operation between corporations, the trade unions, their suppliers, and the financial community. The central feature of the German system was the high value attached to training, and the objective standards of excellence which prevailed in the pantheon of German champions, such as Daimler-Benz, BMW, and Porsche in the up-market segments, or Volkswagen for the mass markets. Both Opel (GM) and Ford Europe were incorporated under German law. By contrast, the industries in France, the UK, and Spain had been plagued in the past by poor labour relations, a low corporate commitment to training, regular interference by governments and political parties, and volatile financial conditions. The turning-point came at the end of the 1970s, and the early 1980s, when Europessimism prevailed. None the less, employment in the automobile industry in Germany moved ahead, while the sector in the rest of Europe shed 460,000 jobs. By 1986, the market had polarized between six high-volume producers—GM, Ford, VW, Renault, Peugot, Fiat—and the specialized up-market producers. The boom at the end of the 1980s enabled some privatization to go ahead, and major investments were made in new technologies. But work-forces remained on lower pay and with lesser skills, relative to German workers. In France, one-third of the sector's labour force were without diplomas in 1990.

EC trade law is derivative of GATT. Indeed, the EC's '1992' strategy to complete the internal market was launched alongside the Uruguay Round. Corporate policies, no doubt anticipating impending changes, became more offensive in challenging inherited market agreements. Ford and VW, for instance, penetrated Fiat's fiefdom in Italy, sharply reducing the latter's domestic market share. They also became associated through partnerships or joint ventures with Honda, Nissan, Mitsubishi, or Toyota with a view to improving their specific competitive positions on their main European markets. Indeed German corporations, with trade association support, promoted their own export drives and retail outlets abroad, particularly into Japan, where Germany's up-market automobile producers accounted for 85 per cent of total EC producer sales in Japan in 1989. Meanwhile, as Mason points out, the British government turned to Japanese producers to regenerate its own industry.

Continental corporations remained extremely reserved about Japan's government and corporate trading practices. They had observed as the Big Three US producers saw their Japanese competitors' share of the US market rise from about 5 per cent in 1974 to 30 per cent by 1990. Japanese corporations had established production facilities there, and brought with them some 350 component manufacturers. With the negotiated fall of the dollar after 1985, Japanese exports were diverted to European markets, prompting calls by the CCMC for a freeze on Japanese market share to 10–11 per cent of the EC's future internal market, and local content regulations on inward Japanese investment. The ratio of units exported to imported (on a global basis) was 60 : 1 for Japan, as against 2 : 1 for Germany, Europe's automobile export champion. The build-up of Japanese facilities in Britain stimulated further anxiety, not least for the future of the 1,000–1,500 European subcontractors. With the slow-down in 1990 in the European economy, Continental producers faced a combination of harsher Japanese competition and higher fixed costs.

A key factor in shifting the German producers towards a grey area in the EC negotiations with Japan was the move up-market of the Japanese producers. BMW, Daimler-Benz, and Porsche had done well on the US markets with the rise of the dollar in the early 1980s; their penetration of the Japanese market was hindered by the high taxation on large cylinder automobiles in Japan. In Spring 1989, once the domestic manufacturers were set to enter the sector, Tokyo lowered the tax. German market shares in Japan's market began to dip, while the Lexus, Infiniti, or Acura outsold established German names on the North American markets within a year or two of the launch.

The implicit restraint on Japanese trade and investment in automobiles, contained in the July 1991 accords, could only have been reached by a change in French policy. This was forthcoming with the development of President Mitterrand's policy to bind Germany into a European Union, as Germany moved to unity. Indeed, the creation of the ACEA—which Mason so well recounts from the Brussels perspective—occurred in February 1991, as the two inter-governmental conferences on political and monetary union were underway and when France had advanced proposals for closer military co-operation among the member states, and particularly with Germany. The automobile story is one strand in this wider picture. The struggle for alignment with Germany was fought within the French policy community between French nationalists and Europeanists. The nationalists, represented in the automobile story by M. Calvet, favoured the continued use of the veto in the automobile association, a hard line on Japanese trade and transplants issues, and a barely concealed concern about the prospect of German hegemony in Europe.

As long as the split within the French camp endured, the automobile manufacturers proved unable to respond to the Commission's 1990 proposals. Nor could the Council give a negotiating mandate to the Commission. There was a spectrum of splits within national policy communities. London, for instance, agreed with Tokyo that the accord should include no quota on transplant production, or any trade-off between direct trade from Japan and output from factories of Japanese corporations. But there was also the realization that the combination of a UK welcome mat to Japanese inward investments, and threats of Continental trade protection, maximized the UK's attraction to Japanese producers. Fiat, sometimes labelled the thirteenth member state of the EC, had benefited since 1972 from the veto system in the CCMC, which the French had created in part as a counter to Ford and GM's European production strategies. No agreement had been reached on the few remaining standards, which would have permitted the development of a European automobile. Yet the rhetoric of Fiat and Rome was for completion of the internal market.

The crunch came, as Mason recounts, in October 1990, when the European automobile producers presented Calvet with a letter outlining their common position to the Commission. The text responded to nearly all of Calvet's demands. Calvet, like Thatcher at the Rome Council that month, refused to sign. Like her, he was ditched. The formalities of the new Europe under negotiation required a move away from a minimum consensus, accommodating to whichever interest adopted a minimalist position, to the threat of a majority vote to isolate the recalcitrant. The ACEA, set up in February 1991, represented a blow to industrial Gaullism in that it was predicated on majority voting.

State interests remain predominant in EC foreign economic policy-making, despite the apparent blow to industrial Gaullism as seen in the case of automobiles. This may be illustrated by reference to the ACEA. The opening was held in Munich. Voting on a majority basis provides an effective blocking power to the German-based manufacturers. In other words, it is possible to argue that the style of industrial Gaullism in automobiles was the veto, the avoidance of which required readiness to negotiate a minimum consensus. The style of industrial federalism is majority voting, the avoidance of which requires whichever state or interest has a minimalist position to move towards the (German-based) majority, or to anticipate the penalties of isolation. This procedure lends itself to an inflated rhetoric of togetherness and harmony, while state or corporate interests remain as multiple and as difficult to reconcile as ever.

Indeed, the July 1991 automobile accord illustrates at once the content, style, and limits of EC foreign economic policymaking. The content is spelt out in the figures on market share, or in the monitoring arrangements for EC markets. The style is one of fractious harmony, whose central feature is the use of intra-EC disagreement as a weapon in EC external relations. Japanese corporations may resent the implicit production quotas on their investments in Britain, but there is always the Damocles sword hanging over their heads that EC governments or competitors may interpret the clauses of the accords to place restraints on trade. The limits are illustrated by another 'non-dit' in the accords as to how the EC is to treat Japanese-owned output, produced in the USA, and exported into the EC. Here the structural power is wielded by the USA. The Maastricht accords on monetary union, and a common foreign policy, postpone any substantial further initiatives until 1996–7. Until then, the Bundesbank, as Europe's central bank and prime partner for the New York Federal Reserve Bank, disposes of European monetary conditions. NATO remains the sole, but inadequate guarantor of post-Cold-War Europe's security.

Both Maastricht and the automobile accord are horses from the same stable. The one is 72 pages long, and the other is six sentences, but both leave more than ample room for interpretation. The reason is that distrust prevails among European states and corporations, which are also divided about policies towards the rest of the world. Hence the special way in which the European political system uses the future, and the élitist and non-transparent way in which policy is formulated in Brussels. The EC uses the future, as in Maastricht or in the terms of the transition period in the July 1991 accords, both as a place to locate differences which are now unresolvable in the hope that they may be resolvable some time in the future, and as a binding or implicit commitment to act now in ways compatible with the EC's longer-term aims about which disagreements remain rife. The EC remains élitist because it represents a special form of interstate diplomacy, and therefore gives rise to dissatisfaction on the part of those who would like to see a Europe where all politics is domestic, and to antagonism on the part of those who wish to preserve the specific citizenship identified with inherited statehood. Europe is truly open to the post-Cold-War winds of change.

Is there any lesson for the USA, then, in Mason's key points that state interests dominate in EC foreign economic policymaking as regards the deal, and that it contains an implicit restraint on Japanese EC market shares? The USA is a federation; the EC is not. The USA may act explicitly; the European states can only do so when they agree. Usually, they agree, implicitly, to disagree.

PART IV
IMPLICATIONS

12

Does Ownership Matter? Answers and Implications for Europe and America

Dennis Encarnation and Mark Mason

Do Japanese multinationals in Europe operate differently? Compared to what? Historically? Cross-sectionally? With what consequences for economics and politics? For corporate strategy and government policy? In Europe and elsewhere? As a result, can we conclude that ownership matters?

To answer these overarching questions, we draw liberally from the otherwise diverse papers collected in this benchmark volume. In the end, we conclude that ownership can—and does—matter. But our conclusions require careful qualification, given the often competing facts and analyses presented above, in earlier chapters. Specifically, from a corporate perspective, important differences remain in both the structure and performance of Japanese multinationals abroad, even as they rapidly evolve along an otherwise common path charted earlier by their US and European counterparts. Such persistent differences cannot be discounted as mere 'vintage effects', vestigial remnants reflecting an earlier stage in a multinational's evolution, but instead may actually grow larger with the proliferation and maturation of Japanese investment abroad. Next, from a government perspective, ownership again matters, as individual European states and the European Community as a whole continue to enact numerous policies that specifically respond to the much-vaunted Japanese challenge. From these responses we see an emerging European policy model that has important implications for Japan's future relations, not only with Europe, but also with the USA.

While answering the several questions posed in this benchmark volume, each of our contributors has had to address, at least implicitly, a common set of conceptual, definitional, and measurement problems. At the centre of these problems is the categorization of a multinational as 'Japanese', distinct from either its 'American' or 'European' counterpart. Any such categorization, of course, is blurred by the cross-national mixture of equity shareholdings through joint ventures; by the internationalization of equity markets in a multinational's home country; and by the global proliferation of strategic alliances that may entail no actual exchange of equity shares. Undaunted by these complexities, however, the preceding papers follow the common practice of relying on the classification schemes employed by their principal data sources, typically government agencies charged with gathering (often inadequate and messy) data on the inflow and outflow of FDI.[1] These agencies define the national origin of foreign investors in terms of a minimum threshold of equity ownership. That minimum, it is assumed by academic researcher and government official alike, correlates with foreign managerial control, which in turn grows proportionately (albeit, imprecisely) with foreign shareholdings. So ownership becomes a proxy for control—a proxy that more closely mirrors reality when multinational corporations secure majority shareholdings in their foreign subsidiaries.

1. EMERGING SIMILARITIES, PERSISTENT DIFFERENCES

Majority shareholdings in foreign subsidiaries have become a common feature in the on-going evolution of American, European, and Japanese multinationals. In marked contrast to minority-owned or equal partnership joint ventures, majority subsidiaries grant these multinationals unrivalled managerial control over the foreign exploitation of their firm-specific advantages: in product and process technologies, in sales and service, in governance and organizations. These tangible and intangible assets seem especially important in advanced industrial markets, and in a few industries—such as automobiles and electronics, as well as financial services—that attract a large share of US, EC, and Japanese investment. While so-called greenfield investments account for a sizeable proportion of this investment, the rate of mergers and acquisitions (M&As) has grown more rapidly. Here, the Americans have led the way, followed by the Europeans and, more recently, the Japanese. As a result, according to our several authors, much of the strategy and structure of US, European, and Japanese multinationals has followed a common evolutionary path.

Our authors go on to report that many of the foreign operations of these multinationals have also followed a similar path. For American, European, and Japanese alike, FDI has become the principal means for securing market access abroad. In fact, through their majority subsidiaries, they record far more foreign sales than do all exporters based in the USA, the EC, or Japan. Most of these foreign sales come either from the local market hosting a multinational's investment, or (in Europe) from geographically proximate markets; by contrast, far more limited sales are generated from a subsidiary's shipments back to its parent's home market, or from widely dispersed third-country markets. To supply such local and regional markets, American, European, and Japanese multinationals increasingly rely on offshore production, and not just on imported goods

[1] For a review of these various data sources, see S. Thomsen, 'Appendix', in D. Julius, *Global Companies and Public Policy: The Growing Challenge of Foreign Direct Investment* (London: Royal Institute of International Studies, 1980).

sold through proprietary distribution channels overseas. These distribution channels, plus the import requirements of offshore production, all illustrate that foreign investment need not displace trade, but instead may complement that trade, by increasing its value while also altering its composition and direction. And these import requirements may initially be quite large, since offshore production typically begins with the largest American, European, and Japanese multinationals, only later extending to their several multinational suppliers. In sum, then, many of the foreign operations evidenced first by the Americans immediately after World War II have been gradually extended to both the Europeans and (more recently) the Japanese.

This common evolution of foreign investment strategies, according to our authors, is most clearly evidenced in the bilateral operations of American and European multinationals. Specifically, in the USA, EC multinationals have finally begun to operate much like US multinationals in the European Community. For example, with their bilateral investments concentrated in majority subsidiaries, both American and European multinationals have significantly expanded offshore production in each other's home market. Of course, these US and EC expansions did not occur simultaneously: for the Americans, the value of local production in Europe greatly exceeded the value of US exports to that growing market as early as the 1950s; while for the Europeans, it would take another two decades (into the 1970s) before local US production even exceeded EC manufactured exports to the USA. And it would take two more decades (into the 1990s) before American and European multinationals would approach parity: Today, US and EC subsidiaries each sell in the other's home market five times more than either EC or US exporters ship across the Atlantic. Much of this trans-Atlantic trade, moreover, is controlled equally by American and European multinationals, principally through intra-company shipments between multinational parents and their majority subsidiaries. In short, the trans-Atlantic model of foreign investment and related trade has become quite symmetrical: the same strategies implemented successfully by the Americans in Europe have also come to be implemented successfully by the Europeans in the USA.

While the historical evolution of Japanese multinationals has generally begun to parallel this USA–EC model, important differences do remain. For example, in marked contrast to either the Europeans in the USA or the Americans in Europe, Japanese multinationals still sell in each of these two markets far more manufactured goods through international trade than they do through local production resident in these markets. Indeed, even after the rapid expansion of such production over the past decade, by the early 1990s Japanese manufacturing (including assembly) in the USA still lags by at least two decades behind comparable manufacturing by the better-established Europeans; while in the EC, that Japanese lag approaches four decades in comparison to the local production of the well-ensconced Americans. In the EC, at least, these ratios are not likely to decline rapidly, since the USA and South-East Asia continue to attract much larger shares of Japanese investment in offshore manufacturing. Rather than rely on offshore production, Japanese multinationals generate most of their EC and US sales from substantial investments in local distribution. Initially much of this investment came from Japanese general trading companies (*sogo shosha*), but today the trading arms of Japanese manufacturers also figure prominently. Together, these investments in offshore commerce remain much larger than those recorded by either the Americans in Europe or the Europeans in the USA. After investing in proprietary distribution channels, Japanese multinationals go on to exercise, through intra-company trade between parents and subsidiaries, unrivalled control over both USA–Japan and EC–Japan trade.

Seeking to understand why Japanese multinationals continue to operate differently, several of our authors (as well as their discussants) argue that such persistent differences reflect 'vintage effects', that the newcomer Japanese are still at a much earlier stage in multinational evolution than are the middle-aged Europeans or the older Americans. For sure, 'vintage effects' have seriously confounded earlier analyses of Japanese multi-nationals, leading whole schools of thought to conclude that the evolution of Japanese multinationals was unique when compared specifically with the Americans.[2] This earlier research reported, for example, that Japanese multinationals preferred minority-owned joint ventures to majority share-holdings; that general trading companies actively participated in many of these joint ventures; that Japanese direct investments enhanced trade far more than did comparable US investments; and that the Japanese shied away from mergers and acquisitions overseas because M&As were sup-posedly alien to corporate strategy back home in Japan. Even if accurate at the time reported (itself a questionable assumption), these earlier differences between Japanese, American, and (by inference) European multinationals had, by the early 1990s, withered away. And by this same

---

[2] The 'uniqueness' of Japanese multinationals has long been associated with K. Kojima, but is not limited to his work, as the following citations suggest: R. Wakasugi, *International Trade, Foreign Direct Investment, and Japanese Industrial Organization* [*Boeki-Chokusetsu toshi to nihon no sangyo soshiki*] (Tokyo: Toyo Keizai Shimposha, 1989), esp. 119–27; R. Komiya, *The Contemporary Japanese Economy* [*Gendai nihon keizai*] (Tokyo: University of Tokyo Press, 1988), esp. 221–95; S. Sekiguchi, *New Developments in Foreign Investment* [*Kaigai toushi no shintenkai*] [Tokyo: Nihon Keizai Shinbun-sha, 1979]; T. Ozawa, *Multinationalism, Japanese Style: The Political Economy of Outward Dependency* (Princeton, NJ: Princeton University Press, 1979), esp. 227–8; K. Kojima, *Direct Foreign Investment: A Japanese Model of Multinational Business Operations* (London: Croom Helm, 1978); M. Yoshino, *Japan's Multinational Enterprises* (Cambridge, Mass.: Harvard University Press, 1976), esp. ch. 5; Y. Tsurumi, *The Japanese Are Coming: A Multinational Spread of Japanese Firms* (Cambridge, Mass.: Ballinger, 1976); S. Sekiguchi and M. Matsuba, *Japan's Direct Investments* [*Nihon no chokusetsu toshi*] (Tokyo: Nihon Keizai Shinbun-sha, 1974).

logic, additional progress along a common evolutionary path should also diminish other, more persistent 'vintage effects'.

Alternatively, however, the withering away of such 'vintage effects' may actually exacerbate some of the remaining differences between Japanese multinationals and their American or European counterparts. Looking first at industrial organization, consider the establishment overseas of Japanese *keiretsu*, especially so-called vertical *keiretsu* linking Japanese buyer-parents with their affiliated Japanese suppliers. Since Japanese investment in the USA is typically of an older vintage than Japanese investment in Europe, such peculiar characteristics of industrial organization common to the Japanese back home have had more time to be established in the USA than they have in Europe. Indeed, time matters, for only after the Japanese buyer-parents of these *keiretsu* invest overseas do we find the arrival of their affiliated Japanese subcontractors. Such sequential investments are already well underway in the USA—most notably in automobiles, but also in electronics—thus exacerbating the differences apparent in the US operations of European and Japanese multinationals. A similar sequencing of Japanese investments is just beginning to occur in the EC, where Japanese buyer-parents still greatly outnumber their affiliated Japanese suppliers. The slow arrival of these more labour-intensive suppliers may help to explain why Japanese subsidiaries in each of these European industries remain far more capital-intensive than their US counterparts. While such capital intensities will probably decline as Japanese investment in Europe grows, structural differences between American and Japanese multinationals in Europe will probably blossom—and not wither—over time.

The growth of Japanese direct investment not only alters the industrial organization of Japanese subsidiaries abroad; it also alters the performance of these subsidiaries. Consider, for example, the rapid expansion of intra-company trade following the growth of Japanese direct investment. Even as US imports from Japan have levelled off in recent years, intra-company shipments from the parents of Japanese multinationals to their foreign subsidiaries continue to grow at the expense of more arm's-length transactions between unaffiliated buyers and suppliers. Similarly, much of the growth in US exports to Japan can be traced to the growth of Japanese direct investment in the USA, where Japanese subsidiaries ship an ever greater proportion of all US exports to Japan. By comparison, intra-company shipments between the parents and subsidiaries of Japanese multinationals account for a smaller—albeit sizeable—share of EC trade with Japan. But that share is likely to grow along with increased Japanese direct investment in Europe. In short, the rapid growth of intra-company trade, like the rapid growth of overseas *keiretsu*, suggests once again that persistent differences between Japanese multinationals and their US or European counterparts may actually increase as Japanese investments proliferate overseas.

In addition to 'vintage effects', a second explanation of persistent differences in Japanese strategy and performance overseas, compared to the operations of American and European multinationals, focuses on wide variation in the market access enjoyed by foreign investors across the Triad. Looking specifically at Japan as a host to such investors, we find an extension of the trans-Atlantic model discussed above: when American and European multinationals operate outside each other's home market, their operations follow a markedly similar evolutionary path. In Japan, this means that both US and EC direct investments remain limited, and are concentrated in minority foreign-owned affiliates. What few majority subsidiaries do exist generate just about the same paltry level of Japanese sales as that generated by EC- and USA-based exporters. By contrast, Japanese multinationals operating in either the USA or the EC have come to pursue many of the same foreign investment strategies denied in Japan to both the Americans and Europeans—but actively implemented by the Americans and Europeans when they invest back and forth across the Atlantic. Among the many explanations of these persistent differences in market access, comparable differences in government policy figure prominently.[3] And it is these asymmetries—in both policy and outcome—that individual European states and the Community as a whole mean to reverse.[4]

2. AN EMERGING EC POLICY MODEL

Seeking expressly to redress these asymmetries, Europeans have begun to fashion a new policy model in reaction to the Japanese challenge.[5] That model differs dramatically from America's response to earlier surges in Japanese investment and trade. Indeed, by consciously drawing lessons from these earlier US responses, the EC enjoys 'second mover advantages' in its formulation and implementation of foreign investment and related trade policies. Such policies, in turn, readily find legitimacy in a European social contract that permits strong state intervention in national economies and across the Community as a whole. The result is a response to the Japanese challenge that simultaneously seeks to manage both international trade and foreign investment. For EC policymakers, then, ownership clearly matters.

[3] On the development of Japanese government policies towards inward FDI, see M. Mason, *American Multinationals and Japan: The Political Economy of Japanese Capital Controls, 1899–1980* (Cambridge, Mass.: Harvard University Press, 1992).

[4] For comparable asymmetries in USA–Japan economic relations, see D. Encarnation, *Rivals beyond Trade: America versus Japan in Global Competition* (Ithaca, NY: Cornell University Press, 1992), esp. 1–31, 183–202.

[5] For an earlier description of this emerging EC policy model, see R. Gaster, 'Protectionism with Purpose: Guiding Foreign Investment', *Foreign Policy* (Fall 1992), 91–106. For a more fully developed analysis of this EC model, see M. Mason, *Europe and the Japanese Challenge: The Political Economy of Capital Controls in the European Community* (forthcoming).

But not all foreign owners are treated equally—a fact amply demonstrated in the automobile industry, where this emerging EC policy model has been most fully articulated. That model, it seems, expressly discriminates against Japanese automobile manufacturers who invested aggressively in European distribution and production during the 1980s. Well over two decades earlier, of course, US automobile manufacturers had also employed comparable strategies to secure EC market access. But unlike the Japanese, the Americans generally have received national treatment from their European hosts, who now prefer to discriminate among different foreign investors. Such discrimination, moreover, is being actively encouraged not only by European-owned automobile manufacturers, but also by Ford and GM, whose European subsidiaries serve as conduits of vital information regarding the efficiency of earlier US responses to Japanese trade and investment. For Ford and GM, then, Europe serves as a critical testing-ground for alternative responses to the Japanese challenge.

In marked contrast to their earlier US experiences, for example, Nissan and other Japanese carmakers have discovered to their dismay that EC member states, despite their disagreements, are often quite keen to regulate the local operations of Japanese transplants. Even the UK, the principal host and vocal advocate for Japanese FDI in the Community, actively seeks to manage both foreign investment and related trade through the visible imposition of local content and related performance requirements. Similarly, other EC member states have also imposed on Japanese investors stiff conditions which they do not extend either to their own national champions or to other foreign (principally US) subsidiaries operating in their markets. Thus, national policies in EC member states openly discriminate between different investors, and thus establish a common principle with important implications for subsequent Community-wide actions.

But inevitable disagreements among powerful member states over how best to implement this common principle across the entire Community subsequently forced the European Commission to negotiate somewhat ambiguous arrangements with the Japanese. These 1991 arrangements imposed both explicit and implicit limits on Japanese trade and investment for the remainder of the decade: explicitly, they imposed ceilings on the total number of cars that Japanese carmakers could export to specific member states and across the entire Community; while implicitly, these arrangements warned Japanese transplants not to concentrate their intra-European exports on restricted member markets. Thus emerged a new, second principle in the European policy model, which sought to regulate foreign investment along with international trade.

Already, this emerging EC model is having a powerful effect on economic policy debates in the USA. For example, the US automobile industry, apparently emboldened by European precedent, reportedly asked the newly elected Clinton Administration to combine tighter restraints on Japanese automobile imports with new restrictions on the total number of vehicles produced in the USA by Japanese transplants. And beyond automobiles, in semiconductors and other more high technology industries, Laura Tyson—Chair of President Clinton's Council of Economic Advisers— advocates a 'cautious activism' that seeks, like the European policy model, to regulate both international trade and foreign investment. In a variant of that model, Tyson proposes that the new Administration adopt the following policy: 'When a foreign investment threatens to impair our economic or our defense security by concentrating market power in the hands of a few [foreign] suppliers, that investment should be carefully reviewed and in some cases modified or blocked altogether in favor of a national solution.'[6] A similar 'national solution' Tyson also proposes for equally threatening foreign trade. At least for Tyson, then, ownership crucially matters in the government's management of trade and investment.

Of course, Tyson's prescriptions run counter to a long tradition in US economic policymaking, which advocates the free flow of both goods and capital. One such advocate is Robert Reich, Labor Secretary in the same Clinton Administration. Here, Reich clearly stands opposite Tyson in policy debates involving questions of foreign ownership.[7] For as Reich argues: 'If we hope to revitalize the competitive performance of the United States economy, we must invest in people, not in nationally defined corporations. We must open our borders to investors from around the world rather than favoring companies that simply fly the US flag.'[8] Far from embracing Tyson's 'cautious activism', Reich's policy prescriptions actually *solicit* foreign investors by boosting the quality and performance of the US labour force. For Reich, then, ownership apparently does not matter.

The Europeans clearly disagree. And they offer an alternative response to the Japanese challenge. Can the Americans learn anything from this emerging European response? Or should they simply reject the EC policy model as either undesirable or unworkable across the Atlantic? Before answering these questions, however, Americans must recognize their unique position in the Triad: when confronted with superior foreign competition in automobiles, electronics, and other industries, Japan and Europe—but not the USA—have each pursued a not so 'cautious' activism toward trade and investment. From this perspective, then, the USA and not its two Triad partners stands apart as the real outlier.

---

[6] L. Tyson, *Who's Bashing Whom: Trade Conflicts in High-Technology Industries* (Washington, DC: Institute for International Economics, 1992), 44.

[7] To illustrate this debate, see R. Reich, 'Who is Us?', *Harvard Business Review* 68 (Jan.– Feb. 1990), 53–64; L. Tyson, 'They are not Us: Why American Ownership Still Matters', *The American Prospect* (Winter 1991), 37–49.

[8] Reich, 'Who is Us?', 54, 56, 63; see also 'Who are They', ibid. 69 (Mar.–Apr. 1991), 77–88.

INDEX